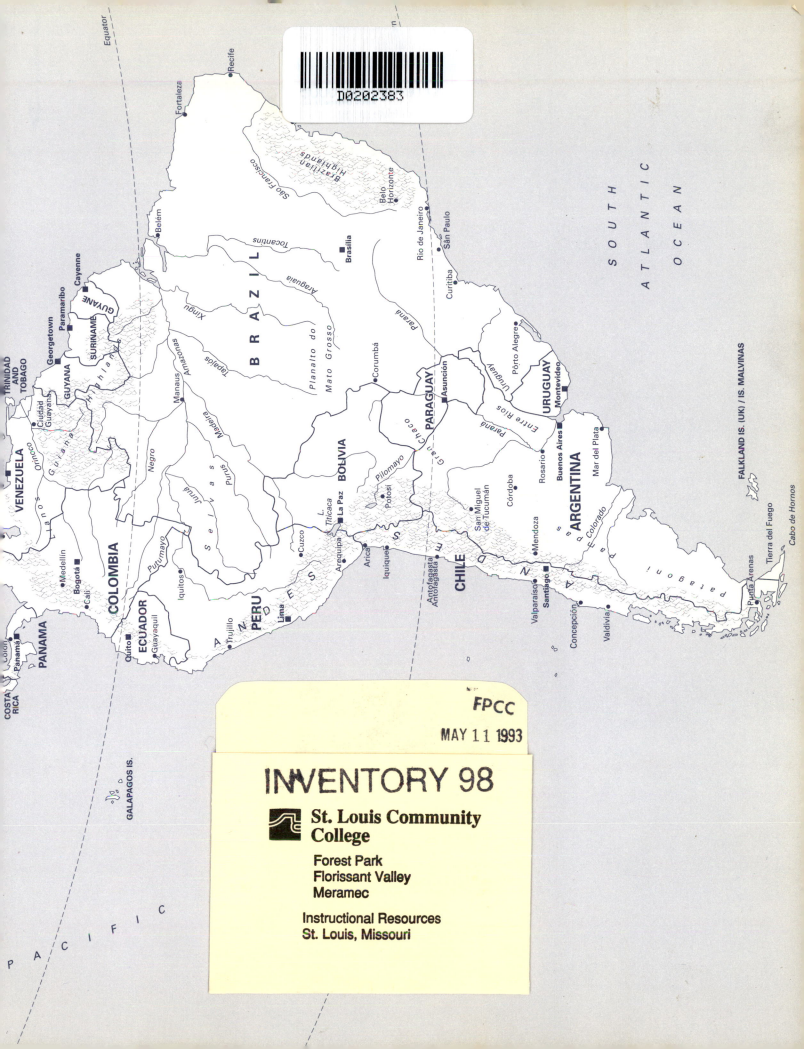

The Cambridge Encyclopedia of *Latin America*
and the Caribbean

The Cambridge Encyclopedia of Latin America

and the Caribbean

General editors

Simon Collier

PROFESSOR OF HISTORY,
VANDERBILT UNIVERSITY

Thomas E. Skidmore

CÉSPEDES PROFESSOR OF HISTORY
BROWN UNIVERSITY

The late Harold Blakemore

SECRETARY, INSTITUTE OF LATIN AMERICAN STUDIES
READER IN LATIN AMERICAN HISTORY,
UNIVERSITY OF LONDON

SECOND EDITION

CAMBRIDGE
UNIVERSITY PRESS

Published by the Press Syndicate of the University of Cambridge
The Pitt Building, Trumpington Street, Cambridge CB2 1RP
40 West 20th Street, New York, NY 10011–4211, USA
10 Stamford Road, Oakleigh, Victoria 3166, Australia

First edition published 1985
Reprinted 1986, 1987, 1989
Second edition published 1992

Printed in the United States of America

A catalogue record for this book is available from the British Library

Library of Congress cataloging in publication data

The Cambridge encyclopedia of Latin America and
the Caribbean/general editors. Simon Collier,
Harold Blakemore, Thomas E. Skidmore. – 2nd ed.
     p.   cm.
Includes bibliographical references and index.
ISBN 0 521 41322 2
1. Latin America – Encyclopedias.
2. Caribbean Area – Encyclopedias.
I. Collier, Simon. II. Blakemore, Harold.
III. Skidmore, Thomas E.
F1406.C36 1992
980' . 03–dc20 92–14496 CIP

ISBN 0 521 413222 hardback 2nd edition
(ISBN 0 521 26263 1 hardback 1st edition)

A CAMBRIDGE REFERENCE BOOK

Editor: Peter Richards
Project editor: Stephen Adamson
Design: Dale Tomlinson/Judith Robertson
Maps: Swanston Graphics
Picture research: Liz Eddison
Index: Susan Moore

CONTENTS

MAPS

CONTRIBUTORS

AEA — ALAN ANGELL
St Antony's College, Oxford

JLA — PROFESSOR JOSEPH L. ARBENA
Clemson University

GA-B — DR GERTRUD AUB-BUSCHER
University of Hull

BB — DR BEN BOX

DB — DAVID BATTMAN
Control Risks Information Services

GB — PROFESSOR GORDON BROTHERSTON
University of Essex

GHAB — DR GEORGE BANKES
University of Manchester

HB — THE LATE DR HAROLD BLAKEMORE
University of London

RB — THE LATE DR RICHARD BOULIND

VB-T — PROFESSOR VICTOR BULMER-THOMAS
*Queen Mary and Westfield College,
University of London*

WB — DR WARWICK BRAY
*Institute of Archaeology,
University of London*

CC — DR COLIN CLARKE
Jesus College, Oxford

CMC — DR CHALMERS CLAPPERTON
University of Aberdeen

EC — EDUARDO CRAWLEY
Latin America Newsletters

FC — DR FRANK COLSON
University of Southampton

GC-S — PROFESSOR GORDON CONNELL-SMITH
University of Hull

PARC — PROFESSOR PETER CALVERT
University of Southampton

PEBC — DR PETER COY

SC — PROFESSOR SIMON COLLIER
Vanderbilt University

JPD — DR J.P. DICKENSON
University of Liverpool

MD — PROFESSOR MARCO DÍAZ
*Universidad Nacional Autónoma de
México*

MDD — MALCOLM DEAS
St Antony's College, Oxford

EFE — DR EDWIN EARLY
Portsmouth Polytechnic

ABF — DR AUGUST BLAKE FRISCIA
New York University

DJF — DAVID FOX
University of Manchester

JF — JAN FAIRLEY

JRF — PROFESSOR JOHN FISHER
University of Liverpool

JVF — DR J. VALERIE FIFER
*Goldsmiths' College,
University of London*

VF — DR VALERIE FRASER
University of Essex

AG — DR ANNE GREENE
*Centre for Strategic and
International Studies, Jakarta*

DG — THE LATE PROFESSOR DOUGLAS GIFFORD
University of St Andrews

RNG — DR R.N. GWYNNE
University of Birmingham

TFG — PROFESSOR THOMAS F. GLICK
Boston University

AH — PROFESSOR ALISTAIR HENNESSY
University of Warwick

HH — HUGH HOLLEY
Lloyds Bank Group Economics Department

PH — DR PETER HULME
University of Essex

PTJ — PETER T. JOHNSON
Princeton University Libraries

AK — PROFESSOR ALAN KNIGHT
St Anthony's College, Oxford

JK — DR JOHN KING
University of Warwick

KFK — PROFESSOR KENNETH F. KIPLE
Bowling Green State University, Ohio

FL — DR FRANCIS LAMBERT
University of Glasgow

JL — PROFESSOR JOHN LYNCH
University of London

JCL — J.C. LANGLEY

RBLeP — PROFESSOR R.B. LE PAGE
University of York

WL — DR WALTER LITTLE
University of Liverpool

JSMacD — PROFESSOR JOHN MacDONALD
King's College London

AMcF — DR ANTHONY McFARLANE
University of Warwick

DRM — PROFESSOR DAVID MURRAY
University of Guelph, Ontario

EM — PROFESSOR EMILIO F. MORAN
Indiana University

GM — PROFESSOR GERALD MARTIN
Portsmouth Polytechnic

KM — PROFESSOR KENNETH MEDHURST
University of Bradford

NM — PROFESSOR NARCISO MENOCAL
University of Wisconsin-Madison

NMN — PROFESSOR MARY NOEL MENEZES, RSM

TM — TONY MORRISON

DN — THE REVEREND DAVID NICHOLLS

FN — FELICITY NOCK

JJN — PROFESSOR JOHN J. NITTI
University of Wisconsin-Madison

LN — DR LINDA NEWSON
King's College London

JO-S — PROFESSOR JUAN ORREGO-SALAS
University of Indiana

AMAP — A.M.A. PALAUS

DAP — DR DAVID PRESTON
University of Leeds

FP — DR F. PARKINSON
University of London

GP — DR GEORGE PHILIP
London School of Economics

IR-U — PROFESSOR INA ROSENTHAL-UREY

LSR — DR L.S. REBELO
King's College London

MRR — DR MICHAEL REDCLIFT
Wye College, University of London

CTS — PROFESSOR CLIFFORD T. SMITH
University of Liverpool

DLS — PROFESSOR DONALD L. SHAW
University of Virginia

RS — PROFESSOR ROBERT STEVENSON
University of California at Los Angeles

SBS — PROFESSOR STUART B. SCHWARTZ
University of Minnesota

TES — PROFESSOR THOMAS E. SKIDMORE
Brown University

EMT-H — DR ELIZABETH M. THOMAS-HOPE
University of Liverpool

DV — DOMINGO VALENZUELA
BBC World Service

DW — DAVID WINDER
Ford Foundation, Mexico City

JTW — JAMES WINPENNY

SELECT GLOSSARY

AIFLD	American Institute of Free Labour Development	LAFTA	Latin American Free Trade Association (Spanish acronym: ALALC)
Altiplano	extended high plateau (Bolivia, Peru)	LAIA	Latin American Integration Association
Ancom	Andean Pact Countries		
AP	Acción Popular/Popular Action (Peru)	latifundio	large estate
APRA	Alianza Popular Revolucionaria Americana/ American Popular Revolutionary Alliance	*licenciado*	holder of the academic degree of licencia (Spanish America)
ARENA	National Renovation Alliance (Brazil)	llano	plain
		MDB	Brazilian Democratic Movement
cacique	see p.326	mestizo	of mixed Spanish/Indian blood
CACM	Central American Common Market	minifundio	smallholding or subsistence plot
campesino	country-person or peasant	MNR	Movimiento Nacionalista Revolucionario/National Revolutionary Movement (Bolivia)
CARICOM	Caribbean Community		
caudillo	see p.325		
CECLA	Special Latin American Co-ordinating Commission	mulatto	of mixed European/African blood
		OAS	Organization of American States
civilista	political supporter of civilian as opposed to military rule	*obraje*	textile workshop (Spanish America)
		ODECA	Organisación de Estados Centroamericanos/Organization of Central American States
CLAT	Latin American Confederation of Workers		
comercio libre	open trade	OECD	Organization for Economic Co-operation and Development
conquistador	conqueror		
CORFO	Corporación de Fomento de la Producción/Production Development Corporation (Chile)	OLAS	Organization for Latin American Solidarity
		OPEC	Organization of Petroleum Exporting Countries
coronel,coroneis	literally 'colonel', 'colonels', i.e., local political boss(es) (Brazil)	ORIT	Inter-American Regional Organization of Labour
ECLA	Economic Commission for Latin America; also known as CEPAL, Comisión Económica para la América Latina	pampa(s)	plain(s) (Argentina)
		PAN	Partido Acción Nacional/National Action Party (Mexico)
ejido	communal landholding (Mexico)	PDC	Partido Demócrata-Cristiano/Christian Democratic Party (Chile)
encomienda	see p.192		
engenho	sugar mill (Brazil)		
ERP	Ejército Revolucionario del Pueblo/People's Revolutionary Army (Argentina)	PRI	Partido Revolucionario Institucional/Institutional Revolutionary Party (Mexico)
estancia	ranch	PSD/PDS	Social Democratic Party (Brazil)
estanciero	rancher	PTB	Brazilian Labour Party (Brazil)
FSLN	Frente Sandinista de Liberación Nacional/Sandinista National Liberation Front	*ranchero*	smallholder
		SELA	Latin American Economic System
		selva	jungle
gaucho	semi-nomadic cowboy of Argentine pampa (seventeenth century to late nineteenth century)	*serrano*	mountain-dweller
		sertão	the hinterland of north-east Brazil
		sierra	mountain range
GSP	US Generalized System of Preference	UDN	National Democratic Union (Brazil)
hacienda	landed estate	UNCTAD	United Nations Conference on Trade and Development
IDB	Inter-American Development Bank		
IMF	International Monetary Fund	UP	Unidad Popular/popular Unity (Chile)
junta	committee		

LATIN AMERICA – the expression first came into use in France just before 1860 – refers to the eighteen Spanish-speaking republics of the western hemisphere, together with Portuguese-speaking Brazil (which is by far the largest Latin American country) and French-speaking Haiti.

SOUTH AMERICA is the big southern land mass of the American continent, which is really a double continent.

CENTRAL AMERICA – the area lying between, and linking, North and South America – is normally taken to include the small republics of Guatemala, Honduras, El Salvador, Nicaragua, Costa Rica and Panama, together with Belize.

MIDDLE AMERICA (or MESOAMERICA) is a term sometimes used to denote the area covered by Central America and Mexico together. It should be noted that Mexico is geographically a part of the North American land mass.

THE CARIBBEAN usually refers to the islands of the Caribbean Sea, but sometimes also to the adjacent mainland countries.

THE WEST INDIES are the Caribbean islands, especially (in Anglo-American parlance) those of the non-Latin Caribbean.

The Physical Environment

Tectonic history and structure

Latin America and the Caribbean are a mosaic of distinct structural units varying considerably in age and size and linked together by tectonic movements of recent geological time. The main composing units are the South American continent, the Caribbean ocean basin, the Lesser Antilles island arc, Old Antillia (Greater Antilles islands and parts of eastern Central America), western and southern Central America and Mexico north of the Balsas depression. The evolution of these units can best be understood by applying the modern concept of Plate Tectonics which states that the Earth's crust is composed of discrete slabs or plates that are continuously in motion with respect to each other. Six crustal plates have been involved in the tectonic and structural evolution of Latin America and the Caribbean.

MAIN STRUCTURAL TRENDS

Beginning in Mexico and moving through Central America and the Caribbean into South America, the main structural trends are as follows.

1 Mexico north of the Balsas depression consists mainly of the Mexican Plateau, a tilted block of upland defined on its eastern, southern and western sides by prominent fault zones. Declining from 2500 m in the south to 1200 m in the north, the plateau is an area of low mountain ridges and shallow intermontane basins bearing two dominant structural trends; a north-west–south-east alignment in the eastern (folded limestone) and western (volcanic) cordilleras is one trend and this is sharply truncated in the south by the younger west–east Neovolcanic zone. The latter is typified by large active and inactive central volcanoes like Popocatépetl (5500 m), Colima (3900 m) and Ixtaccíhuatl (5250 m).

2 The Balsas depression and structure lines dominating mountain ranges in eastern Guatemala and Nicaragua and in the Greater Antilles also have a west–east alignment and may be tectonically related to the Neovolcanic zone.

3 Southern Mexico and Yucatán are two independent blocks of ancient crystalline and Mesozoic limestone respectively and lack clear structural lineation. They appear to be plate fragments moved into their present positions by fault dislocation and shearing.

4 The Central America volcanic axis extends south-eastwards continuously for 1300 km from the Guatemala–Mexico border to western Panama. It cuts across and partially mantles the adjacent and older west–east structures of Old Antillia. Constant volcanic activity for more than 20 million years has constructed volcanic uplands and chains of volcanoes in Guatemala, El Salvador, Nicaragua, Costa Rica and western Panama. More than thirty active volcanoes lie along this axis.

5 The Lesser Antilles is an 800-km arc of young volcanicity, having grown during the last 10 million years at the eastern edge of the Caribbean crustal plate where it is being underthrust by a portion of the Atlantic plate. The arc includes the highly dangerous volcanoes of Mont Pelée, Martinique, and La Soufrière, St Vincent.

6 Along the Pacific coast of Costa Rica and both coasts of eastern Panama mountain ranges seldom exceeding 1000 m altitude curve to the Andean system of north-west Colombia. Distinct from the volcanic axis of central Costa Rica and western Panama, these appear to share a common origin with the Colombian Andes and result from subduction processes at the complex junction of three crustal plates – the Cocos, Caribbean and South American.

7 The Gulf of Mexico is an abandoned ocean basin which has become isolated by the development of the Caribbean plate and has remained tectonically quiescent for about the last 40 million years; it has been an immense sediment trap since that time.

8 The Caribbean Sea occupies an ocean basin developed by sea floor spreading between 40 and 10 million years ago; floored by basaltic rock, it forms an independent crustal plate bounded on the east and west by the volcanic arcs of Lesser Antilles and Central America respectively and on the north and south by the Balsas–Greater Antilles zone of crustal shearing and the Caribbean coast ranges and shear zones of Venezuela respectively. The plate seems to be moving slowly towards the east.

9 South America is the continental part of the large crustal plate presently being created along the mid-ocean ridge of the South Atlantic. It has a much longer history of structural evolution than most of Central America and the Caribbean and is a complex assemblage of many different formations developed over more than 3000 million years. Basically, the continent is dominated by three major types of structure: up-warped and faulted massifs composed of pre-Cambrian crystalline rocks thinly covered with some Palaeozoic and Mesozoic strata; down-warped basins in the same pre-Cambrian basement filled with more than 4000 m of Palaeozoic, Mesozoic and Cainozoic sedimentary rocks; and great chains of folded and thrust rocks composing the Andean cordilleras and Caribbean coast ranges. The up-warped ancient massifs are largely composed of metamorphic and igneous rocks like gneiss, schist

Previous page
Tributary of the River Amazon curving through the rainforest. The Amazon has the largest of the world's tropical forests, and its protection has become a leading concern of ecologists.

Mt Condoriri, Cordillera Real, Bolivia. The Cordillera of the Andes contains some of the world's highest mountains after the Himalayas.

and granites which crop out extensively in areas known as the Guiana and Brazilian shields; such rocks form the pre-Cambrian basement that probably underlies the entire continent and which developed over almost 3000 million years. The ancient massifs of the shields have been deeply weathered and dissected due to prolonged exposure to the elements, giving rise to spectacular residual topography in granitic areas such as eastern Brazil and the Guianas where sugar-loaf inselberg landforms occur. The shield areas are dominated by dissected plateau country in which tributary streams draining to major river basins have become deeply incised as a result of geologically recent uplift, but impressive structurally controlled scenery includes the fault line escarpment of east-central Brazil and the extensive plateau basalt terrain masking the southern edge of the shield in southern Brazil, northern Uruguay and north-east Paraguay; the Iguassú Falls plunge over the edge of this formation. Smaller ancient massifs forming uplifted plateaux are present in the southern hills of Buenos Aires and in Patagonia.

Down-warped portions of the continental pre-Cambrian basement are occupied by the immense sedimentary basins of the Orinoco, Amazon, Paranaíba–São Francisco and Paraná. Originating more than 600 million years ago, these have been periodically inundated with marine and terrestrial sediments which now exceed 4000 m depth in places. The most recent pulse of sedimentation and subsidence was during the last 15 million years as the Andes formed, resulting in a thick cover of late Tertiary and Quaternary sediments on top of older strata. The present course of the Amazon became established between 15 and 8 million years ago as the Andes were elevated across drainage routes to the

Pacific and the Gulf of Guayaquil; this river system has not only deposited over 3000 m of sediment in the basin but has also built out an immense sedimentary cone over the continental shelf and slope; the estimated rate of sedimentation during the last 2,200,000 years is 50 to 115 $cm/10^3yr$. The majority of exposed strata in the basins and the thin sedimentary cover rocks fringing the shields show signs of only gentle tectonic disturbance, mainly in the form of large-scale warping, and hence are typical of the relatively quiescent tectonic environment of continental interiors. In South America such little disturbed strata extend west of the shield massifs and sedimentary basins as gently sloping plains. These stretch as a belt parallel to the Andes for almost the entire length of the continent from the llanos of Venezuela to the steppes of Patagonia and form an intermediate structural–topographical zone before the Andean province. The multiple ranges of the Andes continue for more than 6500 km from the shores of the Caribbean to the tip of Tierra del Fuego. This remarkable mountain barrier is much narrower (*c.* 300 km) and higher than the mountains of western North America. Aconcagua (6960 m) is the highest peak in the western hemisphere and the Cordillera Blanca of Peru and the Cordillera Real of Bolivia each contain many peaks exceeding 6000 m in altitude. The geological structure and history of the Andes is quite complex and to describe them as a single continuous unit is incorrect. There are distinct lithological, structural and age differences along their length and across their breadth. In general, the Andes are composed mainly of folded, thrust and faulted sedimentary and volcanic strata extensively intruded in places with immense linear masses (batholiths) of granitic rock; zones of metamorphic

MAIN TECTONIC AND STRUCTURAL FEATURES

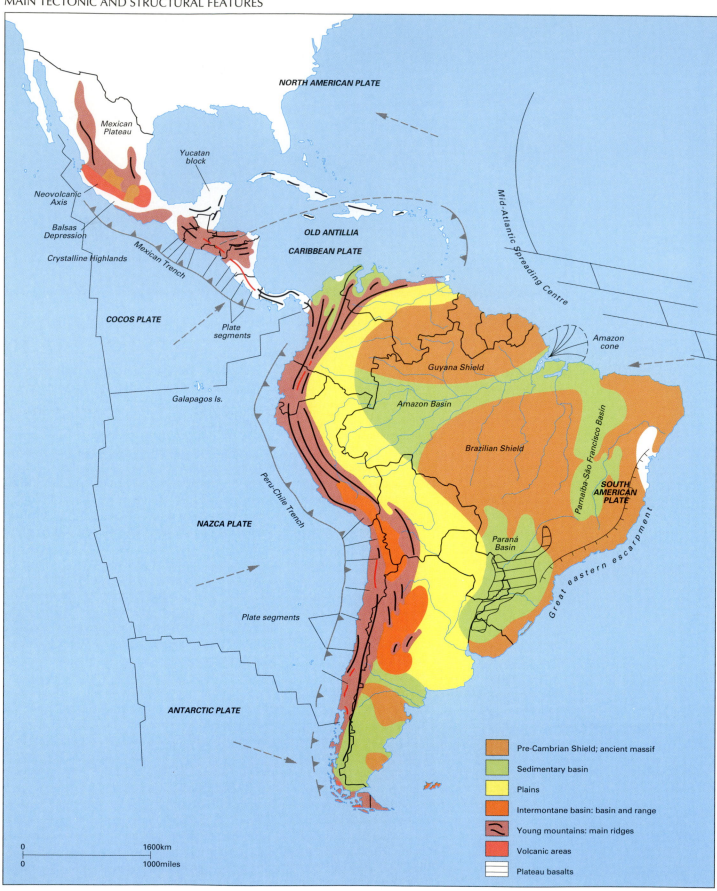

NORTH AMERICAN PLATE

Mexican
Plateau

Yucatan
block

Neovolcanic
Axis

Balsas
Depression

Crystalline Highlands

Mexican Trench

OLD ANTILLIA

CARIBBEAN PLATE

COCOS PLATE

Plate
segments

Galapagos Is.

NAZCA PLATE

Peru-Chile Trench

Plate segments

ANTARCTIC PLATE

Mid-Atlantic Spreading Centre

Amazon
cone

Guyana Shield

Amazon Basin

Brazilian Shield

Parnaíba-São Francisco Basin

SOUTH
AMERICAN
PLATE

Paraná
Basin

Great eastern escarpment

	Pre-Cambrian Shield; ancient massif
	Sedimentary basin
	Plains
	Intermontane basin: basin and range
	Young mountains: main ridges
	Volcanic areas
	Plateau basalts

0   1600km
0   1000miles

rock are also present. The number of structurally distinct ranges varies along the length of the Andes. In Colombia there are three principal ridges, the western, central and eastern cordillera and a minor range of coastal hills; the eastern cordillera swings eastwards into Venezuela and the western can be traced into Panama. Southwards the Andes are continued in Ecuador by only two principal ranges, although the low coastal hills may be structurally linked with those of Colombia. A change in alignment occurs at the Peruvian frontier, south of which three closely spaced principal ranges extend south-eastwards as far as the latitude of Lima. South of here the eastern cordillera swings farther inland away from the central cordillera but continues southwards in Bolivia and Argentina while the central and western cordillera extend parallel with the coast into Chile and Bolivia. The immense down-faulted basin of Lake Titicaca and the Bolivian Altiplano occupies the unusually wide gap between the eastern and central cordillera. The basin has been filled with more than 5000 m of fluvial, volcanic and glacial deposits. The three-fold structural assemblage of cordillera continues into Chile and Argentina but by latitude 28°S the eastern cordillera becomes more diffuse and splits into faulted basin and range topography; south of 34°S only two cordillera compose the Andes, the most westerly of which is lower and becomes an archipelago of coastal islands before curving south-eastwards to terminate in Tierra del Fuego.

Other important differences in the structure of the Andes include the predominance of Palaeozoic sedimentary strata in the eastern cordillera (although granitic intrusions of Mesozoic age occur in places), the predominance of Mesozoic volcanic, sedimentary and igneous rocks in the western cordillera and the abundance of Cainozoic to present-day volcanic rocks, sediments and igneous intrusions in the central cordillera. The distribution of active volcanoes is also not uniform; they occur in southern Colombia and Ecuador, southern Peru and along the Bolivia–Chile border and in the southern part of middle Chile; in other segments of the Andes volcanicity has either become recently extinct or has been extinct for a few million years.

STRUCTURAL EVOLUTION

Although the structural evolution and tectonic history of Latin America and the Caribbean has been a continuum it is perhaps helpful to consider it in two sections: from the Cambrian to Triassic period and from the Jurassic to the present.

At the end of pre-Cambrian times South America was part of an assemblage of 'southern' continents (nowadays referred to as Gondwanaland) and lay on the opposite side of the globe from its present location in an 'upside-down' position; the 'northern' continents lay some distance away across an ocean basin. Central America and the Caribbean did not exist at this period.

Developments in the Cambrian–Triassic period (600–200 million years ago)

Major structural events affecting South America during this period may be summarized as follows.

CROSS SECTION THROUGH SOUTH AMERICA FROM THE PACIFIC TO THE AMAZON BASIN IN THE LATITUDE OF SOUTHERN PERU

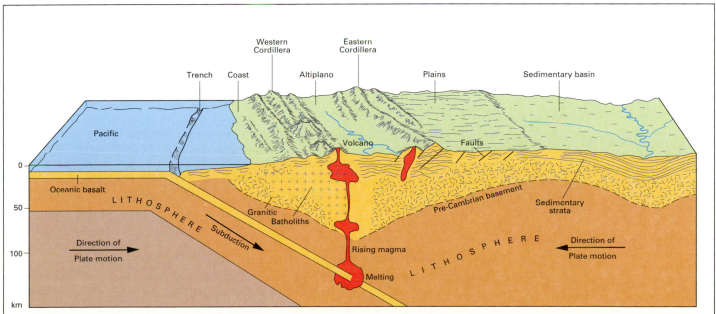

TECTONIC HISTORY: CARBONIFEROUS-PERMIAN TIMES TO THE END OF THE JURASSIC PERIOD

Pangea landmass around 200 million years ago (Carboniferous – Permian times); Caledonian structures had been created earlier as Laurasia and Gondwanaland collided. Central America and the Caribbean do not yet exist. Large continental ice sheet lies over southern continents. Present-day positions of Lesser Antilles (LA) and South Sandwich (SS) Island arcs are marked to indicate relative positions of continents 200 million years ago.

End of Jurassic period c. 135 million years ago. North Atlantic and Caribbean have opened but the South Atlantic is just beginning. The Hot Spot marked is only one of a larger number which caused crustal doming and cracking. The one indicated probably caused the floods basalts shown on the map, p. 14.

1 Periodic marine sedimentation along the western margin of the land mass and a Pacific Ocean connection into down-warped basins of the interior.

2 Development of large ice sheets during the Silurian and Carboniferous–Permian periods as Gondwanaland moved across south-polar latitudes from one side of the globe to the other.

3 Gondwanaland collided with the northern continent Laurasia in Silurian times, forming the Caledonian mountain system extending from south-west North America to north-west Europe.

4 Subduction of Pacific Ocean floor along western South America in Permian times with volcanism, folding and faulting of Palaeozoic rocks, creating early Andean structures. Subduction and probable continental collision at the southern margin of Gondwanaland (South America/Africa with India/Antarctica/Australia) during the upper Triassic period, producing folded structures exposed in the hills south of Buenos Aires and the Drakensbergs of South Africa. Most of the Earth's continental crust was now joined up to form the Pangea super-continent.

5 During the upper Triassic period massive plumes of heat rising from the mantle bulged up the crust of the continental mass, cracking open the surface to release vast quantities of basaltic lava and beginning the break-up of Pangea which continues in today's movements of continents and ocean basins.

Jurassic period to the present day

Stresses set up by prolonged up-doming of the Pangea continental crust at the end of the Palaeozoic era began a period of active tectonic disturbance which continues to the present day. By the late-Jurassic period (150 million years ago) the lithosphere broke all along the western side of Pangea as parts of the Pacific Ocean basin began to subduct beneath the super-continent. Heat generated at depth by this activity produced masses of molten magma that rose upwards to form arcs of volcanic islands, the roots of which partly compose the western cordilleras of South America. The northern margin of South America/Africa separated from North America as crustal fracturing and then ocean-floor spreading opened up the Gulf of Mexico and the southern North Atlantic. Thus a proto Caribbean and Central American domain came into existence for the first time. By early Cretaceous times (100 million years ago) North and South America had widely separated and, although Africa remained joined to northern South America, a great dome in the crust had developed and split in the region of eastern Brazil and a gulf like the Red Sea opened up to form an incipient South Atlantic ocean basin. During the late Cretaceous period (90–60 million years ago) subduction of the Cocos plate beneath the Caribbean basin and adjacent parts of the North and South American plates produced the Greater Antilles arc across the position of present-day Central America. Meanwhile, subduction of the Nazca plate formed a second volcanic arc in the Andean province, the roots of which are now exposed in places as great granitic batholiths in the western cordilleras. By the Eocene period (c. 40 million years ago) considerable tectonic developments had occurred in the Caribbean. The Greater Antilles arc had migrated eastwards and

TECTONIC HISTORY: EOCENE TIME TO THE PRESENT

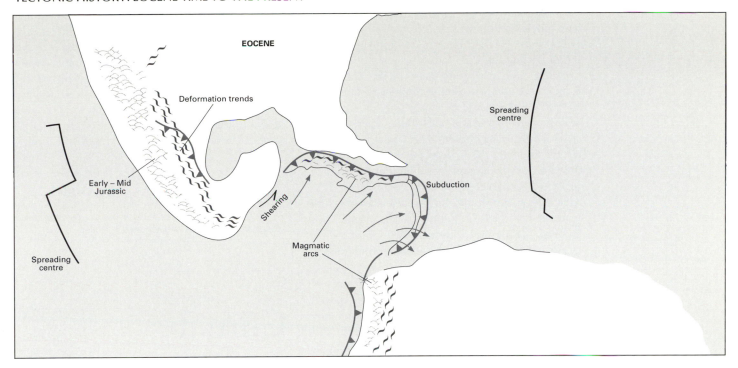

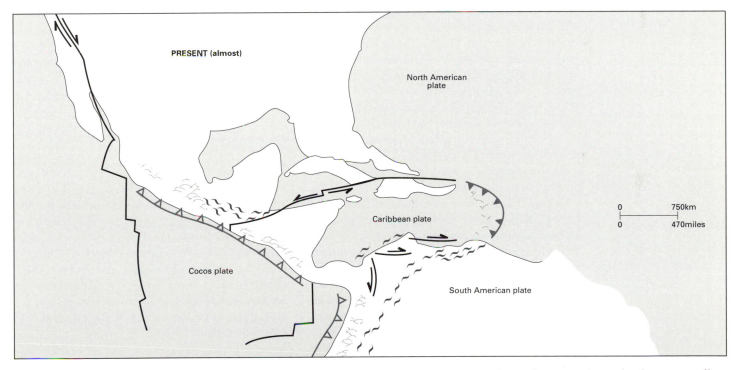

Top
About 40 million years ago.

Above
The pattern initiated soon after Eocene time: subduction of Cocos plate forms a land-bridge in Central America.

widened south-eastwards, shearing past the Yucatán escarpment until it collided with the Florida–Bahama limestone mass; ocean-floor spreading moved part of the arc south-eastwards to collide with northern South America, forming the Caribbean coast ranges. Meanwhile, subduction beneath the southern North American plate produced volcanic activity and fold structures with the north-west to south-east trend now exposed in the Mexican Plateau.

By the mid-Miocene period (about 15 million years ago) the present-day geometry of the Caribbean plate and hence of most of Central America began to finalize. As the Greater Antilles arc complex collided and extinguished against Florida, convergence of the Pacific and North American plates produced master shear faults which sliced Cuba from Haiti-Dominican Republic and also defined the Caribbean plate edge along northern Venezuela;

jostling between the Cocos, North American, Caribbean and South American plates ignited two new subduction zones, resulting in the volcanic arcs of the south Mexican Plateau, Central America and the Lesser Antilles.

While such events occurred in the Caribbean domain, even more violent tectonics were unfolding along the western side of South America. About 15 million years ago in the mid-Miocene period there began a third major phase of magmatic activity which affected not only the Andean zone but also much of the whole continent, causing substantial warping and elevation. Remarkable volcanic activity burst out in the Andes as uplift and folding disturbed the rock sequences; immense volumes of acidic magma, rich in silica, poured out of fissures and spread mobile incandescent flows of ash over wide areas of terrain to depths exceeding 500 m, particularly in Peru, Bolivia and Chile. The ash eruptions continued until about 4 million years ago when they ended and were replaced by the growth of large andesitic central volcanoes, indicating a change in the magmatic chemistry. This was accompanied by the main pulse of regional uplift that created the present mountainous topography; prior to this time only low mountains rose above a widespread rolling plain close to sea level. Magmatic swelling of the crust uplifted the gentle plain by 3500–4000 m, forming the Altiplano; it also caused extensive folding and thrust faulting which compressed strata into anticlinal-synclinal structures, and formed the parallel ranges of the eastern cordillera. Some units of terrain, formerly part of the low-lying denudation plain, were differentially uplifted along major fault systems to form the most scenically spectacular ranges of the Andes, such as the Sierra Nevada de Santa Marta in Colombia, the Cordillera Blanca in Peru and the Cordillera Real in Bolivia. As the central and western cordillera were elevated, intense erosion removed huge volumes of sediment, exposing the great plutonic intrusions (batholiths) and in-filled down-faulted intermontane troughs with vast quantities of sands, gravels and conglomerates. Although the basic structural pattern and high elevation of the Andes had probably become established by 6 to 4 million years ago, with final details developing since then, it is perhaps worth emphasizing that the evolution was probably differential along the various structural segments of these mountains. The present uneven distribution of active volcanoes indicates that this still characterizes tectonic activity in the Andes. East of the active tectonic edge of South America much of the continent has remained tectonically quiescent but not quite immobile. Broad-scale warping and localized faulting has occurred during the last few million years, perhaps as a response to disturbances of underlying thermal

circulation by deep (*c.* 700 km) penetration of the relatively cool slabs of Pacific Ocean crust, their inclination down the subduction zone taking them far eastwards beneath the continent. This possibly accounts for the widespread late Cainozoic uplift which affected the shield massifs, basins and plains as well as the Andean region; together with lowering global sea level related to growth of the Antarctic and other ice sheets, this has produced a condition of geocraty – in other words a time of much land above sea level.

CMC

Further Reading: W. F. Jenks, ed., *Handbook of South American Geology*, Geological Society of America, Memoir 56 (1956); W. Zeil, *The Andes: A Geological Review*, Beiträge zur Regionalen Geologie der Erde (Stuttgart, 1980)

Climate

There is a great diversity of climate in Latin America and the Caribbean, varying in type from tropical to cool temperate. Principal reasons for such diversity include the latitudinal range, the pattern and movement of atmospheric pressure cells and related wind systems, the influence of adjacent oceans and seas and the altitude and alignment of mountains.

DETERMINING FACTORS

Latitude

The location of more than three-quarters of Latin America and the Caribbean within tropical latitudes means that the climate is predominantly tropical at low altitudes. This ensures high average annual temperatures (over 20°C) and abundant rainfall in most places; but most characteristic is the relatively small annual *range* in temperature, that is the difference between the average temperature of the warmest and coldest months. Since this is usually less than 1°C there are no distinct summer and winter seasons with respect to temperature. The diurnal range (commonly 15–20°C in tropical mountains) is normally much greater than the annual range, hence the expression, 'Night is the winter of the tropics.' Outside tropical latitudes, in much of northern Mexico and south of Paraguay, the annual temperature range increases markedly poleward, demarcating definite summer and winter seasons. With increasing latitude there is also a higher number of days in the year with killing frosts. The high southerly latitudes of southern South America are in the cool temperate

MEAN ANNUAL PRECIPITATION, OCEAN CURRENTS, TRACKS OF POLAR AIR AND HURRICANES

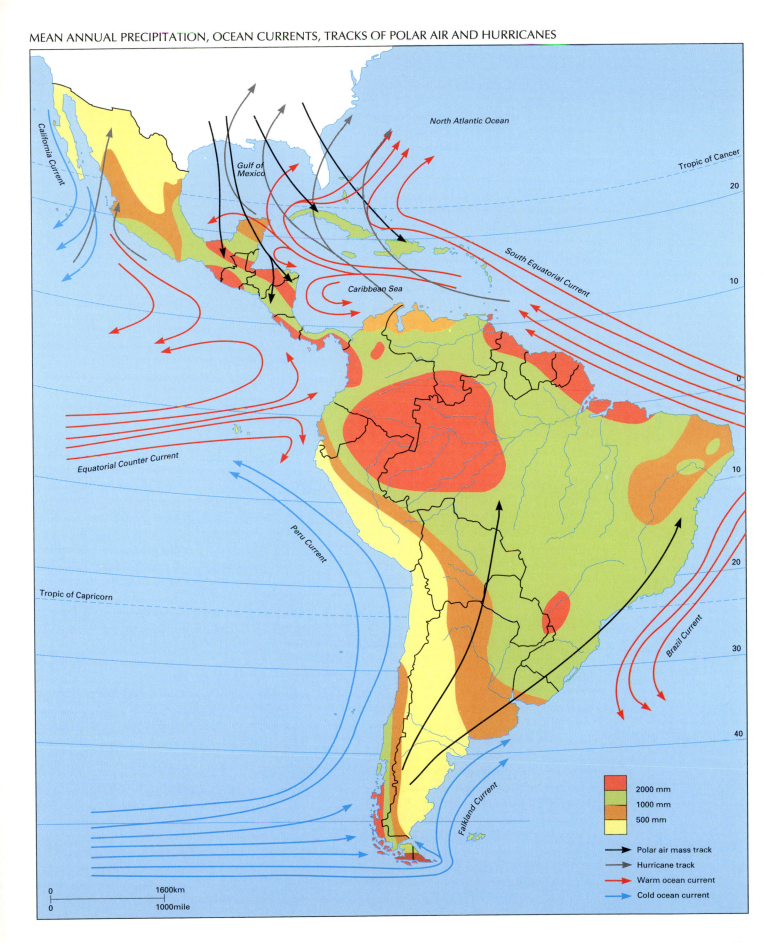

North Atlantic Ocean

Tropic of Cancer

California Current

Gulf of Mexico

South Equatorial Current

Caribbean Sea

Equatorial Counter Current

Peru Current

Tropic of Capricorn

Brazil Current

Falkland Current

20

10

0

10

20

30

40

	2000 mm
	1000 mm
	500 mm

➤ Polar air mass track
➤ Hurricane track
➤ Warm ocean current
➤ Cold ocean current

0   1600km
0   1000mile

zone where mean annual temperatures may be less than 10°C and where mountain ice caps exist.

Pressure systems and air masses

Weather patterns in Latin America and the Caribbean are fundamentally influenced by pressure systems at three scales. At the largest are the four vast high-pressure cells at mid-latitudes in the neighbouring oceans and the zone of low pressure along the inter-tropical convergence. Anticyclonic circulation of air around those in the Atlantic directs trade winds towards the Caribbean and eastern South America from the north-east, east and south-east; winds associated with the Pacific cells trend more parallel with the coasts of Mexico and most of South America. As the inter-tropical convergence zone moves slightly northwards and southwards seasonally with the sun, the strength and location of the pressure systems also change. This influences the second scale of pressure system which involves cyclonic depressions originating along the zone of convergence of polar and tropical air. When these develop, mainly in the respective winter seasons north and south of the equator, they bring outbursts of cooler polar air into the Caribbean and the South American continent. South of latitude 40°S travelling depressions generated along the polar front in the south-east Pacific bring notoriously stormy weather into southern Chile and Patagonia. At the smallest scale are the tropical hurricanes which develop mainly over the warm waters of the Caribbean; intense thermal convection and very low atmospheric pressure over a localized area cause violent circulation of air and, accompanied by extremely high winds and torrential rain, the hurricanes may travel over long distances.

Water masses and ocean currents

Since the temperature and moisture characteristics of air masses are derived from the surfaces over which they originate, and as most air masses affecting Latin America and the Caribbean come from oceanic source regions, the nature of the seas and oceans surrounding the area are of critical importance in understanding the climate.

The Caribbean Sea and the Gulf of Mexico are warm, practically inland seas fed by warm off-shoots of the Atlantic north-equatorial current. With surface water temperatures ranging from 22–28°C, these water masses are like hot cauldrons over which air travelling with the north-east trades becomes hot and moist. On the Pacific side of Central America are two contrasting water bodies: a northern extension of the equatorial counter current provides warm, moist air for the southern part of Central America, whereas the relatively cold southward flowing Californian

---

El Niño

El Niño is a warm, southward flowing current which raises sea surface temperatures off northern Peru and Ecuador in the early months of each year, reducing levels of inorganic nutrients and photosynthesizing plankton in the normally cold ocean and thus disrupting the food chain.

Every few years El Niño is stronger and warmer than usual and, accompanied by heavy rain, penetrates unusually far south. In these *años de abundancia* (years of abundance), the agriculture of northern Peru can benefit from the warmer and wetter climate. In most respects, however the climatological and ecological impact is both malign and widespread. The intense El Niño of 1982–3 saw heavy rainfall and floods in northern Peru and Ecuador while southern Peru and Bolivia experienced extreme drought, and the effects were felt as far away as California, the Philippines, and Australia. Damage to bird life and fish stocks was also considerable: the 1982–3 anchovy catch off Peru amounted to less than1 per cent of that in the previous year. The warm tropical water of El Niño results from changes in the circulation of the entire Pacific Ocean basin caused by unusually weak westward-blowing surface winds.

---

current ensures cool year-round temperatures in western Mexico. A similar situation occurs along the west coast of South America from Chile northwards to the Peru–Ecuador border where the cold Peru current exerts a cooling influence on the coastal air masses. Because mild oceanic air from the Pacific Ocean passes over a cooler surface it is not able to absorb moisture and hence becomes a stable and dry air mass, inducing arid conditions immediately onshore. East of the Andes tropical regions are affected by hot, moist air masses moving in from the equatorial Atlantic with the north-east and easterly winds and, since moderate ocean temperatures persist as far south as the Plate estuary, southern Brazil, Paraguay, Uruguay and northern Argentina all experience sub-tropical to warm temperate conditions. South of the River Plate the cool Falkland current exerts an influence and moderates the temperatures of southern Argentina.

Altitude

Since air temperature decreases with altitude at the rate of about 1°C per 165 m of elevation, it follows that even on tropical mountains there will be an altitudinal zonation of weather and climate. This fact is keenly recognized by people living in mountainous parts of Latin America and the Caribbean where altitudinally distinct climatic belts have long-established Spanish names – the *tierra caliente*, *tierra templada* and *tierra fría*, meaning the hot, temperate and cold land respectively; in particularly high areas a fourth zone, the *tierra helada* or icy land, may be present. In an environment like the Andes with such a relief amplitude there may be three or four types of climate within a horizontal distance of only 40 km.

Tierra caliente lies between sea level and 800 m altitude and thus covers all the coastal lowlands, large plains and interior basins and low mountain and foothill areas. The zone is characterized by high daytime temperatures (30–33°C) and cool night-time conditions (20–24°C) for most of the year with only small differences between the summer and winter months. Frosts are unknown and rarely do night temperatures descend below 15°C.

Tierra templada lies roughly between 800 and 1000 m altitude and constitutes the tropical highlands of Central America and northern South America; the term could also be applied to parts of the Guiana and Brazilian shields. Warm daytime temperatures (24–27°C) prevail, although hot afternoons with temperatures rising to 32–35°C sometimes occur in the summer months. The difference between summer and winter temperatures increases polewards so that in the Mesa Central of Mexico and in the southern Brazilian escarpment periods of cold and occasional night frosts are not uncommon during mid-winter months.

Tierra fría lies above 1800–2000 m and is thus widespread throughout the Andes but in Mexico occurs only in the higher basins and mountain slopes. This is a zone of warm pleasant days (24–27°C) and cold nights (10–12°C). Frosts are common during the winter months and at the upper limit of the zone.

Tierra helada lies above 4000 m and extends over the higher cultivable slopes of much of the Andes and higher parts of the Altiplano. Daytime temperatures during the dry season may often exceed 15°C but, because of the altitude and clear night-time skies, temperatures plummet below freezing most nights.

CLIMATE TYPES

These main climatic variables have produced a variety of distinctive climatic types in Latin America and the Caribbean, classified in detail by the Köppen system which has been generalized for the figure on p. 23 and the following description.

Tropical wet climates have high temperatures all year round, the average for each month being above 18°C and there is no pronounced dry season; this corresponds with the *tierra caliente* or hot tropical lowland. Such conditions pertain to the north-eastern (windward) side of the Caribbean Islands, most of the eastern half of Central America and southern Mexico, the north-east coast of South America, upper Amazonia and the interior valleys of Colombia. Many of these areas experience a short drier period during cooler months. Annual precipitation usually reaches over 2000 mm and relative humidity is frequently high (over 75 per cent).

Tropical wet-and-dry climates have temperatures similar to the tropical humid types but are distinguished by a definite dry season of four to six months during the cooler part of the year; this dry season may not be entirely rainless but is sufficient to induce a seasonal rhythm to vegetation growth. In the Caribbean and Central America this type is characteristically developed in the lee of the trade winds along southern and western coasts and in interior basins lower than 1000 m; it also covers the biggest portion of South America, extending across most of the Guiana and Brazilian shields and into eastern Bolivia and northern Argentina. Annual rainfall varies from 750–1500 mm in this zone.

Tropical highland climates correspond generally to the *tierra templada* and *tierra fría* – tropical highland zones. There are only scattered patches in the Caribbean Islands, and in Central America they are confined to the mountain ranges of the Mexican Plateau and volcanic highlands. They occur throughout the Andes and in parts of the great eastern escarpment of Brazil. Because of the altitude at least one month in the year averages below 18°C. Within the tropics seasonal temperature differences are slight but they increase with increasing latitude, as in Mexico where the northern half of the Sierra Madre Occidental has cold winters, often with snow, followed by warm summers. Throughout parts of the central and eastern cordillera of the tropical Andes this zone is characterized by a wet season and is known as *invierno* (winter) even though it is in the southern summer. Increased cloudiness induces lower temperatures and above 4000 m snowfall commonly occurs.

Subtropical climates are typified by mild winters, hot summers and either no dry season or a short, dry summer season. They occur in a small area of north-east Mexico and over a much larger area of south-east South America where they comprise the humid pampa of Argentina, Paraguay and Uruguay. This is a truly temperate climate in which the average summer temperature is around 28°C and the winter average seldom drops below 10°C. During the winter

MEAN JANUARY TEMPERATURE

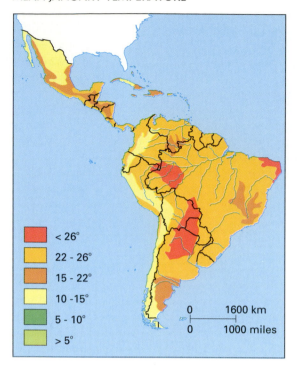

🟥	< 26°
🟧	22 - 26°
🟫	15 - 22°
🟨	10 -15°
🟩	5 - 10°
🟩	> 5°

0 ——— 1600 km
0 ——— 1000 miles

MEAN JULY TEMPERATURE

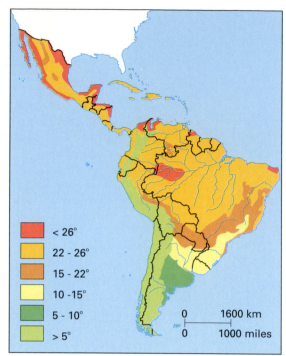

🟥	< 26°
🟧	22 - 26°
🟫	15 - 22°
🟨	10 -15°
🟩	5 - 10°
🟩	> 5°

0 ——— 1600 km
0 ——— 1000 miles

season, however, occasional outbursts of cool polar air from North America and from Antarctica may cause spells of more bitter weather in Mexico and south-east South America respectively. Rain normally falls each month but the total amount is relatively low at 500–1000 mm.

Warm temperate climates are characterized by mild, rainy winters and cool, dry summers or by mild winters, cool summers and no dry season; they are restricted to the so-called 'Mediterranean' part of central Chile and to the part of Argentina south of the Plate estuary around Mar del Plata. At Valparaiso on the coast of Chile the coldest months (June and July) average 11.25°C and the warmest months average 17.6°C. Santiago is more extreme because of its location in the Central Valley and averages 7.6°C and 20.4°C for those periods. Rainfall increases steadily southwards from the Atacama Desert until by the latitude of Santiago it totals 350 mm, produced by the interaction of cold polar and warm Pacific air.

Dry climates are the semi-arid and arid types. They are absent from the Caribbean but occur in the northern interior and north-west of Mexico where they are related to the persistence of dry, stable air from the Pacific and rain-shadow effects of the mountains. In South America, however, beginning at the Peru–Ecuador border, arid and semi-arid conditions affect much of the coastal cordillera and some interior basins of the Andes continuously southwards to central Chile. The Andes are an effective barrier pre-

venting moist Atlantic air masses reaching the Pacific coast. Warm, moist air moves over the cold Peru current and becomes chilled in its lower layers; during the southern winter months this cool, damp air moves slightly onshore from a south-westerly direction as a coastal mist and brings rather unusual and miserable conditions to the Peruvian desert. During the rest of the year and for most of the time in northern Chile the air movement is more parallel or offshore in alignment and this leads to clear, dry conditions which reach their greatest intensity in the Atacama Desert. This is one of the driest places on earth, where so little rain falls that average precipitation figures are meaningless; in some places east of the coastal plateau no rain has ever been recorded. Nevertheless, there are temperature and humidity differences between the coast and the interior, the former having higher humidity and greater cloudiness and hence a lower temperature range.

Cold montane climates are characterized by continuously cool or cold weather with no warm season and are caused either by exceedingly high altitudes (above 4500 m) or by exposure to polar cyclones in the high latitudes of southern Chile and Argentina. In the tropical Andes the abundance and warmth of diurnal sunshine is offset by the effect of altitude and shade; many of these climatic types are close to or above the regional snowline. A low altitude type occurs in southern Chile where south of 40°S the climate deteriorates progressively until it has become one of the stormiest and most unpleasant in the

CLIMATE TYPES

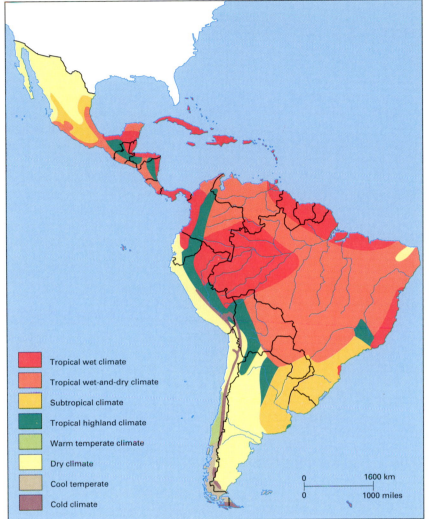

- ■ Tropical wet climate
- ■ Tropical wet-and-dry climate
- ■ Subtropical climate
- ■ Tropical highland climate
- ■ Warm temperate climate
- ■ Dry climate
- ■ Cool temperate
- ■ Cold climate

0 1600 km
0 1000 miles

Natural disasters

Because of their tectonic and climatic setting, the high amplitude of relief and dense concentrations of population, Latin America and the Caribbean are subject to a variety of natural processes that often have disastrous consequences. They can be grouped into three main categories, tectonic, meteorological and geomorphological.

TECTONIC DISASTERS

Interaction between six crustal plates in the tectonic domain of Latin America and the Caribbean results in a great deal of seismic (earthquake) and volcanic activity distributed in distinct linear belts. Earthquakes occur because the energy of frictional stress between sections of crustal rock being forced past each other is periodically released by a sudden slip, causing a violent shaking of the Earth's crust. The 'stick-slip' points may be at shallow (<100 km),

world. At Chiloé island, for example, almost 40 per cent of the weather is classified as stormy and may average little more than 50–60 days each year with sunshine. The regional snowline descends rapidly southwards until it is at 700 m in Tierra del Fuego; in Patagonia the Andes are able to support two large ice caps and in places glaciers terminate in the Pacific Ocean. Precipitation reaches 5000 mm, summer temperatures average little more than about 8.3°C and winter months 3.8°C, and there are few hours of sunshine and few hours when wind is not blowing. Drier lee-side sites, such as Punta Arenas, may have only 490 mm rainfall, however.

The climatic types described above indicate the variety that exists in Latin America and the Caribbean. These are extremely generalized and simplified, however, and it should be emphasized that a much greater range of climates actually exists and at various scales; this is particularly significant when attempting to understand soils, natural vegetation and especially land use.

CMC

Coastal desert, Peru. Most of the coastal area of Peru and about one third of that of Chile is occupied by desert, with settlement concentrating in valley oases.

intermediate (100–300 km) or deep (300–700 km) levels (focal points) within the crust. Latin America and the Caribbean count for approximately 17 per cent of the world's total seismicity. In Central America the Cocos plate and the overriding Caribbean plate are broken to eight discrete segments 100–200 km long. Transverse breaks in the crust separate segments of overriding lithosphere that have greatly differing volcanoes, topography, structure and geologic history. Structural depressions infilled with volcanic and alluvial sediments typically mark the transverse breaks in the volcanic axis. Dense rural settlement, urban development and many large cities have developed in such apparently prime localities which unfortunately lie exactly above the zones of most active crustal slippage and the generation of what are termed 'large shallow' earthquakes. The cities of San José (Costa Rica), Managua (Nicaragua), Santa Ana and Ahuachapan (El Salvador) and Guatemala City and Quezaltenango (Guatemala) are located near the intersections of transverse and longitudinal depressions, the loci of moderate-size shallow earthquakes; such earthquakes have repeatedly destroyed Guatemala City (9 times) and San Salvador (14 times) as well as razing most of Managua to the ground in 1972.

In South America the subducting Pacific plates are also broken by transverse shear zones into discrete segments which behave differentially in space and time. At present the most tectonically active segments are indicated by the coincidence of higher seismicity and active volcanicity, although no part of the Pacific coast can be deemed entirely free from earthquakes. In the northern Andes (Colombia and Ecuador) most earthquakes occur in a belt along the Pacific coast from the Panama–Colombia border to the mouth of the Guayas River, but others may occur inland where prominent shear faults (e.g. the Bocono fault) and graben occur. That which took place on 12 December 1979 at Tumaco in south-west Colombia (magnitude 8) was the largest in South America since 1942; it had been forecast that one would occur to fill the seismic gap detected for that plate segment. In the central Andes (Peru and Bolivia) major seismicity is concentrated along the coast of southern Peru, destructive shallow-intermediate tremors frequently occurring in Arequipa province. More northerly parts of Peru also suffer periodically as in 1970 and 1974 when the Chimbote and Lima areas were respectively shaken. In the southern Andes north of Antofagasta intermittent but extremely large earthquakes at intermediate depths (120 and 220 km) offshore produce destructive tidal waves (*tsunami*) and in central Chile activity along the Coast Range fault is the cause of infrequent but very destructive earthquakes. Southern Chile is another region where large earthquakes offshore severely shake the landward area and produce devastating tidal waves.

Earthquakes have three main damaging effects; they cause buildings to collapse, killing people inside or in the streets; they generate rock-falls and landslides in mountainous areas, causing considerable destruction and death on roads and in settlements; and at the coast the displacement of the sea bed offshore creates tidal waves which devastate low-lying coastal areas.

Volcanic disasters are relatively infrequent in Latin America and the Caribbean despite the number of active volcanoes. There are six well-defined zones of present volcanicity, Lesser Antilles, Mexican volcanic axis, Guatemala–Costa Rica, southern Colombia–Ecuador, southern Peru–northern Chile and south Central Chile. Most activity is characteristically explosive because of the chemical make-up of

In September 1985 a major earthquake struck Mexico City, causing large-scale destruction and around 20,000 fatalities.

VOLCANOES AND SEISMICITY

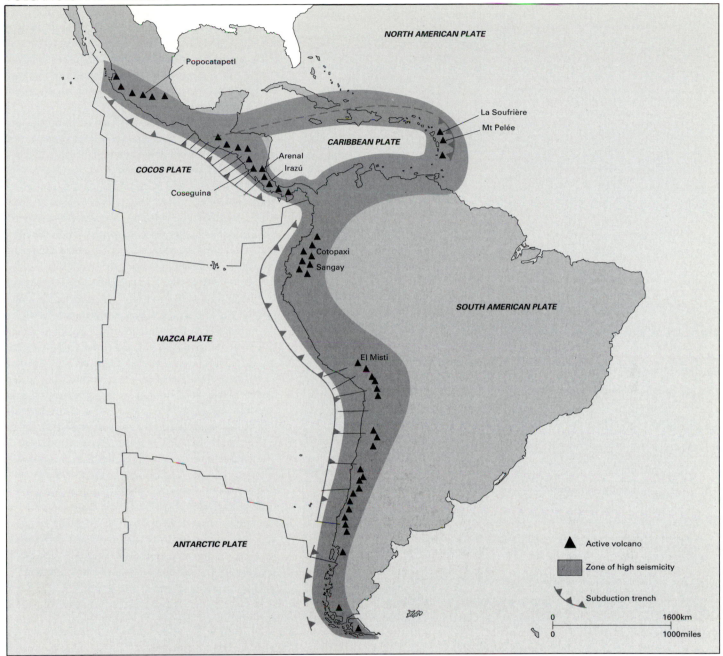

the molten rock (magma). Generally known as Andesitic (intermediate) and Rhyolitic (acidic), magma generated in these regions normally contains much silica (more than 50 per cent) which, together with other compounds, makes the magma viscous, slow moving and relatively cool (750–850°C) at the surface. Because of this, magmatic volatiles escape out of solution only with great difficulty and gas bubbles develop extremely high confining pressures as the magma approaches the surface. Thus, when the magma erupts, pent-up gases escape explosively, pulverizing lava into incandescent fragments (tephra) and throwing out masses of large blocks and

dense glowing clouds of magmatic froth. The most devastating eruptions in Latin America and the Caribbean have involved activity of this nature. For example, in 1835 Cosegüina on the Gulf of Fonseca in north-west Nicaragua erupted with explosions that were heard as far away as Kingston, Jamaica, and Bogotá, Colombia. The exploded debris partially buried villages and farmland in the surrounding area over a radius of 160 km.

A great loss of life resulted from powerful eruptions of three volcanoes during 1902 when a total of approximately 37,500 people were killed. In that year the volcano Mont Pelée on Martinique (Lesser

Poas volcano, Costa Rica, with smoke billowing. Much of Mexico, the Caribbean and western South America is an earthquake zone, with numerous active volcanoes.

discharged so much tephra that the nation's coffee crop and economy were seriously affected. Six volcanoes in Nicaragua are currently in various states of activity: Concepción, Santiago, Momotombo, Las Pilas, Cerro Negro and Telica; ranging from vigorous emissions of gas to explosive discharges of ash with minor lava flows, the activity is seldom destructive and is more an inconvenience.

In South America the majority of volcanoes that have erupted in historical times are too remote from densely settled areas to have caused major calamities. However, eruptions of Cotopaxi (Ecuador) in 1877 and Nevado del Ruiz (Colombia) in 1985 melted ice and snow which mixed with tephra to produce large mud flows that descended rapidly downslope to overwhelm considerable areas of settled and cultivated land. Probably one of the potentially most dangerous volcanoes in the whole of South America is El Misti in southern Peru which has not had a major eruption in historical recollection but which appears to be a young volcano in a state of temporary dormancy. Rising above the large and beautiful city of Arequipa, the volcano could cause an appalling loss of life and property if it were to erupt explosively.

A much milder form of eruption has been typical of the Mexican volcanic axis. Eruptions at Jorullo between 1759 and 1774 and at Paricutín between 1943 and 1952 produced new volcanoes that developed and became extinct after fifteen and nine years duration respectively. The products built up cinder cones 380 m and 410 m high respectively and thick (245 m) lava flows which buried farmland and, in the case of Paricutín, the villages of Paricutín and San Juan de Parangaricutiro. Such activity does not have the sudden devastating explosiveness of the more acidic volcanoes and no lives are normally lost, but El Chichon exploded in 1981 and killed 2000 people.

METEOROLOGICAL DISASTERS

Because Central America and the Caribbean are located at the poleward margin of the tropics, they are vulnerable to atmospheric disturbances originating in both low and middle latitudes and invasions of frost-producing polar air from higher latitudes. Prolonged droughts occur in central Mexico, flood-producing excesses of rainfall periodically occur throughout Central America and the Caribbean and summer hailstorms damage crops in the highlands of Mexico and Guatemala. Much more destructive, however, are the tropical hurricanes and mid-latitude cyclonic storms. Caribbean hurricanes develop between July and October, when there may be five to twelve affecting areas shown on the map, p. 19. Originating over warm waters of the Atlantic, Caribbean

Antilles) burst open and discharged a dense emulsion of incandescent lava droplets and hot gases which raced downslope and over the town and harbour of St Pierre, instantly suffocating 30,000 inhabitants. Twenty-four hours later La Soufrière volcano on the neighbouring island of St Vincent, 150 km distant, erupted in a similar fashion killing over 1500 people. During the same year an eruption of Santa Maria (Santiaguito) volcano in Guatemala took 6000 lives. Elsewhere in Central America only two other volcanoes have been a major problem in recent decades. In Costa Rica, Arenal exploded exceptionally violently in 1968 after prolonged quiescence and threw bombs on to a nearby village, killing 64 people; and from 1963 to 1965 Irazú volcano just south-east of San José

and Gulf of Mexico, hurricanes (c. 150 km across) move slowly westward or north-westward and eventually re-curve to the north and north-east to be dissipated in mid-latitudes. High winds cause enormous destruction of life and property, both directly and through the creation of large tidal waves along coasts, while torrential downpours frequently flood large areas of land. Pacific hurricanes are much less dangerous but cause destruction along the west coast of Mexico, as in November 1961. Mid-latitude cyclonic disturbances commonly develop between November and March when incursions of northern polar air into the tropics are common. Along the polar front heavy rain storms are followed by cold northerly winds and accompanying destructive frosts. They affect the Gulf coast of Mexico and the Caribbean coast of Guatemala and Honduras where extensive sections of banana plantations may be destroyed.

South America is much less susceptible to extreme meteorological events than other continents, suffering less from drought and floods than Africa and India, but problems occur at local and regional scales, for example mid-latitude polar fronts bring cold frost-producing air to affect parts of Brazil and Paraguay, where much of the coffee crop can be lost, as in July 1981. The Brazilian north-east has suffered recurrent severe droughts over the past century, prompting mass migration to the coast and southern Brazil. Such a drought struck in 1977 and was still holding in early 1984. The year 1963 can be taken here to illustrate climatic disasters which may occur in any one year in South America. During the winter months, May–October, serious droughts affected southern Brazil, Paraguay and northern Argentina; crop yields were greatly reduced and there were water shortages and power cuts in Rio and São Paulo. Dry conditions allowed fires to spread and in Paraná state, Brazil, around 30,000 people were made homeless. Exceptionally severe frosts afflicted the same general region and some 650 million coffee trees were destroyed. Frosts destroyed up to half the vine harvest in central Chile, storms and heavy rain caused damage farther south; floods in south coastal Peru affected several towns, droughts impaired rice crops farther north while exceptionally heavy rains caused problems in the Andes. The Caribbean area was swept by hurricane Flora which caused the loss of several thousand lives and the destruction of tens of thousands of homes (mostly in Haiti), the destruction of half of the cocoa crop in Tobago and most of the bananas in several of the smaller British islands. In 1982–3, the periodic El Niño climatic phenomenon of the central Pacific caused floods and landslides in coastal Ecuador and northern Peru, killing 600; it also produced severe droughts in Central America and Mexico.

GEOMORPHOLOGICAL DISASTERS

Much destruction can result from large-scale falls of rock and ice and from the slumping or flowing of large masses of soil and rock; both phenomena may be triggered off by earthquakes and torrential rains. Because such disasters involve the downslope mass displacement of debris, they occur mainly in areas of steep slopes and high relief such as the Andes and some highland areas of the Guiana and Brazilian shields. As precipitous rock faces in the Andes experience stress release, rock expansion may periodically cause the loosening of very large slabs which crash destructively into the valleys below. Should these be accompanied by overlying ice and snow then highly mobile debris avalanches develop, covering long distances very rapidly and devastating everything in the way. The Cordillera Blanca in Peru is notorious for such events; one in 1941 ripped through part of the town of Huaras, killing over 4000 people; one in 1962 obliterated small settlements and part of Ranrahirca village, killing 3500 people; and that triggered by the 1970 earthquake took 5000 lives in the same area. Another process leading to large-scale slumping and/or flowage involves the presence of steep unstable slopes and the build-up of high pore-water pressure in unconsolidated overburden and along less permeable beds in underlying strata. Destructive mud flows can result from prolonged torrential rainfall as around Rio and other regions of steep relief in Brazil and in many parts of the Andes. The sudden downslope discharge of large volumes of mud and/or wholesale rotational slumping of large sections of mountainside can devastate wide areas of terrain, taking many lives. Scars left by two gigantic prehistoric landslides are present at the edge of the Altiplano in southern Peru (at Chuquibamba north of Arequipa) and in Bolivia (at the southern outskirts of La Paz); these cover thousands of square kilometres and may have occurred during a period of late Quaternary climatic change when more rain fell in these regions. Should an event of such magnitude take place in a settled area today, thousands of lives would be lost.

CMC

Further Reading: T. Y. Canby, 'El Niño's Ill Wind', *National Geographic*, Feb. 1984, pp. 144–83; C. M. Clapperton, 'The Glaciation of the Andes', *Quaternary Science Reviews*, 2 (1983), 83–155; J. P. Cole, *Latin America* (London, 1970); P. James, *Latin America* (New York, 1969); R. C. West and J. P. Augelli, *Middle America* (New York, 1966)

Jaguar (Panthera onca) on a tree branch. This big cat, native to the Americas, is found in woodlands and savannahs from the southern USA to Aregentina.

Flora and fauna

Central and South America, tropical Mexico and the Caribbean islands constitute the Neotropical realm, one of the major zoo-geographical regions of the world. Within these limits and touching adjacent areas including the southern United States, particularly Texas and Florida, the animal and plant life is rich in species. Many of the families are unique to the New World, and of these a large proportion are exclusively South American. The diversity stems from the wide range of habitats in a land of rivers, tropical forest, mountains and grasslands coupled with the unique geological history of the isolation of the subcontinent.

THE EFFECTS OF CONTINENTAL ISOLATION

About 200 million years ago the enormous continent of Pangea began to divide into two super-continents of which the southern part, Gondwanaland, was made up of South America, Africa, India, Antarctica and Australia. Then, about 130 million years ago, South America began to move away from Gondwanaland and its marsupials and extraordinary early mammals evolved in total isolation. North America, on the other hand, remained part of the northern continent, Laurasia, for perhaps as long as another 50 million years. Resulting from this prolonged connection, the northern hemisphere mammals, including monkeys, some rodents and the large carnivorous cat predators, evolved separately and only reached South America when the land masses were linked.

The isolation of South America and its subsequent re-connection to North America produced some remarkable animal types. Some orders of mammals are exclusively South American: three of these are now extinct, including the Litopterna or hoofed herbivores, some of which resembled horses or camels. The other order, the opossum rats, includes survivors such as the little-studied rat-sized marsupials of the dense Andean forests and southern Chile. While Neotropica offers a large variety of obscurely evolved curiosities, many of the mammals are among the most unusual in the zoological world, none more so than the Edentates, an order including armadillos, sloths and anteaters. These peculiar animals form part of the relic fauna of South America which, as the fossil record reveals, included ancestors on a much grander scale than modern types. A glyptodont of a million years ago was a massively armoured armadillo-like beast; some possessed heavy club-like tails, and their remains are commonly found in the southern part of South America, particularly in the recent sedimentary deposits of the pampas and Patagonia; their beautifully patterned carapaces have survived well. Likewise, in the same places, the remains of bear-sized ground sloths are not uncommon. One of these sloths, the *Megatherium*, was massively built and reached a length of 6 m. *Megatheria* were browsers, standing on their hind feet to reach branches and leaves of the trees that once clothed this now desolate place.

By contrast, modern sloths are much smaller, and renowned for their agonizingly slow movements. They usually live in the forest upper level or canopy, seldom venturing to the ground. When they do, they manage a slow crawl, of little more than 1 km per hour. As they are well camouflaged and their coarse grey hair is often tinged green with microscopic algae, sloths are relatively safe from predators.

Armadillos, on the other hand, are ground dwellers, but are good burrowers, digging into even hard earth in a rapidly accomplished defence that complements the hardened bony scutes of their shell. The third Edentate family, the anteaters, comprises both arbooreal and ground-living forms. A typical, though hard-to-find rainforest inhabitant is the 25-cm-long pygmy or silky anteater with a strongly prehensile and gripping tail which it can use as a fifth limb. This rare animal is almost defenceless and seeks safety in the higher levels of trees. Inhabiting the open plains and forest edges, a giant anteater up to 5 m long is armed with powerful claws on its forelimbs which it uses for ripping open termite nests. Less spectacular, medium-sized and equally at home on the ground or in the trees, is the *Tamandua* anteater, also equipped with a nearly hairless prehensile tail.

Many Neotropical mammals have evolved with similar prehensile tails, a clear indication of their long arboreal ancestry. Some New World monkeys have tails with a powerful, almost hand-like grasping ability, while spider monkeys have tails equipped with highly developed special pads resembling a soft palm. Among the other groups of mammals, one rodent, the prehensile-tailed porcupine, is a good climber; so too is the kinkajou, one of the two living carnivores with a prehensile tail.

*Nine-banded armadillo (*Dasypus novemcincus*). There are about twenty species of armadillo, all noted for their snouts and bony-plated shells.*

Of all South American mammals, the Edentates are probably the best known of those that evolved during the isolation of the subcontinent and began to spread northward as the isthmus and Central America formed. Sloths now occur as far north as Costa Rica and Honduras; anteaters, the pygmy species especially, as far north as Mexico and the nine-banded armadillo to the south United States including Texas and Oklahoma.

Also of the ancient fauna, the marsupials, including opossums, flourished during the isolation of South America and many different forms evolved. Some, like the common opossum (*Didelphis*), have survived, and this species has reached far into North America with a none too specific habitat. The meat-eating marsupials, many of them hyaena- or wolf-like, with short legs and large skulls – at least one had large stabbing canine teeth – were the only carnivorous mammals in ancient South America and are now extinct. Others, like the tiny mouse opossums, are some of the least conspicuous members of the Didelphidae and different species inhabit forests, arid places and even houses.

MIGRATIONS FROM NORTH AMERICA

When the land connection was formed with North America, the movement southward was suddenly far stronger with bats, deer, tapirs and particularly predators, including bears, otters, dogs and cats, moving into every part of the diverse southern land which was already well stocked. The incoming predators met the established marsupial carnivores, and being more successful in evolutionary terms they have occupied their place in the ecology.

Among the most successful of the newcomers were the Cricetid rodents: the hamster family, and rats and mice of the Old World. Once these mammals found their way into the rich and complex habitats of South America, a remarkable evolutionary explosion occurred, which is probably unparalleled in any other part of the world. Now, at least fifty genera can be identified with countless species and subspecies of Cricetids occupying many habitats from the swamp lands bordering the Amazon to high, cold and arid plateaux in the Andes; some even occur in the barren south as far distant as the Straits of Magellan. Not all are hamster- or rat-like. The forests are well populated with Cricetid climbers, endowed with specially adapted paws. And there are many marsh dwellers with webbed feet or jumpers that have well-developed kangaroo-like thighs. All these, and there are many more, highlight the evolution of species to fill many ecological niches or an adaptive capacity which has reached record proportions.

More than 3500 species of birds have been recorded and described in the Neotropical region and that amounts to more than two-fifths of all the known bird species of the world. South America alone has over 2900 species, making it outstanding as the 'bird continent'. The reason is perhaps two-fold. An influx of tropical northern families, including barbets, thrushes, motmots and wrens added to those already enjoying the existing variety of habitats. Then a factor that strongly influenced speciation was a changing climate brought by the ice ages, creating near-arctic conditions in the north and severely cooling the southern part of the globe.

Particularly in the warm and humid Amazon region, where rich forests were flourishing much as they had done for millions of years, the cooling induced clear ecological change. As the rainfall was reduced, the forests shrank to patches restricted within a grassland vegetation something akin to savanna. The effect of this change is most noticeable among birds and some butterflies, and recently these have drawn the attention of researchers. Within these so-called Pleistocene refuges, many species evolved in isolation, each becoming significantly different from species of the same genus in another refuge. When the ice retreated and the humid conditions returned, the forests spread once again, and when the populations mixed again interbreeding was impossible. The result is obvious in an abundance of species. Now the Neotropical forests are virtually unbroken from southern Mexico to northern Argentina.

Many species of birds followed the spreading forest, though in a few areas where the original isolation has been maintained, some original refuge species are strongly represented. On some isolated mountains of Venezuela, Colombia and Brazil, species occur many hundreds of kilometres from the mainstream of their distribution in the Andes, as they were cut off when the climate changed, leaving wide expanses of savanna. (Pleistocene refuges are becoming increasingly important for researchers and conservationists, and Brazil has selected some of these unusual areas as national parks or forestry reserves.)

THE NEOTROPICAL REGION

Tropical rainforest

Neotropical habitats are immensely varied, ranging from dry tropical forests of Mexico southward to the ice-bound mountains of Tierra del Fuego, or mangrove-fringed Atlantic shores of Brazil to the desert coast of Peru. Between these limits are the many specialized habitats of the largest tropical rainforest on the planet. The Amazonian and Guyanan forests contain the most diverse ecological communities with the largest collection of plant and animal species on the planet. Altogether about 900 tons of living plants per acre have developed in these regions as the result of constant high temperature and rainfall. Though by no means uniform in character for the vast area of the Amazon region, the rainforests tend to have certain well-defined characteristics. The number of species of trees is immense: as many as 117 in a square kilometre; most frequently encountered are Brazil nuts, rubber trees (*Hevea*), species of myrtles, laurela, acacias, bignonias and palms. Strongly characteristic too of many of these are odd flange-like structures or buttresses which perhaps may have a supportive function, though such an assumption is by no means certain. Some palms though, including *Iriartea*, have numerous stilt roots while other trees have multiple smaller buttresses.

Of the ancient flora the only survivors are a few gymnosperms, like the rare podocarpus found in some higher montane forests, or the climbing *Gnetum*. Otherwise the tropical forests abound with the more recent angiosperms that evolved in the same period as the insects. Often the pollination of these plants is closely tied to insect visitors.

With all-year-round near unchanging conditions, the tropical rainforest offers unparalleled evolutionary possibilities. Plants in the tropics do not flower in regular seasons, and so there is a constant supply of nectar, fruits, young shoots and other foods to be exploited by animals of every form. The temperature is ideal for cold-blooded animals (those unable to regulate their body temperature). Insects are especially abundant and have become the food supply for many birds. Some of these, like the ant-birds, or certain

Buttress roots of the Ojé strangler – Ficus Antihelminica – in the Amazon rainforest

Giant spider (fam. Theraphosidae). Such 'bird eaters' are part of the characteristic fauna of the floor of the rainforest.

woodcreepers, follow the hordes of army ants, carnivorous ants moving slowly through the forest. These ants, descended from wasps, feed largely on other arthropods such as crickets and spiders.

The presence of large numbers of birds and insects increases the possibilities of cross pollination, and insects naturally help to recycle the forest debris. Thus the rainforest can be reckoned as a powerhouse of life where the number of species seems boundless. Adding to the already diverse habitats within such a forest are the various levels, perhaps as many as five between the ground, where decomposition is rapid, and the canopy exposed to the sky where sunlight induces rich growth and where photosynthesis occurs. In this carbon cycle oxygen is produced, to be used again by the same plants.

Between the two extremes are lower, shade-loving trees including the palms, mauritia and euterpe, and below them at the next level are many herbacious plants. Calliandras, heliconias and hirtellas are typical of the Amazon region. Growing in the crowns of the tallest trees are stranglers such as *Ficus* or *Clusia* species, their seeds deposited there by birds. As a seed develops, the young plant sends out aerial roots to descend (by geotropism) to the ground. (Once the root has a firm hold, the plant grows rapidly in the crown and its bulky roots may ultimately envelop and 'strangle' the tree.) Sometimes the strangler fills the entire crown and the host eventually dies. Lianas, on the other hand, are more like weak-stemmed trees: they find a hold on the rainforest trees, and, by a variety of biological means, hoist themselves to the sunlight. Some have sharp, recurved spines and the plant can jack its way up the tree. A few of these plants have stems as bulky as a man's thigh, others

are flattened and ribbed, and, like stranglers, their flowers and seeds usually form high in the canopy, out of normal sight.

Animal life has a foothold at every level, even subterraneously. An ever growing wealth of plant material supports countless millions of insects. Butterflies may be eyecatching, but the less gaudy sauba or leaf-cutting ants can defoliate a tree, taking all the leaves, bit by bit, to an underground nest that may occupy many cubic metres. Nothing escapes their ravages, so even flowers are cut into tiny pieces to be turned into a mulch in which the ants grow a fungus to be eaten by both young and mature ants. Similarly, ants in the grasslands cut grass and build underground gardens, the only visible sign on the surface being a small entrance.

The floor of a tropical forest is an arthropod world, with termites, scorpions, spiders, isopods, millipedes, centipedes – some almost 25 cm long – sheltering beneath decomposing wood. There is a clear trend towards gigantism, and some spiders, notably the Theraphosidae or 'bird eaters', can reach a span of 25 cm, with a body over 9 cm long. Beetles such as *Dynastes* can be the size of a child's clenched fist and butterflies, like the spectacular blue morphos with a span of 15 cm, flash brilliantly and can be seen from more than a kilometre away. Sometimes for no obvious reason hundreds of thousands of butterflies gather in moist places on river banks or occasionally migrations of what must be millions of a single species take days to pass one point. The American naturalist William Beebe reported such migrations during his work in the Guianas early this century.

How many species?

No area on earth has a more spectacular diversity of plant and animals than tropical Latin America. Half our estimated five million species are found here, and the continuous growing season and immense range of available habitats, particularly within the rainforest, generate plant and insect species so fast that a new species of orchid can evolve in as little as fifteen years.

Ecuador, not much larger than Britain but encompassing extreme ecological variation between coastal plain, Andes and Amazonia, illustrates speciation at its most profuse. It is reckoned to have 20–25,000 plant species (five times more than, say, California), of which 4–5,000 are not found elsewhere. Some 3,000 species of orchid alone are known, compared with fifty in Britain and 153 in the whole of North America. There are in addition 1550 species of birds (17 per cent of the world total), 280 species of mammals, 345 of reptiles, and 358 of amphibians.

Frogs and toads are well represented by many species, the tree frogs being particularly well adapted to the forest. Other frogs live among the debris on the forest floor, or within the natural reservoirs of rain water captured in the tight leaf rosettes of certain bromeliads. Other amphibians, the curious caecilians, have a burrowing habit and are rarely seen. Similarly snakes and other reptiles are not immediately obvious, though there is an abundance of species. Some, like the vine snakes (*Oxybelis*), are bootlace thin and beautifully adapted to a life among spindly climbing plants. At the other extreme, the largest water boas or anacondas may attain a girth of a man's body or more, and live in swampy places. Other snakes, particularly the brightly coloured coral snakes and the false corals, are adapted to life underground, with their flattened heads and small eyes.

Fresh water life

South American rivers and lakes are richly endowed with fish, and as many as 2000 species occupy niches in the immense Amazon, itself with one-fifth of the world's fresh water. Others have adapted to survival in places baked dry by intense sun (for example, killifish in the Chaco). Catfish species are numerous and often taken as an important food source: the larger specimens attain gargantuan proportions. One species of the Amazon and Orinoco can weigh as much as 180 kg, so a fully grown specimen needs two men to carry it. These monsters, living on the river bed, have the reputation of attacking swimmers, though perhaps they are doing no more than scavenging. At the other extreme, a tiny 5-cm-long near transparent catfish, the candirú, is a danger as it may enter the urethra, its backward-facing spines preventing simple removal. Many of the catfish are heavily and grotesquely armoured, others are beautifully coloured with leopard-like spots or a variety of dark bands. The reputation of the piranha as a man-eating fish is exaggerated, though, as a carnivore, it is always potentially dangerous.

The important food fish, the pirarucú (arapaima or paiche are other names), is a relative of salmon and trout, measuring 3 m in length. This superb fish provides such high-quality meat that its numbers are declining everywhere and it has disappeared totally from some places. It is easily caught (by harpoon) as it comes to the surface to gulp air. But the trade in pirarucú simply underlines the importance of the tropical rivers as a resource, and as more access roads open, refrigerated or ice-packed trucks are hauling tons of fish to urban centres. Particularly rich fishing times are during the seasons of low water; at these times some tributaries of the Amazon are so densely packed with fish (charachoids) that local fishermen can scoop them with pails and plastic bowls. Man is not the only predator: the giant catfish follow the mass upriver.

The life of the lakes, rivers and estuaries is everywhere diverse and extraordinary. Numerous species of freshwater turtle were abundant a hundred years ago, but their numbers have declined as they are much used as a food; there are now plans to farm some of the larger types. Reptiles related to crocodiles – in South America the caimans and a variety of curious and seldom seen denizens, among them manatees or sea cows – are relatively common, though hunting has reduced both numbers and their size. River dolphins occur far upriver, even at the foot of the Andes over 3000 km from the Amazon mouth; another species exists in the Plate system.

Non-forest species

The same pattern of variety and high proportion of endemic families is repeated throughout Neotropica. Both the number of species and individuals is limited by geographical and climatic conditions. Along the Andes, in the cooler heights of the mountains or in the far south, there are fewer species; for example, at the equator as many as 163 hummingbird species have been listed, though in Tierra del Fuego only one, the Green-backed Firecrown, is resident. With such limiting factors, the vegetation changes too, with species of plant families becoming dwarfed and assuming a compact alpine form. One outstanding exception to the rule is the bromeliad, *Puya raimondii*, with its flower spike reaching to 6 m. This is the world's largest flower spike, and bears many thousands of individual flowers. Growing in the barren plateaux, the *Puya raimondii* is a micro habitat occupied by many species of birds and insects. This plant is a native of only a few places in the central Andes and may be a relic of the ice-age flora that has survived as it is well adapted to the semi-arid environment of the cordilleras.

Among the other arid lands, pure deserts are numerous in Neotropica. None are large but some, like the Atacama of northern Chile (and parts of Bolivia and Argentina), are exceptionally dry. Plants have adapted and among the numerous cacti there are a few remarkable species. One from the Atacama grows beneath the surface and gets enough light through the opalescent sand for its photosynthesis. Occasionally the desert is itself modified by local conditions: on the west coast, within sight of the Pacific, condensing fog can induce rich plant growth in certain places. These *lomas* are tiny oases of fertility and attract many species of birds and insects not commonly occurring in the desert. Man, too, is there, using the *lomas* for small patches of farmland, growing corn or grazing cattle.

Geography

The importance of the physical environment to the people who live in it hardly needs to be underlined. It limits the range of feasible activities which may be altered and reassessed by changing technologies and capital investment. Resources and their possibilities are continually reappraised in the light of technological, social and economic change, as becomes abundantly apparent where there have been repeated adjustments over a long history going back far beyond the impact of Europeans on the Americas, as in parts of Mexico and the central Andes. Colonial empires which once gave direction to geographical change – in the nature and distribution of economic activities and population – were replaced in the nineteenth century by export economies. In the twentieth century, however, urbanization and industrialization have tended to shift the growth points of spatial organization to the urban-dominated regions which are, in Latin America, most frequently, though not always, the capital cities of old colonial administrations and their republican successors. This is partially a geographical consequence of the shift from outward-directed development, characteristic of the nineteenth and early twentieth centuries, to inward-directed development of more recent decades.

It is often possible, within the Latin American countries, to see at least three categories of region in this sense: advancing areas of urban and industrial growth with a good network of communications, an agriculture vitalized by urban markets, and above-average levels of literacy, welfare and income. South-east Brazil, the Puebla–Mexico City–Guadalajara axis in Mexico, the Buenos Aires–Córdoba axis in Argentina and Greater Lima and the coastal region of Peru are examples of this kind of area. Secondly, there are relatively stagnant or depressed areas, often quite densely populated but remote from the advancing areas, which may have experienced a former prosperity or levels of development adjusted to a local rather than a national economy, which have been bypassed by growth elsewhere: the south-central sierra of Peru, parts of southern Mexico, north-east Brazil are examples. Thirdly, there are the sparsely populated regions in which potential resources exist to be developed, exploited (and sometimes destroyed) but which offer hopes for expansion as yet unrealized. The interior lowlands of South America and the Brazilian west seem to offer such possibilities. But the form which such development is taking, in terms of its social and ecological consequences, is very often a matter of grave concern throughout the international community. Latin America still has vast areas for potential settlement.

The majestic Andean condor (Vultur gryphus) has the largest wing-span (up to three metres) of any bird currently living on the planet.

Of the major habitats, though, grasslands have a special economic importance, especially the pampas of Argentina or llanos of Colombia and Venezuela. These open seas of grass were once home to specialized mammals including armadillos and many rodents. The pampas have long been turned into ranch and farmland, so only pockets of the endemic flora and fauna survive. Within the other grasslands north of the Amazon and across the Orinoco drainage there is a fauna very much reflecting the closeness of the Amazon region. Gallery forests along the rivers contain many monkeys, parrots and toucans, many of which have circum-Amazon distribution. The rivers here once contained many turtles and caiman, but their numbers have declined sharply with the opening up of the region. On a broad front, almost all the way across South America, development plans clearly mean that great changes are occurring all the time. But so, too, are attitudes and new national parks and forestry reserves have been established in recent years.   TM

Further Reading: M. Bates, *The Land and Wildlife of South America* (New York, 1965); J. Dorst, *South America and Central America: a Natural History* (London and New York, 1967); R. J. A. Goodland and H. S. Irwin, *Amazon Jungle: Green Hell to Red Desert* (New York, 1975); T. Harper Goodspeed, *Plant Hunters in the Andes* (London, 1961)

PRINCIPAL PHYSICAL FEATURES

Metres
5000
3000
1000
500
200
Sea level

0   1600 km
0   1000 miles

THE ANDEAN REGION AND COASTAL MARGINS

Though not the oldest geological feature of the South American continent by any means, the Andes are the framework around which the geography of the continent is moulded. Relief is complex, reflecting a varied geological and geomorphological history, and general statements are difficult to make. Between Chile and Argentina there is a single, continuous range, rising to Aconcagua (the highest peak of South America), and presenting a difficult barrier for modern communications; in Bolivia and southern Peru, western and eastern branches diverge to enclose within them the high plateau generally known as the Altiplano and constituting the only substantial area of inland drainage in Latin America to Lake Titicaca at 3812 m above sea level and Lake Poopó in Bolivia. In Ecuador, well-defined western and eastern ranges of the Andes are separated by intermontane basins, but in northern and central Peru this clarity is absent, and although the western cordillera is massive and continuous, intermontane basins, fault-guided troughs and discontinuous high massifs follow no single orientation and make it difficult to identify a single eastern range. Structure and drainage define a simpler general pattern of relief in Colombia, however, with a clear division of western, central and eastern ranges, the latter continuing into northern Venezuela.

Towards the Pacific margins, fragments of ranges older geologically than the main Andean front – in northern and southern Peru and in northern and central Chile – give shape to the coastal zone and define the western limits of relatively low basins filled or partially filled with the debris of erosion from the main Andean chain, as, for example, in the neighbourhood of Ica in southern Peru, or on a grander scale in the Central Valley of Chile. But elsewhere the low-lying coastal fringes of the Pacific are largely composed of alluvial or fluvio-glacial materials derived from the erosion of the Andean chain.

Andean landforms

At a very general level, the characteristic landforms of the Andes fall into five groups. Glaciated landforms characterize the highest massifs in the tropical Andes, with features of Pleistocene glacial deposition reaching down to 3500 m in northern and central Peru (where modern glaciers are to be found at 5000 m). Modern snow levels and glaciers reach their maximum low-point in southern Bolivia and northern Chile, but south of this point glaciated features and modern glaciers are to be found at steadily lower levels to reach sea level itself in southern Chile. Volcanic landforms – active and recently extinct volcanoes,

calderas, associated lava flows and deposits of volcanic ash – are characteristic of northern Chile, Bolivia and southern Peru and reach classic proportions in Ecuador. These are the most dramatic manifestations of Andean landforms, but in the central Andean region as a whole, and particularly in Bolivia and southern and central Peru, one of the most universal features is the existence of high-level erosion surfaces (at c. 4500 m in southern Peru), occasionally warped and at times overlain by volcanic ash or lava. Complex erosion surfaces such as this, and others at lower levels, mark stages in the uplift and warping of the Andean region. Structural troughs and intermontane basins, partially filled with alluvial and lacustrine deposits and sometimes with deposits of volcanic ash, vary in size and altitude from the Altiplano to relatively small areas like those which are strung out between the east and west ranges of Ecuador, but their importance in the human geography of the central Andes is immense, for unlike the high-level erosion surfaces, they are below the upper limits of arable agriculture and are generally densely populated, supporting nuclei of rural settlement and major provincial towns or cities such as Quito, Cuenca, Huancayo or Ayacucho. In the humid areas of the Andean region, notably in Venezuela, Colombia, Ecuador, and in eastern Peru and eastern Bolivia, the landforms are those of tropical weathering and erosion, with intricately dissected steep slopes of bewildering complexity, rapid erosion and frequent landslips, tending to make communications much more difficult to build and maintain than in the arid Andes or where erosion surfaces and intermontane basins provide more uniform surfaces. Finally, there are the river valleys, often deeply and spectacularly incised into the surrounding landforms. The Upper Marañón or the Apurimac are excellent examples, again adding to the difficulties of communications across the Andean region, particularly where they lie parallel to the high ranges.

Settlement and cultivation

One most important consequence of these patterns of relief is the tendency for nuclei of population to be highly concentrated in the agriculturally productive valleys, intermontane basins and on alluvial or erosional benches at intermediate altitudes. Small, but densely populated zones tend, therefore, to be separated from each other by high-level surfaces, high ranges, or deep river troughs. There is a degree of local isolation and a need for self-reliance in basic food and raw materials which were certainly not broken down by the railway, and have not been totally broken down by modern road-building.

Secondly, given the enormous variety of local and regional climates within the Andean region as a whole, together with the implications this variety has for natural vegetation and for potential crop production, it is not surprising that one of the enduring features of the Andean region as a whole is its capacity for producing a wide variety of products from relatively small areas which offer complementary ecological riches. The territory of single communities, or single landowners, may commonly include land with an altitudinal range of 1500 m, and sometimes much more than this. Complementary production of irrigated maize, subtropical crops, temperate grains such as wheat or barley, rootcrops such as potatoes, and high-level pasture can take place within a few kilometres. Different plots of land within the same holding may sometimes cover this range, though more commonly traditional mechanisms of exchange between neighbouring communities secure a variety of products for consumption from very different ecological zones. In the Inca empire ethnic groups with their 'core' area at intermediate altitudes had 'colonies' at both higher levels (to produce salt, animal products, high-level arable crops and especially potatoes) and at lower levels (for coca, maize, manioc and forest products). High-level groups around Lake Titicaca (the Lupaca, for example) had 'colonies' at lower levels both in the Bolivian *yungas* and on the Pacific slope of southern Peru.

Viewed on a larger scale, it is evident that different ecological zones within the Andes have been given different social and economic values at different times and in different areas. In pre-Colombian times the sub-humid intermontane basins at intermediate altitudes from Venezuela through Colombia to Peru and north-west Argentina, together with the arid, but irrigable coastal zone of Peru, supported intensive irrigated and terrace agriculture focused on the cultivation of maize, chief among a whole repertoire of indigenous crops adapted to various ecological levels. Dense agricultural populations in the Andean region were associated with the most developed of the South American cultures, including of course that of the Inca empire. It is indeed within the heart of that empire, in the sierra regions of Ecuador, Peru and Bolivia, that ethnic Indians still form a majority of the population. The Spanish colonial empire, relying as it largely did on Indian labour, did relatively little to change the pre-existing general distribution of population except in a few areas where African slave labour was used in plantation agriculture. But the expanding commercial world of the nineteenth century ultimately saw a significant reassessment of ecological zones with the downward shift in Colombia, Venezuela and Ecuador for the cultivation of coffee and cacao. From the 1940s the movement down from the mountains accelerated with the conquest of malaria. In Venezuela the Andean region of the

north-west is the poorest and most depressed region of the country and a region of out-migration. In Ecuador, the balance of population is steadily shifting towards the coastal zone in spite of the capital's location in the sierra. In Peru the sierra as a whole is a region of out-migration both to the coast and, to a much lesser extent, to the eastern regions. And in Bolivia, too, growth of population has been much less rapid on the Altiplano than in the eastern regions, even though, as in Ecuador, the capital city is on the edge of the Altiplano itself.

In part, this trend reflects the fact that in some areas Indian peasant-farming communities have pressed traditional methods of cultivation to and even beyond their limits in order to sustain the increasing rural population over the last generation. Farms are fragmented, pastures overgrazed and cultivated land pushed to apparently impossible slopes. Soil exhaustion and soil erosion are all too evident.

In the Andean region the major motif is of high contrast between adjacent micro-regions. On the coastal margin, the pattern is simpler, reflecting in the main the regional contrasts of climate. In Chile the gradation is from a wet, cool climate and broad-leaved evergreen and deciduous beech forests of the south, through the cool temperate, almost West European conditions of south-central Chile to the favoured 'Mediterranean' climate of the Central Valley, grading northwards into semi-aridity and then to the arid coastal zone of the Atacama and of Peru. In northern Peru and southern Ecuador there is, however, a sharp transition to hot and humid equatorial climate supporting rainforest under natural conditions, reaching its maximum development in the Pacific coastlands of western Colombia, which is the wettest area in the Americas, receiving up to 7000 mm a year. The Caribbean margin of the Andean region, however, is one of sharp contrast between hot and humid climates supporting tropical forest in north-west Colombia and the surprisingly dry climates of the Guajira peninsula and parts of northern Venezuela, including the Coro peninsula and the region to the south of it.

Regional development

Patterns of regional development imposed upon the complex mosaic of contrasting ecologies in the Andean region and its margins have increasingly depended both on the exploitation of resources and on the leadership of rapidly expanding metropolitan cities, and regional capitals – seats of government and bureaucracy, preferred locations for industrial development, especially of import substitution industries, and magnets for the concentration of purchasing power and of population. In Peru, regional patterns of growth have focused essentially on Greater Lima, the coastal zone and the hinterland of Lima in the central sierra of Peru. The geographical basis of the relative progress of the coastal zone rests on its irrigated agriculture and the exploitation of mineral and marine resources. Irrigation is made possible, in this naturally arid region, by the Pacific-flowing streams draining from the relatively well-watered Andes of central and northern Peru. Commercial agriculture has been facilitated since the sixteenth century by the ease of accessibility to coastal ports, and from the 1940s by the Pan-American Highway. It is a region dominated formerly by highly productive farming for export, particularly of sugar and cotton, and although these are still important exports, coastal agriculture is increasingly oriented to production for domestic urban markets, particularly that of Lima itself. Wine and brandy are specialities of long-standing in the Ica area, but production of fruit, vegetables, staff-fed dairy cattle, maize and potatoes is of increasing significance. Coastal ports, notably Callao and Chimbote, have generated industrial activity from the fishing industry, booming from the 1950s, but declining in the 1970s and 1980s as a result of overfishing of the *anchoveta*, the raw material for exports of fishmeal to Western Europe and North America. The coast has benefited, too, from the exploitation of mineral resources on the Pacific slopes – oil in the far north-west, iron ore and low-grade copper ores to the south of Lima, near Arequipa and Matarani. Development of phosphates in the north at Bayovar is seen as the basis for further industrial growth. The hinterland of Lima in the Central Sierra is also the area in which much of Peru's copper, lead, zinc and silver have been exploited since the nineteenth century, and is well connected to Lima by road and rail. But the Lima market, and local mining activities have also encouraged the commercialization of agriculture in the

Central Sierra for dairying, grains, potatoes and vegetables. Secondary urban centres have grown rapidly in recent years, and both Arequipa and Trujillo are important industrial centres, partly as a result of encouragement by government, but it is Greater Lima which has come to dominate Peruvian economic and social geography, with a population currently estimated at 5.5 million or about a quarter of Peru's total population, and over half of Peru's industrial activity.

Whereas the Spanish conquistadors rejected both Cuzco, heart of the Inca empire, and Jauja, briefly considered, in favour of Lima as a capital nearer to the coast and the life-line to Spain, Quito, in what was to become Ecuador, was retained from Inca times as capital for colonial government in spite of its distance from the coast. This fact has been of enormous importance in the regional development of Ecuador. Coastal Ecuador, like coastal Peru, was the location for export production from the late nineteenth century, but given its hot, humid equatorial climate, development focused on cacao, coffee, bananas and rice for the domestic market. Development has spread northwards to Esmeraldas, but Guayaquil, the major colonial port for Quito and the terminus of its railway link to the sea, was the main urban focus for external trade. Guayaquil, traditionally the commercial and banking centre, with a reputation for its liveliness and business enterprise, has continued to grow. Quito, always the seat of government and headquarters of the conservative landowning oligarchy of the sierra, has the metropolitan advantages which flow from the presence of government and an expanding bureaucracy and the concentration of purchasing power, It shares with Guayaquil the major part of industrial growth in Ecuador. By contrast functions dominated by Lima alone in Peru are in Ecuador shared between twin primate cities. The coastal zone of Ecuador remains the scene of new settlement and colonization, of highly commercialized agriculture and of immigration, but in the sierra Indian peasant farming, haciendas and the activities of regional urban centres, strung out like beads from Cuenca in the south to Loja in the north, are enlivened by the commercial possibilities inherent in Quito's expansion.

Bolivia, too, has its capital firmly located in the predominantly Indian highlands of the Altiplano, a region of dense Indian settlement near Lake Titicaca with a more humid and slightly more equable climate than the rest of the Altiplano, which becomes more arid, harsh and more sparsely settled towards the south-west. Since the agrarian reform began in 1952, Indian peasant farming has become significantly more prosperous and more commercially oriented towards the urban market presented by La Paz. But

Atacama Desert, Chile. This is the driest of the world's deserts, with only sparse vegetation. In some parts of the Atacama no rainfall has ever been recorded.

Altiplano and Cordillera Real, Bolivia. The altiplano, or high plateau, of southern Peru and Bolivia, with elevations of upwards of 3000 metres, is the highest area of settlement in Latin America.

the spatial organization of Bolivia is more complex, aligned broadly on two axes: one of long standing from La Paz through Oruro to Potosí and associated with the exploitation of mineral resources; the second of more recent development from La Paz through Cochabamba to the boom city of Santa Cruz. The fabulous wealth in silver of Potosí, largest town in the Americas around 1600, and later at Oruro, was replaced in the late nineteenth century by tin-mining, until recently the major legal source of Bolivia's foreign-exchange earnings and the *raison d'être* of the western railway system linking La Paz with Arica and Antofagasta, Lake Titicaca and the Peruvian system. But the mining sector has been less dynamic than the eastern settlement round Santa Cruz and north of Cochabamba where production of tropical and subtropical products (notably sugar, rice, coffee, coca) and cattle have flourished in the context of oil and natural gas production. The centre of gravity of Bolivian development is shifting fairly rapidly from the Altiplano and the mining centres to the new east. Cochabamba, located in the centre of this axis, and in a zone of intermediate altitude, is well placed to benefit from industrial and commercial growth. But La Paz is still the primate city, and resource-based development elsewhere has by no means robbed it of economic leadership.

In the broadest sense, Colombia's make-up is similar to that of Ecuador and Peru – coastal margin, Andean ranges and eastern interior lowlands. In Colombia two structural troughs separating the three main ranges are lower in altitude than further south and more importantly are followed by partially navigable river systems – the Cauca and the Magdalena – draining directly into the Caribbean. Within the relatively open landscapes of the Colombian sierra there are larger areas appropriate for the production of temperate and tropical crops than further south, but the coastal regions tend to be hostile, swampy regions of forest or savanna. In spite of the early strategic importance of Cartagena, chief port until the rise of Barranquilla, the focus of government remained at Bogotá, always relatively difficult of access from the coast and from other parts of the country. Partly because of this, several urban centres of substantial regional importance developed. Medellín, focus of an early gold trade and then a centre from which agricultural colonization spread southwards, was the city to gain most from the expansion of coffee production; it then developed as an industrial city. Cali and Bucaramanga are the other urban poles which, with Bogotá, define a quadrilateral which contains over half the centre's population, with the country's highest incomes.

VEGETATION

Mountain vegetation	
Conifer forest *(pine, spruce and larch)*	
Mixed forest, mid-latitudes *(broadleaf and conifer)*	
Prairie *(long grass)*	
Steppe *(short grass)*	
Savannah *(grass and scrub)*	
Tropical rain forest *(selva)*	
Monsoon forest *(moist deciduous)*	
Dry tropical forest *(semi-deciduous)*	
Dry tropical scrub and thorn forest	
Desert vegetation *(xerophytic shrub, grass and cactus)*	

0   1600 km
0   1000 miles

Finally in Venezuela, the tripartite arrangement of coast, sierra and interior lowlands is repeated again, though the mountains are lower in altitude and less of a barrier except in the west, and the Guiana shield to the south of the Orinoco gives a fourth dimension. The coastal zone is complex with contrasting environments from the steaming rainforest south of Lake Maracaibo to the semi-aridity further east. Oil and its exploitation have elevated Maracaibo to be the second largest city, but it has always been the capital, Caracas, which has benefited most from the oil revenues, so that Venezuela, like Peru, offers one of the best South American examples of urban primacy, though industrial development is spreading southwards from Caracas and westwards to the older industrial area around Valencia, and even further west at Barquisimeto. There has been substantial progress, too, in the settlement of the inner flanks of the Andean range draining to the Orinoco and in the creation of a new urban–industrial complex at Ciudad Guyana, based on resources at the northern margin of the Guiana Highlands – iron ore, bauxite and hydroelectricity.

Chile is the exception among Andean countries, in that it is the coastal zone which is overwhelmingly dominant. Much of the Andean massif is uninhabitable, and the territory extends only to the crestlines of the Andean chain, except in the south. Chile's geographical differentiation is latitudinal and defined in terms of climate and vegetation. It is the Mediterranean climate of the Central Valley which was attractive for agricultural settlement from the early colonial period and which provided the bulk of its exports until the advent of mining. It is still the most densely populated zone of Chile, though expansion southwards towards Valdivia was accomplished from the nineteenth century with the assistance of a certain amount of immigration. The far south has few possibilities except for tourism, extensive sheep-raising and perhaps greater oil production. The north is desert, lacking the irrigation possibilities of coastal Peru, since the aridity of the high Andean ranges supplies few streams with adequate water for large-scale irrigation. Yet it is the desert which has produced the resources to sustain the Chilean economy: nitrates in the late nineteenth and early twentieth centuries; copper from Chuquicamata and El Salvador and elsewhere in the twentieth century, and iron ore from near Coquimbo. But the desert environment has precluded the generation of large and diverse settlements around the mining areas. Further south, Concepción has grown as a regional capital with coal and steel production nearby, but it is Santiago which, like Lima in Peru, has been the main beneficiary of urban and industrial growth. Efforts at regional development, such as the establishment of Arica as a free industrial zone, have failed to reduce significantly the primacy of Santiago.

Amboro forest, in the Andean foothills, Bolivia. Bolivia, Peru and Ecuador all have landscapes of this type on the eastern side of the Andes.

THE INTERIOR AND ATLANTIC LOWLANDS

Four well-defined lowland zones separate the Andean region from the ancient massifs of eastern South America: the Orinoco basin, the Amazon basin, the lowlands of the Paraná–Paraguay system, and the Atlantic-facing lowlands of the Argentine pampas and Patagonia. There is a corresponding differentiation in their ecology according to climate and vegetational patterns: the Orinoco basin has a highly seasonal rainfall regime which supports predominantly grassland vegetation of the savanna type with galería forest along the better-watered of its rivers; the Amazon lowlands are the largest area of surviving equatorial rainforest in the world, with rainfall all the year round, but with some marked features of seasonality in the incidence of rainfall, and with the highest totals tending to occur along the western margins of Amazonia; further south there is a gradual transition, with many areas of swamp vegetation, to savanna grassland and thorn scrub of the Gran Chaco, with a highly seasonal rainfall regime and a climate which, while the hottest part of South America in the southern summer, is liable in winter to occasional bursts of cold air drawn along the lowland corridor from the south. The natural grasslands of the pampas have a more equable temperate climate in which rainfall occurs throughout the year but with a summer maximum, but totals diminish westwards towards the semi-arid margins of the Andes. Soils are fertile, characterized by chernozems developed on the thick deposits of wind-blown loess derived from the Pleistocene of the Andes. But to the south, rainfall becomes scarce and summers cool in the arid desert of the Patagonian plateau, with its harsh landscapes of volcanic lavas and glacial moraine.

With the very important exception of the Argentine pampas, the interior lowlands are sparsely populated and relatively undeveloped – the empty heart of South America. Why this should be so is partly a result of its varied ecological character, but it is perhaps even more bound up with the cultural history of South America, not least of its pre-Columbian heritage. The indigenous cultures of the Amazonian rainforests were ethnically and linguistically highly fragmented. Their material cultures were based on shifting agriculture and the hunting and fishing of a wide variety of fauna. Population was sparse (though less so in the sixteenth century than it was to be later) and groups were probably separated by unoccupied forest. Intelligent use was made of the distinction between relatively fertile, regularly flooded soils of the *varzea* and the leached, mature and fragile soils of older terraces – the *terra firme*. But the indigenes were neither docile nor numerous enough to provide a massive labour force for Spanish or Portuguese settlers, nor were there prospects of rich mineral wealth or raw materials to attract settlement. The forest and its inhabitants were ruthlessly exploited for rubber and cinchona in the nineteenth century, but it was not until recently that a serious attempt has been made by Brazil to exploit the potential resources of the area.

The building of the Transamazonian Highway and its feeder roads is in part strategic and military in conception, aiming at completing the occupation of national territory to its frontiers with the Andean states, and it is also, of course, economic. Large-scale clearing of forest and its replacement by more rapidly maturing, consolidated stands of timber or, more commonly, its replacement by grazing for cattle, together with plans for mineral exploitation of iron ore, tin, manganese and bauxite, have aroused grave apprehension of an ecological disaster. Equatorial soils are fragile – mineral nutrients are locked in the bio-mass rather than in the soil itself – and forest clearance has demonstrably resulted in rapid soil deterioration, apart from fears as to the contribution of large-scale deforestation to the global problem of the 'greenhouse' effect, and on the future of the indigenous groups that have still survived, and other fears as to the social consequences of unbridled exploitation for peasant settlers and immigrant workers. Furthermore, the forest is subjected to a two-fold attack: from Brazil on the one hand, and from the Andean states on the other. Colombia, Ecuador, Peru and Bolivia are also concerned to validate their political boundaries by frontier settlement and see economic possibilities in the production of cattle as well as tropical crops from the eastern flanks of the Andes, where on the whole soils are richer than in the lowlands proper. Eastern colonization is more important to Bolivia than to other Andean states, lacking as it does a Pacific coast and alternative sources for such products; and it is here that eastern colonization has moved fastest in recent years. Everywhere there is potential conflict of interests between small-scale peasant farmers moving into the lowlands by a process of spontaneous colonization, and large-scale projects encouraged by governments or financed with abundant capital backing. Cacao, coffee, bananas, palm oil, sugar, rice and beef are among the potential products to supply domestic markets and even export revenues, but in the Andean states it is cocaine, derived from the leaves of the coca shrub, that has been the source of high and illegal profits in recent years, and it is also oil and the prospects of oil that have raised high hopes, partially realized in Ecuador, Peru and Bolivia.

To the north and south of the rainforest, the plains of the Orinoco and the basin of the River Paraguay

Grasslands and hills of Cuchilla Grande, Uruguay, in the temperate zone of South America. This pastoral scene could almost be in England.

seem to offer fewer possibilities of intensive development. Seasonal flooding of the Orinoco plains inhibits more intensive use of the natural savanna grasslands than the extensive stock-raising to which it is now devoted. Further south, seasonal flooding and vast areas of marshland alternating with thorn scrub on sandy soils discourage settlement in the Paraguay basin, shared among Brazil, Bolivia and Paraguay, though there is some development along the tenuous link from Brazil to Corumbá and thence to Santa Cruz in Bolivia. Patagonia, with limited possibilities for extensive sheep grazing and arable crops where irrigation is possible, and with the descendants of its Welsh colonies still retaining an ethnic identity, is also an area of limited potential.

The empty heart of South America is thus, in one sense, a frontier of settlement, though one of hardship and of elusive possibilities, but it has also been a frontier zone in a political sense, in which rivalries between Spain and Portugal for control of the interior were worked out far away from the region itself. On the Spanish side, the religious missions to pacify and 'civilize' the Indian communities were one expression of a colonial strategy adopted to contain the Brazilian Portuguese – in the Orinoco basin in

Venezuela, in eastern Peru, the Mojos region of north-east Bolivia, and also in the Jesuit 'state within a state' in the region of modern Paraguay. After independence, large slices of territory changed hands, with a greater significance, perhaps, on the maps than on the ground. Peru lost territory in the Amazon basin to Brazil, and gained from Ecuador (as late as 1941); Bolivia lost territory to Brazil in exchange for concessions, and the Bolivian border with Paraguay was only settled in 1938 after a long-drawn-out and exhausting war.

In complete contrast to the lack of development in the interior plains the remaining lowland region – the Argentine pampas and its surrounding lowlands to the north in the lower Paraná – Paraguay and to the north-east into Uruguay – is intensively settled and constitutes the major productive areas of Paraguay, Uruguay and Argentina itself. Until the eighteenth century this, too, was a region as sparsely populated as the interior lowlands further north, its natural grasslands the habitat of a sparse Indian hunting population and of semi-wild cattle controlled by nomadic gauchos. The major exception was the sedentary agricultural Indian population, largely Tupi–Guaraní, of what is now Paraguay, organized into village life by the Jesuit missions (until their expulsion in 1767). Accessibility to the Atlantic by way of the River Plate estuary became of major significance from the late eighteenth century, and the economic revolution on the pampas which brought the railways, immigrant settlers from Europe, meat production for the European market and intensive arable farming only came after the mid-nineteenth century. Over a long time-scale, Argentina offers the best example of the movement down from the mountains, for in 1750 the major settled areas were still in the old north-west, in the irrigated, semi-arid intermontane basins from Salta and Jujuy southwards to Tucumán and beyond. By 1900, the pampas were effectively settled and were now the economic core of Argentina, linked to the old north-west by a chain of towns which still form the major economic axis of the country from Buenos Aires to Rosario and Córdoba. Settlement and agricultural development of the pampas is limited westwards by increasing aridity, but the northward expansion of settlement for the production of livestock and a range of subtropical crops was still proceeding in recent years, particularly in the Argentine Mesopotamia between the Paraná and the River Uruguay. Eastern Paraguay is still an active area of new settlement, in which immigrant stock farmers play an important role. More obviously even than in the Andean countries, however, it is Buenos Aires which demonstrates the role of the metropolis as a major engine of growth, concentrating over 10 million people or over a third of the total population of Argentina, and its major industrial and commercial focus. On a smaller scale, Montevideo stands in an even more striking role in relation to Uruguay with over 40 per cent of the country's population.

But in the rest of the interior lowlands there is no coherent urban network and only isolated urban centres acting as the focus of regional development: Belem, Manaus and Iquitos on the Amazon; Pucallpa in eastern Peru; Rondonia as a centre of new settlement in south-west Brazil; in Bolivia, Trinidad and especially Santa Cruz.

THE ANCIENT MASSIFS AND THEIR ATLANTIC MARGINS

Eastern South America is composed essentially of two unequally sized ancient massifs – the Guiana Highlands and the Brazilian Shield – divided by the lower Amazon basin. Although the geological structure is complex, the major physiographic features are those of an eroded plateau tilted towards the north-west with a relief of rolling country broken by residual ridges and escarpments of more resistant rocks and sinking imperceptibly towards the lowlands of the Amazon and the basin of the River Paraguay. To the east and south-east the plateau is at its highest, falling to the Atlantic by steep escarpments, such as the Serra do Mar between Rio and Santos or the Borborema in the north-east. With a rainfall that is increasingly seasonal in summer to the south of the Amazon basin, the interior of the plateau displays a transition from rainforest to tall grass savanna and to the *campos cerrados* of savanna with xerophytic trees and shrubs. But towards the Atlantic coast, rainfall amounts are higher, and more continuous throughout the year, supporting evergreen tropical forest under natural conditions and Araucarian pine forests or subtropical evergreen forests to the south. But in the interior of the north-east there is a sharp transition between the moist Atlantic coast and a dry, hot climate supporting the thorn scrub cactus and grassland vegetation known as the *caatinga*.

Compared with the Andean region, the interior plateau had little to offer to the initial Portuguese settlers. The relatively scattered Indian population, at a lower level of cultural development, lacked the homogeneity, docility and the skills which attracted the Spanish settler further west. Except in the south, soils are poor and easily eroded or exhausted, though extensive cattle-raising supported a sparse and scattered population and still does so. Above all, there were no obvious sources of precious metals until the discovery of gold and diamonds in the late seventeenth century brought settlement to Minas Gerais. Given its Atlantic orientation and colonial settlement from Portugal, it was almost inevitable that the east, with its humid climate, should be developed earliest. Indeed, although the distribution of population is changing, with a continued shift towards the interior, the general pattern is one in which most of the population and all of the large cities, with the exception of Brasília, Manaus and Belo Horizonte, lie within 160 km of the Atlantic coast.

Three major features, then, characterize the human geography of Brazil. One is the imbalance in its population distribution; the second is the scale and rapidity of the economic advance that has taken place in the south-east, and the third, stemming in part from the first two, is the inequality of regional development.

It was coffee which brought wealth, population and commerce, first to Rio and later to São Paulo (and its port at Santos) from the early nineteenth century. Rio de Janeiro, with its magnificent harbour, had grown with trade to the gold-mining areas of Minas Gerais, became the focus of the court and then capital of Brazil, and prospered with the coffee trade, later sharing pre-eminence with São Paulo as the coffee frontier moved south-west on to the fertile *terra roxa* soils on the interfluves of the upper Paraná system. It

Aerial view of the Transamazonian Highway, Brazil. The construction of such roads began with the founding of Brasília and was a particular dream of the military governments after 1964.

was coffee which ultimately financed the building of a railway system comparable in density and pattern to that of the pampas, and attracted European immigrants from the late nineteenth century. It was the commerce in coffee which financed early industrial development in São Paulo for a significant internal market. But industrial development, encouraged by the use of high-quality iron ore reserves to produce steel, first at Volta Redonda on any scale, has spread more widely in the industrial triangle of the south-east, defined roughly by Belo Horizonte, São Paulo and Rio de Janeiro. Brazil's industrial complex, backed by the largest internal market in Latin America, and contributing substantially to its export sector, is now wide-ranging in its variety of industrial activity, and is largely responsible for generating an average regional per-capita income which is far above the average for Brazil as a whole.

At the other extreme, the north-east, while densely populated, is the most economically depressed and impoverished region of Brazil, with an average per-capita income of only a fifth of that of the Rio de Janeiro area. Sugar plantations, worked by slave labour in the humid coastlands of the north-east, generated wealth for a few in the sixteenth and seventeenth centuries, but with impoverished soils and low yields in many areas it has never recovered prosperity, while retaining sharp inequalities in income distribution. The juxtaposition of large estates and smallholdings is one manifestation of

inequalities of income, which persist in spite of attempts to bring industrial development to the cities of the north-east. Further inland, in the 'polygon of drought', irrigation schemes, as a response to the shortage and unreliability of rainfall, have failed to relieve rural poverty; nor have resettlement schemes in the Amazon basin had much effect.

Just as the Transamazonian Highway and its colonization schemes (Brazil's 'march to the west') attempt to settle the interior, so the foundation of Brasília as capital (inaugurated in April 1960) represented a bold, imaginative attempt to create an urban growth pole which revitalized the interior plateau, still in general underpopulated and devoted to shifting cultivation and extensive cattle-raising. The elegant formal planned city has, in fact, generated a host of informal unplanned satellites which exemplify the social inequalities of the country as a whole.

MIDDLE AMERICA AND THE CARIBBEAN

Within this vast and complex region it is, broadly speaking, Mexico which conforms to a continental scale both in the characteristics of its physical environments and its economy. But in Central America proper and the Caribbean islands it is fragmentation which is the keynote in a physical, economic and political sense.

Mexico contains within its borders a rich variety of natural conditions. In the south, humid tropical and naturally forested lowlands on both Atlantic and Pacific coasts (with the exception of northern Yucatán) rise to the dissected highlands of the southern range, moderately well-watered and enclosing tectonic basins such as those of Oaxaca and Chiapas. The Volcanic Axis, crossing the country from east to west, includes snow-capped cones such as Orizaba (5750 m) and Popocatépetl (5452 m), but the important areas for settlement and agriculture are again the tectonic basins enclosed within the ranges, including the Valley of Mexico at *c.* 2500 m above sea level. To the north, the coastal lowlands, widest near the US border, are better watered on the Caribbean shore than towards the Pacific, where there is a rapid transition towards the desert coasts of the north-west and the peninsula of Baja California. Inland the western branch of the Sierra Madre is more continuous, higher and more massive, and also more highly mineralized than the eastern branch, and they enclose within them the plateaux and range-and-basin country of northern Mexico, becoming increasingly more arid to the north and west. Irrigation has made possible more intensive and modernized agricultural settlement in some areas of the north, particularly near the US border and on the Pacific coast, but the north as a whole is relatively sparsely settled, and in many areas overgrazed and badly eroded.

Minerals have played a fundamental role in Mexico's development. Silver at Guanajuato, Zacatecas and San Luis de Potosí drew the Spaniards northwards to frontier regions beyond the Aztec empire, and silver has continuously played an important role in the external economy from the sixteenth century, though copper, lead, zinc, sulphur, and iron ore (combined with local coal for an expanding steel industry at Monterrey) have in this century supplemented silver, and all are now overshadowed by oil production from new Gulf offshore fields.

But it is Mexico City, once the capital city of the Aztec empire, which dominates the human geography of the country. Likely to be the world's largest city in 2000 and with an estimated population of about 17 million people in 1990, it sprawls far beyond the lake margins where it originated as Tenochtitlán, creating vast problems of housing, traffic congestion, pollution, water supply and drainage, but containing a wide range of engineering and consumer goods industries. An industrial–urban axis has emerged parallel to the Volcanic Axis and extending from Puebla to Guadalajara, with Mexico City as its central focus. Although relatively poor areas exist near and within this prosperous industrialized zone, regional development in Mexico conforms to a pattern in which the northern border zone near the United States and the metropolitan region represent the highest levels of income and welfare, but the far south, with a high proportion of Indian population and relatively remote from urban or international markets, is the poorest region.

Fragmentation is the keynote of Central America and the Caribbean, though in rather different ways. Wet, forested lowlands and a confusion of dissected highlands with volcanic peaks and small-scale basins at varying altitudes define a region from Panama to Guatemala which has been accessible mainly by sea, though capital cities, except for Panama, are located in interior basins initially carrying a moderately dense Indian population. At independence, such unity as there was in Spanish colonial administration disappeared and the region fell apart into what are now seven independent states, each quite small, ranging from Belize (150,000 in 1979) to Guatemala (6.8 million in 1979), and with wide-ranging per-capita incomes, from that of Honduras, which shares with Bolivia the distinction of the lowest per-capita income in mainland Latin America, to Costa Rica and Panama, which rank in the top ten. Political profiles have ranged equally widely, from the harshest of personal and military dictatorships, like that of the Somozas of Nicaragua (up to 1979) to the relatively stable democratic structure of Costa Rica. The Central American Common Market (CACM) represents only the most recent, and now fading, attempt of many in the last 150 years to achieve a regional grouping of these small and economically vulnerable units.

The Caribbean islands present a distinctive pattern of fragmentation of a different kind. They comprise a series of island arcs ranging from the substantial highland massifs of the Greater Antilles to the low coral islands of the Bahamas or the volcanic peaks of Martinique, for example. Colonial rivalries of Spain, Holland, France, Britain and Denmark imposed very different political structures on the islands until their decolonization in the twentieth century, through Guadeloupe and Martinique are still departments of France and Puerto Rico is a dominion of the United States. Indigenous Indian populations were replaced by slave labour to work the plantations which made fortunes for the planters and merchants of the colonial powers in the eighteenth century. Sugar above all, but also coffee, tobacco, cotton and bananas, and more recently tourists, and minerals such as bauxite from Jamaica, support the precarious and vulnerable external economies of political units too small to generate an internal market for much industrialization. As in Central America, political regimes vary widely. Attempts at co-operation and regional groupings tend to founder in the face of island particularisms, and while old colonial links are suspect, the basis for new groupings has not yet arisen. But for many of the islands, emigration overseas has provided something of a safety valve: from the islands to the neighbouring continental mainland, but, more commonly, from Puerto Rico to the United States; from Cuba of political dissidents to the United States; from the former British West Indies to Great Britain, Canada and the United States.

CTS

Further Reading: H. Blakemore and C. T. Smith, eds., *Latin America: Geographical Perspectives*, 2nd edition (London, 1983); R. and D. F. Bromley, *South American Development* (Cambridge, 1988); P. E. James, *Latin America* (New York, 1969); A. Morris, *Latin America* (London 1987); P. R. Odell and D. A. Preston, *Economies and Societies in Latin America* (London, 1978); D. A. Preston, ed., *Latin American Development* (London, 1987)

Environmental conservation in Latin America

The growing worldwide concern with environmental deterioration has not bypassed Latin America. There is abundant evidence that Latin America, while not the worst case of environmental degradation, is experiencing a number of large-scale processes that threaten the long-term productivity of many regions. Two types of environment have been identified by specialists as particularly problematic: steeply sloping lands and tropical moist and rainforests.

The areas with steeply sloping land cover large proportions of Latin American countries. Table 1 reminds us that the areas are not insignificant: from 40 per cent of the total national area of Colombia to a high of 80 per cent for several countries in Central America. Even when the population does not live on the steep sloping lands, it lives and farms in the intermontane valleys below those steep lands. Increasingly, the poor have been forced to move into steep areas because of land concentration in the more favourable lands at lower altitudes.

Steeply sloping lands are vulnerable to rapid loss of soil and of their future productive potential. The elegant terraces and irrigation systems that were constructed in Pre-Columbian times have in up to 75 per cent of all cases fallen into disuse with a consequent decline in their productive potential. The costs of building, maintaining, and managing steep terraces is high and agrarian policies have not favoured the rural sector in ways that would ensure the steady investment in soil conservation and terrace maintenance that would be required.

The management of steeply sloping lands presents many challenges. To reduce soil loss, one of the most serious negative results of non-terraced agriculture in these areas, it is necessary to plant vegetation in strips on slopes and terraces, and to build up structures that can counter erosive forces, like embankments and other means to reduce the speed of water-flow down the slope. How to do so without removing the surface from productive use is one of the great challenges to conservation work in Latin America and elsewhere.

Efforts to revive Pre-Columbian techniques of hill-side terrace farming and raised-field farming have been undertaken in Peru. The costs of new terrace construction (about $2,000 dollars per hectare) compare favourably to the initial costs of opening coastal desert to irrigated agriculture and other alternatives to land use. New bench terraces produce yields 54 per cent higher than non-terraced land in the same localities. Raised-fields – areas of land that have been prepared through the transfer and elevation of earth – could also serve to put back into production areas now thought to be too poor for cultivation. However, this technique was abandoned long ago and will have to be treated as a new technology in

Eroded hillsides between Sucre and Cochabamba, Bolivia. Inadequate farming methods and the abandonment of terrace agriculture have led to many scenes such as this.

TABLE 1

Proportions of national area, arable land, and population on steep lands of tropical America

Country	National area	Arable land	National population
Colombia	40%	25%	15%
Costa Rica	70%	25%	20%
Dominican Rep.	80%	15%	15%
Ecuador	65%	25%	25%
El Salvador	75%	40%	30%
Guatemala	75%	30%	40%
Haiti	80%	70%	50%
Honduras	80%	15%	15%
Jamaica	75%	50%	15%
Mexico	45%	20%	15%
Panama	80%	10%	15%
Peru	50%	25%	25%

Adapted from Posner and McPherson, 1981.

AREAS OF TROPICAL DEFORESTATION

MEXICO

BELIZE
HONDURAS

GUATEMALA

EL SALVADOR

NICARAGUA

COSTA RICA

PANAMA

VENEZUELA

GUYANA

SURINAME

GUYANE

COLOMBIA

AMAPÁ

ECUADOR

RORAIMA

MARANHÃO

AMAZONAS

PARA

B R A Z I L

PERU

ACRE

RONDÔNIA

MATO GROSSO

GOIÁS

BOLIVIA

PARAGUAY

CHILE

ARGENTINA

URUGUAY

Tropical Forests

Deforested Areas

0   1600 km

0   1000 miles

terms of how it is re-introduced among Latin American farmers.

Fortunately, most conservation procedures and structures are within the technical competence and capital range of most small-scale farmers. Farmers are often familiar with a vast array of surface management techniques that they can use – when incentives are adequate. Thus, the problem of managing steeply sloping land is not a lack of techniques but a lack of appropriate incentives to the farm-level farmer.

In the moist and rain forests of Latin America the problems are quite different. The lowland forests have the highest rates of biomass production on earth and the tropical American rainforests are the largest in areal extent. Removing the vegetation through deforestation can bring about severe environmental problems at both local and global scale. In 1987 alone, it is reported, 8 million hectares of forest were burned. Primary concern has focused on the effects of this destruction on species diversity and on atmospheric chemistry. One-half of the world's biota is said to make its home in the tropical American forests, and many of the species are endemic (i.e. occur in very restricted territories). The removal of vegetation through burning, the most common method, releases vast amounts of carbon dioxide which have made Brazil one of the largest contributors to atmospheric carbon dioxide and possibly to global warming – second only to the industrial countries' contribution from fossil fuel use. Removal of such vast areas of tropical vegetation in the Amazon and in south-eastern Mexico and Central America, it is believed, will bring about changes in the hemisphere's hydrological cycle and climate change of such magnitude that the forests may not be able to re-establish themselves.

A section of the rainforest is being cleared for agriculture or ranching in Rondônia, Brazil.

TABLE 2
Land use in Rondonia
(in square kilometres)

| Year | Crops | | | |
	Annual	Perennial	Pasture	Forest
1970	323.7	127.2	410.1	15,031.1
	2%	0.8%	2.5%	92.1%
1975	1503.9	457.6	1645.2	26,681.4
	4.9%	1.5%	5.3%	86.6%
1980	2425.8	1701.8	5101.8	41,461.1
	4.6%	3.3%	9.8%	79.4%
1985	3153.3	2,238.0	15,611.5*	39,903.7*

Source: IBGE 1987 in Mahar 1988:35.
*Estimated.

The causes of this deforestation vary from country to country in Latin America but they are largely associated with policies that favour the conversion of forest land to pasture. This is rooted in colonial legislation to encourage occupation of the frontier lands. Such legislation considers any removal of native vegetation to constitute an 'improvement' and becomes the basis for claims to land tenure over such areas. Because such legislation has not been explicitly spurned by new legislation, litigation has tended to favour cattle ranchers who have greater legal resources than do the conservation organizations.

In countries like Brazil, where tax holidays were provided to encourage the occupation of the Amazon, the process proved devastating. The conversion of forest to pasture took place at a rate of approximately 8 to 10 thousand square kilometres per year in the 1970s and increased to 35,000 square kilometres in the late 1980s. Cattle ranches currently cover at least 8.4 million hectares and average 24,000 hectares each. Some of these ranches are larger than 500,000 hectares, and employ on average one cowboy for every 300 hectares – resulting in very low labour absorption capacity.

The process of moist and rain forest deforestation, which was promoted by generous fiscal incentives and tax holidays, is now driven also by land speculation. Average land prices have skyrocketed in areas with adequate road access, especially in areas like Rondonia, Brazil. Table 2 illustrates the steady path of forest to pasture conversion. Annual and perennial crops have remained largely stagnant by comparison. As farmers sell their land in southern Brazil to large-scale producers of cash crops for export, like soybeans, they have available cash to buy larger landholdings in the Amazon. Because the capital gains tax on land sales is rarely if ever collected, there is strong incentive to engage in speculative land sales.

The environment and indigenous people

Numbering around 17,000 and with their own distinctive language and social structure, the Yanomami of Northern Brazil are self-sufficient hunter-gatherers living scattered through the rain forest in groups of 10–20 families. From the 1960s they came under increasing pressure from logging companies and mining prospectors backed by a military government. Highways, forest clearance, airstrips, and large-scale military intervention along the 3,000 km northern edge of the Amazon basin brought ecological disruption and disease, particularly malaria.

Then, because immense mineral reserves were rumoured, in 1988 the Yanomami homeland around Surucucus Hill suffered a prospecting rush of Klondike proportions. Boa Vista, the regional capital, became a frontier town of bars and brothels.

In November 1991, after the first presidential elections in Brazil for a generation, the government of Fernando Collor de Mello set aside 9.4 million hectares of traditional Yanomami territory as a legal homeland. As a result the Yanomami now stand a decent chance of surviving into the next century.

Besides cattle ranching, timber extraction is growing in importance each year with the decline in the productivity of Asian and African tropical forests. In the most recent statistics, four of the six states in the Brazilian Amazon depended on wood products for more than 25 per cent of their industrial output. In Rondonia and Roraima timber products account for 60 per cent of output. The number of licensed mills has increased eightfold since 1965. In addition, the development of pig-iron production in the Carajás region will result in the conversion of forests in that region into charcoal to fire the pig-iron factories. Already the demand from the approved projects requires 1.1 million metric tons of charcoal annually, and is expected to double when projects under evaluation are approved by the Amazon Development Agency. The impact of hydroelectric projects has also been felt. Tucuruí in the eastern Amazon flooded many prime lands and its energy has not led to the electrification of rural areas as originally promised. Instead, the energy has benefited several aluminium industries and much of the energy has been transmitted to southern Brazil.

Alternatives to current processes are readily available but will require a level of political will that has yet to express itself. Collection of capital gains taxes on land sales, as well as collection of property taxes, could do much to take away the incentive to speculate with land. The process of deforestation is clearly tied to tax holidays and fiscal incentives, all of which should be immediately removed from all projects. They have largely proven to be income transfers to the already wealthy.

Positive approaches to management of these areas suggest greater attention to agroforestry, wildlife management, ecotourism, rediscovery of traditional systems of land use and conservation and restoration of already cleared areas. Conservationists are seeking ways to develop sustained yield approaches. One report has found that forests in the central selva of Peru regenerated quickly when clearing took place in narrow clear-cut strips and proposes this be widely applied for sustainable tropical lowland forestry.

Efforts by NGOs (non-governmental organizations) such as the World Wildlife Fund and the Nature Conservancy, Environmental Defense Fund have begun to pay off. Several 'debt-for-nature swaps' have been agreed on in countries like Costa Rica and Bolivia which provide some external debt relief while ensuring that parks will be set aside and staffed with the interest from those loans. Few people realize, for example, that between 1977 and 1981 new national parks and protected areas were created totalling more than 11,830,000 hectares in Bolivia, Brazil, Ecuador and Venezuela. These are poorly staffed and generally unprotected. Unless action is taken there will be much more destruction than conservation of the Latin American environments in the immediate future. A growing number of conservation organizations have begun to appear throughout Latin America with remarkable ability to act and attract media attention. Their alliance with international organizations has proven effective in mobilizing support and political pressure.

This article has focused on the two most serious problem-areas of Latin America in terms of their extent. The environmental problems of urban growth and pollution, and of coastal pollution and petroleum drilling, to be found throughout Latin America, present dilemmas which face many other parts of the developing and developed world. Of specific importance in the Latin American case, continuation of population growth, of government policies that encourage misuse of the land, and which are more responsive to the needs of the few will continue to threaten the environment. There are some encouraging signs of change but they still lack an adequate level of political will in response to popular demand.

EM

Further Reading: J. Browder, ed., *Fragile Lands of Latin America* (Boulder, Colorado, 1989); E. Moran, *The Human Ecology of Amazonian Populations* (Petropolis, Brazil, 1990); G. Wilken, *Good Farmers. Traditional Agricultural Resources Management in Mexico and Central America* (Berkeley, 1987)

The Economy

Agriculture

Latin America and the Caribbean is distinctive among Third World regions in having a relatively small proportion of the population engaged in agriculture and fishing. Although in Latin America farming only accounts for one in three employed people, compared with two in three in all developing countries, it is nonetheless the main livelihood of many families. Together with fishing, in Latin America it takes place at two very different scales. On the one hand, large numbers of small-scale farmers and fishermen produce in aggregate large quantities of foodstuffs for their own or local consumption which may not even provide work for all the family. On the other hand, large quantities of valuable foodstuffs are also grown on a small number of much larger farms, predominantly for export. This is illustrated by the fact that Brazil produces the largest quantity of bananas in Latin America, almost all of which were consumed in Brazil, yet Ecuador, a much small country, is a leading Latin American and world exporter of bananas.

AN AGRICULTURAL GEOGRAPHY OF LATIN AMERICA AND THE CARIBBEAN

In Mexico and Central America the rural population is concentrated in the highland chain which forms the backbone of the continent. The native Indian populations found predominantly in these areas are mainly small-scale farmers who produce maize, beans and pumpkins for their own use. In some highland areas there are middle-sized and large farms where excellent-quality coffee is grown, largely for export. Intensive farming of livestock, tomatoes, fruit and vegetables for the USA market is increasingly important in certain areas of highland Mexico. Agricultural development of the lowlands, apart from colonization areas and the Yucatan peninsula in Mexico, Belize and Guatemala, is dominated by commercial farming, particularly by US corporations, which provides large quantities of bananas as well as cattle for export.

In the Caribbean, subsistence farming on the hilly islands has always occupied large areas but commercial farming is also important in the lowlands, producing fruit, especially bananas, for northern markets on plantations and middle-sized farms. In Cuba and parts of the Dominican Republic sugar is produced on large farms for export.

The farm population of western South America is densely concentrated in the highland zone which runs from eastern Venezuela to southern Chile and Argentina. Agriculture is carried on at all levels, even as high as at 3900 m in the Central Andes. Smallholdings predominate, and potatoes, maize and beans are the main food crops grown. The rearing of sheep, pigs, cattle and camelids (llamas and alpacas) is important for both small- and large-scale farmers. The lowlands to the east of the mountains are thinly populated although there are growing colononization areas on the fringes of the mountains. The number of Indians and non-Indian farmers in the lowlands east of the Andes form a very small proportion of the Andean countries' population. The coastal regions of Ecuador, Peru and Chile contain areas where commercially oriented farming is important. In Ecuador coffee, cacao and bananas are produced for export: in Peru, with the aid of irrigation, cotton and sugar are grown. Central Chile, between the coastal hills and the Andes, has productive farmland supporting a large rural population which has produced an increasingly important quantity of fruit for export during the 1980s.

The temperate farmlands of Argentina, Uruguay and southern Brazil produce grains, meat and, further north in Brazil, coffee, largely for sale to the big cities and for export. The frontier of farming in Brazil has been moving westwards during this century, and is increasingly associated with the spread of cattle farming. In central and north-eastern Brazil good farmland is concentrated, with the population, along the coast as far north as the mouth of the Amazon. While small-scale farming is widespread, cacao and sugar are among the major crops produced for shipment elsewhere. Fishing is practised by most coastal communities in tropical Latin America and on the major rivers and lakes, but few people live exclusively from fishing, and it is normally supplemented by farming. In some countries commercial fishing is important, and in Peru, Ecuador and Chile the export of fish, shrimps and fishmeal comprises between 9 and 19 per cent of the value of exports. In Ecuador shrimp production boomed during the 1980s and it made up 18 per cent of total exports by value in 1988.

TRADITIONAL FARMING SYSTEMS

The majority of those farming in Latin America are not primarily concerned with producing a surplus for sale or with achieving the maximum sustainable yield from their land. They wish primarily to produce enough food to eat and possibly to exchange locally. The methods of production used by these small-scale peasant farmers are ever-changing but their basic system is traditional. Such farmers have

Previous page
Sulphur-crushing plant, San Pedro de Atacama, Chile

AGRICULTURE AS A PERCENTAGE OF GDP

MEXICO
9%

CUBA

DOMINICAN REPUBLIC
15%

BELIZE

HONDURAS
21%

HAITI
31%

GUATEMALA
18%

NICARAGUA
29%

EL SALVADOR
22%

COSTA RICA
17%

VENEZUELA
6%

GUYANA

SURINAME

GUYANE

PANAMA
11%

COLOMBIA
17%

ECUADOR
15%

PERU
8%

BRAZIL
9%

BOLIVIA
19%

PARAGUAY
29%

CHILE
9%

ARGENTINA
14%

URUGUAY
11%

Percentage of labour force
employed in agriculture

Below 18 percent

18 - 40 percent

Above 40 percent

The percentage figures show
the proportion of GDP
represented by agriculture

0   1600 km

0   1000 miles

Two peasants sitting on a cart drawn by water buffalo, Marajó Island, at the mouth of the Amazon

TABLE 1
Agricultural population 1987
(Percentage of occupied labour force in agriculture)

Country	Per cent in agriculture
Mexico	31
Guatemala	52
El Salvador	38
Honduras	56
Nicaragua	40
Costa Rica	25
Panama	26
Caribbean	
Cuba	20
Puerto Rico	3
Jamaica	28
Barbados	7
Dominican Republic	38
Guadeloupe	11
Haiti	65
Martinique	9
Trinidad & Tobago	8
Guyana	23
Suriname	17
South America	
Colombia	29
Venezuela	12
Ecuador	32
Peru	36
Brazil	26
Uruguay	14
Paraguay	47
Chile	13
Bolivia	43
Argentina	11
USA	*2.5*
UK	*2.1*

Source: FAO *Production Yearbook*, 1988.

very little money and do not buy much factory-made chemical produce because of its cost and the uncertainty of the benefits that may result from its use. They are concerned with minimizing risks involved with farming since crop failure could mean hunger. A basic way of farming which ensures some success is to plant a wide variety of crops and often several crops in the same field. Therefore, if one field is hit by a hailstorm, only some of the harvest of a few of the crops is lost. Many crops were first used by prehistoric farmers in Latin America – potatoes and maize originated in the New World. Many different varieties of these and of other crops are used by farmers in any village and each variety has different attributes, perhaps being drought resistant, tolerant of cold, or able to withstand strong winds, so that each hazard does not affect all the maize or beans or potatoes in the same way.

Many of the areas where farming has been longest known in Latin America are hilly and animals were not used to till the ground before 1500. Thus, the means of cultivation involved simple tools – hoes, digging sticks or footploughs – and human labour. Such systems are still commonplace in many parts of highland Latin America. Land is planted in crops usually for one to three years before being allowed to revert to scrub so that the soil may regain fertility; fallow periods can last from five to thirty years, depending on the land available and local practice. Livestock are corralled and brought food, or allowed to graze freely, frequently on land being fallowed where some edible plants have grown. Children frequently tend livestock, while planting is usually an adult male task. Women assist in all tasks and when men are absent they do all save those which are physically impossible.

The system of cultivating different plots each year is often, especially in forest areas, referred to as shifting cultivation; it has been widely recognized as an effective and sensitive method of using land resources in such a way as to ensure that the soil can regain fertility and little erosion occurs. Fertility is assisted by use of animal dung but its collection is seldom meticulous and little use is made of human waste. Crops to which chemicals are applied are frequently those destined for sale. Fishing and hunting are adjuncts to farming in many places and provide a further source of protein. Traditional diets based on a combination such as maize, beans and pumpkins (squash) can be well balanced without the inclusion

THE COLUMBIAN EXCHANGE

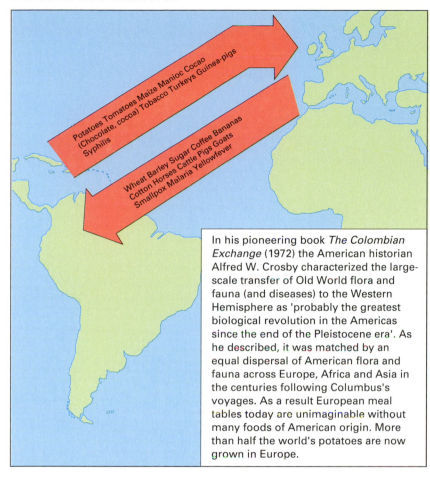

Potatoes Tomatoes Maize Manioc Cocao (Chocolate, cocoa) Tobacco Turkeys Guinea-pigs Syphilis

Wheat Barley Sugar Coffee Bananas Cotton Horses Cattle Pigs Goats Smallpox Malaria Yellowfever

In his pioneering book *The Colombian Exchange* (1972) the American historian Alfred W. Crosby characterized the large-scale transfer of Old World flora and fauna (and diseases) to the Western Hemisphere as 'probably the greatest biological revolution in the Americas since the end of the Pleistocene era'. As he described, it was matched by an equal dispersal of American flora and fauna across Europe, Africa and Asia in the centuries following Columbus's voyages. As a result European meal tables today are unimaginable without many foods of American origin. More than half the world's potatoes are now grown in Europe.

of meat. A range of plants is grown or collected for food flavouring and for medicinal use.

COMMERCIAL FARMING

Most farmers grow some crops and raise animals with a view to selling when the need arises. Livestock, in particular, are regarded as a valuable capital

Coffee plantation, Costa Rica. Coffee is extensively cultivated in the Central American nations, in Colombia and in Brazil. Costa Rica was the first Central American country to grow coffee.

resource since a cow can be sold for cash more or less whenever the need arises. Fully commercial farmers sell a large part of what they grow or rear and buy the necessities of life with the cash received. Many such commercial farmers have small farms and are very poor but their farming system is cash-based and relies on few components. The major crops or products associated with specific Latin American countries such as coffee (Colombia, Brazil), bananas (Ecuador, Colombia), sugar (Cuba, Barbados) or cattle (Argentina, Uruguay) are produced on relatively large farms, employing workers who are paid in cash and use relatively modern methods of production. Grains, especially wheat, are grown throughout Latin America, but they are grown commercially in large quantities only in a few parts. New varieties of wheat developed in the past twenty years are resistant to disease and storm damage, and have proved responsive to the use of artificial fertilizers, but wheat production in general has not kept pace with the demand, inflated by a growing preference for white flours. Argentina is the only country producing sufficient wheat to export.

Major exports of agricultural produce from Latin America have always included fruit and sugar cane from the humid tropical areas. Sugar production occurs predominantly on large estates even where major social reforms have given control of the land to the people. Some mechanization is taking place but sugar production continues to be associated with large amounts of poorly paid manpower. Cuba remains the leading exporter with the Dominican Republic and Guyana also exporting large quantities. Banana-growing for export has traditionally been associated with large estates wholly controlled by one of the few major US fruit companies, particularly in the Central American republics. In Ecuador since the 1950s, and subsequently in Colombia and elsewhere, banana-growing land has passed into the hands of middle-sized farmers – often city-based businessmen. Coffee has long been associated with middle-sized farms in Colombia, Brazil, Guatemala and elsewhere, but these are frequently run as small plantations with a lot of hired labour at harvest time and a sophisticated system of disease control and berry processing to maintain a high quality.

New agricultural exports from Latin America reflect not only changing world demand and prices but also Latin America's low labour costs and climatic advantages over many industrialized countries. Thus, avocado pears, tomatoes and strawberries are all grown intensively in Mexico, largely for export to North America, under conditions closely controlled by US companies; and the highly specialized production of flowers, including orchids, in parts of Central America, and specifically carnations in Colombia, can

Cutting sugar cane, Montero, Bolivia. Sugar is only one of several crops grown in the eastern lowlands of Bolivia, an area to which settlement is spreading from the bleak altiplano.

be expected to spread as air freight services improve their efficiency. The availability of land and feed at lower cost than in the USA has encouraged the development of both cattle ranching, often for low grade minced beef for hamburgers in Central America and Brazil and high quality feedlot-raised livestock, particularly in Mexico. Finally, soya beans have assumed major importance in the past decade in Brazil and, to a lesser extent, Argentina. In 1987 the export of soya beans and associated products (cake and oil) from Brazil was worth more than the export of coffee. Soya beans are grown largely on middle-sized and large farms and the processing is controlled by a small number of mainly foreign companies.

THE ORGANIZATION OF FARMING

At one end of the farming spectrum are large, highly organized units producing tropical fruit for northern hemisphere markets, and at the other are family units producing food crops in addition to hunting and fishing, but with only occasional contact with the money economy. We shall identify the main characteristics of the land tenure, labour system and cropping arrangements for three very broad categories of Latin American farm.

Large-scale commercial farms

Certain crops in Latin America, such as sugar, cotton, wheat and bananas, and livestock, such as sheep and cattle, have customarily been produced on properties needing the labour of many people. In many countries such farms occupy 70 per cent of the farmland but employ only 15 per cent of the farm workforce. Such large farms are frequently owned by large corporations (often foreign-based), by the state, or by powerful families who do not live on the property. It is quite common too for the same family or company to own several such properties, maybe in different areas. Not necessarily all of the available land in these units is used for production. Some potentially fertile land may be held in reserve, particularly where the farm has been established where there are few people. Steep slopes and land that is in any way unsuitable for agricultural production are seldom farmed and frequently protected from grazing or tree felling; these measures help check soil erosion and increase the percolation of the soil by rainfall. Frequently, land in these large units is rented to a number of middle-sized farmers who contract their own labour, if necessary, and pay the landowner with a percentage of their crop or in cash. This was a practice much favoured in southern Brazil and Argentina as a means to get land cleared and/or ploughed for the first time and after an initial period tenants handed back the land ready ploughed or planted with coffee trees. In some areas it is customary to give permanent labourers on the estate a plot of land which they can cultivate for their own benefit. Where land is given as part of the remuneration for labour a range of other services is required besides working on the land, and wages are frequently low.

Large-scale farmers produce livestock and crops for national and international markets, have access to credit from banks and from the government and have the ear of agricultural advisers. They thus have the opportunity to know of and to adopt agricultural innovations and are able to acquire funds to invest in improved techniques and to acquire the new equipment that is difficult for smaller farmers to acquire. Where such large farms are producing for an overseas market the quality of the end product must be high; this demands the greatest care with the preparation of the livestock, bananas or coffee, for instance, in order to meet the consumer standards of the northern industrial nations. Further, the packaging and transportation of the product need care and organization which frequently means either that producer-organizations handle packaging, local and international transport, or that large international companies handle the goods from farm to final market and themselves contract producers to grow what they wish.

In several countries large estates have been acquired by the state as part of a programme of land reform. This has happened to sugar estates in Cuba, to cotton and sugar plantations in Peru and to some estates in Mexico. The consequences of the change in ownership and the creation of an enhanced political status for the labour force have often been profound, but production systems have not necessarily changed; workers have been better paid though not necessarily more productive. Periodic labour shortages, indeed, have often encouraged mechanization. Where the large estates produced temperate crops and livestock the large units of production have not usually been maintained after agrararian reform. The most dramatic change in Cuba that took place at the same time as the land reform was an increase in the range of services available to rural people, in particular education and health care; this has happened to a lesser extent in other countries where effective land reforms have taken place, as in Bolivia and Peru.

For the most part, however, large estates remain important both for the large surpluses they produce, the modern technology that they use and for the relatively small number of people that they employ. Recent years have witnessed the intensification of commercial farming and the establishment of highly capital-intensive farms, not always large in area, producing chickens, pigs, cattle and vegetables in large quantities as well as the feedstuff for the livestock.

Family farms

Family farms are simply defined as those units that give employment only to the nuclear farm family and where extra labour is only occasionally necessary. The essence of family farming is that it fully supports the family without need to have recourse to work elsewhere. Family farms occupy between a quarter and half of the farmland in Argentina, Colombia and Ecuador and employ a similar proportion of the agricultural labour force. In areas of Latin America isolated from markets and where it is difficult to buy manufactured goods, family farming is the way of life

Sheep farm, Uruguay: wool, together with beef, was one of Uruguay's staple exports in the country's era of prosperity, and remains important.

A cattle estancia *in Argentina. The export of beef from the pampas was one of the factors that made Argentina one of the world's richest nations in the 1920s.*

that can provide for most of a family's needs, with goods sold from the farm in order to buy only essential manufactured goods, such farming systems may in fact produce specific staples such as wool or livestock but production is essentially for subsistence. These ways of farming presuppose adequate land resources to enable succeeding generations to farm there too. Because of the cost or difficulty of obtaining new seeds, chemical fertilizers, etc., subsistence farms use a range of traditional and crop varieties and use largely cheaper organic fertilizers. For some cash crops many of the producers are small-scale farmers relying largely on family labour. Coffee, in particular, is often grown by family farmers as the principal means of earning cash; this is the case with tobacco too, and both crops benefit from the level of care that can be applied by family farmers. In pioneer areas in the Amazon basin, along the fringes of the Andes, in the new lands of Mexico's gulf coast and in newly settled areas of northern Argentina, family farms predominate in recently colonized areas; within a decade of initial settlement, however, more successful farmers – usually those with most capital resources – have acquired the land of colonists who have left or gone bankrupt, and family farms do not always retain their importance in respect of agricultural production, although they account for a large proportion of the farms.

Tenure in areas of family farms is varied. In some areas, such as parts of north-east Brazil, many family farms are rented from large, usually absentee, landowners; and the development of grain farming in the humid pampas and coffee in São Paulo was based on the preparation of the land by tenant farmers, most of whom were later displaced. Tenant farming has likewise become less common where some form of land tenure reform has taken place, since tenants are a liability to a large landowner if they cannot easily be replaced. Owner-occupiers predominate amongst family farms even though many may also farm some land that is rented, or sharecropped.

Although the labour force is basically all members of the family, which includes children of maybe eight years of age and over as well as the very old, at times when extra labour is needed others are employed. In many areas the payment of a daily wage and food is now usual, but exchange labour, where kinsfolk or neighbours help in return for eventual reciprocation, remains important in a number of areas and this serves to reinforce and establish links between members of a family-based community.

Land reforms of one sort or another have not affected family farms since they did not monopolize good land nor did they maintain 'feudal' relations with a clearly identified labour force. Indeed, some land reforms have specifically sought to give security of tenure to family farmers by issuing them with land titles, as in the case of Bolivia.

Smallholdings

Smallholders predominate in many Latin American rural areas. By smallholders is meant farm families whose land provides work for less than two people and some of whose household members are therefore forced to obtain work elsewhere or follow non-agricultural activity at home. In countries such as Guatemala, Ecuador, Peru, Haiti, Jamaica and El Salvador more than three-quarters of all farm families live on smallholdings, usually known as *minifundios*. They subsist on such small farm units because they have a variety of sources of income; farming, even on a small scale, provides a good deal of the food necessary for sustenance and it offers a minimum of security which is denied to landless people. Although smallholdings cannot provide enough produce to be sold to pay for all the family's basic needs, many different products are sold according to the needs of the family and the price in the marketplace. The agricultural system of such farmers is closely geared to security of production for family consumption. Thus, traditional varieties of crops are more likely to be grown than new, potentially more productive ones and a wide range of crops is often grown. In mountain areas farmers may have small, widely separated plots at different ecological levels, producing maybe potatoes and other tubers, maize and beans and sweet potatoes, yuca and sugarcane at different altitudes. Livestock are kept for a variety of purposes so cows are also used to plough, and llamas are pack animals as well as wool producers. Many families have a few chickens, guineapigs, or pigs which can not only be eaten but may also be easily sold in a crisis, whereas a ripening crop of bananas or coffee cannot be sold profitably prior to harvest.

By not buying seeds or chemicals or selling the harvest, the farmer avoids the pitfalls of the market-place where prices are determined by external and largely uncontrollable factors and where merchants conspire to minimize the return the farmer gets for his labour.

Although there is little need for outside labour on smallholdings, when some members of the family are working far away, labour may need to be hired. Likewise, many smallholdings are subdivided while the owners work and live elsewhere and other smallholders and family farmers rent or sharecrop these small parcels of land. Where the land is not productive it is not even worth renting and may be abandoned or used for planting trees, as has happened to hillside land in some Caribbean islands.

Many smallholders in Latin America and the Caribbean are desperately poor but, where they have retained their independence, they are often poor largely in relation to improvements in levels of living elsewhere. The continual subdivision of land through inheritance frequently means a shrinking land base from one generation to another even where out-migration is common. The future of the extensive areas of smallholdings, especially in areas of hilllands, is therefore uncertain. In some areas land continues to become concentrated in the hands of a few better-off farmers and merchants as a result of indebtedness and the manipulation of economic and social power; but in other areas such as the Guatemala highlands, the western Andes of Venezuela or the central Andes of Ecuador, Peru and Bolivia, the rate of social and economic change has not led to much change in the role of smallholders.

Fishing

For many coastal communities in Latin America fishing is engaged in both as a subsistence activity and to earn money. Frequently women and children tend the fields while men fish. Where there are good transport systems, fish and shellfish are sold to merchants to deliver them to the main urban markets. Where lobsters and crayfish are caught the price is such that alternative means of collection are devised to overcome the lack of roads, such as small aeroplanes which can land on the beach at low tide.

As with smallholders and family farmers, the level of technology is frequently low, associated with limited capital resources and the minimization of risk. The boats used are hollowed tree-trunks (canoes), and balsa log rafts powered with paddles or a single sail; such boats do not go far from land. Fishermen are frequently subject to domination by middlemen, especially because alternative means of marketing are difficult given the rapid deterioration of dead fish. They are thus as poor as smallholding farmers even though they derive a living from the land as well as the sea.

The beach of a fishing village in northern Peru. Around 1970 Peru was the leading fishing country in world, but overfishing and changes in the coastal current in the 1970s brought a drastic reduction in activity.

Industrial commercial fishing, except in Peru, is city-based and associated with considerable capital investment; it employs a labour force with which factory-style labour relations are maintained. In Peru, until overfishing depleted fish stocks in the 1970s, anchovy fishing for fishmeal caused dozens of small factories and harbours to be established along the coast, in part because of the nuisance caused by the smell and fumes from the processing plants. Fishing on this scale is concerned largely with the export of frozen and tinned fish as well as fishmeal, and northern hemisphere demand for certain seaproducts, such as lobsters and crayfish, encourages the construction of freezing plants near fishing grounds. Shrimp farming under controlled conditions in former areas of mangroves in many parts of coastal Ecuador became important in the 1980s and had overtaken bananas as the most valuable export commodity after petroleum.

MARKETING

Marketing is an important component of agriculture, even where subsistence farming predominates, for exchange of goods customarily takes place between farmers as well as between farmers and merchants or consumers. Marketplaces are an important part of the rural scene in Latin America, but particularly where the scale of farming is such that there is ample demand for intermediaries to collect small quantities of produce. Marketplaces, however, have a variety of functions and while they serve as centres for peasant exploitation through false weights, unfair prices and physical coercion, they are also important social and political meeting grounds. They have long been regarded by non-farmers, especially by local and regional oligarchies, as potentially dangerous and their foundation and development is frequently politically controlled.

The largest volume of agricultural produce in Latin American rural marketing systems is destined for export, but the marketing structures that are involved are frequently simple and bypass local markets; the bananas, coffee, or livestock are passed directly to national wholesalers who are part of or contracted by international marketing companies, and who grade and export the commodity to the northern industrialized countries. External demands for specific commodities articulated by marketing agencies not only stimulate production but also dictate the nature of the commodity produced.

Many rural Latin American areas have marketing systems that function through periodic markets where many small-scale producers sell goods and buy other items that they do not or cannot produce.

The city- and town-based merchants not only collect quantities of farm produce for urban markets but they also sell manufactured goods. Such marketplaces are highly complex systems in which each actor may play several different roles.

A major drawback to rural marketing as far as small farmers are concerned is the extent to which the prices for farm produce rise more slowly than those of manufactured goods and also the large differences in prices at local markets and in cities. In part this is the result of government policy which seeks to minimize the cost of staple foods to the articulate urban proletariat, but it is also a reflection of a labyrinthine market system where multiple middlemen extract profit from dealing with farm produce. The numerous attempts to form co-operatives to overcome this have seldom been successful because of the hostility of merchants, the inadequate training of those who seek to encourage their formation and the deep suspicion with which farmers regard such externally inspired organizations.

MAJOR CONTEMPORARY TRENDS IN FARMING

Over many areas of Latin America large numbers of rural people are leaving for towns, cities, colonization areas and for other countries. This has led to an actual emptying of the countryside in areas as diverse as highland Colombia and lowland Argentina. Such a trend is not only a consequence of the continuing impoverishment of rural Latin America but also a reflection of the penetration of rural areas by urban value systems which demean the rural farmer and exalt the town dweller. Schooling in rural areas, for example, prepares children for urban employment rather than for rural life.

A series of factors combine to decrease the production of a surplus of food crops and cause increased imports of the necessary goods. On the one hand, market systems do not stimulate commercial production of non-export crops, while, on the other, the middle-sized farmer seldom has access to credit and technical knowledge that is adequate to encourage him to produce more of the crops that are needed in urban centres. Large-scale producers are increasingly encouraged to produce export crops for which prices are high. International market systems encourage vertical integration which provides the producer with the comfort of advice and security of a contract with an exporter but at the cost of the option to sell elsewhere. Major changes such as the dramatic recent increase in soya-bean production in Argentina, and especially Brazil, and in chickens and eggs, which may be regarded as by-products of maize and soya-bean production, have broadened the range of agricultural products exported from Latin America. Such changes are important because they signify the rise of a new form of agriculture, frequently known as 'agribusiness', in which either multinational or national metropolitan companies invest capital in high-technology farming of export crops, making use of largely imported technology, cheap labour and often limited investment in land. Thus, Colombia has for a decade been a major exporter of carnations grown expressly for the North American and European markets, and Mexico exports large quantities of strawberries to the United States, largely during the period of highest prices when Californian fruit is not ready.

Perhaps the largest-scale example of agribusiness has been the growth of large cattle ranches in Brazilian Amazonia during the early 1970s. At this time Volkswagen, Armour-Swift and other major multinational companies were encouraged by the Brazilian government to obtain large blocks of land for the creation of cattle farms for the export of meat and meat products to the major population centres in eastern Brazil and to the northern hemisphere. To the overseas investor, Latin American agribusiness may be attractive because of the ready availability of cheap land, low wage rates and the consequent high return of capital invested, which is such that initial investment is often completely recovered within five years.

Finally, the increasing involvement of multinational companies in foodprocessing industries in Latin America often provides a powerful stimulus to production. Thus, while soya beans in Brazil are grown largely by individuals and co-operatives of Brazilian farmers, the milling of the beans is controlled by industrial corporations, predominantly Anderson Clayton, Unilever, Cargill, and Bunge and Born.

The importance of this trend in Latin American agriculture lies less in the land area that is devoted to producing export crops and industrial raw materials than in the priority that governments are thus encouraged to give to a form of farming that enriches very few rural people. Usually this is at the expense of the vast mass of smallholders and family farmers who produce much of the basic food consumed by the working-class majority of urban people.

AGRICULTURE AND THE DEBT CRISIS

The economic crisis of the 1980s affected all Latin Americans but perhaps least those involved in farming. A large part of farm production is still destined for local markets or for farming people themselves, and thus is little affected by the global or national economy. Production from medium-sized and large farms was stimulated by national needs for export to earn foreign exchange to service the accumulated debt. Agriculture's share of Gross Domestic Product grew slowly in the period 1980–86, but this was still three times as fast as GDP as a whole.

The move of people from the land slowed during the 1980s. Urban growth slackened from 0.84 per cent per year in the 1960s to 0.54 per cent in the 1980s. The number of traditional sector farmers increased markedly (by 41 per cent) between 1960 and 1980. The agricultural population in the modern farming sector was better off than that in the traditional sector but much of the employment in export-oriented production is seasonal and poorly paid.

DAP

Further Reading: D. Barkin, *Distorted Development. Mexico in the World Economy* (Boulder, Colorado, 1990); R. Burbach and P. Flynn, *Agribusiness in the Americas* (New York, 1980); J. Foweraker, *The Struggle for Land: A Political Economy of the Pioneer Frontier in Brazil from 1930 to the Present Day* (Cambridge, 1981); W. C. Thiesenhusen, ed., *Searching for Agrarian Reform in Latin America* (Boston, 1989)

Hidalgo covered market, Guanajuato, Mexico. As in many such markets in Mexico a wide variety of produce is on sale.

Mining

MINING AND THE DEVELOPMENT OF LATIN AMERICA

Starting with the search for gold, then silver, the pursuit of metals was an important impetus to the settlement of Latin America. Initially, Spain, and to a lesser extent Portugal, tried to restrict the trade in mining products, as in other staples, to designated ports and routes. However, their weakening hold on the colonies in the eighteenth and early nineteenth centuries led to a relaxation of those restrictions to the benefit of the mine owners and the landed classes and the trend was continued when the same classes came to political power with the independence of most of Latin America in the 1820s. The new countries committed themselves to more open trading policies.

Mining in Latin America had fallen into relative decline, but it was greatly expanded in the second half of the nineteenth century. Three circumstances contributed to this change: there was a growing industrial demand for non-ferrous minerals in Britain, Western Europe and the United States; the costs of transport were significantly reduced by the steamship and the railway, effectively creating a revaluation of Latin American mineral reserves; and the young Latin American countries welcomed capital and technology for mining from overseas as one

way of both realigning political ties and of building a larger national economy. Mining was particularly encouraged in Mexico, Chile, Peru and Bolivia.

A distinctive geographical dualism was created with mines, railways and ports forming the long axis of an island of modernity in a sea of tradition – almost a foreign beachhead in an alien continent – with little exchange between the one and the other.

The laissez-faire attitude of Latin American governments to mining was jolted by the domestic consequences of the Great Depression of 1929. Then the absence during the Second World War of a return flow of manufactured goods for minerals now in demand stimulated governments and individuals to promote local manufacturing and the diversion of domestic capital away from the mining industry. And even when peace returned, and brought with it a high demand for minerals, Latin American countries felt that the controlled prices offered by the consuming countries (whose companies frequently owned the mines in Latin America) were below those a free market would allow. Governments began to adopt a more purposeful policy towards mining.

The state began to exercise more control over the mining industries in the 1950s. In some countries this meant outright nationalization of all or significant parts of the industry. This occurred in Bolivia (1952), Cuba (1959–60), Chile (1971), Guyana (1971), Peru (1973) and Nicaragua (in 1979). Elsewhere the state or national private companies and individuals negotiated majority holdings in existing mining enterprises: this has been the policy in, for

TABLE 2

Significant production of selected minerals and metals in Latin America, 1989 (thousand metric tons)

Selected countries	Bauxite	Aluminium	Copper	Lead	Zinc	Tin	Gold (tonnes)	Silver (tonnes)	Iron ore	Steel crude
Argentina	–	–	–	26	43	–	–	–	580	3900
Bolivia	–	–	–	16	72	14.4	10	173	–	–
Brazil	8250	888	–	19	103	50.2	96.9	–	154,000	25,000
Chile	–	–	1609	–	–	–	26.1	470	8470	609
Colombia	–	–	–	–	–	–	30.7	–	500	–
Guyana	1430	–	–	–	–	–	–	–	–	–
Jamaica	9400	–	–	–	–	–	–	–	–	–
Mexico	–	71	230	175	271	–	–	2120	7400	7700
Peru	–	–	364	193	597	5.1	–	1710	4170	–
Suriname	3400	–	–	–	–	–	–	–	–	222
Venezuela	–	546	–	–	–	–	–	–	19,030	3500
Total Latin America	23,380	1698	2240	436	1137	69.7	229*	5000*	194,150	40,100
% of world production	23	12	26	14	18	32	14	37	20	5

* Estimated.

Sources: Calculated from *Mining Annual Review* 1990 and *Metals and Minerals Annual Review* 1990 (*Mining Journal*, London).

example, Mexico, Brazil, Venezuela and Jamaica. The high degree of foreign involvement in the mining industries gave such moves much popular support. By 1980 there was no country in Latin America where foreign capital effectively controlled output.

Modern mining, like a modern metallurgical industry, is increasingly capital-intensive. Many of the developments in mining in Latin America during the second half of the twentieth century have been in the bulk-mining of low-value minerals using highly mechanized techniques. In the 1970s and early 1980s the risks inherent in entering major new mining ventures were often cushioned by the involvement of the state, and oil-rich states with seemingly stable governments, such as Mexico and Venezuela, were able to enter into significant new mining development thanks to the easy availability of petro-dollars.

THE SITUATION AT THE BEGINNING OF THE 1990S

Latin America was responsible for about one eighth of the value of all non-fuel minerals produced in the world during the 1980s. In 1989 Latin America's mines produced about a third of the world's silver and tin, a quarter of its copper and bauxite, one fifth of its iron ore, one sixth of its zinc and molybdenum, one seventh of its lead, one eighth of its gold, and a tenth of its manganese; she was an important source of certain speciality minerals such as antimony, tantalum and niobium; Brazilian aquamarines, opals and other gemstones and Colombian emeralds are famous. However, the contribution of mining (excluding that of fuels) to the gross domestic product of the region has been declining. At the end of the 1980s it was a little above 2 per cent; in the 1970s it had averaged about 3 per cent and in the 1960s about 4 per cent. Mining accounted for about 8 per cent of the continent's industrial activity in 1989 and gave direct employment to over half a million people, or about 1 per cent of the total workforce.

Most metals mined in Latin America are still destined for export, and metals make a larger contribution to the external trade of Latin America than they do to its internal economy. They represented about one quarter of the non-petroleum trade of the region in 1983–7. Iron ore (2.3 per cent of total trade in 1983–7) and copper (1.8 per cent) were the third and fourth export staples of the continent (after petroleum (30 per cent) and coffee (7.6 per cent); exports of iron ore and bauxite are now of growing importance.

The mining industry of Latin America is based upon a relatively restricted portfolio of minerals, and these are unevenly distributed over the continent.

The major copper ore bodies are found on the western slopes of the Andes in central and northern Chile and southern and central Peru, and in north-western Mexico where they form an extension of those in Arizona and Utah. They are of the porphyry type deposits in which the copper is disseminated widely and more or less uniformly, oxidized near the surface and the deeper deposits sulphides. Iron ore deposits are more widespread. They include ancient sedimentary 'iron formations', often several hundred metres thick, in which local enrichment to create high-grade (50–55 per cent Fe content) ores has taken place to produce residual ores which are earthy in texture: most of the iron ore mined in Brazil and Venezuela and some in Mexico is of this nature. Another set of deposits is of igneous origin: concentrations of magnetite which have replaced other rocks in the contact zones of metamorphic activity. Deposits of this type are typical of western South America and Mexico – the Marcona deposit in Peru is a good example. The bauxite ores resemble in origin the sedimentary iron ores with aluminium taking the place of iron: the Caribbean islands and the north-eastern quadrant of South America – Venezuela, the Guianas and Brazil – have the main reserves. Primary tin deposits of any size are restricted to veins which thread the high eastern Andes of Bolivia; alluvial and eluvial deposits occur in adjoining Brazil. Some gold is mined in situ in the highlands of the ancient Brazilian Shield but most is won from past and present alluvial deposits, particularly in Amazonia. Zinc, lead and silver are often associated either in veins or disseminated amongst limestone or similar deposits: Mexico and Peru are the leading producers.

This uneven distribution means that the mining industry is highly significant in the economic life of some countries and insignificant in others. The leading mining country in absolute terms is undoubtedly Chile. In 1980, it ranked sixth in the world table of major mineral producers, and has confirmed this position thanks to the premier role played by copper. Brazil (eleventh) has since leap-frogged Peru (tenth place) and Mexico (twelfth); Venezuela (twenty-fourth) has risen and Bolivia (twenty-fifth) fallen. The importance of mining in Chile is underlined when allowance is made for its relatively small population and limited size. The part of the income directly derived from mining of the average Chilean (about $230 in 1989) is comparable to that of the average South African or Australian: it is five times that for the average Bolivian and ten times that of the average Peruvian or Brazilian. Amongst the smaller countries mining generated some $165 in 1989 for the average Jamaican (a figure only surpassed by that provided by tourism), and $115 to the hard-pressed Surinamese. There is a similar variation in the degree

Chuquicamata open-cast copper mine, Chile. 'Chuqui', as the mine is colloquially known in Chile, was for many years 'the largest hole in the ground' in the world.

of dependency of the national export trades upon metallic minerals. Bolivia still gains half its legitimate overseas earnings from its mines and smelters. For Chile, without a drug trade, the fraction is slightly higher; for Jamaica, Guyana, and Peru a little less; but for large Brazil and oil-rich Venezuela and Mexico the proportion sinks below 10 per cent. Nowhere else does the trade in non-fuel minerals remain a significant fraction of the national total, although regionally and locally it may be highly important.

Chile

Since 1982 Chile has been the largest copper producer in the world, with an output of 1.609 million tonnes or 23 per cent of the non-ex-Communist world's total in 1989. Production is rising: it first reached the million mark in 1976, having passed the half-million figure in the late 1950s and the quarter-million level in the late 1920s; new mines likely to come on stream during the mid-1990s will continue the upward trend and Chile should then be providing a quarter of the world's primary copper; her reserves, of about 140 million tonnes, are the largest in the world.

The scale of the Chilean copper industry has endowed it with particular political importance. Prior to 1955 the political arguments were mainly aimed at ensuring that Chile received a fair share of the return from a national resource which would clearly not last for ever. From 1955 the policy changed to one of gaining more state control over the big mines: in the 1960s the big three mines accounted for over 80 per cent of Chile's copper production and consequently a very substantial part of the 8 per cent of the gross domestic product, 60 per cent of the value of exports and 80 per cent of government tax receipts then contributed by copper to the national economy. In the

late 1960s the state acquired a majority holding of the Chilean assets of Anaconda and Kennecott and an agreement, under threat of outright nationalization, of expanded investment and increased refining capacity. In 1971 the Popular Unity government of President Allende nationalized the three big mines and two others (Exotica near Chuquicamata, and Andina). After the overthrow of Allende in 1973, agreement was reached with the US copper companies indemnifying them against the results of nationalization, and they have returned to the country, but not to regain ownership of the big mines. Since 1976 these have been run by the state Corporación de Cobre de Chile (Codelco).

Peru

Cerro de Pasco is the name most widely associated with mining in modern Peru. It housed one of the great silver mines of the continent until the end of the nineteenth century. Since then the hill has been mined away and interest has shifted to the non-ferrous ores associated with the silver mineralization. There has also been a move away from underground and towards open-pit mining methods. Today, most of Peru's lead, zinc and silver comes from mines in the Central Sierra, and most of its copper, iron ore and gold comes from the south.

Peru is the largest source of lead and zinc ores in Latin America and occupies fourth and third positions in the world production of these minerals. But it is lower down in the tables of metal production: only a third of its lead and a quarter of its zinc is actually smelted in Peru.

The importance of copper in modern Peru dates from 1960 when the first shipments of ore were made from the Toquepala deposits. Today the Southern Peru Copper Corporation (SPCC) is the most important copper producer in the country; it remains in private hands with the United States company Asarco its major shareholder. But most of the other significant mines belong to the state: the Compania Minero del Centro (Centromín) is the largest producer of lead, silver and zinc, the Empresa Minera del Peru (Mineroperú) acts as the main purchasing and mining development agency, the Tintaya corporation mines the Tintaya copper deposit, and Marcona – the main iron ore mine – is now worked under the auspices of Hierro Peru. The change to a monetarist economic policy following the 1990 election of President Fujimori presages a lessening involvement of the state in mining and smelting and, in time, more overseas interest in the industry.

Bolivia

Mining in Bolivia offers many contrasts with that elsewhere in Latin America. Tin replaced silver as the

MAJOR MINES OF LATIN AMERICA

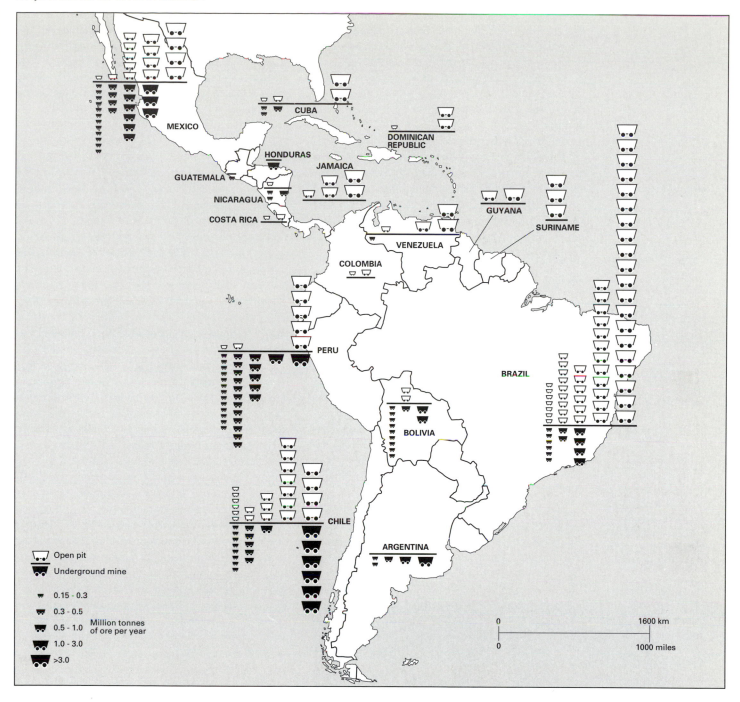

Open pit

Underground mine

0.15 - 0.3
0.3 - 0.5
0.5 - 1.0 Million tonnes
of ore per year
1.0 - 3.0
>3.0

0   1600 km

0   1000 miles

country's staple product at the beginning of the twentieth century and remained so until the 1980s. It is found in veins associated with the granite batholiths which core the eastern Andes, and extracting it has made harsh demands upon Bolivia's miners. Most tin mines are above the 4000-metre contour line, and some above the permanent snowline, where the rarefied atmosphere affects the efficiency of men and machines.

Two thirds of the tin produced in 1985 and two thirds of Bolivia's overall mineral production came

from a dozen larger mines which had been the property of the Patiño, Aramayo and Hochschild interests prior to the revolution of 1952, and which had subsequently been amalgamated to form the rump of the state mining corporation Comibol. These mines had long suffered from lack of investment and expertise and were over their most productive phases when nationalized; they continued to be under-capitalized, poorly equipped, labour-intensive and increasingly economically marginal. Their parlous condition was irredeemably exposed when the tin price collapsed following the bankruptcy of the International Tin Council in 1985, and the majority of Comibol and Bolivia's mines closed. Only those with reserves of minerals other than tin have survived into the 1990s.

There is a second tier of commercial mines in Bolivia that is under private ownership: these include the Porco lead and zinc mines, a gold-leaching operation outside Oruro, some wolfram mines, and two tin dredges.

Bolivia's present dependence on mining (it provided half its legitimate export income in 1990) is a persistent feature of its history. With the dramatic rise in the 1980s of Brazil as a major new source, and with the slackened world demand for tin, the metal seems destined to play only a relatively modest economic role during the rest of a century in which it has been Bolivia's dominant commodity.

Mexico

Mexico's mines provided 3 per cent of the country's GDP in 1950, but during the 1980s their contribution was down to 1.3 per cent, although mining still gave employment to some quarter of a million people. Yet Mexico remains the world's leading producer of silver (2120 tonnes in 1989, or one fifth of the total produced in the non-Communist world). Most of this silver is mined as a by-product of the older non-ferrous metals, and it is these that have superseded silver in economic importance in Mexico during the twentieth century. In terms of total value copper was the most valuable metal until 1930, lead until 1950 and zinc since 1950.

Many of the older mines were developed by foreign capital – British and latterly US. But after 1961 a policy of progressive Mexicanization was pursued with the consequence that by 1980 48 per cent of the capital invested in the Mexican mining industry was

drawn from private Mexican sources and 15 per cent from Mexican public funds; only the remaining 37 per cent came from overseas sources. However, the growing state involvement in the mining industry was reversed in 1989 when President Carlos Salinas unveiled his new economic policy. This included more liberal investment regulations and a deliberate programme of selling off various state-owned enterprises to the private sector.

Brazil

In 1989 Brazil (154 million tonnes) was third to the USSR (241 million tonnes) and China (162 million tonnes) as a world producer of iron ore, and was the leading supplier (113.7 million tonnes, Australia 108.1 million tonnes) to the world trade (422 million tonnes) in the ore. The roots of this situation are in the 1940s when Brazil began to develop a domestic iron-and-steel industry on the back of an export trade in iron ore. Development was put in the hands of the government-owned Companhia Vale do Rio Doce (CVRD) and the deposits south and east of Belo Horizonte in Minas Gerais were attacked. In 1966 the new port of Tubarão, near Vitoria, was opened: it is one of the few ports in the world capable of handling 250,000-tonne ore-carriers, and in 1989 shipped about 55 million tonnes. During the 1970s work began on developing a second major iron ore deposit, at the Serra dos Carajás situated in Pará state. A new 900-kilometre-long railway was completed in 1985 linking the deposits with a new sea terminal at Ponta da Madeira near São Luis in Maranhão. In 1986 13 million tonnes of ore moved down the railway; in 1990 it was working to its full capacity of about 33 million tonnes. The development, to 1987, had cost about $3.8 billion, with CVRD contributing $1.6 billion, Brazilian sources $850 million, the World Bank $365 million and Japanese and European sources the rest. This is part of a more grandiose scheme – the Grande Carajás Project – in which mining and the basic infrastructure serving it is to underwrite the creation of a regional growth pole. As well as the railway, the river ports of Barcarena and Itaqui (capable of taking ocean-going bulk carriers) and the hydro-electric resources of the Tocantin River are key elements in this development.

The remarkable Serra Pelada gold pit lies within the CVRD concession, and although the company was unable to take control of it during the 1980s from the prospectors, or *garimpeiros* (in 1983 at the height of its exploitation there were 40,000 working the diggings, in 1990 15,000), the company began exploiting other gold ores nearby in 1991. Agriculture, forestry and cattle raising will supplement mining. Another giant mineral development of recent years has been that of the Trombetas bauxite deposits, a thousand

Bolivian miners. For much of the twentieth century tin-mining was fundamental to the Bolivian economy. However the world market for tin collapsed in the mid-1980s.

Aerial view of the Carajás iron-ore mine, Brazil. By the early 1980s Brazil was second only to the then Soviet Union as a producer of iron ore.

kilometres north-west of Carajás, discovered by the Aluminum Company of Canada in 1966, and worked since 1979 by Mineração Rio do Norte (in which CVRD has a 46 per cent interest and Alcan 24 per cent).

In 1990 some 8 million tonnes of bauxite were mined at Trombetas, almost 10 per cent of that produced by the market economy countries of the world. The mining of bauxite and the production of alumina are recent growth areas in the Brazilian economy: Amazonia alone has estimated reserves of 4000 million tonnes and cheap hydro-electric power potential. Manganese ore is another recent product of Amazonia with the major source to date being the mines inland from Santana in Amapá Territory; large reserves exist at Urucum near Corumbá in Mato Grosso; and open-pit manganese production started near Carajás with the opening of the railway. Perhaps the most remarkable expansion of mining in Amazonian Brazil in recent years has been in tin: in 1984 Brazil overtook Bolivia as the leading producer in Latin America and by the end of the decade had become the world's largest producer and effectively controlled the international tin price.

There has also been a substantial growth in Brazil's gold production in recent years. This has come from two sources. The first, and most important, has been discoveries made by *garimpeiros*: the frontier regions of Rondônia and Roraima have seen gold rushes during the 1980s and prospectors now produce three quarters of Brazil's enhanced production; with the result that in 1989 Brazil occupied fifth place in the world table of gold producers. The second has been the increased investment in conventional gold mining during the 1980s. Interestingly much of this has come via the Anglo-American Corporation of Brazil, capitalizing on the expertise gained in the geologically similar goldfields of South Africa.

The recent invasion of Amazonia by miners (and others) has created a number of conflicts and unresolved policy issues. One concern relates to the impact of mining on the relationships between the newcomers and the indigenous Amazonian Indians, and on the degree to which the ecological balance of the forests should be disturbed to provide what is becoming an increasingly valuable input into a hard-pressed national economy.

Venezuela

Mining in Venezuela focuses on the iron mines of the middle Orinoco valley. In 1981 proven reserves of iron ore with an iron content of at least 55 per cent were established at 2116 million tonnes and production doubled in the 1980s (reaching 18 million tonnes in 1989). The major mine is a huge open-cast working at Cerro Bolivar. The iron mines and processing plants have since 1975 been in domestic ownership, but many joint mining ventures with US steel firms are in hand. 1983 saw the first production of alumina from the new Interalumina refinery in Ciudad Guayana, a refinery financed almost entirely by domestic funds.

Jamaica, Suriname and Guyana

Jamaica, Suriname and Guyana were the source of one sixth of the western world's bauxite production of 91.9 million tonnes in 1989, a quarter (of 80.8 million) in 1980 and one-third (of 50.7 million) in 1970. In each of the countries the initiative to develop the reserves came from one or other of the Big Four North American companies – Alcan, Alcoa, Kaiser and Reynolds – and with a view to feeding their processing plants conveniently situated in the US and Canada. In recent years the local governments have been trying to increase the benefits accruing to their countries, spurred partly by the example set by the

Industry

OPEC countries, partly to counter inflation, and partly for internal political reasons. Guyana nationalized its industry in 1971. Jamaica and Suriname preferred to increase the export levies charged on the export of bauxite and to enter further into downstream processing: alumina production generates three times the unit income derived from mere bauxite mining. Whereas overseas business confidence in Jamaica had recovered by the end of the 1980s and the major international aluminium companies were expanding refining capacity, in Suriname the two main bauxite producers – Suralco (Alcoa) and Billiton (Royal Dutch Shell) – were holding back on investment. Both Guyana and Suriname have rich resources of hydro-electric power and would like to harness it to produce refined aluminium (worth twelve times as much as the raw bauxite; for although the three ex-colonies produced half Latin America's bauxite in 1990, they produced none of the continent's 1.7 million tonnes of primary aluminium.

Mining elsewhere in Latin America

Important mines or mining prospects in the Caribbean and the Central American isthmus include the nickel mines of Cuba, whose reserves (20 million tonnes in 1989) are equivalent to about twenty years' world supply, the nickel, silver and gold mines of the Dominican Republic, and the Cerro Colorado porphyry copper deposit in the Chiriqui province of western Panama. Colombia is, perhaps, best known for its emeralds, but production figures are unreliable; it is the only significant coal-producing country of Latin America (see 'Energy'). The country is also second to Brazil in Latin America as a gold producer, the gold being won from the alluvium of the rivers of the Antioquia department. In contrast, Paraguay and Uruguay have mineral reserves of little value and Argentina's are relatively small; only Argentina's uranium has attracted any significant (state) investment, and that for strategic rather than commercial reasons. DJF

Further Reading: F. E. Banks, *Bauxite and Aluminum: An Introduction to the Economics of Non-fuel Minerals* (Lexington, Mass., 1978); D. Cleary, *Anatomy of the Amazon Gold Rush* (London, 1990); E. Dore, *The Peruvian Mining Industry: Growth, Stagnation and Crisis* (Westview Press, London, 1988); D. J. Fox, *Mining in Latin America: Contemporary Change in Andean Bolivia and Amazonian Brazil*, Euro-Latin America Research Papers, 1, 1989 (University of Bradford); T. Greaves and W. Culver, eds., *Miners and Mining in the Americas* (Manchester, 1985); R. Mikesell, ed., *Foreign Investment in the Petroleum and Mineral Industries: Case-studies in Investor-Host Country Relations* (Baltimore, 1971); *Mining Annual Review and Metals and Minerals Annual Review* (London, published annually in July by *Mining Journal*)

Latin America is not internationally renowned for its industrial base. This partially stems from the colonial period when industrial development was largely prevented due to tight Spanish and Portuguese control of colonial trade and the privileged position given to Spanish- and Portuguese-endorsed manufacturers in supplying industrial goods. With independence, such controls were lifted but industrial development became closely identified with the expansion of exports – such as nitrates in Chile, coffee in Brazil and beef cattle in Argentina. The growth in exports did lead to significant industrial expansion in some countries, notably Argentina and Mexico, where the industrial sectors contributed 18 per cent and 14 per cent respectively to the domestic product by 1905. The American historian Warren Dean has demonstrated that the timing of São Paulo's industrial growth before 1930 was closely synchronized with good coffee exports, notably in the period between 1907 and 1913. The First World War, making industrial imports more scarce, also stimulated a moderate increase in manufacturing activity.

IMPORT SUBSTITUTION INDUSTRIALIZATION

A major watershed in Latin America's industrial development came in 1929–30 with the onset of the World Depression. Latin American exports declined precipitously from an average of almost $5000 million in 1928–9 to $1500 million in 1933. With the concomitant decline in foreign exchange, Latin America found itself able to finance ever decreasing amounts of imported manufactured goods from industrial countries. Various measures were taken to conserve and ration decreased foreign exchange resources and restrictions were placed on the use of foreign exchange. An array of policies was developed out of the crisis, and an administrative machinery established to carry them out. Latin America changed from a set of free-trade economies to a continent of highly protected economies. Tariffs, quotas, and exchange controls provided protection from foreign competitors by making the entry of foreign goods expensive or impossible. Latin American entrepreneurs, observing the scarcity of goods and the level of protection, began to produce or increase the production of goods previously imported. Industrial production and employment increased as a result; in Chile, industrial employment increased by over 5 per cent a year between 1928 and 1937, but in those sectors that protection particularly favoured, employment rose at much higher rates – 10 per cent per annum in metal products, 16 per cent in textiles and 19 per cent in chemicals.

Such a strategy of industrial development behind high protective tariffs continued to be followed in most Latin American countries after the worst phase of the Depression had improved. It became formalized into a policy known as 'import substitution industrialization' (ISI). Adherents of the policy came to envisage four stages of industrial production within this process of industrialization. The first stage saw the production of basic non-durable consumer goods such as textiles, foodstuffs and pharmaceuticals. This was followed by the production of consumer durable products, such as small ovens, radios and televisions, and the important motor vehicle industry; assembly began with a considerable ratio of imported parts. The third stage was critical in the industrializing process as it had to promote 'intermediate' industries, producing the inputs for companies set up during the first and second stages. Typical industries at this stage were chemical plants making paint, synthetic fibres, dyes and acids, or engineering works producing small motors and gearboxes, or parts industries for durable goods assembly. The final stage of the process promoted the development of the capital goods industry which would manufacture machinery and plant installations. It was the task of the government to plan and synchronize each subsequent stage in the process.

However, as import substitution industrialization progressed through the 1950s and 1960s, it became evident that, despite its theoretical attraction, high-cost industry normally resulted, particularly in the smaller countries where market size was limited. A United Nations study that analysed eleven non-durable and nine durable consumer goods sectors in 1964 concluded: 'the prevailing situation in the region is characterized by high relative prices of manufactured products and this phenomenon cannot but affect the size of Latin America's market for this type of good'.

High costs and high prices behind high protective tariffs were due to a wide variety of factors, but one key structural problem was the lack of economies of scale that small markets permitted, particularly in the critical second and third stages of the import substitution process. As production increases in any operation, per-unit costs will normally decline as fixed costs (e.g. plant and technology) will be spread over more and more units. The decline in per-unit costs with increased production will slacken and even out at some stage (known as the minimum efficient scale) before perhaps rising as output increases still further.

The example of the motor vehicle industry can demonstrate the relationship between economies of scale and import substitution industrialization in Latin America. Table 3 shows vehicle output for each producing country by firm for 1977, when policies of import substitution still dominated manufacturing. It is evident that assembly plant economies were only achieved by firms operating in Brazil (Volkswagen, General Motors, Ford and Fiat). Other countries had firms in which severe cost penalties were operating on their assembly operations. As a result, high-cost cars were being produced and sold to national consumers. A detailed cost analysis of the Chilean motor vehicle industry in 1969 demonstrated that cars were produced at up to three times the cost in the vehicle's country of origin. Cars in both Argentina and Venezuela were being sold at double international levels in the late 1970s.

Such high prices and high costs were not solely the result of a lack of sufficient economies of scale in the assembly of vehicles. In order to promote certain stage-three industries, many governments instituted schemes whereby assembly firms had to purchase increasing quantities of nationally produced components. However, components production can require greater production runs than vehicle assembly in order to achieve maximum economies of scale. Modern engine and transmission plants attain maximum economies of scale at annual production levels of 500,000 per annum (although cost penalties are not great once levels of 100,000 per annum are reached). Again, only the Brazilian assembly industry could offer such a scale of demand. Thus, apart from Brazil, the pattern of the Latin American motor vehicle industry under policies of import substitution has been one of small-scale plants assembling high-cost components for a domestic market limited by the high prices of the finished product.

Developing in the late 1950s and 1960s, the motor vehicle industry occupied a significant and potentially influential position in the process of import substitution industrialization. As an assembly industry, it produced one of the more sophisticated goods of the second stage. However, in terms of government planning, its critical role was to develop a variety of components industries which, through backward linkage, would create additional demand for the national production of such basic goods as steel, alloys, aluminium, plastics and glass. Its eventual high cost caused scepticism about the applicability of import substitution for the efficient production of more sophisticated products and for the ability of the process to advance further than stage two without the aid of very high tariffs. Nevertheless, in this context, such factors as market size and character became crucial as large, rapidly growing markets seemed to provide conditions in which import substitution could prosper.

Chrysler factory, Toluca industrial park, Mexico. Chrysler is one of several mutinational corporations to have set up auto assembly plants in Latin America.

TABLE 3

Distribution of motor vehicle production by country and firm, in Latin America, 1977

	Argentina	Brazil	Chile	Colombia	Mexico	Peru	Venezuela	TOTAL	%
Chrysler	23,434	21,970	–	8275	56,956	7169	32,430	151,234	9.1
Fiat	47,837	77,963	3120	4128	–	–	4889	137,937	8.3
Ford	56,795	130,197	–	–	50,503	–	61,665	299,160	17.9
General Motors	20,897	153,836	2124	–	34,638	–	32,281	243,776	14.6
Mercedes Benz	7845	52,957	–	–	–	–	564	61,366	3.7
Nissan	–	–	–	–	37,066	5270	5223	47,559	2.9
Peugeot/Citroen	34,214	–	5277	–	–	–	–	39,491	2.4
Renault	34,744	–	2568	17,353	27,559	–	5153	87,377	5.2
Volkswagen	–	472,192	–	–	52,143	6075	5340	535,750	32.1
Others	9590	10,127	–	–	20,948	6710	15,752	63,127	3.8
Total	235,356	919,242	13,089	29,756	280,813	25,224	163,297	1,666,777	100.0
Percentage	14.1	55.2	0.8	1.8	16.8	1.5	9.8	100.0	

INDUSTRIALIZATION AND ECONOMIC INTEGRATION

The disadvantages of small market size for import substitution industrialization gave great impetus to schemes of economic integration. The creation of the Latin American Free Trade Association (LAFTA) in 1960 (which came to include most major countries of South America and Mexico) was unable to stimulate much industrial progress due to the limited terms of reference of the scheme and the lack of success in inter-regional trade liberalization. However, schemes involving only small countries achieved greater success.

The Central American Common Market (CACM), created in 1960 and consisting of Guatemala, El Salvador, Nicaragua, Costa Rica and Honduras, gave manufacturers a market of 10 million, up to ten times larger than previous national markets. With a strong commitment to close integration, the CACM had virtually achieved both intra-regional free trade and the imposition of a common external tariff by 1966. Industrial growth not only benefited from a common external tariff that averaged 48 per cent overall and averaged 80 per cent for consumer goods but also from a scheme for the regional allocation of key industries. This scheme was established because certain industries, in order to achieve adequate economies of scale, would need only one plant to serve the whole market of the CACM. In 1961 it was agreed that each member country should benefit from one of these industries. Unfortunately, during the 1970s, the CACM began to disintegrate, partly because of the unequal distribution of industrial growth that had occurred in the 1960s. During the 1980s ideological differences between the Central American countries, combined with internal warfare, virtually signified the total demise of the CACM;

however, the 1990s could see a gradual re-emergence of a common market in the Central American countries as ideological differences lessen, internal warfare ceases and the benefits of intra-regional free trade once again become apparent.

The success of the CACM in boosting industrial growth in small countries in the 1960s probably had an impact in stimulating ideas of economic integration in the Andean countries. In 1969, five Andean countries (Chile, Bolivia, Peru, Ecuador and Colombia) formed the Andean Pact. The main motivator in its formation was Chile, whose industrial development by import substitution had been severely constrained by its small internal market. The prospect of an enlarged market of 70 million attracted all five countries (and later Venezuela in 1973). However, the pace towards integration was inordinately slow during the 1970s and 1980s. The complicated sectoral programmes of industrial development (e.g. motor vehicles, metal goods) had not been implemented by the late 1980s, partly because of the enormous problems involved in organizing import substitution policies on an international scale; for example, the motor vehicle programme envisaged twelve assembly plants dividing up a market of 300,000 vehicles.

However, during the early 1990s, a renewed vigour could be observed in the Andean Group, particularly in terms of promoting intra-regional free trade. In November 1990, the five Andean Group presidents (Chile had left in 1976) signed the La Paz accord which agreed to free intra-regional trade (apart from products on an exception list) by 1992. For Venezuela and Colombia, intra-regional free trade will not be restricted to the Andean Group; both countries are also committed to free trade with Mexico (the so-called Group of Three) by July 1994. Meanwhile, Mexico is well advanced with North

American integration schemes alongside the United States and Canada.

THE LEGACY OF IMPORT SUBSTITUTION INDUSTRIALIZATION

The record of Latin American industrialization in the predominantly import substituting period of 1950 to 1978 is summarized in tables 4 and 5. The association of manufacturing strength with the larger countries of Latin America had become considerably accentuated during the period. In 1950, Brazil and Mexico were responsible for only 42.5 per cent of manufacturing Gross Domestic Product on the continent. By 1978, however, with populations of 120 and 65 million respectively (57.4 per cent of the region's total), 62.4 per cent of Latin America's manufacturing GDP was generated by the two largest countries. Notwithstanding the formation of the Andean Pact, its member countries registered a relative decline in manufacturing GDP from 20 per cent of the Latin American total in 1950 to 17 per cent in 1978; only

TABLE 4
Population, total and manufacturing gross domestic product, level of industrialization, industrial weight within the region and per-capita manufacturing GDP, 1950

	Population thousands of inhabitants	GDP millions of 1970 dollars	Manufacturing GDP millions of 1970 dollars	Level of industrialization (manuf'g GDP as % of GDP)	Industrial weight within the region (%)	Per-capita manufacturing GDP (1970 prices)
Large countries	79,507	27,683	5597	20	42.5	70
Brazil	52,901	14,440	3113	22	23.6	59
Mexico	26,606	13,243	2484	19	18.9	93
Andean Pact (incl. Chile)	36,928	16,471	2600	16	19.8	70
Bolivia	3019	754	104	14	0.8	34
Chile	6019	3914	989	23	6.8	149
Colombia	11,689	4658	585	13	4.5	50
Ecuador	3224	867	137	16	1.0	42
Peru	7832	2774	454	16	3.5	58
Venezuela	5145	3504	422	12	3.2	82
CACM (incl. Panama)	9168	2855	327	12	2.5	36
Costa Rica	866	335	49	15	0.4	58
El Salvador	1940	554	76	14	0.6	39
Guatemala	3054	947	114	12	0.9	37
Honduras	1390	359	25	7	0.2	17
Nicaragua	1109	261	30	11	0.2	27
Panama	809	399	33	8	0.2	41
River Plate countries	20,715	18,270	4640	25	35.2	224
Argentina	17,150	15,699	4103	26	31.2	239
Paraguay	1371	430	68	16	0.5	50
Uruguay	2194	2141	469	22	3.5	214
Total Latin America	146,318	65,279	13,164	20	100.0	90

Source: ECLA

TABLE 5
Population, total and manufacturing gross domestic product, level of industrialization, industrial weight within the region and per-capita manufacturing GDP, 1978

	Population thousands of inhabitants	GDP millions of 1970 dollars	Manufacturing GDP millions of 1970 dollars	Level of industrialization (manuf'g GDP as % of GDP)	Industrial weight within the region (%)	Per-capita manufacturing GDP (1970 prices)
Large countries	*184,898*	*170,140*	*48,172*	*28*	*62.4*	*261*
Brazil	119,477	101,056	30,327	30	39.3	254
Mexico	65,421	69,084	17,845	26	23.1	273
Andean Pact (incl. Chile)	*83,394*	*66,662*	*13,132*	*20*	*17.0*	*158*
Bolivia	5848	2072	325	16	0.4	56
Chile	10,843	10,335	2451	24	3.2	226
Colombia	28,424	19,162	3384	18	4.4	119
Ecuador	7798	4434	905	20	1.2	116
Peru	17,148	10,323	2554	25	3.3	149
Venezuela	13,333	20,336	3513	17	4.5	264
CACM (incl. Panama)	*21,002*	*12,279*	*2198*	*18*	*2.8*	*105*
Costa Rica	2111	2031	461	23	0.6	218
El Salvador	4524	2238	436	19	0.6	96
Guatemala	6623	3783	617	16	0.8	93
Honduras	3362	1166	185	16	0.2	55
Nicaragua	2559	1195	238	20	0.3	93
Panama	1823	1866	261	14	0.3	143
River Plate countries	*32,490*	*43,042*	*13,761*	*32*	*17.8*	*424*
Argentina	26,395	38,011	21,512	33	16.2	474
Paraguay	2888	1553	250	16	0.3	87
Uruguay	3207	3478	999	29	1.3	312
Total Latin America	*321,784*	*292,123*	*77,263*	*26*	*100.0*	*240*

Source: ECLA

the two OPEC countries (Venezuela and Ecuador) managed to increase their industrial weight within the region. But the largest relative decline hit the River Plate countries whose industrial weighting within the continent fell from 35 per cent in 1950 to 18 per cent in 1978. The import substitution process was 'completed' earlier in these countries, but with the high costs of national industry preventing exports and further domestic expansion, such 'completion' brought industrial stagnation; Argentine industry declined by 1 per cent per annum between 1973 and 1978, causing per-capita manufacturing GDP (in constant 1970 prices) to fall from $531 in 1973 to $474 in 1978. The limited success of the CACM is reflected in the slight rise from 2.5 per cent to 2.8 per cent in its contribution to Latin American manufacturing GDP between 1950 and 1978.

However, in general, ISI did promote industrial growth in most countries. There were significant increases in the 'level of industrialization' (defined as the share of the manufacturing product in the total product) from 20 per cent in 1950 to 26 per cent in 1978, and, in per-capita manufacturing GDP, from

$90 in 1950 to $240 in 1978 (both at 1970 prices). The regional variation of these two indices reflected the increasing relative strength of the two larger countries.

ISI brought major structural changes in manufacturing. Industries producing non-durable consumer goods declined in relative importance as the industries producing intermediate goods, consumer durables and capital goods developed. In 1950 non-durable consumer goods represented almost two thirds of total manufacturing production, as opposed to 40 per cent by the late 1970s. In contrast, the relative importance of intermediate products in manufacturing output rose from less than 25 per cent of the total to more than one third during the period. However, it was the consumer durables and investment goods sector where the relative changes were most striking. This sector represented only 11 per cent of total manufactures in 1950 but accounted for more than one quarter of manufactures produced by the late 1970s.

There were, however, great differences here among Latin American countries according to their

Table 6

Industrial production, 1950 and 1975 (percentage of value added in the manufacturing sector)

		Non-durable consumer manufactures	Intermediate manufactures				Consumer and capital manufactures	Total manufactures
		A	B	C	D	B+C+D	E	
Large countries	1950	64	10	10	4	24	12	100
	1975	35	9	21	7	37	28	100
Medium-sized countries	1950	66	10	15	3	28	6	100
	1975	48	9	20	6	35	17	100
Small countries	1950	85	8	6	0	14	1	100
	1975	65	11	14	1	26	9	100

A. Food, beverages and tobacco; textile, wearing apparel and leather industries; furniture and fixtures, except primarily of metal; printing, publishing and allied industries; pottery, china and earthenware, and other manufacturing industries.
B. Wood and cork products, except furniture; paper and paper products, and other non-metallic mineral products.
C. Chemicals and chemical, petroleum, coal, rubber and plastic products.
D. Basic metal industries.
E. Metal products, machinery and equipment.
Source: ECLA

respective sizes. Tables 6 and 7 demonstrate that the process of import substitution became much more 'complete' in the large countries where intermediate manufactures and consumer durable/capital goods sectors accounted for a large proportion of the total value in 1975, than in the smaller countries. The production of non-durable consumer goods, however, expanded considerably in medium-sized and small countries, while the production of intermediate goods expanded significantly in medium-sized countries but less so in small countries.

The most pronounced concentration of industrial growth in the larger countries occurred in the consumer durable/capital goods sectors (87 per cent of continental growth). As table 3 demonstrates, 86 per cent of motor vehicle assembly took place in Brazil, Mexico and Argentina. Furthermore, the govern-

ments of these countries had demanded high integration levels, normally the equivalent of over 90 per cent of parts by value from national sources. The medium-sized countries had been much less ambitious. Meanwhile, the capital goods sector had 90 per cent of its production concentrated in the three largest countries, with Brazil having the technologically most advanced and broadest machinery sector.

ISI did create the basis for significant industrial expansion, particularly in the larger countries. However, the possibility for sustained economic and industrial growth was hampered by at least seven major failings:

1 *Problems of government intervention* · ISI required excessive administrative regulations and these in turn led to bureaucratization, corruption,

Table 7

Estimation of the distribution of the growth of industrial output by branches of activity, 1950–75

	Total manufacturing industry	Manufactures[a]				
		Non-durable consumer goods	Intermediate goods			Consumer durables and capital goods
	%	A %	B %	C %	D %	E %
Large countries	80	71	80	83	86	87
Medium-sized countries	13	17	13	13	13	10
Small countries	7	12	7	1	1	3
Total Latin America	100	100	100	100	100	100

[a] Columns A, B, C, D and E represent the manufacturing branches and groups as indicated at the foot of table 6.
Source: ECLA

uncertainty and delays. These discouraged productive private investment and foreign trade initiatives.

2 *Bias against exports* · The existence of import restrictions led to a higher exchange rate than would have prevailed under a free trade regime, reducing the relative gains obtained from exporting.

3 *Bias against agriculture* · The protection of local industry raised the prices of manufactured goods relative to agricultural products in the home market, and the overvalued exchange rate reduced the domestic currency receipts for agricultural exports.

4 *Under-utilization of installed capacity* · Since import controls did not equally apply to capital goods and since credit for installing machinery was relatively cheap, factories were over-equipped with imported machinery. At the same time, protection in domestic product markets made it possible to earn good profits even at low capacity utilization.

5 *Under-utilization of labour* · Imported capital goods could be obtained relatively cheaply due to the combined effect of over-valued exchange rates, low import restrictions for such goods and subsidized financing conditions. ISI thus became characterized by the location of capital-intensive plant within countries where labour markets contained large numbers of underemployed and low-skilled workers.

6 *Import intensity of ISI* · Although consumer good imports were reduced substantially, this was achieved at the expense of increased imports of equipment and components, resulting in an even greater reliance on foreign supplies.

7 *The slowing down of ISI* · Although initially industry can grow faster than domestic demand for manufactures, Latin American countries soon ran out of import substitution possibilities (as in the case of Argentina). Then manufacturing growth rates become closely linked to those of domestic demand.

THE MOVE TO OUTWARD ORIENTATION

The slowing down of Import Substitution Industrialization became perhaps the major reason for its gradual replacement during the 1980s and 1990s in favour of more outward-oriented strategies reliant upon export growth. Table 8 shows how a reliance on ISI created low or negative rates of manufacturing growth during the 1980s after the high rates of the 1960s and 1970s.

TABLE 8

The slowing down of ISI in the 1980s

	GNP per capita 1988	Average annual growth rate of manufacturing (per cent)	
		1965–80	1980–88
Venezuela	3250	5.8	3.3
Argentina	2520	2.7	−0.2
Uruguay	2470	–	−0.5
Brazil	2160	9.8	2.2
Panama	2120	4.7	0.7
Mexico	1760	7.4	0.2
Chile*	1510	0.6	2.0
Peru	1300	3.8	1.6
Paraguay	1180	7.0	1.3
Colombia	1180	6.4	2.9
Ecuador	1120	11.5	0.6
El Salvador	940	4.6	0.3
Honduras	860	7.5	1.9
Bolivia	570	5.9	−5.6
Nicaragua	–	5.2	0.6

* Outward-oriented policies began in 1974.
Source: *World Bank Development Report, 1990.*

The 1980s in Latin America were dominated by the debt crisis. Coming to terms with it required these countries to undergo severe austerity, which in turn meant a lack of demand for domestically produced manufactured products. The manufacturing sector in most Latin American countries therefore had to face reduced domestic demand. Meanwhile, the legacy of ISI (bias against manufactured exports, under-utilization of installed capacity, over-valued exchange rates) meant that manufacturers could not turn easily to exports. Hence, two generalizations can be made about manufacturing in Latin America in the 1980s. First, manufacturing growth rates were low. Secondly, there was a policy shift to more outward-oriented policies. The only country to switch to export-oriented policies in the 1970s, Chile, was the only country to record much higher manufacturing growth in the 1980s than in the 1970s.

However, it takes time for manufacturing firms to switch from a reliance on safe, domestic markets to struggling in the competitive world of export markets. This is particularly the case for domestic private firms. The switch can take time even if foreign multinationals are prominent in the sector. One could take the example of the Mexican vehicle sector, dominated by six vehicle multinationals (GM, Ford, Chrysler, Volkswagen, Renault and Nissan). Mexico's economic crisis came to a head in 1982 with its declaration of a moratorium on its external debt and a 268 per cent devaluation of the peso against the dollar. This latter measure created an effectively valued exchange rate (after many years of over-valuation) which it was hoped manufacturers would take advantage of. However, exports crept up only slowly from 1982 to 1986. It was not until 1987 that exports suddenly took off, with the export of both engines and assembled vehicles doubling in one year and total value of vehicle exports reaching over $2.5 million. It had thus taken five years for Chrysler to fully modernize its plant in Toluca, for Ford to build a new export-oriented plant in Hermosillo, and for all six multinationals to be maximizing exports from their engine plants.

Thus the shift from inward orientation to outward orientation is a long and difficult process. However, by 1991, the governments of most Latin American countries had announced this shift as policy. The economic growth that had followed the switch of Chile (1974) and Mexico (1982) to outward orientation was sufficient to tempt Venezuela, Bolivia, Peru and Argentina away from years of inward orientation. Some countries, such as Colombia and Brazil, were historically more encouraging to manufactured exports (normally via large subsidies), but these have also been moving to liberalizing trade. Furthermore, liberalization has not only been concerned with trade; measures encouraging foreign investment and facilitating the transfer of technology have also become more popular during the late 1980s and early 1990s.

THE TRIPLE ALLIANCE

The institutional agents of industrialization in Latin America are often referred to as the triple alliance. This is because Latin American industrialization has been distinctive in terms of its reliance on three types of institution: state or public enterprises, foreign multinational corporations, and national private

enterprises. They are more or less equal in terms of their contribution to GDP, but there is evidence of a significant differentiation of roles between these three institutions.

The state or public enterprise, especially in the large and medium-sized countries, focused on developing basic industries, such as iron and steel, oil refining and petrochemicals in the ISI period. In 1978, the production of steel by state enterprises made up 69 per cent of the total in Argentina, 60 per cent in Mexico and Brazil and 80 per cent in Venezuela. The share of state enterprises in oil refining was even more dominant. In Brazil, Mexico, Chile, Colombia, Uruguay and Bolivia, 100 per cent of oil refining was carried out by state enterprises in the 1980s. The contribution of state enterprises to the processing of chemical and petrochemical products was also significant. In Argentina, Brazil and Mexico, large state enterprises came to dominate the processing of basic products, while in Andean Pact countries such as Colombia, Peru and Venezuela all the enterprises processing basic petrochemical products were state-owned.

In the early stages of industrial development the state assumed the role of entrepreneur in basic industries in order to initiate locally the production of goods regarded as essential to accelerated industrial growth. Subsequently, state participation in basic industries also became due to the conviction that such participation was a means of increasing national decision-making power in the industrial sector. In a number of countries, areas within certain industrial sectors have been defined for action by the public and private sectors, with the state reserving for itself the manufacture of basic products. In Venezuela, for example, PEQUIVEN controls the production of basic petrochemical feedstock (ethylene, propylene, ammonia, urea) but sells them to either mixed (state/private) or private firms for further elaboration.

In contrast, the national private firm has become characterized by great diversity in terms of size, technological level and forms of organization. In most large and medium-sized countries, large national conglomerates have developed with a variety of manufacturing interests as well as important tertiary functions in banking, insurance, finance, tourism, commerce and often the media. At the other end of the size range, large numbers of small enterprises are at work, filling the demand gaps left by, or providing low-cost competition for, the large state, national and international companies. Due to labour-intensive methods and low capital inputs, these small enterprises generate a much higher proportion of employment than their production levels would indicate. The organization is simple, based around a single

Barrancabermeja oil refinery, Colombia

entrepreneur (or family), and most small firms are highly susceptible to changes in the macro-economy or the policy shifts of the large companies; as a result they have to be very adaptable and flexible in order to survive.

In terms of their relationship with multinational companies, it is often pointed out that the latter predominate in the technologically more dynamic sectors, leaving the national private firms to specialize in the more traditional industries. The 2700 largest private firms in Brazil, for example, account for 75 per

TABLE 9
The role of private national, multinational, and state firms in the various sectors of the Brazilian economy, 1978

	Private national (%)	Multinational (%)	State (%)
Predominantly national			
Civil construction	100.0	–	–
Communications	100.0	–	–
Supermarkets	98.3	1.7	–
Furniture	97.4	2.6	–
Clothing, shoes	96.9	3.1	–
Retail business	90.0	10.0	–
Heavy construction	88.7	8.5	2.8
Printing and publishing	73.8	26.2	–
Food	66.6	33.4	–
Pulp and paper	59.9	32.9	7.2
Non-metallic minerals	58.0	42.0	–
Predominantly foreign			
Wholesale business	41.4	42.2	16.4
Machinery	41.5	48.8	9.7
Transportation equipment	37.7	53.6	8.7
Heavy vehicles	45.2	54.8	–
Petroleum distribution	11.0	60.8	28.2
Electronics	33.6	66.4	–
Textiles	31.8	68.2	–
Cleaning products	27.2	72.8	–
Plastics and rubber	21.5	76.1	2.4
Beverages and tobacco	23.6	76.4	–
Pharmaceuticals	15.6	84.4	–
Office equipment	13.8	86.2	–
Automobiles	0.6	99.4	–
Predominantly state			
Public services	–	–	100.0
Chemicals and petrochemicals	5.0	15.8	79.2
Steel	27.1	7.9	65.0
Minerals	29.5	12.0	58.5
Transportation	49.6	–	50.4

Source: S. A. Hewlett, *The Cruel Dilemmas of Development: Twentieth Century Brazil* (New York, 1980). These figures refer to the sales of the twenty largest firms in each sector.

Multinational capital and Chilean forestry exports. Logs are being loaded on to a Forestal Colcura truck for the 150-kilometre journey from the Colcura eucalyptus plantations near Lota to the cellulose plant of Forestal e Industrial Santa Fé in Nacimiento. Both companies are owned by an international consortium.

cent of production in the non-durable consumer goods sector but only 33 per cent and 45 per cent in the intermediate and metal goods machinery sectors. Table 9 shows that multinational investment dominates in the automobile, office equipment, pharmaceuticals, tobacco, beverages, plastics and rubber industries. However, such a distinction can be misleading, as national private firms are active in some very dynamic sectors in Latin America. For example, in the motor vehicle industry, national private firms have specialized in components and parts production while leaving assembly and engine production to the multinationals. In Brazil, national firms figure prominently in the furniture, clothing, shoes, printing, food, pulp, paper and cement industries. In Venezuela, the metal fabrication industry is dominated by such national firms as SIVENSA. Nevertheless, throughout Latin America the majority of firms producing in the food, beverages, textiles, footwear, clothing, leather, cement, furniture and pottery sectors are of national private origin.

Direct foreign investment through multinational enterprises in manufacturing became particularly significant in the latter stages of ISI. Thus, while manufacturing activity accounted for 20 per cent of total US direct investments in Latin America in the 1950s, this increased to approximately 65 per cent in the 1960s. Direct foreign investment has mainly been channelled into Brazil and Mexico where import substitution policies were more successful; indeed, during the late 1960s and 1970s, about two thirds of direct foreign investment in Latin America was concentrated in these two countries. During the 1960s and 1970s, most foreign investment originated from the United States (50 per cent in the large countries, 77 per cent in the medium-sized countries, and 69 per cent in the smaller countries). However, during the 1980s, both European and Japanese investments increased. Japanese investment is still prominent in the processing of raw materials (steel, aluminium) but is increasingly shifting to areas of high technology (for example, the motor vehicle sector) and assembly (as in north Mexico). European investment has been significant in high-technology sectors such as motor vehicles, pharmaceuticals and machinery. Thus, the rapid growth of multinational investment in manufacturing in Latin America has taken place in the more dynamic and technologically innovative sectors.

Conflicts of interest between multinational enterprise and the state have been frequent in the region. The state is basically interested in maximizing benefits for its own territory whereas multinational enterprise, in the words of a General Motors chief economist, attempts 'to find ways of achieving the economic efficiencies of world-wide specialization of

SITES AND EVOLUTION OF MEXICO'S MOTOR INDUSTRY

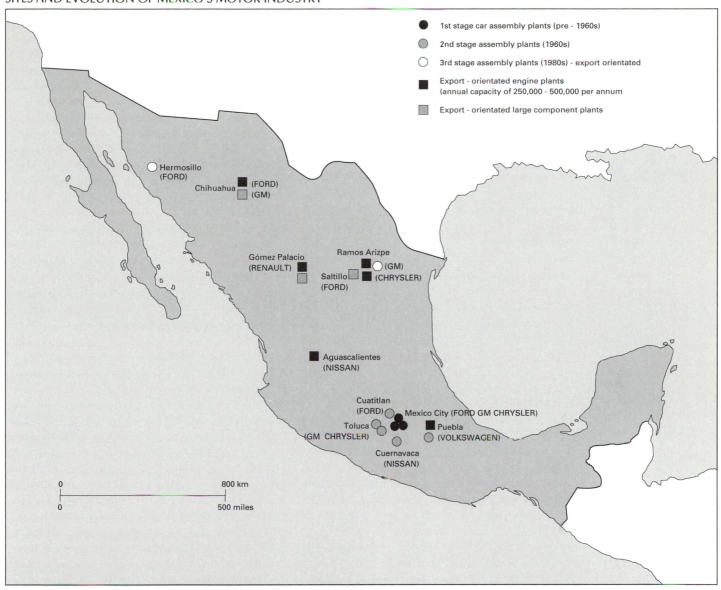

- ● 1st stage car assembly plants (pre - 1960s)
- ◐ 2nd stage assembly plants (1960s)
- ○ 3rd stage assembly plants (1980s) - export orientated
- ■ Export - orientated engine plants (annual capacity of 250,000 - 500,000 per annum)
- ▪ Export - orientated large component plants

Hermosillo (FORD)
Chihuahua (FORD) (GM)
Gómez Palacio (RENAULT)
Saltillo (FORD)
Ramos Arizpe (GM) (CHRYSLER)
Aguascalientes (NISSAN)
Cuatitlan (FORD)
Toluca (GM CHRYSLER)
Mexico City (FORD GM CHRYSLER)
Puebla (VOLKSWAGEN)
Cuernavaca (NISSAN)

0 — 800 km
0 — 500 miles

production and development within the political constraints imposed by national policies'. While the state can control its own enterprises and strongly influence national private firms, it finds it difficult to exert influence over multinational enterprises. Again, there are major contrasts in the experiences of large and small countries. The larger countries can often exert considerable power in bargaining with multinationals as their markets are valuable to obtain and rival companies will compete against each other for tenders. Smaller countries generally have substantially less bargaining power due to their small market size and the often low level of multinational interest.

Within the context of the more recent government policies of export promotion in the manufacturing sector, multinational corporations have begun to play a particularly significant role in boosting exports. One impressive example is provided by the

Chilean forestry exports. During the construction phase of the Mininco plant (seen here in April 1991), 5000 workers were employed on the project. Following the start of production (late 1991) about 350 workers are employed.

motor vehicle corporations in Mexico. For example, Chrysler, GM and Ford increased vehicle exports from nothing in 1983 to 143,000 in 1987 and an estimated 300,000 in 1991 (see map). The great majority of these vehicle exports were to the United States. Meanwhile, four of Mexico's six export-oriented engine plants were producing engines for assembly plants in the United States, while Renault and Volkswagen were having to export engines to Brazil and Europe following the collapse of their US operations.

URBANIZATION AND INDUSTRIALIZATION

Industrialization has been a potent driving force in the rapid process of urbanization experienced in all Latin American countries. Although much of modern manufacturing is based on new technologies and is capital intensive, a significant proportion of the total workforce is either employed directly in manufacturing plants or in 'backstreet' workshops which depend on their orders from subcontracting agreements with modern plants. Furthermore, manufacturing growth should not be underestimated as a factor in the recent and rapid expansion of the tertiary employment sector due to increased demand for commercial and non-commercial services (lawyers, accountants, advertising, banks, financial services, insurance, medical services), and through the demand created by a relatively well-paid workforce.

Industrial growth has, however, been spatially very concentrated within most Latin American countries. In many, the primate city alone contains the great majority of manufacturing employment and value-added. In larger countries core areas or belts of activity have appeared – São Paulo–Paraíba Valley–Rio de Janeiro–Belo Horizonte crescent (75 per cent of Brazilian industrial employment), the Mexico City–Puebla core (55 per cent of Mexican industrial employment), the Greater Buenos Aires metropolis (66 per cent of Argentinian industrial employment), the Santiago-Valparaiso core (66 per cent of Chilean

industrial employment), the Lima–Callao metropolis (75 per cent of Peruvian industrial employment) and the Caracas–Maracay–Valencia axis (75 per cent of Venezuelan industrial employment).

Such concentration is observable at a continental scale, given that these six industrial belts or agglomerations (see maps of Brazilian, Venezuelan and Chilean industrial belts) contain 60 per cent of the continent's industrial employment. Furthermore, it is difficult to see how much spatial concentration can be reduced. The technologically innovative industries, such as motor vehicles, pharmaceuticals, electronic and electrical products, machinery, plastics and office equipment, are heavily concentrated geographically in these major agglomerations. As these growth industries expand, the overall spatial concentration of industry intensifies. In addition, the large metropolitan areas have been able to nurture huge numbers of small, labour-intensive manufacturing enterprises. The only notable area of industrial deconcentration in Latin America at the moment is that of north Mexico, where the neighbouring attractions of the world's largest economy constitute very special factors attracting foreign manufacturing investment.

Industrial concentration derives as much from the historical process of urbanization as from the advantages that large cities can offer industrialists in the form of external economies and a large market. After the early-nineteenth-century division of Spanish America into a mosaic of countries, each country adopted a highly centralized system of government in order to prevent further secession. The resulting concentration of both government and population in one major city had a strong spatial effect on import substitution industrialization as the latter developed in the 1930–80 period. As such industrialization was both closely linked to government planning and orientated primarily towards the national market, a primate city location was advantageous on two very important counts. Not only did a capital city location offer the possibility of close interaction with members of the relevant government bureaucracies but it also gave proximity to the single largest and most affluent market in the country. Meanwhile, the historical development of transport systems, whether railways in the late nineteenth century or motorways in the last thirty years, in focusing on the major city or core area, meant that all other areas of the national market were easily served by plants located in that core area. Such transport advantages and market considerations have, for example, maintained the industrial supremacy of the Rio–São Paulo axis, despite government relocation to Brasília.

Industrial entrepreneurs perceive and probably receive a number of further benefits from a big-city

THE INDUSTRIAL CORE OF BRAZIL

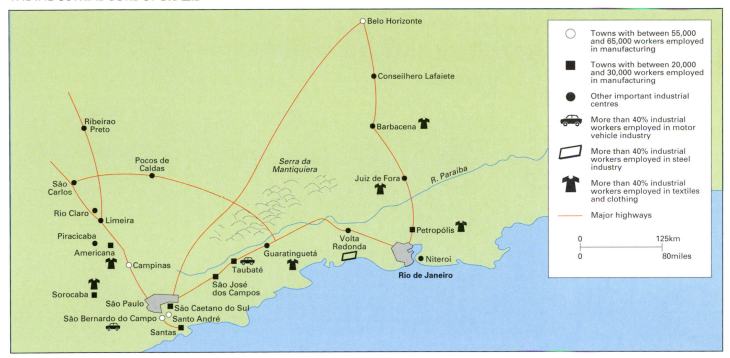

THE INDUSTRIAL BELT OF VENEZUELA

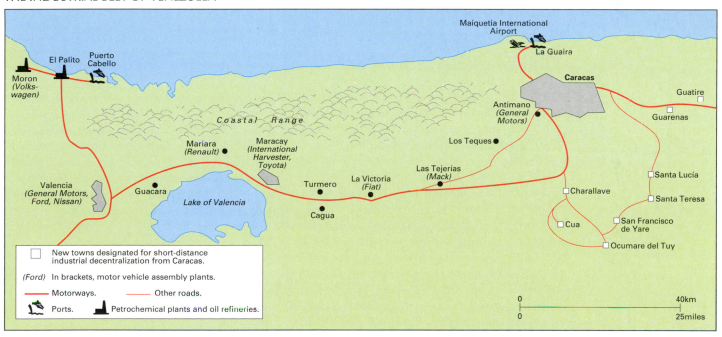

location. In terms of basic costs, labour costs are no higher and sometimes lower than in small urban centres, while the cost of water and electricity is similar, and the supply often more reliable. The entrepreneur can rely on a wide range of external services which may act to reduce his costs, such as stockists, machine maintenance companies and high-order banking and financial services. He can find it easier to subcontract out parts of his operation to small, cheap workshops. At the same time, the executive of the multinational corporation is attracted by such facilities as the international airport, the cosmopolitan setting, varied cultural activities and private schools.

All Latin American countries have regarded industrial growth as a vital component of economic advance. However, the basic mode of industrialization since 1930, that of import substitution, has undoubtedly been more appropriate for the larger than for the smaller countries. Smaller countries

CHILE'S CENTRAL CORE

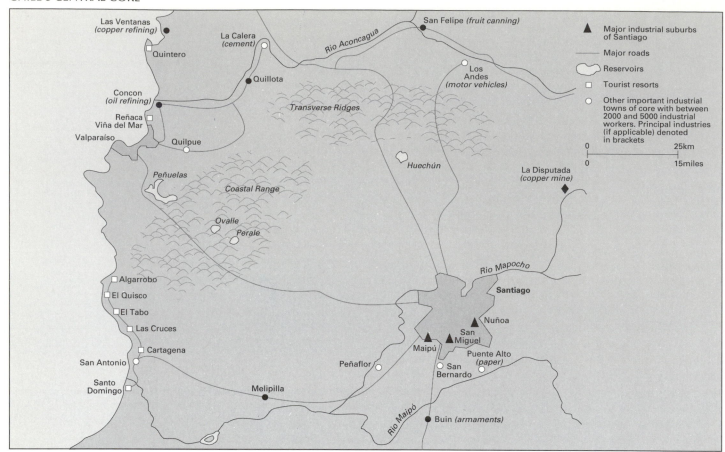

Las Ventanas
(copper refining)
Quintero

La Calera
(cement)

Quillota

San Felipe *(fruit canning)*

Rio Aconcagua

Los
Andes
(motor vehicles)

▲ Major industrial suburbs
of Santiago

— Major roads

Reservoirs

□ Tourist resorts

○ Other important industrial
towns of core with between
2000 and 5000 industrial
workers. Principal industries
(if applicable) denoted
in brackets

Concon
(oil refining)

Transverse Ridges

Reñaca
Viña del Mar

Valparaíso

Quilpue

0   25km

0   15miles

Peñuelas

Coastal Range

Huechún

La Disputada
(copper mine)
◆

Ovalle

Perale

Rio Mapocho

Algarrobo

El Quisco

El Tabo

Santiago

Las Cruces

▲ Nuñoa

Cartagena

San Antonio

San
Miguel

San Antonio

Maipú

Santo
Domingo

Peñaflor

San
Bernardo

Puente Alto
(paper)

Melipilla

Rio Maipó

Buin *(armaments)*

have tried to counteract their market limitations by grouping together in schemes of economic integration. However, their success until now has been distinctly limited due to the unequal distribution of benefits that has resulted, the tension that this has created (CACM) and the elaborate bureaucracy and plans needed to ameliorate such inequality (Andean Group). Meanwhile, the larger countries, particularly Brazil and Mexico, have come to form the industrial powerhouse of the region and have led other countries into adopting industrial policies in which export promotion is stressed. Trade liberalization, however, and the reduction of tariff barriers have been pursued with greater vigour in the smaller countries, most notably Chile, although it has recently been joined by Mexico and Argentina.

The future of industrial growth linked to export promotion will, nevertheless, be difficult. In the context of the international division of labour, there are some industries in which Latin American wage rates are already too high for international competition to be viable – basic textiles, clothing and consumer electronic products. At the other end of the manufacturing spectrum, Latin American industry still has to import much of its technology in some form and will find it difficult to progress in those high-technology

sectors where rapid growth will occur – microchip technology, biotechnology, communications systems. Latin American industrialization linked to export promotion must concentrate on the middle-ground consumer products such as motor vehicles, intermediate products such as chemicals and steel, and any other sector where comparative advantage may be attained – most notably those linked to resources, such as the forestry and fishing sectors in Chile and the oil and aluminium sectors in Venezuela. The future of industrial growth based on export promotion will be a difficult one, but the lesson of the fifty years from 1930 to 1980 has been that 'inward oriented' industrialization can only too easily end in high-cost industry and eventual stagnation.

RNG

Further Reading: W. Dean, *The Industrialization of São Paulo, 1880–1945* (Austin, Texas, 1969); G. Gereffi and D. L. Wyman, eds., *Manufacturing Miracles: Paths to Industrialization in Latin America and East Asia* (Princeton, 1990); R. Grosse, *Multinationals in Latin America* (London, 1989); R. N. Gwynne, *Industrialisation and Urbanisation in Latin America* (London, 1985); R. N. Gwynne, *New Horizons? Third World Industrialization in an International Framework* (London, 1990); R. O. Jenkins, *Transnational Corporations and the Latin American Automobile Industry* (Basingstoke, 1987)

Communications and transport

EVOLUTION OF THE TRANSPORT SYSTEM

Pre-Columbian transport forms were rudimentary. Most overland travel used simple trails, but the Incas developed a more organized road system to control their empire and extract tribute. Their roads across the mountains incorporated spectacular rope bridges, but they had no wheeled traffic. They utilized the llama as a beast of burden but such domestication was uncommon, and dignitaries travelled by litter. The Indians made limited use of water transport though dugout canoes and balsa rafts were constructed by some peoples.

The colonial period

Advances in European shipbuilding and navigation facilitated the long voyages which resulted in the discovery of the Americas and the speedy exploration of the coasts of Latin America. The nature of the contact and the relationship which emerged between the Old World and the New shaped a pattern of settlement and economic activity which has largely survived up to the present day.

Contact was by sea; the points of contact were, therefore, ports, which became major focuses of settlement. Routes pushed inland from them, to the pre-existing Indian settlements of Mexico and the Andes, and to mineral resources and farmlands. Spanish fleets sailed to Veracruz for New Spain, to Nombre de Dios and later Porto Belo for Peru, and to small ports in the Caribbean. The arrival of the fleets was a time for trade fairs and a stimulus to town growth. Overland links remained limited by the adverse terrain, vast distances and poor quality of existing roads.

Even on routes such as those from Veracruz to Mexico City and across the Isthmus of Panama, travel was slow, and the volume of trade low.

The Iberians did, however, introduce two important innovations in land transport: the mule and the wheel. These meant that pack trains and carts could move more goods. Some of the routes used were pre-Columbian, such as from highland Mexico to the tropical lowlands. Elsewhere (as in Peru) new routes linked the ports, other towns and the focuses of economic activity.

During the eighteenth century trade expanded and diversified, internal trade increased, and the road system improved. In Spanish America cart roads linked Buenos Aires and Tucumán, Lima and Paita, and Mexico City to Jalapa and Guadalajara. Else-where mule trains and llamas still provided transport. In Brazil the discovery of gold in Minas Gerais prompted the building of roads over the difficult coastal escarpment, linking Rio de Janeiro to the gold fields and creating the first substantial settlement in the interior of Portuguese America.

Trade in the colonial period linked Latin America with Iberia and later with the rest of Europe. Ships also provided contact between the dispersed coastal settlements, isolated from each other by terrain and distance. Most trails and tracks penetrated inland to interior towns or sources of primary products.

Steam power

Until well into the nineteenth century deep-sea and coastal shipping and generally poor overland links provided the basis for transport and trade. The advent of steam power transformed the transport system as the steamship moved more cargo more rapidly. After the 1870s refrigeration widened the range of products which could be transported.

The railway system developed particularly after 1850, initially in a 'colonial' network designed to facilitate trade between an industrializing Europe and North America and the raw materials and markets of Latin America. Many of the railroads were built by foreign capital – British, French and North American – limiting national control over railway growth. There was consequently little planning to integrate and develop the new republics. Lines ran inland from the ports, linking them to interior capitals such as Quito and Santiago, and to sources of export commodities such as wool, meat, and minerals.

Few lines linked existing coastal settlements, which remained dependent on maritime contact. In the Andes, railroads were constructed to exploit specific resources, such as the copper of Cerro de Pasco in Peru. Elsewhere the railway stimulated development as new areas were made accessible and settlements were created or expanded. The advance of the railways across the São Paulo plateau, for example, is marked by beads of towns along their routes.

Only in a few areas – Argentina, Uruguay, southeast Brazil, Chile and Cuba – did more than skeletal rail networks develop. Argentina and Uruguay benefited from the ideal conditions of the pampas, which facilitated construction of a dense rail network to move grain, meat and wool towards European markets, and in Argentina the network increased from 736 km in 1870 to 12,480 km in 1891. In Brazil after 1867 a dendritic rail net spread across the São Paulo plateau, following the advancing coffee frontier. Lesser nets evolved in the coffee lands of Minas Gerais and Rio de Janeiro, and in the sugar plantations of Cuba. In general, however, there were few international or even interregional railways.

Hunslet locomotive leaving a tunnel and crossing a single track bridge on the Huancavelica line in the Peruvian Andes. The line connects with the Peruvian Central Railway (Lima-Huancayo), whose construction between the 1870s and 1890s was one of the wonders of nineteenth-century engineering.

Much of the system was single track and most countries inherited mixed-gauge systems, inhibiting later integration. Difficult terrain, limited traffic and poor maintenance checked the long-term role of the railway, and then by the 1930s the railways had begun to face competition from the automobile and improved roads, so that their share of freight and passengers fell.

Much of the continent's system then passed into public ownership. The most striking feature of the railways is their spatial concentration; of the 131,000 km built by 1945, three quarters was in Argentina, Brazil and Mexico.

The development of roads and shipping

Governments became increasingly interested in highways from the 1920s onwards. Brazil's president in 1927 noted that 'to govern is to populate, but it is not possible to populate without building roads of all types. To govern, then, is to build roads', and many countries embarked on road-building programmes during the inter-war years. The new highways often paralleled the railways, and served to hasten their decline. The road system offered direct delivery between producer and consumer, rather than the multiple handling of rail transport. Carriage of freight by road has grown to include long-distance, high-bulk, low-value goods, better suited to an efficient rail system. Road building requires less foreign exchange than railway construction and employs many unskilled workers. Road transport's liability has been its dependence on rising oil prices.

Most Latin American countries now have reasonable road networks, some planned as concerted highway systems. In 1928 an inter-American highway was begun, and by 1940 62 per cent of the Middle American and 87 per cent of the South American sections had been built as all-weather road. In contrast, away from federal and provincial highways, municipal roads may be dirt-surfaced, poorly maintained and seasonal.

In the post-colonial period water transport remained significant. Movement of agricultural and mineral produce by rail demanded increased shipping and improved ports, but many Latin American ports were small, ill-equipped and even some major ports such as Buenos Aires, Montevideo, Valparaiso and Veracruz, were little more than unprotected open roadsteads. The principal ports of Argentina – Buenos Aires, Rosario, Bahía Blanca and La Plata – were all improved between 1880 and 1900; Santos, Rio de Janeiro and Montevideo were improved in the first decade of the twentieth century. Much of the overseas trade was carried by foreign ships. As late as 1912 British ships were responsible for more than half of the foreign tonnage in the principal ports of Brazil and Argentina.

The inland waterways of Latin America have had restricted roles as arteries of commerce. The continent appears to have a good inland waterway system, but even the major rivers or their tributaries are often not navigable throughout their entirety. Most rivers of the Brazilian east coast and the Andean republics are short, steep and broken by rapids, and many rivers have markedly seasonal regimes, with depth of water fluctuating greatly. The major systems of the Orinoco, Amazon and São Francisco flow through areas which remain little settled or developed, and only the Magdalena and the lower Paraná–Paraguay system are close to focuses of settlement, thereby playing important roles in the evolving transport systems. In the late nineteenth

MAJOR ROADS AND RAILWAYS OF SOUTH AMERICA

between major cities, aeroplanes gave access to previously isolated interior areas.

THE PRESENT-DAY TRANSPORT SYSTEMS

The railways

The railway system has declined in terms of the share of passengers and goods carried, in some cases absolutely. However, there have been exceptions with freight: Brazil, with the largest rail freight in the continent, experienced an increase from 17,000 million tonne-km of freight to 92 millions between 1970–84, largely due to increased transport of iron ore and other minerals.

For seventeen countries (which together contained over 90 per cent of the continent's railways) the length of track decreased from 125,701 km in 1950 to 109,000 in 1983, with major decreases in Argentina, Brazil and Mexico. Few new lines have been built since the Second World War, exceptions being the Chihuahua-Pacific line in Mexico, the Ferrocarril del Atlántico in Colombia, and an extension of Brazil's network to Brasília.

The high costs of maintenance of lines in difficult terrain and dependence on foreign locomotives, rolling stock and rails have contributed to this decline. Physical decline and falling profits were partially responsible for the nationalization of most of

ANDEAN RAILWAYS, COLOMBIA TO CHILE

century the Amazon provided the basic routeway which sustained the rubber boom, but declined in importance when the boom collapsed.

Airlines

The Brazilian Alberto Santos Dumont was a pioneer aviator before the First World War, and air transport developed rapidly in Latin America after 1918. Commercial air services began to operate in Colombia in 1919 – Colombia's airline AVIANCA claims to be the western hemisphere's oldest – and in Mexico, Bolivia and Brazil by 1927. Foreign airlines such as Pan-American and other, particularly French and German, interests assisted domestic airlines. During the Second World War construction of air bases by the United States in the Caribbean and northern South America provided airports and infrastructure for later civilian air traffic. In the 1940s Latin American airlines increasingly passed to domestic control. In addition to the development of scheduled links

TABLE 10
Railway passenger traffic
(million passenger-kilometres)

	1940	1950	1970	1986
Argentina	4404	13,326	12,828	12,459
Bolivia	125	158	271	657
Brazil	6428	9987	12,351	15,782
Chile	1457	1588	2338	1274
Colombia	457	790	249	178
Cuba	248	556	1130	2200
Ecuador	080	126	085	55
Mexico	1862	3025	4534	5874
Nicaragua	54	100	030	–
Peru	124	241	248	490
Uruguay	272	00–	529	196

Railway freight traffic
(million net tonne-kilometres)

	1940	1950	1970	1986
Argentina	13,028	17,117	13,357	8761
Bolivia	219	249	326	464
Brazil	6075	7605	17,531	103,677
Chile	2031	2102	2533	2555
Colombia	309	615	1173	691
Cuba	726	1055	1625	2155
Ecuador	73	112	56	7
Mexico	5764	9391	22,863	40,608
Nicaragua	11	21	16	–
Peru	299	392	610	1022
Uruguay	395	–	250	204

Source: UN, *Statistical Yearbook 1951* (New York, 1951), pp. 311–12, *1957*, pp. 335–6, *1979*, pp. 541–2, and *1985/86*, p. 709.

the foreign-owned railways – in Mexico in the 1900s, Argentina in 1947 and Brazil in 1957. Few are now profitable, except the ones moving particular commodities such as coal – Rio Turbio (Argentina) and Teresa Cristina; iron ore – Vitória–Minas and Carajás –São Luis; and manganese – Amapã (all in Brazil). Even the growth country, Brazil, has suffered recently from economic difficulties which have delayed progress on its 'coal', 'soya', 'steel' and 'North–South' railway projects.

Road transport

By 1985 the continent had over 2.5 million km of road, although only about one fifth was paved.

Although there are some spectacular multi-lane interurban and interregional highways, much of the system lacks a permanent surface. Brazil, Mexico and Argentina have the largest share of the system, totalling 2 million km of road, though only 7, 46 and

27 per cent respectively is paved. Lack of all-weather roads is a constraint on the marketing of agricultural produce in much of the continent.

The number of passenger cars in South America increased from 4 million to 17 million between 1968 and 1984. Such spectacular growth reflects the switch to road transport, some increase in prosperity, and the establishment of domestic car industries. Though vehicle assembly industries were established in some countries before 1939, manufacture using largely domestic components began after 1950. Most industry is controlled by multinational firms, with Ford,

TABLE 11
Motor vehicles in use (thousands)

	1948	1970	1986
Argentina	508	2194	5244
Bolivia	11	48	80
Brazil	326	3020	11,089 (1984)
Chile	69	326	833
Colombia	55	322	1243
Dominican Republic	6	59	210
Ecuador	7	63	322
Mexico	235	1822	7464
Panama	21	60	287
Paraguay	2	28	–
Peru	41	347	599
Uruguay	75	209	365
Venezuela	82	764	2086

Source: UN, *Statistical Yearbook 1951*, pp. 317–18, *1978*, pp. 547–8, *1987*, pp. 687–8.

Length of roads, 1985

	Thousand km	Percentage paved
Argentina	211	27
Bolivia	41	4
Brazil	1583	7
Chile	79	12
Colombia	75	13
Costa Rica	35	13
Cuba	11	–
Dominican Republic	17	29
Ecuador	36	28
El Salvador	12	14
Guatemala	26	11
Honduras	12	16
Mexico	214	46
Nicaragua	15	11
Panama	11	37
Paraguay	11	19
Peru	57	–
Uruguay	50	20
Venezuela	78	32

Source: J. W. Wilkie & E. Ochoa, *Statistical Abstract of Latin America*, Vol. 27 (Los Angeles, 1989), p. 60.

Urban highway, Brasília. Brazil's brand-new capital, inaugurated in April 1960, was designed for the automobile rather than the pedestrian.

Volkswagen, General Motors and Chrysler accounting for three quarters of total output. Brazil, Mexico and Argentina are the principal producers, Brazil ranking tenth in the world car production in 1985. The number of commercial vehicles in South America rose from 1.9 million in 1968 to 5.2 million in 1984. Over a longer perspective, Argentina, Brazil and Mexico all had less than 65,000 commercial vehicles in use in 1928; by 1984 they each had over 1.4 million. Similar expansion can be seen in the smaller countries – commercial vehicles registered in the Dominican Republic rose from 6000 in 1960 to 60,000 in 1984; in Honduras passenger vehicles registered rose over the same period from 5500 to over 28,500.

Cars, buses and trucks have become increasingly important in private, mass transit and freight journeys, and have come to dominate intraurban and interurban transport. However, away from the major cities and principal highways, the quality of roads and the frequency and quality of vehicles decline.

Latin American road-building programmes have involved the construction of urban motorways and interurban highways in existing areas of settlement; they have also been used to penetrate into frontier areas. The Amazon basin has been the major focus, with roads into the region from the Andean countries, the *Carretera Marginal de la Selva* from Colombia to Paraguay, and the Transamazonia highway running from Brazil's north-east coast to the Peruvian frontier.

A spectacular example of the potential impact of new highways on frontier development is provided by the Belém–Brasília highway, built along the eastern periphery of Amazonia in the late 1950s: it led to the influx of two million people, the growth of new towns and villages, and the opening of new lands to farming and industry. The more recent highway from Cuiabá to Porto Velho has opened up the west Brazilian territory of Rondonia to both small-scale squatting and large-scale colonization.

Such highway-settlement schemes have aroused controversy, because of their consequences for the environment, and have not always created permanent settlements. The Brazilian experience also points to a check on road transport development in Latin America. The latter was based on the assumption of continued availability of cheap petroleum, but the rise in oil prices in the 1970s undermined this, particularly in countries largely dependent on imported oil. It prompted a greater search for domestic oil and alternative fuel sources (in Brazil, the use of alcohol derived from sugar cane), greater emphasis on mass transit, reappraisal of other transport modes, and a slowdown in highway construction.

Nevertheless, there is little doubt that the automobile has increased the speed, volume and flexibility of movement in Latin America in the twentieth century. Roads have provided most countries with a reasonably comprehensive net of communication, even if the quality varies. Yet international links are limited, and the Pan-American Highway remains uneven in quality. Such international highways could stimulate intraregional trade. The Asunción–Paranaguá highway, for example, has had a substantial impact on the scale and pattern of Paraguayan–Brazilian trade.

Shipping

Shipping has always had a significant role in the trade and transport in Latin America. The countries as well

HIGHWAY SYSTEM IN THE BRAZILIAN AMAZON

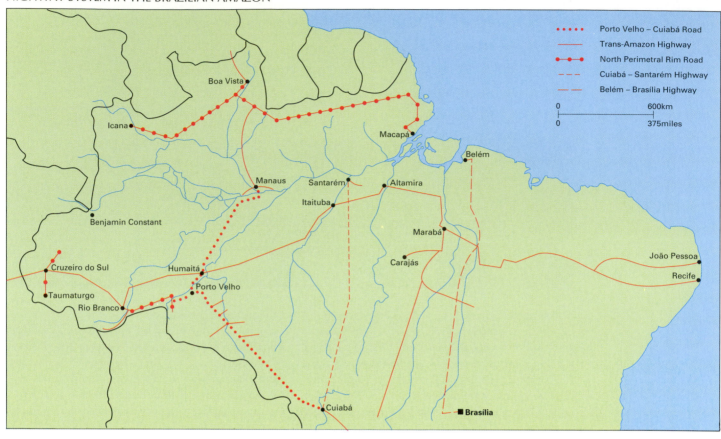

- •••• Porto Velho – Cuiabá Road
- —— Trans-Amazon Highway
- •—• North Perimetral Rim Road
- - - - Cuiabá – Santarém Highway
- – – – Belém – Brasília Highway

as the main clusters of settlement and economic activity within them are separated by 'demographic deserts' so water links around the continent's periphery are substantial.

In the early post-war years shipping was handicapped by an aged fleet and inadequate ports, but in recent years both ports and ships have been modern-

Port of Manaus, Brazil, 1600 kilometres up the Amazon from the Atlantic Ocean

ized, and some countries now have substantial ship-building industries. The industry in Brazil in 1969 launched 105,000 tons of merchant shipping; in 1986 the figure was 493,000 tons.

Shipping fleets have also expanded. In 1969 the continent had a fleet of 10 million gross registered tons; in 1985 it was over 55 million tons, 10 per cent of the world total. The high figure and growth rate is partly distorted by those countries which provide 'flags of convenience' for foreign ship-owners, and in fact the Panamanian-registered fleet accounts for 70 per cent of the Latin American total. Nevertheless, Brazil, Cuba, Ecuador and Mexico doubled the size of their fleets between 1975 and 1985. Brazilian, Cuban, Mexican and Venezuelan ships, for example, have an average age of less than twelve years.

There has been increasing use of containerization and specialized ships – oil tankers, bulk and ore carriers. Much of the fleet is publicly owned, major tanker fleets being operated by Pemex (Mexico), Petrobrás (Brazil) and Yacimientos Petrolíferos Fiscales (Argentina). Oil tankers and ore and bulk carriers provided over half the tonnage of the Argentine, Mexican and Brazilian merchant fleets; oil tankers alone provided almost the same share of the Venezuelan fleet.

Sea transport remains the dominant method of

commodity movement between the countries of Latin America and, except in the case of Mexico, to other markets in Europe, North America and Japan. Although interregional trade accounts for only about one tenth of their total trade, the countries of the Latin American Free Trade Association (LAFTA) have tried to ensure that an increasing proportion of their trade moves in national or LAFTA-member ships.

Modernization and specialization of the merchant fleets has been paralleled by improvements in harbour facilities and cargo handling, movement and storage. In addition specialist ports have been developed or expanded to handle particular cargoes. Examples include Tubarão and São Luis (iron ore), Sepitiba (oil) and Paranaguá (cereals) in Brazil, the oil terminals of Aruba (Netherlands Indies) and Amuay (Venezuela) and the bauxite terminals of Jamaica.

Coastal and inland waterway traffic remain significant, particularly for bulk-cargo, raw materials and petroleum, but the potential of the navigable rivers is still under-utilized. Improvements in the lower Orinoco improved access to the iron ore deposits of Venezuelan Guyana, and the river and its tributaries offer 10,000 km of navigable waterway. In Amazonia, Manaus is accessible to deep-sea vessels, and the river and its tributaries provide 58,000 km of navigable waterways. Traffic on the São Francisco and Paraná systems has increased as their navigability has been improved.

Air transport

Air traffic has become increasingly important in Latin America. Although in 1985 the continent generated less than 10 per cent of world air travel, air travel has expanded rapidly. Between 1975 and 1985 the distance flown by scheduled airlines increased by

Embraer 30-seater 'Brasília' airliner at Itajaí. These Brazilian-made aircraft are now to be seen at airports around the world.

TABLE 12
Merchant shipping fleets
(thousand gross registered tons)

	1939	1950	1970	1988
Argentina	291	914	1266	1877
Brazil	485	698	1722	6123
Chile	172	169	308	604
Cuba	26	–	333	912
Honduras	84	522	60	582
Mexico	30	144	381	1448
Panama	718	3361	5646	40,604
Peru	34	86	378	675
Venezuela	75	157	393	982

Source: UN, *Statistical Yearbook 1951*, p. 320, *1979*, p. 552, *1987*, pp. 711–14.

TABLE 13
Scheduled air services
(million passenger-kilometres)

	1939	1950	1970	1980	1987
Argentina	–	–	2395	8031	8652
Bolivia	4	19	109	944	912
Brazil	31	–	4385	15,572	22,613
Chile	2	54	839	1875	2117
Colombia	–	–	2063	4198	4230
Cuba	–	–	502	932	1997
Mexico	34	626	2939	13,870	17,649
Peru	–	–	789	1974	2670
Venezuela	–	–	1033	4367	5040

Source: UN, *Statistical Yearbook 1951*, pp. 335–6, *1979*, pp. 602–4, *1981*, p. 597, *1987*, pp. 711–14.

60 per cent, passengers carried by 80 per cent, and freight carried more than doubled. Many Latin American countries have higher percentage use of passenger capacity than the United States. Brazil has the most extensive flight network, with over 228 million km flown in 1985, followed by Mexico (185 million) and Argentina (84 million).

The major cities are the principal nodes for domestic and foreign flights, led by Mexico City, Buenos Aires, Rio de Janeiro and São Paulo. The most heavily used routes link Buenos Aires to Córdoba and Mendoza, Lima to Cuzco, Caracas to Maracaibo, Bogotá with Cali, Medellín and Barranquilla, and São Paulo and Rio with Porto Alegre, Salvador, Recife, Fortaleza and Belém and the inland cities of Belo Horizonte, Brasília and Manaus. In Brazil heavy traffic in the south-eastern core led to a pioneering 'air-bridge' of frequent walk-on flights linking São Paulo, Rio de Janeiro, Brasília and Belo Horizonte. Internal airline systems have expanded, which in most cases reinforces the pattern of a centripetal system focusing on the national capital. This is the case in Argentina, Peru and Venezuela. Brazil has, however, built a well-developed grid of services in the more settled eastern half of the country.

Air charter facilities have also become increasingly important in linking remote areas in the interior, and in intracontinental communications. The continent's major cities are therefore connected by a net of scheduled airline services, with routes between Rio, São Paulo, Montevideo, Buenos Aires, Santiago and Lima among the most heavily used. Air freight has also shown spectacular growth.

Air transport development has been accompanied by expansion and modernization of aircraft fleets, the diffusion of small airports and landing strips to small towns and the rural backlands, and the modernization of old airports or the building of new ones in the principal cities.

As well as numerous domestic airlines and charter firms, most countries now operate, and subsidize, flag-carrier international airlines.

Urban transport

Recent improvements in transport have facilitated both movement to the city and mobility within it. The horse-drawn and later the motorized tram, the bus and most recently the private car have made it increasingly possible to separate workplace and home, giving rise to increasing functional differentiation in the city between office, factory and residential areas.

Increasing pressure from journey-to-work has generated growing problems of traffic congestion, and air and noise pollution in the major cities. In an effort to counter this problem and, in some cases, to reduce oil import bills, new mass transit systems have been developed, with underground metro systems now in Mexico City, Rio de Janeiro, São Paulo, Santiago de Chile and Caracas. By far the oldest such system in Latin America is that of Buenos Aires with the first of its five lines constructed in 1911.

Conclusion

Transport is a crucial element in the development process, but Latin America's system reveals limited integration of networks within most republics and even less between them. There are few overland links, and air transport provides the best system of international connections.

Much of the system betrays its colonial and neo-colonial origins and even some recent developments serve primarily overseas rather than internal demands. The persisting pattern of peripheral settlement has deterred links between countries or deep into the interior. The absence, except for Mexico,

Central America and Colombia, of countries with both Pacific and Atlantic coasts may have repressed the urge to build transcontinental routes such as those developed north of the Rio Grande. Transport by land, sea and air provides linkages between what are economic and demographic 'islands'. Despite recent projects, Amazonia and the far south remains poorly served by land transport. Overall provision of transport remains low, whether in absolute terms or measured by density of road and railway per 1000 square kilometres or per capita, when compared with more developed areas.

Nevertheless, transport systems have been substantially improved over recent decades, serving to integrate more fully established areas of settlement and to open up new ones. Roads and air transport have been improved at the expense of railways, and coastal shipping. Also Latin American governments have become increasingly involved in the ownership and operation of transport systems. Most railroads are nationalized, and about 60 per cent of merchant fleets and 40 per cent of airline services are publicly owned. There has also been considerable development in the manufacture or assembly of automobiles, the building of railway rolling stock and ships and, in the case of Brazil, the manufacture of small aircraft suited to local conditions.

These developments have improved mobility and accessibility. At the same time some projects have benefited only small segments of the population. Were investments in prestige projects such as international airlines, jumbo jets and new air terminals, in multilane intercity highways, or ultra-modern underground railways the best use of scarce resources? Do spectacular highways provide new opportunities and resources for a nation and all its people, or do they merely serve the interests of large landholders, big-city capitalists and multinational corporations, as against those of impoverished migrants, indigenous groups and the natural environment?

JPD

Further Reading: J. H. Coatsworth, *Growth against Development: The Economic Impact of Railroads in Porfirian Mexico* (DeKalb, Illinois, 1981); R. E. G. Davies, *Airlines of Latin America Since 1919* (London, 1984); M. H. J. Finch, *South American Steam* (Truro, 1974); C. J. Stokes, *Transportation and Economic Development in Latin America* (New York, 1970)

Indian boatman on Lake Titicaca, with the Cordillera Real in the distance. Areas of great national beauty such as this have the potential to bring in wealth through tourism, providing that political instability does not keep the tourists away.

Trade and tourism

ATTEMPTS AT ECONOMIC INTEGRATION

The outbreak of the First World War severed the traditional pattern of trade between Europe (manufactures) and Latin America and the Caribbean (raw materials), with the result that the United States became the region's major trading partner. Latin America's non-involvement in the Second World War initially created strong demand for its exports, even of manufactures, but its favourable terms of trade were reversed as the United States and Western Europe rebuilt their industries. As shortages of manufactures throughout the world led to rising prices, there was a tendency in Latin America to turn to industrialization for import substitution. However, the industries thus created behind high tariff barriers proved inefficient in supplying domestic markets and could not compete in world markets. They also generated a higher level of capital imports in the 1950s to the late 1960s, which came increasingly not from the United States, but from Western Europe and Japan. At the same time, exports to these areas expanded, while trade with the United States grew at a slower rate.

As a consequence of Latin American trade adopting a more western-industrialized model in the mid-1950s (influenced greatly by the UN Economic Commission for Latin America – ECLA), intraregional trade fell by 25 per cent: exports between the Latin American countries constituted 12 per cent of total exports in 1953, but only 6 per cent in 1961. At the same time imports from the rest of the world grew by 20 per cent between 1953 and 1961. To redress this imbalance, as a result of which raw materials could buy fewer manufactures in 1960, and to replace existing bilateral trade agreements in Latin America, free trade areas and customs unions were established.

FREE TRADE AGREEMENTS

The first of these was the Central American Common Market (CACM), formed under the General Treaty for Central American Integration, in Managua 13 February 1960. It was followed by the Latin American Free Trade Association (LAFTA – Spanish acronym ALALC) of 1 June 1961, which was replaced in 1980 by the Latin American Integration Association (LAIA – ALADI in Spanish). The Andean Pact (ANCOM), a separate grouping within LAFTA, was

TABLE 14
Andean Pact intraregional trade, 1984, 1986, 1988(a) (US$ million)

Year	Importing country	Exporting countries				
		Bolivia	Colombia	Ecuador	Peru	Venezuela
	Bolivia					
1984	25.5		1.2	0.2	24.1	0.1
1986	10.6		1.3	0.2	8.8	0.4
1988	5.9		2.5	0.2	2.0	1.2
	Colombia					
1984	453.4	4.6		44.6	83.3	320.9
1986	198.7	1.9		30.0	45.3	121.6
1988	296.7	13.6		43.5	61.9	177.8
	Ecuador					
1984	75.2	0.1	44.3		28.8	2.0
1986	79.9	0.1	58.9		11.9	9.0
1988	94.1	0.1	53.3		25.2	15.5
	Peru					
1984	67.0	9.6	20.9	6.3		30.3
1986	145.3	22.3	70.9	9.9		42.2
1988	270.2	2.5	80.3	129.0		58.4
	Venezuela					
1984	143.8	1.4	89.9	3.1	49.5	
1986	198.5	0.0	150.2	2.8	45.4	
1988	383.0	0.4	253.0	4.5	125.1	
	Andean Pact					
1984	765.0	15.6	156.3	54.2	185.6	353.2
1986	633.1	24.2	281.4	42.9	111.4	173.2
1988	1,050.0	16.6	389.2	177.1	214.2	252.9

Source: Interamerican Development Bank.

first constituted at Cartagena on 26 May 1969, and the Caribbean Common Market (CARICOM) was formed under the Treaty of Chaguaramas in 1973, to replace the Caribbean Free Trade Association (CARIFTA). Consequently, the level of intraregional trade was high in 1980 as Latin American countries strengthened integration and tried to penetrate world export markets via easy access to international credit for trade financing. However, a combination of factors after 1981 undermined all trading goals: inflation-inspired recession forced industrialized countries to reduce imports; commodity prices fell; Latin American currencies became overvalued and exports lost competitiveness. High real interest rates and rising obligations led to the debt crisis of the early 1980s. In order to service debts, positive trade balances were sought through the promotion of exports and the restriction of imports, including products covered by intraregional agreements. This caused a sharp decline in intraregional trade, which only

began to recover at the end of the 1980s.

The signatories of CACM were Costa Rica, El Salvador, Guatemala, Honduras and Nicaragua. In the 1960s it was regarded as an excellent example of a common market between low-income countries, but progress was upset in 1969 by the severance of links between Honduras and El Salvador after the five-day 'Football War', and Honduras, the least developed of the members, withdrew in 1970. However, in 1973 it made bilateral agreements with all but El Salvador, with whom diplomatic links were eventually restored in 1980. Further limitations in the 1980s were imposed by civil war in El Salvador, Guatemala and Nicaragua (which also underwent a US trade embargo) and by the severity of the debt crisis, especially in Costa Rica. Under these conditions, the common market virtually disintegrated; having grown from $30 million in 1960 to $1,160 million in 1980, the value of intraregional trade slumped to $413 million in 1986. Then two rounds of cuts in the common

TABLE 15

Central American Common Market, intraregional trade, 1984, 1986, 1988[a] (US$ million)

Year	Importing country	exporting countries				
		Costa Rica	El Salvador	Guatemala	Honduras	Nicaragua
	Costa Rica					
1984	114.9		30.8	59.4	8.3	16.3
1986	106.3		33.8	61.3	5.9	5.3
1988	118.7		33.1	68.8	4.8	11.9
	El Salvador					
1984	251.4	44.8		186.8	16.9	2.9
1986	157.1	37.8		108.7	9.2	1.4
1988	201.4	45.6		142.1	10.2	3.4
	Guatemala					
1984	186.6	62.8	94.7		14.2	14.9
1986	102.5	35.7	53.2		5.7	7.8
1988	153.0	54.0	85.2		12.0	1.6
	Honduras					
1984	99.0	44.6	8.9	41.3		4.2
1986	58.2	24.3	8.0	24.6		1.2
1988	52.4	10.4	11.1	29.2		1.7
	Nicaragua					
1984	74.5	19.3	11.6	29.2	14.4	
1986	38.2	9.6	10.5	15.6	2.5	
1988	36.8	14.8	8.1	13.4	1.5	
	Central America					
1984	726.3	171.4	146.0	316.7	53.8	38.4
1986	462.1	107.4	105.5	210.2	23.4	15.6
1988	563.3	124.9	137.6	253.5	28.6	18.6

[a] Preliminary data

Source: Interamerican Development Bank.

TABLE 16
Intra-LAIA trade, 1989–90 (US$ million)

Country	1989			1990 (a)		
	Exports	Imports	Balance	Exports	Imports	Balance
Argentina	2388	1389	999	3070	1396	1674
Bolivia	394	270	124	408	345	63
Brazil	3476	3480	–4	3115	3759	–644
Chile	959	1754	–795	928	1840	–912
Colombia	525	1011	–486	585	1090	–505
Ecuador	313	370	–57	262	459	–197
Mexico	736	702 (b)	34	870	883 (b)	–13
Paraguay	422	300	122	426	444	–18
Peru	578 (a)	497 (a)	81	418	764	–346
Uruguay	588	615	–27	665	687	–22
Venezuela	826	656	170	1141	726	415
TOTAL	11,205	11,044		11,888	12,393	

(a) = estimated; (b) = f.o.b. value

TABLE 17
Intra-LAIA imports, 1981, 1985, 1988 (US$ million)

	1981	1985	1988
TOTAL	12,199	7533	9921
Products subject to LAIA agreement	3143	2309	3919
Percentage of products subject to LAIA agreement to total	26	31	40

TABLE 18
LAIA extraregional trade as percentage of total, 1990 (%)

Bolivia	54
Uruguay	56
Paraguay	63
Argentina	73
Peru	80
Chile	83
Ecuador	84
Colombia	86
Brazil	87
Venezuela	93
Mexico	97

Source: LAIA Secretariat, quoted in *Business Latin America*, 3 June 1991 (a and c), and Interamerican Development Bank, *Economic and Social Progress in Latin America*, 1990 Report, p. 11 (b).

external tariff, the first in 1986, the second initiated in 1987 by Costa Rica, plus increased openness of borders, stimulated trade, which rose to $652 million in 1989. Regional trade in most basic agricultural produce was to be liberalized by the end of 1991, and in all such products by June 1992 uniform prices would be set and tariff barriers removed.

LAFTA was composed of Argentina, Bolivia, Brazil, Chile, Colombia, Ecuador, Mexico, Paraguay, Peru, Uruguay and Venezuela. Trade concessions between members were drawn up without delay, but these were for products that either had already been granted similar freedom, or were unimportant in intraregional trade; by 1980 only 3 per cent of all existing concessions had been made since 1969. A second Treaty on 12 August 1980 – signed, like the first, in Montevideo – replaced LAFTA with LAIA, which has the same members with the same prob-

lems deriving from the different levels of industrialization, but embodies a change of emphasis from economic growth to the defence of trade.

LAIA also had to contend with the problems of the debt crisis and, for the reasons noted above, intra-LAIA imports declined from $12.2 billion in 1981 to $7.5 billion in 1985. Thereafter, intraregional

Milled mahogany planks, piled up for export from Brazil. Though more than half Brazil's exports are now manufactured goods, timber and similar commodities are not neglected.

imports recovered to $12.4 billion in 1990. In 1991 Mexico proposed that the Treaty of Montevideo be revised to broaden the number of goods covered by negotiation and to change the process of bargaining over discounts on tariffs within 'partial' agreements to negotiation of the tariffs themselves.

Seeing that exports from Mexico, Brazil and Argentina represented nearly 50 per cent of total intraregional exports, but that their own contribution was not in the same proportion, Chile, Peru, Bolivia, Colombia and Ecuador signed the Andean Pact at Cartagena (26 May 1969); Venezuela joined in February 1973. Their aim was to coordinate their industrial development and trade liberalization ahead of LAFTA's stalled liberalization policies. Chile left in 1977 in disagreement over the treatment of foreign capital, and other political and commercial disagreements have put additional strains on the pact.

Intraregional exports in the pact constituted 4.7 per cent of its total exports in 1982 ($1.2 billion out of $26.1 billion) and 4 per cent in 1989 ($1.2 billion out of $30 billion). Up to 1981 ANCOM trade had grown at an annual average rate of 22 per cent, reaching $1.3 billion, before the subsequent retrenchment, which was common to the whole region, whereafter trade recovered. Venezuela and Colombia account for over 60 per cent of ANCOM trade, both in terms of their combined sales to the other three members and in each's penetration of the other's market.

In May 1991 in Caracas the ANCOM countries agreed to swift trade liberalization; by 31 December 1991 a free trade zone would be opened and a timetable for a common external tariff (CET) would be formalized. All would have a CET in force by end-1993, except Ecuador and Bolivia, which would have until the end of 1995. Ecuador was also given a slower timetable for other measures. The Caracas declaration directed ANCOM trade away from the model of import substitution and restrictions on foreign investment which had characterized all of Latin American trade in the 1960s and 1970s. The group was therefore following the lead successfully taken by Chile in the mid-1970s of adopting policies of export-led growth, deregulation and attracting foreign capital. Bolivia embarked on a similar route in 1985.

These policies form the basis of the consensus established in Washington by the IMF, World Bank, Interamerican Development Bank (IADB), the US executive branch and others as the reforms necessary to bring Latin America out of the debt crisis, the goal being free trade, achieved by competitive exchange rates and import liberalization. With this in view, in June 1990 President George Bush announced the Enterprise for the Americas Initiative (EAI), which

envisaged a free trade zone stretching from 'Anchorage to Tierra del Fuego'. The Western Hemispheric Free Trade Area, designed to compete with European and Asian trading blocs, would be constructed around a series of bilateral negotiations between the United States and individual, or groups of, nations. The principle was endorsed at the first summit of Spanish- and Portuguese-speaking nations at Guadalajara, Mexico, on 18–19 July 1991. Negotiations were also well advanced at the same time for Mexico to join a North American Free Trade Area with the United States and Canada (NAFTA); among the many other Latin American countries that had signed, or were discussing, free trade pacts with the United States were Chile, Ecuador, Bolivia, Colombia, Venezuela and the other southern cone countries. However, the sheer size of a hemispheric free trade area, with its differences in industrial development and economic stability, and the need for US congressional approval at every stage, may prove to hinder rapid progress. Many Latin American countries, therefore, were seeking partners in regional agreements separate from the longer-established integration movements.

A further free trade group, Mercosur, was formed by Argentina, Brazil, Uruguay and Paraguay at the Treaty of Asunción on 26 March 1991. The founding agreement proposed the free circulation of goods and services, a regional CET for third-country imports and the harmonization of macroeconomic policies. It was due to be in operation for Argentina and Brazil by the end of 1994 and by the end of 1995 for all four. In the transition period, Brazil and Argentina would continue their bilateral integration programme which began in November 1985. Mexico and Central America (excluding Panama) also signed a free trade pact at Tuxtla Gutiérrez on 11 January 1991; Mexico, Venezuela and Colombia (who planned to establish their own free trade zone by July 1994) additionally agreed to open their markets to Central American goods. In September 1991 Chile and Mexico signed a free trade accord, and on 1 July 1991 Venezuela signed a pact with CARICOM granting duty-free access to Venezuela for Caribbean goods for five years.

The Caribbean

Having been formed by Barbados, Guyana, Jamaica and Trinidad and Tobago, the Caribbean Common Market was joined in 1974 by Belize and the members of the East Caribbean Common Market (Antigua, Dominica, Grenada, Montserrat, St Kitts/Nevis, Anguilla, St Lucia and St Vincent). The Bahamas were admitted in 1983. Since most of these nations rely on sugar and tropical fruit for foreign exchange, there is strong competition between them for markets. Moreover, the need to import manufactures from outside the region caused balance-of-payments deficits in all but Trinidad and Tobago which, until the 1980s, could offset import bills with earnings from petroleum products and natural gas.

PATTERNS OF TRADE

Historically, intraregional trade expanded in manufactures (except in CARICOM), while the region's world trade has been mostly in primary commodities. The onset of recession in industrialized countries in the 1980s disrupted this pattern. Falling commodity prices and a tendency for industrialized countries to supply their own primary commodities accelerated a fall in terms of trade for Latin America

that began with the first oil shock of 1973. In 1975 the region's terms-of-trade declined by 16.7 per cent as primary commodity prices weakened and manufactured imports prices rose. In the four following years, price variations led to an overall expansion of exports and terms-of-trade income, but from 1980 to 1989 terms of trade fell by 29 per cent. Overproduction of most traditional agricultural commodities, the use of plastics instead of metals and the decline of heavy engineering in industrial countries all contributed to falling non-oil commodity prices between 1973 and 1990. For the oil exporters (Mexico, Venezuela, Ecuador and Trinidad and Tobago), oil price rises were a constant source of exchange from 1973 until the lowering of OPEC prices in 1983. Thereafter these countries experienced a 37 per cent fall in their terms of trade.

TABLE 19
Origin of Latin American and Caribbean imports, 1983, 1989 (per cent)

Country	United States		EEC		Japan		Canada		Middle East		Western Hemisphere		Other countries	
	1983	1989	1983	1989	1983	1989	1983	1989	1983	1989	1983	1989	1983	1989
Argentina	21.9	17.9	27.3	29.2	6.8	6.3	1.2	0.7	0.2	1.0	32.6	34.0	10.0	10.9
Bahamas	16.4	34.6	8.4	6.3	2.4	13.0	2.2	1.1	21.0	1.1	12.3	5.5	37.3	38.4
Barbados	46.3	35.0	15.8	18.8	4.2	5.7	5.4	7.5	–	0.1	20.4	25.0	7.9	7.9
Belize	41.5	55.6	16.1	17.8	1.4	4.1	1.7	3.0	–	0.1	36.0	12.9	3.3	6.5
Bolivia	28.2	20.2	16.9	13.5	7.3	5.3	0.8	0.9	–	0.1	41.5	54.9	5.3	5.1
Brazil	15.6	20.9	12.5	19.4	3.7	6.6	3.3	2.6	35.3	17.7	14.8	18.4	14.8	14.4
Chile	23.7	19.8	17.2	19.5	5.4	7.7	2.1	2.2	3.0	0.7	29.9	27.2	18.7	22.9
Colombia	35.6	36.4	16.5	19.9	11.1	10.9	3.6	3.9	0.1	0.4	25.4	20.8	7.7	7.7
Costa Rica	37.8	40.5	12.3	12.2	5.3	6.7	1.9	1.3	0.3	0.3	38.7	30.7	3.7	8.3
Cuba	–	0.1	27.0	26.3	6.4	2.2	17.9	5.3	–	–	23.5	41.6	25.2	24.5
Dominica	26.4	21.0	23.9	15.8	7.1	9.6	3.2	4.3	–	–	35.0	14.3	4.4	35.0
Dominican Republic	35.9	41.3	11.3	11.5	4.3	14.4	2.3	1.8	0.1	0.1	42.7	26.5	3.4	4.4
Ecuador	34.0	33.1	23.9	20.8	9.3	13.9	2.7	1.9	0.2	–	19.6	19.0	10.3	11.3
El Salvador	32.5	43.5	11.8	12.9	3.5	3.5	1.5	0.8	–	–	47.3	30.4	3.4	8.9
Guatemala	32.2	39.5	11.5	17.8	4.9	5.1	1.6	1.1	0.1	0.3	45.3	26.7	4.4	9.5
Guyana	21.2	40.1	19.7	18.9	1.5	5.0	2.6	2.0	–	–	52.8	26.1	2.2	7.9
Haiti	63.6	55.1	11.2	13.3	4.3	5.4	2.2	4.6	0.1	0.1	14.3	14.9	4.3	6.6
Honduras	36.1	52.3	14.3	10.2	4.5	9.1	1.2	1.3	0.1	0.1	39.7	18.5	4.1	8.5
Jamaica	39.7	49.4	10.8	12.4	3.4	4.1	4.2	5.6	0.1	0.1	34.3	17.7	7.5	10.7
Mexico	60.5	67.0	15.1	13.0	3.9	5.3	2.5	1.8	–	0.1	3.2	4.2	14.8	8.6
Netherlands Antilles	9.4	18.2	4.9	16.9	1.1	2.9	0.1	0.5	7.1	1.3	75.0	51.6	2.4	8.6
Nicaragua	19.0	0.4	17.0	20.6	2.4	3.6	1.6	3.8	0.2	–	45.1	31.9	14.7	39.7
Panama	32.3	28.0	8.7	14.6	7.8	10.6	1.0	0.5	0.1	0.5	33.9	26.1	16.2	19.7
Paraguay	7.3	17.6	20.7	15.3	4.2	13.0	0.1	0.1	0.1	0.1	50.6	27.8	17.0	26.1
Peru	38.0	33.0	22.0	20.4	10.2	4.1	3.2	2.1	–	0.5	18.3	30.4	8.3	9.5
Suriname	30.0	36.4	23.5	23.6	6.6	2.8	0.4	0.2	0.1	–	34.0	32.3	5.4	4.7
Trinidad and Tobago	42.5	51.6	19.8	15.7	9.5	2.3	6.5	5.3	–	–	14.2	16.1	7.5	9.0
Uruguay	8.4	8.6	15.1	20.6	2.4	3.0	0.4	1.5	4.7	4.9	44.3	49.1	24.7	12.3
Venezuela	46.2	44.6	22.4	28.8	5.7	4.1	5.0	2.2	0.1	0.4	14.4	12.1	6.2	7.8

Middle East includes the following petroleum countries: Iran, Iraq, Kuwait, Oman, Qatar, Saudi Arabia United Arab Emirates.
Western Hemisphere includes all Latin American and Caribbean countries but excludes the USA and Canada.

TABLE 20
Destination of Latin American and Caribbean exports, 1983, 1989 (per cent)

Country	United States		EEC		Japan		Canada		Middle East		Western Hemisphere		Other countries	
	1983	1989	1983	1989	1983	1989	1983	1989	1983	1989	1983	1989	1983	1989
Argentina	9.9	13.0	24.0	28.9	4.4	3.6	0.4	0.9	7.6	4.5	14.1	21.2	39.6	27.9
Bahamas	90.2	41.5	4.5	12.3	0.4	1.3	1.9	2.6	0.4	0.6	1.6	3.9	1.0	37.8
Barbados	52.7	21.1	5.6	14.8	–	0.8	1.5	2.8	–	–	24.0	40.0	16.2	20.5
Belize	38.7	42.8	25.1	31.4	0.1	4.1	9.6	4.8	–	–	26.5	16.6	–	0.3
Bolivia	20.5	19.2	18.1	30.9	1.9	0.3	–	0.1	–	0.1	55.0	43.5	4.5	5.9
Brazil	23.2	23.4	28.9	28.9	6.5	6.7	1.4	2.6	6.9	4.0	10.4	11.4	22.7	23.0
Chile	28.1	19.7	34.5	36.1	9.0	12.5	1.6	0.7	2.4	1.6	12.1	13.1	12.3	16.3
Colombia	28.3	40.7	39.3	26.9	4.4	5.2	0.9	1.3	0.2	1.0	14.0	15.5	12.9	9.4
Costa Rica	31.8	45.2	24.1	25.7	0.6	0.6	0.8	3.8	1.9	0.6	30.6	17.7	10.2	6.4
Cuba	–	–	30.7	30.0	8.0	10.0	4.3	4.0	12.3	5.9	6.9	9.0	37.8	41.1
Dominica	3.0	10.1	44.1	57.9	–	4.8	–	0.3	–	–	53.1	19.1	–	7.8
Dominican Republic	67.4	77.0	11.2	13.5	1.9	1.7	2.1	1.9	–	–	3.7	3.6	13.7	2.3
Ecuador	56.6	45.9	2.6	9.2	1.8	2.5	0.6	0.1	–	–	21.5	27.1	16.9	15.2
El Salvador	38.6	41.0	23.3	22.8	4.9	2.7	1.8	3.9	–	–	25.6	27.5	5.8	2.1
Guatemala	35.0	47.6	17.0	14.5	3.4	3.6	0.5	1.8	3.0	3.9	35.7	21.8	5.4	8.9
Guyana	17.4	29.9	37.3	44.9	8.0	5.7	6.4	6.9	0.1	–	25.6	12.3	5.2	0.3
Haiti	73.5	79.9	22.6	15.5	–	0.3	1.0	1.8	0.5	0.3	1.7	1.5	0.7	0.7
Honduras	55.1	49.9	18.3	19.4	6.0	9.7	0.4	2.2	2.7	1.4	13.3	6.0	4.2	11.4
Jamaica	33.6	37.2	22.7	29.6	1.0	1.2	12.6	13.7	–	–	17.6	9.4	12.5	8.9
Mexico	58.4	63.3	17.9	15.9	6.8	7.1	2.1	2.4	2.4	1.6	7.5	5.2	4.9	4.5
Netherlands Antilles	48.3	39.8	12.3	12.4	0.2	1.5	0.7	0.2	0.4	–	25.4	27.0	12.7	19.1
Nicaragua	22.2	–	32.7	32.6	11.5	6.7	0.4	21.1	0.1	0.1	18.4	17.3	14.7	22.2
Panama	53.7	46.1	14.4	25.5	0.3	0.3	0.9	1.3	1.2	0.6	14.9	22.6	14.6	3.6
Paraguay	8.6	3.6	36.6	35.5	2.0	0.7	0.2	0.2	0.4	0.1	42.0	33.0	10.2	26.9
Peru	37.7	23.0	22.5	28.9	15.9	11.9	2.2	1.7	0.1	0.5	10.4	14.1	11.2	19.9
Suriname	20.6	14.7	38.0	37.3	3.9	3.4	1.1	–	–	–	17.7	8.7	18.7	35.9
Trinidad and Tobago	60.0	54.6	12.5	10.1	0.4	0.9	0.6	1.0	–	0.5	20.4	28.6	6.1	4.3
Uruguay	9.7	11.9	20.5	23.2	1.9	1.4	2.4	4.0	25.1	6.4	23.7	31.7	16.7	21.4
Venezuela	31.1	51.6	21.4	12.4	2.7	4.0	3.8	3.1	0.5	0.1	20.9	21.5	19.6	7.3

Middle East includes the following petroleum countries: Iran, Iraq, Kuwait, Oman, Qatar, Saudi Arabia United Arab Emirates.
Western Hemisphere includes all Latin American and Caribbean countries but excludes the USA and Canada.
Source: *Direction of Trade Statistics Yearbook*, 1990.

To offset falling commodity prices, the region diversified into non-traditional agricultural and manufactured exports. In volume terms, the latter grew at twice the rate of primaries in the 1980s so that, according to the World Bank, by 1986 manufactured exports accounted for 32 per cent of export volume (compared with 12 per cent in the mid-1960s), non-oil commodities were 42 per cent (against 58 per cent) and petroleum 26 per cent (against 30 per cent). The initiatives introduced to widen exports coincided with the lowering of protective barriers to extra-regional trade and with exchange rates becoming more competitive. Thus a number of countries could take advantage of the return to economic growth in the OECD after 1984 (for example, Brazil and Mexico from manufactures, Chile, Mexico and Guatemala from non-traditional agricultural produce). This development must be seen in the context of a slowdown in growth since 1984 in the volume and value of Latin American exports. Foreign sales were hampered by protectionist measures in the EEC and USA and by the technological inferiority of Latin American manufacturing industries compared with their industrialized and newly industrialized competitors.

For the oil-importing countries of the region the import bill for fuels soared after 1973, upsetting what until then had been a relatively stable structure of commodity imports. Increasing fuel costs and inflation in industrialized countries also adversely affected the price of capital and intermediate goods, and of raw materials for the region's manufacturing

Bananas for export from Ecuador. Until the early 1970s, when oil production boomed, bananas accounted for the largest share of Ecuador's export earnings.

The part played by the USA

The United States remains the region's largest market. Between 1961 and 1963 the United States' average share of total Latin American exports was 37.2 per cent; by 1978–80 this had fallen to 33.7 per cent, but by 1989 it had just exceeded the 1961–3 average, at 37.8 per cent. In 1989 fifteen countries depended on the United States for purchasing over 40 per cent of their exports, compared with eight in 1978–80 and twelve in 1961–3. Imports from the United States declined from an average share of 41.8 per cent in 1961–3 to 34.9 per cent in 1978–80, falling still further by 1989 to 25.5 per cent. The purchases of twelve countries in 1989 from the United States were more than 40 per cent of their individual total compared with five in 1978–80 and fourteen in 1961–3.

COMMODITY EXPORTS

Despite the attempts at diversification, many countries continue to rely on one or more commodity exports for over 30 per cent of their export income: Belize (sugar), Bolivia (natural gas), Chile (copper), Colombia (coffee), Dominican Republic (ferronickel), Ecuador (petroleum), El Salvador (coffee), Grenada (nutmeg), Guyana (bauxite and sugar), Honduras (bananas), Jamaica (alumina), Mexico (petroleum), Netherlands Antilles (petroleum), Nicaragua (coffee), Paraguay (soyabeans, cotton), St Lucia (bananas), St Vincent (bananas), Suriname (alumina) and Venezuela (petroleum).

Two groups of banana growers compete for markets. The Union of Banana Exporting Countries (UPEB) comprises Colombia, Panama, Guatemala, Costa Rica, the Dominican Republic, Venezuela and Honduras (which left in 1989, only to rejoin in 1991); Latin America's largest producer and exporter, Ecuador, is under pressure to join. The other group is the Windward Islands Banana Growers' Association (St Lucia, St Vincent, Dominica and Grenada), closely aligned with Jamaica and Belize. Suriname also exports. Despite the preferential access given to Caribbean ex-colonies under the Lomé Agreement, Latin American growers provide 56 per cent of all bananas imported by the EEC, and the creation of a single European market in 1992 threatens the Caribbean further, especially since Latin American bananas cost less to produce and their quality is perceived to be higher. In 1989 the Windward Islands exported $185.9 million-worth of bananas, compared with $370 million from Ecuador, $288 million (Colombia), $275 million (Costa Rica) and $391 million (Honduras – 1990 figure).

Non-traditional agricultural commodity exports include fruit from Brazil (mainly oranges for juice),

industries. Imports grew at an unsteady rate until 1981 ($100.9 billion), whereupon their volume and value fell (to $60.3 billion in 1983) as countries strove to service their foreign debts. The greatest reduction was in the import of manufactures, while the share of imported primary products increased to account for about one third of total imports. Not until 1987 did Latin American imports recover, rising to $69.8 billion in that year and to $84.8 billion in 1989. The merchandise trade balance in 1989 was in surplus by $26.8 billion, $11.6 billion lower than the decade's highest surplus in 1984, but over three and a half times greater than the decade's first surplus of $7.3 billion in 1982 (the trade balance was in deficit by $2.4 billion in 1981). In the mid-1980s imports of capital goods were restricted by the curtailment of direct foreign investment in energy and infrastructure projects.

When imports increased later in the decade it was as the result of trade liberalization policies which reduced import restrictions on the intermediate goods which were needed to supply export-oriented industries, but such policies were not applied uniformly or successfully. Mexico, for instance, opened up rapidly so that imports doubled from $12.2 billion to $23.4 billion between 1987 and 1989, while exports grew by a mere $2.1 billion to $22.8 billion in the same period, reducing a trade surplus of $8.5 billion to a deficit of $644.8 million.

TABLE 21
Contribution of major commodity exports to total value of merchandise exports, 1984, 1990 (per cent)

Country	Commodity	First product 1984	1990	Commodity	Second product 1984	1990	Commodity	Third product 1984	1989
Argentina	Wheat	12	7	Corn	9	3	Meat	5	8
Bahamas	Petroleum	89	63[a]						
Barbados	Sugar	7	13						
Belize	Sugar	35	33	Citrus	10	17			
Bolivia	Natural gas	52	36[b]	Tin	34	13[b]			
Brazil	Soyabeans	10	9	Coffee	10	4	Iron ore	6	8
Chile	Copper	43	50[c]						
Colombia	Coffee	52	22	Fuel oil	13	29			
Costa Rica	Coffee	26	17	Bananas	25	22			
Dominican Republic	Sugar	35	24[c]	Ferronickel	12	40[c]	Dore	15	10[c]
Ecuador	Petroleum	62	46	Coffee	7	17	Bananas	5	4
El Salvador	Coffee	62	46[c]						
Grenada	Nutmeg	12	46[a]	Cocoa beans	23	13[a]	Bananas	16	13[a]
Guatemala	Coffee	32	26	Cotton	7	2	Sugar	6	13
Guyana	Bauxite	44	33	Sugar	34	32			
Haiti	Coffee	26	20[c]						
Honduras	Bananas	32	38[c]	Coffee	23	21[c]			
Jamaica	Alumina	44	45[c]	Bauxite	20	13[c]			
Mexico	Petroleum	67	36	Coffee	2	14			
Netherlands Antilles	Petroleum	98	95[b]						
Nicaragua	Cotton	35	16[a]	Coffee	32	45[a]			
Panama	Bananas	27	28[c]	Shrimp	18	22[c]	Sugar	12	3[c]
Paraguay	Cotton	40	32[c]	Soyabeans	29	35[c]			
Peru	Copper	14	23[c]	Fishmeal	4	12[c]	Zinc	11	6[c]
St Lucia	Bananas	50	67[a]						
St Vincent	Bananas	22	30[a]						
Suriname	Alumina	56	64[a]	Aluminium	12	1[a]	Bauxite	11	6[a]
Trinidad and Tobago	Sugar	1	16[c]						
Uruguay	Wool	17	18	Meat	16	16			
Venezuela	Petroleum	88	75[c]						

[a] 1987, [b] 1988, [c] 1989
Source: *International Financial Statistics*, July 1991.

with exports valued at $1 billion in 1989. Chile ($557 million), which is also a major exporter of wine, and Colombia ($265 million in 1989). Colombia is the world's second largest exporter of cut flowers, after the Netherlands (sales were put at $229 million in 1991); its main market is the United States, with about 15 per cent of exports going to Europe. Ecuador, Mexico and Central American countries are now investing in flower-exporting ventures too. The illegal trade in narcotics from Colombia, Peru and Bolivia has provided a large proportion of each country's foreign exchange earnings (estimated at $300–400 million per year in Bolivia, $1 billion in Peru and $1.3 billion in Colombia in 1989).

Two Latin American oil-producing countries are members of OPEC, Venezuela and Ecuador. In 1990 Venezuela exported 1.9 million barrels per day (bpd), the value of which ($14 billion) represented 79 per cent of its total exports (compared with 93 per cent in 1983). During the Gulf War of 1991 Venezuela replaced the Middle East as a supplier of oil to the United States, a position it hoped to maintain. Venezuela's OPEC production quota in 1991 was 2.2 million bpd, compared with 270,000 from the region's next largest exporter, Ecuador. Ecuador's exports in 1990 were 160,000 bpd, worth $1.3 billion (46 per cent of the total). But the largest oil producer in the whole region is Mexico (2.95 million bpd in 1990); exports of petroleum in 1990 were 1.2 million bpd, earning $10 billion.

Brazil has significant oil output, but insufficient to meet demand, although Petrobrás is aiming for self-sufficiency by 1995. In Peru, which like Ecuador has oil and natural gas reserves in the Amazon jungle, the curtailment of foreign investment in the 1980s caused local demand to outstrip production, ending exports. Colombia also produces oil on the eastern side of the Andes, exporting 200,000 bpd of crude and fuel oil, worth $1.4 billion in 1990; it has also become a major exporter of coal since 1984.

TABLE 22
Exports, imports, trade balance, current account balance, by country, 1981, 1983, 1986, 1989 (US$ million)

	1981				1983			
Country	Exports	Imports	Trade balance	C/A balance	Exports	Imports	Trade balance	C/A balance
Argentina	9169.1	8414.5	754.7	−4634.1	7833.6	4123.1	3710.5	−2440.5
Bahamas	176.9	799.0	−622.2	−88.0	225.1	823.6	−598.4	−37.1
Barbados	162.7	527.2	−364.4	−118.6	272.2	571.5	−299.3	−42.0
Bolivia	912.4	827.7	84.8	−446.8	755.1	496.0	259.1	−126.7
Brazil	23,341.5	22,099.8	1241.7	−11,764.5	21,923.1	15,437.4	6485.6	−6797.8
Chile	3835.8	6512.5	−2676.7	−4732.0	3831.3	2844.6	986.7	−1116.0
Colombia	3157.8	4729.6	−1571.8	−1958.6	2969.7	4464.1	−1494.5	−3006.0
Costa Rica	1002.4	1089.1	−86.7	−407.5	853.2	895.5	−42.3	−280.9
Dominican Republic	1188.0	1451.7	−263.7	−389.4	785.2	1279.0	−493.8	−418.0
Ecuador	2527.1	2353.0	174.0	−1002.1	2348.0	1421.0	926.9	−4.1
El Salvador	798.1	898.4	−100.3	−250.5	757.9	832.2	−74.3	−28.1
Guatemala	1282.3	1544.2	−261.9	−588.3	1090.8	1056.6	34.2	−226.5
Guyana	346.4	399.6	−53.2	−183.7	193.4	225.8	−32.4	−157.5
Haiti	147.2	350.7	−203.5	−141.0	185.5	323.9	−138.4	−106.2
Honduras	783.8	898.4	−114.9	−302.7	698.7	756.2	−57.5	−219.3
Jamaica	974.0	1296.7	−322.7	−336.7	685.7	1124.2	−438.5	−355.0
Mexico	20,056.3	23,961.7	−3905.4	−16,196.9	22,329.3	8564.8	13,764.4	5396.3
Nicaragua	508.2	922.5	−414.2	−591.7	428.8	778.1	−349.3	−559.6
Panama	287.0	1260.8	−973.8	−360.3	304.9	1232.5	−927.6	−202.5
Paraguay	398.6	772.3	−373.8	−373.3	326.0	551.4	−225.3	−248.1
Peru	3248.6	3804.0	−555.4	−1728.6	3018.9	2723.8	295.0	−871.2
Suriname	473.8	507.0	−93.9	−25.2	367.3	402.1	−96.5	−172.4
Trinidad and Tobago	2612.2	1763.4	848.8	374.5	2026.5	2233.4	−206.9	−1003.0
Uruguay	1229.7	1592.1	−362.4	−461.4	1156.4	739.7	416.7	−60.0
Venezuela	19,963.2	12,122.9	7840.2	4002.1	14,570.5	6408.7	8161.8	4427.8

	1986				1989			
Country	Exports	Imports	Trade balance	C/A balance	Exports	Imports	Trade balance	C/A balance
Argentina	6851.3	4391.2	2460.1	−2855.5	9587.0	3822.0	5765.0	−1274.0
Bahamas	293.5	1009.9	−716.3	−18.2	250.1	1,09.3	−859.2	−157.4
Barbados	244.3	522.6	−278.3	−15.8	155.0	597.0	−442.0	−43.5
Bolivia	545.5	596.6	−51.0	−370.1	723.0	521.2	201.8	−24.7
Brazil	22,407.5	14,011.2	8396.4	−5204.2	34,392.0	18,281.0	16,111.0	1424.0
Chile	4198.8	3099.5	1099.3	−1136.8	8080.0	6501.9	1578.1	−905.0
Colombia	5330.9	3409.2	1921.7	381.3	6041.3	4740.3	1300.9	24.6
Costa Rica	1083.7	1043.7	40.0	−79.1	1319.7	1591.8	−272.1	−400.6
Dominican Republic	722.1	1351.7	−629.6	−206.5	925.7	1952.1	−1026.4	−205.3
Ecuador	2186.0	1631.1	554.9	−612.9	2354.0	1685.0	669.0	−441.0
El Salvador	777.9	902.3	−124.4	117.0	497.3	995.5	−498.2	−128.8
Guatemala	1047.5	874.5	173.0	−11.4	1157.9	1514.4	−356.5	−338.0
Guyana	238.7	241.1	−2.4	−112.3	206.8	210.7	−3.9	−130.5
Haiti	196.0	311.6	−115.6	−42.8	155.0	288.9	−133.9	−68.7
Honduras	891.3	874.0	17.2	−147.8	966.7	964.0	2.7	−271.5
Jamaica	589.5	837.4	−247.9	−38.5	970.3	1567.3	−597.0	−233.1
Mexico	16,027.8	11,451.3	4576.5	−1699.9	22,764.9	23,409.7	−644.8	−5449.4
Nicaragua	247.2	726.5	−479.4	−693.2	292.1	632.6	−340.5	−316.0
Panama	359.4	1127.1	−767.7	40.2	300.0	911.5	−611.5	−61.9
Paraguay	573.4	735.8	−162.4	−358.9	1097.2	1171.2	−74.0	−252.7
Peru	2529.4	2582.1	−52.8	−1061.7	3546.0	2029.0	1517.0	668.0
Suriname	336.6	303.5	24.4	−49.2	609.9	470.1	139.8	−15.4
Trinidad and Tobago	1363.1	1209.4	153.7	−441.8	1534.6	1202.5	332.1	−114.6
Uruguay	1087.8	814.5	273.2	67.0	1599.0	1136.2	462.8	153.3
Venezuela	9122.6	7862.6	1260.0	−1471.2	12,049.0	7500.0	4549.0	792.0

Source: *Interamerican Development Bank.*

Macchu Pichu, Peru, one of the most spectacular sights in South America. This small Inca city was not found by the invading sixteenth-century Spaniards, and was discovered only in 1911 by the American explorer Hiram Bingham.

Not only do Latin America and the Caribbean have to confront changing demand for their products, they are also faced with uncertainties in the structure of world markets. Since 1986, the Uruguay Round of GATT has attempted to define methods of further opening up international markets, of reinforcing the standards and rules of multilateral trade, and of managing to include new areas in trade. But the Uruguay Round collapsed in December 1990, the main obstacles being disagreements over liberalization of tariffs in farm products and over trade in services.

A further consideration within GATT is the call for an environmental code to govern trading standards. In September 1991 it ruled that a US ban on tuna fished in Mexican waters by methods which also killed dolphins was contrary to fair trade. (Venezuela was also affected by the ban; a similar case is the destruction of mangroves by Ecuadorean shrimp farming.)

TOURISM

Beaches are the major draw in the Caribbean, together with the increasing popularity of associated watersports. Generally there are few large resorts (such as Mar del Plata, Argentina, or Punta del Este, Uruguay) in Middle and South America, although Mexico is investing in new developments to rival its older resorts of Acapulco and Cancún. In Latin America commercial exploitation of this type of centre is often inhibited by difficult terrain. This is also true for some archaeological sites whose remoteness adds to their mystery, such as the many prehispanic cities found in Peru (for example, Machu Picchu), but in Central America and Mexico the Maya heritage is being exploited on a cross-border basis (the Mundo Maya). However, the region has much to offer the tourist. Latin America's colonial and modern cities provide a contrast with the pre-Columbian cultures, while the continent's landscapes and wildlife offer great scope for environmentally based tourism. The Andean mountain chain embraces Lake Titicaca, the highest navigable lake in the world, primary temperate forests and an alluring lake district in Chile, glacial ranges in Patagonia, and snow-capped volcanoes near the Equator. Mountains, which also stretch through Central America and Mexico, are not the only natural feature; there are also great rivers, like the Amazon, with its surrounding jungle; waterfalls (the Angel Falls, Iguazú), vestiges of cloud forest in Central America, wide open plains, and the world's driest deserts. The preponderance of high land, especially in the tropical zones, makes the climate more amenable than in similar regions throughout the

Bolivia exports natural gas, mainly to Argentina, earning an estimated $220 million in 1991.

The main Caribbean oil industry – that of Trinidad and Tobago – declined in the early 1980s, where previously it had accounted for over 90 per cent of export earnings. Having initially switched emphasis to natural gas production, the government in the early 1990s decided to concentrate on oil refining by reforming the entire sector. The Bahamas imports the crude oil for the refined products, which make up over 60 per cent of export earnings (down from about 90 per cent in the early 1980s). On Curaçao, refining still dominates the economy, accounting for over 90 per cent of exports (the necessarily imported crude oil and products make up two thirds of imports).

Below
*Iguassú (Iguazú) Falls, on
the border between
Argentina and Brazil –
much larger than Niagara.*

Bottom
*Ipanema beach, Rio de
Janeiro. This beach and its
elegant adjacent suburb
were immortalized in the
Brazilian hit song 'A garote
de Ipanema' ('The Girl from
Ipanema'), heard all around
the world in the 1960s.*

world. Within the natural variety there are numerous social attractions: carnival in Brazil and Trinidad, Indian festivals (often overlaid with Christianity), and the countless crafts of every country, which link the present with the past.

After the variable contribution of merchandise trade to the current account balance in the 1970s, and the large deficits of the early 1980s, regional policies helped produce trade surpluses until the end of the decade. However, a continual negative services balance, exacerbated by declining investment income, cancelled out the trade surpluses so that throughout the 1980s the regional current account was in deficit.

Travel (to and from a country) has been the one service sector consistently to record a surplus, except between 1980 and 1982, when exchange rate policies encouraged residents to travel abroad, while reducing the incentives to foreigners to visit the region.

Political and economic factors have discouraged visitors, but not necessarily to the region as a whole. Political instability in Central America, the fear of terrorism and street assaults, weak Eurocurrencies that attract Americans away from Latin America, repercussions of the Falklands/Malvinas and Gulf Wars have all had their effect on tourism. All the same, many countries have a positive travel account, the largest being in islands like the Bahamas, Barbados, the Dominican Republic and Jamaica, but also in Costa Rica, Mexico and Uruguay (the majority of tourists coming from Buenos Aires). Peru's tourist industry experienced strong growth until 1980, when the number of visitors reached 390,200; for the rest of the decade the average was about 200,000 a year. The decline was first owing to many of the factors above, but when Sendero Luminoso guerrillas first killed foreign travellers in 1989, followed by 1991's cholera outbreak, tourism fell by an estimated 70 per cent. In Mexico tourism is the second largest foreign-exchange earner ($3.4 billion in 1989), and the creation of NAFTA should give the sector a further boost with greater access and improved transport links with the United States, whence 87 per cent of the visitors come.

In the Caribbean, development is inextricably linked with tourism, which is a major foreign-exchange earner. For example, in Barbados tourism accounts for 73 per cent of earnings, in the Dominican Republic 51 per cent, and in Jamaica 34 per cent. In comparison, Mexico, the region's only country to figure in the top twenty worldwide earners from tourism (according to the World Tourism Organization), tourism earnings represent 16 per cent of foreign-exchange income. Sixty per cent of arrivals in the Caribbean come from North America, although its share of the Caribbean market is in decline as European visitors grow in number. A continuing problem in the eastern Caribbean, where the islands compete with each other for visitors, has been poor inter-island air services, a subject discussed frequently at Heads of Government summits. A more recent debate has surrounded the loss of hotel visitors to cruise ships, formerly encouraged but which contribute little to island economies. Caribbean tourism undergoes periodic depressions as a result mainly of external factors, as happened in early 1991 during and after the Gulf War.

It is no longer possible to claim that tourist resources are practically inexhaustible, or to disregard the cultural and physical damage associated with

TABLE 23
Service transactions: travel, by country, 1981, 1983, 1986, 1989 (US$ millions)

Country	1981		1983		1986		1989	
	Credit	Debit	Credit	Debit	Credit	Debit	Credit	Debit
Argentina	412.7	1433.9	452.2	505.6	561.9	894.0	763.0	1009.0
Bahamas	635.7	91.7	765.0	95.8	1104.2	131.3	1214.3	183.0
Barbados	262.7	22.1	253.6	21.5	326.1	28.9	504.5	42.5
Bolivia	36.0	50.0	42.0	20.0	35.4	26.6	57.2	58.9
Brazil	235.8	410.3	38.5	429.7	84.5	591.3	1224.0	750.0
Chile	200.5	220.5	98.3	242.7	145.5	319.1	257.0	397.1
Colombia	437.5	286.5	235.2	315.4	417.6	611.2	408.9	620.2
Costa Rica	95.6	48.5	132.8	52.5	138.6	66.5	217.4	87.2
Dominican Republic	206.4	127.8	320.5	87.9	506.5	90.5	912.1	138.6
Ecuador	131.0	260.0	120.0	152.0	133.0	210.0	185.0	163.0
El Salvador	14.1	69.2	24.3	86.3	42.1	74.1	62.4	60.0
Guatemala	30.3	133.5	6.7	89.6	28.9	15.3	108.9	123.5
Guyana	3.7	10.7	4.2	14.0	5.9	13.0	10.6	23.2
Haiti	73.0	30.3	85.0	39.1	84.2	37.5	72.6	33.0
Honduras	30.5	26.8	22.4	20.5	26.0	30.0	28.1	38.1
Jamaica	284.4	13.8	399.3	25.0	516.0	35.1	607.4	54.3
Mexico	3313.4	4084.6	2728.1	1586.4	2992.8	2171.5	4794.4	4247.1
Nicaragua	22.5	15.0	12.5	14.8	13.5	9.6	4.3	1.5
Panama	174.9	65.4	171.8	70.8	204.8	82.9	n.a.	n.a.
Paraguay	80.2	38.0	48.9	44.1	148.3	48.0	100.0	75.0
Peru	263.0	176.9	210.6	191.4	323.8	320.3	360.0	430.0
Suriname	17.5	29.1	4.3	34.5	5.7	11.7	n.a.	n.a.
Trinidad and Tobago	155.3	167.3	86.9	261.4	83.3	165.3	80.9	129.8
Uruguay	283.0	203.1	89.7	259.1	257.7	173.7	227.9	166.5
Venezuela	187.5	2372.5	310.0	1073.3	443.5	543.2	n.a.	n.a.
Latin America	7587.1	10,387.5	6662.6	5733.3	8629.9	6700.7	12,200.9[a]	8831.5[a]

[a] Excludes Panama, Suriname and Venezuela
Source: Interamerican Development Bank.

Market in Barbados

overseas travel. Latin America and the Caribbean have an abundance of attractions for the tourist, but those areas which receive large numbers of visitors are beginning to experience environmental degradation. For example, the Caribbean Sea is being polluted by sewage and shipping discharges, the Inca Trail in Peru is heavily littered; and culturally, the South American Indians' lifestyle is threatened by exposure to Western mass culture. BB

Further Reading: M. Barbera, 'Latin America's Place in World Trade' *Cepal Review*, No. 41 (August 1990), 73–105; D. W. Berensen, M. Carnoy, J. Grunwald, *Latin American Trade Patterns* (Washington, DC, 1975); Inter-American Development Bank, *Latin America in the World Economy, Recent Development and Trends* (Washington, DC, 1975); J. D. Theberge, R. W. Fontaine, *Latin America: Struggle for Progress* (Critical Choices for Americans, Vol. XIV; Lexington, 1977); W. M. Will, 'A Nation Divided: The Quest for Caribbean Integration', *Latin American Research Review*, Vol. 26, No. 2 (1991); J. Williamson, ed., *Latin American Adjustment: How Much Has Happened?* (Washington, DC, 1990); *Economic and Social Progress in Latin America,* Annual report by the Interamerican Development Bank (Washington, DC)

The South American Handbook (edited by Ben Box) and its two companion volumes, *The Mexican and Central American Handbook* and *The Caribbean Islands Handbook,* are published each year by Trade and Travel Publications, Bath, England, and are strongly recommended to all travellers to Latin America and the Caribbean. The long-running single volume *South American Handbook,* covering the whole region, was edited from 1972 to 1989 by the late John Brooks. Under his guidance it became a remarkable compendium of useful information, eulogized by numerous travellers, including the novelist Graham Greene, who once described it as 'the best guidebook in existence'.

Energy

In 1986 Latin America produced 6.5 per cent (451 million tonnes of oil equivalent) and consumed 4.9 per cent (321 million tonnes of oil equivalent) of the world's commercial energy within an area which is approximately 17 per cent of the continental surface of the globe and by a population which is about 8 per cent of the world's total.

Oil and natural gas dominate the commercial energy stage in Latin America: in 1986 these hydrocarbons accounted for 90 per cent of production and 93 per cent of energy consumed. Commercial energy sources – oil fields, natural gas reservoirs, coal deposits and suitable hydroelectricity generating sites – are scattered evenly throughout Latin America. The economic effects of such geographical disparities have been greatly exaggerated by the increases in the world price of oil since 1972. Venezuela remains the largest exporter of energy and at the end of the 1980s was enjoying the highest per-capita income on the mainland of Latin America, but it had also run up the highest per-capita foreign debt in the continent. Mexico has grown in recent years to be the other major exporter of energy; it, too, has used its oil as collateral for huge external loans. Brazil is the major loser in the energy stakes and its net energy deficit (22.3 million tonnes of oil equivalent in 1986) accounts for almost all the energy imported by South American countries and half that by all Latin American countries. Many Central American and Caribbean countries were in a worse relative position than Brazil with only traditional fuels locally available to supplement imported energy: Cuba (with a deficit of 9 million tonnes of oil equivalent in 1986) and Puerto Rico (5.4 million tonnes) suffer most, although arrangements with Mexico, Venezuela, the USA and the USSR have reduced oil's price below the prevailing world price for some countries, though Cuba no longer enjoys such favourable terms from Russia.

Although there has been a notable expansion and diversification of energy sources used in Latin America, there is a limit to its ability to find economic substitutes for oil and natural gas. Fortunately, in 1984 the continent was blessed with 12.1 per cent of the world's proven oil reserves and 5.9 per cent of its reserves of natural gas. In contrast, no other area of the world is so poorly supplied with coal and lignite reserves, with less than 1 per cent of either.

HYDROCARBONS

The petroleum industry has a dominant role both in meeting the energy requirements of the continent

Oil rigs, Lake Maracaibo, Venezuela. Large-scale oil production began in Venezuela soon after World War I and has remained the country's economic mainstay ever since.

and as a trading staple: in the 1980s petroleum exports averaged a quarter of the value of Latin America's total export trade. It also has an important political role. Latin America pioneered the heavy involvement of the state in the oil industry. A precedent was set in 1938 when Mexico nationalized the local assets of the international oil companies and created its own state oil company. Then in 1960 Venezuela promoted the establishment of OPEC, and has continued to play a leading role in what is now the most remarkable cartel in modern economic history.

Mexico and Venezuela produce just over three quarters of Latin America's oil and natural gas, yet house just under one quarter of the population. Three of the world's thirty-five 'super-giant' oil fields are in Latin America: the Bolívar field in Venezuela was the first such field to be identified and has yielded more oil than any other worldwide; the other two in southern Mexico are the most recent to be discovered and have reserves larger than any except the largest Middle Eastern fields.

Mexico

The Mexican oil and natural gas industry has moved through several historical phases: the boom-and-bust of the first third of the twentieth century, a

period of recovery and undramatic growth between 1940 and 1970 and, from 1972, a modern boom following the providential discovery of huge new reserves. Today Mexico is fourth in the world league of oil producers.

From a little over 12 million barrels of crude oil in 1911, Mexico's output soared to over 190 million barrels in 1921: for a brief period in the 1920s the country was second only to the USA as an oil producer and responsible for a quarter of the world's production. But by the late 1920s a decline almost as spectacular as the original boom had set in: in 1931 output (33 million barrels) was only one fifth of that a decade earlier. The decline in production was reversed in the 1930s, thanks to the discovery in 1932 of the Poza Rica field in the Gulf Plain behind Veracruz. In 1938 Mexico astounded the financial world by nationalizing its oil industry. British and American military intervention was contemplated, an international boycott was organized, and capital and skilled labour withdrew. But by then the home market was absorbing 60 per cent of Mexico's oil, the oil industry had ceased to be one primarily serving overseas markets and the effects of sanctions were thus limited. With the advent of the Second World War to divert British attention elsewhere, an agreement to pay compensation to the former owners, and with the

PETROLEUM PRODUCTION

Continental shelf

Petroliferous areas

Oil and natural gas fields

| 0 | | 1600 km |
| 0 | | 1000 miles |

TABLE 24
Proven hydrocarbon reserves in Mexico 1990
(million barrels of oil equivalent)

	Crude oil	Natural gas (liquids)	Natural gas
NE Frontier	16	229	1463
North	418	30	86
Central	1060	248	639
South	669	59	198
South-east	6695	1918	4490
Gulf	25,494	2929	2254
Chicontepec	10,928	1320	5337
Total	45,280	6733	14,467

Source: Pemex (*Memoria de labores*, 1989).

political desire of the United States for hemispheric solidarity, Mexico was gradually drawn back into the international fold.

Exploration, including airborne seismic exploration, was increased in the 1960s and new fields in the swampy forests of Central and Eastern Tabasco, first discovered before 1938, were delineated and developed. In 1971 Mexico produced 177 million barrels of oil but the gap, bridged by imports, between domestic production and demand was widening.

By 1975 Mexico was once again producing oil surplus to its own requirements, and the oil deficit of 1974 ($288 million) had been replaced by a surplus ($141 million) which was to multiply one hundred-fold in the next decade. In 1977 the true scale of the new reserves was first publicized and the new president, López Portillo (1976–82), took the decision to accelerate production. By 1977 the OPEC-induced rise in oil prices had greatly enhanced the value of these reserves and they underwrote the international loans necessary for their development.

A surge in production – from almost 400 million barrels in 1977 to almost 600 million in 1979, to almost 1100 million in 1982 – followed new finds. By 1983 the old pre-1972 fields were responsible for only 10 per cent of Mexico's oil production and the proportion continued to fall; almost two thirds of Mexico's crude oil production in the 1980s came from beneath the Gulf of Campeche, an area which only began to contribute to production in July 1979, and virtually all the rest from the Reforma fields of central Tabasco and northern Chiapas.

By 1989 Mexico was able to refine almost 60 per cent (up from almost 40 per cent in 1982) of the crude it produced as new refineries came on stream and old ones were expanded.

Mexico's earnings from the export of surplus oil (and, since 1980, natural gas) have risen from $1 billion in 1977 to $4 billion in 1979, to around $15 bil-

lion in the years 1982–5, and between $6 and $8 billion in the years of lower oil prices in the second half of the decade. Domestic consumers continue to benefit from relatively cheap energy, in spite of real increases in charges following the more open economic policies of the early 1990s.

Because of its origins Pemex (Petróleos Mexicanos, the Mexican Petroleum Board) has enjoyed a national mystique which has at times obscured administrative chaos and scarcely disguised corruption. Under strong leadership it has enjoyed the same kind of independence of government control that multinational corporations are often accused of enjoying elsewhere: sometimes Pemex has led the government, at other times the reverse. Under the impetus of the new discoveries and the changing world economy, Pemex has generally proved itself sufficiently flexible to adapt to changed political and technological circumstances. Nevertheless, productivity remains low, and overmanning, thanks to the historic privileges won by the petroleum workers' union (STPRM), remains rife.

As a non-member of OPEC, Mexico is not liable to the financial penalties levied by some importers, notably the United States, against imports of oil from OPEC countries. The United States has a strategic interest in the success of the Mexican petroleum industry and it is impossible to divorce such an important commercial association from Mexico's other, wider and frequently ambivalent relationships with the United States.

Venezuela

Venezuela has produced two thirds of Latin America's oil and retains over one third of the continent's reserves. The first concession was made in 1866, drilling began in 1883, Royal Dutch Shell began exploration in 1913, commercial production began in 1919, and by 1927 Venezuela had superseded Mexico as Latin America's leading producer. The significant discoveries were all made in the eastern part of the Lake Maracaibo region. By 1937 Shell and Standard Oil controlled virtually all Venezuela's output then running at 500,000 barrels per day. In 1948, when output reached 477 million barrels, the government was able to pioneer the 50–50 profit-sharing agreement with the companies.

Whereas in 1955 Venezuela remained second to the United States as a world producer and supplied as much of international trade in oil as did the entire Middle East, by 1960 the USSR had usurped that position amongst world producers and the trade of the Middle Eastern oil exporters was growing at twice the rate of that of Venezuela. It was against this background and in response to the imposition by the United States of import quotas on oil, that Pérez

Alfonso, the Venezuelan oil minister, helped set up OPEC. In that same year Venezuela decided to grant no fresh concessions and to establish a state oil company. Thus by 1960 Venezuela had more or less gained control over its oil industry: decisions on prices and production were made by the ministry and most of the income derived from oil was extracted as tax and stayed in the country. The oil companies responded by drastically reducing investment, thereby reducing reserves.

1970 proved to be the peak year of Venezuelan oil production (1.35 billion barrels or 3.7 million barrels per day) and it heralded a period of remarkable change. The financial importance of the industry to the state grew astonishingly as the export price of oil rose from $2 per barrel in 1970 to $14 in 1974 to $35 in 1981 even though production fell (in part in compliance with OPEC policy) by more than a half (to 1.73 million barrels per day) between 1970 and 1985. Government income from oil was $1400 million in 1970; in 1974 it was $8700 million, and in 1980 $12,000 million. This new-found wealth meant that from 1976 Petrovén (Petróleos de Venezuela, the Venezuelan State Petroleum company) began reversing the process of decapitalization which preceded nationalization. In 1980 Petrovén invested ten times as much capital in the industry as had been invested in 1972.

Almost half the country's output, over half its exports and reserves are now of heavy crudes and the proportions are increasing. But, whatever the problems its oil industry faces, oil continued to provide Venezuela with over 80 per cent of its export earnings in 1989 and the average citizen with one of the highest per capita incomes of Latin America.

Other hydrocarbon-producing countries

Brazil's petroleum history is briefer than that of Mexico and Venezuela, but output tripled in the 1980s and by the end of the decade it could claim third place in the Latin American petroleum stakes with a daily output of 0.645 million barrels in 1989.

Most of Brazil's oil comes from eight sedimentary basins and embayments close to the Atlantic coast between Belém and Santos: exploration of Amazonia has so far been disappointing, with only the Solimões basin east of Acre attracting attention. In 1974 oil in commercial quantities was found by Petrobrás in the first of fifteen fields subsequently charted 60 km off the coast of Campos in Rio de Janeiro; in 1976 foreign oil companies accepted invitations to share the risks of exploration (but, in view of the scale of investment, with relatively meagre results).

Argentina is Latin America's next largest producer of crude oil (1989:0.45 million barrels per day) having been overtaken by Brazil in 1985. It is also notable as a major producer of natural gas: at the end of the 1980s it produced more natural gas than any other South American country and production was equivalent to that of its oil. All its natural gas and almost all its oil is consumed within the republic; it produces about as much energy as it uses. Two thirds of its cumulative oil production has come from the Comodoro Rivadavia and Chubut fields in the San Jorge sedimentary basin in Patagonia; a similar fraction of its reserves remains in the same basin.

Argentina's petroleum resources are widely distributed and peripheral to the major national market for energy in and around Buenos Aires.

Oil production in the 1980s remained relatively static: the desire to expand domestic production was hampered by a combination of hyper-inflation, incompetence in YPF, and the lack of creditworthiness of governments, military and democratic, rather than by the lack of seemingly promising areas, particularly offshore, for exploration. The implementation of new economic policies at the end of the decade led to the ending of YPF's privileged monopoly position: in 1990 some 28 secondary oilfields were sold off to the highest bidders as a prelude to bidding for partners to work the major oilfields and opening up the country to private (including foreign) prospecting companies.

Ecuador is producing over twice as much oil as it consumes; it is the only other OPEC member (with Venezuela) in Latin America. Although it has produced some oil in the coastal region of the Santa Elena peninsula, since 1918 it has only been with the discovery of oil in the Oriente in 1967 and the completion of the Trans-Andean pipeline in 1972 that oil (almost overnight) has taken the place of bananas as the country's leading export. The state oil company (CEPE, the Corporacion Estatal Petrolera Ecuatoriana, formed in 1972, and reconstituted as Petróleos de Ecuador in 1989) holds a majority of the shares in the consortium responsible for almost all Ecuador's oil and natural gas production and also its refining capacity.

Trinidad was the most important oil producer in the British Commonwealth prior to the Second World War. Production rose to a recent peak in 1978 but reserves have been depleted and daily output in 1989 (0.16 million barrels) was the same as fifteen years earlier. Oil revenue peaked in 1981 and it took most of the next ten years for the government to adjust to placing less reliance upon it. Half Trinidad's crude and five sixths of its refined petroleum are exported, still providing over half the country's export earnings at the beginning of the 1990s.

Colombia shared with Venezuela the discovery in the 1920s of significant oil deposits and their exploration by foreign companies. Although a state oil corporation (Ecopetrol or Empresa Colombiana de Petroleo) was formed in 1951, the international oil giants have continued their involvement in the country. But production reached a peak of 0.2 million barrels a day in the early 1970s and by 1980 had fallen to the same level as that a quarter of a century earlier; since then output has risen (1989 0.4 million barrels a day) as new reserves have been developed. Colombia returned to being a net exporter of oil in 1986.

Peru Peruvian oil production, which was five times local demand in the 1930s, rose more slowly than demand and by the early 1960s Peru had ceased to be self-sufficient. In 1968 the leading company (a subsidiary of Jersey Standard) was expropriated to form the core of the state petroleum corporation (Petroperú or Petróleos del Perú) already thirty-four years old. The 1980s proved disappointing in spite of substantial efforts by various international oil companies working under contract, and production fell to two thirds its level at the beginning of the decade, obliging Peru to become a net importer again in 1988.

Bolivia's small oil industry around Camiri in the Oriente was nurtured by Standard Oil and continued under the state body (YPFB, Yacimientos Petrolíferos Fiscales Bolivianos) following nationalization in 1937. Gulf Oil expanded Bolivia's reserves in the 1950s and 1960s; it was nationalized in 1969. Although oil production declined in the 1970s and Bolivia ceased to be a net oil exporter in 1978, natural gas production expanded and exports provided half Bolivia's legitimate overseas earnings during the 1980s. Argentina imports Bolivian gas and Brazil is expected to begin importing gas-generated electricity in the early 1990s.

HYDROELECTRICITY

Latin America currently exploits only about 5 per cent of its huge but largely inaccessible hydroelectric potential. Unfortunately, many sites, for example along the eastern flank of the Andes, are remote from demand for electricity, the generating process remains inefficient, and losses in transmission over long distances are large.

The earliest hydroelectricity stations in Latin America date from the late nineteenth century and were situated close to the towns they were designed to serve. Overseas companies usually built them, but they were destined later in life, like other foreign-owned public utility companies, to be nationalized.

Later many Latin American countries, notably Mexico, followed the example of the Tennessee Valley Authority and began generating hydroelectricity as part of a co-ordinated programme of improving rural or regional infrastructure. Fully one third of Latin America's installed hydroelectric power capacity has been built with the help of finance from the World Bank.

Hydroelectricity met 22 per cent of Latin America's demand for commercial energy in 1989 and provided about three quarters of her electricity. The relative contribution of hydroelectricity is growing: consumption doubled in the 1970s and redoubled in the 1980s. In 1986 Brazil was responsible for 58 per cent of the total hydroelectric power generated in Latin America, a proportion which continues to grow; Mexico was in second place (8.6 per cent in 1986, 18.6 per cent in 1970): together they account for two thirds of Latin America's primary electricity output.

Brazil relies more on hydroelectricity as a source of commercial energy than does any other major country in Latin America. In 1986, hydro plants provided 91 per cent of Brazil's electricity and accounted for 84 per cent of its installed electricity-generating capacity; hydroelectricity accounted for 28 per cent of domestic production of commercial energy (compared with 20 per cent in 1970) and met 20.5 per cent (11.8 per cent) of the country's total commercial

Powerhouse, Itaipú dam, Brazil. Constructed in the 1970s and 1980s (nominally as a Brazilian-Paraguayan project), Itaipú is the largest hydroelectric station in the world.

Nuclear power station, Angra dos Reis, Brazil. Nuclear power is less developed in Latin America than in Europe or North America, and its future is in question.

energy consumption. Brazil has an estimated 150 million kW of hydroelectric power potential – one third in the basin of the Amazon, almost one third in the Paraná, a tenth in the São Francisco, and most of the remaining quarter in the relatively short rivers draining the coastal ranges fronting the Atlantic. Construction is expected to be completed in the early 1990s of installations at Itaipú on the Paraná 15 km above its confluence with the Iguassú at the Argentine border; the first turbines began to turn in 1984. This plant will have the largest capacity (11.7 million kW) of any hydro-station in the world. Although it is a joint project between Paraguay and Brazil, Brazil underwrote all construction costs and will purchase all the electricity generated.

The rivers of Amazonia began to be tapped with the opening of the Tucuruí plant on the Tocantins River; the main market for this electricity is the Carajás mining and metallurgical complex. Most of the new capacity has been built by a federal holding company (Electrobrás) created in 1961 to co-ordinate the work of individual states (especially São Paulo); today 98 per cent of Brazil's hydroelectric capacity is in public ownership.

Mexico, in contrast, has moved away from installing new hydroelectric capacity in recent years as cheap domestic oil has become more prolific. 1971 was the last year in which water generated more electricity than did oil; in 1986 two and a half times as much thermal electricity as hydroelectricity entered the national grid.

Argentina increased its hydroelectricity output tenfold in the 1970s and continued the upward trend in the 1980s. The Piedra del Aguila plant (2.1 million kW) under construction on the Limay has benefited from the largest single loan ever made by the Interamerican Development Bank. Joint projects with

Uruguay at Salto Grande (1.6 million kW) and with Paraguay on the Paraná at Yacyretá (2.7 million kW) are underway.

In both Peru and Chile hydroelectricity supplied three quarters of national electricity in 1986 with resources best developed close to the capital cities.

NUCLEAR ELECTRICITY

Nuclear-generated electricity makes a minor contribution to Latin America's indigenous energy production and is likely to remain of little significance. In 1986 only 1.1 per cent of Latin America's electricity came from nuclear power stations. Of the countries in the region, Argentina has the longest experience of nuclear power: its 344-megawatt Atucha 1 heavy-water reactor became operational in 1974.

Brazil's first nuclear plant, situated at Angra dos Reis 100 km south-west of Rio de Janeiro, became operational in 1981, but technical problems led to the withdrawal of production in 1986, and work on two additional neighbouring reactors designed to add a further 2.6 million kW of capacity in the early 1990s has faltered. Mexico has constructed two 650-megawatt reactors supplied by the United States at Laguna Verde in Veracruz, but engineering difficulties, adverse public opinion and the oil bonanza have damped the enthusiasm for this programme. Cuba had plans to add 1.7 million kW of nuclear electricity to the national supply in 1990 from plants at Huragua and Holguín built with Soviet assistance. In general, by the early 1990s Latin America was having second thoughts about the usefulness of developing nuclear electricity capacity.

COAL

Coal is, and has been, remarkably unimportant in Latin America. In 1989 production was equivalent to under 6 per cent of the region's oil and natural gas, and coal production and coal reserves account for only 1–2 per cent of the world's totals. This is after output doubled to 38.5 million tonnes (equivalent to 24.7 million tonnes of oil) in the 1980s under the stimulus of higher oil prices.

Colombia has the largest measured or proven reserves of coal in Latin America (some 4500 million tonnes), is responsible for half the continent's current output, and is expanding production rapidly; coal met a quarter of Colombia's commercial energy demands in 1986, a larger fraction than in any other Latin American country, and since then production of coal (like that of oil) has doubled. Coal is widely distributed in Andean Colombia, particularly in the

Cauca Valley. Production is expected to be 40–50 million tonnes by the end of the century and Colombia expects to be supplying 10 per cent of the steam coal on the international market by the year 2000.

Brazil has large coal reserves but production remained fairly steady at about 6.5 million tonnes during the 1980s. The bulk of its current output comes from Santa Catarina; most new production will come from mines to be developed in Rio Grande do Sul close to the Uruguayan border.

Mexican coal comes mainly from the Sabinas basin in Coahuila in the north-east of the country and primarily supplies the iron and steel mills of Monterrey. Chile is reviving its small coal industry and doubled production (to about 2 million tonnes) in the 1980s.

Argentina has a small coal field at Río Turbio in the Andean foothills of southern Patagonia linked by rail to the coast at Río Gallegos.

TRADITIONAL ENERGY SOURCES

Firewood is the most traditional of Latin America's primary energy sources. As recently as 1945 half the energy used in the region was of this home-grown type. In 1986 the energy equivalent of about 100 million tonnes of coal or 70 million tonnes of oil was provided by firewood – fully one eighth of the total energy produced by Latin America or one seventh of that used. In some countries the overall contribution of firewood to the total national energy output is crucial: in 1975 the reported proportion ranged downwards from poverty-stricken Haiti (90 per cent) through Paraguay (54 per cent), Guatemala (52 per cent), Honduras (48 per cent), the Dominican Republic (44 per cent), Bolivia (43 per cent), Grenada (43 per cent), El Salvador (42 per cent), Ecuador (38 per cent), Cuba (35 per cent), Nicaragua (34 per cent), Barbados (28 per cent) and Costa Rica (23 per cent) to Brazil (20 per cent), and the figures will not have changed much since 1975.

Sugar-cane waste or bagasse is another fuel which in sugar-growing areas is a highly significant domestic source of energy. In Brazil, Cuba, Mexico and elsewhere, bagasse powers the sugar mills which produce not only sugar but more bagasse fuel.

UNCONVENTIONAL ENERGY SOURCES

Solar energy, clearly present in abundance in Latin America, nevertherless remains largely unexploited except through vegetation.

The Dominican Republic has an international solar technology centre. Wind power is used to gen-

Brazil's alcohol experiment

In 1975 Brazil launched a Proálcool programme to distill ethanol from sugar cane in sufficient quantities to reduce the country's dependence upon imported oil. It had as its target the building of about 400 distilleries which were to convert cane from 2–3 million hectares, yielding 10,000 million litres of ethanol. By 1985 it was most of the way to achieving its target, and a market for hydrous ethanol had been created. Although hydrous ethanol has only 60 per cent of the energy content by weight of petrol, it can be used neat, albeit only in cars with specially built alcohol engines. The programme persuaded the domestic car companies to produce enough alcohol-driven vehicles (the millionth alcohol car to be manufactured in Brazil was sold in 1983) to ensure a significant measure of success. In 1985 85 per cent of new cars sold were alcohol-driven.

However, the production costs in 1981 were probably about half as much again as that of imported oil when reduced to a common yardstick of dollar per barrel of oil equivalent. When the price of oil fell, at a time when the exchequer was bankrupt, the heavy subsidies for the programme were withdrawn; by 1989 it had cost some $7 billion.

Although there were about 4.5 million alcohol-fueled cars running on alcohol on the Brazilian roads by 1990, the tide had turned back towards petrol; in 1989, with cost of alcohol to reach $54 a barrel the next year, sales of new alcohol-driven cars represented only 5 per cent of the total.

There is a parallel programme (Proóleo) to find a substitute for diesel: soya beans, sage, sunflower seed, groundnuts and, in particular, the dende palm are targets for experiment.

erate commercial electricity on some of the Caribbean islands, in Patagonia and at other windy, isolated places. Since the mid-seventies Brazil has run a much-publicized programme to run cars on fuel distilled from sugar cane, but this has ultimately proved not to be cost-effective.

CONCLUSIONS

The economies of the Latin American countries were fashioned around cheap energy: the transition in the 1970s to high international oil prices had dramatic effects. For oil-rich, oil-exporting countries like Venezuela the new wealth meant easy access to overseas financing. In Mexico, as in most oil-producing countries, the new bonanza meant that the state became an even more dominant element in the life of the country. The search for, and development of, new reserves led such countries to incur large debts, but

Taxi filling up with 'gasohol', Brazil: Brazil has become a world leader in developing this non-oil fuel.

the debt crisis initiated in 1982 and the halving of the real price of oil from 1986 removed the prop from already faltering national economies. Recently national energy bodies have been subjected to more open market forces: some have been privatized, others enjoined to enter joint ventures with private, often trans-national, companies, some decentralized or dismembered, and almost all required to operate with greater economic efficiency. Increased real energy costs since 1970 have forced the oil-importing countries to adopt policies of substituting indigenous energy for imported oil; Brazil and Colombia, Guatemala, Belize and Barbados have found new oil.

Brazil and Colombia are investing in large coal deposits and almost all countries in hydroelectric projects. But it is unrealistic to expect a significant contribution from unconventional energy sources: few seem to offer the prospect of energy which is cost-effective. A second response has been to promote a more conservative attitude to energy. Latin America has been slow in this area. Energy consumption rose at an annual rate of 3.6 per cent between 1979 and 1989, or twice the rate of the world at large. Forty per cent of commercial energy is consumed by industry in plants, many of which could be modified to be more energy-saving. Thirty-five per cent is consumed in the transport field – seven eighths by road vehicles – and a substitution of public transport for private cars and of bigger trucks for smaller lorries could reduce overall demand particularly for the lighter oils.

It is the poor who have been worst hit by the higher and fluctuating cost of energy. In many parts of Latin America the real energy crisis is the growing shortage of traditional fuels. Thus many poor people have put into reverse the simple process of substituting bought-in kerosene for local firewood. Similar retrogressive moves by growing numbers of people have placed added pressure on the accessible woodlands of Latin America and added further impetus to the forces of ecological instability within the continent.   DJF

Further Reading: British Petroleum Company, *B.P. Statistical Review of World Energy* (London, annual); J. E. Katz and O. S. Marwah, *Nuclear Power in Developing Countries* (Toronto, 1982); Latin American Energy Organization (OLADE), *The Foreign Debt and the Energy Sector of Latin America and the Caribbean* (Quito, 1987); J. W. Mullin, *Energy in Latin America: The Historic Record* (ECLA Santiago, 1978); G. Philip, *Oil and Politics in Latin America: Nationalist Movements and State Companies* (Cambridge, 1982); L. Randall, *The Political Economy of Mexican Oil* (London, 1989); World Bank, *Renewable Energy Resources in Developing Countries* (Washington, 1981)

Banking

The Latin American republics have generally well-developed banking and related financial services, especially in the larger countries. Commercial banking dates back well into the last century. Economic growth in the decades following the Second World War was paralleled by the rapid expansion of banking systems, the establishment of new and specialized institutions and the adoption in the more developed countries of innovations originating in North America and Europe. More recently, financial systems have had to cope with the strains imposed by the debt crisis, economic recession and the intensification of inflation. In many countries this has required significant restructuring to strengthen the banks and improve their efficiency, and has produced a widespread questioning of established orthodoxies of economic control.

THE DEVELOPMENT OF COMMERCIAL BANKING

The first bank so-called in Latin America was in fact an officially inspired enterprise, set up in Brazil on the initiative of the Regent in 1808 after the arrival of the Portuguese court, with the somewhat reluctant participation of Brazilian and Portuguese capitalists. This, the first Banco do Brasil, was liquidated in 1829. The first bank in Argentina, the Banco de Buenos Aires, was founded in 1822, largely on the initiative of Anglo-Argentine merchants, and dissolved by Rosas in 1836. More significant for the development of Latin American banking was the establishment of the second Banco do Brasil in 1851 by the industrialist and financier, the Barão de Mauá, which in 1853 merged with the Banco Comercial de Rio de Janeiro to form the first substantial institution for commercial credit, and the foundation in 1854 of the Banco de la Província de Buenos Aires.

Although these early banks were the result of local initiative, foreign banks were to play the dominant role in the development of banking in Latin America in the second half of the nineteenth century. Their functions were closely related to the growth of foreign trade and investment, the main instruments of the export-led economic development of that period. The foreign banks that were successful provided stability and introduced European banking techniques.

British banks, following in the steps of British merchants and paving the way for British investors, led the way with the establishment of both the London Buenos Aires and River Plate Bank and the London and Brazilian Bank in 1862. Their example was to be followed by other British banks and by banks originating in Germany, France, Italy and other European countries linked to Latin America by trade or the flow of emigration. A name such as the Banco Chileno-Yugoeslavo (subsequently Banco Austral) indicates the origin of banks founded to serve a local immigrant clientele.

Many important locally owned commercial banks in Latin America were established in the last two decades of the nineteenth century. Argentina, by then the most developed country, had over forty banks by the end of the century. After the First

Headquarters of the Banco de la Nación Argentina, Argentina's national bank, Buenos Aires.

World War, when the United States displaced Europe as the principal source of capital and became increasingly important in Latin American trade, US banks established an extensive branch representation in Latin America. Canadian banks became active, especially in the Caribbean area where there were long-established trading interests, and Japanese banks were set up in areas where Japanese immigration was significant. In the development of banking, as in so much else in Latin America, the depression years of the early 1930s marked a watershed.

OFFICIAL BANKING

The mixed economy that has been characteristic of most Latin American countries is reflected in their banking structures. The distinction between privately and publicly owned institutions is by no means wholly functional. State-owned institutions are prominent in commercial banking as well as owning the more important institutions for the provision of long-term finance. Some of the early domestic, commercial and mortgage banking ventures were sometimes created by state initiative or else fell under state control as a result of a financial crisis, and continued thereafter to consolidate their position in the banking structure. This process continued, especially in those countries where the public sector expanded more rapidly than the private. In Mexico all private and mixed-capital banks were taken over by the state in September 1982 by the outgoing administration of President José López Portillo after the onset of the external debt crisis, but were re-privatized by President Carlos Salinas de Gortari.

Argentina has official commercial banks at the three levels of government – federal, provincial and municipal. The Banco de la Nación (founded in 1891) alone accounted for 13 per cent of the total assets of all commercial banks in the mid-1980s and is by far the largest bank in the country, followed by the Banco de la Provincia de Buenos Aires with 9 per cent; all official banks held about 34 per cent of total commercial bank deposits.

In Brazil, banks controlled by the federal government or the states also play an important role in commercial banking. The present Banco do Brasil, in which the government is the principal shareholder, is the largest commercial bank in the country; it is also the largest Latin American bank. In Peru, the Banco de la Nación, in its own right and through the three commercial banks that it acquired in 1970, exercises a dominant influence. Such banks, as well as carrying out normal short-term commercial lending, generally have special functions – in the case of the Banco de la Nación Argentina, the financing of agricultural production and development. The Banco do Brasil and the Banco de la Nación in Peru act as agents of the treasury, and have other functions derived from government policy which they share with the central banks.

During the depression years of the 1930s, governments became more actively involved in encouraging economic activity. In order to remedy the inability or unwillingness of commercial banks to provide medium-term finance for economic development and diversification these governments set up sectoral development banks. In Peru a Banco Agrícola (now Banco Agrario) was established in 1931, a Banco Industrial in 1936 and a Banco Minero in 1941. Similarly, in Venezuela a Banco Agrícola y Pecuario was set up in 1928, a Banco Industrial in 1937 and a Banco Obrero intended to finance low-cost housing in 1941. In Colombia a Caja de Crédito Agrario, Industrial y Minero was founded in 1931. In the larger republics the powerful state-owned banks were directed towards providing larger amounts of medium-term finance for industrial and other development.

Wider in scope than the specialized official banks are development corporations such as the Chilean Corporación de Fomento (CORFO), set up originally to finance reconstruction after the Chillán earthquake of 1939. Other such corporations which have played a central role in the provision of long-term finance for development are the Nacional Financiera in Mexico (1934), and the Banco Nacional do Desenvolvimento Econômico e Social (BNDES) in Brazil (1952). These are funded in various proportions from budgetary allocations, the issue of domestic obligations, and borrowings from the international development agencies or on capital markets abroad. These institutions have in general played a vital role in mobilizing longer-term funds both domestically and abroad for financing electrification, communications and basic industrial development projects in the public sector, as well as for on-lending for private-sector industrial development.

CENTRAL BANKING AND MONETARY CONTROL

In the nineteenth and early twentieth centuries banking was generally as little regulated as other forms of business enterprise. The establishment of an official monopoly of the note-issue, introduction of prudential controls and other general banking legislation, development of clearing systems, and the creation of central banks with the function of controlling the banking system and implementing monetary policy was a gradual process that continued right up to the 1960s.

In the 1920s and 1930s the first central banks were set up, usually accompanied by the first general banking laws. Professor E. W. Kemmerer of Princeton University was active in setting up central banks in the Pacific coast republics in the 1920s, as was Dr Herman Max of the central bank of Chile rather later in the Caribbean area; Argentina's central bank was established in 1935 with the advice of Sir Otto Niemeyer of the Bank of England. In some countries, notably Brazil and Uruguay, central banking functions were gradually assumed by one of the large official banks. The Banco do Brasil and the Banco de la República Oriental del Uruguay operated as both commercial and central banks until the two functions were formally separated with the creation of the Banco Central do Brasil in 1965 and the Banco Central del Uruguay in 1967. Only Panama is now without a central bank, reflecting the fact that the US dollar is the principal currency for transactions, although the Banco Nacional de Panamá acts as financial agent of the government and carries out some co-ordinating functions.

The limited powers of the early central banks were gradually amplified by amendment to their statutes. They, alone, or in conjunction with one or another of the official banks or an official body such as a Superintendency of Banks, now have far-reaching authority to impose credit controls in furtherance of monetary policy, regulate the activities of banks in other ways, administer special credit funds and operate exchange and trade control systems. General banking legislation has established prudential controls designed to ensure solvency and liquidity by prescribing minimum capital requirements, capital/deposit ratios, and other limits on credit creation.

The complexity of controls on bank lending, which has been characteristic of many republics, is related not only to *dirigiste* traditions of government but also to the persistence of deficit financing of the public sector, to high and variable rates of inflation and to instability in the external accounts. Variable reserve requirements, prescriptions of interest rates for different types of operation and various forms of qualitative control designed to channel lending into particular sectors of the economy have been common. The structure of interest rates is often complex; negative rates (i.e. less than the prevailing rate of inflation) have for long periods provided subsidies to certain classes of borrower. On the other hand, the destructive effect on savings and malfunctioning of financial markets caused by very high inflation led to the extensive application of indexation or 'monetary correction' to financial assets and liabilities, most notably in Brazil. Although initially useful, indispensable even as a means of restoring long-term credit and capital markets, indexation tended, in the

Lloyds Bank (formerly the Bank of London and South America), Buenos Aires, a striking modern building set in the heart of the 'City', the financial district of the Argentine capital.

absence of appropriate fiscal and other measures and over a period of years, to institutionalize inflation rather than help to overcome it. After several programmes of monetary reform, Brazil had still not succeeded in eliminating indexation by 1990. The simplification and rationalization of methods of credit control – as with Mexico, in measures adopted at the end of 1988 – is now increasingly seen as a necessary aspect of financial reform.

Central banks enjoy only a very limited autonomy, except for the Banco Central de Chile, which was given full independence as one of the last acts of the outgoing Pinochet regime in 1989. They generally respond to a monetary board or to the national treasury, and the presidency of the central bank is likely to be a political appointment. Nevertheless, they are, by reason of the importance of their functions, the professionalism of their staff and the continuity that they provide, institutions of very considerable prestige both inside and outside their countries, and they have played a key role in the protracted negotiations over the external debt crisis.

FOREIGN BANKS

The role of foreign banks in the nineteenth and early twentieth centuries was crucial. Their share of domestic banking business has, in general, much diminished over the past 40 years. In Brazil, for example, total deposits in foreign banks amounted to about one-third of those in domestic banks in 1929; a decade later the proportion was about one quarter, and by the end of the 1980s was less than 10 per cent. The long-term decline in the relative importance of foreign-owned banks was due to several factors: the changing nature of economic development, which after 1930 was no longer so export-oriented; restrictions on their activities imposed in various countries; and, above all, the rapid growth of domestic banking after the Second World War.

The depression of the early 1930s naturally had serious effects on the business of foreign banks. The largest British bank in Latin America, the Anglo-South American Bank, was deeply involved in the Chilean nitrate industry and fatally weakened by its collapse. In 1936 the process of amalgamating all British banking interests into a single bank, the Bank of London and South America (now absorbed into the Lloyds Bank Group) was completed. Some foreign banks passed into the hands of local shareholders and banks such as the Banco de Italia y Rio de la Plata and the Banco de Galicia y Rio de la Plata are now, despite their names, local Argentine banking institutions. From the Bank of London and Mexico ultimately evolved the present-day Banca Serfin, one of the largest of Mexican banking groups.

In a few of the smaller countries foreign banks are still preponderant, notably in Panama (an important 'offshore' banking centre). In Argentina, official policy towards foreign banks has varied considerably with changes in political regime, but has on the whole been fairly liberal in comparison with most of the other large republics; even so, foreign banks held in 1985 only about one fifth of total peso deposits of the commercial banking system. Elsewhere, conditions are often much more restrictive, though in only a few are foreign banks totally excluded. The latter include Cuba, where foreign banks as well as those domestically owned were nationalized in the early years of the Castro revolution; a similar process of nationalization took place in Chile under the Allende government of the early 1970s, though in this case the successor-regime reversed policy and offered the foreign banks the opportunity to re-acquire their former branches, so that by 1990 foreign banks held about 18 per cent of total local-currency deposits. The general trend towards reduction in the importance of foreign banks was also reversed in Uruguay where a consolidation of the banking system after the crisis of the mid-1960s led to the disappearance of many local banks and to the absorption of others by foreign institutions.

In Mexico the *de facto* ban on foreign investment in banking was made explicit in 1965 when any type of foreign participation in the capital of Mexican credit institutions was prohibited. Only one long-established branch of a foreign bank, Citibank of New York, continued to operate. Foreign banks could, however, set up representative offices in Mexico; these may not carry out any domestic banking transactions, but assist in the negotiation of foreign borrowings and support correspondent banking relations. By the early 1980s some 120 banks maintained such offices in Mexico City, reflecting the large scale of Mexican borrowings in the international markets. In 1990 most of these offices still remained in existence, and as part of the re-privatization and general banking reform programme outlined in that year, minority foreign participation in Mexican banks was again envisaged.

In Brazil both the entry of new foreign banks and the expansion of existing ones remain severely controlled, although many banks, as in Mexico, have opened representative offices. The Andean Pact countries were initially highly cautious about admitting foreign investment. In Venezuela, for example, new investment from abroad in banks, finance companies and insurance companies was forbidden, and the maximum permitted holding for existing banks reduced to 20 per cent. Here again, some relaxation appears probable in the 1990s.

From the 1970s onwards many of the larger Latin American banks have themselves established branches abroad, reflecting their enhanced status within the world banking community, their countries' increased involvement in world financial markets and their own desire to participate in 'Eurocurrency' and other international business. Argentine, Brazilian, Mexican and other banks set up in London, New York and other financial centres in the form of representative offices, branches or participations in consortium banks; while the latter have now mostly disappeared or suspended operations following the collapse of the developing country syndicated loan market, the branch networks generally remain, and 15 Brazilian banks, for example, still have branches, agencies or subsidiaries in New York. Latin American banks have also set up branches in other countries of the region. All the republics except Cuba are members of the IMF, the World Bank group and the Inter-American Development Bank.

RECENT EVOLUTION

The development of banking and related financial services after the Second World War paralleled general economic growth and diversification. In Mexico and Brazil particularly, these decades saw a sustained and substantial growth in the financial service industries, in the volume of transactions and in institutional development in both the public and private sectors. In some other countries, such as Argentina, Uruguay and Chile, political change and related economic instability led to a less ordered evolution of banking systems.

In the private sector the most notable post-war development was the proliferation of non-banking financial companies. Up to the Second World War private-sector financial institutions consisted almost entirely of commercial banks, mortgage and savings banks. Commercial banks were restricted in law or in practice to granting short-term credit. Economic diversification and controls on commercial banking led to the development of other institutions, generally known as *financieras*. These differ widely in character, some carrying out a genuine development banking role by arranging longer-term finance, others specializing in consumer finance. In Mexico and Brazil they increased rapidly from the 1950s onwards, in the former to the point where their combined assets exceeded those of the commercial banks. As with the commercial banks, a small number of *financieras* generally conducted a large share of the total business and were often linked to one of the major banking groups. Other developments have been the formation of savings-and-loan associations in some countries, the introduction of leasing and the spread of credit card operations. The most dynamic of the private sector banks have taken a lead in technological innovations, for example, in the use of satellite telecommunication systems.

While full nationalization of banks has been exceptional, central banks have tried to shape the evolution of the banking system in various ways. In Uruguay and Brazil in the 1960s a determined effort was made to reduce the number of banks in the interest of the efficiency and stability of the system; in Brazil the number was reduced from 328 in 1969 to 108 in 1979. The functions of the various types of *financiera* were defined and their operations regulated. Commercial banks, with their wide deposit base, remain, however, at the centre of the private banking system.

With the world economic recession of the early 1980s and the onset of the external debt crisis that affected so many of the republics, a period of general economic growth that had led to the expansion and deepening of Latin American financial systems seemed to have come to an end. The magnitude of Latin American external borrowing had itself reflected not only these countries' need to supplement domestic savings but also the most serious deficiency of their financial systems – the inadequacies of their long-term capital markets, in turn related to the failure to control inflation.

Serious banking and related industrial failures occurred at this time in Argentina, Chile and other countries. The nationalization of banks in Mexico and intervention or take-over of private banks in Colombia, Peru and even in Chile, the stronghold of liberal economic policies, suggested that the role of the state was becoming more dominant. In the event, it was clear by the early 1990s that this was not the prevailing trend. Realism suggested that the solution of the economic problems of the region would not be helped by the extension of state controls and state ownership: it was in the state industries – and in many if not all of the state banks – that inefficiency was most rampant. Whatever the nominal political philosophy of the government in power, economic liberalism, including the liberalization of markets and 'privatization', looked like becoming the new orthodoxy of the 1990s. Banks in Chile, Colombia and elsewhere that had suffered 'intervention' were to be returned to private ownership, and even opened cautiously to new foreign investment. The biggest reversal of policy was in Mexico, where the gradual sale of government shareholdings in the nationalized banks under a privatization plan announced in 1990 would permit up to 30 per cent foreign participation. The over-riding aim was to strengthen the banking system and to reinforce the natural trend of the market by uniting the whole range of financial services into powerful and resilient business groups.

Brazil, too, has accepted the growth of powerful financial groups as inevitable. Financial 'conglomerates' have emerged from the process of concentration, consisting of commercial bank, investment bank, finance company, leasing, brokerage and other subsidiaries and this process has continued to be seen as a necessary means of strengthening the financial sectors. In both countries not more than half a dozen banking groups have a preponderant share of total business. In establishing the multi-purpose bank, Latin America follows the European rather than the North American example.   HH

Further Reading: P. Drake, *The Money Doctor in the Andes: the Kemmerer Missions, 1923–1933* (Durham, N.C., 1988); A. Hendrie, ed., *Banking Structures and Sources of Finance in Latin America* (London, 1980); D. Joslin, *A Century of Banking in Latin America* (London, 1963); B. Stallings, *Banker to the Third World: U.S. Portfolio Investment in Latin America, 1900–1986* (Berkeley, 1987)

Current developments are best studied in *The Banker, Euromoney, The Institutional Investor* and other specialized financial periodicals. These are not, of course, primarily concerned with Latin American issues, but provide up-to-date coverage of events in the region.

Inflation

THE NATURE OF INFLATION

Inflation is normally associated with rising prices, though where prices are held down by controls, inflationary pressures can surface in other ways, such as lengthening order books, queues, and a growing shortage of goods – known as 'suppressed' inflation.

The change in the price level can reflect an excess of aggregate demand in the economy over the supply of resources. Supply and demand have to be balanced at a new higher price level. Inflation can be viewed as a way of rationing scarce resources among claimants whose initial demand, expressed in money, exceeds the initial monetary value of resources available.

There is another type of inflation which is not obviously due to excessive money demand. 'Stagflation' is when prices rise in the midst of recession, where excessive demand is not the prime cause. This was common in the industrial countries in the late 1970s and early 1980s in the wake of successive oil price rises. It often results from cost increases due to rises in import prices (because of a devaluation, or changes in the terms of trade), wage increases which are insensitive to the state of demand or delayed adjustments to administered (or controlled) prices.

The term 'price level' is not unambiguous. Price changes can be monitored at the wholesale or retail level. Whatever prices are chosen have to be combined into an index to represent changes in the price level as a whole. The compilation of the index is from a 'basket' of goods and services, and whatever basket is chosen may not reflect the spending pattern of particular social groups, hence separate indices are sometimes produced for different social groups. The most sophisticated measure of price changes is the GDP Deflator, a concept in national accounts devised to arrive at 'real' growth in national income, after allowing for price changes. Hereafter we shall use the consumer price index to measure inflation. This is the most easily understood and widely employed measure, and comparable data exist over the period concerned for the countries under discussion.

FORTY YEARS OF INFLATION

Over the last forty years Latin America and the Caribbean have undergone greater inflation than the rest of the world. Tables 25 and 26 show that the rate of inflation in the western hemisphere (excluding the United States and Canada) has exceeded worldwide inflation by a substantial margin. The cumulative results, which show the power of compound interest,

TABLE 25

Inflation since 1953: South America and Mexico (average annual percentage changes in consumer prices)

	1953–60	1961–73	1974–80	11981–85	1986–89
Argentina	26.3	43.5	178.3	382.4	911.1
Bolivia	n.a.	7.5	19.6	2692.4	80.5
Brazil	n.a.	38.5	45.7	153.9	586.1
Chile	n.a.	65.7*	184.1	21.5	17.8
Colombia	7.9	12.1	24.0	22.4	24.0
Ecuador	0.6	5.6	13.8	28.1	46.6
Mexico	6.1	3.7	21.2	62.4	88.1
Paraguay	22.0	4.7	15.3	15.9	25.4
Peru	7.7	9.0	42.5	104.9	1057.3
Uruguay	18.1	52.1	60.1	45.9	67.4
Venezuela	1.3	1.6	10.7	11.1	38.4
Latin America	*15.1*	*22.1*	*43.6*	*99.5*	*191.0*
World	*2.6*	*5.1*	*12.2*	*12.1*	*11.7*

n.a. Not available

*incomplete series

Source: International Monetary Fund, *International Financial Statistics* (Washington DC)

TABLE 26

Central America and the Caribbean: average annual percentage changes in consumer prices

	1953–60	1961–73	1974–80	1981–85	1986–89
Central America					
Costa Rica	1.8	3.6	12.6	37.4	16.5
El Salvador	2.1	1.2	14.7	14.7	23.6
Guatemala	0.8	1.7	11.7	7.7	17.9
Honduras	0.7*	2.6	8.0	7.0	5.3
Nicaragua	n.a.	n.a.	16.7*	66.9	3932.8
Caribbean					
Bahamas	n.a.	5.9*	8.3	5.9	5.2
Barbados	n.a.	8.6*	15.7	7.7	3.9
Dominican Republic	−0.4	3.7	11.1	16.9	23.3
Guyana	1.4*	2.8	12.8	19.7	25.5
Haiti	0.3*	4.9	10.2	9.1	−1.3
Jamaica	2.4*	5.5	21.9	16.9	11.1
Trinidad & Tobago	2.4	4.5	14.8	12.4	9.4
Latin America	*15.1*	*22.1*	*43.6*	*99.5*	*191.0*
World	*2.6*	*5.1*	*12.2*	*12.1*	*11.7*

n.a. Not available

*incomplete series

Source: International Monetary Fund, *International Financial Statistics* (Washington DC)

are startling: an item costing 1 unit (in the 'western hemisphere') in 1953 would cost 579,908 in 1989.

Too much should not be read into the choice of the time periods. 1953 is a convenient date to start since the inflationary effects of the Korean War had largely worn off. In addition, some of the consumer price series reported in 'International Financial Statistics' (those used here) start in 1953 or soon after. There is no significance in the use of 1960 to close this period, except that it enables us to refer to the '1950s,' a period of generally low inflation in which a number of our countries periodically reported *falling* price levels. On the other hand, there was an inflationary watershed around 1973 and 1974, and this is the reason for starting the third period in 1974, since when most countries have regularly experienced double-digit inflation.

Table 25 shows that most of the larger countries (grouped as South America plus Mexico) have seen growing rates of inflation in each successive period since 1953. (Paraguay is an exception, due to the decline from very high rates of inflation in the early 1950s.) Over the whole period the highest inflation has been in Argentina, Chile, Uruguay, Brazil and Peru. Venezuela has usually had lower inflation than elsewhere. The averages conceal violent inflationary episodes in particular countries, such as Argentina continuously since 1975, Brazil 1962–5 and since 1979, Chile 1973–7, Uruguay since 1973, Peru since 1978, and Bolivia and Mexico in the mid-1980s.

Table 26 focuses on the Central American and Caribbean countries. It is apparent that inflation has been very much lower in Central American countries than in their larger South American neighbours. Indeed, in the 1950s inflation was frequently negative in some of these countries. The increase in the tempo of inflation from one period to another has certainly happened, but even in the 1970s Central America experienced relatively low inflation by regional standards. In the 1980s, however, Nicaragua suffered the highest rate of inflation of any Latin American or Caribbean country.

A similar picture applies to the Caribbean countries in the table. The table includes the larger islands (plus Guyana, which it is customary to include in the Caribbean rather than Latin America). Price data for these countries for the 1950s are weak and incomplete, but the patchy evidence suggests very little inflation in that period. Inflation in the 1960s was greater, though still modest by the standards of the hemisphere. It was only since 1973/4 that inflation rose into two digits for most of them, with the highest rates hitting Jamaica, Trinidad and Tobago, Dominican Republic and Guyana.

It is not practical to include data for each of the smaller Caribbean islands. Many of them have only a few thousand inhabitants and price data are frequently weak and incomplete. Many are closely tied to metropolitan powers, and inflation mirrors that in the metropolis or the major trading partner (variously, Britain, France, Netherlands and the United States). Nor is Cuba discussed, since it is not a market economy and comparable price data do not exist.

With persistent high inflation, as in Argentina and Brazil in the 1980s, currency reform can sometimes only be achieved by eliminating three zeros and starting afresh.

A VARIETY OF CIRCUMSTANCES

Before discussing the theoretical causes of inflation, it should be obvious that its incidence has varied widely in the region, even between apparently similar countries. This should already warn readers against accepting any single, or simple, explanation of inflation. For instance Argentina and Brazil have both undergone substantial industrial development during this period, for much of the time under military regimes, yet Argentina has had the higher inflation. Both countries have had much higher inflation than the other industrially developed country, Mexico. Inflation in Jamaica and Trinidad has been very similar, despite the latter's status as an oil producer. On the other hand, inflation in the major oil producer, Venezuela, has usually been low.

Is inflation imported? Clearly, the enormous rises in petroleum prices after 1973 and 1979 hit virtually all our countries, save the oil producers. But the more 'open' economies, with a larger trading sector, had comparatively low inflation over the whole period (e.g. Bahamas, Barbados, Panama, El Salvador). For those inclining to the 'cost push' explanation of inflation, trade union pressure would be one of the major stimuli to rising prices. Certainly the political power of unions in Argentina, Jamaica and Uruguay has helped to sustain inflation (though whether it caused it is another matter), but inflation has reached high levels in Brazil too, where trade unions cover only a minority of workers.

Another mechanism for propagating inflation, indexing prices to the cost of living, has been extensively practised only in Brazil, and to a much lesser extent in Colombia. The impact of indexation on inflation is a matter of some dispute, and the bald statistical record is open to different interpretations. Brazil has had high inflation throughout the indexation period, and although the rate declined from the peak in 1964, it surged to high levels again in the late 1970s and 1980s. Colombia, on the other hand, has never suffered the extremes of inflation.

It is also clear that the type of government is too simple an explanation of variations in inflation. Over this period most Latin American countries have had spells of government either directly by military regimes, or by civilian governments with the crucial support of the military. But authoritarian governments are not always or necessarily better than their civilian counterparts in controlling inflation. Mexico, Venezuela, and Colombia – ruled by civilian governments throughout this period – have had relatively low rates of inflation, while Brazil and Argentina have persistently shown much higher rates under both military and civilian governments. It could be argued, as in Chile and Brazil, that the intervention of the military to end a period of increasingly unstable civilian rule succeeds in getting inflation down over the ensuing few years, but thereafter it seems that deep-rooted factors supervene to determine long-term inflation (cf. Brazil since the early 1970s).

CAUSES OF INFLATION

As in other countries, there has been considerable debate in Latin America and the Caribbean about the causes of the inflation which has been such a prominent feature of their economic life. But whereas in other countries the debate has polarized between 'monetarists' and 'Keynesians', or in earlier, simpler days, between theories of 'demand pull' and 'cost push', in the western-hemisphere developing countries the division has traditionally been between monetarists and structuralists. It is worth outlining these latter two positions.

BOLIVIA: AN EXAMPLE OF INFLATION AND STABILIZATION IN THE 1980S

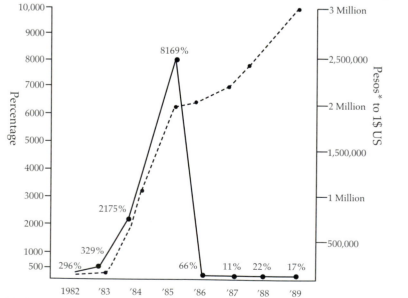

* In January 1987 six zeros were removed from the peso to create the new boliviano.

The monetarist explanation

Monetarism is more than a mere emphasis on the relation between the supply of money and the rate of price increase. This is, after all, a truism. It is not difficult to associate inflation with an increase in the quantity of money or the speed with which it changes hands (its 'velocity of circulation'). This can result from increased note issue by the Central Bank, increased credit from the commercial banks, and more government borrowing from the banking system (e.g. to cover a budget deficit). These, however, are the *means* by which inflation is transmitted to prices, and tell us nothing about how the inflation arose, or how it can be reduced.

Monetarists stress the importance of firm central-bank control over the liquid assets of the commercial banks in order to restrain credit expansion. They abhor the government's printing money to finance budget deficits. They advocate fiscal restraint in order to prevent the emergence of budget deficits. If the latter is inevitable, they advocate financing in non-inflationary ways, such as issuing public bonds (rather than borrowing from the banks).

More fundamentally, monetarists place greater faith in market mechanisms than in the use of direct administrative controls. Thus, they advocate 'realistic' interest rates, reflecting the 'real' returns on capital necessary to induce the required amount of savings. The foreign exchange rate should be determined by market forces, instead of being fixed for long periods at 'unrealistic' levels. Price control should, in general, be dropped, otherwise there is the risk of prices being fixed too low to induce sufficient supplies of the goods in question. Consumers should, as a general rule, pay the economic cost of their goods and services. The alternative is either the reduced supply of those goods and services, or the growth of consumer subsidies which enlarge the budget deficit. Monetarists claim that the strains and bottlenecks which accompany rapid growth and structural change would be greatly eased by allowing more scope for the operation of the price mechanism.

The structuralist view

Structuralists, on the contrary, view a degree of inflation as an inevitable concomitant of development in countries subject to structural changes. Attempts to eliminate inflation by firm monetary and fiscal policies bring on ills that are worse than the original malady, namely arrested growth, unemployment, and increased foreign dependence. They favour 'supply side' measures to control inflation, such as state investment, land reform, controls over private investment and foreign firms, etc.

Take food prices as an example. It is argued that agriculture is not able to respond to the rapidly increasing demand for food from a growing and urbanizing population. Landowners may lack motivation because of outmoded attitudes or tenurial forms. Complementary factors (machinery, seeds, fertilizer, and credit) may be lacking, together with know-how or enterprise. Hence food becomes increasingly scarce, causing price increases, consumer subsidies and/or imports.

Foreign exchange is another increasingly inevitable bottleneck, according to this view. The attempt to raise the growth rate, and push through industrial development, exacerbates a growing shortage of foreign exchange. Exports are sluggish, consisting as they do of primary products the demand for which is not responsive to income or price changes. The demand for imports by a growing population and expanding industrial sector rises rapidly. Neither exports nor imports are responsive to price changes such that movements in the exchange rate would bring about. Faced with a growing imbalance in foreign receipts and payments, the government is pressured into devaluation. This merely gives another twist to the inflationary spiral, since there is little effect in boosting exports or checking imports, the rise in the latter's price is passed on into wages and prices, and a further incentive is given to replace imports in a high-cost and inefficient manner.

It is argued that deficit financing is another 'structural' element feeding inflation. The choice of development strategy made by governments of developing countries often entails high public spending. On the other hand, the tax base is limited by the inequitable structure of incomes and wealth and by the smallness of the productive sector. At the same time, the poorer countries have limited recourse to such non-inflationary financial sources as overseas borrowing or the issue of domestic bonds. Hard-pressed governments start borrowing from the banks to cover the deficit in their budgets, and may even print money. Whatever the ultimate prime mover, the process normally shows in a budget deficit, which propagates further inflation.

A reconciliation

There is clearly a difference of view between these two schools about the ability of developing countries to cope with rapid growth and change without undergoing the tensions that show up in inflation. But there is also an implicit difference in the priority that the two schools accord to controlling inflation as opposed to modifying growth policies.

Structuralists, faced with a 'trade-off' between inflation and growth, would prefer more of both, while monetarists would choose less of both. This is, of course, a gross simplification, since some structuralists would recommend 'supply side' measures to improve the economy's response to growth, and possibly devices like indexation to take the sting out of inflation. On the other hand, many monetarists would align themselves with 'gradualist' approaches to the control of inflation that did not jolt output and employment too severely, and would direct public and private investment into the more obvious bottlenecks. Indeed, monetarists tend to argue that in the long run there is no conflict between inflationary control and growth since a degree of price stability is essential for economic progress.

Reviewing the Latin American experience before the 1980s it is clear that prices and market forces were neglected by policy makers, leading to an exacerbation of structural distortions and the loss of opportunities for output, employment and exports. When price signals –whether to farmers, banks or exports – are suppressed by price controls, legislation on interest rates, over-valued exchange rates etc., these sectors are discouraged and the myth of 'structural rigidities' arises. However, the greater play of market forces leads to a different kind of economy and society, such as one with a larger farm sector, more open to the international economy, with more private investment, etc. The fundamental difference between the two schools may be traced to the kind of sociopolitical regime they wish to see in place.

REMEDIES?

If there were no cost involved in reducing inflation, in the sense of difficult policy trade-offs to be faced, then there would be little point in delaying anti-inflationary policy. But as the above discussions show, observers differ in the priority they place on reducing inflation, where this involves costs for output, employment, growth, and even social stability. All observers would, however, agree that the most outrageous inflationary episodes (Brazil 1963–4 and since 1979, Argentina since 1973 and especially 1976, Chile 1973–6, Uruguay 1972–6, etc.), where prices were virtually doubling every year (in some cases more), were simply not sustainable and drastic measures were called for.

There are, of course, ways of living with inflation. Individual people try to cope with inflation in various ways, such as resorting to the Black Market, taking on extra jobs, and smuggling. People differ in their opportunity to do this. Alternatively governments may try to link as many prices as possible to the index of inflation, so that suffering and distortion are mitigated. The most comprehensive attempt at 'indexation' took place in Brazil after 1964, although it was also tried in Chile and Argentina. Interest on government securities, tax obligations, deposits in invest-

ment banks, and housing finance have all formally been linked to the official cost of living index, and minimum wages have been indexed on a looser fashion.

Brazilian indexation, though widely applied to important sectors, has not been universal and, as applied to wages, has not maintained purchasing power for the lowest-paid workers. It certainly had an early and favourable impact on the growth of savings, which helped government finance and home ownership. More recently, though, it has been argued that indexation has helped to perpetuate inflation, not least because the government has only been able to finance its index-linked obligations by raising further finance in inflationary ways. This is an important argument for those who believe inflation is essentially 'inertial'.

Since inflation is associated with price increases, it is tempting to think that price controls can form the cure. But, by making the supply of the goods and services in question increasingly unprofitable, price controls create scarcities or else they are simply evaded. Price controls can therefore only be effective for a limited period, as part of an attack on inflationary expectations.

The rapid growth of money supply 'causes' price rises in a proximate sense, just as petrol thrown on to a flame 'causes' a blaze, but we need to ask what makes people throw petrol on to flames if we are seeking a full explanation. The control of the money supply may be lax, and it may be irresponsible, but in many cases the creation of money results from the need to finance a budget deficit when all other, non-inflationary, means have been tried. In short, the excessive expansion in the money supply may contribute to inflation in its own right, but often it merely reflects the exigencies of public finance.

Unbalanced budgets are invariably a feature of inflation. Financing the gap between revenue and spending sometimes takes inflationary forms, namely borrowing from the banking system (which is then used to expand credit) or even printing new money to pay the government's bills. Balancing the budget has a pivotal part in any anti-inflationary measures. However, the budget is the result of pressures from different political, social and economic groups. A government that feels in peril will not have the will nor the power to take 'obvious' budgetary measures.

Thus ultimately the worst outbreaks of inflation in Latin America over the last forty years have arisen from the lack of a political consensus about how the burdens and benefits of development should be distributed or how the costs of an exogenous 'shock' should be shared. Commonly, a series of events arises (such as a fall in export prices, leading to a decline in government revenues and a balance-of-payments deficit) which demands some remedial action by the government, but where none of the parties concerned is willing to bear the sacrifices (higher taxes, reduced government spending, higher food prices and utility tariffs, devaluation, higher interest rates, etc.). Each group tries to maintain its former share of the national cake, and in the process the aggregate pressure of demand on resources causes mounting inflation. Although sound 'technical' measures can go a long way towards preventing excessive inflation, the ultimate causes, and cures, for inflation often lie in the political domain.

INFLATION, RECESSION AND DEBT

High rates of inflation, which before the 1980s afflicted only a minority of Latin American countries, have now become widespread. The problem of inflation in the 1980s was given a further twist by the debt crisis which crippled the flow of new capital to the region and forced each republic to adopt both stabilization and adjustment programmes in an effort to generate the resources needed to service their foreign obligations. All republics have been affected, but not all have responded in the same way. Let us begin with the experience of the three largest republics: Argentina, Brazil and Mexico.

The contrasting experiences of Mexico, Brazil and Argentina

Even before the 1980s, Argentina and Brazil had suffered from high rates of inflation while price stability in Mexico had begun to break down in the 1970s. The debt crisis in the 1980s, however, forced all three countries to adopt measures which exacerbated inflationary pressures; on several occasions during the decade all three republics recorded monthly rates of inflation which exceeded annual rates in the 1970s.

The first twist to the inflationary spiral was given by exchange rate depreciation. In an effort to generate a trade surplus (i.e. exports greater than imports) that could be used to meet debt service payments, all three countries pursued real exchange rate depreciation aggressively and this forced up the domestic price of all traded goods and services. Additional measures were taken to curb imports and this redirected demand towards the domestic market, which led to an increase in the price of non-traded goods and services.

The second consequence of the debt crisis was the increase in the size of budget deficits, as governments were forced to borrow domestically – often by printing money – in order to obtain the resources needed to service the public external debt. These deficits,

which reached over 10 per cent of GDP in Argentina between 1981 and 1984, contributed heavily to inflationary pressures. Furthermore, the nominal rate of interest was driven sharply higher, adding to the prime costs of firms and encouraging those that could to raise their prices.

Faced with accelerating rates of inflation, all three republics have adopted a variety of stabilization programmes. The most successful by far has been Mexico, where the key to success was the stabilization of the exchange rate in December 1987; the monthly rate of inflation fell immediately and this in turn pushed down nominal interest rates. By mid-1989 Mexico had become the first country to qualify for debt relief under the Brady Plan (named after the US Secretary to the Treasury in the Bush Administration) and the announcement brought a further sharp fall in nominal interest rates. In turn, this lowered the government's internal debt servicing costs, thus allowing Mexico to reduce the public sector financial deficit.

The partnership between government, business and the unions has been a very important factor in the reduction of Mexican inflation, which fell from 132 per cent in 1987 to 20 per cent in 1989. Mexico has also benefited from the growing rapprochement with the United States, which has raised the very real possibility of a Free Trade Agreement between the two countries and led to special treatment for Mexico in terms of access to foreign capital. Finally, the return of flight capital – attracted by the interest rate differential between Mexico and the USA and the government's commitment to the fight against inflation – has helped to maintain the stability of the exchange rate, despite the fact that Mexican inflation remains significantly higher than world inflation.

Despite repeated attempts under different names, Argentina and Brazil have had little success in curbing inflation. Unlike Mexico, they have been unable to stabilize the exchange rate for any length of time. Although monthly rates of inflation have dropped each time a stabilization plan has been adopted, the fall has not been sufficient to justify the maintenance of a stable exchange rate, since exports have quickly suffered from overvaluation of the currency. Budget deficits – swollen not just by debt interest payments, but also by massive state subsidies and inflated payrolls – have remained stubbornly high, although major efforts were made by new presidents at the start of the 1990s to reduce the level of subsidies through programmes of privatization.

In all three large republics industry is highly oligopolistic and prefers to respond to cuts in nominal demand by lowering output rather than prices. Mexico, however, sharply reduced its tariffs in the 1980s, eliminated virtually all non-tariff barriers and also liberalized foreign trade to the point where even oligopolistic domestic firms were being forced to compete with imports. In Argentina and Brazil, on the other hand, the process of trade liberalization has proceeded much more slowly so that many firms have not had to compete with imports. However, with a common market in Latin America's southern cone (embracing Argentina, Brazil, Paraguay and Uruguay) expected to be completed by 1995 and with new administrations at the start of the 1990s taking important steps towards trade liberalization, oligopolistic firms in Argentina and Brazil have begun to face the same competition from imports as industry in Mexico.

The smaller countries

Inflation in the smaller countries, many of which have no formal system of indexation, has had particularly severe social, as well as economic, costs. Real wages have fallen sharply, income distribution has become more unequal and new (often fragile) democratic governments have sometimes found it difficult to persevere with policy reforms in the face of popular protest.

Nevertheless, the success of some stabilization programmes has shown that inflation can be tamed even under such adverse circumstances.

Many of the smaller countries (see tables 25 and 26) had little problem with inflation before the debt crisis struck the region in the 1980s. By the second half of the 1980s, however, only a handful of countries – all with open economies and fixed exchange rates – had kept inflation down to the levels found in their main trading partners. Some countries, notably Nicaragua and Peru, even had to grapple with hyperinflation – a process in which prices rise by at least 50 per cent every month.

As with the large republics, the acceleration of inflation in the smaller countries in the 1980s owes much to the debt crisis and the responses it provoked. The crucial change has been exchange rate devaluation. Many of these countries had pegged their currency to the US dollar for years (in some cases decades), but debt problems and the need to boost exports as well as curb imports have eliminated exchange rate stability almost everywhere. Since smaller countries are typically more open than larger ones, currency devaluation rapidly produces an increase in prices, which requires further devaluations, and so on. Real depreciation, i.e. a fall in the currency by more than the difference between domestic and foreign prices, is then only made possible by a decline in real wages.

In a few smaller countries, inflationary pressures have been exacerbated by huge budget deficits; Nicaragua and Peru, for example, and Bolivia before 1985 suffered from a manifest failure by governments to cover a sufficiently high proportion of their public expenditure with tax revenue. In general, however, the contribution of budget deficits to inflation in small countries has been less than in large republics. Small countries are more likely to be able to cover part of their deficits by non-inflationary borrowing from abroad (e.g. from official sources), and international financial agencies (e.g. the IMF) have had greater success in limiting the size of the deficits in the first place.

Just as exchange rate depreciation has been the main cause of the rise in inflation, so has currency stability been the principal factor in successful stabilization programmes. The introduction of the Boliviano in 1985, for example, and its subsequent (relatively) stable value was a major factor in the success of the Bolivian stabilization programme, while the adoption of a crawling peg (mini-devaluations) in the mid-1980s brought inflation in Costa Rica down from nearly 100 per cent a year to a more manageable 10 to 20 per cent. In both cases, governments were able to draw upon the goodwill of the international community to build international reserves in defence of the new value of the currency.

The overriding need to continue the shift of resources towards the export sector has forced the smaller countries to persevere with currency depreciation despite the social costs and the damage to price stability. Rather than seeking to peg the currency, the emphasis has shifted towards targeting public expenditure to protect the living standards of the poorest groups. Similarly, tax and public expenditure reform is seen as an important part of the anti-inflation strategy in order not only to lower budget deficits, but also to free resources for helping the poor. Trade liberalization through tariff cuts is also seen by many as a way of lowering inflationary pressures. Significantly, virtually all Latin American countries had joined, or applied to join, GATT by the beginning of the 1990s.   JTW/VB-T

Further Reading: W. Baer and I. Kerstenetzky, eds., *Inflation and Growth in Latin America* (Illinois, 1964); M. Bruno, G. Di Tella, R. Dornbusch and S. Fischer, eds., *Inflation Stabilization* (Cambridge, Mass., 1988); J. Sheahan, *Patterns of Development in Latin America* (Princeton, 1987); R. Thorp and L. Whitehead, eds., *Inflation and Stabilization in Latin America* (London, 1979); S. Wachter *Latin American Inflation: The Structuralist–Monetarist Debate* (Lexington, 1976); J. Williamson, ed., *Latin American Adjustment: How Much Has Happened?* (Washington, DC, 1990)

External debt

The overwhelming economic event for Latin America and the Caribbean in the 1980s was an external debt crisis of a pandemic nature. The region had prospered in the 1970s with economic growth of some 6 per cent per year, stimulated by the abundant availability of foreign commercial bank debt. But, precipitated by the capital flight of the Mexican peso in early 1982, and then compounded by the Argentine-British war of the Falklands later that year, creditor perceptions of the region turned adverse. With the withdrawal of new finance the region was plunged into severe debt-servicing problems and near-defaults on its $200 billion of commercial bank debt.

ANTECEDENTS OF THE DEBT CRISIS

In what has been identified as 'The First Latin American Debt Crisis', seven newly independent Latin American nations issued over £20,000 in bonds in the City of London during 1822–5. British financiers and merchants were the underwriters, who then sold the debt in the form of bearer bonds to investors in London. However, the new countries – Chile, Colombia, Peru, Brazil, Argentina (Buenos Ayres), Mexico, Guatemala – proved unable to muster the public finance to service these bonds. By 1829, of the original £20,000 of the 1822–5 bonds nearly £19,000 were in default. Protracted negotiations and reschedulings ensued, but bondholders recovered little, and Latin America lost its ability to borrow in London until another generation of financiers and investors rediscovered the region in the 1860s.

The Latin American loan boom of the 1860s ended in a further crisis during 1873–5 as most borrowers were forced to default in the midst of world-wide depression. A revival of world trade in the 1880s led to another resurgence of lending to Latin America. Yet another interruption followed with the 'panic' of 1890 in London as Argentina proved unable to meet its outstanding debts to the Baring Brothers merchant bank. However, confidence was restored in the late 1890s by improving export markets and another high tide of lending took place as British, German and French banks competed for loans. By 1914, total Latin American external debt had reached $2 billion and the region was poised for another loan surge after the First World War.

In the period after 1918 and the retrenchment of Britain as a creditor nation, the next burst of lending to Latin America came from US markets. Between 1919 and 1931, US banks were the leading underwriters of Latin American government bonds, of which some $2 billion were sold in the United States between 1920 and 1930. A smaller amount of $269 million of Latin American bonds were sold by British and European banks.

However, the international depression of the early 1930s and the troubles the Latin American countries experienced in their export sales caused the region to lag in servicing of bonded debt. By the mid-1930s almost 70 per cent of Latin American national government bonds were in default. Collection efforts to recover on the defaults were desultory. Since the US banks had kept only very small holdings in their own portfolios, they took no role in trying to make recoveries of the debt. These fruitless endeavours were attempted by bondholders 'protective' councils, with the US government refusing to get directly involved.

Foreign direct investors were in the forefront of providing the bulk of capital inflows for Latin America in the 1950s. A desire to participate in the Latin American wave of import substituting industrialization (ISI) was a primary motivator, as investors took advantage of locating behind protective barriers in domestic markets.

Following the decade of direct investment, the next wave of Latin American finance was in 1961–5 with official creditor government loans. During this half-decade over 40 per cent of the external financial resources for Latin America came from bilateral government loans, especially from the United States.

THE NEW ERA OF BANK LENDING

The share of commercial bank lending among total financial resource flows to Latin America increased rapidly from only 9 per cent in 1970 to 35 per cent in 1972. By the next year the bank share of Latin American financial flows had jumped to 43 per cent. Two major institutional changes were behind this shift. First was the emergence of the Eurocurrency market and the development of syndicated lending. The other was the OPEC oil price shocks of 1973 and 1979 and the role the banks seized in intermediating surplus revenues from oil-producing countries to the net oil-importing nations.

Latin America viewed the availability and low-cost of bank credit as a spur to faster economic development, and the banks perceived the region as creditworthy in view of substantial new investments and rising export and economic growth. Thus, about two thirds of all new bank lending to the non-oil-producing developing countries during 1975–80 went to Latin America. Total long-term commercial bank debt to Latin America rose from less than $15 billion in 1970 to almost $120 billion by 1980. Bank financing was directed at both the oil-exporters of Venezuela, Mexico and Ecuador as well as the net oil-importing countries of the region. The share of bank debt within the total long-term debt consequently increased from 53 per cent to 69 per cent. In addition, some $68 billion of short-term bank credits to Latin America had accumulated by 1980. Thus, of the total Latin American debt of almost $243 billion in 1980, over three quarters was owed to commercial banks. Debt to official creditors was only 13 per cent of the total; bonds, suppliers credits and others represented the 9 per cent balance.

The increasing reliance on external bank finance and high investment rates produced a fast 5.9 per cent average annual real growth rate in Latin America during the 1970s. In per capita GDP terms, the region realized a substantial growth of 3.3% per year, comparing quite well with other developing countries. But despite these gains, strains began to appear.

THE 1982 DEBT CRISIS

The resort to bank lending in Latin America was viable until world economic conditions changed and servicing of the debt became difficult. After 1979 there was a substantial increase in international interest rates, which hit Latin America especially hard since most bank debt was in variable rate form. Coupled with world recession in 1981–2 and commodity price declines, the banks changed their credit-worthiness perceptions of the region and started to withdraw from new lending in 1982. The precipitating events were a run on the Mexican peso in early 1982 and the Falklands/Malvinas war between Argentina and Britain in April 1982. A sensational announcement on 20 August 1982 by the Mexican finance minister that the country could not meet coming loan maturities marked the beginning of the debt crisis. It was a crisis that was perceived as a threat to the financial solvency of the Latin American countries as a whole, and as a similar threat to the solvency of many commercial banks – not to mention the international financial system itself – if massive and simultaneous defaults occurred in the region.

After the Mexican meeting with the banks in late 1982, and the formation of a 'Bank Advisory Committee', the other major Latin American debtors followed suit. Brazil met with its creditors in December 1982 and Venezuela in March 1983.

By this time, the entire region was experiencing problems of debt and debt servicing with the commercial banks.

The Mexican Bank Advisory Committee set the pattern for debtor–creditor relations to work out the crisis. The banks tried to persuade the countries to maintain current interest payments, while rescheduling the bunched debt maturities over a longer period and providing new money to meet cash flow 'gaps'. As this process was extended to nearly all Latin American countries, the reschedulings and concerted or forced new money loans helped to avert a solvency crisis. The banks – with the strong support of the International Monetary Fund – essentially provided the relief needed to prevent the countries from declaring formal defaults. And by their doing so, the threat to the international financial system was lessened.

Between 1983 and 1985 a total of twenty-eight reschedulings, refinancings and deferments was negotiated between the banks and the Latin American countries. The reschedulings totalled almost $134 billion, representing about half of bank debt outstanding in 1982. In addition, the banks provided about $33 billion of new money commitments, of which all but $1 billion for Colombia was in the form of concerted lending. Further aid was provided in 1985 in the shift to longer-term reschedulings, the 'Multi Year Rescheduling Agreements', or MYRAs. These agreements included more maturities to be rescheduled and repayments stretched to as long as fourteen to fifteen years with lengthier grace periods. Important relief was also provided by the 'Paris Club' reschedulings of principal and interest by creditor country governments. Altogether $8 billion of official debt was rescheduled in fourteen agreements between 1983 and 1985.

Painful recessions were endured as Latin American economies adjusted to the lesser availability of bank and other types of finance. The current account deficit of the balance of payments was cut from over $40 billion annually in 1981–2 to less than $1 billion in 1984. This was accomplished through a curtailment more of investment than of consumption. Imports dropped almost 40 per cent from 1981 to 1984 and economic output fell 4 per cent between 1981 and 1983. Meanwhile exports went up only 1.5 per cent. But it was the import compression that allowed the region to generate the trade surpluses needed to service interest payments. This produced a net outward transfer of resources since interest payments abroad were far greater than the net capital inflows, in contrast to the period before 1982, when the region had enjoyed a net inward transfer of resources from the large availability of bank finance.

The Latin American investment-to-GDP ratio declined from 20 per cent to 16 per cent between 1982 and 1985. By this latter year output per capita was 8 per cent below the 1980 level. Whether measured in terms of output or investments, the adjustment to the constrained debt situation certainly pushed the region into recession.

THE BAKER GROWTH WITH ADJUSTMENT PROGRAMME

Rescheduling and concerted lending from 1983 to 1985 were merely the first phase of the debt strategy undertaken by creditors and debtors. Marking a clear second phase was a proposal from the US Secretary of the Treasury, James A. Baker, in October 1985 for a new initiative on growth-oriented policies, rather than on recessionary adjustment. This was to be a programme of renewed economic growth linked to national structural reforms and provisions of new finance by the commercial banks and the international financial institutions – notably the World Bank and the Interamerican Development Bank (IADB) in the case of Latin America.

On the Baker list of the fifteen countries recommended for his Initiative, ten were in Latin America; for the most part it was a Latin American programme. The basic premise was that countries with the appropriate market- and export-oriented policies could grow their way out of the debt problem, and they would receive continued net financial flows from the commercial banks and official agencies while they were making their structural adjustments. The general targets were: a net lending increase of $20 billion for the 1986–8 period for the commercial banks, and for the World Bank and the IADB a 50 per cent increase in their annual gross disbursements from $6 billion to $9 billion over the same period. The macroeconomic expectation was that GDP would rise 4.5 per cent to 5 per cent per year for the period, to be made possible by adequate finance and structural reforms in each country.

The Baker goals were partially realized by the multilateral institutions but not by the banks. Moreover, growth-with-new-debt policy was slowly eroded by the decision of some smaller banks to withdraw from lending altogether. Bank debt was traded on secondary markets at substantial discounts, casting doubt on the logic of new lending. The decision by Citicorp/Citibank, the leading US bank, in mid-1987 to set aside 25 per cent of its reserves for possible loan losses took the impetus off new lending. Why would a bank lend new money to a country when it could require the provision of reserves? A second erosion of new lending was represented by the Mexican government proposal in late 1987, in conjunction with J. P. Morgan and with support of the US Treasury, to exchange up to $20 billion of the country's debt at a discount for Mexican government bonds. From this point on debt reduction became an accepted element in the banks' strategy, although with the caution that it should be voluntary and not mandatory.

Banks became particularly responsive to debt reduction by means of equity conversions, in which they could acquire shares in a business enterprise. Instead of providing voluntary new money, the banks chose to reduce some $35 billion of debt in the ten Latin American countries of the Baker programme through loan sales, write-downs, charge-offs and equity conversions. These increased options led the banks to develop the 'menu' approach by which each bank could choose to exit from further lending or rescheduling, convert debt into bonds or equity, or even provide new loans if they desired. But for several Latin American countries that failed to get sufficient finance or relief from the menu approach, arrears on interest payments became a back-door type of financing. Used notably by Argentina, Brazil and Ecuador, arrears to commercial banks started accumulating and reached $8 billion by the end of 1987.

Because of reductions and conversions, the Latin American loan exposure to commercial banks declined $6 billion between 1986 and 1988. This was despite concerted new money packages of $12 billion during the period. But some analysts contend that the voluntary debt reductions and conversions by banks represented a lessening of the debt and debt service of the countries, so it should be recognized as a contribution to financial relief. Further, the banks – especially in the United States – believed they had made sacrifices for Latin American debt in the form of lower share prices, actual loan losses, forced asset sales, and lowered investment ratings for their securities. Costs were also borne by Latin America itself.

Economic growth declined during the period of the Baker programme. A lowering of oil and commodity prices particularly affected economic activity. For the ten Latin American countries the rise in GDP averaged only 3.6 per cent during the period, while the per capita income rise was 1 per cent. For the entire region the record was worse – a three-year average of 2.6 per cent and stagnant real income.

THE BRADY DEBT REDUCTION PROGRAMME

The third phase of the Latin American strategy was ushered in by another US Treasury Secretary, Nicholas F. Brady, on 10 March 1989. He shifted the emphasis from growth to debt reduction, endorsing debt and debt service reduction for bank debt on a voluntary basis. He added that the IMF and World Bank were to support debt reduction through 'set asides' of their loans to guarantee principal of bank debt converted into bonds. Interest payments were also to be partially guaranteed. The Brady proposals were eventually endorsed by the major creditor governments and by the IMF and World Bank.

TABLE 27
Latin America and the Caribbean: economic performance and external debt

	1970	1980	1983	1985	1990
	(Percent changes)				
Real Gross Domestic Product (GDP)	4.8	5.3	−2.7	3.5	−0.5
Per capita GDP	2.2	2.8	−4.8	1.2	−2.6
Consumer prices	12.3	56.1	130.5	274.1	1492.5
	(Billions U.S. $)				
Total external debt	27.7	242.5	360.9	389.9	428.6
IMF credit	0.1	1.4	8.8	14.5	20.8
Short-term debt	–	68.3	61.2	44.5	68.8
Bank debt, long-term[a]	14.9	119.9	209.1	229.4	208.8
Multilateral debt	3.0	14.0	21.7	.8	56.9
Bilateral debt	5.2	16.5	23.9	32.5	58.1
Bonds	1.2	9.6	16.2	17.8	–
Suppliers and other	3.3	12.8	20.0	20.4	–

[a] For 1990, as of September, and includes short-term debt.
Sources: Economic Commission for Latin America and the Caribbean, IMF, World Bank, Bank
       for International Settlements

TABLE 28
External debt, balance of payments and international reserves, 1990
(billions U.S. $)

	Bank Debt	Total Debt	Debt as Percentage Exports	Trade Balance	Current Account Balance	Total Internal Reserves
Argentina	35.2	56.8	418	7.3	0.7	3.5
Brazil	79.6	122.5	338	11.6	−3.5	9.6
Chile	9.1	19.5	193	1.4	−1.0	4.6
Colombia	7.3	17.8	212	1.5	−0.5	4.0
Ecuador	6.5	11.7	370	0.8	−0.4	0.6
Mexico	61.1	98.3	237	−2.0	−4.5	8.3
Peru	8.6	22.0	522	0.8	−1.3	0.9
Venezuela	24.2	34.4	165	9.6	6.7	11.0

Source: The Institute of International Finance, Inc.

The justification of debt reduction *per se*, as articulated by the IMF and the World Bank, was that the debt overhang – defined as debt that cannot normally be serviced – acts as a potential tax on investment in the country. Prospective investors, domestic as well as foreign, are thus deterred. Once the overhang is eliminated, confidence is restored and investor expectations brighten. Increased investment then leads to rising economic growth.

Commercial banks reacted sceptically at first to the Brady proposals. They noted that the problem of Latin America was not the debt but the lack of policies that would foster exports, new investment, domestic savings and the return of flight capital. Another concern was the size of the debt reductions being proposed, since some countries' secondary debts were selling at substantial discounts of 50 per cent or more. However, despite these reservations, the banks did

enter into Brady-type negotiations with Mexico in 1989, considered the 'pioneer' country for debt reduction and a country that the US government strongly supported for geo-political reasons.

The Brady debt reduction agreements

Through the first half of 1991, four countries had concluded debt and debt service reduction agreements with commercial banks, reducing their aggregate bank debt by some $11 billion.

Mexico was the first 'Brady' country as it adhered to IMF–World Bank programmes and concluded agreements in early 1990 with the commercial banks. These provided for three options: bank debt to be exchanged for thirty-year bonds with a 35 per cent discount on the principal; debt to be exchanged for thirty-year bonds, at reduced interest rates; and a new money option for banks that wished to invest further in the country. The agreements resulted in reduction of almost $7 billion in Mexico's commercial bank debt and the provision of $6.4 billion in new bank finance. The principal of the bonds was collateralized with US government zero-coupon bonds, and interest payments were also supported with IMF–World Bank funds. However, purchasing the collateral cost Mexico $7 billion, borrowed largely from the IMF, World Bank and the Export–Import Bank of Japan.

Costa Rica's agreement of May 1990 was to buy back a large portion of bank debt at deep discount and convert the remainder into bonds. The buyback was for cash at an 84 per cent discount, retiring almost $1 billion. Banks that offered 60 per cent of their debt for buybacks could exchange the remainder for twenty-year bonds at reduced interest rates.

Initiating far-reaching economic reforms in early 1989 Venezuela presented a full five-options menu to the banks late in 1990. The choices for the banks were buybacks, new money bonds, discount bonds with a 30 per cent reduced principal, reduced interest par bonds, and bonds with lower and then higher interest rates. Because of the run-up of oil prices prior to the Venezuela agreement, most banks selected par-value bonds with reduced interest rates, and more than $1 billion of new money bonds was also taken. The 30 per cent discount bonds were taken by fewer banks than expected, partly because oil income was boosting Venezuela's reserves and partly because many banks felt debt reduction *per se* was not needed. Thus, bank debt reduction was only $1.9 billion.

In February 1991 Uruguay completed its debt reduction agreement with the commercial banks. This included a cash buyback of bank debt which retired about one third of this indebtedness.

The responses to structural reform and debt

reduction were most clearly seen in Mexico. Foreign and domestic investment rose substantially, and $5 billion of flight capital returned in 1990. Venezuela also experienced an economic revival in 1990, although greater oil income from the Gulf crisis provided much of the impetus.

Chile and Colombia – special cases

Beyond the Brady countries there are the special cases of Chile and Colombia, which have demonstrated steady and good management of their economies, maintained creditworthiness and avoided formal debt reduction exercises. Chile completed debt rescheduling with banks and voluntary Eurobond financing in early 1991 without a Brady agreement. But the country had already reduced its stock of debt by $8.8 billion during 1985–9 through debt to equity conversions and cash buybacks. For Colombia, a cautious attitude toward external debt and low indebtedness ratios at the start of the 1982 difficulties kept it out of formal reschedulings. But the debt crisis affected its access to new bank loans and it had to obtain financing for rollover purposes through tightly managed bank 'club' deals.

OUTLOOK FOR DEBT

As of April 1991 Argentina, Brazil and four smaller Latin American economies were still to complete debt negotiations with their bank creditors. These countries represented over 51 per cent of commercial bank debt and 55 per cent of GDP in Latin America. While the general debt crisis might have been considered to be ended for countries that had achieved debt agreements and begun to return to the voluntary lending markets, for this set of countries the problems were still legion.

Argentina was paying partial interest payments to banks, while in Brazil negotiations were continuing on a scheme to settle arrears on a 'cash and bonds' arrangement, with interest payments also paid at a partial rate. The creditors' priorities for both countries were on handling arrears and current interest payments first, reducing bank debt through the conversion into equity of privatized state enterprises, and then turning to the issue of debt and debt service reduction on the remaining stock of bank indebtedness. Thus, for both Argentina and Brazil, the treatment of the stock of debt and a Brady-type reduction would take considerable time and depend on economic stabilization efforts and compliance with IMF and World Bank programmes.

Although both Argentina and Brazil were heavily indebted to the banks, some analysts have contended that for these two countries the problem is not the debt overhang but the need to generate adequate fiscal resources and achieve structural reforms. Yet large stocks of debt had to be treated, and ultimately a reduction and conversion of bank debt – along the lines of the Mexico and Venezuela agreements – was to be expected.

A group of smaller countries in Latin America also faced resolutions of their debt and arrears problem. Ecuador was on the threshold of negotiations with its bank creditors in mid-1991, with issues centring on the level of partial interest payments being made, a debt buyback, and the settlement of arrears. For three remaining countries with deep-seated economic problems – Peru, Panama, the Dominican Republic – the resolution of their bank debt problems loomed even more distant.

External debt and development outlook

A reasonable projection would assume that eventually all of the Latin American countries will reach agreements with their creditors, and solutions will be found so that the bank debt problem is put behind them and the region can proceed with renewed economic development. As alternative sources of finance through the securities markets, foreign investors and domestic savings are accessed, the outlook for economic growth should be considerably better than the 'lost decade' of the 1980s when per capita income dropped almost 10 per cent.

Both the IMF and World Bank have projected average growth for Latin America of 4 to 5 per cent per annum, assuming that the debt burden is no longer a constraint on investment and that sound economic policies are continued. Commercial banks will continue to play a role in the future, but it will be a supportive one to provide trade and project finance and asset-based lending for the better-performing economies. It is unlikely that the star role of the banks in the debt-led growth of the 1970s can be repeated. Multilateral and bilateral institutions and the securities markets are clearly poised to increase their share of Latin American financing. And the return of flight capital is expected as confidence in economic stability is regained.   ABF

US Treasury Secretary Nicholas Brady addressing an IMF/World Bank meeting in Berlin, September 1988

Further Reading: F. G. Dawson, *The First Latin American Debt Crisis: The City of London and the 1822–25 Loan Bubble* (New Haven and London, 1990); R. Devlin, *Debt and Crisis in Latin America: The Supply Side of the Story* (Princeton, 1989); B. Eichengreen and P. H. Lindert, eds., *The International Debt Crisis in Historical Perspective* (Cambridge, Mass., and London, 1989); E. J. Frydl and D. M. Sobol, 'A Perspective on the Debt Crisis, 1982–1987', in the *Seventy-Third Annual Report of the Federal Reserve Bank of New York* (New York, 1987); J. D. Sachs, ed., *Developing Country Debt and Economic Performance: Country Studies – Argentina, Bolivia, Brazil, Mexico* (Chicago, 1990)

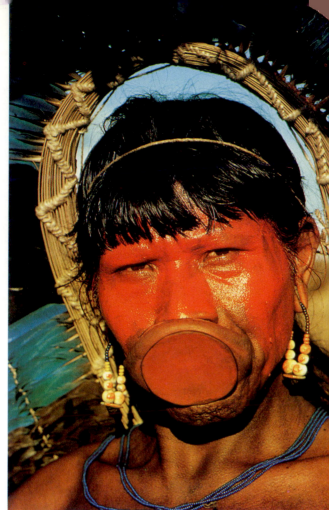

The Peoples

Pre-Columbian settlement and population

America was settled first by people who migrated from Asia via the Bering Strait probably between 25,000 and 40,000 years ago. They travelled south, arriving in South America about 20,000 BC and reaching Tierra del Fuego by 9000 BC. The earliest areas occupied were the uplands and upland slopes of the Mexican plateaux and the Andes, where man first hunted Pleistocene mammals, such as mammoths, mastodons, wild horses and ground sloths. As these mammals became extinct, as a result of climatic changes and over-exploitation, the Indians began to hunt deer and the wild ancestors of the llama and alpaca, and to collect wild berries, seeds and roots. From about 8000 BC they began to occupy the coasts and lowlands. On the coasts the Indians caught fish, shellfish and sea mammals and gathered wild plant products, but the lowland savanna and tropical rain-forest areas offered little in the form of wild food resources so that their occupation occurred at a later date and was restricted to the river valleys and coasts, where a broad spectrum of wild plants and animals was to be found. Since these hunting and gathering bands were dependent on wild food resources they were forced to move in response to the seasonal availability of different sources of food; those bands which were more dependent on fishing, which generally provides more reliable sources of food, were less nomadic, often remaining in the same place for several months of the year. They lived in caves or erected temporary camps in the open. Because of the limited sources of food, the population was dispersed in small groups of under one hundred, but generally less than thirty people. When food resources were scarce the group would disperse and forage in smaller units composed of one or two families, whereas when resources were abundant they would come together in larger numbers and remain sedentary for longer periods. The population density that could be supported by hunting, gathering and fishing was probably only one person per 25 to 50 sq km. By the time of the Spanish conquest these bands were to be found mainly in areas which were either too cold, wet or arid for agriculture, for example, northern Mexico, southern Chile and Argentina, and eastern Brazil.

EARLY AGRICULTURE

There is evidence of the beginnings of plant and animal domestication by about 7000 BC. At Tehuacán in south-central Mexico and at Tamaulipas in north-eastern Mexico there is evidence of seed-crop cultivation in semi-arid areas, whilst at Ayacucho in the central Peruvian Andes there is evidence of the cultivation of temperate seed crops and the domestication of the llama from about 5000 BC. By 4000 BC seed crops were being cultivated on the semi-arid coast of Peru and it has been suggested that the cultivation of root crops began in the Amazon basin about 5000 BC, although the first definite evidence of their cultivation comes from northern Venezuela and is dated at 2700 BC. Agriculture provided people with more productive and reliable sources of food; it enabled larger populations to be supported and thus laid the basis for the development of more complex societies and ultimately states. The growth in population associated with the development of agriculture was not only related directly to the increase in food supply, but also to the settled way of life which was made possible by more reliable sources of food. A sedentary mode of existence has the advantage of reducing both the dangers of miscarriages and the average number of years between child births; in a nomadic society children tend to be more widely spaced because of the difficulty of carrying more than one infant. Thus, the population did not expand dramatically with the beginnings of agriculture but with the establishment of permanent villages. This is demonstrated in the archaeological record of Tehuacán, where agriculture

Previous page clockwise from top left Mulatto selling fried papaya, Cartagena, Colombia; Kayapo Indian Chief, Xingu, Brazil; Citizen of Petén, Guatemala (originally from Belize); Young rider, Lo Barnachea, Santiago, Chile

Agricultural terraces at Colca canyon in the Western Cordillera of the Andes, Peru

began about 5000 BC, but village life was not established until 3000 BC and the population did not increase dramatically until 500 BC.

Horticulture was probably the first type of agriculture practised, followed by a form of shifting cultivation of either seed or root crops. The latter form of cultivation requires that, after several years of cultivation, plots are abandoned to fallow in order that they may regain some of their lost fertility. This means that although shifting cultivation supports larger populations than hunting, gathering and fishing, the density of the population is limited by the need for fallowing. Characteristically, populations associated with this type of cultivation formed permanent or semi-permanent hamlets and villages of several hundred, and occasionally up to 2000 people. Such communities were common in the Amazon and Orinoco basins at the time of the conquest; but in other areas, where agriculture was practised, more intensive forms of cultivation had been developed.

Amongst the techniques introduced to intensify and expand production were irrigation and the construction of *chinampas* (artificial islands, constructed in shallow lakes), ridged fields and terraces. It has been estimated that whereas under shifting cultivation about 10 to 20 hectares of land are required to support a family, with irrigation and *chinampas* the amount is reduced to three quarters and half a hectare respectively. Similarly, ridged fields, which were constructed to extend cultivation into seasonally flooded areas, could have supported about 1000 people per sq km, whilst terracing extended cultivation on steep slopes, particularly in the narrow valleys of the Andes. The increase in the size of the population that could be supported was accompanied by the beginnings of social stratification and political organization. Chiefdoms formed with populations of between 5000 and 20,000 people, or even more. For example, the five Chibcha chiefdoms (in what is now Colombia) each contained about 60,000 people. Minor ceremonial and civic centres emerged to serve outlying villages, thus indicating the beginnings of differentiation in the size, form and functions of settlements. At the time of the Spanish conquest chiefdoms were to be found in Central America, Colombia, Ecuador, Bolivia and the Greater Antilles.

POPULATION

In Mesoamerica and the Andes chiefdoms were short-lived and were gradually transformed into states, which were characterized by the presence of a hierarchy of classes and a complex political organization, which wove populations of tens and even hundreds of thousands together into large social units.

States were characterized by the presence of towns and cities. These may be distinguished from the earlier ceremonial centres by their larger size, the presence of a substantial residential population and the existence of distinct suburbs inhabited by different professions and social classes. These major towns and cities formed the apexes of extensive hierarchies of settlements ranging down to small villages and hamlets. The most notable of the early towns were Tiahuanaco in highland Bolivia and Teotihuacán in central Mexico, the latter with an estimated peak population of 50,000 to 100,000. At the time of the Spanish conquest the two major cities were Tenochtitlán, capital of the Aztec empire, and Cuzco, centre of the Inca empire, but they differed in size and form, as well as the functions they performed. Tenochtitlán had a highly concentrated population of between 150,000 and 300,000, whereas Cuzco possessed about 100,000 to 200,000 people and consisted of a core area, where the nobles, bureaucrats and priests resided, with the rest of the inhabitants living in residential settlements around the city. Whilst both cities performed administrative and religious roles, Tenochtitlán was also a major manufacturing, trading and military centre, giving it a more metropolitan character than Cuzco.

From the first peopling of the New World the population increased, although there were short-term fluctuations caused by natural disasters, famines and warfare. Famines were not only caused by natural disasters but by population increase outstripping the ability of the land to support it given the available technology. Shortages of food were probably a contributory factor in the collapse of the Maya civilization after AD 900 whilst Sherburne F. Cook and Jeffrey R. Parsons have shown that in central Mexico there were fluctuations in the population in the immediate pre-conquest period. In the latter area evidence for soil erosion and famines at that time suggests that the population was reaching saturation point to the extent that even if the Spanish conquest had not occurred, there would probably have been a decline in the Indian population. Population pressure is seen by many as the cause of the incessant warfare and political instability that characterized Mesoamerica and the Andes for about five hundred years before the conquest. Similarly, the annual sacrifice of between 10,000 and 50,000 victims, mainly war captives, by the Aztecs, whilst ostensibly to honour the gods, also served to control population expansion. Disease, which became a major factor in the decline of the Indian population in the colonial period, does not appear to have caused major fluctuations in the population in pre-Columbian times. Although the Indians suffered from a number of gastro-intestinal and respiratory infections, as well as syphilis, they had built

DISTRIBUTION OF CULTURAL TYPES

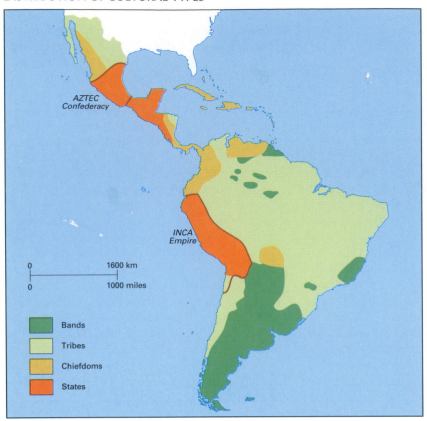

AZTEC
Confederacy

INCA
Empire

0   1600 km
0   1000 miles

■ Bands
□ Tribes
□ Chiefdoms
■ States

up a high resistance to them and they were free from severe epidemics.

There is still considerable controversy over the size of the population of Latin America and the Caribbean on the eve of the Spanish conquest. Estimates vary from 7.5 million to between 80 and 100 million and the variations reflect not only the type of evidence used but also the methodology and basic philosophy of researchers. There is a wealth of documentary evidence available for making such estimates. It includes accounts of the early conquistadors, soldiers and explorers, later administrative reports, including counts made for the assessment of tribute and labour services, church and missionary records, as well as some native accounts and recorded traditions, the most notable of which are the Aztec codices. Despite the wealth of evidence there are considerable problems of interpretation which in part account for the divergence of estimates. For example, there are difficulties in estimating the total population from the numbers baptized or fighting in battle, or paying tribute. Archaeological, ecological and cultural evidence has also been used to reconstruct the nature of the resources and technology, settlement pattern and social structure of Indian groups, which by comparison with similar present-day cultures may be used to give general indications of the size of native populations. Estimates of the native popula-

tion for small areas may be calculated using a wide variety of source materials, but such a task would be extremely time-consuming for the whole subcontinent and therefore a number of projection methods have been used. These generally involve the detailed examination of the demographic history of a small area, which is then taken to have been similar in areas with comparable cultures and environments. Often the rate of decline established is projected backwards from dates for which the demographic evidence is more reliable. The estimates of researchers have also been influenced by their interpretations of the nature of New World cultures and of history. Those who believe that the present is superior to the past and would emphasize the European contribution to Latin American culture are likely to underestimate the size of the native population and its decline as a result of European activities in the early colonial period, whilst those wishing to emphasize the native contribution and criticize the destruction brought about as the result of European domination are likely to exalt the native cultures and to come up with high population estimates. These views may strongly influence the interpretation of the evidence, for example, in judging whether the accounts of the early observers were exaggerated and in assessing the impact of disease.

Alfred L. Kroeber estimated that the aboriginal population of Latin America was a conservative 7.5 million, in the belief that the Indian population had grown at a regular rate since the time of the conquest and that the accounts of the early observers were exaggerated. Julian H. Steward accepted Kroeber's latter conclusion and, on the basis of evidence provided by the contributors to the *Handbook of South American Indians*, concluded that the aboriginal population of Latin America was 14.4 million. His estimate is not dissimilar to that of the Argentine scholar Angel Rosenblat, who, on the basis of documentary evidence, has estimated that the population was 12.3 million. These three authors have provided the three lowest estimates of the native population which alternative approaches have suggested are too low. Karl Sapper, on the basis of the resources and available technology of the Indians, suggested that the population was between 35 and 45 million, whilst Henry F. Dobyns, reviewing the demographic history of the hemisphere, concluded that insufficient account had been taken of the devastating impact of disease and suggested that the Indian population had been twenty to twenty-five times greater at the time of the conquest than at its nadir, which occurred at different times in different parts of Latin America. His estimate for Latin America was between 80 and 100 million and this high estimate is generally supported by Woodrow Borah, who has worked extensively on the demographic history of Mexico and the Caribbean.

Aymara Indians, with Mt Illimani in the background, Bolivia

Turning to estimates of the Indian population of specific areas there has been an equal diversity of opinion. For Mexico estimates range from Kroeber's 3.2 million to Dobyns's 30 to 37.5 million, whilst the most detailed study has been undertaken by Sherburne F. Cook and Woodrow Borah of central Mexico, which they estimate had a population of 25.2 million. This figure has been challenged on methodological grounds by William T. Sanders, who on the basis of archaeological, ecological and documentary evidence has estimated that the Aztec empire had between 5 and 6 million, and the whole of Mesoamerica only 12 to 15 million. Similar variations are to be found amongst estimates for the central Andes. They range from Kroeber's 3 million to Dobyns's 30 million, although the most frequently cited estimate is John H. Rowe's of 6 million. A recent review of the documentary evidence by Cook has led him to estimate 6 million for Peru alone, whilst a reworking of much of the evidence used by John H. Rowe has led C. T. Smith to suggest that the population of the central Andes was 12.1 million. Daniel E. Shea, on the other hand, believes that the decline in the population in the central Andes was less than in Mexico, partly due to the lesser impact of disease, and he has constructed a mathematical model to describe the demographic changes in the sixteenth century,

coming up with a conservative estimate of 2.0 to 2.9 million. A number of other regional estimates have been made of parts of Central America, Colombia, Argentina, Brazil and Amazonia. Reviewing the conclusions reached in all these regional studies, William M. Denevan has estimated that the aboriginal population of Latin America was 52.9 million, which falls mid-way between the range of estimates.

POPULATION DECLINE AFTER THE CONQUEST

Whilst Dobyns has suggested that the Indian population declined by a ratio of 20:1 to 25:1, that is by 95 to 96 per cent, between the time of contact and the population nadir, it is clear that there were regional and temporal variations in the rate of decline. Cook and Borah have calculated that in central Mexico between 1532 and 1608 the Indian population declined more rapidly on the coast, where the depopulation ratio was 26:1, than in the plateau area, where it was only 13:1. A similar difference in the decline of the Indian population on the coast and in the highlands has been identified by Smith in the central Andes, where the depopulation ratios between 1520–5 and 1570 were 58:1 and 3.4:1 respectively. Denevan also regards

TABLE 1

Estimates of population in pre-Columbian America on the eve of the Spanish conquest

	Kroeber 1939	Rosenblat 1954	Steward 1949
Mexico	3,200,000[a]	4,500,000	4,500,000
Central America	100,000[b]	800,000	736,000
Caribbean	200,000	300,000	225,000
Andes	3,000,000	4,750,000	6,131,000
Lowland South America	1,000,000[c]	2,035,000	2,898,000
Total	7,500,000	12,385,000	14,490,000

	Sapper 1924	Denevan 1976	Dobyns 1966
Mexico	12–15,000,000	21,400,000	30,000,000– 37,500,000
Central America	5– 6,000,000	5,650,000	10,800,000– 13,500,000
Caribbean	3– 4,000,000	5,850,000	443,000– 553,750
Andes	12–15,000,000	11,500,000	30,000,000– 37,500,000
Lowland South America	3– 5,000,000	8,500,000	9,000,000– 11,250,000
Total	35–45,000,000	52,900,000	80,243,000–100,303,750

[a] Includes Guatemala and El Salvador.
[b] Honduras and Nicaragua only.
[c] Includes Costa Rica and Panama.
[d] Colombia, Ecuador, Peru, Bolivia, Chile.

Dobyns's depopulation ratios for the highlands as too high, but maintains that they are not high enough for the tropical lowlands, which he suggests declined at a rate of 35:1. It is also clear that they are not high enough for the islands and fringing mainland of the Caribbean, where the Indian population became extinct within a generation. Clearly the timing of the decline varied with the date of contact, although it is possible that diseases reached areas ahead of the Spaniards. Thus many Indian groups living in the remote tropical lowlands did not come into contact with Europeans until the seventeenth and eighteenth centuries, by which time the Indian population in other parts of Latin America had begun to recover. Unfortunately less research has been done on this aspect of Indian demographic history, but it would appear that the recovery began first in Mexico in the middle of the seventeenth century, while increases began to be registered in Central America in the last decades of the seventeenth century, but they did not occur in Peru until the second half of the eighteenth century.

Causes of the decline in the Indian population were manifold, complex and interwoven. Two major causes were identified by contemporary observers: disease and the systematic killing, overwork and ill treatment of the Indians, an interpretation often described as the 'Black Legend'. Epidemic diseases introduced from the Old World were undoubtedly a major factor in the decline of the Indian population, which had no immunity to them. The most notable killers were smallpox, measles, typhus, plague, yellow fever and malaria. There are numerous accounts of the populations of villages and whole areas being reduced by one-third or a half as a result of epidemics, including the Aztec capital of Tenochtitlán whose population was halved as a result of a smallpox epidemic in 1520. Many Indians were killed in military encounters with the Spanish, whilst under slavery, the *encomienda* and later the *repartimiento* Indians were forced to work in poor conditions for long hours, with little or no pay and under threat of punishment for shortcomings. Bartolomé de las Casas, one of the most outspoken critics of Spanish activities in the New World, estimated that by 1560 40 million had died from such causes. Although few contemporary observers attributed the decline in the Indian population to the cultural changes that occurred as a result of the Spanish conquest and colonization it is clear that they were considerable. Spanish demands on Indian lands, labour and production led to food shortages and famines, whilst the breakdown in social organization of Indian communities and the psychological impact of the conquest led to a decrease in the fertility rate, contributed to by an increase in birth control, abortion and infanticide. As the Indians became integrated into the socio-economic life of the empire, *mestizaje* or racial mixing became a more significant factor in the decline of the Indian population, particularly in the towns, haciendas and mining centres. The recovery of the Indian population in many parts of Latin America may be accounted for by the abolition of the worst excesses of exploitation in the early sixteenth century by the introduction of the New Laws in 1542; by the increased immunity of the Indian population to the newly introduced diseases; by improvements in the Indian diet brought about by the introduction of livestock, although they were by no means uniform; and by the Indians generally reaching a new cultural equilibrium by adapting to the realities of Spanish conquest and colonization.

LN

Further Reading: S. F. Cook and W. Borah, *Essays in Population History, 3 vols.* (Berkeley and Los Angeles, 1971–4) A. W. Crosby, *The Columbian Exchange: Biological and Cultural Consequences of 1492* (Westport, Conn., 1972); W. M. Denevan, ed., *The Native Population of the Americas in 1492* (Madison, Wisconsin, 1976); N. Sánchez–Albornoz, *The Population of Latin America: A History* (Berkeley and Los Angeles, 1974)

Iberian colonial settlement

The study of Iberian migration to Latin America in the colonial period is for a variety of reasons of great importance to historians. First and foremost it is impossible to understand the origins and the nature of the societies which emerged in Spanish America and Brazil between the sixteenth and the early nineteenth centuries without detailed information on the motives, attitudes, and culture of the continual waves of Spaniards and Portuguese who crossed the Atlantic to the New World to form the apex of the sociopolitical pyramid created there in the colonial period. The investigation of the patterns of migration, the numbers of migrants, and their regional and class origins in the Old World is an essential part of the process of evaluating their behaviour in America. Consideration of these latter questions is also of significance for historians of peninsular Spain and Portugal, who desire to quantify and assess the impact on the mother countries of the drain of people to Latin America. The more that is known about the age, sex, occupational and regional distribution of emigrants, the easier it is, for example, to correlate emigration with other factors provoking economic decline in certain regions. This process, in its turn, throws light upon the more general question, relevant for all studies of migration, of whether the immigrant is pushed out by adverse conditions at home or pulled in by opportunities overseas. Finally a proper understanding of migration to Latin America in the colonial period provides a context and an antecedent within which historians of the nineteenth and twentieth centuries can study the massive trans-Atlantic migrations which occurred in the century before the Great Depression.

COLONIAL SPANISH SETTLEMENT

It is perhaps not surprising that more is known about the actual numbers involved in this latter period of migration than for the colonial period. Recent estimates suggest that some 11 million Europeans migrated to Latin America between 1824 and 1924 (compared with 48 million to North America), and that half of them went to Argentina, and one third to Brazil. The majority – an estimated 38 per cent between 1854 and 1924 – came from Italy, although Spain and Portugal, which had enjoyed a virtual monopoly of colonial migration, remained in second and third places, with 28 per cent and 11 per cent respectively. An interesting feature, also present, as we shall see, in the colonial period, although to a lesser degree, was that 40–50 per cent of the immigrants to Latin America in the national period (the period since independence) eventually returned to their countries of origin. The data available on the numbers of migrants who left Spain and Portugal for Latin America in the colonial period is, by contrast, much less precise, particularly for the seventeenth and eighteenth centuries; for the sixteenth century, however, a reasonably clear picture has emerged, at least for Spanish migration, largely because of painstaking research into detailed passenger registers preserved in the Archive of the Indies in Seville.

As soon as the enormous economic and political potential of the discoveries made by Christopher Columbus and subsequent explorers impressed itself upon the Spanish crown it took steps to impose a rigid control upon migration to America, in the hopes of excluding heretics, Jews, foreigners, and other undesirables from contact with its new Indian subjects. The control was relaxed for a few years in the reign of Charles I, who experimented with the policy of admitting his non-Spanish subjects, but after 1538 non-Spaniards were strictly forbidden to settle in or even visit America. The policy could never be enforced with total rigidity, despite the fact that throughout the Habsburg period most shipping for the empire left from the single port of Seville: determined foreigners could bribe officials or obtain decrees of naturalization, while the very volume of trade which rapidly developed between Seville and

Recruitment of Spaniards for the conquest of Peru, from Guamán Poma, La nueva corónica

Latin American surnames

Spanish Americans, like Spaniards, have *two* official surnames; their father's, which comes first, and then their mother's (maiden name), which comes second. For most everyday purposes (and on most occasions in this Encyclopedia) the first surname is used on its own, e.g. Fidel CASTRO, rather than Fidel CASTRO RUZ. When the first surname is very common, some people use both surnames all the time, e.g. the Chilean president (1956–52) Gabriel GONZALEZ VIDELA, who doubtless wanted to distinguish himself from all the other people in the world called González. In the old days, the conjunction 'y' ('and') was used to link the two surnames, e.g. José ORTEGA Y GASSET, but this has become less common in the Spanish-speaking world.

Marriage brings further complications. A Señor (Mr) Francisco AGUIRRE might marry a Señorita (Miss) Maria ROMERO. The bride will be known henceforth as Señora (Mrs) Maria ROMERO DE AGUIRRE. Their children, of course, will be called AGUIRRE ROMERO.

Brazilians who, of course, are Portuguese-speaking have a different system. The mother's maiden name comes first, the father's (or principal) surname second, e.g. the Brazilian statesman Getúlio VARGAS. Senhor (Mr) VARGAS married a girl called Senhorita (Miss) Darcy SAMANHO. She became Senhora (Mrs) Darcy SAMANHO VARGAS. Their children (they had five) had the surnames SAMANHO VARGAS. (*Note:* the linking 'de' ('of') found in Spanish American married women's surnames – as in Romero *de* Aguirre, the example shown above – does not appear in Brazilian married women's surnames.)

It should not be forgotten that surnames in Latin America, as elsewhere, can sometimes be double–barrelled, e.g. Argentina's finance minister (1976–81) José Alfredo MARTINEZ DE HOZ (full name: MARTINEZ DE HOZ CARCANO), or Brazil's military president (1964–7) Humerto CASTELLO BRANCO (full name: DE ALENCAR CASTELLO BRANCO).

Don and *Doña* (or *Dom* and *Dona* in Brazil) are simply polite and nowadays slightly old-fashioned forms of address or reference, used (as with the title 'Sir' in Great Britain) before Christian names (never surnames), e.g. Don Francisco, Doña Maria, Dom Getúlio, etc. This use is still fairly common but is by no means universal any more, and conventions on this point differ from one Latin American country to the next.

America provided another loophole, for the ships engaged in it were often crewed by non-Spaniards – notably Portuguese and Italians – many of whom remained in the New World after voyaging there. But tens of thousands of *bona fide* Spanish emigrants faithfully went through the complex bureaucratic procedure required for obtaining licences of embarkation, and it is the surviving records of their applications, coupled with the lists of departing passengers prepared for the Council of the Indies by officials in Seville, which provide the best sources for researchers. The general consensus which has emerged from an examination of these records is that a maximum of 300,000 people migrated from Spain to America between 1492 and 1600; a similar result is obtained by the alternative method of multiplying the number of ships which sailed by the average number of passengers carried by a sample of them. From one standpoint the total may seem surprisingly small – by contrast up to 300,000 people were entering Argentina each year at the height of the migration boom of the national period. On the other hand it represents an average annual outflow from Spain of some 3000 people for over a century. Population in the mother country was probably rising in the sixteenth century, to reach about 8 million by 1600, but the majority of migrants were young, vigorous males, often with artisan skills, while an increasing percentage of those who populated the mother country were economically inactive. A detailed examination of no less than 55,000 individuals known to have sailed to America between 1492 and 1600 (undertaken by Peter Boyd-Bowman) also reveals that certain regions of Spain, notably Andalusia, Extremadura, and Castile, bore the brunt of the population outflow, whereas provinces in the north and the east were affected to a much smaller extent.

In the seventeenth century, as Spain itself declined and Spanish America grew richer, the pace of migration was accelerated, although not dramatically, and it also began to draw in an increasing number of northern Spaniards, traditionally thought of as more industrious and resourceful than their Andalusian counterparts. The estimate of 450,000 for the century as a whole, proposed by Antonio Domínguez Ortiz, is generally accepted, and is broadly confirmed by the ship-counting method, referred to above, which produces a figure of some 200,000 for the first half of the century. This relentless annual drain of 4000–5000 people was clearly a contributory factor of some significance in the economic and demographic recession which afflicted Spain in the seventeenth century, particularly as it removed men, and an increasing number of women, who were in the age group capable of producing children. But it has to be kept in perspective: great plagues in Castile in 1597–1602 and 1649–52 each cost half a million lives, the expulsion of the Moriscos from Valencia in 1609–14 accounted for the loss of at least 100,000 peasants, and between 1635 and 1659 the war in Flanders was costing an estimated 12,000 men a year. As

Spanish missionaries attempting to introduce Catholicism in Venezuela (from Theodore de Bry, America)

the vicious cycle of depression was accelerated by these and other catastrophes the attractions of migration to America must have become increasingly evident to poor yet ambitious Spaniards who saw little prospect of bettering themselves in the mother country.

LATER SPANISH MIGRANTS

In attempting to assess the volume of migration in the eighteenth century from Spain to America, we have to rely upon fleeting glimpses and unsubstantiated suggestions, for virtually no primary research has been undertaken into the subject. It is recorded, for example, that in 1742 the viceroyalty of New Spain (modern Mexico and Central America) contained some 450,000 whites, of whom 29,000 were Europeans. Over 80 per cent of this immigrant group were male Spaniards, many of whom would marry into local families, thereby creating space for further waves of male migrants from the mother country. There is a substantial amount of literary evidence to suggest that the traditional influx of Basques and other northern Spaniards into the commercial sector accelerated in the last third of the eighteenth century: the number of peninsular Spaniards resident in Mexico City, 1182 in 1689, had doubled by 1792. In this period travellers in various parts of Spanish America commented upon the deep-seated hostility between creoles (whites born in America) and *peninsulares* or *gachupines*, as European Spaniards were described, caused primarily by the belief of the former that their native lands were being invaded by shiploads of parsimonious northern Spaniards, anxious to exploit the economic and commercial boom which characterized

Spanish America as a whole in the second half of the eighteenth century. By the turn of the century the European-born constituted only 2 per cent of the population of Mexico City (2500 out of 137,000), according to the German traveller Alexander von Humboldt, whereas creoles accounted for 48 per cent (65,000); but the newcomers comprised the dominant entrepreneurial class, active in commerce and mining, whereas the creoles were represented primarily in landholding and in the bureaucracy. The most senior positions in government, the army, and the Church were reserved for Europeans, however, particularly in this late colonial period, when the Bourbon kings of Spain made a determined effort to increase the actual authority of the crown in its far-flung American possessions. Spanish writers of the period confirm the impressions of visitors to America: the influential José de Campillo suggested in a work of 1742, for example, that some 14,000 people a year were emigrating, and that over the centuries about a million Spaniards must have gone to America, and Gerónimo de Uztáriz commented that most emigrants to America in his time were from Cantabria, Navarre, Asturias, Galicia, and Burgos. Andalusians continued to go in significant numbers to certain parts of South America, and we also know of colonization schemes which took some 5000 Canary Islanders to Santo Domingo, Texas, and Florida between 1700 and 1764. No historian has yet hazarded a guess at total emigration to America in the eighteenth century, but it must have been at least as large as that of the seventeenth century, and was probably larger, particularly in the relatively peaceful and prosperous years between 1763 and 1796. The final great influx occurred, ironically, in the aftermath of the Napoleonic Wars, as Ferdinand VII despatched large contingents of European troops to America in an ultimately vain attempt to defeat the revolutions for independence which had begun in 1810: General Pablo Morillo, for example, took an expedition of 10,500 men to Venezuela in 1815, thereby almost doubling an immigrant population estimated to have numbered 12,000 in 1800.

The exact number of Europeans resident in Spanish America by the early nineteenth century is difficult to ascertain, partly because most population counts indiscriminately lumped creoles and *peninsulares* together as 'Spaniards' (*españoles*). Humboldt suggested 200,000–300,000, although this was probably an overestimate: his separate figure of up to 80,000 in New Spain compares with a modern estimate of a mere 15,000, which, in its turn, is perhaps too small. A figure of 150,000 for Spanish America as a whole is probably about right; in 1570, by contrast, there had been a mere 60,000. But at this earlier date the European Spaniards had outnumbered, albeit

Portuguese settlers punishing slaves on a Brazilian sugar plantation, early nineteenth century (from a lithograph by Deroy after Rugendas)

slightly, the creole element in a total white population of some 115,000, whereas by the end of the colonial period the 150,000 Europeans were swamped by a creole population of more than 3 million. By 1800 the creoles themselves formed a distinct minority of the total Spanish American population of 16.9 million, in which the largest racial groups were 7.5 million Indians and 5.3 million of mixed descent (mestizos). Many of them, moreover, were somewhat less white than the upstart immigrants whose social superiority they resented. But the creoles insisted on their 'Spanish' identity – in speech, dress, manners, and so on – in order to preserve their own supremacy over the Indian, mestizo, and black masses. When in 1810 there began the revolutions which brought independence to all the mainland of Spanish America by 1825, many creoles initially fought against the rebels, such was the strength of creole conservatism and allegiance to the crown; most (though not quite all) *peninsulares*, on the other hand, championed the cause of the mother country. The consequence was that the attainment of independence in most of the new states was swiftly followed by the forced expulsion of those European Spaniards who had not already left voluntarily: many went, with their capital and expertise, to the surviving Spanish colonies of Cuba and Puerto Rico, which were to enjoy unprece-

dented prosperity as sugar producers in the nineteenth century, whereas those who had been in government service, whether civilian or military, tended to return to the peninsula to join the scramble for office there.

PORTUGUESE MIGRATION TO BRAZIL

If firm data on Spanish colonial migration to America is patchy, that relating to Portuguese migration to Brazil is almost non-existent, although general patterns can be identified. Systematic attempts to send settlers to Brazil did not begin until 1534 when, in an attempt to counteract a growing French presence there, John III established a dozen hereditary captaincies, and entrusted the *donatários*, or lord proprietors, to whom they were granted, with the responsibility for settling them and defending them against both Indians and European interlopers. At this time the population of peninsular Portugal was at most 1.4 million. Emigration was already a well-established feature, particularly from the northern provinces of Minho and Douro – one convincing estimate suggests that on average in the sixteenth century some 2400 people a year, mostly young, unmarried males, left for overseas. But the majority of them headed for the proven riches of the East, despite the high risk of shipwreck or disease during the eight-month voyage to India, rather than to dangerous Brazil where, in these early decades of colonization, the dangers of ending up in a Tupinambá cooking pot loomed large, at least in popular imagination. One consequence was that the Portuguese crown adopted a more liberal policy than its Spanish counterpart in relation to the admission of foreigners to America, allowing in all who professed to be Christian (i.e. Catholic) rather than attempting to restrict permission to Portuguese nationals. The latter predominated – although, paradoxically, many were Jews – but considerable numbers of Dutchmen and other non-Iberians were also to be found in Brazil in this early period. The union with Spain (1580–1640) ushered in the more restrictive policy already in force for Spanish America, but, by way of compensation, substantial numbers of Spaniards began to go to southern Brazil, particularly to the area around São Paulo. The old policy was reintroduced after 1640, with Dutch and English traders and adventurers being the principal beneficiaries, but major gold strikes in the 1690s ushered in a more mercantilist policy, which was to persist for the remainder of the colonial period, of restricting migration from Europe to Portuguese. The forced migration of black slaves from Africa to Brazil, which far exceeded white migration, was, of course, a separate issue, although one which was to have a profound effect on the nature and composition of colonial society in Brazil.

The introduction of both whites and blacks to Brazil is known to have increased substantially in the last quarter of the sixteenth century, primarily as a response to the boom in sugar cultivation in the area around Bahia. By 1600, it is usually suggested, there were about 100,000 non-Indians in Brazil, of whom 30,000 were whites and 70,000 blacks or of mixed descent. Migration continued at a moderate pace in the first half of the seventeenth century, when significant numbers of newcomers were deportees, but began to accelerate in the second half, when contraction in the East, caused by Dutch rivalry, coupled with recession in the metropolis, made Brazil a more attractive prospect. By 1700 the non-Indian population of Brazil had grown threefold to 300,000, of whom roughly 100,000 were nominally of Portuguese, and 200,000 of African origin. How many of these 100,000 were born in Portugal it is impossible even to guess, although it has been estimated that an average input of 500 immigrants a year from the mother country over the previous two centuries would have been sufficient to produce a white population of this size. Throughout this period the population of Portugal itself seems to have remained remarkably stable, despite the toll of migration,

famine, epidemics and other disasters, at about 1.5 million. Migration to Brazil undoubtedly multiplied in the first two decades of the eighteenth century, reaching a peak of 5000–6000 a year, in response to rich gold strikes in Minas Gerais. It remained substantial in the second half of the eighteenth century, too, as the mineral boom was followed by the revival of the sugar industry and rapid development of cotton and tobacco cultivation. The increasing attention which the mother country paid to Brazil saw the influx of substantial numbers of administrators and soldiers, particularly after 1750, and there was also a marked increase in the number of private emigrants anxious, as in Spanish America, to establish themselves in the commercial sector. The attitude of the crown fluctuated from an attempt in 1720 to limit the outflow by requiring all migrants to obtain government passports to ambitious schemes in the mid-century to send 4000 peasant families from the overpopulated Azores to the provinces of Santa Caterina and Rio Grande do Sul, in southern Brazil. Demographic growth in Portugal itself, where the population numbered 3 million by the end of the eighteenth century, more than compensated for the loss to Brazil. But by this period the population of the colony was also growing dramatically, reaching 3 million by 1798, of whom 1 million were of white descent (a tenfold increase since 1700), 1.5 million slaves, and the remainder Indians and free coloureds. By 1818, on the eve of the attainment of independence, total population had increased to almost 4 million, primarily because of a substantial increase in the black population.

The final decade or so of colonial rule in Brazil was a period of unprecedented prosperity, primarily because of the forced migration there in 1807–8 of the Portuguese royal family and thousands of its followers anxious to escape the Napoleonic invasion of Portugal. With the final defeat of Napoleon in 1815 the majority of these newcomers realized, as had generations of earlier immigrants, that they preferred to remain in Brazil rather than return to the mother country, thereby setting in train a complex series of political events which was to lead the heir to the Portuguese throne to declare Brazilian independence in 1822, with himself as the country's first emperor, Pedro I. The transition was much more peaceful than in Spanish America, primarily because most Portuguese residents in Brazil, like Brazilian whites generally, were willing to support a movement which preserved monarchical legitimacy and social stability. A small number of Portuguese returned to the peninsula immediately after 1822, and rather more in 1831, when Pedro was overthrown (to be replaced as emperor in due course by his son Pedro II), but the majority recognized that slave-holding, patristic Brazil offered the safer haven for the relatively easy life to which they had grown accustomed.

The general phenomenon of re-emigration was one which certainly existed throughout the period of Iberian colonialism in America, although it is absolutely impossible to measure it. A detailed study of the 168 conquerors of Peru who were with Francisco Pizarro in 1532 shows that no less than 74 of them (44 per cent) eventually returned to Spain, and it may also be assumed that some of the 36 (21 per cent) whose destiny cannot be ascertained also did so. A substantial proportion, probably a majority, of the senior administrators, soldiers, and churchmen sent out to the Americas over the next three centuries would have remained there for fixed terms rather than in perpetuity, while many merchants almost commuted across the Atlantic, particularly in the eighteenth century. On the other hand, the attitude of many ordinary migrants who financed their own journeys was probably similar to that of a tailor, Alonso Morales, who wrote in 1576 from Puebla (Mexico) to his cousin in Extremadura:

> Your brother and I keep shop here and are doing well. . . . So you would give me great pleasure in leaving that misery there and coming here, because it would be greatly to your advantage. . . . Get my brother Pedro to come with you, and leave that wretched country, because it is only for people who have a lot of money, and here, no matter how poor a man may be, he never lacks a horse to ride and food to eat.

Men such as this, who probably constituted the vast majority of Iberian colonial migrants to Latin America, were never likely to return to Europe. Wealthy merchants, landowners, miners, and administrators frequently did return to Spain and Portugal to display their American-acquired wealth in somewhat vulgar ostentation until the very end of the eighteenth century. When they began to cease to do so in the first decade of the nineteenth century, because retirement to Rio de Janeiro or Mexico offered greater security and comfort than return to Lisbon or Madrid, the shift was symbolic of the fact that the American empires of Spain and Portugal had outgrown the mother countries. Independence was the inevitable outcome.   JRF

Further Reading: I. Altman, *Emigrants and Society: Extremadura and Spanish America in the Sixteenth Century* (Berkeley and Los Angeles, 1989); P. Boyd-Bowman, *Patterns of Spanish Emigration to the New World (1493–1580)* (Buffalo, NY, 1973); J. Lockhart, *The Men of Cajamarca* (Austin, Texas, 1972); D. J. Robinson, ed., *Migration in Colonial Spanish America* (Cambridge, 1990)

African slave migration

From small beginnings in the 1440s until its demise in the second half of the nineteenth century, the atlantic slave trade carried one of the greatest forced migrations of history: that of African peoples taken into slavery in the Americas. Estimates of the volume of the slave trade vary widely, but there is no doubt that it uprooted millions of people and involved a significant depopulation of the African continent. Of the slaves taken in Africa, an unknown number perished before embarkation for the Americas and many more died in the harsh conditions of the transatlantic crossing. Probably about 9.5 to 10 million survived to become slaves who, with their descendants, came to constitute an important, sometimes preponderant element of the American regions in which they were settled.

The Atlantic slave trade was first developed by Portuguese traders during the second half of the fifteenth century, taking black captives from sub-Saharan Africa as part of a trade in several commodities. Until the mid-sixteenth century the traffic in slaves – which soon came to dominate commerce with Africa – was primarily geared to meeting demands for unfree labour in the Old World. Between 1441 and 1550, more than half of the slaves extracted from the coasts of West Africa were destined for the labour market in Europe, particularly in the Iberian peninsula, or for use in the emergent plantation economies of the Atlantic islands. However, in quantatitive terms, the slave trade to the Old World was to pale into insignificance compared to the formidable flows of human cargoes which swept across the Atlantic to the Americas after about 1550. Henceforth, the Atlantic slave trade assumed patterns of growth and distribution over time and space which responded to the rhythms of economic development in the areas of European settlement and dominion in the Americas. The principal patterns of temporal and spatial expansion in the African migrations generated by the slave trade may be traced in table 2.

In terms of distribution over time, the estimates given opposite suggest that slave immigration into the Americas passed through several distinct phases, in which changes in the scale of the slave trade were associated with variations in the distribution of slave imports between regions. The first broad phase of growth took place during the second half of the sixteenth century, when the number of slaves arriving in the Americas surpassed those who went to Old World destinations. At this stage, most of them went

TABLE 2
Slave imports into the Americas, 1451–1870

Importing region	1451–1600	1601–1700	1701–1810	1811–70	Total per region
Old World (Europe, Atlantic Islands, São Tomé)	149,900	25,100	–	–	175,000
Spanish America	75,000	292,000	578,600	606,000	1,552,100
Brazil	50,000	560,000	1,891,400	1,145,400	3,646,800
British North America	–	–	348,000	51,000	399,000
British Caribbean	–	263,700	1,401,300	–	1,665,000
French Caribbean	–	155,800	1,348,400	96,000	1,600,200
Dutch Caribbean	–	40,000	460,000	–	500,000
Danish Caribbean	–	4000	24,000	–	28,000
Total	274,900	1,341,100	6,051,700	1,898,400	9,566,100

Source: Philip D. Curtin, *The Atlantic Slave Trade: a Census*, p. 268.

to the Spanish colonies which, between 1451 and 1600, took some 60 per cent of slaves landed in the Americas. Towards the end of the sixteenth century, the Portuguese settlements in Brazil gave a new impetus to African immigration and, by the early seventeenth century, Brazil emerged as the major market for black slaves. Over the century as a whole, Brazil absorbed about 42 per cent of all slaves brought to the Americas. In the latter half of the seventeenth century, the slave trade spread away from the Iberian powers' colonies into the possessions of North European nations in the Caribbean. The English West Indies, in particular, offered a new and important market in the latter half of the century when, in a burst of growth, they absorbed almost as many slaves as were taken into the Spanish colonies over the century as a whole. The emergence of new slave markets in the Caribbean presaged the great era of growth in the eighteenth century. Not only did Brazil continue

SOURCES AND DESTINATIONS OF THE AFRICAN SLAVE TRADE TO THE AMERICAS

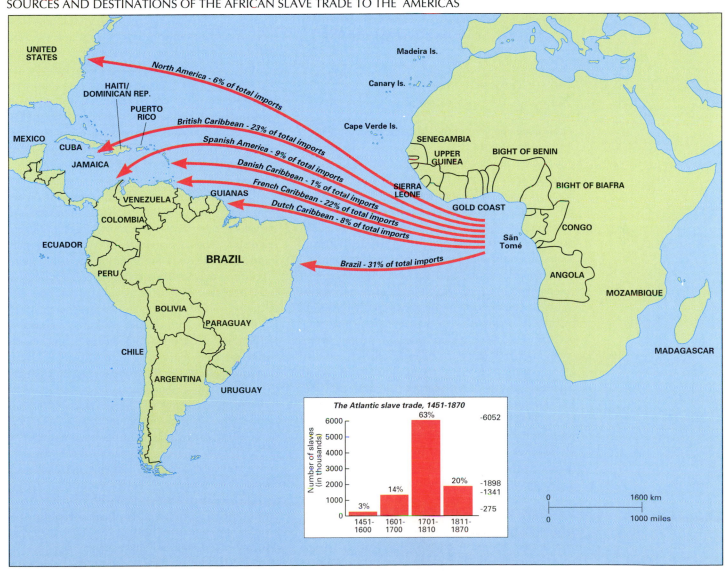

139

to take in growing numbers of Africans, but demand in the Caribbean islands pushed the trade to unprecedented levels. The French and British islands alone accounted for about 45 per cent of total American slave imports during this period, while the additional demand of the Spanish, Dutch and Danish islands ensured that the Caribbean region received more than half of the six million slaves landed in the Americas during the period 1701–1810. Thus, the major phase of African slave migration (in which about 60 per cent of all slaves carried to the western hemisphere were landed) was closely bound up with developments in the Caribbean and in Brazil. Not surprisingly, these were the areas in which African immigration had greatest impact on social and economic development, for between them they had absorbed about 80 per cent of all African migrants to the New World. Even when the trade entered into its final, declining phase in the nineteenth century, Brazil and the Spanish Caribbean islands continued to exert their baneful influence by keeping the institution of slavery and the currents of the slave trade alive long after they had been suppressed elsewhere.

THE ECONOMIC IMPORTANCE OF SLAVES

These developments in the scale and spatial spread of African slave immigrants corresponded with changing requirements for manpower in the Americas. Already familiar with the use of African slaves, Spaniards took them as personal servants on their early expeditions of conquest and later extended the employment of slaves to meet a variety of special needs. By the end of the sixteenth century, African slaves and their half-caste offspring had become an important element in both Spanish and Portuguese colonial societies, and were almost as numerous as the white settlers themselves. The settlement and occupational patterns of nascent Afro-American society varied from region to region. African slaves were mainly located in areas where Amerindian labour was inadequate for the needs of white colonists. In the highlands of Mesoamerica and South America, where the Spaniards encountered dense Amerindian peasant populations whose labour could be used in agriculture and silver mining, black slaves were used chiefly as skilled artisans and domestic servants, and formed a relatively small part of the population. The main areas of African resettlement were in the tropical lowland regions of the Caribbean islands and the mainland coastal zones, where indigenous peoples were far fewer in number and where Africans provided a substitute labour force in both rural and urban areas. Here African

slaves were used in a variety of occupations, including gold mining, but the main source of demand arose from the development of plantation agriculture, producing tropical crops for overseas markets.

The pre-eminent export crop was sugar, and the primary centre of its production was Brazil. By the late sixteenth century Brazil had become Europe's principal source of sugar, and the establishment of plantations on the rich alluvial soils of its north-eastern coastal centres greatly accelerated the transmission of African slaves to the Americas. Moreover, where Brazil had shown a way, others followed. When the Dutch were expelled from Brazil in the mid-seventeenth century, they transplanted the techniques of sugar cultivation on slave-based plantations to the Caribbean islands, where their rapid dissemination among the colonies of the new imperial powers soon undermined Brazil's lead in world sugar production. By the early eighteenth century, Jamaica had become the world's single largest sugar producer, foreshadowing the emergence of the English and French West Indies as the core of a transoceanic commercial system founded on sugar and slaves, a system which extended to include the Spanish islands, especially Cuba, in the latter half of the century. Thus most of the Africans who were forcibly resettled in the Americas were destined to work on the land, as labourers in plantations producing sugar and, on a lesser scale, tobacco, cacao, indigo, cotton and coffee.

As the slave trade expanded in response to these growing demands, so its organizers sought out new sources of supply on the African continent. When Portuguese traders initiated the trade in the later fifteenth century, slaves were mostly taken from the region of Senegambia on the West African coast immediately south of the Sahara. Gradually slaving expeditions extended the catchment area for slaves as the Portuguese established new bases farther south in the regions of modern Guinea and Sierra Leone. During the sixteenth century, this area – known as the 'Guinea of Cape Verde' – was to become one of two major zones for slaving; the other was much farther south, on the Central African coast, just beyond the mouth of the Congo River.

During the seventeenth century, Central African sources grew in importance, and Spanish America took an increasingly large proportion of its slave migrants from Angola. After the 1640s, Iberian control of the trade faced rising competition from Dutch, English, French and other northern European slavers and the pattern of African supply became more complex as the slavers of different nations concentrated on different regions in Africa. The vagaries of contemporary statistics preclude accurate identification of the ethnic origins of African slaves but, as the slave trade entered its phase of greatest expansion in the eighteeth century, a rough pattern of development may be discerned. The West African coastal regions from Senegambia to the Bight of Biafra continued to be exploited, but with greater intensity, mainly by English and French traders seeking slaves for their Caribbean colonies. However, while West Africa still supplied about 59 per cent of the eigtheenth-century Atlantic slave trade, Central and East Africa opened new frontiers for growth. Over the century as a whole, the trade in these areas was dominated by the Portuguese and the majority of slaves entering Brazil came from the region of Angola. Slave migration from this region was further expanded in the 1780s, when British and French slavers stepped up their purchases of human cargoes drawn from among the Bantu-speaking peoples of the Central African hinterlands. In the late eighteenth century, growing numbers of slaves were also taken from East Africa, in a trade organized by the Portuguese from stations established in Mozambique, and were sent mainly to Brazil and southern South America. This shift towards Central and East African sources became more pronounced during the decline of the slave trade in the nineteenth century, when the great bulk of slave exports derived from the region just north of the Congo River, from Angola and, to a lesser extent, from south-eastern Africa through Mozambique.

ADJUSTMENT TO THEIR NEW SOCIETIES

Drawn from such diverse regions, Africans sent to the Americas came from a wide range of economic and cultural backgrounds, including peoples from forests and savannas, from matrilineal and patrilineal societies, from simple tribal organizations and from stratified kingdoms, with many forms of religious life. Uprooted from their native habitats and thrust together in an alien environment dominated by whites, Africans were not able simply to reproduce their societies in the New World. Although imported slaves tended to be young, their introduction into new disease environments led to high rates of morbidity and mortality, while the generally high ratio of males to females discouraged a high rate of natural increase among African migrants. These factors, together with the breakup of African families and communities during and after shipment to slave markets, inhibited the physical and cultural reproduction of African social traditions. Instead, Africans were forced to submit to a system of social and economic stratification in which they, as slaves, were relegated to the lowest position, and excluded from full participation in the societies in which they were made to live.

As slaves, Africans were universally regarded as units of private property, disposable chattels who were subject to the ownership rights of their masters and deprived of the civil rights which the law bestowed on free persons. Although the laws of slave societies expressed the interests of slaveowners, slaves could not logically be regarded merely as inanimate objects devoid of recognized human needs for physical and spiritual sustenance. Consequently, the absolute power of slaveholders could be restrained, either by special legal codes laid down by governments, or by customs and conventions which emerged from local practices governing master–slave relations. In the Catholic cultures of Latin America, slaves were theoretically afforded rights to marriage, to protection from cruelty, and, under special circumstances, to manumission by self-purchase. In contrast, in the Protestant cultures of the West Indies and British North America slaves were supposedly denied such opportunities and treated with greater severity in more rigidly segregated societies. However, the recognition of the slave as a moral personality did not release him from a servile status, nor did it necessarily influence the treatment that he received. In practice such differences in legal and cultural norms were less important in influencing the status and treatment of slaves than were more specific conditions, such as the type of economic activity in which the slave was engaged, the size of the productive unit in which he lived, and market conditions for the commodity which he produced. Thus, although slavery was not a homogeneous institution, differences in the character of slave regimes cannot be attributed solely to broad cultural differences between the host societies; strong regional and temporal variations were of equal, if not greater significance.

The importance of African slave migrants for the development of major regions in the Americas was not merely economic; Africans and their descendants

Diagrammatic drawing of slaves packed on board a slave-ship (from an early nineteenth-century print)

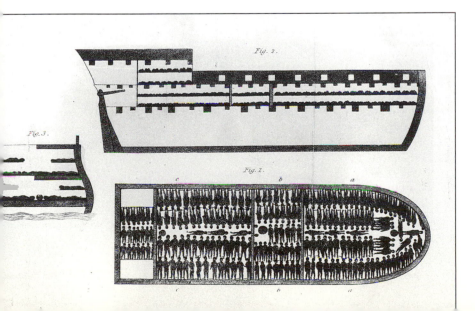

also contributed to the formation of distinctively American cultures. Despite the deep trauma of capture, transportation and enslavement, with the consequent severance of family and community ties, slaves did not lose all contact with the cultures of their past. In Brazil and in the Caribbean islands, where the plantation was the central social and economic institution, where there was a constant influx of Africans, and where blacks and mulattos formed the largest element of the population, there appeared many of the most vigorous Afro-American cultural forms. African influences manifested themselves in music, language, work techniques, and, perhaps most importantly, in religious beliefs and practices. Little is known of the history of African cultural survivals before the eighteenth century; however, from that time at least there were distinctive religious cults in Brazil and the West Indies, fusing with, and competing against, the Christianity of dominant white society. Cults such as Obeah and Myalism in the Anglophone Caribbean, Vodùn in Haiti, and Candomblé, Xangô and Macumba in Brazil, all testified to the transmission of African patterns of worship.

The response of Africans and their offspring to slavery also took more tangible shape in various forms of open rejection of, and resistance to, white society. Not only did individual slaves flee from servitude, but runaway slaves also formed their own communities, known as *maroons*, *palenques* and *quilombos*, which were *de facto* autonomous polities beyond the authority of white-controlled governments. Organized rebellions by plantation slaves, seeking the redress of grievances suffered at the hands of their masters, were also common throughout Latin America and the Caribbean, though they rarely resulted in concerted movements for emancipation. Only in Haiti did slave rebellion form the basis for a revolutionary movement which in 1804 replaced colonial government with an independent republic headed by an ex-slave.

The end of slavery

Elsewhere, an end to slavery came more gradually and was bound up with the decline and cessation of the slave trade. Although the slave trade had already passed its peak by the early nineteenth century, a crucial step towards abolition was taken in 1807, when Britain outlawed the slave trade in its colonial possessions and thereby inaugurated a movement to end the flow of slaves across the Atlantic. During the Spanish American wars of independence, creole independists followed this lead, with attempts to abolish the trade in Venezuela and Mexico in 1810, in Chile in 1811, and in Buenos Aires in 1812. More-

over, many slaves won their freedom through military service during the struggles for independence. But a definitive end to slave trading and slavery awaited the establishment of republican governments and increased British pressure to outlaw the trade. Chile, Central America and Mexico, where slavery was of marginal economic importance, were among the first Hispanic republics to emancipate their slaves, in 1823, 1824 and 1829 respectively. In the British Caribbean, abolition came in 1834, an example followed by the French in 1848, and the Dutch in 1863. In Venezuela, Ecuador, Colombia and Peru, where slaveholders were politically influential, complete abolition was delayed until the 1840s and early 1850s. In Brazil and the Spanish Caribbean islands of Puerto Rico and Cuba, slavery endured even longer. In Puerto Rico, abolition was finally decreed in 1878; in Cuba, it was not fully enacted until 1886, while Brazil remained the last area of slavery in Latin America until the 'Golden Law' of 1888 proclaimed unconditional emancipation.

The termination of African slave migration to Latin America and the Caribbean was, then, a slow and uneven process. Even after provisions were made to free newborn slaves, and international agreements were made to end the slave traffic, an active clandestine commerce sustained transatlantic and intra-American transfers of slaves until the 1870s. Their main destinations were the coffee zones of Brazil, where expanding coffee plantations sustained a market for slaves, and Cuba, where sugar plantations continued to draw on new, illicit supplies of slaves from Africa until the early 1870s. Thus, though greatly reduced by the mid-nineteenth century, the slave trade died hard. So long as the economic conditions which had created markets for African slaves persisted, then both the commerce in slaves and the institution of slavery endured. To exploit the resources of Latin American and Caribbean territories required supplies of manpower which, when not available locally, were brought from abroad. Thus, when the long waves of African slave migration finally subsided in the second half of the nineteenth century, new waves of free European migrants were gathering force, signalling the emergence of new configurations in the world economy and resulting in the next great era of transatlantic migrations to the New World.   AMcF

Further Reading: R. Blackburn, *The Overthrow of Colonial Slavery 1776–1848* (London, 1988); P. D. Curtin, *The Atlantic Slave Trade: A Census* (Madison, 1969); D. Eltis, *Economic Growth and the Ending of the Transatlantic Slave Trade* (New York, 1988); J. C. Miller, *Way of Death: Merchant Capitalism and the Angolan Slave Trade 1730–1830* (Madison, Wisconsin,1988)

Immigration since 1850

Immigrants are the unsung heroes of Latin American history. Although every Latin American country is, to a greater or lesser extent, a nation of immigrants, their contributions to society are only rarely acknowledged. There is nothing comparable in Latin America to the United States myth of immigrant pioneers conquering and taming an intractable wilderness.

In comparison with the 33 million Europeans who emigrated to the United States in the classic period of mass migration (1800–1930) only some 7 to 9 million went to Latin America, and these were concentrated in Argentina and Uruguay with their populations of predominantly European descent and in Brazil, Chile, Costa Rica, Cuba and Venezuela whose populations were more mixed. Elsewhere, the European strain stems from the earlier migrations of the colonial period and has since been diluted by miscegenation.

POLICY AMBIGUITIES

Owners and hands on a nineteenth-century Argentine cattle estancia

The uneven pattern of immigration settlement in the independence period was conditioned by labour needs, climate and politics. Where ownership of land was concentrated in the hands of a few families and where Indian or African slave labour was available, there was little incentive to attract land-hungry European peasants, for whom the United States offered clearer opportunities to own land, for social advancement and political and religious freedom. Nor were immigrants attracted to tropical regions with their risks of disease, or to countries racked by incessant political feuding.

Even in Argentina where, from the last quarter of the nineteenth century, economic development was in large part due to immigrants, attitudes towards immigration remained ambivalent, both on the part of immigrants themselves and governments. For many immigrants Latin America was an El Dorado where fortunes could be made quickly and then used to buy position and prestige in their country of origin. The low identification of many first-generation immigrants with their host country (by 1914 under 2 per cent of immigrants to Brazil had been naturalized and in Argentina only 3.2 per cent) was partly caused by the generous terms offered them by governments desperate for their labour. A foreigner could obtain most of the benefits of citizenship without becoming a national, at the same time keeping the protection of his consul. By contrast, in the United States naturalization was a prerequisite for voting and thus political parties had an interest in encouraging immigrants to become naturalized so that they could vote, whereas in Latin America restricted franchises or dictatorial governments removed this incentive and the majority of immigrants remained on the margin of politics.

Even where governments were anxious to attract immigrants, official attitudes towards them were divided. Welcomed for racial reasons (northern Europeans were preferred) as a means of 'whitening' the racial stock, they were also sometimes distrusted as carriers of pernicious democratic, socialist or anarchist doctrines. This distrust can be explained by the prominent role played by immigrants in labour organizations. Germans founded the first Argentine socialist party. Spaniards introduced anarchist ideas into Buenos Aires, and Italians dominated the first labour unions in São Paulo. As the number of immigrants increased in the first decade of the twentieth century, so restrictive legislation (such as deportation for organizing strikes) was used to enforce social control. Immigrants, in short, were regarded as a source of docile, cheap labour rather than as positive contributors to the nation's social and political life. However, for the second and third generation there were few barriers to political ambition, as is attested by many presidents with non-Hispanic surnames – such as Carlos Pellegrini and Arturo Frondizi in Argentina, Arturo Alessandri and Eduardo Frei in Chile, and Juscelino Kubitschek and Ernesto Geisel in Brazil, not forgetting General Alfredo Stroessner in Paraguay.

Economically, though, the immigrants' contribution was crucial – they were important not only as a source of cheap labour on the Argentine wheatfields or on the coffee plantations of São Paulo, but also as entrepreneurs. Lacking the social inhibitions of the creole elite, many made successful careers as businessmen and industrialists: families such as the di Tellas in Argentina, the Matarazzos in Brazil, the Gildemeisters in Peru and the Hochschilds in Bolivia could be mentioned as examples.

Although governments in the early nineteenth century attempted to foster immigration through colonization schemes, most of these proved impracticable. In Argentina, the interests of labour-intensive agriculture were sacrificed to those of the cattle barons. In Brazil and Cuba, colonization schemes failed in the face of opposition from the plantocracy and from the reluctance of Europeans to migrate to a slave society (similar to the situation in the southern United States). In Guatemala, an ambitious project to colonize jungle land in the New Liverpool experiment in the 1830s and 1840s collapsed. More successful were the German colonies of southern Chile, north-eastern Argentina and southern Brazil. In these cases, flourishing communities with a distinctive German culture were established in regions largely unsettled by creoles. The success of these colonies vindicated those who argued that northern Europeans made the best settlers in frontier regions. Numerically, though, northern Europeans were few,

although the financial influences of the British and the cultural influence of the Germans and French were out of all proportion to their numbers. In Chile, Argentina and Brazil foreign merchants and entrepreneurs, especially British, contributed to these countries' economic growth, founding in the process dynasties of Anglo-Chilean, Anglo-Brazilian and Anglo-Argentine families who were reluctant to forsake their British connections and become completely assimilated. In other countries, too, there were smaller 'Anglo' communities with their own schools and clubs, as in Peru where their reluctance to become assimilated contrasts with the small Italian entrepreneurial elite whose influence in Peruvian economic growth has been insufficiently appreciated. The Italian contribution, however, was most apparent in Argentina and Brazil in the period of mass immigration during the thirty years before 1914.

ARGENTINA

Argentina was the immigrant country *par excellence*. In the 1840s future president Domingo F. Sarmiento, who had been greatly impressed by a visit to the United States, foreshadowed many later attitudes in favour of immigration, arguing that the 'barbaric' interior could only be tamed by the 'civilizing' influence of cosmopolitan, Europeanized cities, whilst his political rival Juan Alberdi coined the much repeated phrase *gobernar es poblar* (to govern is to populate). In Buenos Aires, which had grown from the *gran aldea* (the great village) of the 1860s to become the 'Paris of the southern hemisphere' by 1914, some three quarters of its inhabitants were foreign-born.

Immigrants to Argentina – nearly half of them Italians, about one third being Spaniards – were drawn into four main activities: shepherding, cattle pasturing, wheat growing and harvesting, and urban occupations. The gradual establishment of political stability after the fall of Juan Manuel de Rosas (1852) created better conditions for immigrants; the Constitution of 1853 guaranteed their legal position. An expanding sheep economy attracted Welsh, Irish and Basque shepherds, some of whom became founders of wealthy families. As sheep pushed cattle further westwards, so the need for pastures to fatten cattle before shipment attracted farmers, mostly Italians, who grew alfalfa as sharecroppers on limited tenancies. Wheat growing first developed in the 1860s in agricultural colonies of Swiss and Italian peasant farmers in the littoral provinces but, when wheat moved south into the pampas, labour for the harvests was frequently provided by transitory *golondrinas*

British clocktower, Buenos Aires, donated by the British community in Argentina to mark the one hundredth anniversary of the May Revolution of 1810

even more so in the grain port of Rosario. The threat posed by an influx of poor non-Hispanic immigrants to traditional values generated nativist responses by the creole elite which took one form in the cult of the gaucho as the symbol of *argentinidad*. One way in which immigrants sought cultural identification with their newly adopted land was to form gaucho clubs and to enact rituals of gaucho life during weekend trips into the pampas.

As the number of Spaniards emigrating to Argentina increased, Spanish intellectuals attempted to strengthen cultural links through the ideology of *hispanismo* which emphasized the spiritual unity of all Hispanic peoples. But this was not regarded too seriously by most Argentines who continued to be bemused by British economic power, French culture, and German science and militarism.

Although Argentina's pre-1914 prosperity was largely due to the labour of immigrants, they were frequently regarded as money-grabbing materialists and were sometimes the butt of satirists. To escape the obloquy attached to commerce, second- and third-generation sons of immigrants sought prestige by entering the hitherto creole-dominated professions of law, medicine and politics. The army, too, was an important ladder of social mobility, as shown by the high proportion of generals with Italian antecedents.

BRAZIL

In Brazil, efforts had been made during the imperial period (1822–89) to encourage immigration by subsidizing agricultural colonies, following the eighteenth-century precedent set by the Portuguese crown of establishing colonies of Azoreans in Santa Caterina. However, few of the Swiss and German colonies founded in the 1830s and 1840s survived. It was not until after the Paraguayan War (1865–70) and the run-down of slavery that immigrants entered in any numbers and, once slavery had been abolished in 1888, the trickle became a flood. Between 50 and 60 per cent went to the state of São Paulo (in the 1890s the percentage rose to 80 in some years), where the coffee boom created a continuing demand for labour. Most of this was provided by Italians, at first mostly from northern Italy, from whence came many of the missionaries who were the earliest links. Transport costs were subsidized by the São Paulo state government under the *colono* system by which immigrants together with their families replaced slaves on the coffee plantations. By careful housekeeping *colonos* could save enough money to buy land on which to produce food for the growing towns or, alternatively, to move into the cities to

(swallows) from southern Europe who were able to work on the Argentine harvest during the European winter. One consequence of this type of seasonal migration was an imbalance between the sexes, which contributed towards Buenos Aires becoming one of the most notorious centres of the white slave trade.

Those migrants who stayed provided labour for the construction boom, meat-packing factories, flour mills, docks and urban services of the rapidly expanding coastal cities. By 1914, 41 per cent of the 2,358,000 foreigners living in Argentina were in Buenos Aires, 49 per cent were in the littoral and Córdoba provinces and the remaining 10 per cent were in the rest of the country. Immigration accelerated the division of the nation into a modern, cosmopolitan, urbanized and economically dynamic coastal region and a traditional economically retarded (and less populated) interior.

Italians, in particular, made their mark in Buenos Aires with their own districts, their contributions to the local argot (*lunfardo*) and the local cuisine, and become artisans or shopkeepers. Portuguese immigrants tended to prefer Rio de Janeiro and provincial towns where they dominated commerce and shopkeeping, often rousing nativist hostility during economic depressions, as in the 1890s. Between the 1880s and 1950s, 31 per cent of all immigrants were Italians and 30 per cent Portuguese, followed by Spaniards (13.8 per cent), Japanese (4.5 per cent), Germans (4 per cent) and thirty other nationalities with smaller percentages. The coffee boom, made possible by the *colonos*, provided the profits which fuelled the industrial development of São Paulo, turning it into a cosmopolitan financial centre.

The First World War and the early 1920s marked a change in the pattern of immigration. During the war many Italians returned to fight on the Italian front (many immigrants had come from the Veneto, the main war zone in Italy). After the war the establishment of immigration quotas by the United States diverted much of the migrant flow from war-torn central and eastern Europe to South America. Poles, Russians, Jews and central Europeans as well as Turks and Syrians swelled the small communities of these nationalities which pre-dated the war. In Brazil, one of the most important groups was the Japanese whose agricultural skills contributed to developing marginal land in São Paulo and frontier regions in Paraná and Amazonia. Japanese immigration was distinctive insofar as the Japanese government both encouraged and supervised the emigration process.

PATTERNS OF IMMIGRATION

A major contrast between Latin America and the United States has been the reluctance of immigrants in the former to move into frontier regions. Apart from a few cases, such as Scottish sheep farmers in Patagonia, the Welsh colony in Chubut (dating from 1865), Germans in southern Chile, north-eastern Argentina and southern Brazil, the Japanese in Amazonia and religious groups like the Mennonites in Paraguay, most immigrants have settled in cities. Although in the 1880s Argentina passed legislation modelled on the United States Homestead Act of 1862 which granted settlers free land on condition it was cultivated, it proved ineffective due to the entrenched power of big landowners, land companies and political corruption. In Brazil, the Land Law of 1850 had been specifically designed to seal off the frontier to prospective settlers by making the price prohibitive and confining its distribution to the plantocracy. In this way immigrants would not be diverted away from the plantations where their labour was needed.

After Argentina and Brazil, Uruguay and Cuba were the countries most affected by large-scale immigration. In the former, Argentine experience was replicated. Montevideo became a city of immigrants – a high proportion of whom were Italians and French – with over one third of the country's population. However, the experience of Cuba was distinctive, firstly because, as it was a Spanish colony until independence in 1898, Spaniards occupied a privileged position in society, monopolizing posts in the bureaucracy and commerce. The Cuban case also illustrates, in exaggerated form, the tendency for the regional attachments of the Iberian peninsula to be perpetuated in the Americas, exemplified by powerful regional clubs of Galicians, Catalans and Asturians. Few Spaniards except *isleños* (Canary Islanders) moved on to the land (Fidel Castro's father, a Galician, was one who did). Secondly, the early years of the nineteenth century created an inexhaustible demand for labour. This was met by rising imports of African slaves until the threat to the racial balance in the 1850s compelled the authorities to seek alternative sources of manpower. As Europeans were reluctant to migrate to a slave society, over 100,000 Chinese coolies were imported between the 1840s and 1870s as semi-free contractual labourers, thus providing a bridge between slavery and a free-labour system. Some remained after their contracts expired and entered traditional Chinese occupations in restaurants, laundries and market gardens and were assimilated into Cuban society. A similar case occurred in Peru where Chinese coolies had been imported during the guano boom in the 1860s so as not to drain off Indian labour from highland haciendas, and where a small Chinese–Peruvian community took root.

With the abolition of Cuban slavery in 1879 the flow of Spanish immigrants increased and even after the fiercely fought war of independence (1895–8) Spaniards continued to enter until by 1930 some 16 per cent of Cuba's population were Spanish. This number dropped after the 'Cubanization' law of 1933 limited the number of foreign employees in any firm to under 50 per cent. Spaniards then either returned to Spain or became Cuban citizens. The absence of any large non-Hispanic immigration has meant that Cuban links with Spain are probably closer than those of any other Latin American country.

The Cubanization law was one expression of rising nationalism throughout Latin America in the aftermath of the Great Depression. This was reflected in restrictive immigration legislation and in nationalization policies designed to hasten the assimilation of groups who had hitherto been on the fringes of national life. Newspapers published in foreign languages perpetuated divided loyalties as did schools where teaching was conducted in a foreign language. In Brazil, the threat posed by self-contained German communities prompted an active policy of Brazilianization as well as the imposition of quotas restricting each nationality during any one year to 2 per cent of the number admitted between 1884 and 1933, and also stipulating that 80 per cent of each national group should be agriculturalists, reflecting Getúlio Vargas's ambition to settle the interior.

The restrictions of the 1930s changed the character of immigration. Previously the majority of immigrants were poor, whereas in the 1930s the political exiles who now became an important component were often intellectuals and professionals. The most important group were those from republican Spain. Every country in Latin America derived some benefit from this new type of migration and none more so than Mexico, which had previously attracted few Spanish immigrants. Spaniards now made substantial contributions to universities, publishing and the arts.

After the war the immigrant flow revived, especially to Venezuela to which Italians were drawn by the economic boom. Argentina continued to attract Spaniards of whom 60 per cent returned to Spain even though Franco was still in power.

Russian immigrant grandmother, Uruguay

With few exceptions immigration into Latin America has been from southern Europe, thus perpetuating many of the values of a Catholic, family-oriented traditional culture. For those choosing to go to Latin America the term 'New World' did not have the connotations of a religious or political utopia associated with the United States. In Latin America the utopian dreams of sixteenth-century Franciscan missionaries and of patriot leaders such as Simon Bolívar evaporated in the confused anarchical early years of independence. Lacking the magnetic pull of free land, or of religious or political freedoms, Latin America tended to attract those who glimpsed possibilities of a future in economic activities despised by the creole elite. Opportunities may not have been as many or as varied as in the United States, but recognized success stories should not obscure the many failures, one of which has lately been documented in a classic immigrant autobiography edited by the late Juan Marsal.

Scholarly attention has so far focused on the statistics of migration and on immigrants' economic influence; little research has been done on social and cultural aspects such as the complex processes of assimilation, the incidence of intermarriage between creole and immigrant, on immigrants' racial attitudes, on the phenomenon of the returnee and on the wider questions of cultural influences. Is it possible to speak of a 'melting pot' in the case of Argentina as some historians have done? Or can Argentina's political difficulties be related to the early political marginalization of immigrants? These and many other questions need (and will surely receive) investigation by historians.

Compared with immigration studies in the United States, those in Latin America are in their infancy. Considering that the Americas share a common experience of immigration from Europe, this is a puzzling omission and one that needs to be rectified for a proper understanding of the continent's historical development.   AH

Further Reading: N. Sánchez Albornoz, *The Population of Latin America* (Berkeley, 1974); E. Fishburn, *The Portrayal of Immigration in Nineteenth-Century Argentine Fiction, 1845–1902* (Berlin, 1981; *Biblioteca Ibero-Americana* no. 29); J. Marsal, ed., *Hacer la América: una autobiografía de un immigrante español* (Buenos Aires, 1969); M. Mörner and H. Sims, *Adventurers and Proletarians: The Story of Migrants in Latin America* (Pittsburg, 1985); C. Solberg, *Immigration and Nationalism: Argentina and Chile, 1890–1914* (Austin, Texas, 1970)

Latin American migration (regional and abroad)

Massive migration to present-day Latin America from Spain and Portugal from the sixteenth to the eighteenth century is, of course, a major feature of the continent's history, but far less attention has been given to contemporary intracontinental and international migration in the region, although it is of considerable economic, social and political importance.

Migrants can be of several types, depending on their reasons for migrating, length of stay, economic intent and legal status in the host country.

The main categories are political refugees, unskilled (largely rural) workers seeking employment in more prosperous countries, and professionals looking for better prospects than they have at home.

Professionals who migrate, often legally, include doctors, nurses and engineers, all of whom have left Argentina, Chile, Colombia, Venezuela, and the Dominican Republic in significant numbers. Many such professionals seek citizenship in the United States, although 7 per cent of Venezuela's migrant population comprises professionals from other Latin American countries, including large numbers of engineers employed in the oil industry. This transnational migration has been attributed to low fees, salaries and benefits, insecure employment and lack of equipment.

POLITICAL REFUGEES

Political refugees originate from most of the region. During and after the Castro revolution in Cuba many Cubans fled to the United States. Largely members of the managerial and professional classes, they were given political asylum. Then in 1969, under a US–Cuban 'family re-unification' agreement, an additional 250,000 Cubans were admitted to the USA. Smaller migrations of less skilled workers continued until Cuba severely restricted emigration. A final wave occurred in 1980, when large numbers of unskilled and semi-skilled workers, the so-called 'Marielitos', escaped by boat. More than half of all Cuban migrants to the United States live in Florida.

Since 1978 political upheavals in Central America have created massive numbers of displaced persons whose legal status as political refugees varies. At the height of the Somoza regime, Nicaraguans left their country in significant numbers, and with the onset of civil war in 1980 many of the elite then fled to the United States, where they were accorded refugee status. Temporary refugee status was also granted in 1990 to half a million El Salvadorans who fled the civil war there, bringing the total of the country's population that has emigrated since 1980 to 16 per cent. In addition to those in the United States, others have gone to Argentina, Costa Rica, Honduras, Guatemala, and Nicaragua; Nicaragua grants rights accorded citizens to refugees from El Salvador, and to Guatemalans fleeing internal strife. Honduras is estimated to have 35,000 immigrants from El Salvador and Nicaragua alone. The State of Chiapas in Mexico receives large numbers of peasants from northern Guatemala who resettle across the frontier and engage in agricultural work, but because Mexico has no official policy on political refugees, their status is ambiguous. After Allende's fall in Chile in 1973, Peron's in 1976, and military coups in Brazil and Uruguay, many nationals of each of these countries left for neighbouring countries, but have returned home as more sympathetic regimes have come to power.

MOVEMENTS OF UNSKILLED WORKERS

By far the most significant transnational migrations in Latin America have been those of unskilled, mainly rural workers. The countries that are most developed – the United States, Argentina and Venezuela – have each received massive numbers since 1950, the majority coming from Mexico, Colombia, Uruguay, Bolivia and Chile. Chile has, in fact, experienced significant economic development since 1960, but it has been unable to absorb its unskilled workers because of slow industrial growth. Much of the migration is illegal – a phenomenon that has grown sharply because of the opening of new frontier areas to colonists, greater road-building, and the increased movement to urban areas of rural nationals, whose places are then filled by transnational migrants from poorer countries.

Large-scale migration from Mexico to the United States began in the 1880s with the expansion of Mexico's railroads. The Mexican Revolution of 1910 and religious wars in Central Mexico in the 1920s caused many agricultural workers to flee to the American south-west. From 1942 to 1964 several million Mexican workers were issued temporary contract labour permits under the Bracero Program, over 4 million alone in the programme's final decade. However, the termination of the programme in 1964 did not diminish the flow, and current estimates of the number of undocumented workers vary for any given year from 2 to 10 million, the likelihood being that there are about 2–3 million present at any given time. A small number have legal permits, the rest do not. Most migrants go to California and Texas, where they were primarily employed on the land, but now mainly work in urban areas in construction, petty industry and the service sector, including domestic service for women. The majority are not accompanied by their families and return to Mexico after a stay of from six to twelve months. In 1987, the United States granted amnesty to persons who had resided in the United States for more than ten years.

The primary Latin American destination in the 1970s was Venezuela. It has a small native population of about 20 million, but there are an estimated 4 million foreign workers. Large-scale migrations began in the 1940s when Venezuela's economy expanded dramatically because of oil. In the 1960s, there was a labour shortage especially in agriculture, as the country's own rural population began to migrate to the urban areas to take advantage of new employment opportunities, which also attracted skilled workers from Europe as well as North and South America. Colombian workers, who have been common in Venezuela since 1890 in the coffee plantations of the border states, have come in large numbers to fill the agricultural jobs. Thirty per cent go to Caracas, but over half remain in the frontier zone, particularly the states of Tachira and Zulia, where they work in coffee, sugar, and cattle-raising, forming a semi-permanent population that swells in the harvest season. Smaller numbers of rural workers come from Cuba and Ecuador, and skilled workers from the Dominican Republic.

Argentina, Uruguay, and Chile are the most industrialized countries in the Southern Cone, but only Argentina attracts significant flows of immigrant labour. Between 1970 and 1980, 140,000 migrants entered Argentina from the four other Southern Cone countries, plus another 7,000 from Brazil. The steady flow from Uruguay intensified in 1960 amongst skilled workers, rising to 10 per cent of Uruguay's working population in 1970–74, many of whom were employed in construction in Buenos Aires. With the advent of a democratic regime in 1985, many of them have returned home.

Migrants from Paraguay, with its large rural population, work in the border cities of Argentina, mainly in construction. Between 1950 and 1980 over 4,000,000 Paraguayans have sought work at some time in Argentina and in southern Brazil, where they harvest maté, or in the developing regions of the Brazilian Mato Grosso. On the other hand, in 1991 250,000 Brazilians were living in Paraguay, primarily farming cotton and soy.

Migrants from Bolivia come mainly from the Altiplano and Valle regions of the Western Highlands where 85 per cent of the population lives. Most are landless agricultural workers or owners of plots of less than 110 hectares. Their favoured destination is Argentina, where it has been estimated that there are as many as 1 million Bolivians. Many are employed in the 'zafra', or annual harvest; of these, several thousand remain throughout the year to work in other agricultural regions where tobacco and vegetables are raised. Many of them hold work permits.

Emigration from Chile was heightened after the collapse of the Allende regime in 1973, women going to work in Argentina as maids; both men and women to work there in fruit orchards, vineyards, and sheep farming. But compared to migration rates for other Southern Cone countries, Chile's current rate of migration to Argentina is low.

Migration from Puerto Rico and the Dominican Republic represents a different pattern from those of other Latin American countries. As members of a United States Territory, Puerto Ricans enjoy the status of US citizens. Puerto Rican migration began before the Second World War, but increased significantly after the war ended, to the extent that in the 1950s there were 225,000 Puerto Ricans in the United States, 83 per cent of them in New York state. Migration dwindled in the sixties, but rose between 1970 and 1980, during which time the number of Puerto Ricans in the United States came to number 2 million, or 35 per cent of the island's population. Approximately 30 per cent of all Puerto Rican migrants return to the island, once they have had the education or made the capital they want. They tend to occupy semi-skilled or unskilled jobs during their stay and experience low job mobility.

The exodus from the Dominican Republic rose sharply after the collapse of the Trujillo regime in 1961. Unlike other regions of high emigration, many who left were primarily skilled, white collar workers and professionals affected by the economic crisis there in 1965. Many choose citizenship in the United States; others seek and find high-wage employment in Venezuela and Argentina.

COMMONWEALTH MIGRATION TO GREAT BRITAIN

Large-scale migration from the English-speaking Caribbean islands to Great Britain was especially notable in the period between the British Nationality Act of 1948 (which allowed West Indians to settle freely in Great Britain) and the Commonwealth Immigrants Act of 1962, the first of a series of measures restricting immigration from the so-called 'New Commonwealth' (i.e., territories other than the old 'white Dominions'). The Census of 1951 showed some 15,000 West Indians living in Great Britain. Ten years later the number had risen to nearly 172,000. An important current of migration from the Indian subcontinent (India, Pakistan) also set in during this period.

The 1962 Act was strongly criticized on the grounds that it reflected thinly disguised racialism. Not least among the critics was the opposition Labour Party, but after being elected to government in 1964, it introduced a still tougher act in 1968.

The largest contingent of Caribbean migrants came from Jamaica, the most populous English-speaking island. But some of the smaller islands felt the impact of emigration even more sharply than Jamaica; for example nearly one third of Montserrat's tiny population left for Britain. By the late 1980s some 3 million inhabitants of Great Britain belonged to the 'ethnic minorities' – just over half of them being of Indian or Pakistani origin. Since the restrictive legislation of the 1960s, natural increase rather than immigration has been the main factor in the growth of the West Indian and Asian populations of the United Kingdom.

Bolivian migrant working at the sulphur mine on the Aucanquilcha volcano, Chile, the highest mine (6100 metres) in the world

THE OPERATION OF 'PUSH' AND 'PULL' FORCES

The dramatic rise since 1950 of unskilled labour migration can be attributed to unequal development and the expansion of the global economy. As industrial capital and technology from developed nations in Europe and North America penetrates Latin America it creates a greater demand for cheap industrial labour, particularly in construction and commercial agriculture.

Labour migration can be seen as a response to both 'push' and 'pull' forces that expel workers from poorer countries and attract them to more developed ones. Push factors include rapid population growth in the rural areas, competition for jobs, diminishing opportunities in the agrarian sector due to mechanization, a disproportionate number of underproductive small plots relative to large landholdings ('minifiundismo'), maldistribution of income, low or irregular wages and rising expectation. Pull factors include the need for cheap labour to implement development, more employment opportunities, a higher rate of exchange for foreign currency and better services and educational opportunities.

THE EFFECTS AND FUTURE OF UNSKILLED WORKER MIGRATION

There are important consequences for both sending and receiving countries. Receiving countries profit from the 'brain-drain' by acquiring skilled and professional personnel without bearing the cost of their training. Seasonal unskilled temporary workers are an asset because receiving countries are spared the cost of reproduction, maintenance, and transportation of such workers. Illegal migrants willingly take menial, low-paying jobs with no promise of advancement, jobs that native workers are not eager to fill. On the other hand, those who oppose the presence of such workers argue that they depress wages, hinder unionization, strain social services, perpetuate low-skill jobs, and contribute to hyperurbanization.

Many argue that emigration of unskilled workers acts as a 'safety-valve' for less developed countries. It absorbs unemployable labour, especially in agriculture, brings in foreign capital in the form of wages, provides income for investment and savings for returning workers, and reduces pressures on internal migration to urban centres. Others dislike it as a solution to internal economic problems, arguing that it enables governments to avoid or reduce efforts to improve rural conditions, create equitable distribution of income, relieve poor housing conditions, and implement economic and social reforms.

Migration policies in Latin America, as well as the United States, the primary non-Latin receiving country, reflect a preference for selective migration to protect the wages of skilled nationals. There is a tacit agreement not to restrict emigration except in the case of Cuba. In 1986 new United States legislation attempted to prevent employment of 'undocumented workers', but by the early 1990s it had proved ineffective in deterring illegal immigration, which totalled well over a million annually, the vast majority from Mexico, Central America and the Caribbean.

Ministers of the Andean Pact countries have approved an Article to create an office of migration to deal with migration problems, workers' rights, and repatriation. However, although the 'Instrumento Andino de Migración Laboral' was proposed in 1975, it has not been ratified by Colombia and Venezuela. These two countries have a series of accords dating from the 1940s that deal with visas and labour permits. Colombia also has accords with Ecuador, although the latest, proposed in 1977, has not yet been approved by the latter. These aim at regulating the rights of labour migrants as well as of agriculturalists who resettle in newly opened trans-border areas.

Colombia is one of the few countries in Latin America with a well-defined labour migration policy (Cuba is another). Created in 1945, this aims to minimize the impact of emigration by both reducing and channelling the flow of workers. It calls for planned development in regions of high emigration and provides assistance for workers seeking employment elsewhere. It also creates contracts for work in overseas countries such as Saudi Arabia and maintains substations along its frontiers to assist migrants. Colombia is also the only country to use income from labour contracts to build low-cost housing.

Venezuela's migration policy has changed from an open one before 1960 to one which is both open and selective. Current policy reflects the government's changing perceptions of its development needs. Long a receiver of European migrants, Venezuela's policy for Latin American migrants now resembles more closely that of advanced industrial nations like the United States and Canada, and in 1980 it created a General Aliens Register to grant temporary renewable work permits.

Argentina's current policy is an attempt to integrate immigration with its development goals. In the last decade, it has experienced severe economic decline and immigration policy has become more restrictive as a way of reducing internal unemployment.

International migration in Latin America is likely to increase over the next decade in conjunction with unequal development in the region. Despite the discovery and exploitation of oil reserves, Mexico cannot generate enough jobs to absorb its growing working-age population. High rates of migration to Venezuela and Argentina are likely to persist, but at a somewhat lower rate. The pattern of migration across borders of small-scale agriculturalists may ebb somewhat as they succeed in newly established frontier colonies. Central American migration will almost surely abate as stability returns to that region. But by and large it can be expected that the overall pattern of international migration that emerged in the 1950s will continue into the next century.

IR-U

Further Reading: J. Balan, *International Migration in the Southern Cone* (Washington, DC, 1985); F. D. Bean and others, eds., *Undocumented Migration to the United States* (Washington, DC, 1990); B. Levine, ed., *The Caribbean Exodus* (New York, 1987); A. Portes and R. L. Bach, *Latin Journey: Cuban and Mexican Immigrants in the United States* (Berkeley, 1985); D. Rieff, *Going to Miami: Exiles, Tourists and Refugees in the New America* (Boston, 1987)

Contemporary size and distribution of population

The population of Latin America, some 150 million at the end of the Second World War, nearly trebled by 1990, as table 3 shows, when it reached 448 million, well above North America or Western Europe. In the next two decades its growth is projected to slow down so that the total will probably not exceed 629 million by the year 2010.

In the mid-1950s Latin American population growth (2.7 per cent) was faster than in Africa (2.2 per cent) or Asia (1.9 per cent) because the region had experienced an earlier start in the reduction of mortality while the birth rate overall (43 per thousand) was the same as in Asia, although not as high as in Africa (49 per thousand). In the mid-1970s rates of growth in Africa, Asia and Latin America were converging (2.7, 2.3, 2.5 per cent per year respectively). In Africa and Asia, this was the result of falling mortality and little or moderate change in fertility. In Latin America the rate of growth was relatively

TABLE 3
Population of Latin America by regions, size and growth[a] (population in thousands)

Total	1950	%	Growth 1950–1990	1990	%	Growth 1990-2000	2000[b]	%	Growth 2000-2010	2010[b]	%[b]
Latin America	165,880	100.0	2.5	448,076	100.0	1.9	538,439	100.0	1.6	628,766	100.0
Central America	37,241	22.4	2.9	117,676	26.3	2.1	145,135	27.0	2.1	172,935	27.5
Caribbean	17,045	10.3	1.7	33,685	7.5	1.4	38,546	7.2	1.2	43,291	6.9
Tropical South America	86,123	51.9	2.7	248,126	55.4	1.9	299,975	55.7	1.6	351,712	55.9
Temperate South America	25,471	15.4	1.6	48,589	10.8	1.2	54,784	10.1	1.1	60,828	9.7

[a] Average annual percentage growth = birth rate minus death rate plus immigration minus emigration
[b] United Nations projections based on 1990 data and recent trends
Source: United Nations *World Urbanisation Prospects 1990.*

steady because crude birth and death rates declined by similar margins. At present, Latin America's crude birth rates are 29 per thousand and crude death rates are 7 per thousand. The current rate of growth is 2.1 per cent per year, slightly higher than Asia's 1.9 but far below Africa's 3 per cent.

In the mid-1980s in both tropical South America and Central America (including Mexico), where the great bulk of the continent's population is concentrated, birth rates continued their downtrend. Although the already low death rates may be expected to fall a little more, there is no doubt that population growth will continue to slow down from the extraor-

Colorado Indian from the western lowlands of Ecuador. The name is taken from the red (colorado) paint used on the hair and body. Not many Colorados now wear their hair in the traditional way.

dinarily high rate of 2.7 and 2.9 per cent per year respectively in the period up to 1990 to 1.9 and 2.1 per cent per year towards 2000. In tropical South America growth may be as low as 1.6 per cent per year before 2010, while remaining at 2.1 per cent per year in Central America.

Well before the Second World War, temperate South America had modest growth as a consequence of its low, Western-European-style birth rates. Indeed, if it had not been for massive infusions of European immigrants and the very low death rates in Argentina, Chile and Uruguay, the population of these quite exceptional countries would not have grown even as gently as it did over the period 1920–60. Their maximum post-war growth rates, 1.9 per cent per year, occurred in the 1950s when immigration peaked, but this fell away to 1.3 per cent per year in the late 1970s. In sharp contrast, tropical South America's annual growth remained at 3 per cent per year until the 1960s and declined to 2.5 per cent per year in the late 1970s. This continuing decline is extremely important in itself because tropical South America now has nearly 250 million people. Whereas the tropical countries were multiplying at practically double the rate of the temperate countries in the 1980s, this is likely to slow down to just over 50 per cent higher by 2000.

Immigration from other continents has not been a weighty factor in South America overall since the 1950s when there were large inflows to Brazil and Venezuela as well as to the temperate countries. Neither emigration from South America nor intra-regional migration among its countries has been large enough to make an appreciable difference over the four decades to 1990, except in the relatively small populations of French Guiana, Guyana and Suriname.

The strongest rate of population upsurge is in Central America, where the population reached nearly 118 million in 1990. There, too, the pace of growth seems to be slackening. The considerable emigration from Mexico and its neighbours to the United States, including a large illegal movement (estimated at between 1.3 million and 2 million breadwinners, plus their families) may have brought down Central America's – and Mexico's – rates of growth slightly more in the 1980s than in the 1970s.

Post-war emigration made a definite difference to the recent growth and present size of population only in the Caribbean and the smallest circum-Caribbean countries. In any case, Caribbean population growth was already the lowest in Latin America in the early 1950s. In 1965–70, when Great Britain was fairly open to Commonwealth immigrants and the Nether-

lands was open to Suriname's people, the combined outflow from the Caribbean and associated circum-Caribbean countries amounted to more than a quarter of natural increase. At that time, birth rates in the Caribbean and associated circum-Caribbean countries had gone up and death rates were down to European-style minimum levels. Without mass emigration, the resultant population upsurge would then have reached the continent's high average rate of growth. The American and French territories still have free access to their metropoles and their population growth is slowed down in consequence. But even without such massive emigration, which is now impossible from Suriname and the British Commonwealth countries, the Caribbean's subsequent growth would have not stayed so high because family planning has become widespread through official programmes and commercial distribution.region.

Table 4 presents the population and its growth rates for countries with more than 250,000 inhabitants in 1950, and table 7 the smaller populations.

TABLE 4
Population of countries: size and growth (population in thousands)

	1950	% Growth 1950–1990	1990	% Growth 1990–2000	2000[a]	% Growth 2000–2010	2010[a]
Central America							
Costa Rica	862	3.2	3015	2.1	3711	1.6	4366
El Salvador	1940	2.5	5252	2.5	6739	2.3	8491
Guatemala	2969	2.9	9197	2.9	12,222	2.6	15,827
Honduras	1401	3.3	5138	2.9	6846	2.4	8668
Mexico	28,012	2.9	88,598	1.9	107,233	1.6	125,166
Nicaragua	1098	3.2	3871	3.1	5261	2.7	6824
Panama	893	2.5	2418	1.8	2893	1.4	3325
Caribbean							
Bahamas	79	3.0	253	1.5	295	1.2	334
Barbados	211	0.5	255	0.4	265	0.6	280
Cuba	5850	1.5	10,608	0.8	11,504	0.6	12,155
Dominican Republic	2353	2.8	7170	1.9	8621	1.4	9903
Guadeloupe	210	1.2	343	0.6	365	0.4	380
Haiti	3261	1.7	6513	2.1	8003	2.1	9835
Jamaica	1403	1.4	2456	1.1	2735	1.0	3011
Martinique	222	1.1	341	0.6	362	0.4	378
Puerto Rico	2219	1.1	3480	1.0	3826	0.8	4156
Trinidad & Tobago	636	1.8	1281	1.5	1484	1.3	1687
Tropical South America							
Bolivia	2766	2.5	7314	2.9	9724	2.8	12,820
Brazil	53,444	2.6	150,368	1.8	179,487	1.5	207,454
Colombia	11,946	2.6	32,978	1.8	39,397	1.5	45,645
Ecuador	3310	2.9	10,587	2.3	13,319	1.9	16,083
Guyana	423	1.6	796	1.1	891	1.2	1005
Paraguay	1351	2.9	4277	2.6	5538	2.3	6928
Peru	7632	2.6	21,550	2.0	26,276	1.8	31,047
Suriname	215	1.7	422	1.6	497	1.3	564
Venezuela	5009	3.5	19,735	2.3	24,715	2.0	30,006
Temperate South America							
Argentina	17,150	1.6	32,322	1.2	36,238	1.0	40,193
Chile	6082	2.0	13,173	1.5	15,272	1.2	17,182
Uruguay	2239	1.0	3094	0.6	3274	0.6	3453

The smaller populations of Latin America are presented in Table 7.
[a] United Nations projections based on 1990 data and recent trends.
Source: United Nations *World Urbanisation Prospects 1990*.

DISTRIBUTION AMONG REGIONS AND AMONG COUNTRIES

Owing to the marked divergences among the various countries' rates of growth, the distribution of population across the continent is shifting quite dramatically in the second half of the twentieth century and into the early twenty-first century (as table 4 shows). Between the Second World War and the current decade, the demographic centre of gravity shifted northward as Central America's population expanded. More than a quarter of the whole continent's population now lives along the isthmus, one fifth in Mexico alone. It should not be forgotten that Brazil's 150 million and Colombia's 33 million together make up more than 40 per cent of the continent's total: Latin America's population as a whole still lives mainly near the Equator. Certainly for the next two decades, the demographic trends of the continent will depend above all on what happens to the birth rates of Brazil and Mexico which already hold more than half the inhabitants.

The temperate countries made up only one sixth of the continent's total population at the end of the Second World War. In the early 1990s these three countries stand at one tenth of the total. The Caribbean's share of the total has been falling too. Cuba, which held half the archipelago's population, has been falling behind over the last four decades, although the upsurge of the Dominican Republic and Haiti has partly counterbalanced the shrinking of the Caribbean's percentage of the continent's total population.

CONTEMPORARY SIZE AND DISTRIBUTION OF THE POPULATION

Persons per square kilometre
0   0.4   2   10   40

0   1   5   25   100
Persons per square mile
■ Cities with population over 5 million
● Cities with population over 1 million

While projections of future population have often proved inaccurate, and certainly cannot tell us much about the next generation, current trends do point to a small expansion of Middle America's population, possibly to 28 per cent by 2010, with Mexico alone still accounting for 20 per cent of the total population of Latin America. Tropical South America probably will grow more slowly, reaching no higher than 56 per cent of the total continental population, with Brazil contributing one third of the total Latin American population. The Caribbean population will continue to shrink in relation to the rest, down to 7 per cent of the continent's total, with Cuba's decelerating population growth setting the pace. Temperate South America is on the way to being less than 10 per cent of the total population. Thus more than four fifths of the total population will be living in tropical South America and in Middle America by the year 2010, according to current trends.

DENSITY

In 1950 the Caribbean was the most thickly populated region of Latin America, as table 5 shows. Haiti had 118 people per sq km. Population pressure was even higher in some of the smaller countries, particularly Barbados with 491 per sq km and Puerto Rico with 249 per sq km.

The second most densely settled region was Central America, particularly El Salvador, which by 1990 at 250 per sq km had far outdistanced any other Central American country. It is now denser than Haiti and indeed most of the Caribbean, apart from Trinidad and Tobago (250 per sq km), Martinique (309 per sq km), Puerto Rico (391 per sq km) and Barbados (616 per sq km) – which will probably remain the most heavily populated into next century. Cuba is far more sparsely populated than any of the other larger islands; it was already in a demographic class of

TABLE 5
Population densities: selected countries and regions (inhabitants per sq km)

	1950	1990	2000[a]	2010[a]
Latin America	*8*	*22*	*26*	*31*
Central America	15	47	58	70
Costa Rica	17	59	73	85
El Salvador	92	250	320	404
Guatemala	27	84	112	145
Honduras	13	46	61	77
Mexico	14	45	55	64
Nicaragua	8	30	40	52
Panama	12	31	38	43
Caribbean	73	144	164	184
Barbados	491	593	616	651
Cuba	53	96	104	110
Dominican Republic	48	147	177	203
Guadeloupe	123	201	214	223
Haiti	118	235	288	354
Jamaica	128	223	249	274
Martinique	201	309	329	343
Puerto Rico	249	391	431	467
Trinidad & Tobago	124	250	289	329
South America	6	17	20	23
Tropical South America				
Bolivia	3	7	9	12
Brazil	1	2	3	4
Colombia	10	29	35	40
Ecuador	12	37	47	57
Guyana	2	4	4	5
Paraguay	3	11	14	17
Peru	6	17	20	24
Suriname	1	3	3	3
Venezuela	5	22	27	33
Temperate South America				
Argentina	8	12	13	15
Chile	8	17	20	23
Uruguay	13	17	18	19

[a] United Nations projections based on 1990 data and recent trends.
Source: United Nations *World Population Prospects 1990.*

its own, with low birth rates and slow population growth, long before Fidel Castro took power.

Population densities in South America remain low: Colombia and Ecuador, the densest South American countries, have 29 and 37 people per sq km respectively. Ecuador will forge ahead but probably will not exceed 60 inhabitants per sq km by 2010. Colombia's population growth is slackening, however, and should not exceed 40 per sq km by 2010. Venezuela's density is not likely to exceed 33 per sq km.

The low population densities of South America can be explained in part by the vast tracts of rainforest around the Amazon and Orinoco, the large stretches of the Andes which are not arable plateaux, the major fraction of the temperate countries in the wastelands of Patagonia and Tierra del Fuego, and the

high percentage of land devoted to cattle grazing in Brazil, Venezuela and the temperate countries.

On the whole, it cannot be said that Latin America is overpopulated, relative to area and resources. El Salvador, Haiti and the Dominican Republic are the exceptions, because they lack emigration outlets and a good mineral resource base, and because their birth rates continue to be high. The Caribbean islands of the British Commonwealth also have problems in that population growth is no longer siphoned off to Great Britain. Rapid mass urbanization has taken much of the direct population pressure off the land in almost all countries: Haiti and Guyana are notable exceptions.

RURAL–URBAN DISTRIBUTION

One of the most conspicuous manifestations of modernization throughout Latin America and the Caribbean has been the concentration of rural–urban migrants in vast squatter settlements in and around the cities in recent decades. These countries had been predominantly rural up to the 1950s, with the exception of Argentina, Chile, Uruguay and Venezuela, which had already developed large primate cities serving as both capital and principal seaport.

While important rural majorities persist in a number of the poorer countries, Latin America as a whole has shifted from a continent largely populated by villagers to one with the majority concentrated in huge metropolitan centres. Certainly, the rapidity of the post-war urbanization of Latin America and the size of its great cities make it more urban than Africa or Asia. Of the world's twelve cities of 10 million or more inhabitants in 1990, four are in Latin America: Mexico City (20.2 million), São Paulo (17.4 million), Buenos Aires (11.5 million) and Rio de Janeiro (10.7 million). Lima has passed the 6 million mark. Mexico City will probably reach 25.6 million by 2000, followed by São Paulo with 22.1 million.

Rural–rural movement has not been a major component of population redistribution, except for particular parts of particular countries where lowland areas have been made attractive by the elimination of malaria, the construction of roads and the introduction of new agricultural techniques such as irrigation. Yet the larger highland–lowland migrations to newly opened-up agricultural areas in Bolivia, Ecuador and Mexico have been dwarfed by the master trend towards metropolitan agglomeration. The large movement from the arid lands of north-eastern Brazil to the factory farms of São Paulo's rural hinterland is unique.

While the temperate countries and Venezuela have stayed ahead of the other · countries in the

TABLE 6
Rural-urban distribution of population: trends 1950–2010

	1950 % urban	1950–90 % urban growth	1990 % urban	1990–00 % urban growth	2000[a] % urban	2000–10 % urban growth	2010[a] % urban
Latin America	42	3.9	72	2.5	76	2.0	*80*
Central America	40	4.2	66	2.8	71	2.3	75
Costa Rica	34	4.1	47	3.2	53	2.9	59
El Salvador	37	3.0	44	3.6	50	3.7	56
Guatemala	30	3.6	39	4.0	44	4.2	51
Honduras	18	5.7	44	4.7	52	3.8	59
Mexico	43	4.3	73	2.6	77	2.0	81
Nicaragua	35	4.6	60	4.1	66	3.4	71
Panama	36	3.6	53	2.8	59	2.4	65
Caribbean	34	3.2	60	2.2	68	1.8	74
Barbados	34	1.2	45	1.7	51	1.9	58
Cuba	49	2.6	75	1.5	80	1.0	83
Dominican Republic	24	5.3	60	3.1	68	2.2	74
Guadeloupe	42	1.6	49	2.0	55	1.6	62
Haiti	12	3.9	28	4.1	35	4.2	42
Jamaica	27	3.1	52	2.2	59	2.0	65
Martinique	28	3.6	75	1.2	79	0.8	83
Puerto Rico	41	2.7	74	1.6	79	1.2	82
Trinidad & Tobago	23	4.6	69	2.3	75	1.8	79
South America	43	3.9	75	2.4	80	1.9	83
Tropical South America							
Bolivia	38	3.2	51	4.2	58	3.9	65
Brazil	36	4.5	75	2.5	81	1.9	84
Colombia	37	4.2	70	2.5	75	2.0	79
Ecuador	28	4.7	56	3.7	64	2.8	70
Guyana	28	2.1	35	3.1	42	3.0	50
Paraguay	35	3.7	48	4.0	54	3.5	61
Peru	36	4.4	70	2.7	75	2.2	79
Suriname	47	1.7	48	3.0	54	2.5	61
Venezuela	53	4.9	91	2.6	94	2.1	95
Temperate South America							
Argentina	65	2.3	86	1.4	89	1.2	91
Chile	58	2.9	86	1.8	89	1.4	91
Uruguay	78	1.0	86	0.8	87	0.8	89

[a] United Nations projections based on 1990 data and recent trends
Source: United Nations *World Urbanisation Prospects 1990*.

continuing rural–urban shift, the rest have rapidly followed suit over the last four or five decades as this profound transformation has swept across the continent. By 1990 the rural population had shrunk to a minority of the inhabitants of several countries, notably Brazil and Mexico, the demographic giants of the continent. This is also the pattern in all of the countries with a population of 250,000 or more, with the exception of El Salvador, Guatemala, Honduras, Cuba, Haiti and Guyana. The continent is now nearly three quarters urban. Urbanization in the Caribbean does still lag behind the other regions, but three fifths of the archipelago's inhabitants now live in towns and cities.

This era of immense rural–urban population redistribution is drawing to a close: henceforth the great majority of Latin Americans will be urban born; indeed a large and growing fraction is being raised in large metropolitan areas. The reservoir of potential rural migrants to the towns and cities has shrunk. Moreover, the city-born population is itself now growing more slowly. Up to the 1970s the birth rates in the towns and cities had been boosted by the continuing influx of countrywomen, and also the natural increase of the city-born population had been rising because the urban death rates were still declining. At present, little improvement can be expected in urban death rates because they are close to the minimum possible under foreseeable public health conditions. Moreover, the age composition of the population born in the metropolitan areas of Central America and tropical South America is now already

TABLE 7
Small populations of Latin America: 1990 population and growth rates[a]

Areas with no more than 250,000 inhabitants	Population (thousands)	Growth 1990–2000	Growth 2000–2010
Central America			
Belize	187	2.1	1.5
Caribbean			
Anguilla	7	1.3	1.2
Antigua and Barbuda	76	0.4	0.4
Aruba	60	−0.3	0
British Virgin Islands	13	1.4	0.6
Cayman Islands	25	3.4	2.3
Dominica	82	0.6	0.7
Grenada	85	−0.2	0
Montserrat	12	0.8	0.7
Netherlands Antilles	188	0.7	0.7
Saint Kitts and Nevis	44	0	0.4
Saint Lucia	150	1.7	1.3
St Vincent and the Grenadines	116	0.9	0.9
Turks and Caicos Islands	10	1.8	1.6
US Virgin Islands	116	1.5	1.2
South America			
Falkland Islands (Malvinas)	2	0	0
French Guiana	98	2.9	2.1

[a] Estimates for 1990–2000 and 2000–2010 projected from last decade's rates, assuming that American and French areas will continue to have unrestricted emigration to their metropoles and assuming severely restricted emigration to Britain and the Netherlands.
Source: United Nations *World Urbanisation Prospects 1990*.

following the pattern established in temperate South America and Cuba. As urban fertility falls, the urban population tends to age, raising mortality and thereby slowing down urban population growth.

By 2010 probably some 80 per cent of the continent's people will be living in urban areas, despite the decelerating urbanization. In percentage terms Venezuela will continue to be the most urbanized country in Latin America, followed by the temperate countries where only a tenth of the population will still be rural.

In 1950, the countries which had been slowest to urbanize were Honduras in Central America, Haiti, the Dominican Republic and Trinidad and Tobago in the Caribbean, and Guyana, Ecuador and Bolivia in tropical South America. By the year 2000, only three countries in Latin America – Honduras, Haiti and Guyana – will remain more than 50 per cent rural. By 2010 this is likely to be true of only Haiti.

THE SMALLEST POPULATIONS

Belize and French Guiana have vast areas which could be opened up to absorb double their populations. Consequently, they expect the fastest population growth over the next two decades. The only other potential for rapid growth, implied by recent trends, is in the Cayman Islands and in Turks and Caicos Islands, which is due to a boom in international banking activities and tourism. The other ex-British-colonial populations shown in table 7 would have real problems of population pressure because their emigration outlet to Great Britain closed by 1971. However, these countries already have long-established family planning programmes.   JS MacD

Rural families migrating to the city often end up in shanty towns such as this one in Managua, Nicaragua.

Current ethnic profiles and Amerindian survivals

The survival of the original inhabitants of what has become Latin America can be gauged by assessing the vitality of their traditional cultures. Key features of Amerindian cultures are, of course, their languages of which more than 1650 different ones have been discovered. This multiplicity of languages makes it possible to assert with some confidence that the Spanish and Portuguese conquerors of the New World did not intrude upon a homogeneous culture but upon many different ways of life and, indeed, that they encountered many ethnic types within a Mongoloid race now popularly known as 'Indian'. Evidence of the persistence of this aboriginal American population has often been sought in the modern national censuses of the countries of Latin America and also in the detailed descriptions of tribal and peasant societies within these countries. National census takers have attempted to differentiate between members of the population by using as criteria their appearance and the languages they habitually speak. The problems in this approach are obvious: judgements as to the skin-colour of a respondent, for example, may be subjective, arbitrary or unrelated to the survival of his culture; on the other hand, whilst the speaking of an Indian language may be evidence of the persistence of other aspects of the related cul-

ture, a shift to Spanish or Portuguese speech by a full-blooded Amerindian does not necessarily denote a surrender of self to an Iberian way of life. The most useful linguistic evidence derives from national censuses which have been able to distinguish between those speakers of native languages who spoke no Spanish or Portuguese - what one might call the 'hard-core' of Amerindian survival - and those bilingual Amerindians who spoke both an American and Iberian language, i.e. those who had taken the first step away from a purely native culture.

Further attempts were made, by Mexico, Peru and Ecuador, to differentiate the population on the grounds of their material culture. All respondents to the census, for example, were asked if they customarily ate maize bread, an Amerindian characteristic, or wheaten bread, a European trait. The replies suggested that native cultural patterns have remained much more widespread than a purely linguistic count would lead one to suppose. Yet even this seemingly much more searching survey method remains open to question: for instance, peasant respondents to a census are quite as capable as the census taker of perceiving the status differences which may be made between, say, those who claim to wear sandals (Amerindians) and those who claim to wear shoes (Europeans) and are liable to present answers which will suit their own social aspirations. Thus even delicate soundings of the cultural depths of a population may be doomed to underestimate the values and norms it really maintains. The fraternal mood of post-colonial Latin America, moreover, has tended to frown on status and ethnic distinctions despite the reality of frequent repression; increasingly, governments find it ideologically inconvenient to differentiate between their citizens, which does not help analysts assess the likely future fate of the continent's

Schoolteacher, Nicaragua

Indians, southern Andes of Colombia

aboriginal populations. There are two propositions in the literature about them: some say that they will all slowly lose their identity under the weight of incoming migrants; others say that the Amerindians are the fastest-growing element in the fastest-growing population in the world. What is the reality?

HISTORICAL BACKGROUND

Any assessment of the current significance of the Amerindian element in Latin America must start with the native American populations before the Spanish and Portuguese discovery and colonization of the continent. They were not evenly spread, but concentrated in and around two agricultural empires in what now are Mexico and Peru, with thin dispersals in the central forests of the Amazon basin and on the savannas of what are now Argentina in the south and the Guianas in the north. The shock of military conquest was to reduce these figures very drastically, not so much due to deliberate slaughter but due to contact with the endemic diseases carried by the Europeans to which the Amerindians had not been able to develop any hereditary immunity. By the seventeenth century the aboriginal populations had begun to recover but they had, by now, to confront successive waves of migrants from two directions: Europeans, in search of lands upon which to settle,

and Africans, brought in as slaves. Once again the demographic dispersal of these incomers was uneven: for three centuries the Africans were to take over the role of labourers in the islands, and in the coastal areas of the Caribbean and of north-eastern Brazil; whilst the Europeans sought landed property in the more favoured and accessible agricultural and herding valleys, extending and increasing their hold on arable and grazing land as the opportunity offered. The physical survival of the Amerindians in this period of colonization depended partly upon their ability to compete with African labour on the tropical coastlines and partly upon their determination to hold on to their traditional lands. Certainly a demographic catastrophe, which was immediate and almost complete, overtook the natives of the Antilles: before mainland Mexico was pacified, the large island which is now Cuba was virtually depopulated and today in the whole of the West Indies there are not thought to be more than a few hundred Amerindians. Similarly, on the plains of the River Plate region the Amerindians and their cowboy descendants fought the encroaching immigrant herdsmen until well into the nineteenth century, but were usually defeated or absorbed. Conversely, in the inhospitable northern deserts and mountain ranges of Mexico, peoples like the Yaqui and the Tarahumara and, in inaccessible recesses of the mountains and forests, peoples like the Araucanos were able to maintain their traditional

Fisherman, North-East Brazil

ways of life. By far the most successful physical and cultural continuity with their Aztec and Inca forebears has been preserved by the populations of the great heartlands of Amerindian civilization, the mainly Nahuatl- and Maya-speakers of Mexico and Guatemala on the one hand, and the mainly Quechua- and Aymara-speakers of Peru, Bolivia and Ecuador on the other hand. The weight of sheer numbers has had much to do with the persistence over time of these two classic groupings, the one bestriding the isthmus of Central America and the other holding the mountain ranges of western South America. The early protection of the Indian afforded by the Roman Catholic Church may just have been enough to help the survivors through the aftermath of the conquest. Thereafter a paternalistic Spanish crown attempted to mitigate the effect of subjugation upon the indigenous populations by 'commending' their Indian souls to the care of Spanish landholders and by appointing local governors with specific instructions to protect the natives and to promote their welfare. Unfortunately these Spanish *encomenderos* and *corregidores de indios* were more enthusiastic about enriching themselves than justifying their custodianship. However, they lived among the subject peoples and the descendants of the two groups have remained together ever since; from this close association over four centuries of Europeans and Amerindians has arisen the classic Latin American of today. In more modern times the sympathy and encouragement of the agencies of some

national governments have facilitated a revival of self-respect and pride in their distinctiveness of today's representatives of great cultural traditions. The populations of today's Latin America are growing apace and a correlation has been observed between low rates of growth, say between 1.5 per cent and 2.2 per cent, and small concentrations of Amerindians, as occurs for example in Argentina and Chile, whereas most Latin American countries have much higher growth rates, between 2.4 and 3.5 per cent, and many of these have large concentrations of Amerindians, for example Bolivia, Ecuador, Guatemala, Mexico and Peru. This reasoning has led some writers to suggest that the demographic explosion in the Latin American part of the whole continent is currently being led by the 'red man' whose home it was before it also became the home of the white man and the black man. Accepting this thesis of an Amerindian-led human increase, one can postulate a dynamic Indian population of 20–30 million today for the Spanish-speaking part of the whole continent.

ETHNIC PROFILES

In Latin America, the powerful argument of 20–30 million recognized Amerindians serves to demonstrate indigenous survival; as relevant are four centuries of miscegenation. It is ethnocentric, or at least anachronistic, to believe that the offspring of unions

AMERINDIAN SURVIVAL AROUND 1980
Estimated number at 1980 and percentage growth rate

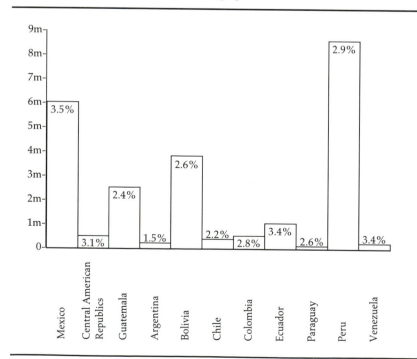

CURRENT ETHNIC PROFILES

	Amerindians	Europeans	Africans/mulattoes	Mestizos
ARGENTINA	>1%	97%	–	2%
BOLIVIA	54%	14%	–	32%
BRAZIL	<1%	50%	50%	–
CHILE	5%	25%	–	70%
COLOMBIA	1%	20%	29%	50%
COSTA RICA	0.5%	92%	–	7.5%
ECUADOR	40%	15%	5%	40%
EL SALVADOR	10%	1%	–	89%
GUATEMALA	54%	4%	–	42%
HONDURAS	5%	1%	2%	92%
MEXICO	10%	15%	–	75%
NICARAGUA	3%	10%	11%	76%
PANAMA	5%	14%	14%	67%
PARAGUAY	3%	20%	1%	76%
PERU	46%	12%	–	42%
URUGUAY	–	90%	2.5%	7.5%
VENEZUELA	2%	20%	8%	70%

between Europeans and other races will always identify with the former. Assuming for the moment that a child of mixed parentage has some sense of belonging to both, what is the magnitude of this factor in respect of Amerindians? What is the proportion of persons of mixed ethnic descent, generally known as mestizos, in the modern populations of Latin America? Is it significant anyway? At this juncture it is necessary to emphasize that the term 'mestizo' is an analytical one only: it is unusual for a person to so describe himself; it is, however, important for the debate about Indian survival to be able to gauge partial survival as well. In the history of the transmission of Indian culture, the mestizo is the muted witness. If one looks at each geographical area of Latin America in turn, the clear ethnic profiles of the continent can be discerned. Of the River Plate, out of a population of over 30 million today, Argentina counts less than 200,000 as 'Indian', although it has been estimated that perhaps 20 per cent of the remainder are of mixed European and Amerindian descent; male immigrants heavily outnumbered female immigrants at first and the settlers who contested the pampas also dispossessed the Indians of their women, but between them they produced some of the cowboys of today's pampas. Out of nearly 4 million Paraguayans, around 3 per cent are Amerindians and a large proportion of the remainder

An anthropologist with newly contacted Nahua Indians, Peru

Right
Maya Indian woman in Guatemalan highlands

are adjudged mestizos. Indeed the people of Paraguay fulfil the prediction of some Latin American savants that a 'cosmic race' is emerging in their countries; a large part of the population makes use of the language of the Guaraní Indians and Spanish is spoken with a Guaraní accent. Uruguay, by contrast, is alleged to be 'the whitest country in Latin America' with only 5 per cent of mestizos.

Of the Andean countries, the highest proportion of Amerindians live in Bolivia: more than half the total population; perhaps 32 per cent of the population are of mixed ethnic origin with only a vestige of African descent. Peru has a larger Amerindian element in absolute numbers. In Andean countries citizens of mixed ethnic origin may be referred to as *cholos*, *cholitos*, or *montubios*, although these terms may occasionally also designate an urbanized Indian; they number perhaps 42 per cent of the total in Peru. In Ecuador census takers have not distinguished convincingly between Amerindians and mestizos, but there is general agreement that it is one of the most 'cosmic' nations with persons of direct European and African descent contributing at the most 20 per cent to the total population. Colombia's large population is estimated to be half mestizo, with one fifth of the population directly descended from Europeans and over a quarter descended from Africans. Chile has the smallest number of Amerindians in the Andean region, and an insignificant number of citizens of African descent, but 70 per cent of its million inhabi-

tants are estimated to be of mixed European and Amerindian descent.

The giant of South America, in all senses, is Brazil. Some element of African descent is claimed for nearly half of its huge population. Official sources give vague and various reports of Amerindian numbers. The Amazonian coastal Tupi have been decimated, the riverine tribes in contact with Europeans driven away and the Cintas Largas of the Mato Grosso ravaged by intrusive diseases. Paradoxically, ever since independence from Portugal, the offspring of unions between Portuguese and Amerindians, *caboclos*, have retained an honoured place in the romantic imagination of some Brazilians who take pride in tracing their Amerindian descent.

Venezuela lies on the north coast of South America and its population is the result of a three-way fusion of its indigenous tribes with Spanish adventurers and with African slaves, to which has been added in this century a large influx of Europeans attracted by the discovery of oil. In consequence, one in six persons is foreign-born, so that 20 per cent of the inhabitants count as white, 8 per cent count as black, 70 per cent are 'mixed' and a mere 2 per cent are Amerindians. The three former Guianas (now

Maya Indians, Guatemalan highlands

including Guyana and Suriname) have comparatively small populations whose Amerindian elements are being absorbed culturally by the ethnic groups of Asian and African descent which surround them, so that these countries have most in common ethnically with the islands of the Antilles like Jamaica and Trinidad, both of which have significant Asian elements. Apart from Cuba, three quarters of whose people are of European descent, and Bermuda with a 40 per cent European element, the mode for the islands is to have small, predominantly black populations counted in tens or hundreds of thousands: thus 82 per cent of the English-speaking Bahamians are of African descent; as are 84 per cent of the Spanish-speaking Dominican Republic; 90 per cent and 92 per cent in Barbados and Jamaica; and virtually 100 per cent of French-speaking Haitians. In the islands, then, Amerindian language and culture were long ago extinguished.

Belize, on the Central American mainland, has often been associated with the Antilles because of the large African and small European elements among its inhabitants, yet important indigenous groups persist there – black Caribs and Mayas with their separate languages. Of the seven remaining countries of Central America, four face the Caribbean and these coastal lowlands have supported many people of African descent in the past who have worked on the banana plantations; hence their significant numbers in Honduras, Nicaragua and Panama, although those in Costa Rica have been absorbed into the general population: apart from a few thousand Amerindians, the Costa Rican population is designated as entirely white. Honduras, Nicaragua and Panama have larger Amerindian nuclei within a mestizo population.

The remaining Latin American countries either face away from the Caribbean, or have massive aboriginal populations, or both. Predominatly mestizo El Salvador has a small Amerindian minority. Perhaps two fifths of the Guatemalan population is Amerindian, an element which has had peculiarly harsh treatment. Mexico's large population includes several million Amerindians.

AMERINDIAN SURVIVALS

For the whole of Latin America, then, one can arrive at a figure for inhabitants positively identified as Amerindians which approximates the credible total

Woman from Olinda, near Recife, Brazil

Quechua girl and child, Peru

calculated by some historical demographers as being alive at the time of the Spanish conquest. It is not sufficient, however, to say that an Amerindian physical presence is almost back to where it was despite four centuries of attrition and depredation. Through miscegenation there have arisen many millions of Latin Americans with memories of, and potential attraction towards, a way of life which belonged to their own forebears and of which they are constantly reminded by their purely Amerindian cousins. These mestizos often uphold the values of their Amerindian heritage, even if they do so subconsciously. Although they may have become acculturated to the life-style of the Spanish side of their ancestry in terms of dress, language, technological skill and even in terms of religion, there are aspects of their social organization which disclose the conservation of an indigenous tradition which is uniquely theirs. This tradition is, in the main, the inheritance bequeathed to them by the great agricultural civilizations of the Incas, the Mayas and the Aztecs, which often includes: the collective exploitation of land, which seems to reflect European anarchist thinking but which has developed quite separately; the ritual accumulation of life-long personal bonds, which has taken on the outward appearance of Iberian godparenthood but whose purpose often relates to purely Latin American needs; the devotion to a whole series of supernatural beings, who have Christian names but who are better understood in terms of a non-western past; the ritualized remembrance of, and hospitality towards, deceased relatives, which has more in common with Oriental ancestor-worship than with All-Souls' Day; the reverence for, and cultivation of, transitory political leaders, which harks back to the pre-conquest treatment of an Inca or of a Montezuma rather than reflecting the respect due to the holder of an elective office; and so on.

We must recognize that the great nations with an organized past and with an Amerindian and mestizo present have a continental culture which is qualitatively different from that of the conquistadors who briefly impinged upon them. This culture appears hybrid only insofar as it displays an alien form and has an alien terminology; the important thing is that at its heart is an Amerindian content which is as different from any other major cultural pattern as it is ingenious. But Europeanized Mexicans and Peruvians also must recognize their own roots: there is a Brazilian saying that 'O gato que nasceu num armazém não é biscoito' ('The cat born in a store is not a biscuit'); the time has perhaps come for the biscuit to stand up and proclaim that he is not a cat either.

So, by reason of the strong inference that in many countries the Indians are not only participating in population growth but are actually leading it, and by reason of the recognition of the genetic and cultural inheritance from past Amerindians it is possible to claim that the survival of the Amerindians, at least in some form, is secure. That, however, should not cause one to be complacent about what is still happening to some small tribal societies, particularly in central South America, which are threatened by misguided 'emancipation', economic development and unpremeditated contact with other human beings. Paradoxically, the onrush of civilization brings more ills to non-immunized and hitherto isolated societies than it cures. The choice for governments with primitive humans in their care is a stark one: integration or reservation. If secluded and vulnerable communities are not integrated officially and with safe deliberation, they may become integrated unofficially to their cultural and physical cost, as has already happened to the Eskimo (Inuit) and to the Australian Aborigine. If their lands are not reserved to them, these may be encroached upon and indigenous peoples may become vagrants, derelicts and dispossessed. Perhaps the most promising road being followed is in Mexico, where the Indigenist Institute brings the benefits of western civilization to the Tarahumara, to the Tzeltal, to the Mixtecs and to many others; it brings education and modern medicine and offers only gradual and voluntary integration into the wider nation. Precipitate incorporation of hunter–gatherer peoples into a state society, on the other hand, is the threatened fate of many dwellers of the Amazon region. This option, presented in the guise of emancipation, has long been recognized by the great Brazilian Indianists as a recipe for the exploitation, degradation and destruction of the very people whom government has a duty to protect.

PEBC

Further Reading: D. C. Chaplin, *Population Policies and Growth in Latin America* (Lexington, 1971); R. Darcy, *The Americas and Civilization* (London, 1971); S. H. Davis, *Victims of the Miracle: Development of the Indians of Brazil* (Cambridge, 1977); M. Mörner, *Race Mixture in the History of Latin America* (Boston, 1967); N. Sánchez-Albornoz, *The Population of Latin America* (Berkeley, 1974)

Bolivian schoolchildren

History

Previous page
*Depiction of the action at
Maracaibo, Venezuela in
July 1823 when the
Spaniards were dislodged
from one of their last
redoubts in northern South
America.*

The first human cultures

In physical appearance, blood grouping, and the form and arrangement of the teeth, the American Indians demonstrate their origin in eastern Asia. The initial colonization of America took place during the final glaciation, at a time when much of the earth's precipitation remained on land in the form of ice sheets, causing a fall in sea level which converted the Bering Strait into a temporary land bridge between Siberia and Alaska. The precise date of man's arrival in America is still uncertain. The first immigrants were few in number, mobile in their habits, and have left little trace of their presence. The oldest archaeological sites so far discovered in Latin America are in Mexico, at El Cedral (San Luis Potosí) where stone tools and extinct animals are at least 30,000 years old, and at Tlapacoya (Puebla) with lakeshore camp sites of around 20,000 BC. In South America a handful of dubious artifacts from the deepest strata at Pikimachay (Flea Cave) in the Peruvian Andes are dated *c.* 18,000 BC, but there is no reliable evidence until the late Pleistocene (13,000–9000 BC) when sites suddenly become abundant.

MAIN ARCHEOLOGICAL SITES

To this period belongs Taima Taima (Venezuela) with a dismembered mastodon skeleton and a date of at least 11,000 BC. Further south, the more recent deposits at Pikimachay are dated around 12,000 BC, and Guitarrero Cave, in the Peruvian Andes, falls somewhere within the eleventh millennium BC. By 10,000 BC, at latest, man had reached south-east Brazil (the Arroio dos Fósseis and Alice Boër sites) and as far south as Los Toldos in Patagonia.

During the closing millennia of the Pleistocene Ice Age, all of Latin America, except perhaps the Amazon basin, was populated by small bands of foragers who lived by hunting game and collecting wild plant foods. This is the era of the spectacular mammoth-kill sites in the Basin of Mexico, though evidence from cave shelters indicates that the bulk of the meat supply came from smaller animals, including rodents and birds. At the kill site of Tagua Tagua, Chile, charcoal fragments in the archaeological stratum suggest the use of fire-drives.

Occupation was not exclusively in caves and rock shelters. Open-air camp sites are documented by scatters of stone tools, while chipping debris indicates the localities where the raw material was quarried. Usually all evidence of structures has disappeared, but at Monteverde (south-central Chile) a habitation zone of some 3000 sq m became covered by a layer of peat which has preserved organic materials of 12,000–10,000 BC, or even older. This site gives an idea of what has been lost under less favourable conditions. Archaeologists have unearthed implements of bone, wood and stone, as well as a structure with wooden posts and several hearths. Nearby were five butchered mastodon skeletons and evidence of fresh-water shellfish and plant foods.

Oldest pottery in the Americas?

In December 1991 it was announced that an international team of archaeologists (headed by Dr Anna C. Roosevelt of the Field Museum of Natural History, Chicago) had discovered fragments of pottery with painted decorations between 7000 and 8000 years old near Santarém in the Amazon basin. Hitherto northern South America (modern Ecuador and Colombia) has been considered as the location for the earliest ceramic-making in the Western Hemisphere. The earliest pottery from there dates from around 4000 BC while the earliest North American pottery goes back to around 2000 BC. The Santarém findings are likely to prompt a revision of the view that pottery (and agriculture) spread to the Amazon lowlands from the Andes, and probably indicate that human settlement along the Amazon in prehistoric times was much more extensive than has so far been assumed.

By the late Pleistocene, distinct regional traditions of stone working had emerged, each with its characteristic technology and range of forms. Ignoring the variability in the shape of the tools, and concentrating more on their function, we can identify spear and dart points, knives and cutting tools, scrapers for whittling wood or cleaning hides, and a range of artifacts used for engraving, chopping, mashing, pounding and hammering. Guitarrero Cave has also yielded fragments of basketry and netting, but the archaeological record of this early period remains biased and incomplete.

THE BEGINNINGS OF AGRICULTURE AND VILLAGE LIFE

Between 8000 and 7000 BC the Pleistocene Ice Age came to an end. Mammoth, mastodon, horse, ground sloth and several other large mammals became extinct. Ice caps and glaciers retreated. Sea levels rose to approximately their present heights, drowning the old Pleistocene coastlands and encroaching as much as 70–100 km in parts of Peru, with consequent loss of all archaeological sites in this area. These climatic changes brought with them changes in vegetation, until gradually the modern landscape began to emerge. In these new conditions, techniques of food procurement had to be modified and the first experiments with farming took place.

Between 8500 and 2000 BC American Indians brought into cultivation a wide range of crops. Of these, maize, potatoes and manioc/cassava became worldwide staples after the European conquest of America in the sixteenth century, and many others (beans, pumpkins and squashes, sweet potatoes, peanuts, chilli peppers, pineapples, tomatoes, avocados, tobacco and cacao, or chocolate) are widespread in the Old World today.

By comparison, animal resources were scanty. Mexico has contributed the turkey to international gastronomy, but it was only in the Andes, where the ancestors of the domestic llama and alpaca were native, that stock raising became important with the development of herding and pastoral economies on the high *puna* grasslands. This process of domestication began as early as 4500–4000 BC. At much the same time, in Peru and Colombia, the domestic guinea pig became a cheap, and easy to rear, source of meat.

The figure below, which is typical of the general pattern in all regions, demonstrates that agriculture was adopted only slowly. There was no single centre of origin. The people of each region experimented with the plants and animals that were locally available, and which they had already collected or hunted

PLANT AND ANIMAL DOMESTICATION IN THE TEHUACAN VALLEY, CENTRAL MEXICO, 10,000 BC TO THE SPANISH CONQUEST, BASED ON EVIDENCE FROM ARCHAEOLOGICAL EXAMINATION

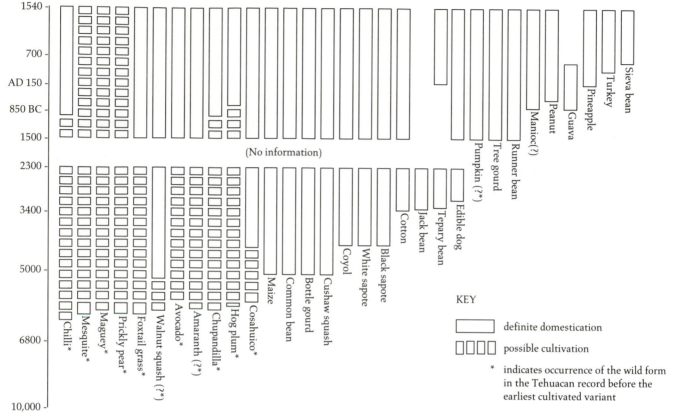

KEY

definite domestication

possible cultivation

* indicates occurrence of the wild form in the Tehuacan record before the earliest cultivated variant

for thousands of years. At first the cultivated crops were no more than a supplement in a diet based on game and wild plants. Gradually, however, in response to new selective pressures and to genetic manipulation by man, improved races of plants were developed from the less productive wild forms. Useful species were transferred from one region to another, and more and more effort was devoted to gardening at the expense of foraging. New food-processing techniques were discovered (e.g. freeze-drying the bitter Andean potato to convert it into storable *chuño*, or the washing of certain seeds to leach out toxins), and irrigation increased productivity still further, until eventually the balance changed, and farming came to provide the bulk of the diet.

It seems that the 'agricultural revolution' was not a sudden revolution at all, and can be explained without recourse to population pressure, environmental change, or any other 'prime movers'. Instead, the change from foraging to farming can be seen not as a matter of conscious planning for thousands of years ahead, but rather as the cumulative outcome of a series of short-term decisions whose long-term consequences could not have been appreciated at the time. This process of agricultural development took place in many different environments and each region has its own individual history.

Some of the most detailed evidence comes from highland areas with dry caves in which foodstuffs are preserved. These have been investigated in the Ayacucho basin of Peru and in the Mexican states of Tamaulipas, Puebla and Oaxaca. In these regions the early post-Pleistocene inhabitants were omnivorous foragers who organized their lives around the seasonal harvests of wild plants and the movements of animals. Desiccated human faeces contain grass seeds, roasted maguey cactus, roots, chili seeds, and fragments of worms, grubs, snails and grasshoppers. For much of the year the community was split into small bands of only a few families, and the corresponding archaeological sites include winter hunting camps and caves occupied seasonally in localities where collection of wild plants could be combined with small-scale cultivation. During the months of abundance, camp sites are bigger and the scattered bands came together in larger groups. In arid zones of this kind, settled village life was impossible without effective agriculture, and it was not until 2500–1500 BC that villages of pottery-using farmers made their first appearance.

In the moist tropics of America preservation is poor, and the evidence suggests a greater emphasis on root crops and on forest products such as palm nuts. From Amazonia we have no information before

2000 BC, but studies of pollen grains and phytoliths (silica skeletons of plant cells) from deep cores at Lake Gatún (Panama) show what sort of thing must have been happening in the rainforests during these critical millennia. Human intervention first appears at Lake Gatún around 2800 BC, with small-scale forest clearance and shifting cultivation which included maize. By the time of Christ, manioc was also grown.

A major controversy surrounds the origin of cultivated maize. Some botanists believe that its ancestor is a wild form of maize which is now extinct. Others maintain that maize derives from its closest living wild relative, a weedy grass (with edible seeds) called teosinte. Teosinte does not grow south of Honduras and, if this plant gave rise to all known races of maize, the implication must be that Mesoamerica is the region where maize cultivation began. If, on the other hand, the ancestral form is a wild maize, South America comes into contention as a possible source of origin.

Leaving aside the problem of origins, there is agreement that maize is a highland plant, not initially adapted to tropical lowlands. Finds of maize cobs, or maize phytoliths, at lowland sites show surprising antiquity: 2000 BC at Cuello (Belize), the fifth millennium BC at Cueva de los Ladrones (Panama), and around 6000 BC at the sites of the Vegas culture in coastal Ecuador. These dates indicate a long period of genetic adaptation, which in turn pushes back the age of the first experimental cultivation in the highland centres of origin.

The consequences of the changeover to agricultural life were not the same everywhere. In dry inland areas settled life had to await the development of high-yield crops and efficient farming technology; elsewhere, and especially in coastal, riverine or lakeshore environments providing food throughout the year, sedentary life preceded effective farming. Zohapilco, beside the lake that once filled the Basin of Mexico, had year-round occupation as early as 5500 BC, and Santa Luisa (Veracruz) was probably a riverine village by 3000 BC. The huge shell mound at Angí (Nicaragua) is dated 5650–3650 BC and may represent an early sedentary occupation of the Caribbean coast.

The most precocious development of settled life during the pre-ceramic period was in coastal Peru. This desert coast has virtually no rainfall and no indigenous crop plants, but the waters of the Humboldt current are rich in fish, birds, sea mammals and shellfish. These wild resources, supplemented by a little cultivation of introduced crop plants, allowed permanent villages to develop soon after 3000 BC.

By 2500, canal irrigation made farming more productive, and maize was introduced from the Andes to the littoral. Farming villages have been discovered all along the coast, and a few sites were already developing into regional centres of government. El Paraíso covered more than 50 hectares, with 3000–4000 inhabitants living in complexes of masonry rooms whose construction required some 100,000 tons of rock. Sites like Aspero and Piedra Parada had massive public buildings on terraced platforms, dominating the dwellings of the ordinary people. Some cemeteries of this period were large (2500 graves at Rio Seco), and at Asia, on the south coast, there was a clear distinction between rich and poor burials. Late pre-ceramic society was neither homogeneous nor egalitarian, and was controlled by some form of organized government, religious or secular, with the power to call out labour for public works. Andean Peru was also participating in these developments, with temple sites at La Galgada on the Pacific slope, Huaricoto in the high Andes, and Kotosh on the eastern side of the watershed.

These three Andean sites, and several of the coastal ones, continued in occupation after 2000–1800 BC, when pottery was introduced – and the future pattern of Peruvian civilization now becomes clearly recognizable.   WB

Pre-Columbian Mesoamerica

ORIGINS

When he entered the city of Tenochtitlán with Hernán Cortés on 8 November 1519, Bernal Díaz del Castillo, the conquistador and chronicler, was astonished by the opulence and beauty of the Aztec capital. In fact he was witnessing the end of an extraordinary episode in human development which, in a mere four millennia, had transformed man's conditions of life from primitive village agriculturism to a degree of urban concentration and sophistication unsurpassed by societies of comparable technology elsewhere in the world. The area where this occurred is known as Mesoamerica, a term with both geographical and cultural connotations. It covers central and southern Mexico, Guatemala, Belize and the northern parts of El Salvador and Honduras. Here man has found the conditions and resources favourable for the creation of cultures which, despite regional and evolutionary variations, display common characteristics ranging from diet and domestic architecture to mythology and religion. Here, at the end of the archaic period man formed small settled communities by the edge of lake, river and sea and began the experiment in sedentary living that led to Tenochtitlán.

EARLY CIVILIZATIONS

The history of that experiment is conventionally divided into three phases which, borrowing from Old World archaeology, are called Pre-classic (or Formative), Classic and the Post-classic. Recently an alternative terminology, free of analogies with the eastern Mediterranean and more suggestive of the complex ebb and flow of Mesoamerican cultural development, has been devised. In this usage three 'horizon' periods, in each of which the influence of one dominant culture – Olmec, Teotihuacán or Aztec – extended over the whole of Mesoamerica, are alternated with 'intermediate' periods of greater diversity when regional influences prevailed.

Our knowledge of the early stages of this process is derived entirely from archaeology and the physical sciences, and is predictably sketchy. As written records in the form of stone inscriptions became a significant source of information during the first

millennium AD, detail can be filled in up to the time when native manuscripts and Spanish chroniclers provide a full, if occasionally garbled and conflicting, history of the last centuries of Indian civilization before the conquest.

As a starting point, it is convenient to take the introduction of pottery (although some sedentary settlements in Mesoamerica date back to the pre-ceramic period). The first primitive fired-clay figurine, found in a hearth at Zohapilco, a lacustrine site in the Valley of Mexico, has been carbon-dated to about 2300 BC, but it is only some centuries later that domestic pottery emerges. It is simple and undecorated but the lack of a truly primitive antecedent has led to doubts whether pottery-making was of local invention or was imported from South America. It is safe to say, however, that early in the second millennium BC several different wares came into use in the central highlands and in the semi-tropical lowlands of the Pacific and Atlantic coasts.

Archaeological evidence suggests that population density at that time was very low and that seasonal nomadism was only gradually transformed into a sedentary life. The earliest settlements were small hamlets of one-roomed houses built of poles and

PRE-COLUMBIAN MESOAMERICA

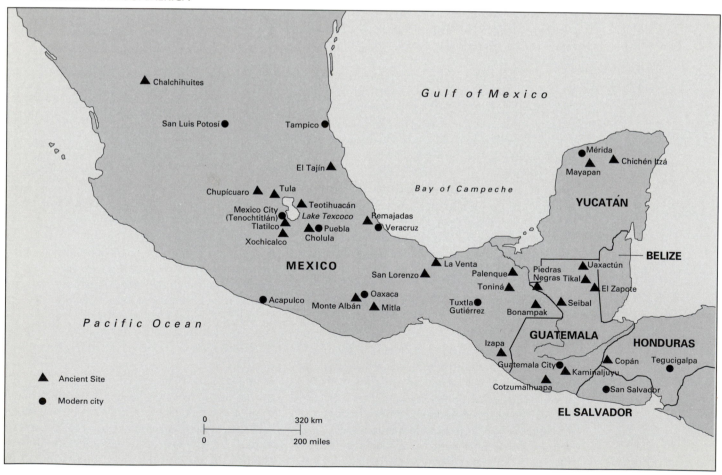

Olmec head, carved from basalt

sists for some 500 years but has not yet been fully explained. Military conquest, proselytism and trade exploitation may all have played a part, but the location of Olmec settlements at key intersections of trade routes suggests that the security of an Olmec trade network handling such materials as obsidian and jade was a major factor.

Within its lowland heartland Olmec culture is most conspicuously manifested in colossal monolithic heads, altars and stelae of basalt and in ceremonial architecture on a grand scale. At San Lorenzo, large mounds, courts and pyramids built of earth bear witness to the importance of state and religion. A slightly later site, La Venta, has similar architecture with an earth-built pyramid of unprecedented height (110 m). The absence of household refuse and remains suggests that La Venta may have functioned as a ceremonial centre rather than an urban settlement, but its satellite population has been estimated as 18,000. The human effort required to construct the public works and to import stone from a distance of 80 km for the many large sculptures indicate a degree of population concentration, social organization and discipline unprecedented in Mesoamerica to that time. We can only guess how the society functioned but its sanctions were, in part, religious. The motifs on pottery and bas-relief sculpture reflect an intricate system of belief, some of which appears to anticipate the themes that were elaborated into the complex of later Mesoamerican religion. The jaguar and the serpent are central to Olmec iconography and their stylized traits are incorporated in images which recur repeatedly in modified form and are well known to us in their Aztec versions. The secular arts are manifested in well-made pottery figurines, notably the 'baby face', whose puffy childlike features and downturned mouth have been dubiously identified as the product of the union of human and jaguar.

DIVERSIFICATION

The 'First Intermediate' period, which coincides roughly with the first millennium BC, was introduced by a waning of Olmec influence outside the heartland. It was accompanied by a renewal of local traditions in the arts and, it may be assumed, local political autonomy. Processes which were to lead to the great classic cultures asserted themselves in highland Mexico, the Valley of Oaxaca and the Maya area. Population growth was persistent if erratic and was accompanied by the occupation of previously uninhabited lands and the emergence of a more complex hierarchy of urban settlements. The move into marginal lands was accompanied, perhaps made possible, by improvements in technology, with the

thatch, with daub-and-whattle walls and compressed-earth floors, often on a low earth platform. Their inhabitants cultivated maize and other crops domesticated in the archaic period and they supplemented their diet by hunting and fishing. Their tools were of stone or of perishable materials. Burials with offerings occurred and structures with stucco floors may have constituted a simple form of public architecture. Social organization was simple, but elites and site ranking appear early in the archaeological record as does regional diversity, most clearly expressed by pottery variability; ecological conditions must also have produced wide variations in subsistence patterns.

Beginning about 1400 BC a striking change occurred with the diffusion through much of Mesoamerica of the distinctive style of pottery and decorative motifs of the Olmec (whose early type site, San Lorenzo, was located in the tropical lowlands of south-eastern Veracruz). The evidence of Olmec influence stretching from the highlands of central Mexico to the Pacific coastal plain of El Salvador per-

introduction of irrigation and terracing to what had previously been subsistence ground-water agriculture.

The differentiation of human settlements which had already begun continued with a proliferation of small urban communities and the rapid expansion of some villages into regional centres with stone-built public architecture. By the middle of the first millennium BC Monte Albán in the Valley of Oaxaca had an estimated population of 10,000–20,000 with an immense plaza surrounded by impressive buildings decorated with stone sculpture. A similar population is attributed to Cuicuilco, a contemporaneous site in the Valley of Mexico, with a circular pyramid some 80 m in diameter.

Elsewhere in Mesoamerica urban development on a substantial scale continued in the south-west at sites such as Kaminaljuyu and Izapa and began in the Maya lowlands at Tikal and El Mirador.

These trends were accompanied by the crystallization of a cultural pattern which was to persist to the end of the pre-Columbian period. Social structure responded to the need for leadership and control with the consolidation of ruling elites whose existence is confirmed archaeologically by wide differences in housing standards and grave offerings. Religion, already a pervasive force in the Olmec culture, came to dominate society quite literally in the temples that formed the ceremonial centres of any sizeable community and was more generally expressed by a ubiquitous religious symbolism. Increasing wealth brought craft specialization which in turn nourished a long-distance trading system of ancient origin that assured the exchange of the specialized products of the different ecological zones of Mesoamerica. Material progress was accompanied by intellectual achievement: the earliest certain evidence of hieroglyphic writing and calendrics, both intimately related to the religious system, comes at this time from the Valley of Oaxaca.

Together with these elements of cultural similarity a note of diversity is struck by the regional art styles that developed during the First Intermediate period. Distinctive pottery originated in the Valley of Mexico, at Chipicuaro and in western Mexico. At Monte Albán the Zapotec styles of pottery, sculpture and architecture took form. The stone sculpture of Izapa and the south-west Pacific coast exploited a rich

Uxmal: the 'Soothsayer Pyramid' and 'Nuns' Quadrangle'

tradition of religious and ritual iconography while, further south, Usulután lent its name to a decorative technique for pottery that spread through the Maya area. However, none of these styles imposed itself on all of Mesoamerica; the threshold between this period and the Middle Horizon is marked by the emergence of a culture which succeeded in doing so.

THE DOMINANCE OF TEOTIHUACÁN

Teotihuacán was, in many ways, an unlikely candidate for primacy in Mesoamerica. It lies 48 km north of Mexico City in an area that was marginal to human settlement until about 500 BC. Even when, in the next two or three centuries, small communities formed around its fresh-water springs, they were dwarfed by the well-established town of Cuicuilco. It is said that the site is a holy one, a shrine built over a sacred spring, which may explain its rapid growth and, more miraculously, the obliteration of Cuicuilco by eruption of the volcano Xitle near the turn of our era. Be that as it may, at about that time Cuicuilco fades from the scene and the population of Teotihuacán is estimated at an astonishing 50,000. The main axis of the city was laid out and the two great pyramids of the Sun and Moon were largely built. Simultaneously a population decline occurred in the rural areas of the Valley, suggesting that the growth of the city was the result of a policy of enforced urban concentration. The expansion continued, although at a slower pace, for 500 years and by about AD 650 some 125,000 or more persons were living in an area of 20 sq km of ceremonial centre, residential compound and craft workshop, making Teotihuacán the largest city of Mesoamerica and the most populous until the latter days of Tenochtitlán. This extraordinary trajectory, the meticulous urban planning of the city with its astronomically oriented grid and modular structures, the monumental public works and the organization needed merely to sustain a population of this size all indicate incontestable political control backed by powerful sanction. Although overt violence is never depicted at Teotihuacán and there is little evidence of physical compulsion, it is increasingly clear that the arts of the metropolis contain many indirect references to war and blood sacrifice. These have been chillingly corroborated by the excavation of mass sacrificial burials in the Pyramid of the Feathered Serpent, one of the site's main structures.

Teotihuacán's growth was fuelled by the successful exploitation of economic resources on a huge scale. The immediate stimulus was the development in the swampy area around its many springs of intensive raised-field agriculture, the antecedent of the productive *chinampa* system of the Aztecs. Its location astride important trade routes and in the immediate vicinity of the richest Mesoamerican deposits of fine obsidian was decisive for its subsequent expansion and prosperity. This obsidian, a volcanic glass used to produce tools of razor sharpness, was traded in exchange for the staple commodities required by the city's increasing population and for the necessities and luxuries which were not available in the Valley. There is early evidence of obsidian workshops in Teotihuacán and its typical products are found in archaeological deposits throughout Mesoamerica.

Teotihuacán remains along the main Mesoamerican trade routes and evidence of more permanent contact and even settlement as far afield as Kaminaljuyu, in highland Guatemala, suggest that by the fifth century AD at latest the city had become the hub of a vast trading network that stretched from Chalchihuites in the north to El Salvador in the south. The Teotihuacán presence is often associated with the symbolism of their most prominent deity, the rain god later known as Tlaloc, giving that presence a religious dimension. There are also more tenuous grounds for thinking that Teotihuacanos were assimilated into the early ruling lineages of several Mayan centres.

Coinciding roughly with the Teotihuacán florescence, other societies of more regional compass developed vigorous and brilliant cultures. The most noteworthy were the Maya, who occupied the southeast of Mesoamerica. Their art and architecture, notably finely carved stone stelae, polychrome pottery and the corbel arch, challenge comparison with those of Teotihuacán while their intellectual achievement in elaborating hieroglyphic writing and one of the world's most complex and accurate calendrical systems surpasses that of the metropolis. However, they did not approach Teotihuacán's genius for organization and control. Their political system is best described as that of the city-state, no one of which seems ever to have succeeded in dominating the Maya area. Their settlement pattern was much more dispersed than that of the central highlands and their cities were relatively smaller. Tikal, for example, had an estimated 45,000 inhabitants at the height of its power. They, nevertheless, created a civilization considered by many to represent the highest achievement of the Americas.

The other main focus of regional culture in the Middle Horizon period continued, as in the preceding period, to be the Valley of Oaxaca where Monte Albán, with a peak population estimated at 30,000, became the leading city in the southern highlands. Its pre-eminence rested in part on conquest but it entertained peaceful relations with its more distant neighbours. Monochrome grey pottery and urns in the form of deity effigies, local variants of familiar

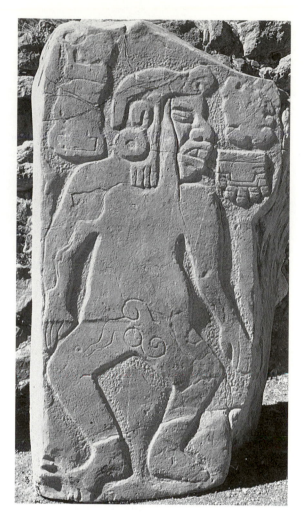

Carved figure, Monte Albán

This may be a symptom of a wider Mesoamerican deviation from a simple theocratic tradition to the callous exploitation of credulity that characterized the militaristic states that closed the last chapter of pre-Columbian history.

The ultimate decline and depopulation of Teotihuacán occurred about AD 750 against the background of these many regional readjustments. Much

---

The Mayan calendar

The Maya were the only fully literate culture of the pre-Spanish New World. Hundreds of stone carvings survive from Mexico, Guatemala and Honduras bearing block-like glyphs designed to be read in double columns.

As the function of public monuments was to commemorate victories in battle or the birth, accession, or the death of a ruler, a calendar was clearly necessary. Among the Maya this took the form of a complex dating system based on permutations of a 260-day sacred cycle with a solar year of 365 days. Though originally developed by the Olmec and used by all the peoples of ancient Mesoamerica, it was the Maya who raised calendar computation to its greatest level of refinement.

At the root of the system was a ancient 260 day count, the Almanac Year, based on a permutation of twenty named days with thirteen numbered 'weeks'. Alongside this ran an approximate Solar Year of 365 days, made up of eighteen 'months' of twenty days each, rounded off by an extra five-day span of ill omen (the *uayeb*). The meshing of the two cycles produced a fifty-two-year Calendar Round, the span of 52x365 days between the occasions when a day in one cycle met the same day in the other. Any date could be precisely placed within a fifty-two year period by this means.

For the long term, the Maya used the Long Count calendar, a five-cycle system which worked from a definite starting date of 13 August 3114 BC, a date probably regarded by the Maya as that of man's creation. In order of size the periods are *baktun* (144,000 days = 392.25 years), *katun* (7,200 days = 19.7 years), *tun* (360 days), *uinal* (20 days), and *kin* (1 day).

Each period glyph on an inscription is accompanied by the numerical coefficient by which it is to be multiplied. This is recorded as a bar-and-dot numeral, each bar having the value of five and each dot one. A date was expressed as a sequence of five coefficient plus period glyph units, the whole adding up to the total number of days since the starting date. Long Count 90.10.5.4.3 thus indicates (9x144,000) + (10x7,200) + (5x360) + (4x20) + (3x1), in all a total of 1,369,883 days since 13 August 3114 BC, ie. 20 September AD 639.

Mesoamerican creator and fertility gods, are characteristic of its distinctive art style which also shows some traces of Teotihuacán influence in the two centuries after AD 300.

Early in the second half of the first millennium a waning of Teotihuacán influence is apparent throughout Mesoamerica. The metropolis itself continued to flourish for another two centuries or so, renewing itself with major architectural projects and innovations in pottery and painting, but its artifacts are less traded and its iconographic motifs fall into disuse outside its near frontiers. The reason for these changes remains to be clarified but they seem to reflect inroads into the Teotihuacán monopoly of long-distance trading by rising centres such as Xochicalco and the outpost states.

Even before the grip of the centre was seriously weakened, new cultural vigour was displayed at the periphery. On the Gulf coast, El Tajín, and on the Pacific coast of Guatemala, the Cotzumalhuapa area, exemplify a reassertion of regional differentiation. Although widely separated, both are notable for their depictions in stone sculpture of a form of the Mesoamerican ballgame involving human sacrifice.

the same fate attended the other great cities of the Middle Horizon period shortly thereafter. By the end of the ninth century Tikal, Palenque and Copán had been abandoned as was Monte Albán. For El Tajín the end was delayed until about AD 1100. The reasons for this widespread collapse of advanced urban cultures remain obscure. Both ecological and social factors may be cited without any certainty as to their relative importance: among them possible causes are the depletion of local resources, economic imbalance, disintegration of the regional trading system, rigidity of the social structure, internal disaffection and external aggression.

The Second Intermediate period, following the fall of Teotihuacán, was a time of complex ebb and flow in the movement of peoples and balances of power throughout Mesoamerica which have not yet been fully documented but of which an outstanding feature was successive waves of 'barbarian' invasion from the nomadic tribal areas to the north. The first of these may have contributed to the ending of the Middle Horizon period; the last, that of the Aztecs, ushered in the Late Horizon, the concluding phase of pre-Columbian history.

Carved figure at the Toltec Temple of Warriors, Chichén Itzá

The immediate consequence in the Valley of Mexico was a redistribution of population towards north and south. The growth of Tula, later the Toltec capital, dates from this period. To the south, Xochicalco and Cholula also probably attracted Valley inhabitants. Cholula, while long influenced by Teotihuacán, had a somewhat cosmopolitan culture with ties to the Mixteca in the south and the Maya area to the east. It was to become the centre of the Mixteca–Puebla style, the last brilliant florescence of polychrome pottery decoration and codex illustration, which left its mark on the arts of the Toltec and Aztec and the mural paintings of the Maya. At this time, however, it seems to have suffered a partial eclipse possibly following invasion by the Mexicanized Maya of Tabasco, the Olmeca–Xicalanca or Putun. Their aggression within the Maya area has been blamed for hastening the collapse of the classic sites and for paving the way for the Toltec conquest of Yucatán. In the central highlands to the west they have been identified in the last centuries of the first millennium at Cholula and the nearby fortress sites around Cacaxtla. If their role was as mischievous as history suggests, their enjoyment of their spoils was shortlived as they were soon displaced by the Toltecs.

THE TOLTECS AND THE AZTECS

Although they are not always consistent and on occasion confuse myth with reality, the native codices and early Spanish chronicles, in which the history of the last five centuries of pre-Columbian Mesoamerica is recorded, give a vivid picture of the rise and fall of the two peoples that successively dominate that history: Toltecs and Aztecs. They speak of the Toltecs as composed of two main ethnic groups, which accords well with our knowledge of the northward drift of Valley population and of nomadic invasion at the beginning of the Second Intermediate period, and record the deeds of their pre-eminent leader Quetzalcoatl. Enlightened rule and the spread of Toltec power are credited to him as are more mythical deeds of which the most dramatic involve his exile from the Toltec capital at Tula, followed by wanderings which take him to Cholula and then further east to found a new kingdom. Archaeology has confirmed much of this story. Toltec rule was consolidated over most of central Mexico in the period AD 900–1150 and its collapse seems to have been precipitated by internal schism. The most spectacular Toltec remains lie 1500 km to the south-east at Chichén Itzá which bears a remarkable resemblance to the ceremonial centre at Tula and whence people of presumed Toltec affiliation dominated northern Yucatán for perhaps a century after the fall of Tula.

The terminal phase of pre-Columbian history centres once again on the Valley of Mexico. The Toltec collapse left the way open for further waves of

ulous, and possibly more memorable, than any city of the Americas or Europe. We can only guess what might have followed had Europe failed to discover the New World.   JCL

Further Reading: N. Davies, *The Ancient Kingdoms of Mexico* (London, 1982); W. Sanders and B. J. Price, *Mesoamerica: The Evolution of a Civilization* (New York, 1968); L. Schele and M. E. Miller, *The Blood of Kings: Dynasty and Ritual in Maya Art* (New York, 1986); M. P. Weaver, *The Aztecs, Maya and their Predecessors*, 2nd edition (New York, 1981); 3rd edition forthcoming

Pre-Columbian South America

CULTURE AREAS OF SOUTH AMERICA

By the second millennium BC in South America different areas had begun to develop distinctive cultural characteristics. The major distinction was between the Andean cultures, especially the central Andean ones, and those of the Amazon basin. The archaeological record for the central Andes is much more comprehensive, especially for the coastal desert where much inorganic material is preserved, than for the Amazon. By the time of the European conquests the area of highest cultural development was Tawantinsuyu (often spelt 'Tahuantinsuyo' in Spanish texts), the name that the Incas gave to their empire.

THE CENTRAL ANDES

This area comprises both highland and coastal Peru along with the Lake Titicaca basin. Here developed the cultures that culminated in Tawantinsuyu.

During the period between about 2300 and 1500 BC the earliest permanent villages were founded in the Peruvian highlands. On the coast settlements moved inland and the earliest irrigation systems were built. Towards the end of this period pottery appears in local styles throughout much of Peru except the far south. The actual techniques of pottery-making probably came from further north, since the earliest South American ceramics have been found in Ecuador, Colombia and Brazil. The oldest Peruvian pottery, about 2000 BC, has been excavated in the Upper Amazon basin. At Kotosh, a temple near

Chichén Itzá, Temple of Warriors

northern incursion which were chiefly remarkable for the speed with which the primitive nomads assimilated the culture of those they displaced in the Valley. Seven Chichimec tribes had thus established small kingdoms when their tardy kinsfolk, the Aztecs, made an unwelcome appearance on the scene after a long migration. Despite many hardships and efforts to expel them, the Aztecs persisted in the Valley and finally in AD 1325 established themselves at Tenochtitlán in the unpromising swampy reaches of Lake Texcoco.

Even in their humble beginnings, the Aztecs considered themselves a chosen people destined to military greatness under the tutelage of their god Huitzilopochtli. A naturally combative disposition was reinforced by a religion based on the concept of a universe whose very existence depended on a continuous supply of sacrificial blood which only wars could satisfy. Conquest became a condition for human survival and a spiritual duty as well as a source of wealth through the tribute exacted from the subject peoples. The result was the expansion of the lacustrine hamlet in less than 200 years into an empire created and maintained by military power. By the time Tenochtitlán fell to the Spaniards on 13 August 1521, its empire extended over most of central Mexico between the Tarascans to the north-west and the Maya to the south-east. The city itself had by that time some 250,000 inhabitants and was laid out on a grid of canals, streets and causeways, with elaborate hydraulic works, ceremonial centres, palaces and markets. It was described by Cortés as being as large as Seville or Córdoba and was in fact more pop-

CHRONOLOGICAL TABLE

Dates	Central Andes	Northern Andes	Southern Andes	Tropical Forest
Spanish conquest	Spanish conquest	Spanish conquest	Spanish conquest	European conquest
1500	Inca empire Chimú	Inca empire Chibcha	Inca empire Fortified towns	
1000			Tiahuanaco influence	
500	Huari Pacheco Conchopata Tiahuanaco Moche culture Nazca culture			
AD BC				
500	Chavin influence		Pottery-making cultures	
1000	Chavin de Hauntar			
		Machalilla Phase		
1500	Garagay Huaca de los Reyes Cerro Sechin Kotosh – pottery			
2000				
2500				
3000		Pottery (coastal Ecuador and Caribbean lowlands)		Pottery (Amazon)

the headwaters of the Huallaga River, the earliest pottery has been dated by radiocarbon to about 1800 BC. The most common shapes are open vessels resembling cups and vases. Stirrup-spout bottles, consisting of a chamber with a stirrup-shaped handle set on top, appear for the first time in the central Andes. This form continued to be made in north Peru right up to the Spanish conquest. Decoration consisted of bands of fine incised lines filled with white, red or yellow pigment. This early Kotosh pottery is too elaborate to be considered an initial stage.

During the second and first millennia BC a tradition of erecting large public buildings, often regarded as ceremonial centres, also continued developing. These are thought to have been built by 'corporate labour' which consisted of construction gangs drawn from extended families or communities. The work would have been directed by a higher authority. Sometimes actual sections built by different groups of workers can be seen in these structures. This system of construction for large buildings was to continue right up to the Spanish conquest. The central coast was the main area where many early ceremonial centres were built by this method. Most of them, like Garagay near Lima, were artificial hills built of

clay and irregularly shaped stones in the shape of an animal, possibly a feline. The 'head' faces west, the tail east and the abdomen north. The abdomen is the most important part, having stairways and terraces at the end of a large plaza bounded by elongated platforms which may represent the legs.

A tenoned head depicting one of the forms of a fanged being at the temple of Chavin de Huantar

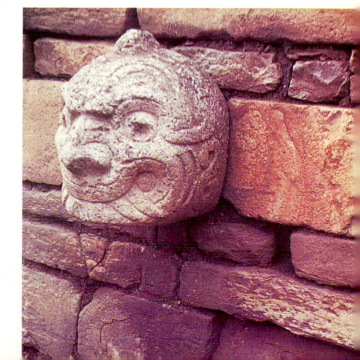

PRE-COLUMBIAN SOUTH AMERICA

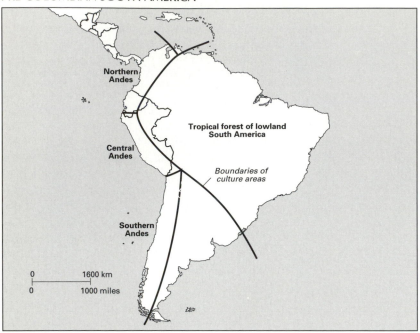

Between about 1200 and 1000 BC the first monumental stone sculpture in Peru was erected at the ceremonial centre of Cerro Sechín on the north-central coast. The large stones depict entire human beings, possibly warriors, while the smaller ones show trophy heads, human heads or parts of human bodies. These carvings all seem to concentrate on various aspects of warfare or rituals involving dismemberment. These themes reappear in later Peruvian art.

Central Andean pottery, especially that from tombs, has been used by North American archaeologists to construct a chronological scheme. This begins with an Initial period about 1800 BC followed by three 'horizons', termed Early, Middle and Late, characterized by varying degrees of cultural and political unification. In between came periods of regional cultures termed the Early and Late Intermediate periods.

Early Horizon

The Early Horizon is marked by an elaborate art style whose principal motifs involved felines, people with feline attributes, serpents, birds of prey and other animals. Elements of this style spread through most of Peru except the far south and have been found on murals, pottery, goldwork, textiles and shells. The most elaborate forms were on stone sculpture at the temple of Chavín de Huantar in the northern highlands. Until a few years ago it was thought that this art style emanated from Chavín itself and spread throughout much of Peru as a religious cult.

The most widespread of the Chavín deities is the 'staff god'. He is shown as a standing feline in human form with outstretched arms, snakes for hair and an elaborate staff in each hand. He could have been a sky god associated with the cyclical movements of the stars and planets.

Recent archaeological fieldwork and analysis have shown that there were significant local variations in this art style. The 'mythical beings' varied from place to place. According to radiocarbon dates, the Early Horizon began about 1500 BC on the central and north coast at ceremonial centres like Garagay and Huaca de Los Reyes near Trujillo. Chavín itself did not become established until about five hundred years later and only reached its height between 600 and 300 BC when it influenced both the highlands and south coast.

Therefore the Early Horizon was really a religious phenomenon which arose in several centres in different areas. There seem to have been regular contacts between them, producing a shared body of ideas.

Early Intermediate period

Towards the end of the Early Horizontal regional cultures with their own art styles began to emerge throughout the central Andes. In particular the Nazca culture, typified by its distinctive pottery style, emerged towards the beginning of the Christian era on the south coast of Peru. Most is known about these people through their polychrome pots which depicted everything from mythical beings with trophy heads to farmers and crops. The trophy heads suggest that ritual decapitation was practised.

A Moche stirrup-spout bottle

At the beginning of the first millennium AD another distinctive regional culture variously called Mochica or Moche (the latter after the name of the village on the north coast where it was first identified) emerged. Like Nazca it was distinguished by its fine pottery, but the emphasis was on sculptured form and fine line drawing rather than polychrome painting. Although Moche pottery has been found from the valley of Lambayeque in the north to that of Nepeña in the south, its style is not exactly the same in each valley. Pottery scenes show similarly dressed Moche warriors fighting each other using wooden clubs with stone heads and metal spikes. Other features are trophy heads and dismembered human limbs. Boundary walls have been found along the northern edges of the Santa and Moche valleys. There may have been a loose alliance of chiefdoms with one in each valley. Evidence from tombs shows that some people were more wealthy than others since they had more and better quality possessions deposited in their graves.

Both the Moche and Nazca employed irrigation to grow crops like maize and beans. In addition the Moche erected substantial mud-brick structures using corporate labour. An example is the Huaca del Sol which may have functioned as a sacred burial mound where occasional religious ceremonies were performed.

Middle Horizon: Tiahuanaco and Huari

While the Moche and Nazca cultures flourished, Tiahuanaco (or Tiwanaku), on the eastern side of Lake Titicaca, began developing as a large ceremonial centre. Excavations have shown that most of the temples there were built between AD 200 and 500. The main stone carving set up was a gateway on the lintel of which was carved a figure with a radiating headdress of puma heads and a staff held vertically in each hand. The figure has been said to represent Viracocha, the creator god of Peruvian mythology.

A locally modified version of this Tiahuanaco god has been found about 600 km to the north on smashed oversize urns at Conchopata near Ayacucho. This version seems to have been adopted by the people of Huari (or Wari), an ancient city of walled compounds about 25 km north-east of Ayacucho, between about AD 550 and 700. Another important religious centre was at Pacheco on the south coast. Here oversize urns of a religious or ceremonial type have been found painted with polychrome representations of a male and female version of the god depicted on the Conchopata urns. Maize ears feature prominently as appendages on both these variations of the Pacheco god.

It has been argued that during the eighth century AD the political and religious influence of Huari spread in the form of an empire through much of highland and coastal Peru in what is termed the Middle Horizon. However, there is little concrete evidence for such an 'empire' outside southern Peru since there were no administrative centres beyond the immediate vicinity of Huari. Also outside the southern highland Huari pottery is relatively rare and hardly ever occurs in domestic refuse. Almost all the evidence for Huari–Tiahuanaco influence has come from the style of offerings, especially pottery in tombs. In fact the cultural unity of the Middle Horizon seems to have been exaggerated. The reality appears to have been a series of regional states or spheres of influence like Tiahuanaco and Huari. What unifying forces there were in the Middle Horizon seem to have ended about AD 800, with Huari itself being abandoned by AD 900.

Late Intermediate period

With the disappearance of Huari and Tiahuanaco influence after about AD 1000 regional cultures developed, especially along the coast. These are known archaeologically through their artifacts and architectural remains together with some Spanish documentary records. Some powerful states arose along the coast and these were encountered by the Incas when they were establishing their empire in the

The Huaca del Sol at Moche, a large mud-brick pyramid built by the Moche people during the first half of the first millennium AD

sixteenth century. In particular we know most about the north coast.

The Chimú became established in the Trujillo area about AD 1200. By the time of their conquest by the Incas in the 1460s the Chimú had established an empire that stretched from the frontier with Ecuador to the Rimac valley on the central coast, a distance of over 1000 km. The capital, Chan Chan, situated at the mouth of the Moche valley, covers an area of over 6 sq km. The site is dominated by ten large enclosures or *ciudadelas*, rectangular or rectilinear in shape, with exterior walls between 200 and 600 m long and up to 10 m high. They were almost certainly the residences of various Chimú rulers.

The Chimú were ruled by a line of dynastic kings of which the first is supposed to have come from the Lambayeque area. Like the Incas, they maintained that before their appearance Peru had been ruled over by a series of hereditary chiefs. The Chimú governed through a system of hereditary local nobility. There was a strict division between nobility and commoners as well as a distinct hierarchy. Women were granted nearly equal rights with men. The marriage ceremony stressed the equality of both parties. Chimú society seems to have been organized along the lines of the *ayllu* (described by the Spaniards as a related group of kinsmen or a lineage descended from a common ancestor). These Chimú *ayllu* had particular names that were handed down in the male line from father to son.

The Chimú legal system was very strict. The punishment for disrespect to shrines consisted of burying the prisoner alive with the bones of other offenders and of unclean animals. Adulterers were thrown from cliffs. Stealing was regarded as very serious and the punishment of thieves was not just a civil but also a religious matter. This gives the impression that property may have been regarded by the nobles as being owned by divine right.

The Spaniards recorded ten different stages of life in the Chimú kingdom from childhood through the adult span to old age. The stages of childhood and youth continued until the twenty-fifth year when an individual was considered to be a full citizen and a warrior with rights to his own home and community fields. From fifty to sixty he was regarded as 'half old', having only to do light work. After sixty he had to pay no tribute and could not be called on for war service.

When a Chimú died there was a five-day period of mourning. Then the body was washed and buried with the knees drawn up. It was wrapped in cloth to form a bundle on top of which a stuffed false head covered with a face mask was placed. The location and type of burial depended on one's status. The ordinary people of Chan Chan were buried in unlined graves in a cemetery just south of the city. The rulers were interred in specially built platforms, one of which is usually found inside each *ciudadela*. At one of the smaller burial platforms found in Chan Chan large

numbers of skeletons of young women have been recently discovered. They were probably the wives and other ladies of a Chimú ruler who were sacrificed to accompany him.

The Late Horizon: the Incas

The Incas, according to archaeological evidence and legends, were originally one of a number of small tribes in the Cuzco area. They appear to have settled in Cuzco about AD 1200 under the leadership of their legendary founder Manco Capac. However, it was not until about AD 1438 that they gained ascendancy in the Cuzco area and started expanding. First under Pachacuti, they under his son Topa Inga, and finally under Guayna Capac, their empire eventually stretched from the present-day border of Colombia with Ecuador to the Maule River in central Chile by about AD 1520.

The Inca emperors ruled by divine right as representatives of the Sun on earth. They claimed direct descent from the Sun through Manco Capac. The Inca emperor or Sapa Inca had absolute power and in theory considered all the men in his empire his sons and all the women his wives. He governed through an elite class of nobles some of whom were of royal blood while others were 'Incas by privilege'. Both

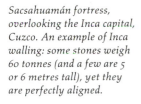

Sacsahuamán fortress, overlooking the Inca capital, Cuzco. An example of Inca walling: some stones weigh 60 tonnes (and a few are 5 or 6 metres tall), yet they are perfectly aligned.

Ceremonial raft (Gold Museum, Bogotá). The Chibcha of Colombia were the finest goldsmiths of pre-Columbian America.

groups belonged to the Inca class and could wear the types of headband and earplugs worn by the Inca himself. The nobles of royal blood formed lineage groups called *panaca* which consisted of all the descendants of a ruler in the male line. 'Incas by privilege' were not Incas by birth although some were related through alliances and political marriages to Inca rulers before Pachacuti came to power in 1438. These Incas by privilege spoke Quechua, the official language of Tawantinsuyu. Many of them were sent to different parts of the empire to set an example and to indoctrinate the local people with Inca culture.

Inca society was stratified, with the commoners at the bottom and the Inca royal family at the top. Within the empire the social structure was essentially one of small local groups, each with its own ancestor cult. In addition, groups of colonists or *mitimas* were established in certain areas but some seem to have remained under the control of local rulers (*curacas*) of the districts whence they came.

Inca society was also divided by age groups. Twelve standard age divisions were made for the purposes of census and tax assessment. The transition from one age grade to another did not occur at a certain time since the Indians kept no exact record of their age. More important were obvious changes in physical condition such as puberty. The most significant age grade was that of adulthood which was entered at marriage and lasted as long as both parties could do a full day's work.

Most commoners were agriculturalists who paid their taxes in labour or *mita*. Archaeological evidence suggests that they were rewarded with a maize beer called *chicha*. The *mita* was used to build and maintain roads, erect public buildings and provide food and cloth for imperial storehouses. Specialist craftsmen paid their *mita* by working at their trade. Transport for goods was on the backs of men and llamas since there were no wheeled vehicles in pre-Columbian South America.

Inca laws were recorded on *quipus*, a system of knot records also used to keep accounts, since there was no writing in pre-Columbian South America. There was a wide range of laws extending from Municipal Law, concerning tribal rights, to *Mitachanacuy*, which regulated the distribution of work so that everyone did their fair share. Punishments for individuals were physical and there were neither fines nor imprisonment. The type of punishment received depended on the rank of the individual. Women in Inca society had a lower legal status than men: husbands were justified in killing their wives for adultery while wives who killed adulterous husbands were hanged by the feet until dead.

Tawantinsuyu represented a degree of organization and sophistication which was not matched elsewhere in pre-Columbian South America. It included many pre-Inca elements which were inherited or taken over from conquered peoples like the Chimú. For example, many of the gold ornaments that Pizarro and his companions had melted down when they kidnapped Atahualpa were very likely made by metal workers brought from Chan Chan. Tawantinsuyu had been in existence for just over sixty years before it fell to the Spaniards. In fact it had already shown signs of considerable strain and was only just recovering from a civil war. If the Spaniards had not conquered it, then sooner or later it could well have disintegrated into regional cultures.

NORTHERN AND SOUTHERN ANDES

In the southern Andes, comprising southern Bolivia, Chile and highland Argentina, farming and pottery-making cultures became established by the middle of the first millennium BC. During the first millennium AD there were signs of influence from the high plateau of Bolivia and more complex societies developed. In the latter half of the first millennium AD the northern parts of this area came under the influence of Tiahuanaco. However, most of the south Andean region appears to have remained culturally, and probably politically, autonomous. At this time pottery and other crafts flourished.

After about AD 1000 settlements were concentrated in fortified towns and villages and there was some aesthetic decline. These fortifications were particularly apparent in the northern part of the area, suggesting warfare between towns or small regional states. The Incas made their presence felt in this area by armed force between 1450 and 1490.

The northern Andes comprise the highland and coastal areas of what is now Ecuador and Colombia. Some of the earliest pottery in South America, dating to about 3000 BC, has come from coastal sites in Ecuador and the Caribbean lowlands. There are also similarities between some of the decorated bowls of the Machalilla phase (*c*. 1500–1000 BC) of Ecuador and those of the Pre-classic cultures of Mesoamerica. This Mesoamerican influence continued right up to the conquest of Ecuador by the Incas in the sixteenth century. Seaborne trade, using large rafts, seems to have been the most likely explanation for this phenomenon.

As is the case in the southern Andes, the pre-Columbian peoples of the northern Andes never developed an empire on the scale of Tawantinsuyu. The political organization of the northern Andeans, like the Chibcha of Colombia, encountered by the Spaniards, was based on chiefdoms. The Zipa, one of the Chibcha chiefs, had his capital at Bogotá. When the Spaniards saw the Chibcha in 1537 they were impressed at the size of their population and their numerous palisaded towns and villages. In addition they not only had palaces and temples but also a prosperous agriculture and thriving internal trade.

TROPICAL FOREST OF LOWLAND SOUTH AMERICA

This area includes the tropical forests of Venezuela, the Guianas and the Amazon basin. The archaeology of this region still has considerable gaps in it although much research is currently being carried out. Pottery appears early and was in use at the mouth of the Amazon by 3000 BC. The first European explorers reported substantial Indian settlements, particularly along the banks of the Amazon and its tributaries. The main food was manioc, supplemented by game and fish. The level of cultural and political sophistication reached here did not match that of the central Andes. However, Inca armies made no significant headway into the Upper Amazon and did, in fact, recruit bowmen from that area to serve in their own forces.   GHAB

Further Reading: G. Bankes, *Peruvian Pottery* (Princes Risborough, 1989); R. W. Keatinge, ed., *Peruvian Prehistory* (Cambridge, 1988); B. J. Meggers, *Ecuador* (London, 1966); G. Reichel-Dolmatoff, *Colombia* (London, 1965)

The Spanish conquests, 1492–1580

AMERICA IN THE 'AGE OF DISCOVERY'

The hundred years from 1450 to 1550 were an 'age of discovery' without precedent in world history. This was the dramatic moment when European civilization began, in J. H. Parry's words, 'to think of the world as a whole and of all seas as one'. In principle, other civilizations might have initiated this decisive historical shift. In several far-ranging expeditions between 1405 and 1433, the great Chinese admiral Cheng Ho conducted imposing fleets of large junks – the world's biggest and best ships at the time – on voyages of reconnaissance to places as far from China as Aden and the Persian Gulf. These impressive Chinese forays were abruptly halted by the reigning Ming dynasty. Had they continued, modern history might well have looked very different. As it was, the initiative thus abandoned in the East was taken up in the West – by the rising states of the Atlantic coast of Europe, especially Portugal (the true pioneer-nation in this respect) and Spain. These two countries were the first to take advantage of the vital late-medieval innovations in ship-design and navigation that made long-range oceanic seafaring feasible. Their quest for new trades, for new territories, and for new converts to Christianity opened the way to an astonishing period of maritime exploration and (on the heels of exploration) imperialism. It was, by any standard, one of the great turning points in history. The world is still living with the consequences.

Three supreme maritime feats stood out in this age of discovery. In 1492–3, the Genoese seafarer Christopher Columbus (1451–1506), backed by the Spanish crown, led an expedition of three ships across the Atlantic to the outlying islands of the then unknown American continent. In 1497–9, the Portuguese commander Vasco da Gama (*c*. 1460–1524), in a technically more audacious voyage, sailed to and from India by way of the southern tip of Africa – the culmination of a Portuguese national effort reaching back over eighty years and associated in its earlier phases with Prince Henry 'the Navigator' (1394–1460); an impressive monument to him now stands on the Lisbon waterfront. Just over two decades later, the globe itself was circumnavigated for the first time by a ship from Ferdinand Magellan's notable expedition of 1519–22. Magellan

(1480–1521), a Portuguese subject working for Spain, did not survive this altogether spectacular journey; he was killed in the Philippines en route. The honour of becoming the first navigator to sail round the world thus fell to the Basque sea-captain Juan Sebastián del Cano (*c.* 1486–1526), who guided the remnants of Magellan's party back to Spain.

Columbus was not the first European to set foot in the western hemisphere – the intrepid Norse sailors of AD 1000 can claim certain priority – yet he was in a real sense the true discoverer (from the European standpoint) of America. The Norse voyages had no after-effects in history; the Norsemen lacked the numbers and the resources to found lasting settlements. They had been forgotten by the fifteenth century, except perhaps in Scandinavia. By contrast, immense and long-lasting consequences flowed from Columbus's first journey of 1492–3. Columbus himself made four voyages in all. On the third and fourth of these (1498–1500, 1502–4), he reconnoitred part of the South and Central American coastlines. Other navigators, including the Florentine, Amerigo Vespucci (1454–1512) – whose Christian name was later to be given to the new-found landmass in the west – established that a huge western continent, undreamed of by Europe, lay on the map of the world. Columbus's purpose had been to prove the existence of a direct, westward ocean route from Europe to Asia – had his geographical opinions been correct, Japan would have been roughly where Mexico is – and he never fully grasped that what had been disclosed as a result of his efforts was truly a 'new world'. 'Our world,' wrote the sixteenth-century French essayist Montaigne (quoted here in Florio's contemporary translation), 'hath of late discovered another,…no lesse-large, fully peopled, all-things-yeelding, and mighty in strength than ours.' Europeans' mental horizons were ultimately to be greatly

Statue of Christopher Columbus, Buenos Aires. The monument was donated by the Italian community in Argentina around 1910. The sculptural group at the base symbolizes Civilization, Science and Genius.

Columbus first sets foot in the New World

Columbus's own journals were lost, but Bartolomé de Las Casas had access to them, evidently transcribed a good deal of material, and used them in his large -scale Historia de las Indias *(probably written in the 1550s, though only published in 1875). His abstract is probably close to the original text.*

Friday 12 October 1492
After sunset [Thursday 11 October] the Admiral returned to his original west course, and they went along at a rate of twelve miles an hour. Up to two hours after midnight they had gone 90 miles, equal to 22½ leagues. As the caravel *Pinta* was a better sailer, and went ahead of the Admiral, she found the land, and made the signals ordered by the Admiral. The land was first seen by a sailor named Rodrigo de Triana . . . At two hours after midnight the land was sighted at a distance of two leagues… The vessels were hove to, waiting for daylight; and on Friday [12 October] they arrived at a small island of the Lucayos, called in the language of the Indians, *Guanahani.* [Watling Island: Lat. 23°55'N, Long. 74°28'W]. Presently they saw naked people. The Admiral went ashore in the armed boat, and Martin Alonso Pinzon, and Vicente Yáñez, his brother, who was captain of the *Niña.* The Admiral took the royal standard, and the captains went with two banners of the green cross, which the Admiral took in all ships as a sign, with an F [Ferdinand] and a Y [Isabel] and a crown over each letter, one on the one side of the cross, and the other on the other. Having landed, they saw trees very green, and much water, and fruits of diverse kinds. The Admiral called to the two captains, and to the others who leaped on shore . . . and said that they should bear faithful testimony that he, in presence of all, had taken, as he now took possession of the said island for the King and for the Queen . . .

Source: The Journal of Christopher Columbus (during his first voyage 1492–93) and Documents relating to the Voyages of John Cabot and Gaspar Corte Real, translated with notes and an introduction by Clements R. Markham (London, 1893).

Model of Columbus's flagship, Santa Maria, *which was in fact lost during his first voyage in 1492–3*

ing venture yet mounted by a European nation. Spain's intentions in America were thus clear from the outset. The Spanish urge to conquer territory was deep-rooted. It came in large part from the turbulent medieval history of the Iberian peninsula, and in particular the long struggle of the Christian kingdoms (with Castile always to the fore) to expel the Muslim invaders who had overwhelmed the Visigothic kingdom of Spain after AD 711 – the *Reconquista*, 'reconquest', as Spaniards called this struggle. The last Muslim redoubt in Spain, the Moorish kingdom of Granada, was subdued by the Catholic Monarchs only a few months before Columbus's first voyage. The cult of honour and the martial virtues – so movingly expressed in the final stanzas of Spain's finest fifteenth-century poem, the *Coplas* of Jorge Manrique; so immortally satirized later on in the most famous of all Spanish books, *Don Quixote* – was well developed in late-medieval Spain. It provided strong psychological reinforcement to the Spanish conquistadors who marched and fought their way across the vast, alien landscapes of America in the sixteenth century.

Spanish colonization was at first confined to the main Caribbean islands, starting with Hispaniola (1494), and spreading from there to Puerto Rico (1508) and Cuba (1511). This was merely the prelude to an astonishing sequence of conquests. Of the scores of expeditions, large and small (generally fairly small), that penetrated the American mainland over the next few decades, two were particularly momentous, for they brought about the downfall of the two most populous and sophisticated native American states. In 1519 Hernán Cortés (1485–1547) and some 600 followers landed in Mexico. Two years later, the once-powerful Aztec confederacy was in ruins, its ruler, Montezuma II, dead, its beautiful capital, Tenochtitlán, reduced to providing the foundations for a new Spanish city. A similar catastrophe befell the Inca empire of Peru, overwhelmed in the early 1530s by Francisco Pizarro (c. 1470–1541) and, at the outset, around 150 men. The Inca emperor, Atahualpa, was garrotted. Thus, in the course of fifteen years, two great Amerindian societies were devastatingly assaulted by a handful of Spanish adventurers. These appalling events were the most incredible of the sixteenth century – among the most incredible, surely, in world history.

From newly conquered Mexico (New Spain, as it became known to the Spaniards) and Peru, subsidiary expeditions of conquest spread out across adjacent territories – into northern Mexico, Yucatán, Central America, Quito (the Incas' 'northern kingdom'), Chile, and what are now Bolivia and north-west Argentina. Meanwhile, separate expeditions incorporated other areas of America into the now fast-

stretched as a consequence of the discovery of America. So too, and rather sooner, were their political and economic horizons. For discovery was to be followed immediately by conquest.

THE SPANISH CONQUESTS

For Spain, recently united under its 'Catholic Monarchs', King Ferdinand of Aragon and Queen Isabella of Castile, the New World offered an alluring field for territorial expansion. Columbus's second expedition, to the island he named Hispaniola (now shared by two countries, the Dominican Republic and Haiti), consisted of seventeen ships carrying around 1400 men (no women), horses, cattle, pigs, farm implements and seeds. It was probably the biggest coloniz-

SPAIN		PORTUGAL	
1492–3	COLUMBUS'S FIRST VOYAGE to the Caribbean.		

	1493	The Papal Bull *Inter Caetera* divides the world into Spanish and Portuguese zones of conquest, settlement and trade.	
	1494	TREATY OF TORDESILLAS. Spain and Portugal adjust the Papal line of demarcation to a longitude 370 leagues west of the Azores.	

SPAIN		PORTUGAL	
1493–6	COLUMBUS'S SECOND VOYAGE. Establishment of a Spanish colony on island of Hispaniola. Foundation of *Santo Domingo*, oldest Spanish-speaking city in western hemisphere (1496).		
1508–9	Conquest of Puerto Rico by Juan Ponce de León.	1500	Pedro Alvares Cabral discovers Brazil while on his way to India.
1509–13	Small mainland colonies established.		
1511	Conquest of Cuba by Diego Velásquez.	1500–30	Brazilwood (dyewood) trade established along the coast of *terra do brasil*, 'brazilwood land'.
1513	Vasco Núñez de Balboa crosses Panama isthmus and becomes first European to see the Pacific.		
1519–21	CONQUEST OF MEXICO by Hernán Cortés. Fall of Aztec confederacy. Destruction of Tenochtitlán and foundation of *Mexico City* (1521).		
1522	Pascual de Andagoya reconnoitres Peruvian coast and learns of existence of Inca empire.		
1523–40	Various expeditions conquer Yucatán and Central America.		
1529	The Welsers (Augsburg bankers) undertake colonization in Venezuela under licence from Emperor Charles V (King Charles I of Spain).		
1531–5	CONQUEST OF PERU by Francisco Pizarro. Fall of Inca empire (1533). Foundation of *Lima* (1535).	1532	Portuguese colony at São Vicente.
1535	First viceroy of New Spain (Mexico) assumes office.	1534	Captaincy system introduced.
1535–7	Expedition to River Plate by Pedro de Mendoza. Foundation of *Buenos Aires* (1536) and of the upriver colony at *Asunción*, Paraguay (1537). Buenos Aires later abandoned (1541).		
1536–8	Conquest of Chibcha kingdoms of New Granada (modern Colombia) by Gonzalo Jiménez de Quesada. Foundation of *Bogotá* (1538).		
1540–2	Francisco Vásquez de Coronado leads an expedition (the most notable of several in this direction) to parts of what is now the United States, reaching as far as the modern Kansas.		
1540–1	Pedro de Valdivia undertakes the conquest of Chile. Foundation of *Santiago de Chile* (1541).		
1542	The New Laws of the Indies. Peru designated as a viceroyalty.	1549	First governor-general of Brazil appointed, with his capital at *Bahia*.
1544–8	Rebellion against Spanish authorities by Spanish settlers in Peru.		
1550–1	The Valladolid Debates.		
1567	Foundation of *Caracas*, Venezuela, by Diego de Losada.	1554	Foundation of *São Paulo*.
1580	Re-establishment ('second foundation') of Buenos Aires by Juan de Garay and colonists from Asunción, Paraguay.	1567	Foundation of *Rio de Janeiro*.
		1580–1640	Portugal under the Spanish crown.

expanding empire. Gonzalo Jiménez de Quesada (*c.* 1510–79), in the mid-1530s, advanced from the Caribbean coast into the highlands of what we now call Colombia (New Granada was its colonial name) and there subdued the Chibcha kingdoms. Ironically, perhaps, the single most powerful expedition mounted from Spain itself in these years of far-flung conquest – the one led by Pedro de Mendoza (1487–1537) to the River Plate in 1535 (one of its members was St Teresa of Avila's brother) – yielded little in the way of immediate territory. Here the nomadic Indians of the Argentine pampa held back the advance of the would-be conquistadors, and colonization had to focus for the moment on Asunción, in Paraguay, hundreds of miles upriver from the sea. It was from this modest Paraguayan base, in 1580,

that a party of settlers sailed downriver to re-establish an abandoned Spanish outpost called Buenos Aires – later to become perhaps the grandest of all Spanish-speaking cities. By 1580, all the main segments of Spain's new American empire were in place.

The rapidity and sheer scale of the Spanish conquests never fails to impress those who read about them. Yet the Spanish crown, eager enough to accept the fruits of conquest, played a relatively small part in its organization. After Columbus's voyages, the expansion of Spain's overseas empire was largely the work of small private bands of armed adventurers operating spontaneously. These bands were invariably licensed by the crown (or later the crown's agents in America) but they were organized, recruited and financed (often on borrowed money)

THE SPANISH CONQUESTS

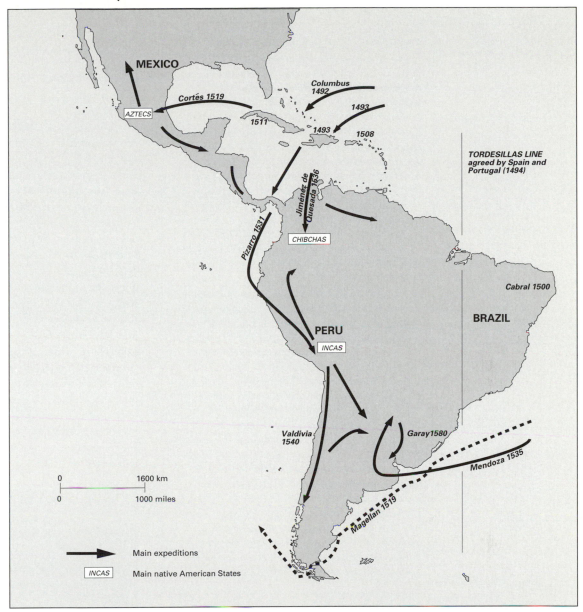

by individual conquistadors or partnerships. At a time when Spanish troops were heavily engaged in European wars, virtually no regular soldiers were used, even if expeditions often contained their share of veterans. At sea, likewise, few if any recognizable warships took part; expeditions used any vessel they could find. The essential element in all the expeditions (there were at least fifty, many of them fruitless) was one of leadership and motivation. Most of the leaders came from the lower fringe of the aristocracy: they were *hidalgos*, to use the Spanish term. One or two, Pizarro for instance, came from lower down the social scale. Often they were impecunious *hidalgos*, eager to acquire the seigneurial style of life to which they felt themselves entitled. A disproportionate number of the most prominent conquistadors

came from Extremadura, the hard, arid region to the west of Castile. Their followers, the majority in any expedition, consisted of a great variety of lower-class Spaniards, including ex-soldiers and a whole gallery of craftsmen, many of them from Andalusia – which was to have consequences for the American variants of the Spanish language. They were sometimes turbulent and unruly; more than one conquistador faced (and some did not survive) mutiny in the course of an expedition.

For leaders and led alike, motivation was all-important. The late medieval cult of honour was here combined – in what proportions it is hard to say – with crusading zeal on behalf of Christendom, and in most cases with sheer greed. Bernal Díaz del Castillo, the doughty footsoldier who later (in old age) wrote a

189

The Conquistadors' invisible allies

Compared with the main European armies of the time the Spanish expeditions of conquest in America were poorly equipped. On his advance into Mexico in 1519 Hernán Cortés took thirteen muskets and a few small cannon. The standard weaponry for the footsoldiers of the conquest consisted of swords, pikes and crossbows. Horses (Cortés had only a few, but more than a third of Francisco Pizarro's followers in 1532–3 were cavalrymen) were at first terrifying to native Americans, but not for long. Some indigenous peoples (e.g., the Araucanians of southern Chile) soon became the Spaniards' equals as fighters on horseback.

Unwittingly, however, the conquistadors bore more deadly weapons. The impact of Old World diseases (especially smallpox) on the previously isolated New World peoples is now commonly recognized as the main cause of the catastrophic decline in the native American population in the sixteenth century. It is less often noticed that disease played an important role in the conquests themselves. The first smallpox epidemic in the Americas began in 1518–19 in Hispaniola, from where it spread to other Caribbean islands and to Mexico. A serious outbreak of smallpox in the Aztec capital, Tenochtitlan, undoubtedly facilitated Cortés's final assault on the city in 1521. The disease decimated the native population of the Panama isthmus in the 1520s and reached the Inca empire before Pizarro. It was the likely cause of the death of the Inca Guayna Capac (1526), which led to the civil war between his sons Atahualpa and Huascar. Had it not been weakend by this conflict – and by the smallpox virus – the empire might have been better placed to repulse the invaders. Old World germs were the conquistadors' invisible allies.

The technological superiority of the Spaniards should not be exaggerated as a reason: firearms undoubtedly gave them an edge at times, while the horse (unknown in America) allowed them a vital degree of mobility. Yet they were always vastly outnumbered by their Indian opponents. The Spaniards were certainly able to take advantage of divisions among Indian peoples; Cortés, for instance, found a small Indian state, Tlaxcala, which was hostile to the Aztecs and had resisted inclusion in their confederacy, and his alliance with the Tlaxcalans was a key factor in his success. Similarly, the Inca empire at the time the Spaniards arrived had recently gone through a civil war; Pizarro was able to play on this to a certain extent in subjugating Peru. In the end, however, it seems to have been the sheer determination (not to say ruthlessness) of the conquistadors that decided the outcome. Indian resistance to the conquests was sometimes fierce enough – the great Inca rising in Peru in 1536 was a moderately close-run thing for the Spaniards – but it was patchy, and only in a few cases *did* it last very long. A conspicuous example of where it did was the remote southern 'frontier' of Chile, where Araucanian Indians maintained their resistance to European domination right into the nineteenth century. But the Araucanians lived on the fringe of an unimportant colony. In the imperial heartlands, as in most other areas, the Indian population was rapidly subordinated to the will of its new European overlords. Sporadic Indian

classic eye-witness account of Cortés's expedition, tells us crisply and without irony that he and his companions went to Mexico 'to serve God and His Majesty the King, to give light to those who were in darkness, and also to get rich – which all of us came looking for'. Here it is worth remembering that the late-medieval cult of honour included the notion that the noblest method of securing wealth was to *win* it, preferably through deeds of valour – deeds of a kind then being extensively chronicled in 'books of chivalry', a type of literature achieving its greatest popularity at the time of the conquest of America. Thus the lure of material gain *and* honour drove the conquistadors to accept extraordinary odds and to submit themselves to heroic feats of endurance.

The speed with which the great native American civilizations were conquered is certainly astonishing.

Hernán Cortés (1485–1547), the conqueror of Mexico

Potosí in a seventeenth-century drawing, showing the legendary 'silver mountain'. In this period Potosí was one of the most populous Spanish-speaking cities.

rebellions, however, continued throughout colonial times.

PATTERNS OF COLONIZATION

Spanish colonization in America was based on (and subsequently focused on) cities. Whenever an expedition conquered a territory, its leader's first action was (with prescribed ceremonial) to found a township – formally a 'city', with a municipal council (*cabildo*) chosen from among the conquerors, a street plan carefully traced out (nearly always on the simple grid-iron pattern), and urban properties distributed among the colony's founders. Spanish settlers aspired to an upper-class style of life; for most, that could best be achieved within an urban setting. The 'urban nucleus' thus became fundamental to the pattern of Spanish imperialism. Nearly all the modern Spanish American republics have capital cities that can trace their history back for well over four hundred years and to their 'foundation' by a particular conquistador. In Mexico, the victorious Spaniards built their capital on the ruins of Aztec Tenochtitlán. In Peru, by contrast, they spurned the old Inca capital at Cuzco, in the mountains, and founded a new one of their own – for ease of communication – on the coast, at Lima. At the outset, these colonial capitals were very modest settlements, but given the Spaniards' desire for a decent urban setting, some of the capitals quickly grew into important centres of wealth and power. By 1580, the year the struggling settlement at Buenos Aires was re-founded, Mexico City and Lima were already very respectable cities.

The colonial cities did not, of course, grow up in an economic vacuum. The Spaniards, as already mentioned, arrived in America with very definite ideas of gaining wealth. The conquistadors were particularly attracted by the lure of precious metals. When offered an estate by the governor of Cuba, Hernán Cortés retorted: 'I came to get gold, not till the soil like a peasant.' In any case, the colonists needed something to export to Spain. In the early stages of colonization, gold was washed from rivers on the Caribbean islands. On the mainland, silver was the precious metal found in greatest abundance. Spectacular silver-strikes occurred around the mid-point of the sixteenth century: in 1545 at Potosí in Upper Peru (now Bolivia), in 1548 and 1558 at Zacatecas and Guanajuato in Mexico. From this time onwards, silver-mining became an important factor in consolidating settlement patterns in the Spanish American empire. Mining centres such as Potosí became significant markets, with large populations, while the need for safe and regular transport of silver to Spain helped determine major trade-routes and the shape of the commercial system in general.

Mines needed labourers. The growing Spanish colonial cities needed to be fed. Spaniards took their tastes in food with them to America; these could not be satisfied by traditional Indian agriculture, so Spaniards established their own farms and ranches. The large native American populations that surrounded the Spanish settlements were viewed as a convenient source of labour for both mining and agriculture. The basic pattern of relations between conquerors and conquered was sadly apparent from the first years of Caribbean colonization. The Spaniards mobilized Indian labour by means of what they termed the *encomienda*. Under this system, groups of Indians – though not (in theory anyway) their lands – were 'distributed' among the leading settlers, who were supposed on paper to Christianize them and 'civilize' them (on Hispanic lines), while in return using their labour or receiving their tribute. (Indians not included in *encomiendas* were required to pay tribute direct to the crown.) As a labour institution, the *encomienda* was of significance chiefly during the first century or so of Spain's colonial rule, but during this period the system was widely abused by colonists. The coercion and exploitation (sometimes very cruel) of the native Americans undoubtedly contributed to the steep demographic decline that now occurred in the New World.

While most settlers (especially, no doubt, the *encomenderos*, the holders of *encomiendas*) regarded their exploitative position as acceptable, some did not. Many conscience-stricken Spaniards (particularly in the religious orders) reacted strongly to the abuses they saw around them, and called on the crown to remedy the evil. The great Dominican, Fray Bartolomé de las Casas (1474–1566), himself a former *encomendero*, spent the latter part of a long life agitating relentlessly on behalf of Amerindian rights. But by the time the crown took steps to reduce the scope of the *encomienda*, in its New Laws of the Indies (1542), it was already too late. The crown's attitude – at least in the short term – had to be tempered by colonial resistance to the legislation. Agitation by ecclesiastics and others did, however, have the effect of bringing the whole question of conquest and its effects on the native population under official scrutiny. In 1550 a ban was actually placed on further conquests while a group of distinguished lawyers and theologians sat down, at Valladolid in Spain, to hear a debate on the rights and wrongs of Spain's imperial activities – one of the more remarkable episodes in the history of imperialism. The debate, in which Las Casas took a prominent part (at one point making a five-day speech), was inconclusive. In any case the conquest was by then largely over.

In the long run, however well-intentioned or otherwise the crown may have been, there was little that could lessen the traumatic impact of the conquest on the native population. The Indian, in W. H. Prescott's deservedly famous phrase, became 'an alien in the land of his fathers'. Indian culture certainly survived, at the level of the local community, but it was now exposed to unprecedented pressures and strains. Not only were Indians now liable to have to supply labour for their overlords, either under the *encomienda* or through other forced-labour systems presently introduced; their lands, too, were steadily encroached on by the newcomers, although it was not until the seventeenth century that the great estate began to assume its place as the dominating feature of the Spanish American rural scene – and even then, much land remained in the hands of the Indian communities. Sometimes the Indian communities adapted to the new circumstances, with a degree of success only now beginning to be recognized by historians. Sometimes they did not. Occasionally, too, humanitarian clerics such as Vasco de Quiroga (c. 1470–1565), an admirer of Sir Thomas More's *Utopia*, tried to set up

Doorway of the palace of the Inquisition, Cartagena, Colombia. The Inquisition started work in Cartagena in 1610, although the building only dates from the early eighteenth century.

model Indian communities – something the Jesuit order accomplished in its province of Paraguay in the seventeenth and eighteenth centuries. These experiments, however, did little to diminish the overall impact of the conquest and its devastating effect upon the Indian way of life.

It must also be remembered that from the start the simple dividing-line between conquerors and conquered was blurred by fraternization and the natural concomitant of miscegenation – racial mixing – that continued throughout colonial times. The conquest, by its nature, was largely a masculine adventure; unions between Spaniards and Indian women were very common; in consequence, mestizos (half-Spanish, half-Indian) made their appearance at an early date. One of their outstanding early representatives was the Peruvian chronicler Inca Garcilaso de la Vega (1539–1616), son of a Spanish conquistador and an Inca princess. Some conquistadors fathered literally scores of mestizo children. One of the conquerors of Chile, Francisco de Aguirre (1508–81), actually recognized at least fifty, and boldly declared (to the displeasure of the Church) that 'the service rendered to God in engendering mestizos is greater than the sin incurred in so doing'. Miscegenation was one of the deepest legacies of the period of conquest, since it did not stop, and led directly to the multiracial societies of today.

AN EMPIRE ESTABLISHED

The age of the conquistadors was fairly brief. The Spanish crown had no intention of allowing these vigorous, ambitious men to rule the colonies unchecked. (For much the same reason, later on, it limited the extent of *encomienda*-grants, fearing that *encomenderos* might become a powerful colonial nobility, difficult to control.) The conquerors fell victim to the centralizing absolutism Spanish monarchs were trying to consolidate, at home as well as across the ocean. A framework of settled colonial institutions was speedily imposed on all the newly conquered territories. In Spain itself, in the aftermath of the conquest of Mexico, a separate royal council (the Council of the Indies) was set up to supervise the government of the new empire. In America, political and administrative jurisdictions were soon defined: both Mexico (New Spain) and Peru were designated as 'viceroyalties' within a decade of their respective conquests. Spanish governors, bureaucrats and (not least) treasury officials took up their places in the emerging structure of imperial government. Surviving conquistadors were edged aside, sometimes paid off with titles or lands. Thus Cortés, who had personally governed Mexico in the years immediately after his triumph, was gradually deprived of his power (though not his wealth), as was Jiménez de Quesada, the conqueror of New Granada, passed over in favour of another governor almost as soon as he completed his conquest. (In Peru, the conquistadors indulged in civil war amongst themselves – Pizarro was assassinated – and briefly rebelled against the incoming Spanish authorities.) Columbus himself, earlier on, had been treated in a similar fashion: the pattern was unmistakable from the outset. Spain's empire was to be an empire, not a patchwork of unruly territories governed by powerful warlords. (That was to come later, after independence.)

The Catholic Church, too, assumed its place – a fundamental place – in the new framework of empire. Generous concessions by the Papacy allowed the Spanish crown a high degree of control over the Church in America. It soon built up an appropriate diocesan and parochial structure. In 1545, with the creation of the archdioceses of Mexico, Lima and Santo Domingo, the colonial hierarchy became separate from that of Spain. The various religious orders (including the Jesuits after their papal recognition in 1540) were present in force in the colonies, extremely active over the next decades (in fact, centuries) in what has been called the *conquista espiritual*, the 'spiritual conquest' of the native populations – an extraordinarily tenacious effort, however it may be judged by a more secular (and relativist) culture. The Spanish Inquisition set up branches in the two

The Spanish fortress at Nacimiento, southern Chile, reconstructed in the mid-eighteenth century. It was a key part of Spain's defences along the Araucanian frontier.

viceregal capitals in 1570–71. It was never quite as active in America as in Spain: it sponsored about a hundred burnings in colonial times.

The commercial system, as it developed, reflected the Spanish desire for control and regulation. The *Casa de Contratación* (Trade House) at Seville was the very earliest specifically imperial institution to be created, opening in 1503. It closely supervised trade between America and Spain. With the great silver-strikes of the mid-sixteenth century – production expanded massively after 1550 – transatlantic trade assumed the shape it was to retain for two hundred years. From now onwards it was based on regular annual sailings of 'fleets' – convoys – to and from a small number of approved ports. Two fleets left Spain each year, one bound for Mexico, the other for the Panama isthmus and northern South America. A single convoy, carrying silver to Spain, completed the round-trip. A subsidiary system operated up and down the Pacific coast of South America. From the 1570s, also, regular sailings between Acapulco in Mexico and Manila in Spain's newly conquered Asian colony, the Philippines, enabled Mexican silver to be traded for Chinese silks. (Year after year the 'Manila galleon' plied its lonely course across the north Pacific, never once sighting the Hawaiian islands, which were discovered only in 1778, by Captain Cook.)

By 1580 Spain's huge American empire was well into its period of consolidation. It had already become legendary. The Spaniards who ruled the empire regarded it, in the manner of successful imperialists throughout the ages, with pride and satisfaction. Other Europeans, it is fair to say, were awed by the magnitude of Spanish acquisitions in the New World, and this awe long outlasted the sixteenth century. Intelligent foreigners were sometimes to reflect on the stability of the empire, with its large mixed population. 'I have marvelled sometimes at Spain,' wrote Francis Bacon, 'how they clasp and contain so large dominions with so few natural Spaniards.' But it was the sheer geographical span of Spain's empire that impressed most Europeans, so that Dr Samuel Johnson, in the eighteenth century, could still ask, with only a light touch of irony:

Has heaven reserved, in pity to the poor,
No pathless waste or undiscovered shore,
No secret island in the boundless main,
No peaceful desert yet unclaimed by Spain?

SC

Further Reading: B. Díaz del Castillo, *True History of the Conquest of New Spain*, trans. A. P. Maudslay (New York, 1956); I. Clendinnen, *Ambivalent Conquests* (Cambridge, 1987); J. Hemming, *The Conquest of the Incas* (London, 1970); M. León-Portilla, *The Broken Spears: The Aztec Account of the Conquest of Mexico* (Boston, 1962); J. Lockhart and E. Otte, eds., *Letters and People of the Spanish Indies, Sixteenth Century* (Cambridge, 1976); J. H. Parry, *The Discovery of the Sea* (London, 1974)

Early settlement of Brazil, 1500–1600

ORIGINS OF PORTUGUESE SETTLEMENT

In the Treaty of Tordesillas (1494) Portugal won from Spain a line of demarcation that meant that from just south of the Amazon's mouth to the present-day state of Santa Catarina, the whole of the coastline of Brazil remained open for Portugal to claim. Portugal was later to acquire the Amazon valley as well as other territories west of the Tordesillas line, and Brazil was to become the largest country in Latin America.

Pedro Alvares Cabral, whose fleet (*en route* to India) made its Brazilian landfall in April 1500, named the land in honour of the Holy Cross. 'Brazil', however, was one of the Middle Ages' favourite legendary islands in the Atlantic, and also the name of an abundant and valued red dyewood which gave the country its name. Dyewood was at first Brazil's only important export. The Portuguese could hardly fail to make profits as the Indians happily yielded up both dyewood and foodstuffs in return for tools, glass, ironware and textiles. King Manoel I (1498–1521) made dyewood a monopoly of the crown, like African gold and Asian spices. The crown also granted rights to such contractors as Fernão de Noronha (1506) who agreed to found a factory, explore the littoral, and pay duty on the dyewood shipped. Within a decade the Portuguese sent 1200 tons to Lisbon, whence most was re-exported to Antwerp, then Europe's biggest emporium.

Isolated and remote, the first Portuguese settlements – 'factories' – could not hold off the French, who attacked Portuguese shipping, made Indian alliances, and offered more exciting trade goods. In 1516 King Manoel riposted with a naval squadron, a move his successor John III (1521–57) repeated in 1526. But the crown was far more interested in exploiting trade – often enforced by sharp practice and brutal interference – than in conquering native societies or settling and organizing territory. Portugal's was almost wholly a trading empire. In it, America came a very poor third, both chronologically and commercially – well below Africa with its slaves and gold, and Asia with its silks and spices. The French were, if anything, keener than the Portuguese to establish forts and factories in Brazil. King John III's strategy to counteract French incursions was to enact continuous settlement of the coastal lands by responsible hereditary proprietors (*donatários*) chartered by the Portuguese crown. This system – half feudal, half commercial – was heralded by the 1530 expedition of Martim Afonso, grantee of the site of the dyewood factory at São Vicente and the true founder of Portuguese Brazil. Settlers were taken there, and both cattle rearing and sugar cultivation were introduced. The plan was to extend the new system all along the coast: in 1534 twelve captaincies were marked out, each occupying 30 to 100 leagues of coastline and stretching indefinitely inland. Only two of these had adequate capital to lead to lasting settlement. In São Vicente, there were six sugar mills and 3000 Indian slaves by 1548. In the north-east, the able soldier Duarte Albuquerque Coelho had the funds to bring in mercenaries and subjugate the Indians of Pernambuco.

The *donatário* system conferred the right to found and charter townships, to administer justice, to collect tithes, and to license sugar mills. Sugar was an ideal crop: Brazil had speedy access to Europe and the capacity easily to outproduce the Atlantic islands. By 1570 there were some sixty mills, producing around 180,000 *arrobas* (2000 tons or so) annually. The north was in the lead, Pernambuco having twenty-three mills and Bahia eighteen. Sugar cultivation attracted Portuguese with a great mixture of skills to Brazil, including a host of craftsmen who set up in business on their own account. The sugar plantations needed skilled husbandmen, as well as foremen and overseers to direct the slaves, clerks and accountants to keep the records, and mechanics to build and maintain the new sugar mills (*engenhos*). The plantations also called into being a superior caste of owners, the so-called *senhores de engenho*, who aspired to great houses and to ostentatious ways of life on their estates. Thousands of Portuguese arrived in Brazil to settle, though many were of low social status: 400 out of the thousand first settlers of Bahia in 1549 were released convicts (*degredados*).

The Indians responded to Portuguese settlement with surprise attacks, in which they burned mills and plantations. The Portuguese enslaved numbers of the Indians, usually by 'ransoming' those captured by other tribes, or by direct raids on villages. As the settlers cleared land for intensive cultivation, the Indians were gradually forced on to the higher hinterland, the *sertão*. Compounded by the prolonged exposure of captives to Old World diseases such as smallpox, measles and influenza – which readily spread from 'tamed' to 'wild' Indians – the trauma shrank the Indian population of coastal Brazil almost as drastically as it had done that of the Caribbean islands. Nor were atrocities by the Portuguese lacking. These were often entirely gratuitous, committed on Indians who would not submit, sometimes even on those who had done so.

Portuguese settlers were thus faced by a diminishing labour force and solved the problem by bringing in African slaves. Black slaves were already resistant to most Old World diseases and fairly inured to heavy labour, and the Portuguese were used to employing them at home. As early as 1552 John III sent Africans to be sold on his account to work the plantations of Bahia. In the 1560s epidemics halved the coastal Indian population, and this encouraged the import of slaves from Africa.

Initially they were west Africans – from Senegambia, the Slave Coast (Whydah, Ardra), Benin and Nigeria (the Yorubas and the Warris) – but after 1550 they began to arrive from the Congo, then from Angola, especially after 1575 when the Portuguese founded Luanda. Though more expensive in the first place, Africans were much more dependable and productive workers than Amerindians. Between 1570 and 1600 Angola supplied Brazil with over 50,000 slaves. The total at work, even at the end of the period, fell far short of that, as plantation slaves had average working lives of only seven years, according to present estimates, and the rate of their reproduction was always pitifully low. By the mid-1580s, one-third of the workforce in the north-east was black: Bahia possessed between 3000 and 4000 slaves, the more prosperous Pernambuco twice that. By 1600, 70 per cent of the blacks in Brazil were engaged in producing sugar.

BEGINNINGS OF ROYAL GOVERNMENT

Profit from sugar, and the partial success of the proprietary system, at last brought about a stronger royal presence in Brazil. In 1549 John III took back the Bahia captaincy for the crown and sent a fleet commanded by Tomé de Sousa, who was appointed Brazil's first governor-general (1549-53). Sousa made Bahia the capital of Brazil, setting up an *ouvidor-geral* (chief justice) to supervise municipal magistrates and a *provedor-môr* (royal factor) to improve the yield of customs and excise. It was Mem de Sá (governor-general, 1558-72) who finally made Brazil safe for the Portuguese, displacing unpacified Indians and lifting the threat posed to the south by the proud colony of France Antartique established by the French on Guanabara Bay (present-day Rio). Mem de Sá's foundation of Rio de Janeiro (1567) secured the area for good.

Brazil's early history bore the distinctive stamp of Portugal's commercial motivation, deepened by the late arrival there of soldiers, officials and missionaries. (The latter were Jesuits, disciplined and self-confident, who tried to keep the Indians away from Europeans and Africans.) Brazil was different in every way from the heartlands of Spanish America, founded upon great pools of native labour. The early enthronement of sugar dispersed the colonists across the land. By 1600 a Portuguese population only 30,000 strong was scattered over fourteen captaincies and 6400 km of coastline. Only in the south did settlement reach at all far inland: round São Paulo the temperate uplands had agricultural and ranching potential. Better still, *paulistas* had unlimited access to flocks of Indians under Spanish Jesuit protection

CAPTAINCIES OF BRAZIL IN THE SIXTEENTH CENTURY

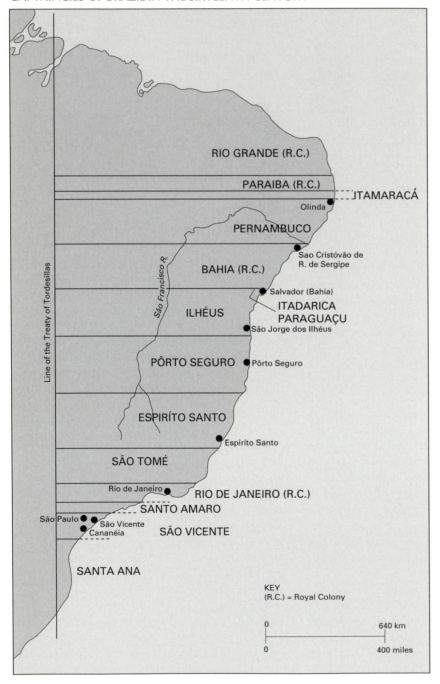

RIO GRANDE (R.C.)

PARAIBA (R.C.)

ITAMARACÁ

Olinda

PERNAMBUCO

Sao Cristóvão de R. de Sergipe

BAHIA (R.C.)

Salvador (Bahia)

ITADARICA
PARAGUAÇU

ILHÉUS

São Jorge dos Ilhéus

PÔRTO SEGURO

Pôrto Seguro

São Francisco R.

Line of the Treaty of Tordesillas

ESPIRÍTO SANTO

Espiríto Santo

SÃO TOMÉ

Rio de Janeiro

RIO DE JANEIRO (R.C.)

SANTO AMARO

São Paulo

São Vicente

Cananéia

SÃO VICENTE

SANTA ANA

KEY
(R.C.) = Royal Colony

0   640 km

0   400 miles

Slaves arriving in Brazil (in a lithograph after Rugendas), nearly three hundred years after the first African captives to arrive in the mid-sixteenth century.

The Spanish American empire, 1580–1808

IMPERIAL CONSOLIDATION

The sense of satisfaction and well-being which pervaded the attitudes of the Spanish crown and its advisers towards Spanish America in the 1580s is neatly encapsulated in a memorial which Francisco de Toledo personally delivered to Philip II in January 1582 on his return to Spain after thirteen years' service as viceroy of Peru:

> What I can truly say to Your Majesty about the state in which I left the affairs of that kingdom is that ecclesiastical matters are controlled by Your Majesty and your ministers…, the Indians receive the necessary religious instruction and their conversion is proceeding well, the authority of justice is established and observed and the liberty which used to reign in that land is restrained, the kingdom is peaceful and without thought of disturbance, the cities have appropriate ordinances and expanding and illustrious public works, the Indians are resettled in large and accessible settlements, free from the tyrannies and oppressions which they used to suffer, supervised by their governors who administer justice in their jurisdictions and defend them from whoever wishes to injure them, the exchequer of Your Majesty is so much richer and fatter, and the kingdom is so rich and prosperous, as the recent fleets and the quantities of silver they have brought back have demonstrated.

along the Paraná River, as well as the back door to the massive silver production of Upper Peru (now Bolivia), an area with which Brazil's peruleiros carried on an illegal trade. Spain, in fact, had relatively little to offer Portugal or its colonies commercially. Even during the union of the Spanish and Portuguese crowns (1580–1640) customs barriers between the two empires remained largely intact. Miscegenation was to become as characteristic of Brazil as it was of Spanish America, and with similar social distinctions and colour bars. Brazilian society in this early era was rural, and culturally dependent. What education was available was almost all given by Jesuits. Colonial Brazil never attained a university of its own. Till 1676 there was no more than one bishop, in the city of Salvador – and he largely an absentee; and till 1677 there was no convent anywhere, though hundreds of them dotted Spanish America.

The main achievement of the Spanish Habsburgs' bureaucratic imperialism in the post-1580 period was a thorough revamping of the judicial system. After 1580 appeal lay from Brazil to the high court in Portugal (*Casa da Suplicação*), while the council of the royal conscience, the *Desembargo do Paço*, was called in to supervise the expanding royal bureaucracy. King Philip II (I, of Portugal) had the laws of the empire collected and they were soon codified (1603).

RB

Further Reading: C. R. Boxer, *The Portuguese Seaborne Empire* (London, 1969); G. Freyre, *The Masters and the Slaves* (New York, 1956); J. Hemming, *Red Gold: the Conquest of the Brazilian Indians* (Cambridge, Mass., 1978)

Spanish monarchs

1474–1504	Isabella of Castile
1479–1516	Ferdinand of Aragon
[Habsburg Dynasty]	
1516–56	Charles I (Emperor Charles V)
1556–98	Philip II
1598–1621	Philip III
1621–65	Philip IV
1665–1700	Charles II
[Bourbon Dynasty]	
1700–46	Philip V
1746–59	Ferdinand VI
1759–88	Charles III
1788–1808	Charles IV
1803–33	Ferdinand VII

SPANISH AMERICA IN 1580

Territory settled by Spain

Territory settled by Portugal

0   1600 km

0   1000 m

Francisco de Toledo, from Guamán Poma, La nueva corónica. *Toledo's viceroyalty of Peru was a key period in the Spanish organization of the territory.*

of Mexico from which Enríquez had governed New Spain, although less spectacular than the Aztec Tenochtitlán which had been destroyed to make way for it, was by 1580 a capital of perhaps 100,000 people, with broad, regular streets, a massive central square, rich churches, impressive public and private buildings, and a complex, sophisticated administrative infrastructure; the capital city of Peru, Lima, or the 'City of the Kings' as it was commonly known in this period, was smaller and less ostentatious than Mexico, primarily because it was a younger city, founded in 1535 by Francisco Pizarro near the coast of Peru rather than on the site of the old Inca capital, Cuzco, which remained as a symbol of indigenous splendour high in the Andes. But Lima had already emerged as the more prestigious of the two viceregal capitals, largely because it controlled the remission to Europe of the silver production of Potosí (in what is now Bolivia). Although only one of three hundred cities founded in Spanish America in the sixteenth century, Potosí, located at a height of over 4000 m in the southern Andes, had an estimated population of 120,000 by 1580; by 1650, at the height of its prosperity, this was to grow to 160,000, making Potosí the largest city in the Hispanic world. Already by 1580 large quantities of silver were being shipped from Callao, the port of Lima, to Spain, as Toledo's memorial indicates, the figure rising from an estimated 4.6 million pesos (peso = piece of eight = dollar) in 1571–5 to 23.9 million pesos in 1591-5.

The very prosperity of Peru by the end of Toledo's viceregency was the material factor which turned

Two years later Martín Enríquez de Almansa, who had succeeded Toledo in Peru in 1581 after serving for twelve years as viceroy of New Spain (Mexico), was able to reassure Philip II that he had succeeded in preserving the stability created by his predecessor. He wrote from Lima in February 1583: 'I wish to begin by first stating that all things in this land are in a good state, with much peace and calm…'

There is an abundance of contemporary evidence which confirms that statements such as these represented not merely the desire of powerful officials to please their sovereign but also a general and genuine pride in the achievements of Spanish soldiers, priests, and administrators on the mainland of Spanish America during the preceding half-century. The city

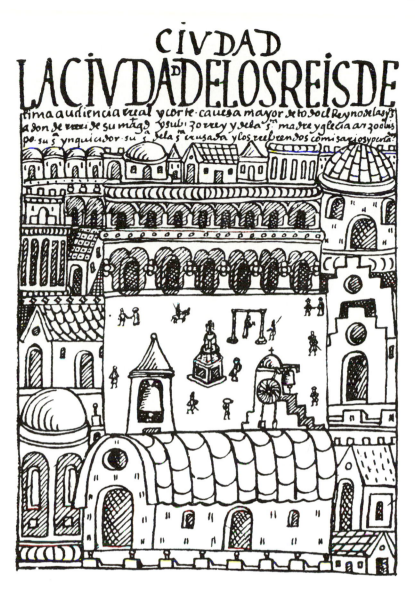

CIVDAD
LACIVDADELOSREISDE

Lima, Peru (from Guamán Poma, La nueva corónica). Lima was already a substantial Spanish city by 1600.

In any case the union of the Spanish and Portuguese crowns in 1580 in the person of Philip II of Spain, while not guaranteeing peace on the frontier between Spanish Paraguay and Brazil, at least provided the Habsburg monarchy with theoretical control of the vast Portuguese overseas empire.

By 1580, the initial phase of exploration and settlement which had characterized Spanish expansion on the mainland of America for more than sixty years had given way to one of consolidation and stability. Spain had emerged from the process with an enormous empire stretching, nominally at least, from California, Texas and Florida in the north, through Central America, the major islands of the Caribbean, and all of South America except Brazil as far as Cape Horn. There remained within these boundaries extensive expanses of territory which Spain claimed but did not or could not subdue, in some cases because of physical barriers, in others because of fierce indigenous resistance. The latter was particularly important in southern Chile, Patagonia, and northern Mexico; the former in the almost impenetrable forests east of the Andes from modern Colombia down to Bolivia. Although frontiers were gradually pushed forward into these inhospitable areas throughout the colonial period, the majority were not effectively incorporated into the republics which replaced the Spanish empire until the latter part of the nineteenth century. Nevertheless, by 1580, and sooner in some areas, what might be defined as the heartland of the Spanish empire in America was secure, settled, and subdued, and men like Toledo, who had made such an important personal contribution to the imposition of the authority of the Spanish crown in these distant lands, were able to take pride in their creation of a lasting colonial structure.

COLONIAL GOVERNMENT

The twin hubs of the Spanish empire in America after 1580 were the viceregal capitals of Mexico and Lima. The viceroyalty of New Spain, which was governed from the former, extended over all Spanish territory on the mainland north of the isthmus of Panama; the viceroyalty of Peru covered all of Spanish South America except for the coast of Venezuela (which was governed from Santo Domingo) until the eighteenth century when two further viceroyalties – New Granada and the River Plate – were created from its northern and southern kingdoms, leaving a rump viceroyalty confined roughly to the territory of modern Peru. Each viceroyalty was further divided into a number of separate areas technically described as kingdoms, each with its own political governor and a tribunal known as an *audiencia* which exercised a

Francis Drake's circumnavigation of 1577–80 into such a profitable enterprise, for the four months which the *Golden Hind* spent off the coast of Peru in 1579 culminated in the seizure of a shipment of silver on its way to Panama. That Drake was able to behave with such impunity drew attention to the fact that the defences of Peru had depended hitherto upon inaccessibility rather than naval or military resources. But attempts at settlement rather than piracy by Spain's potential colonizing rivals in northern Europe had not yet begun. England's first faltering attempts at colonization in America, the abortive Roanoke voyages of 1584 and 1587, were still to come, and the successful settlement of Virginia was to wait until 1607. Portugal, Spain's one serious challenger as a colonial power in the sixteenth century, had confined its American activities to Brazil, a land of vast potential, but one which did not attract Spaniards because of its apparent scarcity of precious metals and its certain shortage of sedentary natives.

Mexico City (Antonio de Solís). Mexico City was the greatest (and grandest) of the viceregal capitals.

mixture of judicial and administrative authority. In the Habsburg period there were four such kingdoms in the viceroyalty of New Spain (Mexico, Guatemala, New Galicia, and Santo Domingo), and six in the viceroyalty of Peru (Peru, Chile, Charcas, Quito, New Granada, and Panama); in the eighteenth century three new *audiencias* were established in South America, with their capitals in Cuzco, Caracas, and Buenos Aires. These colonial divisions were to prove to be of enormous significance for the construction of the independent republics of the nineteenth century, for in most cases national boundaries were drawn along the lines of the old kingdoms: Charcas, for example, became Bolivia; New Granada became Colombia; the kingdom of Quito became Ecuador.

Within the central kingdom of each viceroyalty the viceroy himself acted as political head; within the subordinate kingdoms of his jurisdiction his actual authority varied according to whether they were classified as presidencies or captaincies-general. In the former routine administration was delegated to the president of the *audiencia,* but matters of policy and military affairs were reserved to the viceroy. This, at least, was the theory, but, in practice the president of a remote capital such as Quito usually enjoyed considerable freedom from the control of the viceroy in distant Lima, except in times of crisis or unless the viceroy was particularly vigilant. In kingdoms which enjoyed the elevated status of captaincies-general, usually those considered by the crown to be particularly vulnerable to foreign intervention – Guatemala, Santo Domingo, New Granada, and in the eighteenth century Chile and Caracas – the viceroy's authority was almost entirely nominal, with the captains-general acting like mini-viceroys, directly responsible to the Council of the Indies and the king in Madrid. The viceroys and captains-general who governed Spanish America in the name of the crown were almost exclusively rich, powerful Spaniards sent out to the empire for fixed terms with the prospects of returning to high office and rich rewards in the peninsula. In the Habsburg period, when a common pattern was for a successful viceroy of New Spain to be promoted to Peru, they sometimes held noble titles before appointment, while many others were ascetic churchmen or conciliar lawyers; in the eighteenth century the more pragmatic Bourbons tended to look with great favour upon men with military or naval experience, often on the American frontiers. Several viceroys of Peru in this period were former captains-general of Chile. The viceroyalty of Peru lost its primacy to New Spain as the silver production of the latter multiplied in the eighteenth century, but the salaries attached to both – 60,000 pesos or £16,000 in this period – were the same; those attached to the newer viceroyalties of

New Granada and Buenos Aires were somewhat lower – 40,000 pesos – but still very generous.

Checks on colonial authority

The provision of good salaries for high officials – senior judges were also well paid – reflected a somewhat naive hope in Madrid that corruption might thus be prevented in distant overseas territories. It was commonly accepted in the Americas, in fact, that a viceroy could live well on the fees and presents which his extensive powers generated, saving his salary for his retirement. As the king's representative, a status confirmed by his title, he was head of both civil and military establishments, he supervised the work of treasury officials, and he exercised important powers of vice-patronage (a point stressed by Toledo in his 1582 memorial) in relation to Church appointments; his own patronage covered many minor posts in the colonial bureaucracy, posts for which status-seeking colonists were often willing to pay, and he also appointed to senior posts during vacancies, which were often extensive; in the legislative field he had power on the one hand to issue ordinances for municipalities and for the regulation of certain activities, subject to ultimate royal approval, and on the other to formally suspend the implementation of crown instructions which he deemed to be inappropriate; he presided over the *audiencia* of his central kingdom, and over the municipal council, or *cabildo*, of his capital city. Conscious of the need to provide checks upon the possible abuse of such extensive powers, the crown itself made some provision of deterrents against maladministration. The council of the Indies, established in 1524 as part of the general conciliar system of the Hapsburgs to administer the empire for the crown, had the power to send out a general inspector, or *visitador general*, to investigate the conduct of a viceroy, captain-general, or president who was suspected of serious maladministration. Although effective when applied, this device was used sparingly; much more common, although ultimately less useful in practice than in theory, was the judicial review of conduct, or *residencia*, imposed upon a senior official at the end of his term of office; the Spanish name derives from the requirement that a retiring official remained in residence for a fixed term while a commissioner called for and investigated complaints against him. The files of such cases provide historians with invaluable information about individual abuses, or alleged abuses, which, in the more extreme cases, the crown punished severely. But bribery and influence often rendered the device ineffective, particularly as, on grounds of economy and convenience, the policy was adopted for second-rank administrators of entrusting the inquests to officials arriving to replace those whose conduct was being investigated. According to popular legend, when a provincial governor took up office in the interior of Peru he was usually handed by his predecessor as a bribe a bag of silver which he kept, unopened, to hand on to his own successor in five years' time.

A more effective check upon executive authority in the American capitals, although one which inhibited progressive reforms as well as maladministration, was the complexity of the colonial bureaucracy and of the legislative framework within which it functioned. Treasury ministers, ecclesiastical dignitaries, city councillors, military commanders, and members of closed corporations – of merchants, priests, lawyers, and miners, for example –jealously guarded their prerogatives and privileges, enshrined in a bewildering maze of ordinances and decrees, and could be relied upon to report unfavourably to Madrid upon administrators who attempted to encroach on them. The most powerful and influential watchdogs of all were the judges, or *oidores*, of the *audiencias*. These tribunals not only acted as the superior judicial bodies in their respective kingdoms – appeals to the Council of the Indies were allowed in civil but not criminal cases – but also enjoyed the right to be consulted by the relevant political head in administrative matters. Ultimately the authority of the latter was paramount, but it was generally recognized that the crown would regard with disfavour an administrator who could not work in harmony with his *audiencia*. The sizes of the tribunals varied, but by the eighteenth century they ranged from fourteen ministers in the viceregal capitals to five or six in other cities. In the early Habsburg period strict regulations prohibited the judges from marrying or acquiring property while holding office, but the extension of sale of office in the seventeenth century gradually made it possible for these rules to be evaded and also for rich colonists to obtain appointment as judges in their native cities, where ties of family and influence militated against their impartial administration of justice. Recent research into appointments shows that this state of affairs was at its worst in the first half of the eighteenth century, when colonists attained majorities over peninsular judges in many of the tribunals, usually by purchase. An incoming viceroy found himself confronted upon taking office in what was usually a strange city with a body of entrenched and powerful officials, often allied by family or business ties to other established groups. The consequence was that inertia, corruption, bribery, and easy social relationships became commoner features of the administrative system than did enterprise, integrity, and honesty. It was in an attempt to reverse this state of affairs that the reforming ministers of the Bourbons began after 1750 to implement a determined policy of appointing peninsular Spaniards to these and other important posts in the empire. They did so, however, at the cost of making the colonists feel that their local interests were being subordinated to those of an increasingly oppressive, centralizing monarchy.

Provincial governors

The administration of justice at a local level was delegated to provincial governors known as *corregidores*, who also exercised military and administrative authority within their jurisdictions. Gradually introduced in the second half of the sixteenth century to replace the overmighty *encomenderos*, these officials, who were appointed by the crown, were seen as essential guardians of royal authority. But, although nominally subject to supervision from their superiors in the capital of each kingdom, the *corregidores* themselves often enjoyed virtually unrestricted authority, particularly in remote areas inhabited mainly by Indians. The abuse which provoked most comment from contemporary observers was that known as the *repartimiento*, under which the *corregidor* distributed merchandise to the Indian communities in his province, with the sanction of judicial authority to punish those who were reluctant or unable to pay for the goods which he forced upon them. The practice was defended as a device for incorporating the Indians into the market economy, but its economic benefits were outweighed, particularly in

COREGIDOR DE MINAS
COMO LO CASTIGA CRV

el men te alas casiques pren cipales los corregidores y jueses co poio remor
de la justicia con es feren tes castigos sin tener mi sericordia por dios absp̃o

en las minas   en las

A corregidor maltreating *Indians (from Guamán Poma,* La nueva corónica). *The behaviour of* corregidores *was a major Indian grievance in colonial Peru.*

the eighteenth century, by the fierce resistance which it provoked. After legalizing and attempting to control it in the 1750s, the crown went to the opposite extreme in the 1780s by totally prohibiting the *repartimiento* system as part of a general reform of local government, centred on the introduction of a new class of administrators known as intendants. The latter were usually peninsular Spaniards, committed to efficiency, particularly in the collection of taxes, and to the actual rather than nominal recognition of royal authority. But it was only after a major Indian rebellion, led by a descendant of the Incas who called himself Túpac Amaru, which spread through the Andean area in 1780–3, that the ministers of the reforming Charles III (1759–88) introduced this new system first in Peru (1784) and then in New Spain (1786). In the first decade or so after their introduction the intendants did succeed in reducing forced trade with

the Indians. They also multiplied the yield of tribute, the head tax paid annually to the crown by adult male Indians, by eradicating fraud in its collection. But they were hampered by increasing confusion in metropolitan government after about 1800, which meant that their reports and suggestions were often not answered, and by the fact that their own subordinates, known as subdelegates, tended to co-operate with the creoles (those of Spanish descent born in the Americas) from whose ranks they were recruited, rather than with their more idealistic superiors.

INDIANS, MIXED CASTES AND WHITES

The *repartimiento* system and the Indian tribute were two devices which, besides generating revenue for the crown and its officials, forced the indigenous communities to participate in the money economy introduced by the Spaniards. In order to earn the money to meet these burdens Indians had to produce and sell a surplus – usually of agricultural goods or textiles – or they had to hire themselves out to landowners and mineowners. An even cruder institution was that known as the *mita* (or, confusingly, in New Spain as the *repartimiento*), whereby Indian communities were required to provide fixed quotas of men on a rotation basis to work for either the public authorities or private employers. Rates of payment, maximum distances to be travelled, and similar details were laid down in legislation, but were often ignored. The worst abuses were associated with forced work in the mines. In southern Peru and Bolivia, for example, where Toledo established a rigorous system for the recruitment of 12,000 men a year to work in Potosí, and for a smaller number to work in the mercury mine of Huancavelica, the consequence was a continuous decline in the native population of the contributing provinces throughout the seventeenth century.

NATIVE DEPOPULATION

The debate among historical demographers about the extent of native depopulation in colonial Spanish America is never likely to be settled satisfactorily, because of uncertainty about the numbers already there when the Spaniards arrived. What is clear is that there was extensive demographic decline in the sixteenth and early seventeenth centuries, followed by stabilization, and then gradual recovery in the eighteenth century. However many Indians lived in New Spain in 1519, we do know that there were only about 1.25 million by 1625, but 2.5 million in 1800; in Peru the initial decline may have been somewhat less catastrophic – to 500,000 at the end of the sixteenth century, rising to about 700,000 in 1800. Extensive and casual cruelty, faithfully chronicled by critical Spanish observers, contributed to this disaster, but it was less significant than the impact of European diseases – measles, influenza, smallpox – against which the natives had no natural resistance. The forcible resettlement of hundreds of thousands of families in *reducciones* or *doctrinas*, new communities where they were accessible to missionaries and crown officials, also disrupted traditional life in New Spain and the Andean area, weakening the will to survive of peoples whose world had been turned upside down within a very short space of time. In Peru these dramatic changes in native settlement and the introduction of the *mita* system are associated with the viceregency of Toledo, who imposed a pattern which was to endure for the rest of the colonial period; in New Spain they were introduced over a longer period, but with consequences for native society which were no less catastrophic. It is important to note, however, that, as his 1582 memorial indicates, Toledo regarded his policies for the native population as improvements upon the almost unregulated system of exploitation which he had found in Peru in the 1560s. He at least succeeded in erecting a framework of legislation to protect the Indians from the formal enslavement which many of the conquistadors sought to impose upon them. It is also the case that throughout Spanish America they enjoyed much greater protection from economic exploitation in the colonial period than in the nineteenth century, when republican governments representing the heirs of the conquerors sought to transform them into a mere rural proletariat.

By the end of the colonial period Indians comprised about 7 million of an estimated Spanish American population of 17 million. They formed the base of the social pyramid, despite the fact that Indian society was itself stratified – theoretically the 'republic' of Indians functioned alongside that of Spaniards – with the consequence that individual native leaders, or caciques, could often be men of considerable wealth and status. Technically inferior to the free Indians were the black slaves, numbering perhaps half a million, who were concentrated in the Caribbean islands, other areas of plantation agriculture, such as the coast of Peru, and in the cities of the empire, where they functioned as artisans and domestics. Historians have debated intensively the proposition that Spanish American (and Brazilian) slavery was milder than that of Anglo-Saxon America. The consensus is that where plantation agriculture was organized on uncompromising capitalistic lines – as it was in Cuba from the late eighteenth century for the production of sugar – there was little difference in practice between the two systems, despite the greater benevolence of Spanish legislation and the role of the Church in keeping slave families together. But the urban slave, ubiquitous in Spanish America, probably did enjoy more benevolent treatment, which often compared favourably with that meted out to Indians by whites. The manumission of slaves, moreover, was a common practice in colonial Spanish America, and accounted for the presence of large numbers of free blacks in those areas where slavery itself was important. It is difficult to give a precise figure, but by 1800 freemen of African descent in the region probably numbered about another half million.

The intermediate layer of the social pyramid consisted of a broad band of people of mixed blood, predominantly mestizo (Indian and white), but with pockets of mulattoes (black and white) in tropical areas where slavery was important. The emergence and continuous growth of this mixed population was a product less of the Iberian racial democracy, which historians have often emphasized, than of the irresistible fusion which occurred as relatively small numbers of European immigrants settled amongst large numbers of Indians whom they wished to assimilate for a variety of social, economic and cultural reasons. The leading conquerors of Peru formally married Inca princesses; later generations of Europeans were often less scrupulous about the sacrament of matrimony, but as the white population increased and the recruitment of Indian labour was regulated, so, too, the mixed race population expanded, particularly in the cities, to which Indians flocked from rural areas to avoid conscription for the mines. The definition of a mestizo was often imprecise, reflecting social rather than strictly racial classification: those of mixed descent who lived in Indian communities and wore native dress were 'Indian', whereas those who lived in towns and wore Spanish dress were 'mestizo', unless they became very rich, in which case they would be considered 'Spanish'. In the economically more dynamic parts of the empire, or in areas where centuries of attrition had gradually worn down the resistance of nomadic Indians – central Chile is a good example of the latter – there were by 1800 few surviving pockets of genuine Indian culture; in the Andean area, in Central America, and in southern Mexico, however, large numbers of native communities survived the colonial period to await the onslaught of nineteenth-century liberalism.

The colonial elite

The upper class in colonial Spanish America consisted of a minority of whites, estimated to number 3.2 million by 1800. They were officially designated *españoles*, Spaniards, although only 150,000 of them

– the so-called *peninsulares* – were born in peninsular Spain; the remaining 95 per cent were American Spaniards, or creoles, many of them second- or third-generation colonists whose fathers or grandfathers had gone out to the empire as bureaucrats, soldiers, or private settlers, while others could claim descent from the first conquistadors. It was this white minority, comprising less than 20 per cent of the total Spanish American population, which dominated society, economic life, and government. Its members owned the great haciendas, many of which each employed hundreds of peasants in debt-peonage, the textile factories, and the mines, the ten largest of which were each employing up to 1000 men in New Spain by the late eighteenth century; they staffed the colonial Church, itself a great owner of urban and rural property, sustained by the tithes of the rural population; they filled the honourable professions of soldier, lawyer and university teacher, and were present in tens of thousands in the less prestigious but often more profitable commercial sector. The top echelon could aspire to serve the crown as judges, treasury ministers, and bishops, or could purchase noble titles, while many more obtained employment in government offices as intermediate bureaucrats. Traditionally the most important posts in the administrative hierarchy – viceroy, archbishop, *audiencia* minister, and so on – were reserved for peninsular Spaniards, although the increasing demand of creoles for at least a share of high office in the late colonial period represented not just a remote aspiration but also a desire to return to the situation which had begun to prevail by the early eighteenth century. It would be misleading to suggest that creoles and peninsular Spaniards saw their interests as divergent. In New Spain and Peru, the last of Spain's American colonies to secure independence, they tended to form a cohesive group against the Indian majorities; in Venezuela and the River Plate, where increasing prosperity in the eighteenth century bred a brash self-confidence, the creoles tended to be more ambitious to consolidate their socio-economic status with at least participation in government. Not all European Spaniards in America disagreed with them: first-generation migrants who had left the poorer parts of Spain to make new lives in the empire could be more hostile to the mother country than, for example, creole aristocrats whose families had served the crown for generations. It remains true, nevertheless, that by the early nineteenth century a significant minority of whites in Spanish America was beginning to question the validity of Spain's imperial title. In part this situation was a result of the changes which had occurred in the empire in the second half of the eighteenth century as a result of the application there of the Bourbon reforms.

HABSBURG DECLINE, BOURBON RECOVERY

The traditional chronology of abject decline in seventeenth-century Spain and glorious recovery under a new monarchy in the eighteenth century is increasingly being questioned by historians, who now suggest that the reign of the last Habsburg, Charles II (1665–1700), was less disastrous, and those of his Bourbon successors less dynamic than has usually been asserted. There is still a massive amount of evidence, nevertheless, to confirm that from the standpoint of the metropolitan government the system devised in the sixteenth century to control, defend, and obtain profit from Spanish America had lost much of its efficiency by the end of the seventeenth century. This was not because Spanish America had 'declined', but rather because more of its wealth was being retained in America or diverted into clandestine trade with other nations. By the late seventeenth century Spain still possessed Cuba, Puerto Rico, and the eastern half of Hispaniola (now the Dominican Republic), but most of the other significant islands in the Caribbean had been seized by its northern European rivals: England had Jamaica, Barbados, and St Kitts; the Dutch had Curaçao; the French had Martinique, Guadeloupe, and Saint-Domingue (modern Haiti). Their presence there posed no permanent threat to the security of the mainland of Spanish America, but it virtually destroyed the integrity of the imperial commercial system, devised in the sixteenth century to secure the safe remission of silver from America to Spain and to preserve Spanish America as a closed market for producers of manufactured and agricultural goods in the peninsula.

The hallmark of the Habsburg commercial system was control by restriction. In Spain only Seville (later Cádiz) was licensed to trade with America; in America only Veracruz (serving New Spain), Santo Domingo, and Portobello (serving Peru via the Pacific port of Panama) were licensed to receive the fleets from Andalusia, which were supposed to arrive annually to supply the American market and to take back silver to Spain. The system worked well for the merchant guilds of Seville, Lima, and Mexico, whose members controlled the distribution of merchandise, but it lost its vitality as the colonists turned increasingly to contraband traders to satisfy their demands, often at lower prices than the official channels, and relieve them of their raw materials, including not only silver but also agricultural products. The first Bourbon kings tinkered with the system, replacing convoyed fleets with individual licensed vessels, some of which entered the Pacific, in the early eighteenth century, but it was not until the reign of Charles III that a comprehensive reform of the commercial structure occurred. Alarmed by the British capture of Havana in 1762, during the Seven Years' War, and impressed by its captors, Charles III's ministers gradually extended *comercio libre* (unrestricted trade) within the Spanish empire. Although it was not completely available to New Spain and Venezuela until 1789, the major reform came in 1778 when the principal ports of the empire obtained permission to trade freely with each other and with the thirteen leading ports of Spain.

Seen against the backcloth of the unreformed system, the commercial boom unleashed by the 1778 legislation was a brilliant success: between 1782 and 1796 exports from Spain to America were worth on average four times their 1778 value, and for the first

time for many years goods produced in Spain became more important than re-exports; at the American end mining production doubled in Peru and quadrupled in New Spain in the last quarter of the century. Although silver remained the most important commodity exported to Spain, agriculture, which had always been more important than mining in the American domestic economy, also began to contribute to transatlantic trade, as sugar from Cuba and New Spain, cochineal from Central America, cocoa beans and tobacco from Venezuela, and hides from the River Plate region began to be exported to Europe in ever-increasing quantities. The export of hides through Buenos Aires, to take but one example, rose from 150,000 a year before 1778 to some 1.4 million after 1783, as the capital of the new viceroyalty of the River Plate, created in 1776, entered an era of unprecedented prosperity. Here, as in Venezuela, Chile, and other parts of the empire which had been economic and political backwaters until the ministers of Charles III recognized their potential, the more oppressive fiscal and administrative regime associated with the intendant system was acceptable as long as the mother country was capable of supplying the commercial stimulus which revolutionized economic life after 1778. For two decades it seemed that Spain could, indeed, fulfil this function, despite the fact that the modest industrial growth which it experienced in the second half of the century was overshadowed by that of England. But Spain's entry in 1796 into the French war against Britain – a war which was to persist in different stages until 1815 – threw its transatlantic trade into turmoil, as the British navy blockaded Spanish ports. In a desperate attempt to maintain the flow of commerce with Spanish America, and the revenues which it generated, Spain opened trade to neutral vessels in 1797, but refused steadfastly to accede to the growing clamour from its American subjects for the right to trade freely with the world at large.

The first decade of the nineteenth century was one of growing estrangement between Spain and Spanish America, as the financial demands of the metropolis intensified and the prosperity of the late eighteenth century began to fade. An increasing number of articulate creoles began to apply the same process of rational enquiry which had underpinned the Bourbon reforms to the very relationship between the Spanish crown and its American possessions, and to wonder whether the latter had attained sufficient maturity to follow the precedent set by the United States and establish their independence. The abortive attempt of Francisco de Miranda to mount an emancipating invasion of Venezuela in 1806 demonstrated that only a very small minority sympathized openly with this point of view; the British invasions of

SPANISH AMERICA IN 1808

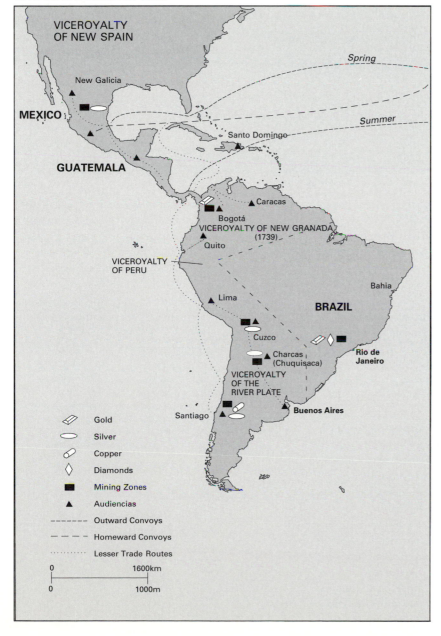

VICEROYALTY OF NEW SPAIN

New Galicia

MEXICO

GUATEMALA

Spring

Summer

Santo Domingo

Caracas

Bogotá

VICEROYALTY OF NEW GRANADA (1739)

Quito

VICEROYALTY OF PERU

Lima

Bahia

BRAZIL

Cuzco

Charcas (Chuquisaca)

Rio de Janeiro

VICEROYALTY OF THE RIVER PLATE

Santiago

Buenos Aires

Gold
Silver
Copper
Diamonds
Mining Zones
Audiencias
Outward Convoys
Homeward Convoys
Lesser Trade Routes

0   1600km
0   1000m

A colonial hacienda near Potosí

Buenos Aires and Montevideo in 1806–7, also dismal failures, emphasized that even fewer creoles were willing to exchange Spanish rule for that of Britain, notwithstanding their readiness to trade with the invader. Both episodes, coupled with the increasing weakness of Spain in Europe, did draw attention, however, to the fact that Spanish America was relying increasingly upon its own military resources for its defence. When, in 1808, Napoleon Bonaparte invaded Spain, deposed Ferdinand VII, and installed Joseph Bonaparte as king in Madrid, the instinctive response of Spanish Americans was to rally to the mother country and support the improvised resistance movement there which held the French at bay in 1808–9. But as news began to arrive in 1810 of the collapse of the anti-French forces, small groups of determined revolutionaries seized the opportunity to depose the peninsular authorities, thus initiating the bloody wars which finally brought independence to the whole mainland of Spanish America by 1825.

A majority of creoles did not aspire to independence in 1808, despite an awareness that the Spanish Bourbons had turned their American possessions for the first time in their history into real colonies, rigorously exploited for the benefit of the metropolis. By 1810 more were becoming aware of the feasibility of securing it, perhaps even the necessity to do so, if Spanish America was not to fall under French control. But when the revolutions for independence began, the immediate reaction of most Spanish Americans was to fight not for independence but to preserve the ties which bound them to Spain. That they did so was a reflection of both their innate conservatism and the strength of the imperial tradition which had persisted for over three centuries.   JRF

Further Reading: L. Bethell, ed., *The Cambridge History of Latin America,* vols. I and II (Cambridge, 1984); C. Gibson, *Spain in America* (New York, 1966); J. Lockhart and S. B. Schwartz, *Early Latin America: a History of Colonial Spanish America and Brazil* (Cambridge, 1983); M. Mörner, *Race Mixture in the History of Latin America* (Boston, Mass.,1967); J. H. Parry, *The Spanish Seaborne Empire* (London, 1966)

Colonial Brazil, 1600–1808

THE GROWTH OF A SUGAR COLONY

By 1600 the essential economic, social, and political patterns of Portugal's Brazilian colony had been firmly established. A population of about 100,000 including some 30,000 whites, 15,000 black slaves, and a remainder of Indians and people of mixed origin lived in and around the twenty or so settlements along the coast. The few cities like Salvador (Bahia) and Olinda were on the coast, serving as administrative control points and as commercial centres for the growing sugar industry. The social and cultural patterns of Portugal were transferred to the colony, but like the European population, tended to concentrate in the larger coastal towns. Salvador, as the capital, also became an episcopal see in 1552 (later raised to archiepiscopal status in 1674) and by the end of the century Franciscans, Carmelites and Benedictines had joined the Jesuits in developing the colony's religious life. Administration and the judicial structure were strengthened in 1609 with the creation of a high court of appeals (*Relacão*) staffed by royal judges. Increasingly, however, social and political forms in Brazil were determined by the colony's economic *raison d'être*, the sugar industry.

Sugar cane, introduced from Madeira and São Tomé, grew well in Brazil and by 1585 some 120 sugar mills (*engenhos*) were scattered along the coast, although two-thirds of them were found in the north-eastern captaincies of Pernambuco and Bahia. By 1600 Brazilian production was probably about 8-9000 tons, and in the next thirty years, aided by the introduction of a new milling system, the number of mills and total production increased rapidly. Brazil became in this period the largest producer of sugar in the Atlantic world, and the colony experienced a vigorous expansion. By 1630 there were 350 mills in operation, and during the next decades sugar constituted over 90 per cent of the colony's export value.

The structure and needs of the sugar industry set the context of Brazilian society. The *engenhos* combined industrial operations with the growing and harvesting of sugar cane because of the need to process the cane immediately after cutting it. Thus each *engenho* was a factory in the field, demanding the investment of large amounts of capital for land, buildings, machinery, oxen, and labour. Those who lacked sufficient capital to set up their own mill often grew cane and supplied it to an *engenho* under a variety of sharecropping or other contractual arrangements. These *lavradores de cana* or cane farmers usually owned their own slaves and sometimes their own land and they hoped eventually to establish mills of their own. Above all, the *engenhos* needed large amounts of skilled and unskilled labour. Technicians and artisans were essential for sugar production. In addition, from the beginnings of the industry in Brazil, the plantations depended on coerced or enslaved labour. Estates with over 200 slaves were not unknown but were exceptional, and an average *engenho* might have ten or twenty free labourers and sixty to a hundred slaves in addition to three or four dependent cane farmers each with their own group of six to ten slaves.

From well before 1600, the Portuguese had turned increasingly to Africa for their supply of labour. In the seventeenth century about 4-5000 slaves a year were imported from West Africa and Angola. Slavery and the Brazilian economy became inextricably linked. 'Without Angola no slaves, without slaves no sugar, without sugar no Brazil,' was a common expression in that century. Brazil remained continually dependent on the slave trade. During the eighteenth century over 1 million slaves were imported from Africa to Brazil. African-born slaves always outnumbered those born in Brazil and the cultural impact of Africa was very strong in the plantation regions.

Slavery and the plantation regime imposed a social hierarchy that eventually characterized even non-plantation regions. The mill-owning families became an aristocracy controlling the social and political life at the local level. Invariably white, this aristocracy was always open to merchants or recent immigrants who by purchase or marriage took on the role of *senhor de engenho*. The planters, and to a lesser extent the merchants, controlled local politics

Portuguese monarchs	
[Aviz Dynasty]	
1481–95	John (João) II
1495–1521	Manoel I 'the Fortunate'
1521–57	John III 'the Pious'
1557–78	Sebastian
1578–80	Cardinal Henry
1580–1640	*Portugal under the Spanish crown*
[Braganza Dynasty]	
1640–56	John IV
1656–67	Afonso VI
1667–1706	Pedro II
1706–50	John V
1750–77	José I [Pombal ministry]
1777–1816	María I
1816–26	John VI

Brazilian slave-market, early nineteenth century (lithograph by Deroy after Rugendas)

through the municipal councils and they shared authority with the thin layer of royal bureaucrats sent out from Portugal who themselves often became linked by personal or business ties to the local aristocracy. Cane farmers were often in effect proto-planters, drawn from the same origins but lacking sufficient funds to set themselves up independently. At the bottom of the social scale was the mass of the population distinguished primarily by its colour and legal status, black and slave. In this sense, the social structure resembled the plantation's organization. A significant portion of the colonial population, however, was composed of people of mixed origin, the result of miscegenation between European, Indians, and Africans, as well as some poorer whites, manumitted blacks and their descendants, and free Indians. These people often performed artisan occupations in the towns or lived as peasants, herdsmen, and free labourers in rural areas. While miners, ranchers or merchants formed the upper class in non-plantation regions, the principles of stratification remained the same.

FOREIGN ATTACK AND INTERNAL EXPANSION

The rise of Brazil from an imperial backwater to a wealthy plantation colony was not without its costs. The union of Spain and Portugal under the Spanish Habsburgs (1580–1640) made the Portuguese empire a prime target for Spain's enemies. The Dutch seized Salvador for a year in 1624–5 before they were dislodged by a joint Luso-Spanish fleet, but they soon returned, taking Olinda in 1630 and then expanding their control over much of north-eastern Brazil. The Dutch West India Company tried to stimulate the sugar industry in Netherlands Brazil by extending credit to Portuguese planters and by regularizing the slave trade, to which end they seized Luanda in 1641. These policies, along with religious toleration extended to Catholics and even to the Portuguese crypto-Jewish population, worked relatively well under the enlightened rule of Governor Johan Maurits of Nassau, but his departure and the recall of loans by the Dutch West India Company combined with nationalistic sentiments to bring about a rebellion against the Dutch in 1645. This movement received the unofficial support of Portugal which by this time was supposedly at peace with Holland and at war with Spain. In 1654, after suffering a major defeat at Guararapes (1649), the Dutch were forced to abandon their last strongholds.

Although the colony was unified once again under Portuguese control, the economic situation at mid-century was gloomy. The revolt and ten years of warfare had destroyed many plantations and disrupted the sugar economy. Matters were made worse by competition from places like Barbados and other West Indian islands, which not only drove down the price of sugar, but also drove up the price of slaves. Despite some recovery in the last decade of the century and the development of another staple, tobacco, the agricultural prospects of Brazil were dim. The second half of the seventeenth century was thus marked by increasing efforts to find new sources of wealth in the colony. Leading the way in this were the frontiersmen from the southern town of São Paulo which, located inland, had turned its fortunes towards the interior. Beginning in the late sixteenth century, bands of these *paulistas*, many of whom were in fact *mamelucos* of mixed European-Indian background, moved into the interior in search of minerals and Indians who (under loopholes in the legislation) could be enslaved. By the 1620s these expeditions or *bandeiras* were raiding Jesuit missions in Spanish-controlled Paraguay and were moving southward on to the plains of Uruguay and northward into the centre of the continent, pushing well beyond the line of Tordesillas that divided the Spanish and Portuguese possessions in America. While the *paulistas* were noted for their independence and arrogance, the crown could not ignore their skills as explorers and backwoodsmen. The great *bandeira* of Antonio Raposo Tavares (1648–52) that traversed the continent had governmental support. The combination of private initiative and governmental sponsorship led eventually to the establishment of a

Portuguese outpost at Colonia do Sacramento on the banks of the River Plate in 1680 and the subsequent settlement of the lands that lay between it and São Paulo. Government-sponsored expeditions also searched for silver and emeralds in the 1670s, with little success, but by 1695 news filtered out to the coast that the *paulistas* had found gold in the interior.

GOLD: A MIXED BLESSING

As news of the gold strikes spread, a great 'rush' quickly ensued. Swarms of men left the coastal towns and plantations and poured into the areas of the gold washings in the region that was soon to be known as Minas Gerais. They were joined by a wave of immigration of some 4–5000 a year who came out from Portugal and the Azores. Since labour in Brazil was associated with slavery, voluntary immigration was matched by an active slave trade fuelled by demand for labour and facilitated by the ability of the prospectors to pay in gold. By 1720 Minas Gerais had some 35,000 slaves. In fact, the discovery of gold in the south-central interior of Brazil caused a decided population shift away from the coast. In 1775 half the 300,000 inhabitants of Minas Gerais were slaves. At this time Minas Gerais had about 20 per cent of the colony's people, making it the most populous captaincy of Brazil.

It took a decade and a civil war to control the wild and raucous miners. The *paulistas* considered the gold strikes to be theirs and hostilites between them and the 'tenderfeet' (*emboabas*) erupted in a civil war (1708–9) in which the *paulistas* lost to their opponents, who were backed by the crown. Rough mining camps eventually evolved into a network of towns around the administrative centre of Vila Rica de Ouro Preto, and an active bureaucracy designed especially to collect taxes and control smuggling was firmly in place by 1730. New gold strikes and finds of diamonds between 1715 and 1735 led to a further movement of population and extension of governmental control. Production of gold rose steadily, reaching a high of over 15 tons of gold between 1750 and 1755. After this point, production began to fall, so that by the 1770s Brazil was once again faced by the problem of declining exports. Even so, the Brazil fleets carried great quantities of gold back to Portugal and much governmental activity in Brazil was devoted to methods of taxation, the creation of colonial mints, and contraband control in order to assure the continued flow of this golden stream to the metropolis.

Gold proved to be a mixed blessing to Brazil and Portugal. At first, it seemed that the movement of population away from the coast and the new demand

GOLD PRODUCTION IN BRAZIL (in tons)

Ouro Preto, Brazil, centre of the eighteenth-century mining boom

for slaves with resulting higher prices would spell the death knell for staple export agriculture, but limitations placed on the slave trade to Minas Gerais and other measures eventually softened the impact of the gold rush. Commercial agriculture survived and, in fact, even at the height of gold production, the value of sugar exports exceeded that of gold. Mining not only opened new regions to settlement but created new demands as well. The new markets in the mining zones caused an expansion of ranching in the northeast, and created a whole new ranching area on the plains of Rio Grande do Sul in southern Brazil. The shift of population into south-central Brazil and the importance of gold in the economy gave Rio de Janeiro, the port closest to the mines, a new importance, which along with its proximity to the southern borderlands on the River Plate, made it a more attractive administrative centre than Salvador. In 1763 the colonial capital was moved to Rio de Janeiro. In Minas Gerais itself a distinctive society developed in the gold-mining towns in which the miners' wealth was used to sponsor the buildings of churches which stimulated a whole range of artisan activities. Like the coast, however, the hierarchy of colour and legal status applied in Minas Gerais as well, where so large a proportion of the population was composed of slaves or free persons of colour.

THE POMBALINE REFORMS

The effects of Brazilian mineral wealth on Portugal were in the long run unfavourable. Militarily and commercially closely aligned with England, especially after the Methuen Treaty of 1703, Portugal paid its balance of trade deficit with Brazilian gold which flowed in large quantities into the hands of English merchants who increasingly penetrated the lines of Portuguese colonial commerce.

The loosening of Portuguese dependence on England, the increase of central authority in Lisbon, and the resuscitation of the colonial empire, especially Brazil, became the primary goals of Sebastião José de Carvalho e Melo, later Marquis of Pombal, who from 1755 to 1777 was prime minister and virtual dictator of the Portuguese empire. He frontally attacked groups whose position or power were in conflict with the regalist sentiments. Thus, the nobility was persecuted and the Jesuits were expelled from all Portuguese lands in 1759. A series of administrative changes and fiscal reforms were instituted by Pombal, designed to increase the flow of wealth into the royal coffers and to weaken the grip of foreign merchants on Portuguese commerce. Realizing that the key to Portugal's prosperity lay in Brazil, he instituted a series of reforms in the colony, appointing vigorous administrators to carry them out. Both diplomacy and warfare were used in the 1760s and 1770s in an attempt to define the extent of Brazil's boundaries with neighbouring Spanish American colonies. His measures like the creation of Boards of Inspection and the use of monopoly companies like the Company of Pernambuco and Paraíba (1750) were designed to increase agricultural exports. Fiscal policies and tax collection in the mining areas were tightened. In all this, however, he did not exclude the colonials. While many Brazilians objected to the constraints of more effective government, elite Brazilian families were not displaced from their traditional positions of authority or prevented from gaining new ones. Brazil had neither a university nor a printing press prior to 1808 and while it did develop a small intelligentsia, their intellectual, professional, and political life was always tightly linked to Portugal. Pombal did nothing to change that pattern.

Certain regions especially benefited from governmental reforms and the conditions created by them. Rio de Janeiro's new importance as the colonial capital was matched by an expansion of its agricultural exports. The vast, previously undeveloped region of northern Brazil became a major target for Pombal's reforms. Created as a separate state of Maranhão (1621), its two principal captaincies of Pará and Maranhão with their respective cities of Belém and São Luiz were for much of their previous history colonial backwaters. The European population was small, efforts to set up a plantation economy had failed (and thus there were few black slaves), and there was little in the region to attract settlement. Despite laws to the contrary, Indian slavery in various forms persisted in the Amazon basin, where the colonists competed with Jesuit missionaries for control of the population.

Pombal's policies were designed to make northern Brazil an integral and valuable part of the empire. A Company of Grao Pará and Maranhão was created in 1755 to promote development of exports. It stimulated the export of cacao from Pará, but its greatest success was in Maranhão where it supplied slaves to a now rapidly expanding cotton economy. Like its sister company of Pernambuco it distributed European goods to the colony and provided a regularized trade, but it was sorely disliked by some merchants in Lisbon and by many colonials. Both companies were abolished shortly after Pombal's fall from power in 1777. In other areas, too, Pombal's reforms were confused or misguided. The system of missions in the far north was replaced in 1757 by the directorate system in which Indians were placed under lay administrators in an attempt to integrate them into the wage labour force and to stimulate their contact with the Portuguese. The directorate system was a disaster for the Indians and failed to produce the desired results. Even in 1800 the Amazonian region remained an area of extractive economy dependent on Indian labour with a predominantly mixed-blood population. Maranhão by that date, however, had developed an active staple economy based on slavery and to that extent resembled more closely the rest of Brazil.

Whatever the deficiencies of Pombal's policies, the decline of gold production and weak prices for Brazilian products created a context in which any reforms were doomed to limited success. Despite the Pombaline measures, the value of Brazilian exports in 1776 was only 40 per cent of their value in 1760. Nevertheless, his policies set the stage for an economic renaissance at the end of the eighteenth century. New staples like cotton, rice, and indigo from regions such as Rio de Janeiro and Maranhão joined more traditional exports of sugar, hides, and tobacco, stimulated by growing demand abroad. In the 1790s with the elimination of Saint-Domingue (Haiti) as a sugar producer, Brazilian production soared, expanding into new regions like São Paulo and intensifying in traditional sugar areas like Bahia and Pernambuco. This economic growth was paralleled by an expansion of the population, growing from about 1.5 million in 1776 to over 2 million by 1800. Much of this population was of African or Afro-American origin, a result of miscegenation and of a slave trade expanding rapidly at the end of the century in response to the agricultural revival. Import levels for slaves in the last decade of the eighteenth century and first decade of the nineteenth were over 20,000 a year. Around 1800 about one third of the Brazilian population was slave, two thirds of the remainder were black or mulatto, and one third was European. There was considerable regional variation in this pattern.

COLONIAL DISSATISFACTION

By 1808 the role of Brazil within the colonial empire of Portugal had changed considerably. In the 1770s almost 75 per cent of the crown's colonial income was generated by Brazil and by 1807 over 60 per cent of all the goods Portugal exported were of Brazilian origin. Brazilian products allowed Portugal to establish a positive balance of trade with the rest of Europe, but this situation in turn caused the metropolis to have a deficit with its own colony which increasingly, if illegally, purchased goods directly from England. With this inversion of the colonial relationship, Brazilians became restive under Portuguese restrictive policies such as the limitation on local textile industries (1785). Agitation grew for free trade and open ports.

The signs of strain in the colonial relationship were showing. Earlier manifestations of nativism like the War of the Emboabas or the War of the Mascates (1710–11) in Pernambuco had not aimed at deep political or social change, but in the spirit of the times such ideas began to emerge in the late eighteenth century. Nevertheless, as several episodes showed, the dissatisfaction of Brazilian planters and merchants over economic policy was always muted by the fear of social unrest in this essentially slave-based society. When, however, in 1807 the prince regent of Portugal and the whole court were forced to flee Napoleon's army by sailing under English protection for Brazil, the economic and political basis of the colonial relation between Portugal and Brazil was already in question. Dom João VI, as prince regent and later as king, was faced with the problem of reconciling the aspirations and power of the Brazilian colony with the needs and interests of Portugal. As the period from 1808 to the declaration of Brazilian independence in 1822 demonstrates, it was perhaps an impossible task.   SBS

Further Reading: C. R. Boxer, *The Golden Age of Brazil, 1695–1750* (Berkeley, 1962); G. Freyre, *The Masters and the Slaves: a Study in the Development of Brazilian Civilization* (New York, 1964); J. Hemming, *Red Gold: The Destruction of the Brazilian Indians 1550-1760* (London, 1978); J. Lang, *Portuguese Brazil: The King's Plantation* (New York, 1979); C. Prado, Jr, *The Colonial Background of Modern Brazil* (Berkeley, 1967); S. B. Schwartz, *Sugar Plantations in the Formation of Brazilian Society: Bahia 1550–1835* (Cambridge, 1985)

The non-Spanish Caribbean islands to 1815

NEW ISLAND COLONIES

When the tide of Spanish conquest engulfed the American mainland in the 1520s and 1530s, the Caribbean island colonies (Hispaniola, Puerto Rico, Cuba) set up after Columbus's voyages lost much of their importance. Even so, the Caribbean sea was part of the vital maritime link between America and Spain; in any case, it lay on the western (Spanish) side of the Tordesillas Line, the line separating Span-

ish and Portuguese zones of dominance. Spain therefore claimed a monopoly on all trade and navigation throughout the West Indies, and sought to enforce it.

The Tordesillas principle was never taken very seriously in other European countries. 'The sun shines for me as for others,' said King François I of France, 'and I should very much like to see the clause in Adam's will that excludes *me* from a share of the world.' Assertive nation-states such as France, England and (a bit later) the newly independent Netherlands were eager to grasp the commercial opportunities they saw in the Caribbean – to grasp them, of course, at Spain's expense. From the 1530s, French privateers were a serious menace to Spanish shipping. In the mid-1550s they even sacked Havana, in Cuba, then virtually undefended – the impressive fortifications visible there today show that Spain quickly took the hint. From the 1560s the English too conducted aggressive trading and raiding forays into the supposedly 'closed' sea, with John Hawkins (1532–95) and, especially, Francis Drake (c. 1543–96), legendary as 'El Draque', inspiring terror in Spain's colonies. After 1600 it was the Dutch who were the most forceful in their assaults on the Spanish monopoly.

The obvious need was for local bases – bases from which to trade, and, if necessary, maraud. With little prospect of wresting major territories from Spain, the European interlopers focused their gaze on the small Windward and Leeward Islands – the beautiful chain of the Lesser Antilles. These were islands the Spaniards had generally left alone, in some cases deterred by the fierce native Carib populations, which, indeed, continued to deter and harass later colonists. In fact, the islands of Dominica, St Vincent and St Lucia were to remain Carib redoubts till the eighteenth century, though increasingly infiltrated by European (especially French) squatters. (As late as the Treaty of Aix-la-Chapelle in 1748 these islands were still declared 'neutral' by the European powers. All eventually became British.) When a French party took possession of Grenada in the 1650s – the first of several invasions of that beautiful island – the local Caribs eventually leapt to their death from a cliff rather than surrender. The village at that spot is still called Sauteurs, 'Jumpers'. (A handful of Caribs survives today on the island of Dominica.)

In the two decades after 1620, England, France and Holland all gained permanent colonies in the West Indies. The English settled on St Kitts (1623–5), Barbados (1627), Nevis (1628), Antigua (1632) and Montserrat (1632). The most important of these was Barbados. France also colonized St Kitts (1625) – the island was long shared by French and English – and in 1635 the French Compagnie des Iles d'Amérique began settling Martinique and Guadeloupe. In the

1630s also, the Dutch secured the trading bases they needed on the small islands of the Curacao group, off the Venezuelan coast, and on the even smaller islands of St Eustatius, St Martin (shared with France after 1648) and Saba, in the Leewards. Denmark, too, became a Caribbean power by colonizing St Thomas and St John in the Virgin Islands in the 1670s. Other European states marginally involved in this story are Brandenburg–Prussia, which held minuscule St Peter (Virgin Islands) for a quarter-century after 1689, and Sweden. Sweden's hopes were long frustrated. Only in 1784 did it gain a base, the island of St Barthélémy, ceded by France in exchange for a concession in Europe. (The island reverted to France after a referendum in 1878. Its capital still bears the Swedish name Gustavia.)

Attacks on the well-established Spanish possessions in the Greater Antilles were not very successful. In the vigorous period of the Commonwealth, England sent a force to conquer Hispaniola – Oliver Cromwell's 'Western Design' – but the attack was a fiasco. The expedition did, however, capture the poorly defended island of Jamaica (1655), English possession of which was recognized by Spain in the Treaty of Madrid (1670). At around the same period, French settlers – ranchers and planters – began infiltrating the depopulated western side of Hispaniola, eventually forming the colony of Saint-Domingue. Spain accepted this *fait accompli* in the Treaty of Ryswick (1697).

SUGAR AND SLAVES

In the earliest phase of island colonization the English and French intention was to foster settlement colonies in which (among other things) tropical crops were produced by predominantly European labour. Tobacco was such a crop in many of the islands, often bought up and marketed by the ever-obliging Dutch, who were much more interested in trade than in settlement. (As the English governor of Jamaica reported in 1673, 'The Dutch have a proverb: "Jesus Christ is good, but trade is better!"') Without the Dutch commercial network (and naval actions against Spain at the critical period) the island colonies might well have perished at birth. History allows no place for gratitude: Dutch predominance offended against the restrictive, monopolistic ideas of 'mercantilism' shared by all early modern empires, and both England (in its Navigation Acts) and France (with Colbert's 'Exclusive') acted later in the seventeenth century to shut the Dutch out from their respective colonial trades.

The heyday of the European settlement colonies was brief. Indentured labour (in the French case

TABLE 1

Sugar production (in tons) and slave populations in four Caribbean island colonies

Barbados			Jamaica		
Year	Sugar	Slaves	Year	Sugar	Slaves
1680	–	38,400	1703	4782	45,000
1712	6343	42,000	1730	15,972	74,500
1757	7068	63,600	1775	47,690	190,000
1792	9025	64,300	1789	59,400	250,000
1809	6062	69,400	1808	77,800	324,000

Guadeloupe			Saint-Domingue		
Year	Sugar	Slaves	Year	Sugar	Slaves
1674	2106[a]	4300	1739	–	117,411
1730	6230	26,800	1764	60,000	206,000
1767	7898	71,800	1791	78,696	452,000
1790	8725	85,500	[Haitian revolution]		
1820	22,300	88,400	1836	8	none

[a] metric tons

Source: Franklin W. Knight, *The Caribbean: the Genesis of a Fragmented Nationalism* (New York, 1978), p.237.

engagé labour) was unable, in the end, to sustain a successful pattern of colonial life. Nor were transported convict labourers satisfactory. Would-be English settlers eventually found the new mainland colonies of North America more attractive than the tropics. The West Indian islands did, however, lend themselves admirably to sugar cultivation. Once again the indispensable Dutch were on hand to get things going, having gained much experience and expertise during their occupation of north-east Brazil. After 1650 there was a general shift in this new direction. It was a change whose importance for the history of the Caribbean can scarcely be overstated: sugar cultivation brought about a profound transformation of the islands' social structure and, not least, their ethnic make-up. The equation of sugar with slavery is a constant in western-hemisphere history. In the seventeenth and eighteenth centuries, more than half the slaves transported from Africa went to the Caribbean. Europe's sweet tooth (particularly England's) exacted a hideous price in human suffering.

The first important slave-based sugar-producing colony was Barbados – the 'brightest jewel in the crown' for the English long before India took over that description. Barbados was later eclipsed by Jamaica, and Jamaica, in its turn, was surpassed by Saint-Domingue, where there were getting on for half a million slaves by the 1780s. Nearly all the islands went over to sugar monoculture. The commercial importance of the sugar colonies was considerable. In 1773, for instance, Great Britain took a quarter of all

Cutting sugar-cane, Jamaica

its imports from the West Indies – double the from the thirteen colonies of North America. At roughly the same period, shipments to and from the West Indies accounted for about one-third of all France's external trade. The Caribbean islands were highly prized by the European powers.

The spread of sugar plantations across the islands soon gave rise to a society that was rigidly divided along lines of colour and legal status. The white minority consisted of a small, powerful elite of planters, along with merchants and professional men, and a miscellaneous group of poorer whites: smallholders, artisans, storekeepers, drifters. All of these, whatever their social status, were free. The overwhelming majority of blacks, by contrast, were slaves – working the plantations, engaged in specialized tasks, employed in domestic service. (Plantation slavery had its own subtle social distinctions.) Alongside the slaves there emerged a class of free mulattoes and blacks – *gens de couleur*, in French colonial parlance – who were sometimes able to acquire property and become prosperous. This group distanced itself from the slave population, but it was usually denied entry to white circles, and its relative success was often resented by the poor whites.

Social tensions of various kinds were thus always latent on the islands, and there were occasional explosions. Slaves themselves periodically rose in desperate revolt. On the Danish island of St John in 1733, for instance, nearly all the local whites were killed. Planters were continuously nervous of such episodes. Another form of black resistance was escape. Where suitably inaccessible terrain was to hand (as in the Cockpit Country and Blue Mountains of Jamaica, or the rugged highlands of Saint-Domingue) runaway slaves – Maroons – were able to live in stable, independent communities that often lasted over several generations. The nucleus of Jamaica's 'Maroon towns' was provided by slaves who ran off when the English arrived: these particular communities held together far longer than similar settlements on other islands, or even in Brazil, where this phenomenon (known locally as the *quilombo*) was familiar in the era of slavery.

BUCCANEERS AND ADMIRALS

Cannon captured from the British in a colonial Venezuelan fort overlooking the Orinoco: the fortifications were orginally constructed around 1680 to ward off buccaneers.

The Caribbean, from the outset, was an arena of intense international competition. Spain made fitful attempts to dislodge its European rivals, ultimately to no avail, and the new colonial powers frequently fought amongst themselves to win territorial or commercial advantages. Islands were often captured and recaptured: Dutch-held St Eustatius – until devastated by Admiral Rodney in 1781, the most flourishing free port in the Caribbean – once changed hands ten times in as many years (1664–74). This extremely fluid political situation allowed ample scope for unofficial enterprise, and in particular for that notorious seventeenth-century activity, buccaneering.

The buccaneers (known by the Dutch as *zee-roovers*, by the French as *flibustiers*) overshadow a whole phase of Caribbean history. These communities of ruthless cut-throats roamed the West Indies, raiding Spanish settlements (regarded as fair game by all), terrorizing local populations, preying on shipping, and sometimes acting as mercenaries in inter-colonial warfare. Like many such fraternities, the buccaneering bands evolved a distinctive subculture, with rules and conventions – the Custom of the Coast. Despite their reprehensible depredations, they were often regarded as useful allies by colonial governors. In practice, they were only really dependable when it came to attacking Spanish colonies.

Buccaneering was at its height between the 1640s and the 1680s. Its most prominent centres were the French-held island of Tortuga (Tortue), off Hispaniola – headquarters of the notorious Jean-David Nau (d. 1668), better known as L'Olonnais – and the township of Port Royal in Jamaica, which long

enjoyed a possibly exaggerated reputation as 'the wickedest town in the world'. Port Royal was the base for the famous (or infamous) Henry Morgan (*c.* 1635–88) – originally an indentured servant on Barbados – who repeatedly raided Spanish settlements around the Caribbean. His final foray was an audacious and brutal assault on Panama City (1670–1). Morgan survived to win respectability, a knighthood, and the lieutenant-governorship of Jamaica. With the inclusion of the West Indies in standard diplomatic negotiations, and with the introduction of more formalized warfare, buccaneering gradually

Colonial fortifications, St Kitts. St Kitts was the first Caribbean island to be settled from England.

Toussaint Louverture (1743–1803), leader of the Haitian Revolution

smaller flurries of Anglo-Spanish warfare. The island colonies once again became pawns in a wider political game – pawns to be seized in war and (as often as not) returned at the ensuing peace conference, when gains and losses were sorted out on a global scale. In the long cycle of Anglo-French wars that started in 1744, to end only in 1815, Great Britain clearly had the edge, and made most of the gains. In the Seven Years' War (1756–63), for instance, the British made a clean sweep of all French possessions (except Saint-Domingue) in the Caribbean, also capturing Havana. Most of these gains, however, were returned under the Treaty of Paris (1763), even though British opinion seriously debated whether to retain Guadeloupe in preference to Canada, which had also been taken from France during the war and was, so to speak, on offer. This was a reflection of the esteem in which the island colonies were held in Europe. There were many in London who thought sugar-rich Guadeloupe a far greater prize than the territory Voltaire had dismissed as *quelques arpents de neige*, 'a few acres of snow'. In the end, broader political considerations prevailed. Canada was taken instead of Guadeloupe.

One reason for the general British superiority in the West Indies was intelligent naval strategy. From the 1740s – in part at the behest of the planters' lobby, influential in British politics – the Admiralty stationed squadrons of warships in the area, with naval dockyards at Jamaica (Port Royal) and Antigua (English Harbour); the latter, now restored, has become a notable yachting centre. (Minor facets of modern Jamaican and Antiguan culture are said to be traceable to this long presence of that most British of British institutions, the Royal Navy.) France did not station a squadron in the West Indies until 1784. Despite short-term reverses in the War of American Independence (1778–83 in its Anglo-French dimension), British pre-eminence in the area was both confirmed and reinforced during the final great struggle with France (1792–1815), at the end of which Trinidad, Tobago, and St Lucia were added to Great Britain's already extensive colonial holdings in the Caribbean.

THE HAITIAN REVOLUTION

In the prosperous colony of Saint-Domingue, France's 'Pearl of the Antilles', plantation slavery produced its own drastic denouement before the end of the eighteenth century. Here the French Revolution of 1789 sparked off one of the great explosions of Caribbean history.

Some of Saint-Domingue's rich planters (*grands blancs*) reacted to the upheaval in France by demand-

lost its impetus. In a neatly symbolic way, Port Royal was destroyed by an earthquake in 1692. Morgan's tomb slid beneath the sea. Buccaneers were last hired as mercenaries in a successful French attack on Cartagena in 1697. After that, little more was heard of them.

Their place was taken, in the eighteenth century, by well-organized navies and the distinguished admirals whose names – Vernon, Ogle, Keppel, Rodney, Hood on the British side; de Bouillé, de Grasse, d'Estaing among others on the French – loom so large in the naval annals of the period. The pattern of events in the West Indies was now largely determined by the long struggle for global mastery between France and Great Britain. There were also

ing colonial autonomy. But, true to form, they strongly resisted the French National Assembly's decision (May 1791) to enfranchise the *gens de couleur,* the colony's mulattoes and free blacks, who were now pressing their claims to equality with some vehemence. While these dissensions were in progress, the ignored slaves of the plantation-rich Plaine du Nord area – perhaps as many as 100,000 of them – rose in sudden massive revolt, burning cane-fields and killing whites (August 1791). It was the start of more than a decade of confused, often very savage conflict. A small army sent from France – accompanied by Jacobin commissioners, hostile to the planters and sympathetic to mulattoes and slaves – merely added to the chaos. Only one thing seemed clear by 1793–4: white supremacy in Saint-Domingue was doomed. Planters all around the West Indies were terrified. Nervous feelings were expressed in the southern states of the newly independent United States.

Encouraged by some of the *grands blancs,* British (and also Spanish) troops invaded Saint-Domingue to restore the status quo. The increasingly shadowy French authorities were obliged to accept the insurgent ex-slaves as their allies. In this situation the numerical strength of Saint-Domingue's blacks was bound to tell. Amidst the bloody turmoil of the 1790s, the initiative passed by stages to a truly remarkable black leader, Francois-Dominigue Toussaint Louverture (1743–1803), himself a former slave from Plaine du Nord. By the end of the decade, having forced the withdrawal of the British (1798) with his now formidable army, Toussaint was supreme in Saint-Domingue, recognized as its governor-general by France, but acting to all intents and purposes as the ruler of an independent country.

By now Saint-Domingue had been devastated by the years of cruel conflict. The plantations lay desolate; the country's 'infrastructure' – not least the superb colonial irrigation systems of the Artibonite Valley and the Plaine du Cul de Sac, important agricultural areas – was destroyed beyond repair. Toussaint did what he could to revive economic activity. His policy on racial matters was conciliatory. He hoped that Saint-Domingue would become if not independent then at least 'a colony forming part of the French empire but subject to special laws' – the 'special laws' including, of course, the abolition of slavery. This posture was not acceptable to France's new ruler, Napoleon Bonaparte. A powerful armament descended on Saint-Domingue, covertly aiming to restore slavery. Toussaint eventually surrendered. He was kidnapped and taken to France, where he soon died in prison (April 1803), though not before William Wordsworth had eulogized him in a famous sonnet.

There's not a breathing of the common wind
That will forget thee; thou hast great allies;
Thy friends are exultations, agonies,
And love, and man's unconquerable mind.

Toussaint's people, too, proved unconquerable. The French army in Saint-Domingue was checkmated by yellow-fever and by renewed black resistance – resistance stiffened by French atrocities and by the news that slavery, briefly abolished on Guadeloupe, had now been forcibly restored there. The cleverest (and also most ruthless) of Toussaint's lieutenants, Jean-Jacques Dessalines (1758–1806), brought the revolution to its triumphant conclusion. At the start of 1804 he declared Saint-Domingue an independent nation, under the old Indian name of Haiti. He also embarked on a policy of killing the remaining whites.

Within a few months of independence, Dessalines had himself crowned as emperor – Jacques I – of the new nation. He was murdered two years later, after which Haiti became divided for a while into two states: the black-led north, under the remarkable Henry Christophe (1767–1820), a Grenada-born leader who later proclaimed himself King Henry I, strictly regimented his subjects, and built monumental palaces and fortifications, the ruins of which are among the most impressive sights in the Caribbean; and the mulatto-led south, under President Alexandre Pétion (1770–1818), whose easy-going policy (if it can be called that) set the pattern for the rural Haiti of the future, with its struggling peasantry and eroded landscapes. After the deaths of Pétion and Henry I, the country was reunited under the mulatto leader Jean-Pierre Boyer (1776–1850; president 1818–43).

SC

Further Reading: C. L. R. James, *The Black Jacobins,* 3rd edition (London, 1980); F. W. Knight, *The Caribbean: The Genesis of a Fragmented Nationalism ,* 2nd edition (New York, 1990); S. Mintz, *Sweetness and Power: the Place of Sugar in Modern History* (New York, 1985); T. O. Ott, *The Haitian Revolution* (Knoxville, Tennessee, 1973); J. H. Parry and P. M. Sherlock, *A Short History of the West Indies,* 3rd edition (London, 1971)

Spanish American independence, 1808–26

The independence of Spanish America was precipitated in 1808 by Napoleon's invasion of Spain, a blow which severed the metropolis from its colonies and created a crisis of authority among its subjects. Demands were made for political autonomy and economic emancipation, and as these were rejected so Spanish Americans took to arms. The forces of liberation advanced across the subcontinent in two movements: the southern revolution crossed the pampas from Buenos Aires and was carried by General José San Martín's Army of the Andes to Chile and beyond; the northern revolution, more closely shadowed by Spain, was led by Simón Bolívar from Venezuela to New Granada, back to its birthplace, and on to Quito and Guayaquil. Both converged on Peru, the fortress of Spain in America, where the last great battle of emancipation was fought at Ayacucho in 1824. In the north, Mexican insurgency followed a course of its own – violent social rebellion, prolonged royalist reaction, and ultimate conservative revolution. By 1826 Spain had lost everything except Cuba and Puerto Rico, and the empire was at an end.

PRECONDITIONS AND PRECURSORS

The Napoleonic onslaught of 1808 was the occasion rather than the cause of independence. Spanish Americans had already begun to possess a pride in their homelands, a consciousness of their own interests and identity, a conviction that they were Americans, not Spaniards. The new Americanism was a more powerful influence on men's minds than the Enlightenment. This inspired in its disciples not so much a philosophy of liberation as an independent attitude towards received values and institutions, a preference for reason over authority, experiment over tradition, ideas which were agents of reform, not destruction, and did not necessarily conflict with loyalism. A number of Americans, however, looked beyond reform. Francisco de Miranda (1750–1816), who had read the works of the French philosophers during his army service in Spain, transformed ideology into revolution. So did Simón Bolívar (1783–1830) whose liberal education, wide reading,

Simón Bolívar (1783–1830), The Liberator

The title 'Liberator' was first conferred on Simón Bolívar in October 1813, by the *cabildo* (city council) of his native Caracas. It was a title he cherished above all others.

Born into an old and rich Venezuelan creole family, Bolívar rose swiftly to prominence as a military commander in the early campaigns of the wars of independence in northern South America. With the Spanish recapture of Venezuela and New Granada (modern Colombia), he spent several months in exile in Jamaica and Haiti, from where in 1816 he returned to the attack in eastern Venezuela at the head of a small expedition. He made an audacious crossing of the Andes to liberate New Granada (1819), which he followed by proclaiming the new Republic of Colombia, embracing Venezuela, New Granada and Quito (modern Ecuador), although it was only with General Antonio José de Sucre's victory at Pichincha (1822) that the whole of this immense territory was freed from Spanish rule. In 1823 Bolívar and the Colombian Army moved south into Peru, in order to defeat the remaining concentrations of Spanish strength in the Andean highlands.

With the wars of independence over, the Liberator returned north, and strove unsuccessfully to preserve his unwieldy Colombian union. He resigned as president in March 1830, and died while on his way into exile as the union dissolved around him. He is reputed to have said, 'There have been three great idiots of history: Jesus Christ, Don Quixote – and myself.'

Five South American nations (Venezuela, Colombia, Ecuador, Peru and Bolivia) owe their independence to Bolívar. In addition to his striking qualities as a general, he also had a powerful political imagination, reflected in a prolific correspondence and in such classic texts as the *Jamaica Letter* (1815). He came to believe that strong executive government (though not monarchy) was the only realistic formula for the new Spanish American republics, and also supported schemes of confederation to unite the now fragmented Spanish American world for common purposes. These ideas were honoured but largely ignored over the next few decades. Nevertheless, Bolívar's dazzling career and his superb command of the Spanish language have given him a supreme place in the ranks of the Latin American liberators.

Bolívar's bicentenary in 1983 was extensively commemorated in his native Venezuela and in the other Spanish American nations. He remains one of the very few men to have had a country named after him.

LATIN AMERICA, 1800–1830

UNITED STATES

CALIFORNIA

LOWER CALIFORNIA

NEW MEXICO

TEXAS

Rio Grande

MEXICO

FLORIDA

Gulf of Mexico

NORTH ATLANTIC OCEAN

Bahama Is.

CUBA

BR. HONDURAS
HONDURAS
GUATEMALA
SALVADOR
NICARAGUA
COSTA RICA
PANAMA

Jamaica

Caribbean Sea

Caracas
Carabobo
VENEZUELA

GUIANAS

ATLANTIC

COLOMBIA

Bogotá Boyaca

NEW GRANADA

GRAN

Pichincha Quito
ECUADOR

PERU

BRAZIL

Junín
Lima
Ayacucho

PACIFIC OCEAN

BOLIVIA

La Paz

(UPPER PERU)

PARAGUAY

Rio de Janeiro

RIO GRANDE DO SUL

CHILE

UNITED PROVINCES OF THE RIVERPLATE

URUGUAY
(BANDA ORIENTAL)

Chacabuco
Santiago
Maipú
Rancagua

Buenos Aires
Montevideo

Patagonia

Falkland Is.
(Islas Malvinas)

- - - Boundary of Mexico 1824

0   1200km
0   750miles

Fr Miguel Hidalgo (1753–1811), a creole priest who led the popular insurrection of 1810 in Mexico.

and extensive travels in Europe opened his mind to new horizons, in particular to French thought and to English political practice. Men of this kind were true precursors of independence, though they were a small minority and probably ahead of public opinion.

Most of the independence movements began as the revolt of one minority against a smaller minority, of creoles (Spaniards born in America) against *peninsulares* (Spaniards born in Spain). Around 1800, in a total population of 16.9 million in Spanish America, there were 13.2 million whites, of whom only some 30,000 were *peninsulares*. But these distinctions were not clear-cut. The function of colonial elites as economic entrepreneurs investing in agriculture, mining and trade, tended to fuse the peninsular and creole groups into a white ruling class, which preferred to co-opt the imperial bureaucracy by marriage and interest rather than confront it. In Mexico the creoles were frustrated to find that there was a limit to their influence, but this did not necessarily make them supporters of independence. In Peru the creole elite, with all its grievances, was slow to be convinced that independence would serve its interests. Everywhere the wars of independence were civil wars between defenders and opponents of Spain, and the creoles were to be found on both sides. Nevertheless, rivalry between creoles and *peninsulares* was a definite part of the social tension of the time.

The creole aristocracy was a powerful group of landowners, office holders and town councillors, who profited from trade expansion between Spain and America in the second half of the eighteenth century to increase their exports. But economic growth menaced as well as favoured them. Spanish monopoly merchants tightened their grip on the import-export trade. At the same time swarms of new Spanish immigrants moved into the American end of the transatlantic economy. No doubt the antagonism between landowners and merchants could be described as one between producers and middlemen, not necessarily between creoles and *peninsulares*. But the fact remained that the merchants depended upon Spain for their monopoly. Spain's war with Britain from 1796, bringing blockade and shortages, enabled Spanish merchants to squeeze the creole producers still more, giving them minimal prices for exports and charging high for imports. They strongly resisted any attack on the colonial trade monopoly, such as trade with neutrals, and pressed Spain to halt it, 'as though', complained the Venezuelan producers in 1798, 'our commercial laws have been established solely for the benefit of the metropolis'. In Buenos Aires the merchant community itself split along Spanish-creole lines, the latter offering better prices to local ranchers and demanding freedom to trade with all countries, and in 1809 urging the opening of Buenos Aires to British trade.

The new wave of *peninsulares* after 1760 encroached on the political preserves of the creoles as well as on their economic position. The policy of the later Bourbons was to increase the power of the crown and to apply closer imperial control to America. This involved reversing a trend of the previous age, reducing the number of creoles in public office, and restoring the *peninsulares* to dominance in the judiciary, the bureaucracy, the Church and the military. In this sense there was a Spanish 'reaction' in the last decades of the empire, and creoles struggled for office not simply to procure a livelihood but as a means of controlling policy and defending their traditional position.

If the creoles had one eye on their masters, they kept the other on their servants. They were intensely aware of social pressure from below, and they strove to keep the coloured people at a distance. Race was complicated by social, economic and cultural interests, and white supremacy was not unchallenged; beyond its defences swarmed Indians, mestizos, free blacks, mulattoes, and slaves. In parts of Spanish America slave revolt was so fearful a prospect that creoles would not lightly leave the shelter of imperial government or desert the ranks of the dominant whites, and this was one of the reasons why Cuba did not embrace the cause of independence at this time. The demographic increase of the 'castes' or mixed races in the eighteenth century, together with growing social mobility, alarmed the whites and bred in them a new awareness of race and a determination to preserve discrimination. This could be seen in the River Plate, in New Granada and Venezuela. In other parts of Spanish America race tension took the form of direct confrontation between the white elite and the Indian masses. In Peru after the great rebellion of Túpac Amaru the highland creoles noticed the way in which they were distrusted and demoted from a security role and their militias demobilized. In Mexico, too, the social situation was explosive, and the whites were always aware of the simmering indignation of the Indians and castes. The pent-up anger of the Mexican masses exploded in 1810 in a violent social revolution, which proved to the creoles what they had long suspected, that in the final analysis they themselves were the guardians of social order and the colonial heritage.

When the Spanish monarchy collapsed in 1808, the creoles could not allow the political vacuum to remain unfilled, their lives and property unprotected. They had to move quickly to anticipate popular rebellion, convinced that if they did not seize the opportunity, more dangerous forces would do so. The creoles did not necessarily begin by espousing the cause of absolute independence. Many of the elite wanted no more than autonomy within the Spanish imperial system. They were prepared to bargain with Spain, but the metropolis would not respond, and the elite soon found that Spanish liberals were no less imperialist than Spanish absolutists. The lesson was learnt quickly in the River Plate; in Chile it was reinforced by the experience of a harsh counter-revolution. And when counter-revolution prevailed, in Venezuela and New Granada as well as in Chile, the property of Creole dissidents was at risk and the whole economy plundered for the royalist war effort. Creole moderates thus joined creole revolutionaries because Spain offered no alternative to imperialism and this was proving to be too expensive.

THE ARMIES OF INDEPENDENCE

The wars of independence were cruel and the battles heroic. But not all Americans fought for political ideals. The creoles had to mobilize blacks, Indians and castes; they did this without relinquishing the instruments of power or allowing any of these classes to wage an autonomous revolution. In general the masses had to be forcibly conscripted into the armies, if they could be caught before fleeing to the hills or forests. The royalists, too, found it difficult to recruit, both in Spain and in America, and their ultimate defeat was due in part to the impossibility of receiving continued reinforcements from home.

Recruits were sought among black slaves, and manumission was offered in return for service in the revolutionary armies. This was a qualified freedom. Even Bolívar, a true humanitarian, tied emancipation to conscription, though without much success. The slaves were not interested in fighting the creoles' war, while it was also clear that they had little to gain from the royalists. San Martín declared that 'the best infantry soldier we have is the black and mulatto'. Former slaves formed a substantial part of the Army of the Andes which liberated Chile – 1500 out of 5000 – and of General Sucre's army which completed the liberation of Peru at Ayacucho. There was a price to be paid for freedom of this kind; blacks, being in the infantry, suffered the heaviest casualties.

The Indians fought on both sides as a matter of opportunism or tried to avoid fighting at all. The Araucanians of southern Chile simply changed their resistance to the imperial power into hostility to the new rulers. The Indians of Peru were plundered by forces of both sides; they were pushed into battle by those who dominated a particular region, to be subsequently punished if the enemy took over. Both sides treated the Indians as serfs, transforming the personal services demanded of them in peace time into military services in time of war. Basically the white minority in Peru feared the blacks and Indians. The people of Lima were panic-stricken when the Spanish viceroy decided to abandon the capital in July 1821; they feared that the slave population might rise against the whites, and that the Indians and guerrillas in the surrounding districts might invade the city, once the Spanish troops had gone. The leading citizens invited San Martín to enter and occupy Lima, and in effect they sought protection rather than liberation. In Upper Peru, too, the creoles feared the

Simón Bolívar, the Liberator (1783–1830), the supreme Spanish American hero of the struggle for independence

Main events in the struggle for independence

1807 Napoleon invades Portugal: Portuguese royal family and court move to Brazil.

1808 Napoleon invades Spain, dethroning King Ferdinand VII. Crisis of authority in the Spanish empire.

1810 Autonomous governments (juntas) established by creole patriots in Venezuela, New Granada, Argentina and Chile. Fr Miguel Hidalgo leads anti-Spanish revolt in Mexico.

1811 Defeat and execution of Fr Hidalgo. Venezuela declares independence from Spain.

1812 Royalist forces defeat First Venezuelan Republic.

1813 Venezuela liberated by Simón Bolívar (1783–1830). Royalists return to the attack under José Tomás Boves.

1814 Ferdinand VII restored to the Spanish throne, determined to crush rebellious colonists. Montevideo captured by patriots. Chilean patriot government defeated by an expedition from the viceroyalty of Peru, focus of loyalty to Spain in South America.

1815 Spanish expedition under General Pablo Morillo 'pacifies' Venezuela and New Granada. Bolívar goes into exile in Jamaica and Haiti. Fr José María Morelos, successor to Fr Hidalgo in Mexico, captured and executed. The whole of Spanish America except for the River Plate is now restored to colonial rule.

1816 João VI becomes King of Portugal and Brazil. United Provinces of South America (Argentina) declare independence. Bolívar lands with a small force in Venezuela.

1817 General José de San Martín (1778–1850) and the Army of the Andes invade Chile from Argentina. Battle of Chacabuco (12 February). An army from Brazil invades the Bands Oriental (Uruguay).

1818 Battle of Maipó (5 April) confirms the independence of Chile. Bolívar liberates part of Venezuela.

1819 Bolívar liberates New Granada at the battle of Boyacá (7 August) and proclaims the formation of the vast Republic of Colombia (Grancolombia) embracing Venezuela, New Granada and Quito.

1820 Liberal revolution in Spain. Six-month truce in Venezuela. San Martín executes a seaborne invasion of the viceroyalty of Peru from Chile, the navy being commanded by the British Admiral Lord Cochrane.

1821 The battle of Carabobo (24 June) confirms the final liberation of Venezuela. San Martín proclaims the independence of Peru but fails to defeat the royalist armies in the Peruvian highlands. Independence of Mexico proclaimed by General Agustín Iturbide.

1822 General Antonio José de Sucre (1795–1830) liberates Quito at the battle of Pichincha (24 May). Bolívar and San Martín confer at Guayaquil: San Martín retires. Independence of Brazil proclaimed by Prince Pedro of Braganza, son and heir of João VI: he becomes Emperor Pedro I of Brazil.

1824 Campaigns of Bolívar and Sucre in the Peruvian highlands. Battles of Junín (August) and Ayacucho (December) conclude the wars of independence.

1826 Last Spanish garrisons in South America capitulate to the patriots.

1830 Dissolution of the Republic of Colombia into the three states of Venezuela, New Granada (later renamed Colombia) and Ecuador (the former Quito). Death of Bolívar (December).

emancipation of the Indians. The local elite of mine owners, landed proprietors and office holders turned against the liberating armies from Buenos Aires and then supported the security forces against the patriot guerrillas. They remained openly royalist until, in 1825, they were forcibly liberated by the Colombian army of General Sucre, thus inheriting an independence which they did not make. Wherever the creoles' fear of the American masses caused them to prefer the protection of the Spanish army, independence could not make progress without external stimulus. Some countries like the United Provinces of the River Plate (Argentina) were in a position to provide this; others like Peru depended on receiving it.

A CONSERVATIVE REVOLUTION

Independence was a political movement, in which a national ruling class took power from the imperial rulers, with only marginal change in economic organization and social structure. Spanish America rejected monarchy but then searched for a powerful substitute. Bolívar, republican though he was, really favoured a form of enlightened absolutism. Appalled by his compatriots' lack of experience in self-government and by the anarchy and social conflict which the wars unleashed, he sought to contain the forces of disorder by imposing a series of authoritarian constitutions. In his superbly analytical Jamaica Letter of 1815 he wrote, 'Events in Tierra Firme [northern South America] have proved that wholly representative institutions are not suited to our character, customs, and present knowledge.' Four years later, in his famous Angostura Address, he proclaimed, 'Complete liberty and absolute democracy are but reefs upon which all republican hopes have foundered… Let the legislature relinquish the powers which rightly belong to the executive.' On more than one occasion, in Venezuela, Peru, Ecuador and Colombia, he was himself persuaded to assume dictatorial powers, in order to resolve anarchy or defeat the Spanish enemy. Bolívar's search for a strong executive outlasted the war. His final constitutional views were enshrined in the Constitution which he wrote for Bolivia in 1826. This document provided for a president with not only life-long tenure but also authority to choose his successor. 'This supreme authority should be perpetual,' he wrote, thus avoiding 'the changing administration caused by party government and the excitement which too frequent elections produce.' This was the realistic Bolívar, his democratic ideals tempered by anarchy and dissent, although it has to be added that he saw strong government as an instrument of reform as well as of authority.

The pioneers of independence, the intellectuals, bureaucrats and professional politicians, soon gave way to the caudillos, the chieftains whose rule was based on personal power (see p.325). While he was originally a war leader, the caudillo also fulfilled other roles. He represented powerful economic interests, often of a regional kind. He was a distributor of patronage, of office and of land, the apex of a patron–client network. The decades following independence were the classic years of primitive caudillism, when Juan Manuel de Rosas in Argentina, José Antonio Páez in Venezuela, and Antonio López de Santa Anna in Mexico ruled whole nations as extended haciendas. Caudillos were created and ultimately controlled by the new ruling class. But even when they were subject to lawful challenge or

replaced by constitutional models, these were highly restricted. The franchise was often limited to those who were literate and possessed property, the legislature was weak, and the executive consisted of extremely strong presidents, as in Chile. But whatever the system of government, it reflected and did not change the prevailing economy and society.

Independence destroyed the colonial monopoly and opened the ports of Spanish America to the trade of the world. This was an inevitable though not unmixed blessing. The wars were destructive of life and property; terror and insecurity caused a flight of labour and capital, which made it difficult to diversify the economy. The principal owners of capital – Church and merchants – had little inducement to invest in industry in the absence of a strong and protected market. It was easier to allow British manufactures to supply national needs. And in the wake of British manufactures came British merchants, shippers and later bankers, who filled the entrepreneurial

---

Simón Bolívar on the future of Grancolombia

The Latin American independence movements were accompanied by feelings of great optimism about their likely results. Rarely were such feelings better expressed than by the liberator Simón Bolívar in the peroration of his great speech at Angostura (Venezuela) on 15 February 1819.

The union of New Granada and Venezuela as one great state has been the uniform wish of the peoples and governments of these Republics. The fortunes of war have ratified this link, so longed for by all Colombians . . . Contemplating the union of this immense territory, my soul ascends to the heights which are demanded by the colossal prospect offered by so astonishing a picture. Flying through the ages yet to come, my imagination fixes itself on future centuries – and, observing from that vantage-point, with admiration and wonder, the prosperity, splendour and life this vast region has received, it seems to me that I see it as the heart of the world . . . I see it serving as the link, the focus, the emporium of the human family; I see it sending to all the corners of the earth the treasures of its mountains of gold and silver; I see it spreading (through its divine plants) health to the suffering men of the Old World; I see it imparting its precious secrets to wise men who are ignorant of its superior knowledge and wealth, showered on it by Nature. I see it seated on the Throne of Liberty, clasping the sceptre of Justice, crowned by Glory, displaying to the Old World the majesty of the modern world.

Depiction of Simón Bolívar campaigning in the Colombian Andes

vacuum left by Spain. Foreign interests, of course, could not completely control national economies. Policy was made by the new rulers and interest groups. These sought to build their particular centre into a new metropolis and to reduce other regions to a continuing dependence upon themselves. The subregions protected their economies by insisting on various degrees of autonomy: Uruguay and Paraguay opted for complete independence of Buenos Aires; the interior provinces of Argentina chose the way of federalism. Elsewhere, as in Mexico, artisan industries were exposed to foreign competition and while they usually continued production they failed to gain the protection which they demanded. The national economies, therefore, were divided originally by internal rivalry, by conflict between agriculturalists seeking export outlets and those who favoured industry or mining. In the end the promoters of exports and cheap imports won the argument, and the British traders were waiting to take advantage.

The basic economic institution, therefore, was the hacienda, a relatively inefficient organization, absorbing too much land and too little capital, and carried ultimately on the back of cheap labour, seasonal or servile. But the hacienda was also a social and political organization, a means of control, a base of the new rulers. The elite of independence relied on their haciendas for economic support. Landowners took over from the colonial urban sectors of mining, trade and bureaucracy, and displaced too the first

republican rulers, those professional politicians and military who had made a career out of the revolution and whose liberal tendencies had to give way to more conservative regimes.

THE NEW RULERS

The polarization of society between an elite of landed proprietors and their associates on the one hand and the rural masses on the other was the characteristic feature of independent Spanish America. Haciendas and their owners were not always financially strong or able to exercise automatic social control. But land was the ultimate asset and on the whole land remained in the hands of a relatively small group of creoles, often bound together by ties of family and kinship, which enabled them to dominate offices, resources and labour. In the course of the wars the composition of the creole elite was modified, as soldiers, merchants and others who profited from the hostilities managed to turn themselves into landed proprietors. In Venezuela, where revolution and counter-revolution decimated the ranks of the colonial aristocracy, the great estates passed into the possession of a new oligarchy, the victorious caudillos of independence, who in fact frustrated Bolívar's plan to distribute land to the troops. The republican governments promoted private property rights in the llanos, deprived the nomadic plainsmen of their traditional communal usages, and reduced them to the status of rural labourers. In the pampas of Argentina a similar process could be observed. The merchants of Buenos Aires began to invest commercial capital in land, acquired vast territorial concessions from a compliant state, and added to them territory won during wars against the Indians. The *estancieros* then inexorably tamed the gauchos and reduced them to the status of hired ranch hands, tied to the *estancias* by anti-vagrancy laws and the threat of military conscription.

After independence, control over labour was greater than before. The slave trade, it is true, was abolished almost immediately throughout Spanish America, but abolition of slavery itself was a slow and difficult process, except in those countries were slavery was already obsolete. In general, the chronology of abolition was determined by the number of slaves in a country and their importance to its economy. Chile abolished slavery in 1823, Bolivia in 1826, Mexico in 1829. Elsewhere it took almost half a century: 1851 in Colombia, 1853 in Argentina, 1854 in Venezuela and Peru. Bolívar regarded it as 'madness that a revolution for liberty should try to maintain slavery', and he urged the Venezuelan and Colombian legislators to decree abolition. But freedom for Venezuela's 40,000 slaves had to await the time when landowners appreciated that slaves were expensive and uneconomical workers, and that a cheaper labour force could be obtained by turning them into 'free peons tied to the estates by anti-vagrancy laws or by a coercive agrarian regime.

The Indians in a sense *were* emancipated, for they were now free citizens and released from the payment of tribute and the obligation of forced labour. The liberals of post-independence, however, regarded the Indians as an obstacle to national development, and believed that the autonomy which they had inherited from the colonial regime should be ended by integrating them into the nation. In Peru, Colombia and Mexico the new legislators sought to destroy corporate entities in order to mobilize Indian lands and release Indian labour. The policy involved the division of communal lands among individual owners, theoretically among the Indians themselves, in practice among their more powerful neighbours. While the prospects of Indians and blacks were little improved by independence, those of the mixed races, the mestizos and *pardos*, were hardly better. The *pardos* struggled for equality with the creoles. They were already free men, ready to use existing avenues of advancement and to acquire property and status. They now sought access to education, office and political rights, from which they had been debarred by colonial law. Their claims could not be ignored, for in numbers alone they were indispensable to the

whites in the wars of independence. Their presence in the army opened the way to promotion up to officer of middle rank. Finally they obtained legal equality. The new republican constitutions abolished all outward signs of racial discrimination and made all classes and castes equal before the law. In effect the new rulers sought to release tension from the colonial social order by abolishing the caste system, which defined social status in law, and substituting a class society, divided by economic criteria. Inequality came to be based not on law but on wealth; for the franchise confined voting rights and therefore full citizenship to property owners. In a few cases the mixed races moved successfully upwards, but the majority were less fortunate.

'Independence', lamented Bolívar, 'is the only benefit we have gained, at the cost of everything else.' Stability, growth, welfare – these had to await the achievement of later generations. Yet victory was not hollow. Spanish Americans had won a hard war, a new freedom, and a place among the nations of the world. The gains were historic and irreversible.   JL

Further Reading: T. E. Anna, *The Fall of the Royal Government in Mexico City* (Lincoln, Nebraska, 1978), *The Fall of the Royal Government in Peru* (Lincoln, Nebraska, 1979); L. Bethell, ed., *The Independence of Latin America* (Cambridge, 1987); B. Hamnett, *Roots of Insurgency: Mexican Regions 1750–1824* (Cambridge, 1986); J. Lynch, *The Spanish American Revolutions 1808–1826,* 2nd edition (New York, 1986)

Brazilian independence

Though Brazilian independence was proclaimed by Prince Pedro of Braganza on the bank of the Ipiranga River near São Paulo on 7 September 1822, there is a sense in which it was not placed beyond all doubt until 1834. By 1834 the idea of a Luso-Brazilian or 'Atlantic Monarchy' was dead, and a powerful group of planters and merchants had begun to rally behind the figurehead of the emperor Pedro II, constitutional ruler of one of the world's great slave-holding nations.

That Brazil emerged as a centralized unitary monarchy was due to four major factors: an overall shift of economic and political power within the Portuguese empire towards Rio de Janeiro, accomplished by 1815; the growth of regional sentiment and political revolt in reaction to rule from either Lisbon or Rio de Janeiro; the destruction of royal absolutism, between 1820 and 1831; and the emergence of plantation oligarchy, affirmed by 1841.

The shift of economic power from Portugal to Brazil had long occurred when Sebastião José de Carvalho e Melo, Marquis de Pombal (1712–82), attempted to forge an Atlantic mercantile empire firmly centred on Lisbon. Though his vigorous reforms certainly reinforced mercantile oligarchy in Lisbon, they also created powerful groups of merchants and planters in many parts of the empire. The expulsion of the Jesuit Order in 1759 destroyed a countervailing force; the expansion of the administration and creation of local militia units provided the means by which local men could become a powerful opposition to Lisbon's rule. Common interests cemented the empire together after Pombal's fall from power in 1777; a boom in sugar and cotton production in the north-east of the colony brought intensive imports of slaves to Brazil. Loyalty to the Metropolis would, so planters and merchants believed, prevent the spread of slave revolution from Haiti. A prominent younger generation of Portuguese leaders, led by Pombal's godson, Rodrigo de Souza Coutinho, sought to make the royal government, led by the regent, João, aware that the economic change brought about by Pombaline reform must lead to the establishment of an Atlantic empire, based perhaps on Rio de Janeiro.

Souza Coutinho's strategy represented the only alternative left to João when Napoleon ordered his armies into Portugal in late 1807, provoking the flight of the royal family to Brazil. The transfer of the court across the Atlantic, to Rio de Janeiro, was followed by the opening of all Brazilian ports to international commerce (28 January 1808). Brazil now traded directly with Britain and the United States, while the pre-eminence of the colony was formally recognized by a measure of December 1815 which created a monarch consisting of two kingdoms Brazil and Portugal. Such concessions to Brazilian interests antagonized merchants in Lisbon and Oporto, who had been deprived of valuable markets and were incited by army officers chafing under the rule of the English Marshal Beresford. In October 1820 a military rising broke out in Oporto, and won support in Lisbon. The new government in Portugal demanded the return of King João VI, and the convocation of a Cortes (parliament).

THE INDEPENDENT MONARCHY

Pedro I (1798–1834), the first emperor of independent Brazil

Though João returned to Lisbon, and a provisional constitution was accepted by the government in Brazil, it quickly became apparent that the majority

in the Cortes were determined to destroy the autonomy ceded since 1808. The Brazilian reaction was not unexpected; the heir to the throne, Prince Pedro, who had stayed in Brazil, immediately became the focus of local opposition to the Cortes. In January 1822 he announced that he would not return to Lisbon, making his famous declaration, 'I remain!', and refused to dismantle the administrative machinery in Rio. The Cortes replied by ordering that provincial governors report directly to Lisbon, abolishing the general treasury in Rio, the prince's State Council, and the Court of Appeals. Pedro's refusal to depart for Lisbon and his subsequent declaration of Brazilian independence were the inevitable reply to such measures. Though the Cortes sent troops to Rio de Janeiro and Bahia they were eventually dislodged by local forces, while Pedro managed to improvise a fleet with which to seize the northernmost provinces of Maranhão and Pará, which had always remained loyal to Lisbon and held out against Rio de Janeiro. Independence was achieved in military terms by the end of 1823.

The shape of the new regime was to be tempered by regional forces. Attempts to coerce the powerful oligarchies established under Pombaline rule had already led to a republican conspiracy in Ouro Prêto, Minas Gerais, in 1789, while others had threatened in Rio de Janeiro in 1794, Bahia in 1797, and Recife in 1801. Pedro's new government was to be mindful of

DOM PEDRO

Kaiser von Brasilien.

Empereur du Brésil.

the necessity to cater to provincial demands for constitutional government, emanating from Pernambuco and Ceará in the north-east, and Minas Gerais and São Paulo in the centre of the country. Appropriately enough he was crowned 'Constitutional Emperor and Perpetual Defender of Brazil' on 1 December 1822.

By inclination a liberal, in practice an autocrat, Pedro I faced difficulties from the outset. In order to consolidate Brazil's independence he had to come to terms with Britain and the Portuguese government before he could obtain recognition from other European powers. In practice this meant assuming the responsibility for debts contracted by Portugal in order to retain its colony, the acceptance of a powerful and privileged British commercial presence, and the abolition of the African slave trade by 1830. None of these measures was popular with local groups, many of whom were actively interested in commerce and beneficiaries of the slave trade. Many resented the assumption of substantial obligations by the fledgling government, and were concerned when the country went to war with Argentina in 1825. Anti-Portuguese feelings among the Constituent Assembly were inflamed when Pedro closed it on 12 November 1823; the monarch's desire to preserve the royal prerogative was confused with his Portuguese origin by a suspicious and determined assembly.

As Portugal was once again under absolutist control after 1823, and Pedro was suspected of dynastic ambitions, so his conduct became more and more suspect to local liberals. Meanwhile the new Constitution, promulgated unilaterally by the emperor in March 1824, was viewed as 'despotic in practice'. The emperor's refusal to consult with the Chamber of Deputies, and his appointments to high office were construed as autocratic and pro-Portuguese by a hostile group with powerful regional interests. They were assisted in their campaign by the evident unpopularity of a government in deep financial trouble, and at odds with the richer provinces of the north-east and Minas Gerais. The destruction of royal absolutism was complete when the army deserted Pedro on 7 April 1831, forcing him to abdicate in favour of his six-year-old son, Pedro II. A regency was set up to govern the country until the young monarch could assume the throne. Five provincial revolutions occurred between 1832 and 1838, but each was contained, thereby insuring the new empire's unity. Pedro I died in 1834, thus removing for good and all the lingering idea of a reunion of Brazil and Portugal. In 1840 Pedro II assumed the throne and began a reign that lasted until the republican coup of 1889.

The most important legacy of independence was ideological and political. The Brazilian elite, composed mostly of planters and merchants, split over the nature of Brazil's ties to Portugal. The pro-Portuguese faction eventually became the Conservative Party, and fought for a strong centralized monarchy in Brazil. The anti-Portuguese faction formed the Liberal Party and argued for a limited monarchy, subject to elected authorities within a federal structure. These two parties came to dominate imperial politics, with conservatism becoming the more influential ideology.

FC

Further Reading: R. J. Barman, *Brazil: the Forging of a Nation, 1782-1852* (Stanford, 1988); N. Macaulay, *Dom Pedro: the Struggle for Liberty in Brazil and Portugal, 1798-1834* (Durham, N. C., 1986); K. R. Maxwell, *Conflicts and Conspiracies: Brazil and Portugal, 1750–1808,* (Cambridge, 1973); A. J. R. Russell-Wood, *From Colony to Nation: Essays on the Independence of Brazil* (Baltimore, 1975)

Modern Latin America: general historical trends

Following the wars of independence, Latin America fragmented into a mosaic of separate nation-states. By 1903, with newly created Panama and an independent Cuba, the number reached twenty. Portuguese America held together, first as an empire and then as a republic. But the former Spanish colonies split up into separate nations, which frequently followed the jurisdictional boundaries of the former colonial administrative sub-units. This section of the Encyclopedia covers the history of the individual countries (or regions). There are, however, some common themes worth bearing in mind when trying to understand Latin America's historical development as a particular region of the world.

The 'national period', i.e. the period since independence, is best divided into three phases: 1820s–70s, 1870s–1930, 1930 onwards.

1820s–70s

The first decades after independence were marked by power struggles, often violent, with 'strong men' (caudillos) assuming a prominent role in many countries. Brazil and Chile were the exceptions, both consolidating stable political systems fairly soon after independence. Some republics (e.g. Argentina, Mexico, Colombia, Venezuela) went through recurrent spasms of civil war. With the old commercial restrictions of colonial times now eliminated. Latin America participated more widely in international trade, the main trading partners being Western Europe and (for the countries around the Caribbean in particular) the USA. Several countries (e.g. Argentina, Chile and Brazil) experienced a spurt in their overseas trade during this phase. Other nations (e.g. Mexico, Colombia, the states of Central America) tended to stagnate economically. Latin America's population remained predominantly rural, illiterate and poor.

The chief foreign influences after independence came from Great Britain, whose ships and traders were now everywhere, and France, whose cultural and intellectual achievements Latin America's elites greatly admired. Despite the evident weakness of the new nations, outside powers generally respected their sovereignty and territorial integrity. Exceptions were the British occupation of the Falkland Islands (Islas Malvinas) in 1833, the US invasion of Mexico in 1846–7 (which resulted in the transfer of vast Mexican territories to the rapidly expanding United States), and the French intervention in Mexico in the 1860s. Spain had retained Cuba and Puerto Rico – and these remained Spanish colonies until the end of the nineteenth century – but made no serious attempt to recapture its former mainland territories elsewhere in Latin America, though in the mid-1860s a Spanish naval squadron in the Pacific attacked both Chile and Peru.

1870s–1930

From around 1870 a second phase of modern Latin America's development began, as the international capitalist economy (centred chiefly, at that period, on Great Britain) expanded and strengthened new global networks of international trade and exchange – a 'world economy' made possible by the steamship, the railway and the electric telegraph. Latin America's exports – foodstuffs and raw materials – now met increasing demand in the European industrial countries (and soon the United States), and many Latin American nations experienced export booms, thereby financing the import of a full range of manufactured goods to 'modernize' transport and urban life. Argentina's growth in this period was spectacular. In other countries, national leaders saw export-led growth and inputs of foreign capital as the key to progress. This seemed a rational calculation.

As national wealth increased (especially in the larger countries), the traditional social structure underwent change. Cities expanded; more people became literate. Embryonic 'middle classes' emerged, as did small urban working classes (and labour movements) in countries where the export booms had created a sizeable market for locally produced consumer goods, which encouraged the beginnings of manufacturing industry. These economic and social changes – the 'social diversification' of the period – inevitably affected political life. The state itself became more organized. Some countries experienced greater political stability as older forms of caudillo rule began to recede. The newly emerging social groups challenged traditional elites for a place in the sun. This was especially noticeable between 1900 and 1930 in political changes in the Southern Cone of South America (Argentina, Chile, Uruguay), but also, in a very different manner, in Mexico, where ruthless 'modernization' during the lengthy regime of Porfirio Díaz opened the way to violent upheaval and a major social revolution after 1910.

While many Latin American nations retained close commercial and cultural links with Western Europe (Imperial Germany now included) during this phase, the rise of the United States as a great power after 1890 created new patterns of influence in the region. This was demonstrated decisively when the United States pre-empted the key role in Cuba's war of independence (1898), when the United States stage-managed Panama's separation from Colombia (1903), and in numerous military interventions in the Caribbean and Central America. (US military interventionism was halted by President Franklin D. Roosevelt in the 1930s.) The First World War – in which twelve out of the twenty republics remained neutral – marked a significant shift. Latin America's external trade was now redirected towards the United States. By the end of the 1920s, also, the United States had supplanted Great Britain as the leading source of foreign capital for the region.

1930 ONWARDS

The world depression, followed by the six years of the Second World War, saw the international economy seriously disrupted. With the contraction of trade, Latin America's opportunities for further export-led growth abruptly dwindled. Furthermore, every country except Argentina and Haiti had to default on its foreign debt. Latin America was therefore cut off from foreign finance. Governments were at first bewildered by the harsher economic climate of the 1930s, but gradually adopted new policies, such as increased government intervention in their economies. Domestic industrialization – 'import-substituting industrialization' (ISI) – was now pushed, although hindered by the inability to import

Mexican poster denouncing the American invasion of Panama (1989)

needed capital goods. The war brought an export bonanza which helped finance industrial growth, so that by 1960 Brazil, Argentina and Mexico had become the most industrialized countries in the developing world. Several middle-sized countries (e.g. Chile, Colombia) were also advancing fast along the same track. (Smaller nations, such as those of Central America, remained dependent on their agricultural or other primary product output.) A particular feature of this process was the role of the state, which created new state enterprises and marketing boards, as well as new financial structures.

The social diversification of the earlier period was accelerated in the era of import-substituting industrialization. The middle classes continued to grow. Organized labour, too, became more important in politics – sometimes on its own, sometimes as one element in a multi-class 'populist' coalition of the type set up by Getúlio Vargas in Brazil or Juan Perón in Argentina. A genuinely pluralistic political party system, on the Western European model, was most evident in Chile. Argentina came to be dominated by the Peronists, who never lost a free presidential election from 1946 to 1983. Brazil's pragmatic party politicians ruled by coalition until the military seized the initiative in 1964, holding it over the next two decades. In Mexico, one-party (PRI) hegemony survived every challenge. Latin America from the 1930s to the 1960s, as in the past, displayed a diversity of regimes: electoral democracies (with women given the franchise everywhere by 1961), dictatorships, and Mexico's unique political system, consolidated in the 1930s by President Lázaro Cárdenas.

The Latin American panorama after 1930 was overshadowed by the unchallenged supremacy of the United States, which by 1945 accounted for half the world's manufacturing output. Every Latin American country had joined the Allied cause before the end of the Second World War, even Argentina, whose military were openly pro-Axis. Already by 1946–7 the United States was pushing Latin America to enlist in the Cold War against the USSR. The intervention of the CIA to help remove a left-wing regime in Guatemala in 1954 was a striking example. The US omnipresence in the western hemisphere prompted new stirrings of nationalism in Latin America, where the desire for autonomous development was increasingly voiced.

US economic hegemony, in fact, was diluted after 1960 or so by the re-emergence of Western Europe as an important trading bloc and investor, by the rise of Japan, and also by more nationalist policies on the part of some of the Latin American governments – as shown in the nationalization of foreign mining and oil companies in Peru, Chile and Brazil. The Cuban revolution of 1959 – expressing the aspiration to autonomy – profoundly influenced Latin America. But if Cuba's example (in the early phase of the revolution) inspired hope in some, it also frightened others into revamping and strengthening their military. That, in turn, led at least indirectly to the new military regimes of the 1960s, as in Brazil and Peru.

In the 1960s – which opened the 'contemporary' era in Latin America — the earlier hopes of progress through industrialization became more muted. Industry failed to produce the many jobs needed by the country-people who migrated to the cities in ever-increasing numbers. Large-scale poverty persisted in nearly all countries (Argentina being the great exception), usually combined with chronic unemployment or under-employment. In addition, the population was rising at an alarming rate, notably in tropical Latin America and Mexico. In consequence there was an increase in social and political tensions (sometimes reflecting class conflicts) with which political systems often could not cope.

While some countries (e.g. Mexico, Colombia, Venezuela, Costa Rica) avoided institutional breakdown or upheaval, others (including well-established democracies like Chile and Uruguay) did not. The new 'institutional military' regimes (sometimes called 'bureaucratic–authoritarian' regimes) of the 1960s and 1970s – Brazil initiated the trend in 1964 – attempted to control or contain social pressures (by repression) in the interests of renewed economic expansion based on an economic policy geared to a market-orientated strategy which would rely on exports. These 'neo-liberal' experiments reached their most extreme form in Argentina (1976–83) and Chile (after 1973). When recession struck, in the early 1980s, this strategy, too, seemed to be discredited, although in the second half of the decade Chile attained rapid growth and by the early 1990s 'neo-liberal' policies were being attempted all round Latin

America. The Peruvian military regime of 1968–80 tried an alternative course, involving social reform. Meanwhile, civil war in Nicaragua resulted in 1979 in the triumph of a new revolutionary regime (voted out of power in 1989), while El Salvador (small and very overcrowded) staggered into a bloody civil conflict, much exacerbated by outside meddling.

The tide of military rule receded in the early 1980s, with many countries experiencing a rebirth of electoral democracy. The new democratic governments, however, could find no easy formula for stimulating economic progress, and the 1980s, clouded also by a crushing burden of foreign debt, turned out to be a 'lost decade' (economically and socially) for the region as a whole, whose GDP per capita fell by nearly 10 per cent. Whatever the outcome of Latin America's unfolding dramas, recent times have certainly presented Latin Americans with large (and mostly unresolved) dilemmas in their quest for political viability, economic progress, and greater social justice.   TES/SC

Further Reading: B. Albert, *South America and the World Economy from Independence to 1930* (London, 1983); L. Bethell, ed., *The Cambridge History of Latin America* (Cambridge, 1985 – in progress), vols. III–X.; T. E. Skidmore and P. H. Smith, *Modern Latin America* (New York, 1992), 3rd edition; R. Thorp, ed., *Latin America in the 1930s: The Role of the Periphery in World Crisis* (London, 1984); C. Véliz, *The Centralist Tradition of Latin America* (Princeton, 1980)

Mexico

Area	1,967,183 sq km
Population	88.6 million
GNP per capita (1989)	$2010
Capital	Mexico City
Currency	Peso

In 1821 the last viceroy of New Spain signed the Treaty of Córdoba which, in defiance of the Madrid government, recognized the independent state of Mexico. It had been a difficult birth. The country had been ravaged by ten years of intermittent civil war: agricultural production had fallen by a half, mining – the export staple of New Spain – by two-thirds. Once flourishing cities like Guanajuato now lay devastated and depopulated. Yet this sacrifice had purchased an imperfect independence. Spanish colonial rule had been overthrown; a feeble attempt at reconquest in

railway
road

0   320km
0   200miles

1829 was easily parried and the old metropolis formally recognized the Mexican Republic in 1836, some ten years after the United States and the major European powers. Thus, a ponderous but stable bureaucracy gave way to a shifting, semi-praetorian regime, in which national administrations came and went at rapid intervals (fifty in as many years after 1821), usually at the behest of the army, and according to scant political principle. But, in the absence of any profound social revolution, the basic contours of colonial society remained intact: independent Mexico, like colonial New Spain, was predominantly rural, illiterate and – compared with the nascent industrial societies of Europe and the United States – economically backward; its citizens were rigidly divided by barriers of class, geography and ethnicity, many of which stayed firm until the twentieth century.

After a brief imperial episode – the regime of Agustín Iturbide, 'Emperor Agustín I' (1822–3) – Mexico assumed a form of representative government, under the federalist Constitution of 1824. But, like most subsequent constitutions, it was chiefly honoured in the breach. Elections were meaningless, and the great majority of the population remained marginal to national politics; the presidential chair lay in the gift of the army which, alone in a fragmented polity, was capable of concerted political action. As for formal political labels, these were only somewhat less fanciful than the Constitution itself.

In theory – and to a limited extent in practice – Liberals confronted Conservatives. The Liberals believed in representative government, federalism, and a moderate curtailment of the power and wealth of the Church. Strongly wedded to the vague notion of progress, and to the more concrete reality of property, they looked to the democracies of Europe and the United States for their inspiration; they espoused free trade and repudiated – on paper, if not always in practice – the paternalism, protection and concern for caste and status which had permeated colonial society. They garnered their support among the small urban middle class, in the traditionally Liberal port of Veracruz, and in the outlying provinces, north and south, where federalism fed on resentment against Mexico City.

The Conservatives favoured centralist (sometimes authoritarian) rule and were more sympathetic to the privileges of Church and army (where, among the creole officers, they enjoyed ample support, just as the Liberals could usually count on a phalanx of provincial caudillos). If, like the sophisticated Conservative intellectual, *político* and historian Lucas Alamán, they entertained economic ideas, the Conservatives leaned towards protection, *dirigisme*, and industrialization, which harmonized with their 'colonial' mentality; and they won support in the populous and devout heartland of Mexico, the Mesa Central. But this ideological polarity was vague and shifting: it offered inspiration to some – like Alamán,

Bust of Benito Juárez (1806–72), the Zapotec Indian who became the supreme figure of nineteenth-century Mexican liberalism and patriotism

or his Liberal counterpart, José Luis Mora – mere alibis to others. Individuals shuttled between the rival camps, impelled by considerations of place and patronage, rather than principle: hence Antonio López de Santa Anna, the hardy perennial of this period, could serve in both Liberal and Conservative administrations; and military opportunists like Mariano Arista could achieve meteoric promotion. Political parties were unknown, the closest approximations being the rival Masonic lodges, whose York and Scottish rites were aligned with Liberal and Conservative factions respectively.

By the 1830s the hopes born of independence were dissipated. Self-government had produced neither stability nor prosperity. Initial British loans had done little more than inflate the national debt, and chronic insolvency now partnered and aggravated chronic political instability. Some Liberals concluded that they must go beyond the mere provision of constitutional norms and demolish those still strong pillars of the colonial regime which blocked the path of progress – in particular the Church (as a political and economic actor) and the army. Yet when, in 1833–4, reformist policies were attempted, the Conservatives rose in rebellion, imposed a new, centralist Constitution (1836), and established an outright Santanista dictatorship (1841–4). For the time being, the reformist thrust had been parried.

Mexico's foreign relations in these early years were overshadowed by the emerging power of the United States. Brief, *opéra bouffe* wars were fought with Spain (1829) and France (1838: the 'Pastry War'), but the chief threat to Mexico's flimsy territorial integrity came from the north where, with the initial encouragement of the Mexican government, North American immigrants braved the Comanche and flocked into the open expanses of Texas. Remote from Mexico City and resistant to Mexican political control, the Texan colonists went their own way until, in the early 1830s, the government belatedly sought to impose its authority, thereby provoking open rebellion. Defeated by superior Mexican forces at the legendary Alamo, the Texans won their independence after defeating Santa Anna's army at San Jacinto (1836). Nine years later, when the US Congress agreed to Texas's admission to the Union, Mexico contested the decision by force of arms. To many in the United States – including the eagerly expansionist President Polk – this was a fine opportunity to assert the Manifest Destiny of the United States of America, and to stake American claims not only to Texas but also to California and the vast tract of intervening territory. Polk launched a two-pronged invasion of Mexico: by land across the Rio Grande to Monterrey and Saltillo, by sea to Veracruz and thence to Mexico City. Its forces outgunned, if

not outnumbered, its treasury empty, and its citizens distracted by governmental disputes and a major Indian rebellion taking place in Yucatán, Mexico had no option other than to sue for peace. By the Treaty of Guadalupe Hidalgo (1848), Texas, California and the entire present-day American south-west – over half the area of Mexico – were ceded to the United States in return for a cash settlement of $15 million.

THE 'REFORMA'

The trauma of military defeat and territorial mutilation did not unify the country; on the contrary, it radicalized domestic politics and deepened existing divisions. A new generation of Liberals now came to prominence: men like the idealistic intellectual Melchor Ocampo, and the stern, honest Benito Juárez; they sought more radical solutions than those of their Liberal predecessors of the 1820s and 1830s and, in particular, they set out to punish what they saw as an unpatriotic and reactionary Church by the wholesale confiscation of ecclesiastical property. The Conservatives, in turn, resisted and began to flirt with the idea of a Mexican monarchy, which alone could act as a dyke against internal dissolution and external pressure.

In 1854 the old Liberal caudillo of Guerrero, Juan Alvarez, initiated a rebellion which toppled Santa Anna's last administration. This, the Revolution of

Mexico's liberal hero

No nineteenth-century president of Mexico was more remarkable, and none has been more honoured in retrospect, than Benito Juárez (1806–72).

A Zapotec Indian, he was born in a small village in Oaxaca state. Orphaned when a child, he made his way to the state capital, where he was taken up by a kind benefactor who enabled him to enter the local seminary. From there Juárez transferred to the newly established (1827) secular Institute of Sciences and Arts to study law. Soon active in Liberal politics, he served on the city council and in the state legislature, finally winning election in 1848 as the state governor. His four-year term was noted for its honesty and reforming policies.

During the final government of General Antonio López de Santa Anna (1853–5), Juárez was exiled with other Liberals to New Orleans. Then, following the triumph of the Liberal revolution of 1855, he was named minister of justice, in which post he was responsible for legislation (the Juárez Law) depriving both the Church and army of their legal immunities. In 1857 he was elected chief justice of Mexico's supreme court, and as such succeeded to the presidency in 1858, with the outbreak of a bitter civil war between the Liberals and their Conservative adversaries. Driven from Mexico City, he and the other Liberals made their headquarters at Vera Cruz, from where in June 1859 he enacted harsh laws to expropriate the extensive property of the Church. Back in Mexico City (January 1861) after the Liberal victory in the civil war, he won election to the presidency.

A large-scale intervention by France (1862–3) succeeded in installing Maximilian of Habsburg as emperor and in forcing the president to retreat to the far north, where he directed Mexican resistance from El Paso del Norte (now Ciudad Juárez). When the withdrawal of French troops spelled an end to this imperial episode, Juárez's grim insistence on national dignity would not allow clemency for Maximilian, who was shot at Querétaro (June 1867) despite protests from Europe's crowned heads.

Juárez won two further presidential elections (1867 and 1871), but was increasingly opposed by dissident Liberals, including Porfirio Díaz, an unsuccessful candidate in 1871. Juárez himself died of a heart attack on 18 July 1872, having held the presidency for fourteen years. For many Mexicans he remains the model of patriotic integrity. He was made the subject of a Hollywood movie (*Juárez*, Warner Brothers, 1939), which was well received in Mexico, with Paul Muni in the title role.

Ayutla, proved to be more than just another political reshuffle of the kind so common in the previous generation. In the wake of the Liberal triumph – though not without the usual internal squabbles – the government embarked on major reforms: the Ley Juárez (Juárez Law) of 1855 which stripped the Church and the military of their judicial privileges and established equality before the law, and the Ley Lerdo (Lerdo Law) of 1856, named after the Finance Minister, Miguel Lerdo de Tejada, which abolished corporate property-owning, thereby converting both Church and village communal lands into freehold, and throwing them on to the real estate market. These measures were further incorporated into the new Constitution of 1857, which went considerably beyond that of 1824 and which, with its commitment to freedom of education, worship, and the movement of men and property, represented an attempt to curtail military and ecclesiastical power and to push Mexico along the path of liberal, capitalist development.

On the other side, the Conservative response was no less vigorous or doctrinaire. The Church excommunicated those who took the oath to the Constitution, and there was an immediate spate of rebellions in the name of 'Religion and rights'. For three years (the War of the Reform, 1857–60) the country was racked by a civil war more sustained and serious than any since the upheaval of independence. Juárez, now elevated to the presidency, led the Liberals as their forces were defeated and driven from the Conservative heartland of central Mexico; thereby he became a

MEXICO'S LOSSES OF TERRITORY, 1836–53

1 Texas: seceded from Mexico 1836 annexed by USA 1845.
2 Territory ceded to USA under Treaty of Guadalupe Hidalgo 1848.
3 Mesilla Valley, sold by Mexico to USA 1853 for $10,000,000 (known in USA as the Gadsden Purchase).

symbol of popular, Liberal resistance, which manifested itself in constant guerrilla harassment of the Conservatives' regular armies. Gradually, the Conservatives were worn down; the Liberal stronghold of Veracruz held out, aided by American naval support and the steamy, malarial climate; by 1860 the assorted Liberal commanders were strong enough to defeat their enemies in pitched battles and install Juárez in the National Palace.

It was something of a Pyrrhic victory. Radicalized by the conflict, the Liberals had decreed the confiscation and sale of all Church property, save the church buildings themselves: while this measure further alienated the devout, it benefited the large *hacendado* rather than the aspiring yeoman farmer, as the Liberals had hoped. Furthermore, the treasury was empty, and the prosecution of the war had involved the seizure of foreign assets, for which reparations were now demanded. With Juárez barely ensconced in the presidency – and the United States coincidentally immersed in the Civil War – Britain, Spain and France mounted an expedition to seize Veracruz and thereby to compel payment. What for Britain and Spain was an exercise in international debt-collection, not unusual for the times, was for France and Napoleon III a *démarche* in global geopolitics. For the Mexican Conservatives' hankering after monarchy now meshed with Napoleon's quixotic desire to boost French influence – and offset that of the United States – in the New World; and the unfortunate Maximilian of Habsburg, the younger brother of the emperor of Austria, was chosen as the standard-bearer and victim of their grand designs.

Reluctant to connive at such plans, the British and Spanish withdrew, leaving the French to march – not without reverses – on Mexico City (1862). Juárez resumed his travels in the north; the Liberals fell back before the Franco-Mexican forces; and Maximilian, installed as emperor (1864), made a valiant attempt to woo his sullen subjects, affecting Mexican manners and – to the chagrin of his Conservative backers – enacting a series of liberal laws covering labour, education, the press and Church–state relations, none of which had much impact. Increasingly dependent on foreign advisers, and on the 30,000 bayonets of Marshal Bazaine, Maximilian's regime was fundamentally precarious, despite its initial successes. By 1865 Napoleon wearied of his Mexican adventure and, with the conclusion of the American Civil War, US influence was brought to bear in favour of the Juaristas. The Liberal forces waxed; Bazaine retreated and was finally ordered to withdraw altogether; in May 1867 the remaining imperialist forces, gathered for a last stand at Querétaro, were obliged to surrender, and the emperor was executed.

But, once again, the patriot hero Juárez faced a sour post-war fate. Liberal hopes of progress and prosperity were disappointed or, at best, deferred: the country's economy was gravely weakened, government finances were in a parlous state (the foreign debt defaulted, the internal debt standing at 300 million pesos), and, now that the forces of Conservatism had been decisively defeated (the one definitive result of thirteen years of fighting), the victorious Liberals fell out among themselves, with radicals wrangling with moderates, demobilized Liberal forces rising in rebellion, and rival presidential aspirants, like Sebastián Lerdo de Tejada and Porfirio Díaz, manoeuvring for ascendancy. In 1872, a year after his fourth re-election to the presidency, Juárez died. Lerdo, the epitome of the smooth creole intellectual, succeeded and, four years later, he attempted his own re-election; this provoked Díaz, a tough, *parvenu* mestizo caudillo from Oaxaca, to rebel, denouncing the re-election and demanding 'effective suffrage'. Díaz's swift triumph was one of caudillo over intellectual, the sword over the pen.

PORFIRIO DÍAZ

But if Díaz's seizure of power bore all the hallmarks of the traditional *coup de main,* it in fact inaugurated a new phase in Mexico's political and economic development. Save for a four-year period (1880–84) when his loyal compadre Manuel González occupied the presidency, Díaz went on to govern Mexico for the following thirty-five years. Potential presidential rivals, initially prolific, were eliminated or won over; local caudillos learned the wisdom of collaborating with the new national caudillo; and Díaz's regular, easily rigged re-elections demonstrated the artificiality of Porfirian 'democracy', even though the façade of the 1857 Constitution remained. Díaz, who never relinquished personal power throughout this period, proved to be a deft, pragmatic *político*. He employed the educated elite – the old liberal cadres, the *licenciados* and intellectuals – and, in particular, he drew upon the expertise of a new generation of technocrats, the so-called *científicos* (literally 'scientists'), who preached a positivist philosophy of economic development and strong government, while they themselves acquired large private fortunes in law and business. Meanwhile – as the *científicos* rationalized – individual rights and the finer points of democracy would have to be compromised for the sake of economic development; and the old Church–state conflict was gradually muted in the interests of social and political stability. Thus, a new, positivistic Liberalism, stressing 'Order and Progress' (or, according to the Porfirian slogan, 'plenty of administration and no politics'), supplanted the old, idealistic Liberalism of Mora and Juárez. Over time, Díaz slimmed and tamed the army (by 1910 it stood at a mere 15,000, compared with over 90,000 in 1867) and he tightened his grip on the provinces, relying on the new railways and telegraph to garner information, transmit orders and, where necessary, suppress opposition. State governorships were in the gift of the president while, lower down, free municipal government wilted in the long shadow of the *jefe político*, the political boss, appointed by the executive, whose job it was to fix elections, silence dissent, and generally keep order to the president's satisfaction.

Above all, the Pax Porfiriana depended upon – and in turn encouraged – Mexico's accelerating economic development. If the old Liberals' political ideals went by the board, their economic hopes now seemed to approach fruition. The legislation of the 1850s, designed to dissolve corporate property and to release individual initiative, now began to have a dramatic, belated effect; and it was supplemented by fresh legislation framed to attract foreign investment and immigration, to colonize virgin territory, and to develop mining, railways and commercial agriculture. The immigrants never came; but the investment flowed in, with the United States providing the lion's share – 1.2 billion pesos of the total 2.9 billion pesos of direct foreign investment accumulated by 1911. Meanwhile (and as the necessary corollary of this investment), Mexico responded to mounting European and American demand for raw materials: the old staples of gold and silver, now supplemented by copper, lead and zinc, and cash crops including coffee, sugar, henequén, rubber and tropical fruits. At the same time, the secular depreciation of the silver-based Mexican peso stimulated exports further. Hence the long economic doldrums of 1820–70 (which had seen only a modest recovery in mining and agriculture, and no major, qualitative change in economic production) now gave way to the brisk breezes of the Porfiriato, and to a new climate which invigorated some, but chilled many.

The government was a major beneficiary. Tax receipts, chiefly derived from customs, rose, enabling the treasury to achieve a genuine budget surplus by 1895. Mexico's international credit was restored. The new wealth also gave the government greater opportunities for patronage, as well as a greater capacity for repression: Díaz wielded a bigger stick as well as a bigger carrot than any of his predecessors. Thus, in compelling order and obedience from the most distant provinces and stiff-necked provincials, Díaz outdid even the prestigious Bourbon viceroys.

As economic life quickened, towns expanded and a relatively prosperous middle class developed, for the time being content to follow the positivist injunction to work and invest, without too much regard for constitutional niceties. Industrial production also rose, and a genuine factory proletariat appeared, chiefly in the textile centres of Puebla, Veracruz and the Federal District. Despite bad conditions, the infant working class was far from militant: it sought practical solutions to concrete problems notably through mutualist (self-help) societies, and early trade unions whose objectives were essentially 'economist', i.e. for bread-and-butter gains. Though anarcho-syndicalism exercised a limited appeal, those workers who participated in politics – such politics as there were – were as likely to listen to enlightened Porfiristas, like the *científico* mayor of Mexico City, Landa y Escandón, or to spokesmen of a revived liberalism. Meanwhile, rising industrial production hit the large artisan sector, which found its oldest and surest defence – Mexico's poor internal communications – crumbling before the onslaught of the railways, which knitted local into national and international markets.

The pressures of change were even greater in the countryside. Landlords (talk of 'feudalism' notwithstanding) had always shown an eye for profits: astute operators like the Sánchez Navarro of Coahuila had amassed considerable fortunes during the nineteenth century. But the limitations of the market – the result of poor communications, lack of capital, and weak demand – imposed severe constraints on production. Now the railways opened up new markets, foreign and domestic capital was more plentiful, and rising demand, home and abroad, created new incentives. The sugar planters of Morelos, the cotton growers of the Laguna, the henequén producers of Yucatán, entered upon a phase of expansion which incurred all the risks and benefits of large-scale production for the market. To secure land and water they dispossessed villages and smallholders (usually quite legally), converting subsistence farmers into sharecroppers, peons or rural proletarians; and, where the local labour supply was inadequate, they relied on *enganchados* ('hooked' debt-peons) and other forms of semi-servile labour. Some haciendas – especially the producers of Mexico's staple, maize – preserved more 'traditional' ways, exercising a paternalist control over their resident workers, and eliciting deference and loyalty in return; but as these tended to decline, the price of food rose, outstripping wages. The prevailing trends – market production, rising land values, and entrepreneurial initiative – penetrated lower in the rural hierarchy too, where go-ahead *rancheros* expanded and prospered, often at the expense of communal village lands, and of the corporate solidarity these had underwritten. Mexico was becoming a more fluid and, in many regions, a more socially polarized society.

Change of this kind could not but generate social protest, particularly as real wages declined. Local protests – against agrarian dispossession, or the rule of unpopular *jefes políticos* – were endemic throughout the Porfiriato; but the regime had sufficient resources to isolate and suffocate such movements. Some rebellions – like those of the Yaqui Indians of Sonora, or the Maya of Yucatán – smouldered for decades, but alone they could not threaten Díaz's position, or the march of Porfirian progress. By the 1900s, however, a new brand of respectable, urban, middle-class protest became evident, in Mexico as elsewhere in Latin America. Such protest had political rather than economic roots. The urban middle class – a burgeoning, literate and prospering class – resented the apparent immutability of Díaz's personal dictatorship, and of the rule of his local minions; they feared for the future when Díaz died; and they compared Mexico's sad political condition with that of 'advanced' countries in Europe or North America, and with the good old days of Juarista Liberalism (days that acquired a roseate hue as they receded in time). Die-hard Liberals pointed critically to the revival of clerical influence and, lamenting Mexico's lack of civic spirit, they reversed the Porfirian motto and called for 'plenty of politics and good administration'.

In the course of the 1900s, this protest gelled into an organized national opposition, the first of the Porfiriato. The Mexican Liberal Party, founded in 1901, initiated the process; but internal splits and government repression soon drove its leaders into exile and pushed the party towards a militant anarcho-syndicalism which had only limited appeal. Subsequently, as Díaz's seventh re-election loomed up (1910), as the Mexican economy was hit by the American recession (1907–10), and as the dictator was quoted as welcoming a democratization of political life (1908), so new parties assembled under the leadership of General Bernardo Reyes, strong man of Nuevo León, and Francisco Madero, scion of a wealthy northern family, who espoused an idealistic brand of socially conscious liberalism. Reyes flattered only to deceive, but Madero and his anti-re-electionists marshalled support in the major cities, even among sections of the working class, and posed a serious challenge to the regime which the regime finally met in the way it knew best: Madero was arrested and Díaz's re-election was rigged.

While most of his respectable followers were now prepared to throw in the towel, Madero escaped to the United States and issued a call to arms (November 1910). Where so many previous local revolts had failed, Madero's revolution succeeded and did so by mobilizing disaffected groups in the countryside, where agrarian tensions and resentment against government abuses were strongest. Emiliano Zapata captained the campesinos of Morelos, where the regime of the sugar planters weighed heavily; Pancho Villa, bandit turned revolutionary bushwhacker, was among the many leaders who sprang up in the rebellious north. Neither Díaz's modest army, nor his vaunted rural police, could meet the challenge, and control of the countryside slipped from their grasp. In May 1911 the president was forced to resign and, after an unusually free election, Madero was voted into the National Palace. It was the start of a great revolutionary upheaval.

THE REVOLUTION (1911–40)

Madero and his liberal experiment lasted only fifteen months. Conservative groups attacked Madero's supposed weakness and his halting steps towards political and fiscal reform; the press took advantage of unprecedented freedom to snipe without mercy or scruple; and the Federal Army which Madero both retained and favoured proved ungrateful and restless. The president's erstwhile revolutionary supporters, looking for quick results by way of agrarian reform, municipal freedom, and changes in the personnel of government, were swiftly disillusioned. Revolutionary leaders like Zapata in Morelos and Pascual Orozco in Chihuahua rebelled anew, now bitterly opposed to the regime they had helped establish. Caught in this political crossfire, Madero found his position increasingly precarious, his popularity ebbing away. His own middle-class constituency, meanwhile, drifted to the right, losing faith in the liberal experiment, fearing social upheaval, and yearning for a strong man who could dominate the situation.

Many thought they had found such a man in General Victoriano Huerta, a career soldier whose minor laurels were augmented and refurbished by a successful campaign against Orozco in 1912. When the predictable military coup occurred in Mexico City in February 1913, subjecting the capital to the 'Ten Tragic Days' of bombardment, Huerta switched to the rebel side, had Madero arrested and shot, and proclaimed himself president. The liberal experiment gave way to the militarist solution. Madero's supporters were purged; civilian politics were phased out; the Federal Army, expanded some fourfold, became the supreme arbiter of the nation's life. But the militarist solution – a crude attempt to recreate the stability of the Porfiriato by means which canny old Porfirio would not have countenanced – was bound to fail. In death, Madero became a martyr, his failings and equivocations forgotten or pardoned. President Woodrow Wilson refused to recognize the

*Emiliano Zapata
(1879–1919), noted agrarian
leader of the Mexican
Revolution*

among themselves. The Constitutionalist Revolution therefore bifurcated, with Carranza and Villa leading hostile factions, each deriving more from expedience and patronage than any clear class divisions. Though the Villistas – allied to Zapata's forces – were more numerous, Carranza enjoyed the services of the revolution's best general, the shrewd Sonoran, Alvaro Obregón. Once a rancher, now a scientific strategist and a smart *político* who won support among the labour unions, Obregón decisively defeated Villa in a series of bloody battles (1915). The last major bout of civil war was over; Carranza's faction ruled, at least in the capital and major cities.

But they ruled a sad country, ravaged by disease, malnutrition, rampant military graft, and continuing rural revolt and banditry. Zapata fought on until his treacherous assassination in 1919; Villa survived to be amnestied in 1920. Meanwhile, the victorious faction sought to bring order out of chaos. A new Constitution was promulgated (1917), in which the liberal political framework of 1857 was supplemented by 'social' provisions: state education, strict curtailment of clerical education and political involvement, protection of the rights of labour, and a declaration of the nation's ownership of land and subsoil deposits, which would afford the constitutional basis for both agrarian reform and the confiscation or regulation of foreign assets. Like previous constitutions, however, this was basically an ideological document – a statement of intent rather than a manual for the practical government of the country.

Aided by providential oil revenue (oil production, beginning in the 1900s, peaked in 1921, when Mexico provided a quarter of the world's supply) Carranza almost lasted out his presidential term. In 1920, however, an inept attempt to foist his chosen civilian successor on the country led to his overthrow and assassination. Obregón, for some time the heir-apparent, became president (1920–4). His successor was a fellow Sonoran, Plutarco Elías Calles, who ruled first as president (1924–8), then as *jefe máximo* ('big boss'), twitching the strings of successive presidents until 1934. Hence, during the fifteen years of post-revolutionary reconstruction and consolidation, the 'Sonoran Dynasty' governed, bringing to bear ideas and policies which clearly betrayed their origin in that prosperous, progressive, Americanized part of the country.

The Sonorans slimmed the army and cut the military budget from almost two-thirds to about a quarter of government expenditure. In the process, they faced serious, recurrent revolts (1923, 1927, 1929), all successfully put down. By way of a counterweight to the troublesome military, the Sonorans angled for support among the urban workers and, to a lesser extent, the peasantry. The Regional Confederation of

regime of Madero's assassin. Popular rebels like Zapata fought on, well aware that Huerta's regime, for all its occasional, verbal reformism, offered them nothing, and their numbers rapidly grew. In the north, Venustiano Carranza, a liberal landlord and Maderista state governor, assumed the leadership of a conglomerate revolutionary movement, which, in the name of 'Constitutionalism', united rebels of different regions and classes in a common front against Huerta. Thanks in particular to the prowess of Pancho Villa and his Division of the North, and to the more prosaic achievements of the Sonoran state forces, the Constitutionalists reduced the cities of the north and began to march on Mexico City. By summer of 1914, with the country's economy and currency now seriously affected by the revolutionary troubles, and his regime politically and financially bankrupt, Huerta was forced into exile.

The victorious Constitutionalists, eschewing Madero's naive tolerance, at once purged supporters of the old regime, silenced press criticism, and sequestered property (including Church property: it was alleged, with some justification, that the Church had favoured Huerta). But they could not agree

Mexican Workers (CROM), established in 1918, became the first national labour confederation: its leader, Morones, held ministerial rank, collaborated closely with government, and amassed great personal wealth; some benefits filtered down to the rank-and-file. The Sonorans approached the question of agrarian reform in a calculating and pragmatic fashion. Obregón distributed a million hectares to landless claimants, Calles over three million; in a few regions, like Morelos, the power of the old landlords was broken. More commonly, however, landlords survived, trimming their sails to the new wind, seeking the shelter of accommodating generals and *políticos*, who were not hard to find. Those agrarian veterans who continued to campaign on behalf of the villages denounced the slow pace of reform, and the impedimenta of corruption and conservatism which stalled its advance.

Not that the Sonorans could altogether be blamed for this. Their commitment to agrarian reform was lukewarm: they saw Mexican agriculture through Sonoran eyes, favouring the dynamic capitalistic entrepreneur over the subsistence peasant. By 1929, Calles declared, the reform had run its course, and it was pronounced a failure. Calles's chosen priorities were different: his objective – his vision – was a strong state, a thriving capitalist economy, and a literate, hard-working, patriotic and obedient people. To this end, the Sonorans expanded rural education, built roads, created a central bank and incurred a bitter civil war (1926–9) in an attempt to curtail the spiritual and educational role of the Catholic Church. Where the nineteenth-century liberals – most of them Catholics – had sought to eliminate the

Church's economic and political power, some twentieth-century dogmatists, Calles included, looked to the virtual extirpation of Catholicism. When the Church resisted implementation of the anti-clerical provisions of the 1917 Constitution, war broke out, most virulently in west-central Mexico, where Cristero rebels (so called because of their war-cry 'Viva Cristo Rey!' – 'Long live Christ the King!') fought the Federal Army tenaciously until a compromise settlement – approved by the Vatican and the bishops, to the disgust of many of the rebels – ended the conflict. Compromise also proved necessary in Calles's squabble with the foreign oil companies, who resisted the constitutional conversion of their freehold rights to leasehold. As this example showed, the economic nationalism of the Sonorans implied greater regulation and taxation of foreign interest, but it in no sense required expropriation or outright rejection; on the contrary, foreign investment increased during the 1920s, and had an important role to play in the Sonoran model of development.

THE END OF THE SONORANS

1928–9 were years of political and economic crisis. In 1928 Obregón was assassinated by a Catholic fanatic, just as he prepared to assume the presidency for the second time. Debarred from immediate re-election, Calles instead convened a revolutionary convention at which a loosely unified 'official' party was, for the first time, created: the National Revolutionary Party (PNR). Its lineal descendants have governed Mexico to the present day. But if the successful

Zapata's entry into Mexico City, 1914

Lázaro Cárdenas (1895–1970), Mexico's great reforming president of the 1930s

either individually or collectively. Over 17 million hectares of land were distributed and, by 1940, ejidal production accounted for nearly half the country's agricultural output. Peasant land-hunger was assuaged, if not eradicated, and the peasantry was firmly incorporated into the governmental system, with revolutionary *políticos* and bureaucrats replacing the old caciques and landlords. At the same time, the era of the sprawling, 'feudal' hacienda was finally ended, although landlords who invested, irrigated and produced efficiently were not only guaranteed against expropriation, but also given state assistance in the shape of roads, grants, and technical advice.

If Cárdenas's agrarian policies were original within Latin America in the 1930s, his support for organized labour was more typical. In his battle against Calles, Cárdenas won the backing of Vincente Lombardo Toledano and labour elements hostile to the CROM. In 1936 Lombardo organized a new, dominant labour confederation, the CTM, which, a year later, became an integral component (along with the peasant CNC) of a newly constituted official party, the PRM. Labour also received more tangible benefits by way of arbitrated wage settlements, and, in the case of the railways, nationalization and a brief experiment in workers' control. More spectacularly, when the foreign oil companies rejected an arbitrated wage settlement, Cárdenas ordered their expropriation (1938): an act which, while it elicited fierce foreign protests, also met with widespread and emotional acclaim among Mexicans of all political persuasions, including Catholic and conservative enemies of the regime. But the oil expropriation was not altogether typical: in other sectors of the economy, such as electricity generating, Cárdenas welcomed increased foreign investment. In foreign policy, too, Cárdenas tempered principle with pragmatism: he proved to be one of the stoutest friends of the Spanish Republican cause, yet he beat the Allies' oil boycott by selling to the Axis powers. Far from being a doctrinaire socialist – as he was sometimes depicted – Cárdenas was essentially a radical nationalist who, by his agrarian reform, his alliance with labour, his consolidation of the party, and his pragmatic economic nationalism, sustained the broad strategy of the revolutionary victors in the changed circumstances of the depression. In doing so, he greatly strengthened the revolutionary state, and laid the groundwork for the post-1940 'economic miracle'.

POST-REVOLUTIONARY MEXICO

Cárdenas's successors, Manuel Avila Camacho (1940–46) and Miguel Alemán (1946–52), gave

institutionalization and demilitarization of the revolution appeared well under way (1929 also saw the last serious military revolt), the shockwaves of the depression now began to affect the Mexican economy. Export earnings and foreign investment slumped; the very model of development espoused by the Sonorans was called into question. Thus, even while Calles still ruled (and Calles had grown more conservative with age), new economic initiatives were attempted: a Five-Year Plan, provision for greater state intervention, a revival of agrarian reform. But these initiatives were greatly expanded under the presidency of Lázaro Cárdenas (1934–40). Cárdenas, though an ally and protégé of Calles, disappointed his mentor; he would not play the puppet, and he favoured more radical policies. In 1934–5 Mexican politics were dominated by a bitter struggle between Calles and Cárdenas, a struggle fought out in the cabinet, in the statehouses, in the labour and peasant unions, and in the streets. Finally, Cárdenas's presidential weight told: Calles and his diehard supporters were ousted, and the *jefe máximo* was sent into exile. Cárdenas now had a free hand, and he had aroused expectations which had to be met.

Unlike his presidential predecessors, Cárdenas was a firm believer in the agrarian reform, and he favoured the creation of *ejidos*, in which land was vested in the community, though it might be farmed

industrialization priority over agrarian reform and political stability over radical new departures. They conciliated the Church and business interests, while marginalizing the left. Close collaboration with the American war effort stimulated growth – at the expense of inflation and falling real wages – and laid the groundwork for the prolonged economic boom of the 1940–65 period, during which GDP grew five-fold, as population doubled. Manufacturing supplanted mining as the economy's pacemaker, and the agricultural sector proved capable of both feeding Mexico's swelling population and contributing significantly to exports. Through the 1950s and '60s, therefore, Mexico experienced a phase of 'stabilized development' which made it something of a model for developing countries within the capitalist world.

This 'stabilized development', which was matched by rising real income from the early 1950s, did facilitate political stability, as the 'economic miracle' underwrote the 'Peace of the PRI'. The official party – which had gained its new name when rechristened the Institutional Revolutionary Party in 1946 – monopolized the presidency, the state governorships, and most of Congress. Only at the municipal level, in specific regions (such as Yucatán, San Luis Potosí, Chihuahua, and Baja California), were opposition parties – chiefly the centre-right Partido Acción Nacional – able to contest the PRI's hegemony and, occasionally, win precarious tenures of office. Pressure groups and aspiring politicians saw the wisdom of working within rather than against the system; business collaborated with a regime whose radical nationalist rhetoric did not match its pragmatic policy; and labour, although capable of dramatic displays of independence (such as the railwaymen's strike of 1958–9, which was strenuously repressed), remained constrained by the official unions and the dominant CTM. Meanwhile, as commercial agriculture flourished, the *ejido* afforded the peasantry a measure of basic subsistence at the price of political subordination to the state, although migration to the USA, or to Mexico's burgeoning cities, became an important escape valve. When the Cuban Revolution sent shockwaves through Latin America, Mexico proved resistant. Rural guerrilla movements capitalized on popular discontent, especially in Guerrero, but the professionalized and depoliticized army readily contained any threat. Mexico had had its revolution (went the official line) and it did not need to import one.

By the late 1960s and early 1970s, however, the system began to falter. The process of import-substitution industrialization lost momentum; industry, constrained by the domestic market, could not compete internationally; and Mexico's population, growing at 3–4 per cent a year, required increasing food

---

Radical Nationalism (from the programme of the PRI (1946)

In 1946 the ruling party in Mexico adopted the name Partido Revolucionario Institucional *(Institutional Revolutionary Party), and issued a statement of aims and principles under the title 'Democracy and Social Justice'*

[The party] will struggle for purification, instilling morality and renewal for the benefit of the Party, the Government, and the groups and forces that act in national life. It recognizes the existence of the class struggle and upholds the right of workers to contend for political power. It will struggle for the application of agrarian and workers' laws and for the promotion of co-operativism . . . It will struggle for a good administration of justice, for a policy of frank support for the democracies and absolute respect for the rights of weak nations, for the constant and irrenounceable sustaining of national sovereignty as the basis of Mexico's international policy . . .

1) The PRI is a national political organization composed of workers and peasants, organized by independent workers, public employees, co-operativist artisans, students, professionals, lesser traders and other groups similar in interests and tendencies, who accept the principles of the Mexican Revolution; and women are considered exactly equal to men. . .
3) The PRI has as its objective: (a) the attainment of power by democratic means and within the law; (b) the uniting of revolutionary sectors for the conquest of their rights and for the best satisfaction of their needs and interests. . .

Source: E. de la Torre Villar, M. González Navarro, and S Ross. eds., *Historia documental de México*, 2 vols. (Mexico City, 1964).

---

imports. In 1968, the year Mexico was to host the Olympic Games, protesting students mounted a campaign for democratization and reform in the universities and in the country at large. The regime resorted to repression and some 300 demonstrators were killed at Tlatelolco, Mexico City. In the wake of this traumatic event, and conscious of the country's mounting socio-economic problems, subsequent administrations tried new departures. President Echeverría (1970–76) renewed the emphasis on redistribution and nationalism, while his successor, López Portillo (1976–82), tried a modicum of political reform, expanding the representation of opposition parties in Congress. Meanwhile, both government and private business borrowed heavily and Mexico's international debt, which had hitherto been rela-

Modern-day Mexico City

tively low, spiralled upwards. The peso was no longer pegged to the dollar, and began a long process of devaluation. Then providentially, it seemed, new oil reserves came on stream in the late 1970s, encouraging the López Portillo administration to embark on lavish development programmes and enabling some politicians to make sizeable personal fortunes.

In 1982 the party ended. Oil prices fell, the peso was devalued 600 per cent and Mexico declared a *de facto* moratorium on its foreign debt, which was among the largest in the developing world. Miguel De la Madrid (1982–8), occupying a weakened presidency, began a policy of retrenchment, privatization and trade liberalization which his successor, Carlos Salinas de Gortari (1988), continued, with considerable success. By the early 1990s, inflation had been checked, non-oil exports had risen dramatically, foreign debt payments had been scaled down, and government finances had been placed on a sound footing. Displaying a new-found confidence, the Mexican government pressed for the creation of a North American Free Trade Zone, embracing Mexico, the US and Canada – a remarkable departure from the economic nationalist orthodoxy which had traditionally characterized 'revolutionary' governments.

These striking new initiatives, however, carried a heavy social cost. Living standards plummeted during the 1980s. Real wages fell, unemployment rose, and social provisions and union benefits were eroded. Migration, the 'black economy', and Mexico's flourishing drug traffic somewhat countered these tendencies, but the outcome was a prolonged recession, probably deeper and longer than that of the 1930s. With this went a predictable political disenchantment. Local organizations – based on communities,

barrios and churches – protested against deteriorating economic conditions and continued political chicanery. The major parties were slow to capitalize on the new ebullience of civil society: the PRI was tainted by power; the PAN appealed chiefly to the prosperous middle class; the left, despite moves towards unity in the early 1980s, remained divided and, in many Mexicans' eyes, suspect. In 1987–8, however, a faction bolted the PRI, mobilized broad support, and mounted the presidential candidacy of Cuauhtémoc Cárdenas, son of the great reformist president Lázaro Cárdenas. Defeated in a contentious election by the PRI's candidate, Carlos Salinas de Gortari, Cárdenas established himself as the leading left-of-centre critic of the PRI, creating a rallying point for dissidents. Since the right-of-centre PAN remains powerful, especially in the north, where it won a state governorship in 1989, Mexico now enjoys an unusual degree of political pluralism, in terms of party strength, if not of the distribution of power. The key question of the 1990s is whether the government's liberal economic policies will lead inevitably to liberal politics, genuine elections, and the possible removal of the PRI from power. If this happens, it will mark a new era in Mexico's history.

AK

Further Reading: R. Hansen, *The Politics of Mexican Development* (Baltimore, 1971); A. Knight, *The Mexican Revolution, 2 vols* (Cambridge, 1986); M. C. Meyer and W. L. Sherman, *The Course of Mexican History, 2nd edition* (New York, 1983); J. Womack, Jr, *Zapata and the Mexican Revolution* (New York, 1970)

The Central American republics

COSTA RICA
Area	50,900 sq km
Population	3.0 million
GNP per capita (1989)	$1780
Capital	San José
Currency	Colón

EL SALVADOR
Area	20,935 sq km
Population	5.3 million
GNP per capita (1989)	$1070
Capital	San Salvador
Currency	Colón

GUATEMALA
Area	108,889 sq km
Population	9.2 million
GNP per capita (1989)	$910
Capital	Guatemala City
Currency	Quetzal

HONDURAS
Area	112,068 sq km
Population	5.1 million
GNP per capita (1989)	$900
Capital	Tegucigalpa
Currency	Lempira

NICARAGUA
Area	119,300 sq km
Population	3.9 million
GNP per capita (1988)	$550
Capital	Managua
Currency	Córdoba

PANAMA
Area	77,082 sq km
Population	2.4 million
GNP per capita (1989)	$1760
Capital	Panama City
Currency	Balboa

THE FAILURE OF UNION

Central America achieved independence as the result of a general reaction to the Liberal revolution of 1820 in Spain. No unified independence movement developed in the captaincy-general itself, and there was no fighting there. Instead, beginning with the declaration of independence in the regional capital, Guatemala City, on 15 September, 1821 the various cities of the region made their own decisions over a period of months. The short-lived empire of Agustín de Iturbide in Mexico (1822–3) sent an army to recapture the isthmus, but with its collapse the disunited provinces were left to work out their own destiny. One, Chiapas, opted to remain with Mexico (1823). The district of Soconuzco, claimed by Guatemala, was occupied by Mexico and in 1825 a plebiscite of its inhabitants ratified its transfer.

Five provinces remained, reaffirming their independence in a second declaration on 1 July 1823. They were Guatemala, El Salvador, Honduras, Nicaragua and Costa Rica, collectively known as the Provincias Unidas del Centro de América. The course of independence had left their leaders strongly polarized between Liberals and Conservatives (locally termed *Serviles*), and while a Constituent Assembly met between June 1823 and January 1825 to draw up the new Constitution of the Federation as a whole, the factions struggled for control of the new state governments that were simultaneously being created. The Constitution of 1824 for the Central American Federation, written under strong Liberal influence, established a federal government reminiscent of that of the United States, limited clerical influence, and among other libertarian provisions, abolished slavery. Under it, elections for president of the Federation in 1825 gave one vote short of an absolute majority to José Cecilio del Valle, author of the Declaration of Independence of 1821, and a distinguished scholar. The Congress, however, as the result of a political deal, chose instead his Liberal opponent, Manuel José Arce.

Arce's government (1825–9) was rapidly recognized by the United States, Mexico, Colombia and other Latin American states, and in 1826 was one of only four to attend Bolívar's abortive Congress of Panama. But it was nearly bankrupt, lacked federal military or police forces, and was constantly embroiled in disputes between the state governments. Guatemala, whose capital was seat of the Federation until 1834, with a population three times that of any other state, focused the hostility of the others. Between 1827 and 1829 the Honduran caudillo Francisco Morazán was able to build on this to wage a successful war against the Federation. Having installed the Guatemalan José Francisco Barrundia as president (1829–30), Morazán then directed a Liberal purge of the Conservatives and their clerical supporters, as the prelude to his own Liberal government (1831–9). It was Morazán who gave Central America the only brief period of unity it has ever known, but

Francisco Morazán, Liberal leader from Honduras who led the Central American Federation in the 1830s

its very success fostered the unity of its conservative opponents. After the Federation capital had been moved to San Salvador, a cholera epidemic in 1837 aroused mob violence in Guatemala which, skilfully channelled by the Indian Rafael Carrera, destroyed

the flimsy unity of the Federation. In April 1838 both Costa Rica and Nicaragua stated that the Federation had already ceased to exist. It ceased formally to do so when fresh elections were not held to renew Morazán's term in 1839, but the fallen leader tried several times to recover his position until he was executed in Costa Rica in 1842.

Between 1839 and 1898 the five separate states (a sixth, Los Altos, formed in 1838, was reabsorbed by Guatemala in 1840) pursued very similar courses. Each underwent longer or shorter periods of dictatorship punctuated by periods of weak, shifting governments, and even civil war. In turn, major political leaders, once in power, succumbed, as often as not, to the dream of recreating Morazán's republic by force, diplomacy or both. In the early 1840s, with the Conservatives in power generally, this seemed quite possible, but localism reasserted itself, and Guatemala under Rafael Carrera (president 1844–65) formally declared its independence in 1847. The following year Costa Rica followed suit, and with, in the main, Liberal governments in power in the three middle states, a brief period followed in which external influences assumed prime importance. Great Britain, entrenched in Belize and claiming a protectorate over the Mosquito Coast of Honduras, disputed control of the trans-isthmian route with the United States. Settled for a generation by the Clayton-Bulwer Treaty of 1850, the dispute led to local concerted action against the activities of the filibustering American, William Walker (a native of Nashville, Tennessee),

THE CENTRAL AMERICAN REPUBLICS

243

to install himself as president of Nicaragua and leader of a new Federation. By 1863 some eight formal meetings had been held to reconstruct the Federation, but all succumbed to opposition or indifference, and the United States in turn had withdrawn from Central American affairs for a generation.

Following revolts which brought Liberal governments to power in Guatemala and El Salvador in 1871, Justo Rufino Barrios, president of Guatemala (1873–85), carried through an astonishing modernization of his country on Liberal lines, and built up his army. On 28 February 1885 he proclaimed the reunification of Central America under his command, but his ally President Zaldívar of El Salvador refused to accept his lead, and Barrios was killed in battle at Chalchuapa on 2 April. Further attempts to confederate all five states in 1887, and to join the central three in an association in 1896, were destroyed by military coups in each case within a period of months. As the more restricted aims of these attempts showed, by this time the traditional independence of Costa Rica and the assertiveness of Guatemala had been recognized as major obstacles. The fact was that in the two generations since independence, the Central American countries had grown not together but apart. Guatemala's conservative and dictatorial regime had consistently been at odds with its Liberal neighbours, but the fact that still more effectively divided it from its neighbours was that before the time of Barrios it lacked so much as a single all-weather cart track. El Salvador's leaders aspired to leadership of the confederation, but this was ruled out by the small size of their state. Honduras lacked unity. In Nicaragua the internal conflict between the Liberals of León and the Conservatives of Granada, which led in 1852 to the choice of Managua as a compromise capital, lasted until the arrival of American adventurers in the 1850s, which forced the consolidation of an oligarchic republican regime. Costa Rica held aloof from the squabble of its northern neighbour, divided from it the more effectively by the perennial boundary dispute over the Guanacaste territory, and insulated from the long-running dispute over federation.

At the beginning of the national period Costa Rica was already an exporter of coffee, while the main export crops of El Salvador and Guatemala were indigo and cochineal respectively. Costa Rica's exports continued to expand, therefore, while the introduction of aniline dyes finally destroyed the already moribund trade of its neighbours in the 1870s.

Justo Rufino Barrios was responsible for the introduction of coffee growing in Guatemala, which had already begun in El Salvador under his namesake Gerardo Barrios (president 1859–63). By the end of the century coffee had become the major export of both countries, and in El Salvador the basis for a new coffee growers' oligarchy, which was able to regulate peacefully the succession to office among its members. The Vaccaro brothers of New Orleans founded (1899) the company that was to make bananas the major export crop of Honduras, and which ultimately grew into the Standard Fruit Company. Alone among the five countries, Nicaragua failed to develop a major export crop in the nineteenth century. It was therefore keenly interested in the alternative possibilities of wealth offered by the use of its territory for an inter-oceanic canal. When, after 1898, reasons of strategy and commerce alike made the United States interested in such a canal, Nicaragua, then under the rule of the Liberal José Santos Zelaya (president 1893–1909), offered one of the two best possible routes.

AMERICAN DOMINATION

United States sponsorship of the revolution for Panamanian independence from Colombia (1903) not only destroyed Nicaraguan hopes, but created a new, sixth state, which, although historically part of South rather than Central America, focused American influence in the area. While work on the canal went on from 1904 to 1914, the United States came rapidly to exercise a hegemony which European powers could no longer challenge. The United States, in fact, came to sponsor a new departure in the long-running debate over unification. In 1902 President Zelaya had acted as host at Corinto to a conference of heads of state on the resolution of differences between the republics. A tribunal was set up to arbitrate disputes (though not boundary disputes) and Guatemala failed to accede to the treaty. In 1906, when an attempt by exiles to overthrow the dictator of Guatemala, Manuel Estrada Cabrera (president 1898–1920), escalated into a full-scale war between Guatemala and El Salvador, President Theodore Roosevelt, urging an immediate settlement, sent the US warship *Marblehead* to the coast of El Salvador. The ceasefire signed on board between the two states was followed in September 1906 by a conference at San José, Costa Rica, which reaffirmed the Corinto Pact, and created a Central American Bureau. Zelaya, who had refused to attend the conference, took advantage of a boundary clash with Honduran forces to overthrow the president of that country early in 1907; and was on the point of war with El Salvador when the United States again intervened. Together with the president of Mexico, Roosevelt invited all five presidents to a peace conference in Washington, at which a ten-year peace programme for the region

A steam-shovel at work on the Panama Canal, c. 1910. Construction of the canal took ten years.

was agreed and subsequently ratified. At its core was the creation of a Central American Court of Justice (1908) with its seat in Costa Rica, the first permanent international court in the world. Annual meetings of ministers were held from 1909 to 1914.

Neither the 1907 treaty nor the Court of Justice had any practical effect, however, for after 1910 the United States under President Taft ceased to encourage unification. In that year, Taft's administration actively aided the overthrow of Zelaya and his successor José Madriz. Nicaragua became a virtual protectorate of the United States; and in 1912 its new president, Adolfo Díaz, who had requested and received the support of a detachment of United States marines, agreed to the Bryan–Chamorro Treaty by which the United States gained the right to build a canal in Nicaragua. This treaty was not regarded with favour by the other republics. Nicaragua now withdrew from the Central American Court, which ceased to function at the end of its ten-year life (1918).

Throughout his long rule, which became harsh and vindictive after an attempt on his life in 1907, the Guatemalan president Estrada Cabrera pursued a similar policy of friendship with the United States, which reinforced the effect of the American presence in Panama and Nicaragua. Honduras, freed for the moment from intervention, enjoyed political stability until 1920, while El Salvador, under the rule of the Meléndez–Quiñónez families, was, except for the assassination of Arturo Araújo in 1913, to enjoy an orderly presidential succession from 1898 to 1931. Ironically Costa Rica, where a well-established pattern of smallholding, rich soil, and an educated population had helped to facilitate the emergence of democracy, incurred the disapproval of President Woodrow Wilson when the Minister of War, Federico Tinoco Granados, seized power in 1917 in a

near-bloodless coup. Within two years he was forced to resign by American non-recognition and political opposition at home, and the 1871 Costa Rican Constitution was restored. This blatant external pressure, in turn, brought about the last serious attempt to federate Central America once more, appropriately enough on the occasion of the centenary of Central American independence.

In increasing hostility to the domination of the United States, a Union Party had been growing up in the five republics. When the Guatemalan Congress declared Estrada Cabrera insane in 1920, the Unionists seized their opportunity. A conference at San José drew up a new pact for unification. Nicaragua, however, refused to accede to it while the other states did not accept the Bryan–Chamorro Treaty. Costa Rica, fearful of United States influence, also refused to ratify the pact. The three northern states, still not deterred, formally created their new common Constitution on the appointed date. Within weeks it was destroyed by the overthrow in a military coup of President Carlos Herrera of Guatemala. His successor withdrew from the Federation in January 1922 and was speedily recognized by the Harding administration in the United States. That administration then proceeded to sponsor a new Treaty of Peace and Amity between the five republics, but this served only to preserve the dominant position of the United States.

By now that position was effectively ensured by sheer economic power. The First World War had ended the likelihood of an effective European challenge to the growth of United States interests, though German investment, encouraged by Estrada Cabrera, remained strong in Guatemalan coffee until 1944. The new force in the region, however, was that of the US businessman Minor Cooper Keith, who had first become interested in bananas while building a railway in Costa Rica in the 1880s. In 1912 he welded together the two northern states with his International Railways of Central America (IRCA), while serving as vice-president of the United Fruit Company of Boston (founded 1889) which grew the bananas that provided the freight. In 1929 United Fruit effected a merger with the Cuyamel Fruit Company of Samuel Zemurray, who controlled the largest fruit interests in Honduras. United Fruit (UFCo), known familiarly as 'El Pulpo' (The Octopus), thus emerged as a formidable foreign political influence in the region. Its influence, moreover, continued to be felt after 1933, when the United States abandoned direct intervention in Central America.

Nicaragua still lacked a major export crop. Its railway system was confined to the west of the country; it connected with that of Honduras only by sea, and had no link with that of Costa Rica. It was under United States control until 1924, as was the management of the national finances, while the presence of United States marines guaranteed the continued tenure of the Conservatives. When in 1925 the Coolidge administration withdrew the marines, factional fighting among the Conservatives offered the Liberals, led by Juan Bautista Sacasa, the chance to seize power. In 1926 the United States again intervened to ensure the second term of President Adolfo Díaz (1926–9). This second intervention was challenged by a guerrilla movement led by the dissident General Augusto César Sandino, whose name was later to be given to a more successful movement than his own. The marines, who proved unable to capture Sandino, were withdrawn finally in January 1933 in the first and most decisive evidence of Franklin Roosevelt's 'Good Neighbour' Policy. Sandino, however, remained an independent force under Juan Sacasa (president 1933–6) until he was murdered while leaving the presidential palace after dinner (1934), at the orders of the commander of the American-trained National Guard, Anastasio Somoza García. In 1936 Somoza pressured Sacasa himself into resignation and assumed a direct control of Nicaraguan affairs which ended only with his assassination in 1956.

DEMOCRACY, DICTATORSHIP, REVOLUTION

The Great Depression of 1929, the indirect cause of United States withdrawal, caused great hardship in the export-orientated economies of the region. Political repercussions were immediate. Guatemala ended nine years of democratic government early in 1931. Jorge Ubico's (1931–44) stern and unimaginative rule systematized the exploitation of the rural Indians under local officials who lived in fear of his sudden visits on a powerful motorcycle. In El Salvador, General Maximiliano Hernández Martínez (1931–44) shot down thousands of peasants early in 1932 in a confrontation with trade unions, and established a rigorous dictatorship. In Honduras, Tiburcio Carías Andino, fairly elected in 1932, ended elections for sixteen years till his voluntary withdrawal in 1949. Only Costa Rica continued to maintain a democratic system of government throughout the Second World War, though all five countries leapt to the side of the Allies in 1941 at the news of Pearl Harbor.

Stimulated by Allied propaganda, the citizens of Guatemala and El Salvador deposed their presidents by massive general strikes and demonstrations in 1944. Guatemalans chose ex-university professor Juan José Arévalo (1945–50), a proponent of 'spiritual socialism', who survived numerous attempted coups in the course of introducing social security programmes, legalizing trade unions and sweeping away the restrictive bonds on the Indians. His successor, Colonel Jacobo Arbenz, relying increasingly on the aid of a small group of Communist activists, incurred the direct hostility of the United States when he attempted to expropriate the unused banana lands of the United Fruit Company for redistribution. He was finally overthrown by the army when he attempted to distribute arms to workers to resist an invasion of exiles aided by the United States. Since that time, with the exception of the four-year term of Mario Méndez Montenegro (1966–70) the presidency has remained either in military hands or under strong military pressure. At the same time, confronted by a number of guerrilla movements inspired by the Cuban revolution of 1959, the army has fought back with help (since the mid-1960s) from a number of right-wing paramilitary 'death squads' whose activities have effectively eradicated all possible bases for a democratic system. The country's large indigenous population has suffered badly from repression.

In El Salvador no civilian leader emerged on the fall of Hernández Martínez and a series of coups merely consolidated the power of the army as an institution. The reforms of Major Oscar Osorio (1949–56) and his successor José María Lemus (1956–60), though considerable, represented moves by the country's oligarchy to forestall trouble by keeping up with the 'New Deal'-inspired moves then taking place in neighbouring countries. When Lemus was deposed by younger officers and students in 1960, a second coup quickly restored the control of Conservative officers. A series of coups in Honduras after the retirement of Carías similarly led after 1963 to an army nervous of some Cuban-style revolution

Dr Oscar Arias, President of Costa Rica (1986–90) and winner of the Nobel Peace Prize for 1987

arrogating power to itself. It was therefore two military regimes that found themselves drawn in 1969 into the bizarre episode of the 'Football War' (Guerra de Fútbol), also called the 'Soccer War'. It took its title from its origin in a disputed decision in the third qualifying round of the World Cup, but its root cause was the social tension aroused by the migration of workers from overcrowded El Salvador into Honduras, and in a brief thirteen days it killed some 2000 before being ended by a cease-fire arranged by the Organization of American States (OAS).

The Football War arrested at a critical point the growth of a new sort of regional organization for unity, the Central American Common Market (CACM), created in 1960 under the auspices of an earlier regional organization, the Organization of Central American States (ODECA) set up by the Treaty of San Salvador of 1951. Honduras withdrew from CACM in pique, and for twelve years (until late 1980) the two governments, largely because of internal instability, were unable to sign a peace treaty. When it came, it was only because by that time El Salvador had become the scene of a civil war between left- and right-wing forces, both emulating events in neighbouring Nicaragua the previous year.

There the assassination of the elder Somoza had given way to a dynastic succession rarely paralleled in the Americas. His sons Luis (1956–63) and, after 1966, Anastasio ran Nicaragua as virtually a family business, brooking little in the way of opposition. But after the devastating Managua earthquake (1973), the family's blatant greed and the brutality of its national guard led to a massive popular revolt by an alliance of middle-class, church and left-wing groups, led by the Sandinista National Liberation Front (FSLN), and supported from outside by Costa Rica

and Panama as well as Cuba. The victory of the Sandinistas in 1979 produced a revolutionary regime whose radical social policies (reminiscent of those in Cuba's 'socialist transformation') and anti-American rhetoric soon made it a target for the incoming Reagan administration in the United States. The declared policy of Washington was to check the spread of revolution in El Salvador and to back a Nicaraguan counter-revolutionary force (the *contras*), operating across the frontier from Honduras.

With renewed armed conflict in Nicaragua and fighting in El Salvador and Guatemala, mediation was unsuccessfully attempted after 1983 by the 'Contadora' countries (initially Colombia, Mexico, Panama and Venezuela). In August 1987 Costa Rica's Oscar Arias (president 1986–90), in a brilliant manoeuvre, persuaded his fellow Central American presidents to accept a comprehensive peace plan. Arias won the 1987 Nobel Peace Prize. His scheme was only partly successful, but one of its consequences was an effective cease-fire in Nicaragua, followed by a new round of elections, won by the right-wing candidate Violeta Chamorro (1990), with the still-powerful Sandinistas becoming the opposition. In January 1992, moreover, a cease-fire and a peace plan were agreed by the contending parties in El Salvador.

The role of Costa Rica in maintaining democratic ideals in Central America can hardly be overstated. It is an ideal that has been strong at least since 1948, when a democratic revolution led by José Figueres (president 1953-58 and again 1970-74) resulted in the

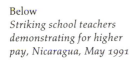

Below
Striking school teachers demonstrating for higher pay, Nicaragua, May 1991

Colombia, Venezuela and Ecuador

Salvadorean guerrillas taking part in a parade barely 30 kilometres from the country's capital, June 1991

outright abolition of the Costa Rican army. The country relied on the Inter-American Treaty of Reciprocal Assistance to check invasions from Somoza's Nicaragua in 1949 and 1955. However, the Arias plan has yet to be fulfilled in all its expectations, federation is seldom mentioned, and the CACM is effectively in limbo. Central America remains proof that language and historical, geographical and cultural ties do not in themselves imply unity.
PARC

Further Reading: V. Bulmer-Thomas, *The Political Economy of Central America* (Cambridge, 1987); P. Calvert, ed., *The Central American Security System: North-South or East-West?* (Cambridge, 1988); J. Dunkerley, *Power in the Isthmus: A Political History of Modern Central America* (London, 1988); T. L. Karnes, *The Failure of Union: Central America 1824–1960* (Chapel Hill, Tennessee, 1961); R. L. Woodward Jr, *Central America: A Nation Divided,* 2nd edition (New York, 1985)

Gran Colombia, whose coasts stretched from the Orinoco delta on the Atlantic to the north of Peru on the Pacific, was the successor state to the old Spanish imperial divisions of the viceroyalty of New Granada, the captaincy-general of Caracas, the *audiencia* of Quito and the province of Panama (Gran Colombia is the name used by most historians, in order to distinguish the larger state from the modern Colombia, which covers only the old New Granada). Formally established by the congress that met in Cúcuta, in present-day Colombia, in 1821, it was an imposing diplomatic façade, and served its purpose in securing men, resources and diplomatic support for the final stages of the War of Independence, but the hold of its government in Santa Fé de Bogotá over the lands and peoples outside the old viceroyalty of New Granada was precarious. Vice-President Francisco de Paula Santander (1792–1840), who was the head of government while Bolívar was on campaign (1821–7), found his authority frequently challenged. Bolívar himself on his return from Peru made concessions, particularly to feelings in Caracas, and finally removed Santander from office. Gran Colombia was well on the way to dissolution by the time his death in December 1830 removed the last obstacle to the emergence of not one but three new states. These were now more firmly based on the demarcations that three centuries of experience had found to be practical, and which, with the exception of the separation of Panama from Colombia, were to persist to the present day. Like many subsequent crises, the break-up of Bolívar's political creation coincided with depression and financial crisis, and default on the substantial loans that in the mid-1820s Gran Colombia had raised on the London market.

Economic development from independence

Colombia, Venezuela and Ecuador in 1830 possessed certain common characteristics. They had scant and scattered populations: the conventional estimates gave Colombia 1,500,000, Venezuela 900,000 and Ecuador 500,000. These populations were heavily rural: Bogotá, Caracas and Quito all numbered somewhere around thirty thousand inhabitants at this time. Communications were everywhere poor, particularly in Colombia and Ecuador, two of the most mountainous countries in the world. Local wealth and economic potential disappointed the expectations of the early 1820s. All three populations were racially mixed, though distinctively so. All three republics inherited from Spain three cardinal institutions, the Church, the judiciary and the army, again in distinct degrees: as Bolívar had pessimistically predicted, 'Venezuela a barracks, Colombia a law-court, Ecuador a convent'.

The largest share of Gran Colombia's population lay in Colombia. It was then settled mostly in the colder highlands of the interior, and it did not represent a large capacity in international trade. Colombia's per-capita exports were to remain among the lowest in Latin America throughout the nineteenth century: in 1830 its main export was gold from the mines of the provinces of Antioquia, El Choco and Cauca. Colombia was one of the world's leading gold producers before the discoveries in California and Australia, but it had little else to offer and its annual export of specie was less than a peso a head. Mining, like so much else, did not respond to foreign hopes at the time of independence. Expansion of exports came in the late 1840s first with tobacco, particularly from the district of Ambalema on the upper Magdalena River, which also brought with it the establishment of regular steam traffic on the river. To tobacco was added cinchona bark, the source of quinine, which grew wild in certain parts of the country and for which an always erratic demand collapsed entirely in the early 1880s when plantations were established in Ceylon and the Dutch East Indies. Coffee began to be exported from Colombia in visible quantities in the 1860s and by the end of the century was the leading export. But as a coffee exporter Colombia did not overtake Venezuela as South America's second producer after Brazil until well into the twentieth century.

The 1920s were the first decade of relative optimism and prosperity since the short-lived buoyancy of the 1860s and 1870s, coffee being supported by bananas from Santa Marta and petroleum. Those supports were also to fall away, and coffee has obstinately remained the mainstay of Colombian international trade. Coal and other mineral resources are more likely to rival or replace coffee in the future than the more publicized marijuana and cocaine.

The slow development of exports was reflected in small state revenues, slow improvement of communications (Colombia had less than 1000 km of railroad by 1900), tardy development of banking and finance and little foreign investment. It also kept Colombian trade in native hands to a degree not common in Latin America. Colombia received little immigration and the few immigrants who did settle in the country were absorbed into native social, commercial, religious and political practices. The largest single group of immigrants has been the Lebanese, who began to arrive in the last years of the nineteenth century. Foreign cultural influences up until the 1920s were predominantly French and British, though Bogotá's isolation and clerical–legal tradition ensured the persistence of creole–Hispanic elements, again to an unusual degree. Great Britain maintained a predominant position as Colombia's leading trading partner until the First World War. The beginnings of native industry can be traced to the end of the last century, though they have no continuity with the artisan weaving and hat-making of Boyacá and Socorro. Modern textile factories came to be concentrated around Medellín, where capital and market expertise derived from the coffee trade of the Antioquia frontier, and before that from the control of foreign trade Antioqueño merchants exercised through the gold production of the province.

At the time of independence Venezuela and Ecuador were the world's leading producers of cacao. The crop's dominance was supplanted in Venezuela by coffee, first grown in the centre of the country around Caracas and then in the western Andean states. Coffee remained Venezuela's leading export until it was overtaken by petroleum after the First World War. Foreign trading houses were more prominent than in Colombia, particularly those of north German origin, but these merchants were well integrated with the local community and in most respects can be considered to be native. The country also exported hides, some cattle and a certain amount of gold from the Guayana region and the llanos. The presence of asphalt and petroleum had always been known, and the earliest commercial production of petroleum dates from over a hundred years ago. The First World War and troubles in Mexico brought Venezuela's potential into prominence, and development by British and United States companies was then rapid. President Juan Vicente Gómez (1908–35) was more successful than he has usually been given credit for in balancing foreign interests against each other and in imposing terms on the companies, but much of what was gained was absorbed in corruption, and the effect on the rest of the economy was to make Venezuela entirely dependent on petroleum; its agriculture was weak and what little industry existed was stifled by its strong propensity to import. These patterns have persisted. General Gómez for reasons of political security did not encourage immigration, but his successors reversed this policy and since the 1940s Venezuela has attracted large numbers of immigrants from Spain, Portugal and Italy, and from other South American and Caribbean states, particularly from Colombia. Venezuela may be said to have originated the idea of OPEC (Organization of Petroleum Exporting Countries), and has aspired to greater influence as a result in hemispheric, and in particular in Caribbean affairs. Venezuela also possesses in the Cerro Bolívar in Guayana immense reserves of iron ore.

The development of cacao exports from coastal Ecuador provided the country with a relatively continuous expansion of its foreign trade in the nineteenth century, though this expansion started from a small base and for long had little effect on the upland sierra. The sierra provinces possessed a textile industry based on the semi-servile system of the *obraje*, but this was already in decline in the eighteenth century in the face of increased imports and imperial readjustments such as the decrees of *comercio libre*. It declined further in the nineteenth century. Hat making in the coastal region of Montecristi and in Azuay expanded, and gave the world the Panama hat. Despite the eventual completion of the Quito–Guayaquil railway in 1908, twentieth-century development was undramatic until the advent of, first, bananas and then petroleum after the Second World War.

COLOMBIA

Area	1,138,338 sq km
Population	33.0 million
GNP per capita (1989)	$1200
Capital	Bogotá
Currency	Peso

Slow economic growth in the nineteenth century was in all three republics reflected in politics. Colombia emerged as an independent nation under the liberal guidance of Francisco de Paula Santander (president 1832–6). Despite his prestige and political industry,

he was succeeded by an opponent, José Ignacio de Márquez, a 'moderate' of more conservative stamp. Márquez himself was faced by a series of populist–federalist revolts, the most important being that of the clerical south around Pasto led, in self-defence against the revived charge of having murdered Bolívar's faithful lieutenant Marshal Sucre in 1830, by General José Maria Obando. These were eventually defeated and Generals Pedro Alcántara Herrán (1841–5) and Tomás Cipriano de Mosquera (1845–9) governed under a more conservative, centralist and authoritarian constitution. The Conservatives were defeated by a revived Liberalism in the elections of 1849, and a period of conflicting radicalisms and Conservative resistance followed under the presidencies of José Hilario López (1849–53) and José Maria Obando, returned from exile and briefly president (1853–4). Under his faltering direction, conflict between the artisans, allied with the small military element, and free-trade radicals produced a short-lived coup d'état by General José María Melo. A united reaction of Liberals and Conservatives against this restored civilian rule, first all-party under President Manuel María Mallarino (1854–7), then Conservative under President Mariano Ospina Rodríguez (1857–61). Ospina's administration planned to consolidate Conservative rule by relying on a clergy reinforced by the return of the Jesuits, but it was frustrated by the rising in the Cauca of former President Mosquera, protesting against Ospina's allegedly unconstitutional interference in provincial affairs.

Mosquera's victory – apart from the removal of Melo, the one example of a successful advance on Bogotá by a provincial army that the history of Colombian civil wars can show – reinforced federalist currents that had been active for two decades, and which reflected the country's geographical and cultural diversity as well as the fiscal weakness of central government and the current fashions of democratic philosophy. Both Liberals and Conservatives had been federalists in competition with each other. The Constitution of Rionegro, which, with modifications, lasted from 1863 to 1885, divided the country into nine 'sovereign' states which did, indeed, exercise wide autonomy. The Church was disestablished and lost its properties. The powers of the presidency were much reduced, and the presidential term reduced to two years. The local governments produced by this system reflected in their competence the wealth or poverty of the state concerned, and defenders of the system argued that it produced governments suited to local conditions and reduced the scope of conflict. It could not however produce order or guarantee prosperity, and it broke up with the economic down-turn of the early 1880s. Free-trade radicalism, whose lead-

Bogotá, Colombia – a city of between four and five million by the end of the 1980s

COLOMBIA, VENEZUELA AND ECUADOR

ing figures were Manuel Murillo Toro (president 1864–6), Santiago Pérez (president 1874–6) and Aquileo Parra (president 1876–8), had failed to keep its promises.

The Constitution of 1886, which was the basis of Colombian political life until 1991, was the product of the 'independent' Liberal positivist Rafael Núñez (president 1882–4 and 1885–94) and the Conservative Miguel Antonio Caro, first Núñez's vice-president and then president himself from 1894 to 1898. Rafael Núñez's 'Regeneration' promised to bring peace and progress through centralization, a restricted suffrage (the Constitution of Rionegro had laid down manhood suffrage, which its Liberal manipulators consistently and necessarily rigged through fraud and the federal army), a Church restored to recognition and influence, a larger army, and a less doctrinaire economic policy, which would include recourse to paper money. It also promised guarantees and participation to the opposition, promises which it failed to make good, and looked forward to an economic revival, which failed to occur. Its too exclusive composition can account for the short Liberal rising of 1895, and the same fault combined with a pronounced slump in coffee prices led to the 'War of a Thousand Days' (1899–1901), with its heavy price in destruction and the indirect consequence of the loss of Panama, which aided and abetted by the United States declared its independence

from an impotent Colombia in 1904. President José Manuel Marroquín, a harmless Conservative *littérateur* whom Theodore Roosevelt in the heat of that separation referred to as a well-known South American bandit, was followed in the same year as president by General Rafael Reyes, who extended his term of office until hostile opinion drove him abroad in 1910.

Reyes admired Porfirio Díaz of Mexico; Colombia's lack of resources on the whole frustrated his attempt to bring progress through 'plenty of administration and no politics', but he achieved some success in cleaning up the financial chaos left behind by the last civil war. He also gave the Liberal Party some participation in government, an essential element in national peace which was continued under his 'Republican' or coalition successor Carlos E. Restrepo (1911–14), and under the Conservatives José Vicente Concha, Marco Fidel Suárez, Pedro Nel Ospina and Miguel Abadía Méndez, the successive presidents before party division and the Depression brought the Liberals to power in 1930.

This was the first peaceful change of party in power in the history of the republic. The Liberals had maintained in opposition, in the civil wars and after, a certain popular appeal, a tradition emphasized by leaders such as General Rafael Uribe Uribe (assassinated 1914) and General Benjamin Herrera (d. 1924). This tradition was muted under the prudent coalition government of Enrique Olaya Herrera (1930–4), but was fully exploited by Alfonso López Pumarejo (1934–8), in the 'Revolución en Marcha' ('Revolution on the March'). The Liberal Party introduced modern social legislation and encouraged the labour movement. The pace was not maintained by the following government of Eduardo Santos (1938–42), and could not in wartime conditions be revived by Alfonso López Pumarejo in his second term. This ended in scandal, disillusion and resignation in 1945. In 1946 the Conservative candidate Mariano Ospina Pérez was elected president against a Liberal vote that was divided between Gabriel Turbay and Jorge Eliecer Gaitán. On 9 April 1948 the assassination of Gaitán, a complex demagogue who by then had captured the leadership of the Liberal Party, intensified what was already an atmosphere of violent antagonism. The 'Bogotazo' riot the assassination caused was perhaps the most destructive in Latin America's history. Sectarian violence broke out in wide areas of the countryside, and 'la violencia' (as it became known) could not be contained by Ospina Pérez or by his successor, the party's main force and ideologue Laureano Gómez. His increasingly authoritarian rule was ended on 13 June 1953 by a military coup carried out under strong civilian pressure by General Gustavo Rojas Pinilla. His government lasted until 1957; though it at first had some success in pacifying Liberal guerrillas, the army had neither the numbers, the training nor the political understanding needed to govern effectively. It was forced to give way to a Liberal–Conservative coalition, formed by a pact which laid down that the two parties should alternate in the presidency and share public office evenly for four terms – sixteen years. This arrangement effectively ended sectarian violence, though it failed to end rural guerrilla activity under other forms and allegiances. The 'National Front' coalition presidents Alberto Lleras Camargo (Liberal), Guillermo León Valencia (Conservative), Carlos Lleras Restrepo (Liberal) and Misael Pastrana Borrero (Conservative) were opposed by various dissident groups from the two traditional parties, and by the Alianza Nacional Popular movement of General Rojas Pinilla. Since the return of controlled competition in 1974 the presidency has been held by Alfonso López Michelsen (1974–8), son of Alfonso López Pumarejo, Julio Cesar Turbay Ayala (1978–82), Belisario Betancur (1982–6), Virgilio Barco (1986–90), and César Gaviria (1990–). In 1991 a Constituent Assembly wrote a new Constitution, as part of plans to pacify the country through a new accord on the rules of the game and wider minority participation.

The Colombian political tradition can be characterized as follows: by the persistence and dominance of civilian liberalism and conservatism, to a degree unknown elsewhere in Latin America; by the presence of the Church as a powerful component of conservatism until the 1960s; by constant electoral activity, though rates of abstention remain high; by widespread and early politicization of a population without strong racial or cultural barriers against some sort of participation; by the ability of both parties to co-opt emerging leaders, and of the Liberal Party not to be outflanked on the left; by the lack of a single dominant city or region, which has enforced collaboration between cities and regions; by a strong journalistic tradition; and by persistent guerrilla activity, complicated in the 1980s by the disruptive role of the powerful drug-trading 'cartel' based on the city of Medellín.

VENEZUELA

Area	898,805 sq km
Population	18.75 million
GNP per capita (1989)	$2450
Capital	Caracas
Currency	Bolivar

The contrast with Venezuela was not at first so apparent. General José Antonio Páez was as opposed to the presence of Simón Bolívar and the Gran Colombian army of liberation in Venezuela as Santander was to its presence in Colombia. Though a military rising soon ended the presidential career of his successor, the medical doctor José Maria Vargas (1834–6), Páez was careful of appearances under the administration of Carlos Soublette (1843–7). The 'Conservative Republic' allowed wide liberties at first to the Liberal opposition, and the 1840s were a fertile time for the Venezuelan press: the polemical level of the Liberals Antonio Leocadio Guzmán and Tomás Lander and of the Conservative Juan Vicente González was higher than could be attained under the successive authoritarian regimes that followed. The Liberal opposition to Páez exploited the economic claims of hacendados and artisans against merchants and monopolists, and did so with an intensity and efficiency not matched elsewhere in the successor states of Gran Colombia. Páez was strong enough to suppress Antonio Leocadio Guzmán, but had to compromise in the 1847 presidential elections by adopting the candidacy of the neutral and independent General José Tadeo Monagas, strongly entrenched in the east, and, as it turned out, not disposed to be a puppet. Páez's attempts to control Monagas through Congress were frustrated by a popular riot on 19 January 1848 (the first revolution of that year) which Monagas is wrongly credited with instigating; he did take advantage of it. In the ensuing civil war Páez was defeated and went into exile. The Liberal domination of José Tadeo Monagas and his brother José Gregorio did not survive exhaustion of reputation – there was much familial corruption – and worsening economic conditions at the end of the 1850s. Páez's attempt to return to power led to the widespread but desultory *Guerra Federal* (Federal War), in which Venezuelan Conservatism met its definitive defeat at the hands of the Liberals led by Marshal Juan Crisóstomo Falcón, General Ezequiel Zamora and General Antonio Guzmán Blanco. The Liberals declared that the cause of federalism was that of democracy and equality against the *godos*, the Conservative oligarchs, and Zamora in particular gave the war a certain populist élan until killed in battle. Guzmán Blanco became president in 1873, and with short interruptions he ruled either in Caracas or from Paris, until 1888. In theory Guzmán was a Liberal, and he was so more than just in theory in that he believed in systematic material progress, in education and in secular control

of the Church – the never powerful Venezuelan Church was further reduced and humiliated by his government. He ruled as an autocrat, and his grand titles and bombastic self-adulation were part of the scheme that set him above his rivals, just as his buildings in Caracas set his capital above other cities. His powerful political intelligence can be seen in the length of his rule and the degree to which his successors have imitated him. He can also claim a measure of administrative and material progress. His share of the latter made him the first noticeably rich South American in Paris.

Guzmán Blanco's ascendancy was followed by the more transient administrations of Juan Pablo Rojas Paúl (1888–90), Raimundo Andueza Palacio (1890–2), and Joaquín Crespo (1892–8). The last might have been less transient had Crespo not been killed in battle, but none of these figures, all Liberals of no strong definition or imagination, has the significance of Guzmán Blanco or of the leader to emerge in 1899, General Cipriano Castro. Castro invaded from the Colombian border with only sixty men, but his small band of *andinos* (from the western Andean

Caracas, Venezuela: municipal apartment-blocks and more modest housing

region) succeeded in installing their leader in the presidency through a combination of fighting and diplomacy. Castro was debauched and corrupt, but his radicalism and nationalism were not entirely faked, and he was a feared and inspiring leader. He survived a number of risings and an Anglo-German debt-collecting blockade, and only yielded office to his vice-president, General Juan Vincente Gómez, to go to Europe for an operation. Gómez's throughgoing tyranny lasted from 1908 to his death in 1935; had it not lasted so long, his genuine contributions to national order and progress would be less overshadowed by his implacable treatment of political opposition, his cultural sterility and his own, his family's and his entourage's greed. Military power was exclusively entrusted to *andinos*. In public finance, in oil matters, in building a modern army and in the ideological defence of his regime he was served by able men (in oil by Gumersindo Torres, in the army by General Eleazar López Contreras, in intellectual argument by Laureano Vallenilla Lanz), but their efforts were offset by a high price in isolation and stultification. Gómez's death was followed by two increasingly liberal military governments under first General López Contreras, 1935–40, then General Isaias Medina Angarita, 1940–5. General Medina was overthrown by a military coup which installed the first short-lived Democratic Action (AD) governments of Rómulo Betancourt and Rómulo Gallegos, the last overthrown by another coup which evolved into the revived *andino* military regime of Marcos Pérez Jiménez (1948–58). Representative democracy, with an enviable record of civil liberty, has since survived under Rómulo Betancourt (1959–64), Raúl Leoni (AD) (1964–9), Rafael Caldera of the Christian Democrat COPEI (1969–74), Carlos Andrés Pérez (AD) (1974–9), Luis Herrera Campíns (COPEI) (1979–84), and Jaime Lusinchi (AD) (1984–9). Carlos Andrés Pérez was then re-elected, though in economic circumstances that were a marked contrast to the boom of his first period.

Venezuelan democratic policies have their origins in the opposition to Gómez and to Pérez Jiménez. Venezuelan parties are elaborately organized and lavishly financed, and their internal structure preserves something of the authoritarianism of the country's tradition, though recent years have seen stronger pressures for decentralization. Government patronage, derived from oil revenues, is far more pervasive than in Colombia or Ecuador. The army has been carefully integrated into the country's political structure. The social and commercial elite are less openly politicized than is common in the region. The spirit of Venezuelan society is markedly egalitarian, which is not incompatible with rampant consumerism when times are good.

ECUADOR

Area	270,670 sq km
Population	10.6 million
GNP per capita (1989)	$1020
Capital	Quito
Currency	Sucre

Ecuador began its independent existence under a Venezuelan General, Juan José Flores, who contrived to command the greater share of influence with the Guayaquil Liberal Vicente Rocafuerte until the mid-1840s. Ecuadorean governments thereafter were unstable constructs of different local influences, the sierra predominating, until the era of Gabriel García Moreno, a progressive theocrat–Conservative of Guayaquil origins whose sway lasted from 1861 until his assassination in 1875. García Moreno believed in public works, in education and in discipline, whose principal support would be a reformed ultramontane clergy. Some of his most persistent enemies were therefore Ecuadorean clerics, but the most famous was the Liberal polemicist Juan Montalvo. The twenty years after his death were occupied partly by General Ignacio Veintemilla, a military opportunist, and partly by governments which sought a compromise between the interests of upland landowners and the exporting groups of Guayaquil. In 1895 these frail arrangements collapsed in the face of the assault of radical coastal Liberalism led by General Eloy Alfaro, a tenacious and warlike idealist for whom the closest model is Giuseppe Garibaldi. Alfaro's coastal forces won the sierra, and his government and that of his successor General Leónidas Plaza carried through extensive anti-clerical reforms – the Ecuadorean Church had not suffered the earlier Liberal attacks of Colombia and Venezuela. Alfaro, with the American entrepreneur–idealist Archer Harman, also succeeded in completing the Quito–Guayaquil railroad. Unwilling to compromise or retire from politics, Alfaro was murdered by the Quito mob in 1912, and General Plaza emerged as the architect of the coast–sierra compromise that, despite appearances, was to be the persistent note of twentieth-century Ecuadorean politics. The Church had to recognize its reduced position.

General Plaza's compromise was not a guarantee of political tranquillity. In 1922 a Guayaquil strike was suppressed by troops with many deaths, and in 1925 the short-lived July Revolution, a reformist military affair, was seen as the beginning of a new era of social preoccupation. In the 1930s José María Velasco Ibarra began a political career that was to last four decades: he could appeal to coast and sierra; his

Eloy Alfaro (1842–1912), a great liberal and anti-clerical who dominated early twentieth-century Ecuadorian politics

combination of ruthless opportunism and disinterestedness gained him the presidency five times (1934–5, 1944–7, 1952–6, 1960–61, 1968–72). But to concentrate too much on this figure is to exaggerate the instability of Ecuadorian politics. The country has known periods of sober civilian government even under Velasco Ibarra, and with particular success under Leónidas Plaza's son, Galo Plaza Laso, between 1948 and 1952. Recent military governments did not depart from a political tradition that can now be characterized as peaceful, unrepressive and remarkably decentralized: there is more genuine provincial autonomy in Ecuador than in either Colombia or Venezuela. A measure of agrarian reform has removed the worst features of exploitation from the countryside, and indigenous groups have found new forms of political expression. Civilian rule was restored in 1979. President Jaime Roldós was killed in a plane crash in 1981, and his term was completed by Oswaldo Hurtado. Subsequent presidents have been León Febres Cordero (1984–8) and Rodrigo Borja (1988–).

MDD

Further Reading: G. Carl, *First Among Equals: Great Britain and Venezuela, 1810–1910* (Ann Arbor, Michigan, 1980); O. Hurtado, *Political Power in Ecuador* (Boulder, Colorado, 1985); J. Lombardi, Venezuela: *The Search for Order, the Dream of Progress* (New York, 1982); M. Palacios, *Coffee in Colombia, 1850–1970: An Economic, Social and Political History* (Cambridge, 1980)

Peru and Bolivia

At independence, Peru's population was about 1,200,000, more than half of them Indians, with an additional 50,000 black slaves; Bolivia's population was estimated at 1,100,000, nearly three-quarters of them Indian.

The early years of independence brought no peace to either Peru or Bolivia. Deeply conscious of former imperial glory, Peru was anxious to extend its authority into the new neighbouring states of Bolivia and Ecuador. In 1828, Peru's General Gamarra invaded Bolivia to begin a thirteen-year period of intermittent but extremely bitter fighting between rival national armies facing each other across the high, broad plateau surrounding Lake Titicaca, known as the Altiplano. No lasting gains were made by either side: Peru failed to capitalize on the pro-Peruvian breakaway movements in and around La Paz; Bolivia failed to win the Pacific port of Arica. This rare desert oasis on the world's most arid coastline had been the traditional port for Upper Peru in colonial times, but as it was located within the boundaries of *Lower* Peru, Arica did not become part of Bolivia at independence. Peru was adamant in its refusal to part with Arica.

Ambitious, quarrelling generals and rootless guerrillas in both countries found civilian life little to their liking. Violence, political intrigue, and the chaotic conditions in the mines plunged much of Peru and Bolivia into turmoil during the critical early decades of independence. The successful attempt by Andrés Santa Cruz in 1836 to form a Peru–Bolivian Confederation lasted only three years. Santa Cruz had held power briefly in Peru before being installed as president of Bolivia in 1828, but the Confederation never inspired the confidence internally that Britain and the United States displayed towards this larger unit. If Chile had not in any case put an end to the union in 1839 at the battle of Yungay, the Peru–Bolivian Confederation would almost certainly have collapsed from within. At that time, overland transport and methods of communication throughout a region virtually the size of Europe were poor or non-existent. Much of Peru and of central and eastern Bolivia remained hostile to the idea of association.

1840S–1880S: GUANO, NITRATES, AND THE WAR OF THE PACIFIC

The 1840s began an important new phase in the fortunes of Peru and Bolivia with the economic exploitation of their coastal guano deposits. It was a phase which was also to reveal their weakness under the

PERU AND BOLIVIA

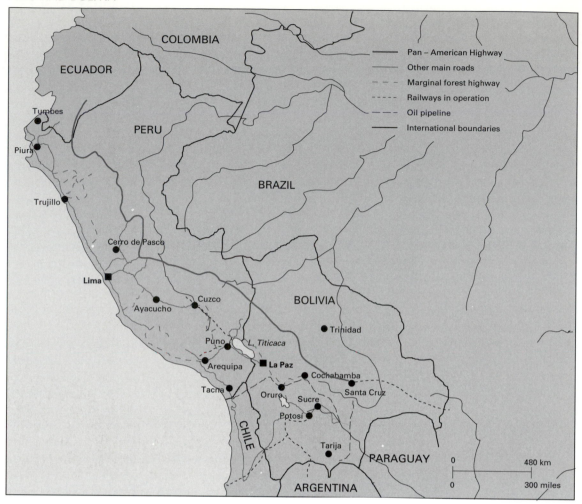

Legend:
- Pan – American Highway
- Other main roads
- Marginal forest highway
- Railways in operation
- Oil pipeline
- International boundaries

growing pressure of Chilean expansion. The thick beds of dried dung produced by the millions of sea birds feeding and nesting along the desert coast were soon in great demand as a rich source of natural fertilizer for Western European agriculture. Guano, which was state-owned, rapidly became the mainstay of Peru's economy. Most Chilean settlement lay well to the south, but the Atacama's new wealth was located right by the ocean, on the coastal cliffs and islands, and thus it was within easy reach of Chilean ships.

Bolivia became the first to experience the effects of vigorous Chilean exploitation of the guano deposits. Bolivia had inherited about 560 km of the Pacific coast but managed to maintain only the one small port of Cobija along this barren shoreline, separated by hundreds of kilometres of desert and mountain trail from the main Andean centres of population. As a result, Bolivia was powerless to prevent Chilean, or any other foreign exploitation of its guano deposits – in fact such exploitation was periodically encouraged by Bolivia's caudillos as the only way of obtaining a share of the profits.

Until the 1870s, Bolivia's buffer location tended to insulate Peru from the more immediate effects of Chilean expansion. Indeed, in 1866, differences between them were temporarily forgotten when Ecuador, Peru, Bolivia and Chile formed a defensive alliance against Spain during the latter's ill-judged attempt (1865–6) to reassert its authority in the region by seizing Peru's guano-rich Chincha Islands. Fears of Spain were short-lived, however, and Chileans were soon exploring the Atacama Desert for new sources of wealth. As the thickest and purest guano deposits became exhausted, exploitation of the desert's nitrate beds intensified. These lay well preserved just below the surface in the desert interior. Chilean prospectors had made important discoveries of sodium nitrate and silver in the Bolivian section of Atacama in the late 1860s, and with the backing of British capital, Chilean development of the region, and its new port of Antofagasta, proceeded without interruption. British and Chilean interests, working under concession, were now increasingly active in Peruvian territory. The Atacama Desert was fast becoming the focus of a new world-trading monopoly in natural nitrate. Commercial uses included dynamite as well as fertilizer production, and the huge potential in profits from nitrate was eagerly pursued as the guano revenues began to decline.

Chile seized control of the main Bolivian centres in the Atacama by armed occupation in 1879 and then proceeded to challenge the authority of Peru. The ensuing War of the Pacific (1879–82) was to demonstrate Chile's skilful use of sea power in its bid for the leadership of Pacific South America. The 'Nitrate War' was a fight for possession of the land's economic wealth but it was a victory for sea transport, and for the greater flexibility of attack and co-ordination possessed by the state which controlled it. Lima itself, far beyond the nitrate region, was occupied by Chilean forces in 1881, and remained so until 1884. Bolivia lost its entire coastline, Peru its nitrate province of Tarapacá, and the port of Arica. Peru's Tacna province was not retrieved from Chilean occupation until an arbitration award by the United States in 1929 resolved what had become a wearying fifty-year dispute between Chile and Peru over the ownership of Tacna and Arica.

Defeat in the War of the Pacific, therefore, marked a humiliating end to the distinctive second phase in Peruvian and Bolivian history. Peru's President Ramón Castilla had provided nearly twenty years of skilful administration and political stability until his retirement in 1862, but after that, internal rivalries and incompetence had seriously weakened the state at a critical stage of its development. Increasing cor-ruption in the handling of the 'windfall' guano and nitrate revenues, and in the manipulation of foreign loans, rocked successive governments. Sales of guano had financed an ambitious and costly programme of railway construction in the Andes between 1868 and 1874, masterminded by the North American engineer, Henry Meiggs. Peru's first civilian president, Manuel Pardo, was elected in 1872 but deteriorating conditions permitted only a few of his important economic and public works policies to be implemented.

Bolivia's problems at the end of the Pacific War more than matched those of Peru, as the country looked back on thirty years of almost continuous violence and disorder, particularly under the inept, often vicious rule of Presidents Manuel Belzú (1848–55), Mariano Melgarejo (1864–71) and Hilarión Daza (1876–79) – the 'barbarous caudillos' as they were later called by Bolivian writer Alcídes Arguedas. The loss of the littoral to Chile, together with territorial concessions to Brazil in 1867, emphasized Bolivia's internal and diplomatic weakness.

1880S–1930S: FOREIGN INVESTMENT AND THE BEGINNINGS OF MODERNIZATION

Peru

Under the firm control of General Andrés Cáceres (1885–90), Peru negotiated the transfer of its external debts to a newly formed London-based company known as the Peruvian Corporation (1890). In

ORIGINAL CLAIMS OF PERU

ORIGINAL CLAIMS OF BOLIVIA

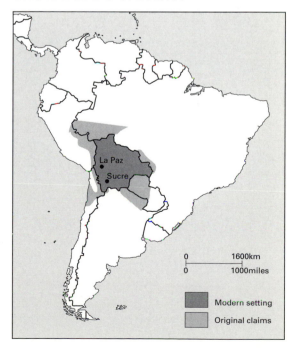

return, the Corporation took over the operation of Peru's railways (and the linking steamship line on Lake Titicaca), acquired free use of seven ports, and received additional cash payments and guano revenues. In the era after the Pacific War, political parties, including Civilist, Constitutionalist, Liberal, and Democratic became more important in Peru, though all were still dominated by the oligarchy, including the so-called 'forty families of Peru' – mainly landowners and mineowners. Bankers, lawyers, industrialists, and military officers were also prominent.

Area	1,280,219 sq km
Population	21.6 million
GNP per capita (1989)	$1010
Capital	Lima
Currency	Inti

Peru's economic and trading prospects slowly improved, and in the early decades of the twentieth century, United States business interests began to challenge Britain's hitherto dominant role. Many American bankers by now regarded South America as a fruitful field for investment, and offered loans for new railway and port construction, and for much-needed urban reconstruction and development. New

An hacienda owner and workers in the Chumbivilcas region of Peru, c.1945

public buildings, parks, public utilities, streetcars, lighting, water supply, sewerage, and a host of other improvements were much in demand in order to make life in the city centres (especially Lima) smarter, safer and more efficient. At the same time, Peru's President Leguía (1908–12 and 1919–30) was actively encouraging North American companies such as W. R. Grace (shipping, sugar estates and sugar-refining, textiles), Standard Oil (later its subsidiary the International Petroleum Company), and the Cerro de Pasco Copper Corporation to expand their operations. Augusto Leguía's determined handling of economic policies became increasingly dictatorial; the emerging middle class began to complain that a civilian caudillo was no more acceptable than a military one. There were growing demands for greater freedom of the press and for civil rights; growing dissatisfaction with the traditional concentration of power in the hands of a few wealthy landowners, and with the total failure to improve the lot of most of the Indian population.

In 1924, Victor Raúl Haya de la Torre founded a new political party while in exile in Mexico; this was APRA (American Popular Revolutionary Alliance). Conceived originally as an international party, APRA was influenced by the Mexican revolution, as well as by bolshevism and socialism. It was strongly critical both of the neglect of the Indians, and of the

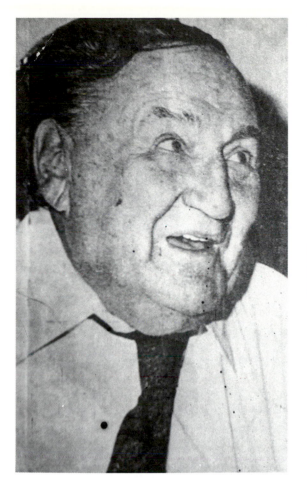

Víctor Raúl Haya de la Torre, Peruvian politician and thinker, founder of APRA

could now reach the Pacific coast relatively quickly, especially along the 1120 km, British-owned Antofagasta and Bolivia Railway. La Paz was also linked by rail in 1905 to Lake Titicaca's steamship service, and so to the Peruvian railway system. Attention was now focused on the western part of the country. As Bolivia's railway and commercial centre, La Paz's dominant position in Bolivian affairs could no longer be challenged; in 1898 the Liberals triumphed, and La Paz finally seized the role of capital from the colonial and Conservative city of Sucre, which was increasingly isolated in the central Andean sierras.

Area	1,098,581 sq km
Population	7.3 million
GNP per capita (1989)	$620
Capital	La Paz
Currency	Boliviano

The new railways were thus the key to a rapid expansion in mining and mineral exports, especially with the demand for tin from the US canning and automobile industries. American business and banking interests were now increasingly attracted to Bolivia, as they had been to Peru; the extraordinary rags-to-riches story of the Bolivian 'tin baron' Simón Patiño emphasizes the enormous power exerted by the three leading local tin magnates (Patiño, Hochschild and Aramayo) on the country's internal and external affairs. In politics, the Republican Party (founded 1914) won power in 1920. The administrations of Bautista Saavedra (1921–5) and Daniel Salamanca (1931–4) were marked by regional rivalries and growing unrest among the Indians and the poorer classes. Coalitions between different Republican and Liberal wings became increasingly fragile as political and economic crisis deepened in the 1930s.

Most Bolivians or Peruvians, meanwhile, were ignorant of their eastern lowlands. The wild-rubber boom had spread from Brazil, to flourish in upper Amazonia between 1890 and 1912. Brazilian expansion into the rubber forests had resulted in boundary changes at the expense of both Bolivian and Peruvian territory. Conflicting territorial claims in these densely forested 'backyard' regions of the interior also involved Colombia and Ecuador, and national passions were easily aroused. The atrocious conditions under which many of the forest Indians, and others, were forced to collect rubber were first brought to light by an American engineer in 1909, and subsequently by a British Foreign Office investigation into the Peruvian Amazon Company, registered in London, and working in the forests along the Putumayo River. But by the time the report was

power of the North American corporations in Peruvian life. The party failed to establish a wider continental base, but in Peru its radical views attracted an immediate following among liberal middle-class people and most of the working class. Apristas were an immediate target for abuse from the conservative sections of society, among them the landowners, the Church and the army. Foreign investors, and all those whose fortunes were tied to them, were suddenly wary. Haya's own career was uneven, and interrupted by periods of exile or imprisonment, but APRA remained influential as a party of the people.

Bolivia

Bolivian politicians like those of Peru, mortified by their country's swift and total defeat in the War of the Pacific, made strenuous efforts in the 1880s to put their house in order. A two-party system developed: power was held by Conservatives (1884–99) and Liberals (1899–1920). By far the most important development for the country at this time was the extension of railways up to the Bolivian Altiplano from Chilean territory. The line from Antofagasta reached the tin- and silver-mining centres of Uyuni in 1889, Oruro in 1892, and Potosí in 1911. The Arica–La Paz railway was completed in 1906–13. Bulk mineral exports

published, the rubber boom was over. Though fortunes were made by a handful of 'rubber barons' in the forests, that whole region remained remote and mysterious to most of the population of Bolivia and Peru.

The sparsely peopled interior nevertheless produced a major crisis for Bolivia in the 1930s, this time in the south-eastern plains of the Chaco. With the loss of a direct Pacific outlet confirmed by the War of the Pacific, outlets via the Amazon and the Paraguay–Plate waterways, despite the great distances involved, became sensitive issues. There was a genuine desire to secure guaranteed routeways to the Atlantic for an isolated *oriente* (eastern territory) not linked to Bolivia's western rail network. National honour was inevitably felt to be at stake in maintaining inherited claims in the south-east, and rumours of extensive petroleum deposits under the Chaco between the Andean foothills and the Paraguay River did the rest.

Skirmishing between Bolivian and Paraguayan border outposts developed in 1932 into the costly Chaco War; it dragged on until 1935, and eventually left Paraguay in possession of most of the disputed area, and the great Chaco Boreal. The shock to Bolivia's morale, disillusion with its institutions, and shame at the appalling front-line role that the thousands of Bolivian Indians from the high Andes had been forced to play amid the heat and alternating drought and flood of the plains, were to have a much more profound effect on Bolivian politics than the country's earlier defeats.

THE 1940S TO THE 1970S: REFORM AND REVOLUTION

During the Second World War, US demands for vital minerals (e.g. tin, zinc, copper, silver, lead, tungsten and vanadium), as well as for sugar, cotton, rubber and quinine, stimulated the economies of both Peru and Bolivia. After the war, the unrest and self-questioning returned to the most articulate and politically active sections of Peruvian and Bolivian society.

In Peru, the Apristas (or People's Party) were increasingly blamed for the failure to stabilize the country in its post-war recession. Food prices rose, and promised reforms were shelved. General Manuel Odría assumed the presidency in 1950, and lost no time in confirming his intention to banish the Apristas and rule on traditionally authoritarian lines. Peru's balance of trade improved dramatically with increased US and other investment in new mines, oil wells, highways, power plants, factories, and in the cotton and sugar estates. The Korean War (1950–3)

helped to increase both prices and demand for raw materials.

After Odría's retirement in 1956, the desire for change re-emerged, along with inflation, anti-American sentiment, and rising protest at the vulnerability of key areas of the Peruvian economy to US import quotas and pricing policies. A new name appeared in the presidential election campaign, that of the architect Fernando Belaúnde who made an impressive showing. With the last-minute support of the Apristas, the successful candidate was Manuel Prado, but little progress was made in dealing with the country's severe economic problems until 1959 when Pedro Beltrán introduced a strict anti-inflation policy with remarkable success. His promised social reforms, however, were less effective. Beltrán's *Techo y Tierra* (Roof and Land) programme involved improvement of housing and services in the sprawling shanty-towns around the major cities, especially Lima, reduction in the size of the great estates, and resettlement of families in more fertile areas east of the Andes. Progress was slow and in the country as a whole there was still little change in age-old patterns and attitudes.

In Bolivia, meanwhile, matters had been brought to a head with the revolution of 1952. This was a genuine social revolution – quite unlike the 170 or so 'palace revolutions' and coups which had preceded it. The tin miners' leaders had become an increasingly powerful political force since the 1940s as strikes and unrest spread among the thousands of workers over their harsh conditions and low wages. A representative of the radical middle class, Víctor Paz Estenssoro, had founded the National Revolutionary Movement (MNR) in 1941; in 1952, with the backing of the miners and the campesinos, and following the armed rising that started the revolution, he was recalled from exile in Argentina to head the new government. It was a major turning point in Bolivia's history. The social revolution of 1952, and the associated agrarian reform of 1953, had four immediate objectives: universal suffrage (without literacy or minimum-income requirements), the expropriation and nationalization of the mines, the break-up of the large estates, and the distribution of land to the peasants, including new colonization programmes east of the Andes.

Paz Estenssoro (1952–6) was succeeded by his vice-president Hernán Siles Zuazo (1956–60). The widespread popular appeal of the revolutionary, but non-Communist, government encouraged the United States to give strong support to Bolivia. The Bolivian economy was stabilized in the late 1950s and early 1960s with the financial and technical assistance offered by the Alliance for Progress. At the time it represented the highest per-capita injection of American aid anywhere in the world.

Bolivian soldiers taking part in the August 1971 coup d'état that brought General Hugo Banzer to power

Paz Estenssoro was again elected president in 1960, but was overthrown in 1964 by the air force General René Barrientos, himself later killed in a helicopter crash in 1969. The longest single presidential tenure since then has been that of the dictator General Hugo Banzer (1971–8). Bolivia's social revolution, however, was internationally recognized, and its fundamental principles have been maintained by each successive regime. In October 1982, Siles Zuazo was elected president, and Bolivia returned to democratic government after eighteen years of almost uninterrupted military rule.

Peru continued, on the whole, to be more cautious in the scope and pace of its reforms. In 1963, Fernando Belaúnde Terry became president for the first time. He led the Popular Action party which sought to win support from flagging Apristas. Bolivia's social revolution was by then more than ten years old. Belaúnde succeeded in pushing through a bill for agrarian reform in 1964 which exempted the large, efficiently run irrigated sugar and cotton estates along the coast, and the great cattle ranches in the sierras, but included some land redistribution, and more Indian community development projects.

Internal colonization of the eastern tropical forests, still lying virtually empty behind the Andes, was a policy close to Belaúnde's heart. Indeed, Belaúnde was said to slip a geography lesson into every speech. His proposal for an 'edge-of-the-selva highway' (*Carretera marginal de la Selva*) to link the new colonies in Peru with similar settlements in Venezuela, Colombia, Ecuador and Bolivia was bold but over-ambitious. Petroleum production has become increasingly important in the jungles of Peru in recent years, and produced its own transport networks of pipeline, highway and helicopter sites – as well as a revival by Ecuador of an old border dispute. Belaúnde was ousted in 1968, and a more revolutionary policy of nationalization and expropriation was quickly introduced by a new military government, particularly during the presidency of General Juan Velasco Alvarado (1968–75). In 1979, Peru adopted universal suffrage with no literacy requirements. Belaúnde was re-elected to the presidency when the military regime ended in 1980.

THE 1980S: ECONOMIC CRISIS, COCAINE, TERRORISM

The collapse of the world tin market in 1985 had catastrophic effects on the Bolivian economy, causing severe unemployment. A dramatic period of hyperinflation (nearly 12,000 per cent in 1985) was followed by harsh stabilization policies during Paz Estenssoro's third presidency (1985–9) and that of his successor Jaime Paz Zamora (1989–). Meanwhile the issue of drugs and the drug trade attracted increasing local and worldwide attention, as the rapid growth in the international demand for cocaine fuelled a major rise in coca cultivation on the eastern Andean slopes in both Bolivia and Peru. (North American observers estimated that at the start of the 1990s, one third of Bolivia's foreign exchange, and one quarter of Peru's, came illegally from coca and cocaine-concentrate production.) Attempts to deal

Coca leaves on sale, La Paz, Bolivia

with the problem were made by the Bolivian and Peruvian governments. But the Andes–Caribbean–North American trade-route is difficult to police; the small processing laboratories (for cocaine-concentrate) are quickly rebuilt when attacked; and crop substitution programmes meet with little success among peasants for whom coca is the main cash crop.

In Peru, the austerity measures to which Beláunde resorted after 1980 led to widespread strikes. In 1985 APRA won the presidency for the first time ever, with its attractive, youthful candidate Alan García (president, 1985–90). The failure of his economic policies, however, produced a startling victory for an outsider in 1990, when Alberto Fujimori took office as head of an independent coalition. Since 1980 all Peruvian governments have had to contend with an internal terrorist movement, Sendero Luminoso ('Shining Path'), an uncompromising 'Maoist' group which first emerged in the Ayacucho district,

killing officials and peasants loyal to the government, bombing power stations, and attacking soldiers, police and journalists. Several thousand Peruvians died in attacks and reprisal raids in the 1980s, with the guerrilla threat constituting a major national crisis. Peru's severe economic difficulties were compounded in 1991 by a large-scale outbreak of cholera.

JVF

Further Reading:

Peru
H. F. Dobyns and P. L. Doughty, *Peru: A Cultural History* (New York, 1979); V. K. Fitzgerald, *The Political Economy of Peru 1956–78* (Cambridge, 1979); S. Stein, *Populism in Peru* (Madison, 1980); R. Thorp and G. Bertram, *Peru, 1890–1977* (London, 1978); D. Werlich, *Peru: A Short History* (Carbondale, Ill., 1978)
Bolivia
J. Dunkerley, *Rebellion in the Veins* (London, 1984); J. V. Fifer, *Bolivia: Land, Location, and Politics since 1825* (Cambridge, 1972); H. S. Klein, *Bolivia: The Evolution of a Multi-Ethnic Society* (New York, 1982)

Chile

Area	756,629 sq km
Population	13.2 million
GNP per capita (1989)	$1770
Capital	Santiago
Currency	Peso

Chile won a unique reputation in nineteenth-century Spanish America for its untypical and durable tradition of political stability. Part (though only part) of the explanation for this lies in favourable geographical and social circumstances. The effective national territory in the 1830s was still fairly compact (see map opposite). The social structure was simple: a small, predominantly land-owning elite coexisted with the vast unlettered mass of the labouring poor. The Chilean heartland was dominated by great estates (haciendas) worked by a 'tied peasantry' of *inquilinos* (tenant-labourers) and by seasonal or itinerant peons. Political stability may to some extent have reflected the social stability of the countryside, where most Chileans lived. Ownership of land was the clearest badge of upper-class status until well into the twentieth century.

THE 'MODEL REPUBLIC'

The earliest governments after independence (1818) did not last very long. The enlightened dictatorship (1817–23) of the liberator Bernardo O'Higgins (1778–1842) was followed by several years of rule by Liberal politicians. Then, in the short civil war of 1829–30, a Conservative alliance seized power under the direction of the sardonic Diego Portales (1793–1837: chief minister 1830–1, 1835–7). The political system created by the Conservatives, partly embodied in the Constitution of 1833, was based on a strong presidency, strictly centralized administration, and the wholesale fixing of elections, a practice which lasted till 1891. Under the first three Conservative presidents (each of whom served for ten years, or two consecutive terms) repression – mild by twentieth-century standards – was also a weapon in the government's armoury. But with all its early blemishes, the system held together, surviving the test of both external and internal warfare: in 1836–9 Chile fought and defeated the short-lived Peru–Bolivian Confederation, while in 1851 and 1859 the inflexible Manuel Montt (1809–80: president 1851–61) was unsuccessfully challenged by armed rebellions. In the 1860s and 1870s, however, a tradition of genuine

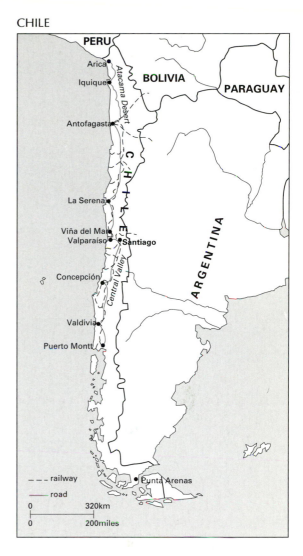

political tolerance was firmly established, the Liberals gradually displacing the Conservatives as the dominant party and Chileans of all parties coming to look on their country as the 'model republic' in Latin America.

Thanks to expanding exports of copper, silver and wheat, the value of Chile's external trade showed roughly a tenfold increase between 1825 and 1875. This export-based expansion, strongly encouraged by the government, brought signs of incipient modernization. Banking and insurance developed from the 1850s onwards. Starting in 1851, railways began to revolutionize internal transport. (By 1930, there were nearly 9000 km of track in Chile; about 65 per cent of the system was state-owned.) A modest industrial effort also got under way in the 1860s and 1870s. But economic expansion faltered very seriously in the mid-1870s, when Chile's grip on overseas markets suddenly weakened. The ensuing fiscal crisis, of great severity, coincided with a growth of international tensions, stemming from Chile's border disputes with Argentina and Bolivia. The latter dispute led to the War of the Pacific (1879–83), which pitted Chile against Bolivia and Peru: a sequence of brilliant campaigns gave the country total victory, a definite superiority complex, and possession of the Peruvian and Bolivian deserts, rich in nitrate, for which there was growing demand abroad as fertilizer. For the next half century the export of nitrates (with British interests playing a major role) provided the basis for a further cycle of economic expansion, with massive revenues accruing to the Chilean state.

In politics the 1880s saw an attack on presidential power by party politicians. A dynamic president, José Manuel Balmaceda (1840–91: president 1886–91), sought to resist this trend, but he was overwhelmed in civil war (1891). His suicide in defeat marked the start of a new 'parliamentary' period (1891–1924) in which Congress replaced the presidency as the key political element. The achievements of the 'parliamentary' governments were not negligible: transport was improved, the cities beautified, and education much expanded during these years. (In 1875, 77 per cent of the population was illiterate; by 1930 this was down to 44 per cent.) Nevertheless, the regime failed to appreciate the magnitude of the social changes which economic growth had by now induced. A swelling bureaucratic-professional middle class (the bureaucracy itself grew from around 3000 in 1880 to nearly 33,000 in 1925) and a militant labour movement, born in the cities and also in the harsh nitrate deserts, were both denied their legitimate place in the sun by the oligarchic politicians of the time. The 'social question' now began to loom large: the contrast between mass poverty and ostentatious opulence seemed to some to cry out for attention.

ALESSANDRI AND IBÁÑEZ

In 1920 a prominent 'parliamentary' politician, Arturo Alessandri (1868–1950: president 1920–5, 1932–8) was narrowly elected to power on a flamboyantly proclaimed programme of reform. The 'Lion of Tarapacá', as he was nicknamed, was the nearest thing to a 'charismatic leader' twentieth-century Chile has known; but with Congress obstructing him, his reforming plans ran rapidly into the sands. In September 1924 the hitherto quiescent military intervened, and Alessandri left the country, though a second military intervention then restored him briefly to power. He stayed long enough to push through a new Constitution (1925) which somewhat enhanced presidential powers, but his ambitions were soon thwarted by those of his minister of war, Colonel Carlos Ibáñez (1877–1960: president 1927–31, 1952–8), who subsequently established a mildly repressive dictatorship, responsible for some important administrative changes, a notable reform of the police, and various public works. The devastating impact of the Depression, however, forced General Ibáñez from power in July 1931. A brief period of near-chaos followed: it included the proclamation of a 'Socialist Republic', though this was very short-lived. At the end of 1932, Arturo Alessandri was re-elected president, and, with support from the right, succeeded in re-establishing the Chilean tradition of stability. Indeed, as a consequence of these upheavals, politics was now more representative than previously, the middle classes and even the urban working class playing a definite part from now onwards. Supplementing the 'historic' parties – Conservatives, Liberals, Radicals – new political movements took the stage in the 1930s. The Communist

THE TERRITORIAL EXPANSION OF CHILE

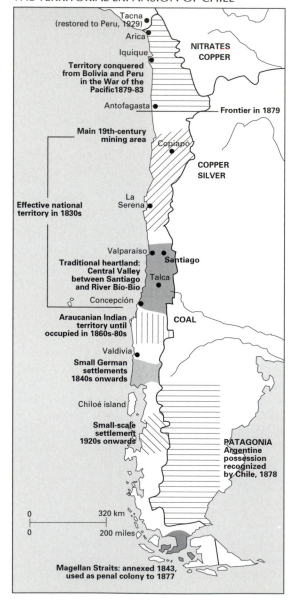

Tacna (restored to Peru, 1929)
Arica
Iquique
NITRATES
COPPER
Territory conquered from Bolivia and Peru in the War of the Pacific 1879-83
Antofagasta
Frontier in 1879
Main 19th-century mining area
Copiapó
COPPER
SILVER
Effective national territory in 1830s
La Serena
Valparaíso
Santiago
Traditional heartland: Central Valley between Santiago and River Bio-Bio
Talca
Concepción
Araucanian Indian territory until occupied in 1860s-80s
COAL
Valdivia
Small German settlements 1840s onwards
Chiloé island
Small-scale settlement 1920s onwards
PATAGONIA Argentine possession recognized by Chile, 1878

0   320 km
0   200 miles

Magellan Straits: annexed 1843, used as penal colony to 1877

Nitrates being loaded at Pisagua (from W.H.Russell, A Visit to Chile, 1890)

Party (founded under another name in 1912) and the new Socialist Party (1933) staked out a space for the Marxist left, stronger in Chile than elsewhere in Latin America. These parties, together with the powerful Radicals, joined forces in 1936 to form a Popular Front, whose candidate, the Radical Pedro Aguirre Cerda (1879–1941: president 1938–41), was narrowly elected president. This was the only Popular Front government to be formed outside Europe. A fourteen-year period (1938–52) of Radical Party ascendancy now began.

The Depression of the 1930s marked the close of Chile's 'nitrate cycle' (synthetic nitrates were now capturing world markets) and left the country in dire economic straits. The role of the state in trying to

direct the country's development had been growing since the late 1920s; it now became a key factor. The creation in 1939 of CORFO (Corporación de Fomento de la Producción, Production Development Corporation), a state development agency later imitated elsewhere in Latin America, gave a much-needed stimulus to industry over the next few years: 'import-substitution industrialization' was now seen as the most promising way forward. (Manufacturing industry experienced particularly rapid growth during the Second World War: by 1950 it accounted for nearly 17 per cent of GDP.) The great steelworks at Huachipato near Concepción (1950) and the formation of a State Technical University (1947) were further signs of this industrial effort.

TABLE 2

Chile: presidential and congressional elections, 1958–73 (percentages of the popular vote)

	1958 Pres.	1961 Congr.	1964 Pres.	1965 Congr.	1969 Cong.	1970 Pres.	1973 Cong.
Right	31.6 *Alessandri*	30.4	–	12.5	20.1	34.9 *Alessandri*	23.6
Christian democrats	20.7 *Frei*	15.4	56.1 *Frei*	42.3	29.7	27.8 *Tomic*	29.1
Radicals	15.6 *Bossay*	21.4	5.0 *Durán*	13.3	12.9	–	3.8
Marxists	28.9 *Allende*	22.1	38.9 *Allende*	22.7	28.2	36.3 *Allende*	34.8
Total vote of UP coalition					[44.2]	36.3	43.9

In congressional elections
RIGHT: combined Liberal and Conservative Party votes in 1961 and 1965, National Party (fusion of Liberals and Conservatives) vote in 1969, and combined National and Radical Democrat Party vote in 1973.
RADICALS: the official Radical Party vote only. (By 1973 the party had split into three groups.)
MARXISTS: combined votes of Socialist and Communist Parties only.
Note: the 1969 figure for UP is the combined vote of the major parties which later that year formed the UP coalition.

The third of the Radical presidents, Gabriel González Videla (1898–1980: president 1946–52) renewed his party's alliance with the left, inviting three Communists into his first cabinet. (The great poet Pablo Neruda, who had lately become a Communist, contributed a catchy ballad to his election campaign.) He later broke with his allies and outlawed the Communist Party (1948), a measure only repealed ten years later. The electorate, temporarily disillusioned with party politics, turned in 1952 to General Ibáñez, widely regarded as a providential 'general of hope'. But hope swiftly faded; the septuagenarian Ibáñez proved incapable of stemming the country's now chronic inflation or of securing stable cabinets. Party loyalties were once again well to the fore in the 1958 presidential election, which saw the narrow victory of the right-winger Jorge Alessandri (1896–1986: president 1958–64), 'the Lion's son', perhaps *personally* the most popular of recent Chilean leaders.

DEMOCRACY AND ITS DISCONTENTS

By 1960 or so many educated Chileans were uneasily aware that neither the 'export-led' expansion of the

Eduardo Frei (1911-82)

nitrate era nor state-led industrial growth after 1930 had really solved the country's most glaring economic and social problems. The economy itself was stagnating, with industry growing very slowly in the 1950s. Average per-capita income was roughly $500 in 1960, but, while a small elite of Chileans was very much better off than this, around half the population lived on $150 per year or less. Despite significant social welfare legislation, mass poverty remained highly visible. If literacy was high (84 per cent in 1960), so, too, was infant mortality. In the countryside the haciendas were still intact; at the other extreme tens (perhaps hundreds) of thousands of peasants owned holdings of less than five hectares. This agrarian structure was not efficient: ludicrously, Chile was now importing food on an increasing scale. But many Chileans were leaving the land; by 1960, in fact, 51 per cent of the population was living in towns of 20,000 inhabitants or more. As elsewhere in the region, industry was unable to absorb the newcomers, with the inevitable consequence of widespread under-employment and the formation of miserable shanty towns (*callampas*, 'mushrooms', in local slang) – most spectacularly around Santiago, the now rapidly expanding capital. A further issue which provoked comment was the vital role of copper in the economy. Three large copper mines, opened up by American corporations in the 1910s and 1920s, produced more than two-thirds of all Chile's copper, and the 'red metal' was the major earner of foreign exchange. That this fundamental national resource should be controlled by foreign interests was obvious cause for concern.

Voices advocating 'structural reforms' to regenerate Chile were therefore not lacking in the early 1960s. At the same time, politics itself was becoming steadily more democratic. Women had received the vote in 1949, and a great effort was now made to increase voter registration. (In 1938, 503,000 Chileans voted; in 1973 more than 3,600,000 did so.) Political mobilization on a large scale was to become a highly conspicuous feature of Chilean life over the next few years. It remained to be seen how well the system could cope with pressures of a kind that had been unimaginable in the simpler world of the 'model republic'. The Marxist parties, now in an alliance led by the veteran Socialist, Dr Salvador Allende (1908–73), were challenged at this point by a dynamic alternative reforming movement, the Christian Democrat Party (PDC) headed by the serious-minded Eduardo Frei (1911–82). In the 1964 presidential contest, the right withdrew from the race and swung its support to Frei, as the lesser of two evils. He won handsomely. The PDC did exceptionally well in the congressional elections of March 1965, in which the right was decimated.

Dr Salvador Allende (1908-73)

system, though at the cost of much confusion. The public sector, already large, was vastly expanded by the takeover of numerous enterprises. The pace of these changes caused widespread economic dislocation: inflation spiralled to over 500 per cent in 1973. Meanwhile, opposition to the UP government became fiercely militant, with public opinion polarizing in a tragic welter of recrimination. The hostility of the United States was manifested both openly, in the withdrawal of aid, and covertly, in the support given by the CIA to opposition groups. By mid-1973, with the latest round of congressional elections resolving nothing, Chile had reached a point of acute crisis. The outcome was perhaps avoidable – but Chilean politicians, prisoners of their own rhetoric, chose not to avoid it.

The crisis was resolved on 11 September 1973 by the devastating intervention of the armed forces. Allende died in his burning palace. The UP was crushed. Democracy was suddenly replaced by a classic police state. The stern, unbending General Augusto Pinochet (b. 1915) quickly established himself as the unchallengeable leader of the military regime. In its first years the dictatorship was relentless in its repression: tens of thousands of Chileans were killed, imprisoned, tortured or exiled, a reign of terror unparalleled in Chile's own past. In its economic stance, the new regime soon adopted an extreme laissez-faire 'model' based on large-scale

THE BREAKDOWN OF DEMOCRACY

Frei and the PDC promised a 'Revolution in Liberty', a possibly over-rhetorical slogan. In the event, they ran the most ambitious reforming government yet seen in Chile. Its achievements included the 'Chileanization' (partial control) of the American-owned copper concerns; a massive educational effort; a vigorous housing programme; the stimulation of grass-roots political activity, not least (at long last) in the countryside; and the initiation of a far-reaching agrarian reform, entailing the compensated expropriation of haciendas. The PDC reforms alienated the right, which now partially revived, while failing to satisfy the Marxist left. In 1969 the Communists, Socialists and Radicals, along with three smaller groups, combined to form a new alliance, Popular Unity (UP). In the three-cornered election of 1970, its candidate, Dr Allende, secured a narrow victory; it was his fourth attempt at the presidency. This democratic election of a Marxist president was unprecedented in world history.

Allende and the UP moved rapidly to carry out their radical programme of 'transition to socialism'. The large copper mines were now nationalized outright (1971). Agrarian reform was greatly accelerated, so bringing the effective end of the hacienda

Right
General Augusto Pinochet (b.1915)

Inauguration of President Patricio Aylwin (March 1990)

Argentina, Paraguay and Uruguay

Argentina

Area	2,776,656 sq km
Population	32.3 million
GNP per capita (1989)	$2160
Capital	Buenos Aires
Currency	Peso

'privatization' and rapid tariff liberalization. This reversed not only the policies of the UP but also much of the state-interventionist trend of recent decades. At the cost of plunging hundreds of thousands of Chileans into destitution, a harsh stabilization plan (April 1975) brought about a drastic reduction of inflation by the end of the 1970s. High growth-rates and success with 'non-traditional exports' (i.e. exports other than copper) – Chilean fruit, for instance, began to appear in British supermarkets – seemed to be heralding a more promising economic future, and the economy in fact recovered well from the serious recession of the early 1980s. In the somewhat more relaxed climate of 1980, Pinochet introduced a new constitution: among other things, this envisaged eight-year presidential terms, the first of which was taken by Pinochet himself.

By the mid-1980s opposition to the regime had become more confident and vocal. A plebiscite (October 1988) denied Pinochet a second eight-year term by 55 per cent to 43 per cent. Under the 1980 rules a presidential election had now to be held (December 1989). The winner (again by 55 per cent) was the PDC veteran Patricio Aylwin (b. 1918), the candidate of a multi-party coalition known as the Concertación. With Aylwin's inauguration (11 March 1990), Chile renewed its historic link with democracy, while politicians on all sides displayed considerable willingness to overcome the legacy of the recent past. SC

Further Reading: A. J. Bauer, *Chilean Rural Society from the Spanish Conquest to 1930* (Cambridge, 1975); H. Blakemore, 'Chile', in H. Blakemore and C. T. Smith, eds., *Latin America: Geographical Perspectives,* 2nd edition (London, 1983), pp. 457–531; B. Loveman, *Chile: the Legacy of Hispanic Capitalism* 2nd edition (New York, 1988); P. E. Sigmund, *The Overthrow of Allende and the Politics of Chile, 1964–1976* (Pittsburgh, 1977)

In the years following the Argentine declaration of independence at Tucumán on 9 July 1816, the United Provinces of the River Plate faced many obstacles in the building of a unified nation. Spread across a vast territory, Argentina's provinces had generally pastoral-oriented economies, were usually under the control of military leaders (caudillos), and were populated with untamed gauchos. Compounding the problem was the fact that the great fertile plains of the pampas were also the hunting grounds of nomadic Araucanian Indians. Within the United Provinces there was a sharp division of opinion as to whether the new republic should have a federal or centralized form of government. The centralists, known as Unitarios, were influenced by enlightened European ideas and wanted to construct a nation on liberal secular and free-trade lines; the federalists were more traditionally minded. At the same time, most interior provinces harboured the realistic suspicion that Buenos Aires, with its privileged strategic position at the mouth of the River Plate, would attempt to assert its dominance over the other provinces.

By the early 1820s, far from achieving national unity, the republic wavered on the brink of anarchy. The liberal–centralist government in Buenos Aires during the early and mid-1820s soon found its reform efforts blocked by provincial hostility. Its strongest figure, Bernardino Rivadavia (named president under the new Constitution of 1826) was obliged to resign (1827).

Out of the ensuing welter of federalist–Unitario civil war there emerged in 1829 a federalist governor in Buenos Aires, Juan Manuel de Rosas. The new leader, unlike his predecessors, enjoyed a broader base of support and had the allegiance of provincial gauchos. Rosas proved to be a strong governor who brooked little opposition from political rivals, the Unitarios above all, and actively promoted the interests of Buenos Aires over those of the interior provinces.

During the period from 1832 to 1835, Rosas relinquished his governorship in order to lead a successful military campaign to drive the Indians further to the south and west of settled areas in the province of Buenos Aires. In 1835 he returned as governor of his province with unlimited powers, setting up a strongly authoritarian (and at times terroristic) regime. At the same time, his government, entrusted with the conduct of foreign affairs, was frequently embroiled in outside conflict in the River Plate waterway and adjacent regions. By 1852, the Rosas regime was in serious trouble, faced with the implacable hostility of its Unitario enemies as well as the opposition of federalists of the interior like the Entre Ríos caudillo, Justo José de Urquiza, earlier the dictator's most devoted henchman.

In addition, a younger generation of Argentines was critical of Rosas for his failure to provide the country with a formal constitution, political freedom and economic development. On 3 February 1852 Urquiza led a combined army of interior forces, Unitarios, Uruguayan Colorados and Brazilians which defeated Rosas at the battle of Monte Caseros, obliging the dictator to spend his remaining twenty-five years in exile in England.

After the fall of Rosas, a constituent convention drew up the Constitution of 1853, and created a Confederation of which General Urquiza was the first president. The refusal of Buenos Aires to join the Confederation led to inter-provincial hostilities in 1859 and again in 1861, at which time Urquiza's army was finally defeated at the battle of Pavón by General Bartolomé Mitre. Buenos Aires and the rest of Argentina were thus finally reunited.

The long boom

National unification provided Argentina with the political stability calculated to attract the large-scale immigration and foreign capital needed to develop the republic's unrealized potential as a major foodstuff supplier of the world. This was the intention of the intellectual reformers now occupying the presidency – the greatest being Bartolomé Mitre (1862–8) and Domingo Faustino Sarmiento (1868–74) – as it was too for the conservative landowning elite of the pampas, who dominated national politics in the last quarter of the nineteenth century and the period up to the First World War. Virtually the entire pampean region was open for ranching and farming pursuits once General Julio A. Roca had finally crushed the pampa Indians in the campaign of 1879–80, opening up 390,000 sq km of land in the southern pampa,

Juan Manuel de Rosas, Argentina's supreme nineteenth-century caudillo

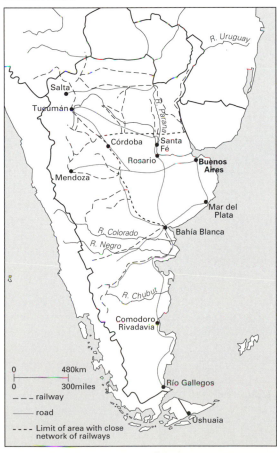

ARGENTINA

R. Uruguay
Salta
Tucumán
R. Paraná
Córdoba
Santa Fé
Rosario
Buenos Aires
Mendoza
Mar del Plata
R. Colorado
Bahía Blanca
R. Negro
R. Chubut
Comodoro Rivadavia
Río Gallegos
Ushuaia

0   480km
0   300miles

- - - railway
──── road
- - - Limit of area with close
      network of railways

most of which was acquired by a small number of landowners.

European immigration rose in the 1860s and continued to grow rapidly in succeeding decades, furnishing the manpower needed for farming and urban occupations. At the same time, the pastoral economy of the pampas underwent change and modernization with the introduction of barbed wire fencing, the sowing of alfalfa for grazing after 1872, the improvement in cattle and sheep breeds, and extensive railway construction from the 1880s onward. By the turn of the century, Argentina was a major exporter of cereal grains and meat products.

To Argentina's export-oriented economy, the economic relationship with Great Britain had a central importance. Not only was the latter a major source of investment capital and the largest foreign investor by virtue of its railway investments, but it was also by far the biggest (though by no means the only) purchaser of the nation's primary products. In particular, the livestock industry, which used the greater part of the land in the pampas, was geared towards the export of high-quality beef to the British market.

The economic expansion of Argentina was matched by demographic changes which Europeanized what had been a small and predominantly mestizo nation. Few countries witnessed such a dramatic transformation within so brief a time span, as the nation's population rose from about 1,200,000 people in 1852 to approximately 8,000,000 by 1914 thanks to the flood of European immigrants to farming areas and to the expanding cities. By 1910, three out of every four adults in the central districts of the city of Buenos Aires were European born.

In spite of these extensive social and economic changes, national political life continued to be dominated by the large landowners of the pampas who had become Latin America's wealthiest social elite. The oligarchic governments of the period relied upon an electoral system which had no provision for the secret ballot and which did not adequately represent the now rapidly expanding middle and working classes of the country. The political scene, nonetheless, was far from static in the 1890s. In 1896, Juan B. Justo, a physician and intellectual, founded the Socialist Party, a movement gaining particular strength in the city of Buenos Aires. Of far greater national significance, however, was the founding of the Unión Cívica Radical in the early 1890s by Leandro N. Alem. This party, which attracted middle-class support but appealed also to other sections of society, took up the cudgels in favour of free and honest elections. With the death of its founder in 1896, the Radical movement turned to the dour but oddly charismatic Hipólito Yrigoyen, who adopted an uncompromising stand by opting for electoral abstention as long as free male suffrage was denied.

By the early 1910s the need for an overhaul of the electoral system was widely felt. Even so, President Roque Sáenz Peña angered some of his fellow Conservatives in 1912 when he pushed through Congress an electoral reform law which at last established multi-party democracy in Argentina. As a result of the new law, Hipólito Yrigoyen became the nation's first popularly elected president in 1916. Radical dominance of the political scene was now a reality, even though the leader's hand-picked successor for president, Marcel Torcuato de Alvear, brought schism to the party by allowing the formation of an Anti-Personalist wing in an unsuccessful attempt to block Yrigoyen's presidential aspirations for a second term.

In the first three decades of the twentieth century, the Argentine economy enjoyed growth and prosperity even though it faced momentary strains caused by the trade dislocations of the First World War and the post-war depression of the early 1920s. Of course, the era of unusually dynamic growth from 1900 to 1913 had ended. In that period, capital formation reached unprecedented levels, railway building was intense and the age of refrigerated beef exports came into its own as British and American companies

Elephant house, Buenos Aires zoo, c.1900. Turn-of-the-century Argentine prosperity sometimes produced exuberantly fanciful architecture.

Ranch-hand on the Argentine pampas.

set up giant meat-packing plants in Argentina. Still, the economy had scope for continued expansion in the 1920s when grain and meat exports reached record levels and manufacturing industry showed steady growth. The long boom had given Argentina the highest levels of prosperity in Latin America.

Depression and war

The world crisis of the 1930s had far-reaching economic and political consequences for Argentina and its export-oriented economy. Fourteen years of representative democracy ended on 6 September 1930 when General José Félix Uriburu staged a military coup, overthrowing the aged President Yrigoyen, who appeared (indeed, was) incapable of dealing with the worsening economic crisis. With Yrigoyen deposed and his party in disarray, the Conservatives were able to return to power and manipulate the electoral process to their advantage. Thus, a loose alliance of National Democrats (Conservatives), Anti-Personalist Radicals and Socialists, known as the *Concordancia*, was able to hold power from 1932 to 1943 with the elections to the presidency of General Agustín P. Justo (1932–8) and Roberto Ortiz (1938–40).

To the Justo government fell the task of developing an economic recovery programme. Within beef-raising circles, wealthy ranchers in particular, there was fear in 1932 that Britain's adoption of the Imperial Preference system would imperil Argentina's access to the all-important British market. Thus, at the urging of influential landowners, the Argentine government negotiated the Roca–Runciman Treaty of 1933 in London which worked to stabilize chilled beef shipments to England in the 1930s, but at the price of offering Great Britain trade, exchange and investment concessions, some of which were bitterly resented by nationalist opinion during this decade and afterwards. The Justo administration made the treaty relationship with Britain the cornerstone of a successful national recovery programme, largely aimed at restoring the economic health of an agrarian sector highly dependent upon overseas markets. The overall thrust of that programme went much farther and included among other things the rehabilitation of the nation's financial system, the construction of a modern highway system and the expansion of those segments of manufacturing industry using domestic raw materials.

While Argentina staged a quicker recovery from the Great Depression than most countries, the *Concordancia* economic programme was never able to recreate the rapid growth or the prosperity experienced before 1930, nor were the burdens of the Depression equally shared by all sectors and groups; moreover, the nation remained profoundly troubled by the disturbed state of world trade and the outbreak of the Second World War in Europe. Within Argentina opinion was divided between pro-Allied and neutralist sentiments, with the government of President Ramón S. Castillo (1940–3) taking the latter line. With the prospect that the *Concordancia* would select as its presidential candidate a wealthy pro-British landowner, the army ousted Castillo on 4 June 1943 and took over the government.

Perón

The military governments under General Pedro Ramírez in 1943–4 and General Edelmiro J. Farrell after 1944 introduced a series of social, educational and labour measures designed to curry the favour of the trade unions, the industrial work force and the Catholic Church. Increasingly, it was evident that the rising star of the military government was the Minister of War and head of the Secretariat of Labour and Social Welfare, Colonel Juan Domingo Perón (1895–1974), who took the lead in helping the trade unions to organize and expand. Within the short span of two years, Perón raised the proportion of unionized labour from 10 per cent to roughly two-thirds of the total work force.

The meteoric rise of Colonel Perón caused alarm in civilian (and some military) circles as well as in the United States where he was considered to be potentially totalitarian and pro-Axis. A faction within the military even went so far as to arrest him; however, the colonel's labour supporters organized a massive

General Juan Domingo Perón (1895–1974), and Eva Duarte de Perón, 'Evita' (1919–52)

demonstration on 17 October 1945 and the Farrell government instantly released him, to the jubilation of his adherents. In 1946 Perón stood for president and defeated decisively the Radical Party politician José P. Tamborini, who was backed by a coalition of Radicals, Socialists, Communists and Progressive Democrats.

In office, Perón created a powerful political organization and introduced measures designed to redistribute income in favour of wage earners, to promote greater industrialization and to nationalize foreign-owned public utilities. At the same time, Perón's ambitious and charismatic second wife, Eva Duarte de Perón, proved to be a major political force in her own right through her close links with the trade union movement, her charitable activities associated with the Eva Perón Foundation and her involvement with the cause of women's suffrage, which was finally sanctioned in 1947. Her death at the age of 33 on 26 July 1952 was a serious blow to the Perón regime.

In terms of accomplishments and the general cohesion of Perón's movement, the years from 1946 to 1949 were probably the high-water mark of the government. The early 1950s, however, were times of great difficulties, in part due to an economic crisis in 1951–2 fuelled by rising inflation, poor agricultural production and lagging economic growth. From 1953 onwards, Perón, already in his second presidential term, began to temper the thrust of his economic and social policies by focusing more attention on obtaining higher productivity and foreign investment. At the same time, the regime's relations with the Church deteriorated, thereby augmenting the discontent present in sectors of the middle class and the armed forces as well as among the landed elite. The gathering political crisis came to a head in June 1955 when units of the armed forces staged an abortive coup, but later, in September, they launched a more powerful insurrection, forcing Perón to flee into exile. Argentina's new rulers declared the Peronist Party illegal and made its leaders and high government appointees ineligible to hold office.

The failure of de-Peronization

Argentina's military government from 1955 to 1958, initially under General Eduardo Lonardi and then under the presidency of General Pedro E. Aramburu, faced diverse tasks such as the control of inflation, the revitalization of the neglected export sector, the attraction of investment funds to promote capital-intensive industries and the return of the country to civilian rule. National elections were held in 1958 in which Dr Arturo Frondizi, the leader of the Intransigent Radical Party and an advocate of reintegrating the Peronists into the political process, won the presidency.

Frondizi preached a policy of 'developmentalism' and assigned a prominent role to foreign capital in developing different areas such as the motor car industry and petroleum production. But doubts about his political reliability lingered within sectors of the armed forces, whose patience was finally exhausted when neo-Peronist parties were able to participate and gain victories in the provincial elections of 1962. Thus, on 28 March 1962, the military in a bloodless coup removed Frondizi from office and appointed in his place José María Guido, the president of the senate. In the national elections of 1963, Dr Arturo Illia of the People's Radical Party gained the presidency, but his government, too, was for no very apparent reason overturned in June 1966 by the armed forces who designated General Juan Carlos Onganía president, with wide-ranging powers.

The Onganía government had long-term authoritarian rule in mind, but was in power at a time when the universities were heavily politicized and when young Peronist groups were starting to show greater militancy towards the anti-Peronist administrations. One of the first acts of the new military regime was its heavyhanded (and gratuitous) intervention in university affairs. In the economic sphere, Minister of Finance Adalberto Krieger Vasena initiated in 1967 a major economic programme designed to achieve monetary stability, to create a domestic capital market and to stimulate economic development by augmenting the production of steel, electric power, road building and housing. In time labour and student groups reacted adversely to the austerity features of the Krieger Vasena plan, and in May 1969 militant workers and students staged a brief insurrection in the industrial city of Córdoba which had to be put down by the army. The uprising in Córdoba led to the resignation of the Finance Minister, and was followed later on, in 1971 and 1972, by more limited labour protests in other cities of the interior.

Internal opposition had left the Onganía government without any credible economic policies. In addition, the political climate became more charged in 1970 when former President Pedro Aramburu was kidnapped and killed by a group of young Peronists who called themselves the Montoneros. With increasing doubts as to the government's ability to dominate events, the armed forces ousted Onganía in June 1970 and replaced him with General Robert Levingston, himself deposed in March 1971 in favour of General Alejandro Lanusse, the new 'strongman' of the Argentine army.

During its period in office the Lanusse government was heir to mounting political and economic difficulties. 'De-Peronization' had proved impossible. Argentina witnessed a growing campaign of kidnappings and terrorist violence from Peronist and extreme left-wing groups. To find a way out of an increasingly dangerous predicament, the Lanusse regime gambled on a return to constitutional rule. Eventually, the military government permitted free elections in March 1973 with the participation of the Peronist Party, although Juan Perón's candidacy for the presidency was disallowed on a technicality. In the election, Héctor Cámpora, a loyal Peronist with good links throughout the entire movement including extreme left groups, was elected president. So began the Peronist Restoration.

Peronist Restoration and its failure

Unable to stop the guerrilla violence or to heal the deep divisions within the Peronist movement, Cámpora soon resigned from the presidency in order to make way for the assumption of that post by Juan Perón, who finally returned to Argentina in June 1973. In the special election of 23 September 1973, Perón received over 60 per cent of the vote with his third wife, María Estela (Isabel) Martínez de Perón, as vice-president. The new president faced daunting political and economic problems. An attempt was made to control inflation through a 'social compact' wherein labour and business agreed to wage-price restraint. There was no headway, however, in ending the wave of kidnappings or killings by urban guerrilla forces or in moderating the growing factional violence between the extreme left and extreme right in the Peronist movement. Perón sided with the more orthodox and conservative sectors of his large and heterogeneous political following; however, he stopped short of ordering an all-out war against the rebellious guerrilla organizations defying his authority.

The 78-year-old president, who was in delicate health, died on 1 July 1974 and was succeeded by his wife, Isabel Perón, Latin America's first female head of state. The unity of the Peronist movement, precarious as it was, disintegrated with the death of its founder as right-wing and left-wing factions engaged in a struggle for power. Furthermore, a rightist death squad established by the Ministry of Social Welfare headed by José López Rega, the Argentine Anti-Communist Alliance, or Triple-A (AAA), began to hunt down and murder persons suspected of extreme leftist sympathies within and outside the Peronist movement.

Throughout its period in power, the government of Isabel Perón proved incapable of coping with the worsening economic and political situation. Inflation went out of control and, by mid-1975, Argentina was at the top of the world inflation league as the consumer price index rose 335 per cent in 1975 and 364 per cent in 1976. In both years the total output of goods and services declined. Government efforts to introduce austerity measures and to restrict wage increases met a chilly response from trade union leaders, who took the unusual action of declaring strikes against a Peronist regime.

The evident failure of the Peronist Restoration gave the military yet another pretext for intervention. When the Montoneros attacked an army base in Formosa province in October 1975, the army demanded and received wide powers to engage in a total war against the well-armed guerrilla forces and, in the succeeding months, the military stepped up significantly its anti-insurgency operations. The armed forces believed that resolute action was needed to forestall the outbreak of a full-scale civil war. Accordingly, on 24 March 1976, the military carried out a coup deposing Isabel Perón and placing her under house arrest. A three-man junta representing the army, navy and air force took charge of the government headed by General Jorge Videla, who was later designated president.

Military rule, 1976-83

Two priorities of special importance to the military were to crush the guerrilla threat and to cure the nation's inflation-ridden and ailing economy. The new Minister of the Economy, José Alfredo Martínez de Hoz, introduced measures to bring down the high rate of inflation and to free areas of the economy from state control or regulation. At the same time, the new economic team, installed in 1976, signalled its intention of transforming the Argentine economy by increasing the economic efficiency of domestic industry, by opening up the economy to international competition and by reducing, when possible, state participation in productive activities.

Military authorities tackled the guerrilla problem by unleasing a campaign known as the 'dirty war' in which tough counter-insurgency methods were employed – often indiscriminately. The initial months of anti-guerrilla operations produced immediate successes. By 1978, the capacity of the several guerrilla groups to wage armed attacks was seriously curtailed. The tactics used in the 'dirty war' exposed Argentina to widespread international censure for its extensive human rights violations.

The military's success in curbing the guerrilla threat was not matched in the sphere of economic policy. While inflation was reduced between 1976 and 1979, the overall rate remained uncomfortably in the general vicinity of about 100 per cent per annum. Economic growth from year to year alternated

between positive and negative rates. Furthermore, by 1980 the general liquidity of the banking and industrial sectors was a source of serious concern.

In March 1981, General Videla handed over the presidency to General Roberto Viola. New economic measures specially tailored to relieve a depressed industrial sector, however, proved singularly ineffective against the backdrop of a worsening recession in Argentina as well as the world economy. But in any case, Viola's ill-health led in November 1981 to his replacement by General Leopoldo Galtieri, an ambitious right-wing nationalist.

Galtieri faced in his initial months in office not only a steadily deteriorating economy but also increasing militancy from the trade union movement, which was at last beginning to challenge the restrictions imposed upon it in 1976. On 30 March 1982, the outlawed General Confederation of Labour organized a mass demonstration in the Plaza de Mayo in Buenos Aires, which produced a clash between the police and demonstrators and which caused many arrests. To contain the spreading worker unrest and to foster a greater measure of popularity, the military junta on 2 April 1982 launched a surprise invasion of the British-held Falkland Islands (Islas Malvinas). As the junta had calculated, repossession of the disputed islands electrified the nation and brought forth, albeit temporarily, a show of unity rare in the annals of the country's post-1945 history. Virtually the entire nation applauded the bold military stroke, and General Galtieri and his military associates enjoyed a sudden rush of popularity in a period of high nationalistic fervour.

During the next two and a half months national attention was riveted upon the confrontation with Britain. The national pride engendered by the reconquest of the Islas Malvinas, however, suffered a severe blow in June 1982 when the British task force re-established complete control of the islands. A shocked and stunned nation began to vent its anger at the military, with the army badly discredited by its incompetent performance. Galtieri was rapidly removed from his twin posts of president and commander in chief of the army.

The restoration of democracy

Defeat in the South Atlantic War ushered in a political crisis almost unparalleled in Argentina's modern history. The army selected one of its own officers as head of state, retired general Reynaldo Bignone (22 June 1982). With the Argentine economy adversely affected by the war, and with mounting civilian pressure for a restoration of democracy, his task was far from easy. In spite of all the problems, President Bignone established a political dialogue with the so-called 'Multipartidaria', a multi-party commission

representing the largest political parties of the land, namely the Peronists, the Radicals, the Intransigent Party, the Christian Democrats and the Movement of Integration and Development. In the end, the military junta was obliged to yield ground to the collective opposition. President Bignone (at the end of February 1983) dispelled all uncertainty when he announced that general elections would be held on 30 October 1983. The military, in effect, were capitulating to popular opinion.

The establishment of a firm election date sparked off frenetic political activity as the major parties in particular campaigned vigorously to expand their membership rolls as well as to prepare for their presidential nominating conventions. The Radical Party united around Raúl Alfonsín, a 56-year-old lawyer and politician who had fired the imagination of many Argentines with his forthright position on human rights as well as his opposition to the South Atlantic conflict. The disunited and faction-ridden Peronist movement, on the other hand, experienced far greater difficulties in agreeing upon its leader and presidential candidate. After a short but turbulent party assembly, the Peronist party selected a compromise candidate, Italo Argentino Luder, a moderate 66-year-old constitutional lawyer.

The elections of 30 October 1983 produced a historic result as Raúl Alfonsín and his resurgent Radical Party convincingly defeated the Peronist opposition by winning the presidency, outright control of the Chamber of Deputies and a respectable number of provincial governorships. For the first time in forty years the Peronist movement was defeated in a free election. Dr Alfonsín was inaugurated as president in December 1983.

Two of Alfonsín's objectives were of paramount importance: the full restoration and consolidation of democracy and the attainment of economic stability and growth. An array of problems, however, faced this administration. While not seeking confrontation, Alfonsín's avowed intention to institute economic and trade union reforms, along with his refusal to absolve the armed forces from human rights abuses during their time in power, only heightened antagonism towards the government from military and trade union leaders. Relations between the government and the armed forces deteriorated further once he gave way to public opinion and sanctioned the trial and conviction of top military junta officers for 'dirty war' crimes. That action, coupled with measures to trim military spending, created such resentment in the officer corps that Alfonsín faced serious unrest in the armed forces and occasional rebellions which forced the government to make embarrassing concessions.

The struggle to stabilize the economy by bringing inflation under control proved to be an unremitting battle. The Alfonsín government tried vainly to gain the support of foreign creditors for the rescheduling of the foreign debt on terms favourable to Argentina, but without the imposition of a tough IMF-style stabilization programme likely to anger the electorate. However, a stabilization programme was finally fashioned in 1985, the Plan Austral, which lowered but failed to eliminate the nation's stubborn inflation that later spiralled even further out of control in 1988.

During Alfonsín's final year in office in 1989, the economic and political horizon for the Radical government was bleak. Its economic strategy was in tatters thanks to hyperinflation. In the presidential elections of May 1989, the Peronist candidate, Carlos Menem, decisively defeated the Radicals led by Eduardo Angeloz. With the economy near collapse, Alfonsín astounded the nation and the president-elect by resigning from office on 8 July 1989, five months before the official end of his presidency. A stunned Carlos Menem hastily took over the reins of government against the backdrop of an appalling economic crisis.

From the outset, the flamboyant and unpredictable Peronist president surprised both the nation and his own party by giving business interests a prominent role in the formulation of economic policy. Eschewing more traditional policy actions such as greater state intervention and income redistribution, Menem preferred a more pragmatic course, emphasizing the fight against inflation and the privatization of state-owned enterprises. The drive to restore the nation's monetary stability acquired great urgency in 1989, as inflation reached a record annual level of 4923 per cent. Austerity policies and the inability of a succession of economy ministers to end the severe economic crisis helped to erode the great popularity that Menem had enjoyed in the initial part of his presidency. Within the military establishment, disaffected officers plotted openly against the President and an unsuccessful mutiny was staged in December 1990. Menem made a major concession to the military at the end of 1990 by pardoning the imprisoned junta officers, an action roundly criticized in civilian circles.

By 1991 the Menem government had a decidedly beleaguered look. While inflation was on a down-ward course (1343 per cent in 1990), the economy was still gripped by stagflation. While Alfonsín and Menem, between them, have presided over the longest continuous period of democracy in Argentina since the 1920s, no magic formula has yet been found to arrest the nation's long-term decline and to capitalize once again on its abundant natural resources. Argentina, Latin America's outstanding early twentieth-century success-story, in the 1990s presents a real challenge to its policymakers and people.

PARAGUAY

Area	406,752 sq km
Population	4.3 million
GNP per capita (1989)	$1030
Capital	Asunción
Currency	Guaraní

Dictatorships and wars

In contrast to many of the Spanish American nations, Paraguay achieved independence from Spain without great bloodshed or prolonged conflict. Initially, the people of the territory refused to heed the call of the Argentine revolutionaries to join the struggle against Spanish authority, and they actually repulsed an army of liberation sent from Buenos Aires in December 1810. Nonetheless, Paraguayan patriots eventually took action on their own, in May and June 1811, deposing the Spanish governor, severing the links with Spain and appointing a junta to rule the new republic.

From the junta emerged a leader by 1814 with the will to build a Paraguayan nation, Dr José Gaspar Rodríguez de Francia, known as El Supremo. Dr Francia took on the character of a populist dictator and sealed off Paraguay from the outside world by prohibiting movement in and out of the country. With foreign trade allowed to stagnate, El Supremo channelled the energies of the nation into the development of domestic activities, particularly cattle raising and agriculture for internal consumption.

The death of Francia in 1840 without an obvious successor created political uncertainty; however, a new leader, Carlos Antonio López, came to the fore in 1844 to become Paraguay's first constitutionally designated president. While less stern than his predecessor, López ruled autocratically and used his office to become the foremost landowner and cattle owner. The new president ended the country's self-imposed isolation and opened up Paraguay to external influences such as trade, immigration and foreign technicians. Paraguay's more outward-looking policies ran

Dr José Gasper Rodríguez de Francia, 'El Supremo' (1766–1840), Paraguayan dictator 1814–40

afoul of the designs of the Rosas government in Argentina, which had closed the River Plate to Paraguayan commerce, and thus López from 1845 sided with the enemies of the Buenos Aires strong man. The eventual fall of Rosas had important implications for Paraguay, as the new leader of the Argentine Confederation, Justo José de Urquiza, renounced in effect any Argentine claim to sovereignty over the nation by recognizing its independence in 1852.

Upon the death of Carlos Antonio López in 1862, the leader's son and vice-president, Francisco Solano López, became president. López, an admirer of Napoleon, came to power determined to make his country's weight felt in the River Plate region. When Brazilian forces intervened in Uruguay in 1864, the decision of the Paraguayan leader to attack Brazil by crossing through Argentine soil only succeeded in uniting the governments of Argentina, Brazil and Uruguay against him, triggering off the War of the Triple Alliance, which lasted from 1865 to 1870. Paraguay was quickly forced back upon the defensive in 1865 and had to mobilize ultimately the entire male population from adolescents to the elderly. Gradually, the allied forces broke through the tenacious Paraguayan defensive redoubts and captured the capital city of Asunción by January 1869. The war ended in March 1870 with the defeat and death of López at Cerro Corá.

The War of the Triple Alliance left Paraguay with a bitter legacy. Not only was the economy in ruins, but the male population had been reduced by ninetenths, making the country (for a generation) a land of women and small children. Paraguay remained under foreign occupation until 1876, with some of its territory annexed.

From 1870 onward, in theory, Paraguay operated under a new constitution, but in practice it entered a new era of chronic political instability as few governments were immune to the threat of uprising or overthrow. Two important political parties were founded in 1887, the conservative Colorado Party and the Liberal Party which first tasted the fruits of power in 1904, becoming the strongest political force. In the decades after 1870, both the economy and population recovered from the catastrophe of war, and a small inflow of immigrants from Spain, Italy, Germany and Argentina made considerable impact on the nation's agrarian and forestry industries.

But national attention could not remain focused merely upon internal matters, as the territorial dispute with Bolivia over the sparsely populated Chaco region now took on growing importance. During the first decade of the twentieth century both Paraguay and Bolivia began to increase their military garrisons in the area. Small army units of the two countries clashed in 1928, and a full-scale war erupted in the

PARAGUAY

Chaco in 1932. Under the able command of General José Félix Estigarribia, the Paraguayan army drove the Bolivians from much of the disputed territory, but the belligerents were thoroughly exhausted and agreed to a cease-fire in 1935. The eventual peace treaty of 1938, signed at the Buenos Aires peace conference, awarded Paraguay about three-quarters of the area in contention in the Chaco.

The new strong men

While a rallying point for the nation, the Chaco War did unleash new forces in the political life of Paraguay. Thirty-two years of Liberal Party rule ended on 17 February 1936 when a group of disgruntled army officers and anti-Liberal politicians overthrew President Eusebio Ayala and appointed Colonel Rafael Franco head of the government. The new president, who was imbued with nationalist and reformist ideas, was in turn deposed by a military revolt in 1937; nevertheless, Franco and his followers, later to be called Febreristas, constituted a reform-minded movement attracting support from student and labour groups, such as they were. The Liberal Party regained control of the government once more when the war hero Estigarribia stood under its banner and won the presidency in 1939. Estigarribia, worried about the social and political climate, assumed temporary dictatorial power in 1940 and obtained the electorate's approval for a new con-

stitution which concentrated all authority in the hands of the executive branch. But the life of the hero of the Chaco was tragically cut short by an aeroplane crash in 1940, and General Higinio Morínigo was designated interim president.

Morínigo, to the surprise of the army officers and Liberals who had installed him as head of state, took on dictatorial powers and restricted political activity for most of his years in office from 1940 to 1948. He experimented briefly with a coalition government in 1946 with Febrerista and Colorado elements, but in the following year he had to put down a bloody civil war initiated by Liberals and Febreristas which left the economy in shambles.

Morínigo gave way to Juan Natalicio González who triumphed in the presidential election of 1948. Neither González nor his immediate successors remained in office very long, but in 1949 the leader of the Colorado Party, Dr Federico Chávez, became a provisional president. Chávez contested and won the presidential election of 1953; however, he was removed from his post by the military coup of 1954 which brought to power the then army commander-in-chief, General Alfredo Stroessner.

Relying on a power base of the army and the Colorado Party, General Stroessner fashioned the longest and most durable regime in the country's history. Initially, he imposed tight restrictions on political activity and found it necessary to repel a series of raids in 1959 and 1960 by exile groups operating from Argentina. But from the 1960s on, the Stroessner government permitted a limited degree of opposition while managing the nation's political scene so that the traditional parties were not able to challenge (in any realistic sense) the dominant position of the Colorado Party. President Stroessner himself, re-elected without trouble at regular intervals, was already Latin America's longest-serving ruler by the 1970s.

During Stroessner's decades in power, Paraguay devoted considerable attention to developing an economy largely oriented towards the production and processing of farm, ranch and forestry products. The state, utilizing foreign loans and aid, engaged in an extensive programme of road building, the expansion of the national merchant marine, the improvement of air facilities and the construction of hydroelectric power plants. Following orthodox and conservative economic policies aimed at maintaining a strong and stable national currency, the Stroessner government in the 1960s and early 1970s opted for moderate economic growth and the gradual industrialization of activities processing domestic raw materials.

In the 1970s, however, the economic circumstances of Paraguay underwent a change thanks to

General Alfredo Stroessner (b.1912), Paraguayan dictator 1954–89

the decision of President Stroessner to undertake, at Brazil's urging, the binational development of the Itaipú hydroelectric project on the Paraná River, one of the largest civil engineering works of this century. The project, which started in 1973, stimulated throughout the rest of the 1970s and the first two years of the 1980s an unprecedented economic boom, expanding the domestic construction industry, providing much employment and producing a massive inflow of foreign currency into the nation's small financial market. From 1976 to 1981, the Paraguayan economy registered one of the highest growth rates in the world, more than 10 per cent per annum, but it became exposed for the first time since the 1950s to a taste of moderately strong inflation. Industrial growth accelerated as did unionization in a trade union movement which the Stroessner government had always sought to control.

The winding down of the Itaipú dam construction project, the delays in the start-up of the similar but small Yacyretá hydroelectric project with Argentina and the political and economic troubles in the important Argentine market all cast shadows on national economic activity as Paraguay's economic growth plunged to an estimated 1.6 per cent in 1982. Also contributing was the worldwide recession which struck in 1981.

With a more sobering economic panorama from 1982 onward, the Stroessner government was confronted with a more restive political scene. The president, however, put an end to conjectures about his political intentions by campaigning and winning his seventh term. In the elections of February 1983, Stroessner obtained 91 per cent of the vote in the usual way; opposition parties boycotted the elections.

From 1983 onwards, the Stroessner government experienced especially testing times. The growing problem of landless peasants and the less robust economic conditions of the decade raised concerns, but it was in the political arena that the government encountered the greatest turbulence. For the first time in many years, unauthorized opposition political rallies were held in Asunción during 1984 and 1985. The dominant Colorado Party was now badly divided, so that by 1987 an open rift had developed between the more reform-minded traditionalists and the militants with close links to Stroessner.

Faced with a heightened challenge to his political authority, the ageing dictator clamped down harder upon the organs of public opinion and tried unsuccessfully to contain the splits in the Colorado Party. With uncertainty about the durability of the regime growing even after its eighth re-election in 1988, and with renewed speculation about the question of presidential succession, the second-in-command of the armed forces, General Andrés Rodríguez, initiated a military rebellion in February 1989 which toppled Stroessner from power, thereby ending a 34-year dictatorship. National elections were held very swiftly (May 1989) and Rodríguez, who headed the Colorado Party ticket, was elected president by an ample majority in an election judged to be the freest since the early 1950s, even though the ruling Colorado Party had a considerable in-built advantage.

In just a few months, President Rodríguez restored press freedoms and began a process of political liberalization. He announced a commitment to democratic transformation of Paraguay through political reform, free elections and constitutional reform. While acknowledging the need of measures to aid landless peasants and the growing urban poor, the new administration acted to implement mildly expansionistic economic measures and moved to create a more open economy by unifying the exchange rate, by reducing selected import tariffs, and by removing some import restrictions. Post-Stroessner Paraguay has thus seen a significant opening in both political and economic terms. The road to confirmed democracy may not prove an easy one, but it is doubtful whether most Paraguayans would wish to revert to the days of the 'strong men' of the past.

URUGUAY

Area	186,926 sq km
Population	3.1 million
GNP per capita (1989)	$2620
Capital	Montevideo
Currency	Peso

Uruguay achieved nationhood in 1828 in part through the diplomatic efforts of the British government, whose mediation brought to an end the conflict between Brazil and Argentina over the territory. For many decades thereafter, the new republic had the character of a buffer state which was neither politically stable nor free of outside interference. It was a sparsely populated land with a rudimentary economy geared to stockraising and with only about a quarter of its 60,000 or so inhabitants living in the port and capital city of Montevideo.

The lawless nineteenth century

Under the constitution adopted in 1830, Fructuoso Rivera became the first president. He relinquished power in 1835 to his elected successor Manuel Oribe, but later organized a revolt against the incumbent. This civil war between the partisans of Rivera and Oribe had historic significance as it laid the basis for

URUGUAY

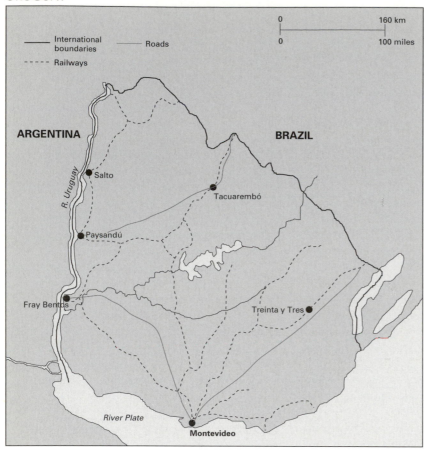

the eventual formation of the two political parties destined to dominate national politics in the nineteenth and twentieth centuries, the Colorados and the Blancos. Rivera's Colorado forces, with the aid of Argentine Unitarios, obliged Oribe and fellow Blancos to take refuge in Argentina under the protection of the dictator Juan Manuel de Rosas.

The fierce Colorado–Blanco rivalry had international ramifications. Oribe's followers, strongly backed by troops of Rosas, besieged the Colorado-controlled city of Montevideo from 1843 to 1852. Even outside maritime powers such as Britain and France found themselves drawn into the conflict occurring in the River Plate waterway. During the nine-year siege of Uruguay's most important commercial centre, pastoral and general economic activity stagnated.

With Rosas's fall from power in Argentina in 1852, the siege of Montevideo was lifted, leaving the Colorados in full control of the country. Their hold remained precarious as a result of the opposition of the Blancos as well as frequent divisions within their own ranks. At the same time, external forces continued to be the arbiters of national destiny. The Colorado leader General Venancio Flores requested Brazil's assistance in the 1850s to protect his presidency and again in 1865 when his forces combined with Brazilian troops to enter Montevideo and topple the government of President Atanasio Aguirre. This latter action so angered the ruler of Paraguay, Francisco Solano López, that it provided the catalyst for the War of the Triple Alliance, pitting Argentina, Brazil and Uruguay against Paraguay.

Flores's assumption of power in 1865 marked the beginning of uninterrupted Colorado political control of the government extending well into the twentieth century. Even so, political turmoil continued to be the rule, with numerous presidents ousted in revolutions occurring in the last three decades of the nineteenth century.

Montevideo, Uruguay in the 1850s, in a painting by Augusto Borget

José Batlle y Ordóñez (1856–1929), reforming president of Uruguay

While very prone to political instability and civil insurrections, Uruguay after 1870 was no longer just a lawless frontier society. In that year, barbed wire was first introduced to fence off livestock ranges. During the 1870s, the social and educational reformer José Varela was instrumental in convincing the government of Lorenzo Latorre to modernize the nation's educational system and introduce universal education. Immigrants had begun to flow into Uruguay in increasing numbers, so that by 1872 one-quarter of the population was foreign born. Economic changes of importance were soon under way as a railway system under the direction of British interests took shape.

Even in the political sphere the warring Colorados and Blancos were beginning to move towards an accommodation of their differences. After the civil war of 1896, the two factions struck a compromise whereby the Blancos gained control of six of the nation's departments while the Colorados were entitled to control the remaining twelve departments. At the turn of the century, therefore, Uruguay was on the threshold of political and economic stability. Large-scale foreign investment went into infrastructure and productive activities, and the construction of the first refrigerated meat-packing plant in 1904 heralded the demise of the salted beef industry and the onset of modern operations processing frozen, chilled and tinned meats for the external market.

The growth of democracy

Uruguay's transition in the early twentieth century from a strife-ridden society to a stable, prosperous nation owed much to a far-sighted Colorado politician, José Batlle y Ordóñez. His influence as president (1903–7 and 1911–15), as well as the force of his ideas on his contemporaries, laid the foundations for a modern, democratic society and for Latin America's first welfare state. Batlle's reforms extended across a wide range of political, social and economic matters. Impressed with the Swiss form of government, he persuaded the Colorado and Blanco parties in 1919 to modify the constitution and to create a plural executive system whereby the president shared his power with a National Council of Administration composed of nine councillors, six from the majority party and three from the opposition party. Extensive social and labour legislation was put on the statute books, including better and shorter work conditions as well as generous medical and pension benefits. State intervention in the economy grew, often at the expense of foreign capital, and public monopolies were authorized to run the electric power network, the telephone system, domestic insurance operations, mortgage banking, the port administration and other diverse activities. The ideas and reforms of Batlle transformed most aspects of national life. Furthermore, Uruguay now enjoyed a good standard of living, with much of the country's prosperity deriving from an export-oriented economy devoted principally to the production of meat and wool products.

The nation faced considerable economic hardship in the Great Depression of the 1930s. In addition, President Gabriel Terra in 1933 circumvented the constitution by taking on special executive powers and ruled as a virtual dictator until he was succeeded by his brother-in-law, General Alfredo Baldomir, the winner of the presidential elections of 1938. Baldomir showed contradictory constitutional tendencies by first postponing the national elections scheduled for February 1942, but then allowing the elections of November 1942 which restored the country to a democratic footing. Later on, in 1951, the electorate voted to abolish the presidency altogether and create a plural executive office known as the National Council of Government, which was composed of nine members, six belonging to the party receiving the most votes and three to the party polling the second largest number of votes. This, for Latin America, was a unique experiment.

The eclipse and return of democracy

In the 1950s the nation's revamped system of government faced formidable economic challenges. High rates of inflation, poor economic growth, stagnant exports of meat and wool products, a less than dynamic manufacturing industry and the problems of funding public expenditures all put great strains upon the operation of Uruguay's welfare state.

General dissatisfaction among the electorate culminated in 1958 with the victory of the Blancos, now known as the National Party, who ended ninety-three years of rule by the Colorado Party. Nevertheless, the Blancos, with their conservative and rural bias, were themselves defeated in the 1966 elections when the Colorados staged a comeback. In that election, also, the voters sanctioned a return to the presidential system and put into office General Oscar Gestido, who became president in 1967, but he died in the same year and was succeeded by Jorge Pacheco Areco.

Progressively in the 1960s, the attention of the country was directed to the emergence of what was to become Latin America's best-known urban guerrilla organization, the Movement of National Liberation, more popularly known as the Tupamaros. This movement, which attracted students, professional people, bureaucrats and others, taunted the government and the police with a series of bank robberies, bombings, temporary seizures of business properties and kidnappings of influential citizens and foreigners, including the British ambassador, Mr (later Sir) Geoffrey Jackson (1971).

With civil authorities making little headway in the fight against the Tupamaros, President Pacheco turned to the military in 1971 in a desperate attempt to smash the guerrilla organization. His presidential successor, Juan M. Bordaberry, who won office as the leading Colorado candidate in the 1971 elections, declared a state of 'internal war' in April 1972. During 1972, the armed forces in a relentless counter-insurgency campaign broke the back of the guerrilla movement, with members or sympathizers imprisoned or forced to flee the country.

Although decisively crippling the Tupamaros, the armed forces showed no disposition to recede into the background. On the contrary, they exerted pressure on President Bordaberry in February 1973 to create a National Council of Security composed of both civilian and military members to deal with matters of security and economic development. In particular, the military wanted the executive branch to embark upon a programme of economic reforms, to root out corruption in government and to monitor the operations of the public administration. With a confrontation looming with the national legislature, President Bordaberry dissolved Congress in June 1973 in a move that soon led to restrictions on political, student and trade union activities. Over a period of time members of different left-wing organizations were arrested. Furthermore, a Council of State was created to assume the legislative function and to rule the country by decree.

While the head of state remained a civilian, a junta of generals and admirals became the real wielders of power. The security forces continued to have free rein for their arbitrary and unchecked repressive activities. In 1976, the military obliged Bordaberry to resign; Alberto Demichelli was appointed as interim president, but he was replaced in the same year by Aparicio Méndez who was to serve as president until 1981. In December 1980, Uruguay held a plebiscite to decide upon a constitutional reform guaranteeing the armed forces a role in national decision making; however, the electorate defiantly rejected the proposal. In August 1981, the Council of State appointed General Gregorio Alvarez president for a three-and-a-half-year term beginning in September 1981.

General Alvarez's government had to grapple with a deteriorating economy in 1981 and 1982 caused to a large extent by the world recession and also the economic downturn in neighbouring Argentina. It was also confronted with the question of charting a return to constitutional rule, an issue which the new president acknowledged in his first speech on taking office.

On 3 June 1982 the Council of State approved a law providing for internal party elections for the following November designed, among other things, to select party officials who would then be in a position to choose presidential and congressional candidates in national elections scheduled for November 1984.

These internal elections furnished once more a rebuff to the government's political aims as candidates critical of military rule gained more votes than the pro-administration politicians. Undeterred by the result, in May 1983, the nation's military rulers began a dialogue with the two main political parties in an effort to work out the details of the elections to be held in the following year. There were several difficult episodes over the next few months, but the 'negotiated' return to democracy eventually succeeded. The first national elections in thirteen years were duly held in November 1984.

With the undisputed leaders of the Blancos and the left-wing Frente Amplio (Broad Front), Wilson Ferreira Aldunate and General Liber Seregni respectively, barred by the military from leading their parties, Julio Sanguinetti's moderate faction of the Colorado Party won the largest popular vote, but it was to be a minority government without a parliamentary majority.

A strong advocate of national reconciliation, President Sanguinetti inherited an economy in the throes of stagflation and with a large per-capita foreign debt to service. Tricky political tasks had to be addressed, such as the full restoration of political party activity as well as the issue of military accountability for acts of repression in the 1970s. In the latter case, Sanguinetti's action in backing an amnesty law in 1986 proved controversial and led ultimately to a national referendum in 1989, which narrowly supported the government view that the book should be closed on the military's human rights violations.

In Sanguinetti's presidential term little headway was made in tackling the nation's stagflation, even though, on balance, economic growth was somewhat better in the second half of the decade. Normal political activity was restored, however, and, in the first truly free election since 1971, Luis Alberto Lacalle's faction of the Blanco Party stunned the Colorados in the national election of 1989 by winning the presidency with 22 per cent of the popular vote. Undoubtedly the most significant feature of the election was the fact that the traditional Blanco–Colorado two-party system now seemed to be a thing of the past as the Frente Amplio firmly established itself as Uruguay's third mass party. That coalition of the left won control of the city of Montevideo.

The Lacalle government that assumed office in March 1990 lacked a parliamentary majority inasmuch as the Colorado and Broad Front opposition parties between them had more members in the council of representatives than the Blancos. Nonetheless, the new President sought to strengthen his political position by entrusting four ministerial portfolios to the Colorados. At the same time, he set out to implement what may prove to be the most far-reaching programme in Uruguay's living memory designed to produce major changes in the economic life of the nation. Among the important objectives of the Blanco government were commitments to reform the state bureaucracy, to privatize the state-owned enterprises, to change certain labour practices, to raise taxes, to eliminate state deficits, and to ease the foreign debt problem. But progress has been slow, and questions remain about the ability of President Lacalle to persuade a rather hesitant nation about the desirability and perhaps the necessity of undergoing a process of extensive and rapid changes to meet the challenges of the 1990s and beyond.   EFE

Further Reading: N. Fraser and M. Navarro, *Eva Perón* (London, 1980); C. G. Gillespie, *Negotiating Democracy: Politicians and Generals in Uruguay* (Cambridge, 1991); J. Lynch, *Argentine Dictator: Juan Manuel de Rosas 1829–1852* (Oxford, 1981); J. A. Page, *Perón: a Biography* (New York. 1983); D. Rock, *Argentina 1516–1987* (London, 1987); C. H. Waisman, *Reversal of Development in Argentina* (Princeton, 1987); R. Roett and R. S. Sacks, *Paraguay: the Personalist Legacy* (Boulder, Colorado, and London, 1991); H. G. Warren, *Paraguay: An Informal History* (Norman, Okla., 1949); J. H. Williams, *The Rise and Fall of the Paraguayan Republic 1800–1970* (Austin, Texas, 1979); H. Finch, *A Political Economy of Uruguay since 1870* (London, 1981); M. I. Vanger, *José Batlle y Ordóñez of Uruguay: The Creator of his Times, 1902–1907* (Cambridge, Mass., 1963); M. I. Vanger, *The Model Country: José Batlle y Ordóñez of Uruguay 1907–1915* (Hanover, N.H., 1980)

The Falkland Islands/Islas Malvinas

Lying some 640 km east of southern Argentina, and on that country's continental shelf, the Falklands consist of about 200 bleak and treeless islands, which have been governed by Great Britain since 1833. The vast majority of their tiny population of around 2000 lives on the two largest, East and West Falkland. The islands gained unexpected international prominence in 1982, when the Argentine military government of General Leopoldo Galtieri sought unsuccessfully by force of arms to realize Argentina's long-standing national claim to them.

The complex history of the dispute between Argentina and Great Britain is critical for understanding the current situation. Mariners from many nations have been credited with the discovery of the archipelago. The British name derives from the designation given to the strait between the two main islands by Captain Strong of HMS *Welfare* in 1690 to honour Viscount Falkland, a high official of the Admiralty. The Argentine name, Las Malvinas, derives from the customary French designation, Les Malouines, after sailors from St Malo, seal-hunters in the South Atlantic in colonial times.

The first real settlement was Port Louis, on East Falkland, established by the French explorer, Antoine Louis de Bougainville, in 1764. Spain, which claimed a historic right to the area, soon protested and the French withdrew in return for compensation in cash. Spain then appointed a governor, and Port Louis became Puerto de la Soledad. During this protracted process, Commodore John Byron – grandfather of the poet – on HMS *Wager* landed on the uninhabited West Falkland, claiming it and adjacent islands for Britain. He established a settlement called Port Egmont. Byron's successor discovered Port

FALKLAND ISLAND/ISLAS MALVINAS

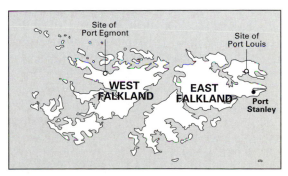

*Sheep-pen on Carcass
Island, Falkland Islands*

Louis, and in total ignorance of the Franco-Spanish accord, ordered its residents to leave.

The critical years were 1770 and 1771. In June 1770, a Spanish frigate entered Port Egmont and expelled the British, bringing Britain and Spain to the brink of war. Spain agreed to negotiate and, in January 1771, agreed to return Port Egmont; however, according to the Spanish ambassador in London. Prince Masserano, this was only after British ministers had made a 'secret promise' to withdraw completely from the islands once the issue had died down in Parliament and public opinion. No positive written evidence of any such promise has ever come to light. In 1774, Britain abandoned Egmont for reasons of economy.

Puerto de la Soledad remained in Spanish hands, administered from 1776 by Buenos Aires, seat of the new viceroyalty of the River Plate. Only in 1806 was the site abandoned. Argentine independence from Spain resulted in the assertion by the successor-state of sovereignty over the islands, whose complex history now took an even more complicated turn.

In 1820, the Buenos Aires government sent Captain Daniel Jewitt, a North American in its service, to raise the national flag at Puerto de la Soledad: this he did, but nothing else. Then, in 1824, a Frenchman, Louis Vernet, long resident in Hamburg and regarded by Argentines as a German, secured Argentine permission to establish a colony on East

Falkland, obtaining additionally, in 1828, the title of governor and, in 1829, usufruct of all the islands. Britain protested, but events there moved faster than its government seemed disposed to do. In July 1831, Vernet seized three ships flying the US flag, and proceeded in one of them to Buenos Aires to prosecute charges of illegal fishing in island waters. Unfortunately for him, the US consul at Buenos Aires, George W. Slocum, had at hand the USS *Lexington*, whose captain, Silas Duncan, was immediately despatched to the islands to throw off the Argentines and declare the territory *res nullius* (free of government), all this with the backing of the US government. Argentina responded in September 1832 with the appointment of Juan Estivier as governor, but his establishment of a penal colony at San Carlos proved abortive when its inhabitants mutinied and murdered him. Argentine attempts to restore order were interrupted by the arrival of HMS *Clio* under Captain Onslow in January 1833. He reasserted British control; in 1834 a British governor was appointed: and the process of British settlement proceeded. The Argentine government protested vigorously at the time, though maintaining relations, and successive Argentine administrations since have regarded the British action of 1833 as illegal, arbitrary, and imperialist.

The British claim to the islands is based on uninterrupted possession for over 150 years and on the avowed intention of the present-day islanders to remain British. That desire, based on principles of self-determination enshrined in the UN Charter, is difficult to refute; on the other hand, the islands' geographical remoteness from Britain and their proximity to Argentina, their sparse population, and neglect by Britain seem to many as powerful arguments for a transfer of sovereignty. Argentine irritation, at what its government and people see as a colonial anachronism, has surfaced from time to time; it was particularly strong during Perón's first presidency (1946–55) and in the 1960s. The United Nations after 1960 sought to reach accommodation between the parties, which, for their part, agreed on specific measures of economic co-operation. Thus, a runway at Port Stanley was built by Argentines; postal, medical and oil facilities were extended to the inhabitants in the early 1970s by the Argentine authorities. In the latter part of the decade, both Labour and Conservative governments in Britain looked to resolve the dispute through dialogue with the islanders and Argentina. They failed; the total incompatibility of British and Argentine claims was finally exposed by the Argentine invasion of April 1982. The war which followed, costing more than 1000 lives, entrenched each country's historic position. For Argentina, the war hastened the demise of an already unpopular military government, but did not affect in any way the national aspiration to recover the islands. Subsequent British inflexibility over the question of sovereignty made an immediate settlement of the dispute impossible. British military manoeuvres in the islands in March 1988 ('Operation Fire Focus') caused much annoyance in Argentina – and also, it seems, in the British Foreign Office, now eager to normalize relations. However, to some extent this was achieved by talks held in Madrid (October 1989 and February 1990) which resulted in a formal ending of hostilities and the restoration of full diplomatic links between the two nations. The issue of the islands themselves remains unresolved.   HB/SC

Further Reading: P. Beck, *The Falkland Islands as an International Problem* (London, 1988); J. Goebel, *The Struggle for the Falkland Islands*, with a preface and an introduction by J. C. J. Metford (New Haven, 1982); M. Hastings and S. Jenkins, *The Battle for the Falklands* (London, 1982); Latin America Bureau, *Falklands. Whose Crisis?* (London, 1982)

Brazil

Area	8,511,965 sq km
Population	150.4 million
GNP per capita (1989)	$2540
Capital	Brasília
Currency	Cruziado

Nineteenth-century Brazil was unlike other Latin American countries. It broke its connections with the mother country, Portugal, by a simple declaration of independence, which preserved the monarchy and the existing social structure and left the economy untouched by the kind of war that occurred in many parts of Spanish America. Prince Pedro, heir to the Portuguese throne, placed himself at the head of the Brazilian independence movement, such as it was, and was immediately acclaimed as emperor (1822).

THE EMPIRE, 1822–89

Pedro was intelligent enough to realize that the monarchy would be strengthened by the grant of a constitution, but he was too autocratic to accept any restraints on his power. As he was faced by politicians who were determined to rule by themselves his reign was stormy. He dissolved the first constituent assembly and himself drew up the 1824 Constitution which gave the emperor preponderant influence; he appointed ministers and provincial officials and was given the 'moderating power' to arbitrate disputes between the other branches of government. Parliament's refusal to accept Pedro's choice of ministers led to a deadlock in government, and the emperor's position was weakened by the loss of a short war against Argentina and his insistence on retaining Portuguese advisers. In 1831 he took the pretext of an army mutiny to return to Portugal, leaving his six-year-old son as emperor.

The abdication was followed by an extremely unstable period – four regencies in nine years. Brazil was saved from breaking up by the Additional Act of 1834, which gave power at municipal level to the local political bosses (*coroneis*), but there was a series of provincial revolts against the central government. Two political parties appeared, the Conservatives, who supported the central government and the rule of the bureaucracy, and the Liberals, who stood for devolving power to the provinces and the extension of civic rights; they then alternated in power amidst armed risings and threats of force.

BRAZIL

Completed roads

0	1600km
0	1000miles

Brazil: population
1810	3,000,000
1850	7,200,000
1900	17,300,000
1930	33,600,000
1960	70,000,000
1980	121,500,000
1988	144,430,000

Under Pedro II, who assumed power in 1840, a constitutional monarchy evolved, combining order, progress, and freedom. This came about slowly as the landowners, the main political class, realized that political disorder might lead to social revolution. But gradually the system began to evolve peacefully; the rigid division between Liberals and Conservatives ended with a coalition government in 1853. After that the emperor used his 'moderating power' to appoint prime ministers and remove them; this was obviously undemocratic but provided for peaceful changes of government, and Pedro II also insisted on freedom of the press and of debates.

1850 also marked the beginning of Brazil's development. Britain forced Brazil to abolish the slave trade in 1850, and thus released capital which went into economic development. Coffee overtook sugar and tobacco as the main export crop; steamers began to improve communications; the formation of limited liability companies made it possible for Brazilians to make other investments than in land. In the 1850s the first railways appeared; the telegraph began to bind the country together, and linked Brazil directly to Europe in 1874. As a result several native entrepreneurs began to develop the country, notably the Visconde de Mauá, who built up a business network extending to Buenos Aires and Paris. Immigration also began to grow, although this was hampered by the continued dependence of the big estates on slave labour. The 'frontier' also moved inland, particularly in São Paulo.

In the end, the monarchy collapsed because it could not adapt itself in time to new social and politi-cal forces, although its actual fall was largely accidental. The emperor's use of the 'moderating power' was called into question after 1868, when Pedro II broke the tradition of bi-partisan governments and appointed a Conservative prime minister. This brought the monarchy into political controversy.

Other factors also weakened the monarchy. In the early 1870s the crown clashed with the Church; young bishops brought up in the spirit of the first Vatican Council opposed the emperor's eighteenth-century latitudinarianism. The army became increasingly opposed to the government, as the emperor refused to increase military expenditure. The abolition of slavery also weakened the traditional landed classes, although the old theory that the empire collapsed when the former slave-owners withdrew their support is too simplistic. Brazilian slavery ended in stages; it began to decline after the abolition of the slave trade in 1850, and became obsolete in the northeast and the south. By the 1870s the remaining slaves were concentrated in Rio de Janeiro State and the east of São Paulo. Slavery was, therefore, associated with declining parts of the country; this is why Brazil abolished slavery peacefully in 1888.

Changes were clearly on the way. The emperor was dying of diabetes, and his daughter Isabel was unpopular. In June 1889 the last prime minister of the empire proposed the creation of a federal system 'which would make the republic unnecessary'. It was never introduced. On 15 November 1889 the commanders of the army demanded the dismissal of the prime minister. This was agreed, but the civilian Republicans (their party had been formed in 1870) went on to proclaim the fall of the monarchy. The emperor was easily captured, forced to abdicate, and sent into exile. Thus the empire fell owing to a series of coincidences, but only because its main sources of support had withered away.

THE FIRST REPUBLIC, 1889–1930

The Republicans came to power by accident and were divided amongst themselves. The triumphant regime was an uneasy coalition presided over by Marshal Deodoro da Fonseca, who had joined the revolution at the last moment for personal reasons. For the first two years the main figure in the government was not da Fonseca but the liberal Ruy Barbosa. He drew up the Constitution of 1891, which gave Brazil a government similar to that of the United States; the states were allowed very wide powers, including permission to form private armies, raise foreign loans, and collect their own customs. He also attempted to develop Brazil (and pay government debts) by printing money, which led to serious inflation. Meanwhile the removal of strong central government led to a return to the chaos of the 1830s in the different states. There were three main groups involved – the supporters of a radical military dictatorship (Jacobins); the civilian Republicans like Barbosa (Historicals); and the mass of ex-monarchist politicians (Adesistas). In 1891 Deodoro was overthrown by a coalition of Historicals and Jacobins, alienated by his autocratic manner and preference for ex-monarchist ministers. He was succeeded by Floriano Peixoto, 'the Iron Marshal', who tried to impose a Jacobin dictatorship, overthrowing state governments and jailing his opponents. The Jacobins combined anti-monarchism and xenophobia with a confused desire to develop the country under an elite of reforming army officers; but they had too little support to do anything, and their harsh methods united both Historicals and Adesistas against them. In 1893 a series of risings, notably in the navy and the southern state of Rio Grande do Sul, put Floriano under pressure. His successor was an elected civilian president representing São Paulo, the most important state in the federation, and by now the main focus of Brazil's increasingly huge export of coffee.

After 1894 the early political parties disappeared, and the struggle for control of the national government was fought out between the oligarchies controlling the different states. These oligarchies varied widely; São Paulo was developed enough to have an opposition party, and Minas Gerais tried to bring in all groups, while Rio Grande do Sul was in the grip of two Jacobin strong men. But they had two features in common; the local bosses (*coroneis*) used the powers of government to keep themselves in power, and they could only be removed by an internal civil war or by the intervention of the central government. As a result there were frequent bloody struggles between local clans for control of the state government and their resources.

At national level peace was precariously maintained; a candidate for president was selected by a meeting of the state governments, who then used their control of the electoral machinery to elect him by 80–90 per cent of the vote. Obviously the states were not equally important; many, especially in the north-east and the interior, were too weak to defy the central government. São Paulo was the wealthiest state; its coffee revenue allowed it to raise larger loans and maintain an effective army; Minas Gerais had the largest population, but was less economically developed; and these two could control the federation if they acted together. Bahia was their most consistent opponent; it had been important under the empire, but had shared in the decay of the north-east. Of the other states only Rio Grande do Sul could play an independent role, but it remained isolated under two dictatorial governors, the last important Jacobins.

After the fall of the military government in 1894 São Paulo provided three civilian presidents. Prudente de Morais (1894–8) restored order and broke the power of the remaining Jacobins; Manoel Campos Salles (1898–1902) restored business confidence by stabilizing the currency; and Francisco de Paula Rodrigues Alves (1902–6) carried out a building programme in Rio de Janeiro and eliminated yellow fever. But this stability was always precarious. The collapse of coffee prices weakened São Paulo's economic supremacy, and in 1906 the state oligarchy had to agree to alternate the presidency with Minas Gerais in return for state subsidies to keep up the price of coffee. In 1910 the states quarrelled over the presidency for the first time; the convention chose a military candidate, Hermes da Fonseca (nephew of Deodoro), and Ruy Barbosa stood against him with the support of São Paulo and Bahia. Hermes won, but Ruy got 40 per cent of the vote – a sign that the state political machines were divided.

The alliance after 1906 between Minas Gerais and São Paulo (irreverently known as 'coffee with cream', after their main products) was always uneasy, though it lasted to 1930. New groups began to enter politics; the working class began to agitate, although unions were very small and handicapped by the foreign origin of their leaders, and general strikes failed. Intellectuals also protested; the Modern Art week in São Paulo in 1922 introduced Brazilians to post-Impressionist work and stimulated a new interest in national music and folklore. Even the oligarchs

Ruy Barbosa (1849–1923), Brazilian abolitionist and statesman

realized the need for change; the presidency increased its power and began to provide social aid by undertaking drought relief in the north-east.

In the 1920s the regime was again under attack from radical army officers. But the 'first republic' did not collapse under attack from revolutionary groups; the struggle among the state oligarchies for the presidency got out of control. The Great Depression hit Brazil extremely hard, and in 1930 the São Paulo elite was divided over the proper policy towards coffee export prices and the exchange rate. The official presidential nominee, from São Paulo, was opposed in the presidential election by an alliance of Minas Gerais, Rio Grande do Sul, and Paraiba, who put up Getúlio Vargas, the governor of Rio Grande do Sul, for President. Vargas lost but was nonetheless placed in office by the military power of the opposition states. Thus the 1930 revolution came about as the result of a quarrel within the elite, though tensions were building up within society. As the governor of Minas Gerais said, 'We must make a revolution before the people make it for us.'

GETÚLIO VARGAS, 1930–45

1930 resembled 1889; the revolutionaries came to power unexpectedly and without a common programme. Most of them were old-guard politicians, whose main aim was to end São Paulo's domination, but there were two more extreme groups. The 'democrats', who were concentrated in São Paulo, wanted free elections and an end to the power of the political bosses; the *tenentes*, the radical army officers, wanted to regenerate Brazil under the leadership of the army. Vargas as president played the various groups off against each other, using his gift of pragmatism to climb gradually to supreme power. At first he handed power over to the *tenentes*, who introduced a mass of social reforms such as compulsory education, labour laws, and attempts at moral improvement, but failed; they were too few, they were divided, and they had no organized popular support. In the end they became members of the political elite or returned to the army.

But the *tenentes* achieved one negative result; they provoked and angered the old politicians. This was especially true in São Paulo. In 1932 the state seceded from the federation; this caused a serious crisis for Vargas, who was forced to promise a return to constitutional government in order to prevent other states joining in. The bargain worked, the rising was suppressed, Vargas treated São Paulo with great leniency, and a constituent assembly was duly elected in 1933. Most of its members were traditional oligarchs, but it carried out several reforms to satisfy the democrats, such as votes for women and proportional representation. Vargas was elected president for four years; the whole episode was a good example of his ability to be all things to all men.

The revolution and the world depression had shaken the power of the landowners; the mass of the people were still largely outside politics, but the middle and lower middle classes, previously employed in professional occupations, were seriously affected. As a result they joined mass political movements, the first to appear in Brazil. The National Liberation Alliance (ANL) was a 'popular front' controlled by the Brazilian Communist Party, but appealing to many progressives and lower-middle-class people; Brazilian Integralist Action (AIB) was a radical nationalist movement which borrowed many trappings from European fascism and was strongly backed by the German minority, but which appealed to middle-class people who wanted to regenerate Brazil. By 1935 these movements had about half a million members (out of an electorate of 2 million), and their demonstrations and street fighting frightened the elite, who were not used to mass political mobilization.

Vargas, as usual, exploited the situation for his

own ends; he frightened the old politicians into giving him more and more power. The ANL was first to fall into his trap; it attempted an unsuccessful coup in November 1935, spearheaded by non-commissioned officers in the army. Many officers were killed and the rebels were very harshly treated; this illustrates the elite's shock at radical mass movements and also Vargas's determination to prevent anyone but himself from organizing mass support. In 1937–8 it was the Integralistas' turn to be crushed by Vargas's political cunning; first he forestalled an Integralista victory in the presidential elections by abolishing the constitution, then he dissolved the movement when it staged an unsuccessful coup (May 1938). After eight years of dividing in order to rule, Vargas was supreme.

From 1937 to 1945 Vargas ran a mild dictatorship, called the New State (*Estado Nôvo*) after Salazar's regime in Portugal. It was not fascist. Vargas never formed a totalitarian political movement and never seriously attempted to be a charismatic dictator; his regime was more like that of an eighteenth-century despot – personal government through an administrative regime of hand-picked experts. He success-

Getúlio Vargas (1883–1954)

fully created the image of a paternal estate owner, 'O Paizinho do Povo' ('the daddy of the people'), while quietly transforming Brazil.

Vargas's chief problems were centralization, industrialization and nationalism. Centralization came first; the president now controlled the whole of Brazil to a degree unequalled since 1889. The states' powers were greatly reduced, an event symbolized by the burning of their flags – from now on Brazil was to have only one flag. The machine of government had been greatly expanded since 1930 with the creation of Labour and Industry ministries; now it was brought under the control of the Public Service Administrative Department (DASP), a body of specially chosen advisers to ministers intended to be the equivalent of the British administrative class. As with much of Vargas's work, the experiment was not entirely successful, but it did unite Brazil more than ever before.

The state also laid the foundations for industrial growth. The government attempted to improve the railways and began the creation of a road network, while the coming of the aeroplane made it possible to link Brazil up effectively for the first time. The regime's great showplace was the Volta Redonda steel mill, which opened in 1941 and was intended to mark Brazil's coming of age in manufacturing. Again, these efforts were partially successful; industry did begin to develop, but the country remained dependent on agriculture for its major exports. The government tried to rescue staples like coffee and sugar by organizing state marketing systems, but they remained largely at the mercy of the international market.

The *Estado Nôvo* also tried to create an atmosphere of popular mobilization and national pride by propaganda and encouragement of sport and folklore. Every radio station spread government information by means of a compulsory 'Brazilian hour', although this inevitably aroused counter-productive ribaldry. The government was more successful in its search for prestige through football, which was rapidly becoming the national obsession, and attempts were made to organize Carnival and to use popular music and art to create a favourable image.

The end of the *Estado Nôvo* was brought about by an external event: the entry of the United States into the Second World War. Brazil followed the North American lead, and benefited from large amounts of aid; in return Brazil patrolled the South Atlantic and sent an expeditionary force to Italy. But it was obviously incongruous for an authoritarian regime to be fighting for democracy, and Vargas began (with his usual pragmatism) to propose a return to constitutional government. From 1942 he began to encourage the organization of the new skilled working class into government-run trade unions, which provided benefits for their members and some degree of protection (although independent workers' action was deterred). This was supplemented by more traditional patronage in the form of gifts to the unorganized poor and the promotion of a cult of Vargas among the unsophisticated. In 1945 the president announced elections for a constituent assembly, and began to build a new political machine. This consisted of two political parties appealing to different bases of support. The Social Democrat Party (PSD) belied its name; it was a conservative coalition of pro-Vargas landowners, who still controlled the rural vote, and businessmen who had benefited from the expansion of the *Estado Nôvo*. The electorate now included a large block of skilled urban workers; Vargas appealed to them through the Brazilian Labour Party (PTB), based on his trade unions. There were also opposition parties, the most important being the National Democratic Union (UDN), a 'liberal' coalition of anti-Vargas landowners and middle-class people who believed in human rights and honest government and saw Vargas as a dictatorial demagogue.

The PSD/PTB coalition won the 1945 elections but, ironically, it did not help Vargas who was at this point overthrown by the army, whose commanders suspected that he intended to keep himself in power yet again; they also feared his appeal to the masses. Nonetheless the election showed the huge changes which had occurred in Brazil since 1930. Then the electorate had been 2 million; now it was 7.5 million. Then most of the electors had voted at the command of the landowners; now there were national political parties (at least in name), and the opposition polled 40 per cent. Leadership had passed to the cities, with their European-style middle and working classes.

THE DEMOCRATIC REPUBLIC, 1946–64

Brazil's experiment with democracy lasted eighteen years, and was stormy as well as short. Only two of the presidents, Dutra (1946–51) and Kubitschek (1956–61), completed their terms at the appointed time: Vargas (1951–4) ended his second term by committing suicide, Café Filho (1954–5) and Quadros (1961) resigned, and Goulart (1961–4) was deposed. The reason for this, apart from the incompetence of the incumbents, was that the Brazilian political system had become less controllable.

The landowners were still a powerful force, and they had been joined by the middle classes and the skilled urban working classes. By the 1960s the unskilled urban workers and the peasants, hitherto voiceless, were also making demands on the system.

In a society that ran on patronage the presidency could only hope to satisfy so many demands when the economy was booming; when resources were scarce the flimsy façade of constitutional government was torn to pieces by the conflicting demands of the different interest groups.

The presidency of Eurico Gaspar Dutra, a conservative general (1946–51), was relatively quiet; the political system had not fully developed and Brazil was prosperous as the result of the Second World War. The two main developments were the banning of the Communist Party, which had shown surprising strength by gaining 9 per cent of the votes in 1946, and the consequent growth of the PTB under Vargas, who appealed to the electorate on the social achievements of his last years in office, and won the 1950 presidential elections by effective use of public relations for the first time in Brazil. He got over 5 million votes, a record in presidential elections, but under half the total vote – another sign that the electorate were voting freely and that the oligarchs no longer controlled the system.

Vargas's second presidency was a failure. The complexity of political life had vastly increased since 1945; the post-war boom was over; the president himself was nearly seventy and his political grip was weakening. Vargas made two major mistakes; he alienated everyone by his mismanagement of the economy and angered his political supporters by his promotion of his *protégé* João Goulart, whom he made Labour Minister and put in charge of the trade unions with all their opportunities for patronage. But Vargas's final downfall was due to his resentment of opposition. In August 1954 an assassination attempt was made on a muckraking journalist, Carlos Lacerda; violence at national level broke the unwritten rules of Brazilian politics, and the armed forces were also angered, since an Air Force major had been killed trying to protect Lacerda. Investigations showed that the killing had been ordered by the president's chief bodyguard; senior officers demanded the president's resignation, and Vargas responded by committing suicide. His death, and the wills issued in his name, created a 'Vargas legend'; he was supposed to have died as a 'sacrifice' protecting the 'poor and humble'. At any rate he had taken vital steps towards modernization and created both a middle class and a skilled proletariat.

But Vargas's suicide had shown up the strains within the political system, and these got worse after his death. Although his political machine showed its durability by winning the 1955 elections, with Juscelino Kubitschek of the PSD gaining the presidency and Goulart of the PTB the vice-presidency, the armed forces had to intervene again to prevent anti-Vargas factions staging a coup. The running of

Dr Juscelino Kubitschek (1902–76), founder of Brasília

Brazil was becoming increasingly dependent on the military.

Kubitschek represented two new forces in Brazilian life; he was the first president of immigrant stock and the first to represent the business community. He had the dynamism and charisma of a super-salesman determined to give Brazil 'Fifty years' progress in five'; and he largely succeeded. Industrial production rose by 80 per cent, the growth rate by 7 per cent a year. Brazil developed a self-sufficient motor industry; structural bottlenecks were ironed out; the nation acquired an international airline and an expanded merchant navy. All this was accomplished with an infectious drive and enthusiasm, aided by the achievements of the national soccer side and the popularity of Brazilian music, dancing, and folk culture. The symbol of the Kubitschek era was the new capital, Brasília, empty scrubland in 1956 and already a masterpiece of modern architecture by 1961. Brazil had finally come of age; it was no longer a string of trading posts along the sea, but a potential world power developing its interior from its own resources.

There was a price, however, to be paid for all this. Kubitschek's boom was built on massive foreign investment and short-term loans, and his waste and prodigality horrified conservative international financiers. Brazil began to achieve 'Fifty years' inflation in five', with a great increase in corruption and mismanagement. Revulsion at this, combined with the influence of ideas about development planned by the state, led to a surprise in the 1960 elections. The PSD/PTB coalition still controlled Congress and Goulart was again elected vice-president, but the presidency was won by Jânio Quadros, an independent candidate backed by the UDN.

Quadros was a new phenomenon in Brazilian politics; he owed his election to public opinion without the backing of a landowner or a political machine. He came to power by championing the ordinary person against the 'establishment' and as councillor, deputy, and governor for São Paulo he had established a reputation for honesty and efficiency. Many middle-class people, particularly intellectuals and civil servants, believed in him and worked hard for his election. He began well, with stabilization of the economy, cuts in expenditure and negotiations with foreign creditors; the only mildly controversial policy was a tendency to friendship with newly independent Third World nations. His award of an honour to Che Guevara was questioned. After eight months in office he suddenly resigned (August 1961), alleging that 'terrible forces' were hindering him from governing. The reasons for this have never adequately been explained; was Quadros under attack from the United States, was he suffering a breakdown, or was he trying to shock Congress into giving him more power? In any case his departure caused a further crisis. The next president was João Goulart; but Goulart was unpopular with the military. A civil war was averted; Goulart became president, but most of his executive powers were given to a prime minister responsible to Congress.

Goulart's presidency destroyed constitutional government in Brazil. He himself was a totally incompetent politician who could not control the nation or even his own supporters; his only claim to prominence was the patronage of Vargas; under his government the economy collapsed and the demands of different sectors of society tore the political system apart. Goulart's ambitions were satisfied when he got the full powers of the presidency restored in 1963, but his supporters included abler men who wanted to carry out radical social change. Leonel Brizola, governor of Rio Grande do Sul, wanted to turn the PTB into a party with a socialist, even a Marxist, programme, while Miguel Arrais, governor of Pernambuco, brought the peasants into political life and used them to break the landowners' stranglehold on local power. Elsewhere Peasant Leagues began to rouse people whom all politicians had previously ignored. Meanwhile inflation rose to 100 per cent and economic growth sank to 2 per cent (against 4 per cent population growth). Brazil seemed headed for disaster.

The final crisis came in 1964, amid a political polarization not seen since the 1930s. Goulart was opposed by most of the governors of the large states, and demonstrations of women organized by the right-wing Catholic organization, 'Tradition, Family, and Liberty', attracted a large number of supporters. Goulart responded by making a demagogic appeal to the poorer urban workers; at a public demonstration in March 1964, he signed decrees nationalizing oil refineries and some land and promised tax changes and votes for illiterates. It was a challenge to the privileged. Preparations for a coup began, and were put into action when Goulart committed what in the eyes of the military was a mortal sin by conniving at the formation of left-wing cells in the navy. The rising of 31 March–2 April met little resistance. Goulart's presidency collapsed with the undignified flight of its leaders; few realized immediately that it was the end of democracy in Brazil for twenty years.

MILITARY GOVERNMENT

The military leaders who came to power in 1964 had negative rather than positive aims; they wanted to 'clean up politics', and only gradually developed ambitions to govern for themselves. But the purge they conducted was so drastic as to make their final takeover inevitable. Most leading politicians were banned from politics for ten years on charges of 'corruption', 'demagoguery', and 'communism' (which were wide enough to cover almost anything). Meanwhile the economy was taken in hand; inflation was gradually reduced to tolerable levels, and growth began to revive, helped by North American official aid and unofficial investment.

A UDN politician who hoped to benefit from military support in the 1965 elections was Carlos Lacerda, governor of Guanabara, the journalist whose attacks had caused the fall of Vargas and who had developed into a political gadfly with a following among the lower middle classes of Rio de Janeiro; but his hopes were shattered when the PSD/PTB coalition won the two most important states, Guanabara and Minas Gerais. The military responded by transferring the election of the president and state governors from the direct vote of the electorate to the indirect vote of Congress and the state assemblies, which could be manipulated more easily. They also dissolved the existing political parts and forced all elected representatives to join one of two new parties, either the pro-government ARENA (National Renovation Alliance), mainly UDN and PSD, or the

Government Building, Museum, and Senate, Brasília

opposition MDB (Brazilian Democratic Movement), the remnants of the PTB after most of its leaders had been banned from politics.

The new political system survived uneasily for four years. Both parties were largely meaningless, and the military only kept the political game going out of a residual shame at setting up an outright dictatorship. Humberto Castello Branco, the first military president, retired in 1967; his successor, Artur Costa e Silva, was selected by the chiefs of the armed forces and then submitted to a compliant Congress for rubber-stamp approval. Costa e Silva was more easy going (and also more corrupt), but he could do little to increase the regime's popularity. The military became more and more touchy at the slightest sign of opposition; they insisted on the imprisonment of a newspaper editor who published an insulting article on Castello Branco's death in a plane crash. On the left the opposition began a guerrilla offensive, stimulated by Cuba's encouragement of such movements.

1968 marked the crisis point at which the military definitely turned to authoritarianism. Government mishandling of student grievances led to a series of massive anti-government demonstrations, supported by the clergy and many middle-class people, which demanded a return to democracy and which were backed by most of the prominent civilians still left in political life. At the same time urban and rural guerrilla groups, particularly National Liberation Action under Carlos Marighela, went into action against the government, which replied with widespread use of torture and the 'death squads' (groups of off-duty soldiers and policemen allowed to kill members of the opposition). The climax came when an MDB deputy called on the people to refuse to celebrate Armed Forces Day because the army had become a 'gang of torturers'. When Congress refused to censure him the military struck back; Congress was closed, ninety-four opposition figures, including Kubitschek and Lacerda, the last civilian politicians of presidential quality, were arrested, and the government took dictatorial powers. The military had wanted to collaborate with the civilians, but they were not prepared to tolerate any dissent.

After 1969 the military ruled without much consultation of the civilian politicians; the press was severely censored and the guerrilla movements ruthlessly crushed. Costa e Silva, paralysed by a stroke, was removed from power in September 1969; the generals, irreverently known as 'the college of cardinals', replaced him with Emilio Garrastazu Médici, who had little power of his own. His government was an alliance between right-wing army officers and civilian technocrats; the Brazilian military, unlike many others, has always worked closely with outside experts and made good use of their talents. The most prominent of the technocrats was the Finance Minister, Antônio Delfim Neto, who created an 'economic miracle' in the early 1970s by raising new loans, paying off old debts, and encouraging foreign investment. These policies were successful for a time. The growth rate went up to 10 per cent a year, the inflation rate went down to 15–25 per cent, and Brazil finally reached 'take-off' point by exporting manufactured goods. Coffee ceased to be the largest single export for the first time since 1850. Prosperity partially reconciled the middle classes to the lack of freedom, and the sense of wellbeing was heightened by the achievements of the national football team; the celebrations of 150 years of independence in 1972 passed amidst a feeling of euphoria – at least for the elite.

'DECOMPRESSION' AND DEMOCRACY

This euphoria did not last. The oil crisis of 1973 brutally revealed the fact that Brazil depended on cheap foreign petroleum and that its exports were vulnerable in a world recession. It also became apparent that social progress had lagged behind economic prosperity and that the price of the 'miracle' had been paid by the poor. In the 1974 elections the opposition MDB won two senate seats, the only serious political posts open to direct election, and nearly won the Chamber of Deputies; it was obvious that the developed part of the nation had rejected the government.

The military bowed to the national mood by electing Ernesto Geisel for the 1974–9 presidential term. Geisel was of German immigrant stock (he was the first non-Catholic president), and favoured a more rationalist and frugal approach to government, seeking a policy which would reconcile the electorate to the regime. 'Decompression', as this was known, involved the gradual relaxation of political repression while a return to democracy was promised – but only for the future. This policy worked reasonably well; the political leaders of the democratic republic returned from exile (in most cases only to die) and the MDB failed to win the 1978 election.

Causing controversy within the armed forces, Geisel imposed João Baptista Figueiredo as his presidential successor in 1979 without any discussion. Figueiredo attempted to continue and develop Geisel's policies. These included an increase in social expenditure and populist gestures such as the president arguing over prices in supermarkets, combined with political sops like the promise of direct elections and an end to the two-party system. (The PSD and the UDN reappeared under other names, while the PTB split into small, largely personalistic factions.)

Political demonstration during the Brazilian elections of 1982

In 1980–1 the most interesting phenomenon was the appearance of an independent trade union movement in opposition to the government-controlled syndicates. The new unionism and its charismatic leader Luis da Silva (Lula) in São Paulo were based on the most modern factories, which perhaps indicated the appearance of something new in Brazilian life.

In the 1982 elections the PMDB (Brazilian Democratic Movement, uniting the old UDN and PTB) won the developed area of the centre-south. In 1984 a new president was elected by Congress after the government had survived mass demonstrations in favour of *diretas já* ('direct elections now!'). The government's conservative candidate, Paulo Maluf, was defeated by Tancredo Neves, for the PMDB. It looked as if Brazil had achieved a peaceful transition to a reformist 'new republic'. But Neves fell ill on the day of his inauguration, dying one month later. His vice-president, José Sarney, on whom great hopes were pinned, took over but his presidency proved disastrous. For a brief period inflation was curbed by the Cruzado Plan (February 1986), and the election of a Constituent Assembly was a triumph for the social-democrat PMDB. But the Cruzado Plan worked for only nine months, inflation rising from 140 per cent in 1986 to 1765 per cent in 1989 despite a second 'Summer Plan'. By 1989 Brazil had had three curren-

cies in five years. Economic failure and a series of scandals destroyed Sarney's popularity and broke up his PMDB-based coalition. The new 1988 Constitution tried to liberalize Brazil, introducing votes for illiterates, trying to protect the environment, and privatizing the state machinery, but it left most power in the hands of the president (as a result of machinations by Sarney). Everything therefore depended on the 1989 elections for the presidency, the first free and direct ones since 1960. With the collapse of Sarney it looked as if the two main candidates were Lula, the charismatic working-class leader of the PT (Workers' Party), and Leonel Brizola, the veteran Rio Grande do Sul and Rio de Janeiro populist. However, the situation was transformed by the appearance of Fernando Collor, Governor of the small state of Alagoas, who presented himself as a radical new force.

Collor won, thanks to backing from the media and the conservative classes combined with strong support in the countryside and smaller cities and in the state of São Paulo. He attempted to cut the government sector and open up the economy. But his 'New Brazil' plan for the economy (involving the freezing of almost all savings and price curbs) was a relative failure and diminished his initial popularity.

Brazil, unlike many other parts of Latin America,

Business district, São Paulo

has generally been successful in avoiding revolution. There has been little political violence at the centre, though more at local level; debate has usually been possible; politicians have generally tolerated each other. This stability has achieved a great deal – economic growth, respect abroad, and a flourishing intellectual and cultural life at all levels. But a price has been paid for this: the persistence of social stagnation and a society whose benefits are all too often confined to the elite. This elite has already accommodated a middle class and a skilled proletariat; it must now bring the unskilled workers and peasants fully into the national society, or all its other achievements will be at risk. The last ten years have seen too many 'last chances' for Brazil.

FL

Further Reading: R. Barman, *Brazil, the Forging of a Nation* (Stanford, 1988); E. Bradford Burns, *A History of Brazil*, 2nd edition (New York, 1980); P. Flynn, *Brazil: a Political Analysis* (London, 1979); T. E. Skidmore, *Politics in Brazil*, 1930–1964 (New York, 1967); T. E. Skidmore, *The Politics of Military Rule in Brazil, 1964–85* (New York, 1990)

Cuba and Puerto Rico

CUBA

Area	114,524 sq km
Population	10.6 million
GNP per capita (1989)	$2509
Capital	Havana
Currency	Peso

The independence of Spain's mainland colonies left Cuba and Puerto Rico as the last vestiges of Spain's American empire. Both islands were placed under the strict autocratic rule of military governors sent out from Spain, and revolutionary conspiracies, not uncommon in Cuba during the nineteenth century, were ruthlessly suppressed. Spain turned down lucrative offers from the United States to purchase Cuba and warded off US-based filibustering expeditions in the early 1850s designed to detach Cuba from Spain and make it an American slave state.

In the latter part of the eighteenth century Cuba had begun its transformation into a slave plantation society, a process completed in the nineteenth century. By the 1860s, Cuba was producing more than 30 per cent of the world's cane sugar. Most of the work was done by African slaves, supplemented by indentured Chinese labourers brought to the island during the 1850s and 1860s. Slavery itself was fed by the Atlantic slave trade, under which an estimated 600,000 African slaves were brought to Cuba in the nineteenth century prior to 1867 when it ended. Puerto Rico received perhaps 10 per cent of the number of slaves brought to Cuba. Spain yielded to British pressure to sign treaties outlawing the Atlantic slave trade in 1817 and 1835, but colonial officials openly connived at continued importations. The largest concentration of Cuba's slave population was located on the island's sugar plantations. These had increased in size by 1860 to the point where many were becoming latifundios and by the latter half of the century were increasingly mechanized.

With the outbreak of a ten-year civil war in the eastern part of Cuba in 1868, Spain at last embarked on some modest political concessions designed to maintain its hold on its Caribbean possessions. The Spanish legislature passed on the Moret Law in 1870, freeing all children of slaves born after 1868 and any slave over sixty. This first step towards the abolition of slavery was followed by complete abolition in Puerto Rico in 1873, but in Cuba abolition became a prolonged social process not finally completed until 1886.

Puerto Ricans were permitted to elect delegates to the Spanish legislature from 1869, but as long as Cubans were in arms against Spanish rule the privilege was withheld from Cuba. The Convention of Zanjón in 1878 ended the civil war, enabling Cubans to elect representatives to the Spanish Cortes in 1879, but it did not bury Cuban dreams of independence. These were to resurface under the extraordinary leadership of José Martí (1853–95), poet, intellectual and

CUBA

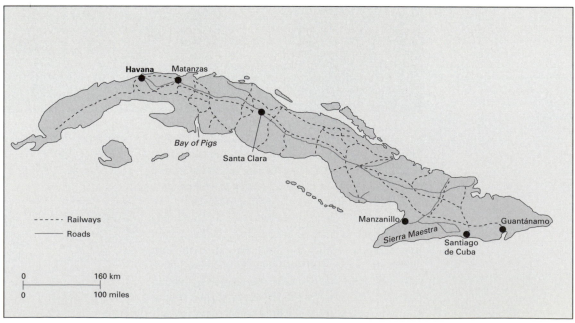

José Martí (1853–95), apostle of Cuban nationhood

revolutionary, who worked from an exile base in the United States in the early 1890s to unite the diverse factions of a Cuban independence movement. His 'Cuba Libre' campaign culminated in an invasion of Cuba in 1895, beginning Cuba's second war of independence. Martí personally led the invasion, but tragically he was one of the first casualties, dying in an ambush in May 1895. For three years fighting raged across the island. Spain was unable to suppress the nationalists and they, in turn, were unable to expel the Spanish. It was the United States declaration of war against Spain which decided the fate of Spanish Caribbean colonies.

Independence

American entry into Cuba's war of independence with Spain in 1898 thwarted Spanish hopes of retaining its most valuable colony, but it also deflected Cuban aspirations for independence from Spain. With Spain's defeat, Cubans found themselves first under American military occupation for four years and then with limited independence granted to them by the United States. The Republic of Cuba, proclaimed in 1902, was constrained by the Platt Amendment passed by the United States Congress. By it the United States claimed the right to naval bases on Cuba, including Guantanamo which the Americans continue to hold. But the provision of the Amendment which clearly made Cuba a protectorate of the United States stated:

> Cuba consents that the United States may exercise the right to intervene for the preservation of Cuban independence, the maintenance of a government adequate for the protection of life, property, and individual liberty.

The amendment was not repealed until 1934 and its psychological effect lingered on until 1959 (and beyond) as a powerful stimulus to the anti-American nationalism of Castro's revolution. American political and military intervention occurred with some regularity before the repeal paralleling the growth of United States economic influence in the island.

American investment in Cuba expanded rapidly in the twentieth century, exceeding one billion dollars by 1929. Even in the late 1950s approximately two-thirds of Cuba's sugar exports went to the United States at prices fixed in Washington under a quota system. In most years these prices exceeded world-market prices, but the arrangement virtually made Cuba an economic client of the United States even after the repeal of the Platt Amendment. Cuba purchased nearly three-quarters of its imports from the United States during the 1950s. American investment in the island, after declining during the 1930s, rose again in the 1940s and early 1950s. Cuba's econ-

omy remained closely integrated with that of the United States until Fidel Castro's revolution. In politics, the island oscillated between authoritarian rule – from 1934 to 1944 the effective 'strong man' being Fulgencio Batista (1901–73), originally an army sergeant – and a somewhat corrupt form of democracy.

By the 1950s Cuba was a society of contrasts. The largest of the Caribbean islands, it had a population of over 6 million people, of whom a million lived in or around Havana. Measured by material standards, it was one of the most advanced states of the Latin American world. More Cadillacs reputedly were sold in Havana in 1954 than in any other city in the world. Cubans in the 1950s, no doubt because of their proximity to the United States, enjoyed the highest number of TV sets per capita of all Latin American countries. Through radio and television Cubans absorbed American culture, and in turn the media perhaps stimulated the forces for change within Cuba; certainly television was a medium which Fidel Castro was soon to exploit very effectively. Yet Cuba suffered from grinding rural poverty, high unemployment, illiteracy and inadequate health care, especially in rural areas. The glitter of Havana's gambling casinos could not hide the glaring social and economic inequalities in the country.

General Batista seized power once again in his coup d'état of 1952, bringing to an end eight years of democratic government under Presidents Ramón Grau San Martín (1944–8) and Carlos Prío Socorras (1948–52). Batista's restoration of dictatorship had profound effects. Of all his opponents none proved more effective in the end than a young Cuban lawyer, the son of a Spanish immigrant. Fidel Castro (b. 1926; prime minister 1959–76; president 1976–) was twenty-six when he launched his first, unsuccessful attempt to topple Batista. Castro had absorbed the nineteenth-century revolutionary tradition of Cuba. He saw himself as the logical successor to José Martí, the man to complete the revolution Martí had begun. In 1953, the 100th anniversary of Martí's birth, Castro engineered a bold attempt to seize the Moncada military barracks in Santiago de Cuba. It failed; Castro was captured and put on trial. The date of the assault, 26 July, provided the name for Castro's revolutionary movement.

Castro's revolution

Castro's overall programme in 1953 was revolutionary, but in no recognizable sense Marxist–Leninist. It called for a return to the democracy of Cuba's 1940 Constitution. Castro used his trial to publicize the evils of Batista's regime and his own revolutionary programme. He received a prison sentence, but was soon pardoned under an amnesty. In 1955 Castro went to Mexico in preparation for a new attempt to overthrow Batista. Here he teamed up with an Argentine doctor Ernesto 'Che' Guevara. Castro's revolutionary band sailed to Cuba in the autumn of 1956 to begin a successful three-year struggle against Batista from the Sierra Maestra mountains in eastern Cuba. On 1 January 1959 the remains of the Batista regime dissolved, and Fidel Castro, to universal popular acclaim, assumed control of the island.

Over the next eighteen months, he revealed to his own countrymen and to the rest of the world just how radical he intended the transformation of Cuba to be. Gone was any thought of restoring the 1940 Cuban Constitution. Instead, the leadership of Castro and the 'revolutionary family' of his guerrilla comrades-in-arms governed Cuba without any formal constitution until 1976. On 1 December 1961, Castro publicly proclaimed his allegiance to Marxism–Leninism. The economic policies of the early revolutionary years reflected this philosophy, especially in the movement towards the collectivization of the means of production. Most important was agriculture and, in particular, the sugar industry. Successive agrarian reform laws steadily trimmed the private sector until it was (by 1977) only 20 per cent of the acreage, although representing much more in terms of production. Co-operatives and state farms replaced private holdings. Where foreign-owned estates or industries existed, they were nationalized, mostly without compensation.

Economic policy during the 1960s was markedly experimental. Che Guevara, Minister of Industry in the early years of the revolution, headed a crash programme to industrialize Cuba, with help from Eastern Europe. Industrialization was part of the larger goal of diversifying the Cuban economy to emancipate it from sugar's historic domination. The strategy of accelerated industrialization was, however, a failure, and it had to be abandoned. Sugar soon controlled the Cuban economy once again. After dramatic declines in sugar harvests during 1963 and 1964, the government targeted a 10-million-ton crop by 1970. This was not achieved, but the frenetic attempt to

---

A Condemnation of exploitation
Extract From The First Declaration of Havana

The General National Assembly of the People of Cuba:
Condemns the latifundio, source of poverty for peasants, and an inhuman and backward system of agrarian production; condemns the starvation wages and iniquitous exploitation of human labour by bastard privileged interests; condemns illiteracy, the lack of teachers, schools, doctors and hospitals, the lack of care in old age that prevails in the countries of America; condemns discrimination against the Indian and the black; condemns the exploitation and inequality of women; condemns the military and political oligarchies who keep our people in poverty and hamper their democratic development and the full exercise of their sovereignty; condemns the cession of the natural resources of our lands to foreign monopolies as a policy of surrender and treason to the people's interests; condemns governments that turn a deaf ear to the people's sentiments and comply with the dictates of Washington; condemns the systematic deception of the people by mass media that respond to the interests of the oligarchies and oppressive imperialism; condemns the news monopoly of the Yankee agencies, instruments of American trusts and agents of Washington; condemns the oppressive laws that prevent workers and peasants, students and intellectuals, and the great majorities in each country from organizing and struggling for their rightful social and patriotic claims; condemns the imperialist enterprises and monopolies which continuously pillage our riches, exploit our workers and peasants, and keep our economies backward, submitting the politics of Latin America to their interests and designs.

In short, the General National Assembly of the Cuban People condemns the exploitation of underdeveloped countries by imperialist finance capital.

Revolutionary militiamen listening to a speech from Fidel Castro, Havana, January 1961

reach the target aggravated the distortions in the island's economy, causing serious repercussions throughout Cuba. The revolution had some success in diversifying the economy, most notably in the expansion of the fishing industry. Nevertheless, the inability of Cuba's socialist economic system to break out of the bonds of a monoculture economy increased the island's economic dependence on the Soviet Union.

The Soviet link was of fundamental importance. Once in power, Castro was determined to establish Cuba's independence from the United States. Nationalization of American holdings and Castro's campaign to export his revolution soon put Cuban–American relations on a collision course. Fearing American retaliation, Castro looked for and found support from the Soviet Union. Relations between Cuba and the United States steadily worsened until diplomatic ties were broken on 3 January 1961. They have never been restored although a small step was taken in 1977 with the establishment of 'interest' sections in both countries. The United States imposed a trade embargo in 1962 which is still in effect.

Meanwhile, American plans to dislodge Castro by force had been set in motion. In April 1961, an inva-

sion of the island by anti-Castro Cuban exiles collapsed on the beaches of Cuba's Bay of Pigs. Castro now requested more military assistance from the Soviet Union to repel any further American attacks. The Soviet Union readily complied and the arms supplied included missiles sent to the island in the autumn of 1962. When he discovered the existence of the missiles, President Kennedy insisted on their withdrawal. The crisis which ensued in October 1962 brought the United States and the Soviet Union to the brink of nuclear war, but it was resolved by a Soviet agreement to withdraw the missiles in exchange for a United States promise not to invade Cuba. Cuban independence was thus assured – though at the cost of a high degree of dependence on the Soviet Union.

United States diplomacy concentrated on securing the support of the Organization of American States for sanctions against Cuba, thus insulating the rest of the Caribbean and the Americas from the spread of Castro's revolution. Under American pressure all but two western-hemisphere countries, Mexico and Canada, broke trade and diplomatic relations with Cuba in the early 1960s. But Castro was equally determined to export his revolution and his 1963 claim that 'the Andes would become the Sierra Maestra of Latin America' shows how far he thought the potential market for revolution extended. The most vivid sign of the failure of this policy was the capture and death of Guevara in Bolivia in 1967.

The second decade of the revolution saw Cuba become more firmly entrenched as a member of the Soviet bloc. Castro publicly supported the Soviet invasion of Czechoslovakia in 1968, a portent of the more docile role Cuba would play in the 1970s. Internally the Sovietization of the island became more pronounced. The Communist Party grew in strength and size. More Soviet and eastern-bloc technicians came to Cuba while growing numbers of Cubans received training in Russia. Central controls were clamped more tightly on education and culture.

The Cuban economy was subsumed into the Soviet economic sphere and Cuba became a formal member of COMECON. Soviet techniques of central planning were introduced. Cuba's financial debt to the USSR, measured in billions of dollars, steadily mounted, as did the island's overall dependence on the Soviet Union. Cuba also received military assistance from the Soviet Union, including sophisticated weaponry such as the MIG-23, and continued to receive the bulk of its oil supplies at prices well below OPEC price levels.

Almost certainly at the suggestion of the Soviet Union, Cuba's leaders focused on the institutionalization of the revolution during the 1970s, using the Soviet model. The post-revolutionary Communist Party had been formally created in 1965 and its first, long delayed, Congress finally occurred, ten years later, at the end of 1975. A new socialist Cuban Constitution was approved in 1976. The Cuban judiciary was reorganized in 1973, the same year that the executive-legislative power in Cuba altered with the creation of a new body, the Executive Committee of the Council of Ministers. The apparatus and power of the state and its attendant bureaucracies have grown, but Fidel Castro continues to place his own unique personal stamp on the direction his revolution takes. In spite of the institutionalization which has occurred, the Cuban revolution is still highly personalized and dominated by Castro.

Cuba's close ideological identification with the Soviet Union was mirrored by developments in its foreign policy. From active assistance to Latin American guerrilla movements in the 1960s, Cuba lined up with the Soviet policy of detente in the 1970s, which for Cuba had the advantage of a greatly reduced threat to the revolution from the United States. Cuba concentrated less on trying to export revolution to Latin America and more on improving relations with key Latin American countries in an effort to reduce its isolation. In 1975 the OAS sanctions on Cuba were lifted and during the decade diplomatic relations were established with a number of Latin American countries. Fidel Castro's foreign policy also concentrated on the Third World in general in the 1970s, and most notably on Africa. Castro and the Cuban revolutionaries had shown considerable sympathy to African liberation movements during the 1960s. In the next decade this sympathy extended to military intervention in support of these movements. The Cuban decision to intervene on a large scale in Angola in 1975 was, from all available evidence, made by the Cubans acting on their own. Approximately 20,000 Cuban troops aided the MPLA forces in their successful struggle to defeat rival movements and claim victory in an independent Angola. Cuban technicians were then sent to Angola to help build the socialist revolution while Cuban army units were gradually withdrawn.

Subsequent to the Cuban military success in Angola, Castro offered military assistance to Ethiopia in its conflict with Somalia and by 1978 thousands of Cuban troops were in the Horn of Africa. Smaller numbers of Cuban military and technical advisers were to be found in a variety of other African countries from Mozambique in the south to Libya in the north. Castro's stress on the Afro-Cuban heritage led to a new and contemporary Afro-Cuban revolutionary connection and helped to propel Fidel Castro into prominence among Third World countries in spite of his ideological alignment with Moscow. A summit conference of world non-aligned nations was held in Havana in September 1979 under Castro's leadership, an event which marked a high point of Fidel's personal influence with the leaders of the non-aligned countries. Cuban actions in Africa also helped to strengthen relations with the Soviet Union for whom Cuba had become an invaluable ally.

Cuban links with neighbouring Latin American countries entered a more difficult period in the 1980s. Colombia broke off diplomatic relations in the spring of 1981. Revolution in Nicaragua and civil war in El Salvador focused world attention on Central America, and Cuba supported the revolutionary government in Nicaragua until its defeat in elections in 1989.

After more than thirty years the revolution is still intact, although facing even more difficult challenges because of the collapse of communism in the Soviet Union and Eastern Europe. Castro remains its unchallenged leader. In some areas the successes have been marked: life expectancy is much greater now for the average Cuban than it was in 1959; birth rates and infant mortality rates have declined, signs

thousand who had left the island in the early stages of the revolution – not least the professional classes. In early 1991 Cuba once again eased restrictions on travel abroad, as an apparent safety valve for the discontent generated by economic austerity measures.

The Cuban revolution has thus created two Cubas: one contained in the island itself where the revolution permeates all aspects of life, and another among the sizeable number of expatriate Cubans, most of whom live in the United States, and for whom exile has become a permanent condition necessitating either accommodation with American culture or assimilation. For the Cuban Revolution and for Fidel Castro, the United States has remained the chief enemy, the personification of the counter-revolution which must be resisted at all costs. It remains to be seen, however, whether the revolution can continue standing alone successfully as the sole example of revolutionary socialism in the Americas.

PUERTO RICO

Area	8800 sq km
Population	3.5 million
GNP per capita (1988)	$5384
Capital	San Juan
Currency	US dollar

Puerto Rico has experienced the colonialism of two imperial powers. Madrid was the real capital of the island until 1898 when a defeated Spain ceded Puerto Rico to the United States and the centre of government shifted to Washington. Puerto Rico's colonial status then gradually evolved to a Commonwealth association with the United States. The name 'Commonwealth' itself came with a new internal constitution in 1952, suggestive of the British Commonwealth, but in reality betokening a very different relationship. Ultimate legislative power continued to reside in the United States Congress, although the island was granted internal democratic self-government.

The American conquest of 1898 imposed the boundaries of the debate on the island's status that continues today. Should the people aspire to full United States statehood or to complete independence? A referendum held in 1967 revealed that 60 per cent of the population were satisfied with Commonwealth status, while 39 per cent wanted full statehood and less than 1 per cent desired independence. The option of full statehood has been intensely discussed in recent years, and a plebiscite is a strong possibility at some point.

Fidel Castro (b.1926)

that Cuba has overcome the problems of rapid population growth confronting many Third World countries; education and health services have been made available to all sections of the population; and illiteracy has been eradicated. These particular achievements are an obvious source of pride to Cubans and impress foreign observers.

Yet the Cuban economy remains fragile and is in fact more vulnerable than ever with the collapse of the Soviet Union in 1991 and the appearance of new regimes in its former territory.

Even before this crisis economic prosperity had eluded the Cuban people. Protests by discontented Cubans escalated in 1980 to the point that the government permitted those who wanted to leave to do so. Up to 125,000 people migrated – most of them to the United States – adding to the several hundred

PUERTO RICO

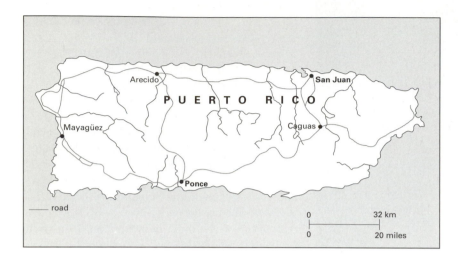

road

0   32 km
0   20 miles

Puerto Ricans were granted collective United States citizenship in 1917, which they continue to hold (although without full representation in Congress). With citizenship came other American imports, and, for a rum-producing island, the first was curious. By the Jones Act that granted American citizenship, the islanders were also required to hold a referendum on prohibition. It passed; and Puerto Rico became 'dry' even before the United States. As United States citizens, male Puerto Ricans became eligible at the same time for the draft and entry into what was then a racially segregated army. Many of the more than 17,000 who were inducted volunteered. None saw any fighting in the First World War, but over 4000 guarded the Panama Canal for the United States during the remainder of the war. It was not until 1948 that the island had a Puerto Rican governor as until then they were Americans, political appointments of the United States president and responsible to him through the American Bureau of Insular Affairs, but not accountable to the people they governed.

American economic control of the island was another consequence of the shift in imperial masters. Sugar, coffee and tobacco had been major export crops in the nineteenth century. Coffee and tobacco production declined after the American takeover, but sugar cultivation, carried out mainly by large American-owned companies, expanded, as did exports to the United States under free trade and American tariff protection. The Depression, however, caused sugar prices to fall drastically with a corresponding blow to the island's economy. Following the Second World War, with the political leadership of Luis Muñoz Marín (b. 1899; governor 1948–64) Puerto Rico rapidly industrialized under 'Operation Bootstrap'. The industrialization experiment, heavily subsidized from the mainland, had many successes,

but by the 1970s serious economic and social problems re-emerged, notably a serious neglect of agriculture, which turned Puerto Rico into a net food importer. Another problem was the capital-intensive nature of the industries, which never generated jobs in the number that Puerto Rico needed. As a result, many Puerto Ricans left the island and tried their luck on the mainland, usually in New York City.

Puerto Rico today is still divided between its Latin American and Caribbean tradition and its American connection. The division has widened appreciably since the Second World War as the other Caribbean islands have become independent and have developed new relationships with each other and with the outside world. However, Puerto Rico shares with them many of the problems of underdevelopment. The challenge for the future will be tackling these as a full State of the Union (should this transpire) without losing its distinct Hispanic cultural tradition.   DRM

Further Reading: J. I. Dominguez, *Cuba: Order and Revolution* (Cambridge, Mass., 1978); R. Guerra y Sánchez, *Sugar and Society in the Caribbean* (New Haven, Conn., 1964); L. A. Pérez Jr., *Cuba: Between Reform and Revolution* (New York, 1988); E. Montejo, *The Autobiography of a Runaway Slave* (New York, 1968); H. Thomas, *Cuba: The Pursuit of Freedom* (New York, 1971); L. W. Bergard, *Coffee and the Growth of Agrarian Capitalism in Nineteenth Century Puerto Rico* (Princeton, 1983); R. Carr, *Puerto Rico: A Colonial Experiment* (New York, 1984); T. R. Clark, *Puerto Rico and the United States 1917–1933* (Pittsburgh, 1975); J. L. Dietz, *Economic History of Puerto Rico* (Princeton, 1986)

Haiti and the Dominican Republic

HAITI

Area	27,750 sq km
Population	6.5 million
GNP per capita (1989)	$360
Capital	Port-au-Prince
Currency	Gourde

In the island of Hispaniola, divided between the new state of Haiti and the old Spanish colony of Santo

Domingo, the early nineteenth century was overshadowed by the effects of the Haitian revolution. After defeating Napoleon's army in 1803, Jean-Jacques Dessalines and his fellow generals proclaimed the independence of Haiti, but in Ocotober 1806 Dessalines was assassinated and Haiti split into two parts. A military oligarchy under Alexandre Pétion (1807–18) governed the south and west, while Henry Christophe (1806–20) ruled the northern state, which became a kingdom in 1811. Haiti was reunited at the death of Christophe in 1820, and two years later the Spanish colony of Santo Domingo was incorporated into the Haitian republic. These early years saw a struggle for land between the former free coloureds (*affranchis*) and the liberated slaves. Pétion and later Christophe made land grants to army officers and many large estates were divided among ordinary soldiers or sold to civilians. Former slaves had deserted the plantations and squatted on vacant lands. Despite efforts by Jean-Pierre Boyer (1818–43) the plantation economy was never to revive and agricultural production throughout the nineteenth century consisted largely of coffee for export and food crops for local consumption.

Internal conflicts led to the fall of Boyer, and in 1844 the Dominicans took the opportunity to declare independence. In Haiti the blacks, who had systematically been excluded from power under Boyer, reasserted themselves and, after some years of unstable and short-lived governments, Faustin Soulouque (1847–59) became president and later emperor. In the sixty-three years which followed, elites struggled for control of the state. One party was composed predominantly of mulattoes, engaged in commerce (though also with landed interests), whose strength was in the capital and in the cities of the south; they were generally francophile and supported the Concordat, reached with the Vatican in 1860. The other party was usually controlled by black generals and landowners. Their support came from Cap Haïtien and from rural areas; they sometimes appealed for US support and were generally anticlerical, being freemasons or protestants. Although each party's leadership was predominantly of one colour, they were never monochrome. Black presidential candidates were often put forward by mulatto politicians hoping to exercise power behind the façade, while disaffected blacks often associated themselves with the predominantly mulatto party. Though the colour issue was rarely absent from politics it was never the sole factor determining alliances. The masses, who were poor, black and illiterate, engaged in sporadic revolts against unpopular presidents, but were seldom able to exert constructive pressure upon succeeding regimes.

Haitian independence was founded on the idea of race. The first constitution (1805) proclaimed that Haitians of all shades were to be known as *noir* and that no *blanc* could own property in the country. Throughout the nineteenth century articulate Haitians defended the black race against European racialists. Nevertheless, among the elites European culture predominated; this was reinforced by the church's commanding role in education after 1860. However, African customs – and particularly the Voodoo religion – prevailed among the masses. The popular language was and remains créole (or Kreyol) – a French-based patois.

HAITI AND THE DOMINICAN REPUBLIC

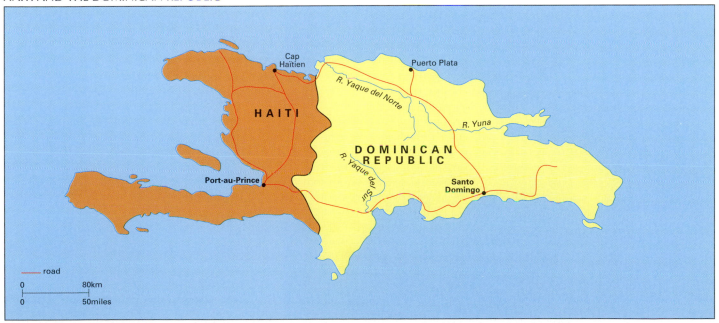

In 1825 France had recognized Haitian independence after Boyer agreed to massive compensation to dispossessed planters. Then later governments contracted further foreign debts, which prompted several external interventions, culminating in the US invasion of 1915, following a period of acute instability after the fall of President Antoine Simon in 1910. The US action was part of a general plan for the strategic and economic control of the Caribbean. A puppet president was installed and the policy of the US administration was concerned principally with making Haiti a safe and attractive field for US investors by ensuring strict debt repayments, improving the infrastructure and strengthening the middle class (which it was believed would lead to stable democracy). However, in the early years the occupation met with military resistance from peasant irregulars under Charlemagne Péralte, and later a growing nationalist movement, encompassing Haitians of different colours and ideological commitments, forced US withdrawal in 1934.

One effect of the occupation was the re-establishment of mulattoes in political power. President Sténio Vincent (1930–41) was skilful in deflecting the challenge of the growing black middle class, but his successor was less astute, and in 1946, after a military coup, a black school teacher, Dumarsais Estimé (1946–50), became president with strong support from the countryside. He was in turn overthrown by

François Duvalier, 'Papa Doc' (1907–71)

Paul Magloire (1950–6), but he represented the return of the old elite, behind the façade of a black president. When he too fell there was a bitter struggle which led to the election of François Duvalier (1957–71), with backing from radical black groups (*noiristes*). Parading an ideology of nationalism and *négritude* (deriving from his involvement with the ethnological movement of the occupation period) Duvalier dealt ruthlessly with opposition groups and drastically reduced the power of the army, the church, the trade unions, the business community and the US embassy. From about 1966 on, however, he came to terms with each of these groups, and his son, Jean-Claude (1971–86), who succeeded him, continued this policy of accommodation.

However, J.-C. Duvalier lost the support of many key black leaders and became more dependent on sectors of the commercial elite. Opposition increased and he fled the country in 1986. The following years saw a succession of military-dominated governments. After the adoption of a new constitution in 1987 an abortive election was held, which ended in violence. A re-scheduled election in December 1990 resulted in a massive majority for Jean-Bertrand Aristide, a thirty-seven-year-old Catholic priest who had recently been expelled from his order (the Salesians) and suspended from officiating. However, he was forced to flee the country in 1991.

Although there has recently been urban growth, associated with the establishment of light manufacturing industries and assembly plants around the capital, the economy is still centred on agriculture, with over 80 per cent of the population living in rural areas. Contending with serious soil erosion, frequent droughts, occasional earthquakes and hurricanes, these peasants eke out a meagre existence. Haiti has the lowest per-capita income in the hemisphere, estimated by the World Bank to be $360 for 1989, less than half that of the neighbouring Dominican Republic. Recent decades have witnessed a huge migration of Haitians to the United States, the Dominican Republic and the Bahamas.

THE DOMINICAN REPUBLIC

Area	48,442 sq km
Population	7.2 million
GNP per capita (1989)	$790
Capital	Santo Domingo
Currency	Peso

Haiti had taken over the Spanish eastern part of the island in 1822, but nationalist sentiment soon also

Generalissimo Rafael Leonidas Trujillo (1891–1961)

gathered momentum in Santo Domingo, and in 1838 a secret society, known as La Trinitaria, was founded by Juan Pablo Duarte and others to work for independence. Encouraged by Britain and France, the Dominicans proclaimed independence in 1844. However, Duarte and the other leaders of the movement, Sánchez and Mella, were forced into exile by Pedro Santana (1844–58 and 1858–61), who became the first president. War with Haiti and a consequent search for foreign protection followed independence, ending in 1861 with the re-establishment of Spanish rule. Soon a new independence struggle led by the mulatto general, Gregorio Luperón (1879–80), broke out, and in 1865 Spanish forces withdrew.

The following sixty years saw a contest between rival generals, often in league with Haitian leaders; the church also played a significant political role. From 1882 the fortunes of the country were in the hands of a black general, Ulises Heureaux (1882–4 and 1887–99), whose dictatorial regime achieved improvements in communications and a growth in coffee production, though at the cost of increased foreign intervention. External loans left the country with enormous debts, the non-payment of which provided excuse for foreign intervention. The United States, which was also interested in a naval base at Samaná and in checking the growth of German influence, established a customs receivership to ensure debt repayment in 1905.

The eastern part of Hispaniola was, compared with its neighbour, relatively undeveloped during the nineteenth century. The economy was dominated by cattle ranching and tobacco growing, together with crops for local consumption grown particularly in the fertile Cibao valley. In the 1870s, partly due to the arrival of Cuban exiles, the sugar industry grew rapidly. Coffee and cocoa plantations were also developed about the same time, while Lebanese and other migrant groups started small manufacturing industries. Towards the end of the century US financial involvement increased considerably.

The assassination of Heureaux in 1899 led to a period of governmental instability, broken only by the regime of Ramón Cáceres (1905–11). In 1916 the United States invaded again, and occupied the country until 1924, encountering some guerrilla resistance. Public works were undertaken and the economic crisis of 1921 led the country into further debt. The occupation set the scene for the advent of Rafael Trujillo (1930–6 and 1940–52) who, after rising through the police force, became army commander in 1927 and president three years later. Thus began thirty-one years of ruthless dictatorship.

The Trujillo era saw a significant expansion of the economy, which became inextricably interwoven

with his personal and family fortune. The population doubled, enormous public works schemes were undertaken and manufacturing industries sprang up. '*El Benefactor*', as he was known, posed as the defender of 'European' and 'Catholic' civilization, and his policy of 'de-Africanizing' the border involved the massacre of 12,000–20,000 Haitians in 1937. During the 1950s Trujillo lost support and there was increasing disaffection on the part of the church and the United States. His attempted assassination of President Betancourt of Venezuela in 1960 and the sanctuary given to such former dictators as Perón, Pérez Jiménez and Batista, led to opposition from Latin American countries. In 1961 a group of military officers, with the complicity of the CIA, assassinated him.

Following the fall of Trujillo a series of short-lived governments culminated in the crisis of 1965, when the United States, fearing a 'second Cuba', invaded. A presidential contest in the following year between two former heads of state, Juan Bosch (1963) and Joaquín Balaguer (1960–2, 1966–74 and 1986–) resulted in victory for the latter, who had US support. His conservative regime lasted effectively until 1978 when he was defeated by Antonio Guzmán (1978–82), a rich agriculturalist with a radical reputation, which subsequently proved to be undeserved. In 1982 (after a short interregnum following

305

Guzmán's suicide) Salvador Jorge Blanco (1982–6) – also of the Partido Revolucionario Dominicano – became president. These PRD administrations were characterized by massive corruption, and in 1986 Balaguer returned to office. He successfully defended his leadership four years later in elections against his old rival Bosch, both men by then octogenarians.

Economic developments in the post-Trujillo era have included the mining of gold, silver and ferronickel, and the establishment of free-zone light manufacturing plants. But Balaguer's ambitious construction of ostentatious public monuments and his lack of any coherent programme have led to a serious economic crisis with spiralling inflation.

For two centuries Dominicans have looked with unease upon their more densely populated neighbour. The 1844 independence movement stressed their European and 'civilized' culture as opposed to the 'barbarous' Haitians. Such racialism has continued to play a significant part in relations between the two states, as many Dominican historians acknowledge. The literary heritage of the country naturally developed out of its Spanish roots but it was not until the present century that literary figures of international significance emerged. Despite possessing the oldest university in Latin America, the education system was quite primitive until reformed in 1880 by the Puerto Rican educationalist Hostos. Today the country has several large universities. DN

Further Reading: I. Bell, *The Dominican Republic* (Boulder, Colorado, 1981); J. Leyburn, *The Haitian People* (New Haven, Conn., 1966); R. W. Logan, *Haiti and the Dominican Republic* (London, 1968); D. Nicholls, *From Dessalines to Duvalier* (Cambridge, 1979); B. Weinstein and A. Segal, *Haiti: Political Failures, Cultural Successes* (New York, 1984); S. Welles, *Naboth's Vineyard: The Dominican Republic 1824–1924* (New York, 1928)

Movements for Latin American unity

The very term 'Latin America' suggests a degree of unity which masks considerable differences in size, natural resources, ethnic composition and degree of political and economic maturity among the republics it embraces. Latin America has never, of course, been united, and both geography and history have encouraged disunity. Thus, relations among the Latin American states have been bedevilled by territorial disputes, some of them unresolved today. In particular, Brazil's size, strategic position and growing power have aroused fear and suspicion among the other republics, especially, until very recently, from Argentina.

Nevertheless, the ideal of Latin American – or, at least Spanish American – unity has persisted from the time of independence to the present day. The idea has been associated, above all, with Simón Bolívar, one of the most revered of Latin America's historical figures, whose bicentenary in 1983 was extensively celebrated in the region. He inspired the Panama Congress held in 1826, which attempted to form a Latin American confederation. Although it was attended by only a few Spanish American countries, and failed to achieve its objective, the Congress is regarded as the precursor of all later attempts to bring about Latin American unity. During the nineteenth century there were further Spanish American congresses, again with limited attendance and no significant achievement. All were concerned with common defence against possible intervention from outside the region.

Then, towards the end of the century, the United States promoted 'Pan Americanism' based, not upon Latin American unity, but rather the concept of a special relationship between the Latin American states and itself. Yet those promoting it claimed that Pan Americanism expressed Bolívar's ideals. The International Union of American Republics was established in 1890, and from it developed the inter-American system which since 1948 has centred upon the Organization of American States (OAS). That system has basically been an instrument of United States policy towards Latin America. Yet it has been within the inter-American system, and *in reaction to* it, that movements for Latin American unity have often developed.

Thus, it was in reaction to United States unwillingness to grant Latin America substantial economic aid that led the governments of the region in 1948 to insist, in the face of United States opposition, upon the creation of the United Nations Economic Commission for Latin America (ECLA) – later expanded to include the Caribbean (ECLAC). It was this body that stimulated Latin American economic integration. Consequently, agreements for a Latin American Free Trade Association (LAFTA), eventually comprising all South American republics and Mexico, and a General Treaty for Central American Economic Integration (CACM) were signed in 1960. Neither was particularly successful. A subgroup, formed in 1969 by the Andean countries of Bolivia, Chile, Colombia, Ecuador and (eventually)

Pan-American Union
Building, Washington DC

Venezuela, had among its objectives not only the liberalization of trade, but joint industrial planning and a common policy for investment. However, progress in the Andean Group was hampered by conflicting state interests and some serious disputes between its members. Meanwhile, Latin American economic integration had been included in the programme of the Alliance for Progress, initiated by the United States in 1961.

Dissatisfaction with that Alliance – and with United States economic aid generally – combined with a significant global development to prompt the states of Latin America to attempt the establishment of a common Latin American position in the international economic order. In 1964 the first United Nations Conference on Trade and Development (UNCTAD) was held in Geneva. The Latin American representatives met beforehand to hammer out a common strategy, and subsequently set up a Special Latin American Co-ordinating Commission (CECLA). This body went on to affirm 'the distinctive personality of Latin America' in its international relations.

In 1975 the Latin American Economic System (SELA) was created as a forum for economic co-operation and consultation. The new organization had two broad objectives: to promote regional co-operation for economic development, chiefly through distinctly Latin American multinational enterprises; and to establish a system of consultation for the adoption of common economic positions in relation to other countries and international organizations. In this SELA was to replace CECLA.

The prospects for further Latin American unity seem mixed. In 1980 a new version of LAFTA, the Latin American Integration Association (LAIA), was launched, largely codifying the practice of LAFTA, and in the mid-1980s some substance was inserted into its framework by a far-reaching commercial rapprochement between Argentina, Uruguay and Brazil. In the course of (and largely as a consequence of) the prolonged debt crisis which gripped Latin America after 1982, many of the *dirigiste* axioms of ECLAC were abandoned in favour of the doctrine of free trade and opening to the rest of the world economy. As a result, Latin America started negotiating bilateral and multilateral free trade areas within the framework of LAIA. Neither the United States nor Canada wants to be excluded and each is now negotiating framework agreements with various Latin American countries.

To counteract any loss of economic sovereignty that such free trade areas entered into with the United States and Canada might entail, Mexico,

Venezuela and Colombia – even prior to these developments – have launched various independent, imaginative and to some extent successful joint diplomatic intitiatives, such as that of the Contadora Group after 1983, signalling the advent of a distinctly Latin American foreign policy. Its scope has been expanding, and its cumulative effect might be to repair the damage done by United States intervention, or to prevent altogether some of its recent excesses. The dream of Latin American unity remains alive.   GC-S/FP

Further Reading: G. Pope Atkins, *Latin America in the International Political System* (2nd ed., San Francisco, 1989); R. D. Bond, 'Regionalism in Latin America: Prospects for the Latin American Economic System (SELA)', *International Organization, vol. 32* (1978); G. Connell-Smith, *The Inter-American System* (Oxford, 1966); R. Hilton, ed., *The Movement toward Latin American Unity* (New York, 1969); J. J. Johnson, *A Hemisphere Apart: The Foundations of United States Policy toward Latin America* (Baltimore, 1990)

Wars in Latin America

Wars between Latin American nations have been relatively uncommon in the period since independence. Internal warfare, as articles on individual countries in this Encyclopedia show, is another matter. War scares have occurred from time to time – as, for instance, between Argentina and Chile in the years 1895–1901 and again in 1978 – but war itself has not usually resulted. The principal international conflicts have been:

THE ARGENTINE–BRAZILIAN WAR, 1825-8

This was the first war between newly independent states in the region. It was started by the invasion (in April 1825) of the Spanish-speaking Banda Oriental (now Uruguay) by the 'Heroic Thirty-Three Orientales', rebels who wished to free their homeland from Brazil, which had occupied the area in 1817, subsequently annexing it and calling it the Cisplatine Province. Argentina proclaimed the incorporation of the Banda Oriental into its own territory, and Brazil retaliated by declaring war. Fighting was intermittent, but February 1827 saw two significant Argentine victories: the naval action of Juncal and the battle

of Ituzaingó. The war ended soon afterwards through British pressure and mediation, which resulted in the creation (1828) of a 'buffer country', the new Republic of Uruguay, in the disputed territory.

THE WAR BETWEEN CHILE AND THE PERU–BOLIVIAN CONFEDERATION, 1836–9

The establishment (1836) of the Peru–Bolivian Confederation by General Andrés Santa Cruz (1792–1865) aroused immediate hostility from the government of Chile, which declared war on the new state. Two Chilean expeditionary forces were sent to Peru. The first of these was trapped by Santa Cruz into withdrawing (Treaty of Paucarpata, 1837). A second and stronger expedition, commanded by General Manuel Bulnes (1799–1866; president of Chile 1841–51), occupied the Peruvian capital, Lima, and went on to win the decisive battle of the war at Yungay, in the Andes (January 1839). The Peru–Bolivian Confederation rapidly dissolved.

THE WAR OF THE TRIPLE ALLIANCE (OR PARAGUAYAN WAR), 1864–70

The background to this war was complex, one of the key issues being control of the upper Paraná River basin, which formed a vital transport line into southwest Brazil. Combat started with a Paraguayan invasion of Rio Grande do Sul, Brazil – an effort by the Paraguayan dictator Francisco Solano López to counteract Brazilian influence in Uruguay. In order to reach Brazil, Paraguayan troops had to cross Argentine territory, which drew Argentina into the conflict. In May 1865, Argentina, Brazil and Uruguay signed a Triple Alliance to defeat López. The empire of Brazil supplied the largest contingents of troops. The Allied army was commanded first by the Argentine president Bartolomé Mitre, and then, from 1867 to 1869, by the distinguished Brazilian general Luis Alves de Lima e Silva, Marquis (later Duke) of Caxias (103–80). Obstructed by the impressive fortress-complex at Humaitá, just inside Paraguayan territory, the Allies' advance up the line of the River Paraguay was slow and extremely costly. The Paraguayan capital, Asunción, fell to the Allied army only in January 1869. López himself was hunted down and killed (1 March 1870). 'I die with my homeland!' he is supposed to have said. Approximately 100,000 Allied soldiers died in the war, which is also believed to have reduced the male population of Paraguay by nine-tenths, making this the most devastating war in modern Latin American history.

WARS IN LATIN AMERICA

MEXICO

CUBA

HONDURAS

GUATEMALA
EL SALVADOR

NICARAGUA

'Soccer War', 1969

COSTA RICA

VENEZUELA

COLOMBIA

ECUADOR

Ecuador-Peru
Conflict, 1941

PERU

BRAZIL

War between Chile
and the Peru-Bolivian
Confederation, 1836-9

BOLIVIA

Chaco War,
1932-5

War of the Pacific,
1879-83

PARAGUAY

War of the
Triple Alliance,
1864-70

Argentine-
Brazilian War,
1825-8

CHILE

ARGENTINA

URUGUAY

| 0 | | 1600 km |
| 0 | | 1000 miles |

British-made tank used in the Chaco War and now on display in Asunción, Paraguay

THE WAR OF THE PACIFIC, 1879–83

This war arose out of Bolivia's threat to confiscate a Chilean nitrate concern operating in the Atacama Desert, then a coastal province of Bolivia. To forestall this move, Chilean forces occupied the port of Antofagasta (February 1879) and the Bolivian littoral. Peru was drawn into the conflict by virtue of a secret treaty of alliance with Bolivia (1873). After several months of naval warfare – the chief battles being those of Iquique (May 1879), a Peruvian victory, and Cape Angamos (October 1879), a Chilean victory – Chile gained command of the sea, and was thus enabled to dispatch large armies to the northern deserts. Two major campaigns gave Chile possession of the Peruvian territories of Tarapacá and Tacna-Arica, after which Bolivia played no further part in the war. A third Chilean expeditionary force, under General Manuel Baquedano (1826–97), was sent to capture Lima, which it did following the bloody battles of Chorrillos and Miraflores (January 1881). If the wars of independence are included, this was the third occasion in the nineteenth century when Chilean soldiers occupied the Peruvian capital. Peruvian guerrilla bands continued the war for two years, but to no avail. Peru finally bowed to the victors' demands in the Treaty of Ancón (October 1883), ceding Tarapacá to Chile in perpetuity and Tacna-Arica for a limited period. (The Tacna-Arica territory became the focus of a lengthy diplomatic wrangle, settled only in 1929.) Bolivia also eventually accepted the cession of Atacama to Chile, and thus became a landlocked nation. The war left bitter feelings of defeat in Peru and Bolivia alike.

THE CHACO WAR, 1932–5

The only major international conflict in twentieth-century Latin America, the Chaco War was a struggle for territory between Bolivia and Paraguay. A number of armed clashes had taken place in the Northern Chaco (an area whose ownership had long been disputed by the two states) prior to the outbreak of war in mid-1932. Although outnumbered by their Bolivian opponents (who were commanded for a time by a German general, Hans Kundt), the Paraguayans, led by the brilliant Colonel José Felix Estigarribia (1888–1940; president of Paraguay 1939–40) – noted for his *corralito* ('encirclement') tactic – succeeded in winning most of the area in contention. International pressure finally brought about a cease-fire (June 1935). Paraguay's victories on the battlefield bore fruit in the eventual peace treaty (July 1938). Some 50,000 Bolivians (the total is sometimes put at 70,000) and some 35,000 Paraguayans died in the Chaco War. Bolivia's loss of territory led to a traumatic soul-searching among the country's elite.

THE ECUADOR–PERU CONFLICT, 1941

Peru had long laid claim to large sections of Ecuador's *Oriente* (Amazon territory), much of which had already been transferred by treaty to Brazil and Colombia. In July 1941 Peruvian forces invaded the Ecuadorian coastal province of El Oro, bombing several defenceless villages and speedily capturing the provincial capital. Fighting continued until October 1941. At the western hemisphere foreign ministers' conference at Rio de Janeiro in January 1942 – with the Second World War uppermost in ministers' minds – Ecuador was persuaded to part reluctantly with a large tract of disputed territory. (There were further border clashes in 1981.)

THE FOOTBALL (OR SOCCER) WAR, 1969

Honduran actions against the large Salvadorean community established in Honduras (driven there by overcrowding in El Salvador) led in 1969 to much ill-feeling between the two Central American states. These recriminations came to a head when the two national soccer teams were playing each other in qualifying games for the 1970 World Cup. On 14 July 1969 the Salvadorean army launched an attack over the border into Honduras, expecting an easy victory. Fighting lasted for several days, some 2000 men being killed, until proposals from the Organization of American States brought this lightning war to a close.   SC

The non-Latin Caribbean islands since 1815

The peace settlement of 1815 at the end of the Napoleonic Wars was a watershed in the island -juggling game of the European powers. Britain emerged supreme once again in the Caribbean, gaining St Lucia, Tobago, Trinidad, Demerara, Essequibo and Berbice; France retained Martinique and Guadeloupe; and Spain kept Puerto Rico and Cuba. By then, the French had been driven from Hispaniola (Haiti/Dominican Republic) not by European rivals or indigenous tribes, but by the very slaves they had earlier imported. Since 1791, the French-held western part of the island of Hispaniola had passed through the hands of Toussaint Louverture, the triumphant leader of the Haitian revolution, and in 1821, the eastern part of Hispaniola declared its independence from Spain as the Dominican Republic. The struggle against European colonialism had thus begun. The liberation of Spanish and Portuguese colonies in South America and the US Monroe Doctrine of 1823 sounded a warning to the colonial powers.

Colonial rule, slavery and the struggle for independence all overlapped from place to place. There was never a static colonial pattern in the development of the West Indian societies. Many bear the imprint of a succession of European masters. The nationality of the colonial settlements was not the line of most significant divide in the region. Except for the administrative elite, the plantation structure provided the most powerful force in the formation of Caribbean 'creole' societies.

BEFORE EMANCIPATION

The economies of the West Indies waxed and waned, but everywhere they were characterized by two common features – monoculture and absentee ownership. Cotton was a principal crop until the early nineteenth century, and tobacco until that century's end. However, the crop which determined the economic value of the region and governed social structure from the mid-seventeenth century was sugar.

Sugar was big business, requiring large inputs of capital for land and machinery, together with vast supplies of labour for harvesting the cane. The plantations, and even entire West Indian territories, became part of a wider international system whose rules were determined elsewhere. Production was geared to the needs of the metropolis and the profits went to the planters, who were often absentee.

The number of African slaves imported into the West Indies corresponded directly to plantation expansion. Their continued arrival from Africa was both cause and consequence of the successes of sugar production. Millions of slaves had been imported into the region between the seventeenth and eighteenth centuries, and by the end of the eighteenth century Barbados and Hispaniola had the highest proportion of slaves to free men that the world has ever known. In those territories where sugar production was not dominant until later in the nineteenth century – Trinidad and British Guiana, for example – slave imports were relatively low.

All blacks were not slaves, though the majority certainly were, for manumission was impossible for most. Yet there were groups of runaway slaves (Maroons) and urban slaves, too, were sometimes able to purchase freedom with savings from their craft income. The most significant group of non-white free persons was the coloureds, many of whom, through their part-white parentage, had escaped the ranks of the slaves. Miscegenation between Europeans and Africans, then between Europeans and mulattoes, occurred at first by an illegal, but at all times an informally accepted, pattern of concubinage. Despite miscegenation, however, the brown groups formed a relatively small proportion of most West Indian populations and the early ratios of black to brown and white at the time of emancipation of slaves have been generally maintained to the present day.

AFTER EMANCIPATION

The plantation was shaken though not shattered by the emancipation of slaves in the nineteenth century. Emancipation did not occur simultaneously throughout the region: in 1834, slaves in the British colonies were freed, but not until 1848 and 1863 did this happen for French and Dutch slaves respectively. With the acts of emancipation affecting various parts of the Caribbean at different times over half a century, the impact necessarily varied.

After emancipation, the former slaves sought to leave the plantations. Many established themselves as independent cultivators forming the origins of the black West Indian free peasantry. Some left their island altogether, even repeatedly, to take advantage of the new circumstances of the labour market abroad and with the objective that on their return, armed

JAMAICA

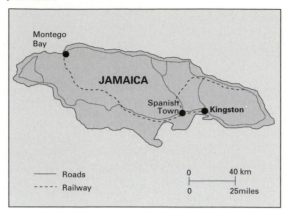

THE LESSER ANTILLES

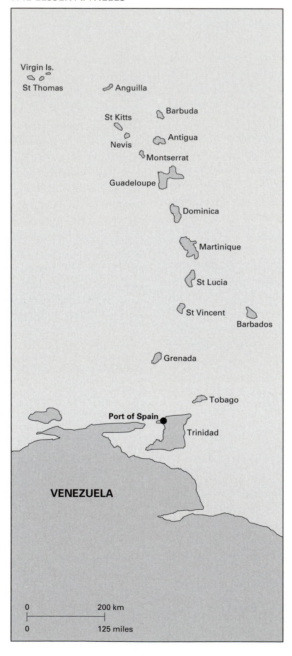

with their savings, they would be independent of planters and all other local employers.

Meanwhile, Caribbean cane sugar was facing stiff competition from European beet sugar. The problems of the planters were greatly exacerbated by their loss of labour, although the illegal importation of new slaves from Africa continued long after the British abolished the trade in 1807. In Trinidad, British Guiana and Surinam, where slaves were no longer available by the time the sugar industry was expanded in the mid-nineteenth century, a labour supply had to be sought elsewhere. India was the principal, though not the sole source of contract labour brought in during the nineteenth century. Portuguese from Madeira went chiefly to British Guiana, Chinese were imported to British Guiana, Trinidad, Martinique, and in even larger numbers to Cuba.

The Asian immigration was significant, not only because of the numbers involved, but also because of its social implications. Only four Caribbean territories – Haiti, the Dominican Republic, Puerto Rico and Barbados – were not included in the new demographic revolution of the nineteenth century. In virtually all other territories, the demographic composition by the end of the nineteenth century comprised a small minority of whites, some mulattoes, a majority of blacks and another segment made up of Indians, Chinese, Javanese or Portuguese in various combinations and degrees of miscegenation. The only other ethnic groups in the West Indian societal mix were Jews (especially in Jamaica and Curaçao), Syrians, Palestinians and Lebanese. Ethnic antagonisms developed in the late nineteenth century which have been carried on to the present day, particularly between the Indian and black communities in Trinidad (and also in Guyana).

THE CONTEMPORARY ERA

Later social influences in the West Indies were not principally from Europe, Africa or Asia, but from North America, especially the United States. As with the former colonial influences from Europe, so those from the United States affected the entire Caribbean, though the extent of Americanization has varied from place to place. The strategic and economic significance of the West Indies to the United States was greatly enhanced towards the end of the nineteenth century, when European and US interests focused upon the need to build a canal across the Central American isthmus. It was to be a vital military and economic link between the Atlantic and the Pacific. The United States was quick to grasp the opportunity of seizing Cuba and Puerto Rico in 1898, following the Spanish–American war, and later became heavily involved in the internal affairs of Haiti and the Dominican Republic. The entire region was further brought under US influence by the establishment of military bases at Guantánamo in Cuba and Chaguaramas in Trinidad. Finally, in 1917, to forestall the possibility of Germany constructing a naval base on the Virgin Island of St John, the United States purchased the island from Denmark, along with St Croix, part of St Martin and St Thomas.

Throughout the early decades of the twentieth century the entire Caribbean region became enveloped by American 'dollar diplomacy'. Sugar interests were consolidated in Cuba, the Dominican Republic and Puerto Rico, and the United Fruit Company expanded to form a vast empire in Central America. A similar pattern developed in oil in Trinidad and bauxite in Jamaica and Guyana, as well as manufacturing and tourism in many territories of the region. Many West Indian lands, and especially those under direct US control, became re-shaped by the process of Americanization.

Caribbean peoples faced problems of identity, which related chiefly to colour and ethnicity, a sense of place and nationality. Modern Caribbean societies have responded to the inherited lack of a meaningful racial identity. *Négritude* as a literary movement emerged in the French island of Martinique in the 1930s in the writings of Aimé Césaire. This movement stemmed chiefly from Cuban literature while the philosophy behind it, glorifying Africa and rejecting Europe, derived from Haitian folklore. Only in Haiti was an African cultural element as fundamental as Voodoo given official support at the expense of European forms. The Black Power movement of the 1970s throughout most of the region was the culmination of the search for an identity through

Mechanized cutting of sugar-cane, Jamaica

the dramatic transformation of the image of the black man. In Jamaica, the eastern Caribbean and Guyana, the result has been a major reversal of racial attitudes which, contrasting with the former situation, has had the effect of alienating the white, light brown, Indian and Chinese groups in society. Exceptions to this reversal of racial attitudes have been the countries of the Spanish Caribbean – Cuba, Puerto Rico and the Dominican Republic.

The West Indian's sense of uncertain racial identity is compounded by an ambivalence about his belonging to the West Indies. All West Indians are relative newcomers and they have tended to lack many of the deep-rooted emotional ties to their country found among indigenous societies. Even peasantries in the West Indies are not closely attached to the land. The 1910s and 1920s saw the rise of Garveyism which pointed towards Africa as holding the only promise for the black man. Marcus Garvey's call for repatriation to Africa did not meet with an immediate response, but later became the rallying cry for the Rastafari cult. Despite all the difficulties surrounding the question of identity in the West Indies, however, nationalism has continued to grow.

Island loyalties can best be seen in terms of autonomy vis-à-vis the rest of the Caribbean. The failure of the West Indies Federation (1958–62) underscored the lack of a regional sense of identity. Anguilla's stand against constitutional inclusion with St Kitts and Nevis, the cause of a minor crisis in 1969, emanated from the same type of separatist sentiment. Aruba objected to independence proposals from the Netherlands because of fears of being subjected to Curaçao.

Post-emancipation diversifications in West Indian agriculture and the twentieth-century development of industry were generally unaccompanied by any significant structural change. Each new crop or industry has occurred within a framework strikingly reminiscent of the original plantation. Control, and in many cases ownership, have been absentee, production has been primarily geared to export needs and the bulk of the profits have been realized outside the region. Despite many changes in welfare for the workers and national government participation, the islands have remained primary-product producers.

Where industrial development included the manufacture of finished goods, only the local provision of assembly plants and cheap labour have been involved. In some territories, ownership has been localized, as in the case of Guyana's bauxite since the 1960s. In Jamaica, the state increased its ownership of shares in bauxite production to 51 per cent in 1977. Even sugar production has been nationalized in most West Indian territories since the 1960s and 1970s. Despite these changes, however, the main issues for

West Indian self-determination relate to economic viability.

Economic growth is frequently, though mistakenly, taken to imply development. It does not imply, nor in the Caribbean does it necessarily include, social development. The bauxite boom years of the 1950s and 1960s in Jamaica were accompanied by a widening of the gap in the distribution of real earnings. Furthermore, unsustained economic growth can coexist with high unemployment rates.

The increasing West Indian populations are inevitably regarded as a problem of over-population in the context of inadequate local resources, accompanied by inadequate re-investment of profits. Between 1960 and 1970 growth rates were approximately 4 per cent throughout the British Commonwealth Caribbean while the population increase was 2 per cent or more. The rate of per-capita growth in the Commonwealth Caribbean, as elsewhere in the region, was therefore limited. In describing 'the problem', many observers have disproportionately blamed the population increases rather than the discrepancies in the growth of different sectors of the economy. Likewise, heavy migration to the towns and cities has been regarded more as a cause than a symptom of national problems. Population increases and the concentration of the poor in the cities merely bring to a head many of the issues inherent in West Indian societies.

Constitutionally the West Indies includes republics, colonies, associated and Commonwealth states, protectorates and departments (in the case of the French possessions). In general, however, independence has been the main political goal since the 1960s. Jamaica and Trinidad and Tobago achieved independence in 1962, and Guyana and Barbados in 1966. Other territories became independent later,

such as the Bahamas in 1973 and Grenada in 1974. Like emancipation, independence is, in a constitutional sense, merely a redefinition of the legal status of the society in relation to the metropolis. Neither brought about an instant metamorphosis of society. Even the earlier example of Haitian independence was a hollow victory in real terms. French colonial masters were replaced by tyrannical regimes and Haiti's people have never been truly liberated.

West Indian societies have not yet rid themselves of their age-old and recurring sense of defeatism. Virtually every generation has been intimidated by threats of impending doom. This absence of national confidence, so typical throughout the region, reflects the precariousness of West Indian fortunes which have traditionally balanced between the internal struggles of the societies on the one hand, and on the other hand, the economic and political pressures of the world outside. Such constant flirtation with defeat and the destruction of national morale place limitations on the development of national independence.

The reconstruction of the social order and social relations in the West Indies is a necessary accompaniment to the wider national struggle against conditions of dependence. These are likely to remain the outstanding issues for the future.   EMT-H

Further Reading: F. W. Knight, *The Caribbean: The Genesis of a Fragmented Nationalism,* 2nd edition (New York, 1990); G. K. Lewis, *The Growth of the Modern West Indies* (New York, 1968); D. Lowenthal, *West Indian Societies* (London, 1972); S. Mintz, *Caribbean Transformations* (Chicago, 1974); E. M. Thomas-Hope, ed., *Perspectives on Caribbean Regional Identity* (Liverpool, 1983)

Michael Manley

Political changes in the Caribbean

The Commonwealth Caribbean

Jamaica became independent in August 1962. The Jamaica Labour Party (JLP) won the elections of 1962 and 1967, but lost in 1972 to the island's other main political movement, the People's National Party (PNP) under Mr Michael Manley, an eloquent advocate of democratic socialist ideas. The PNP won office again in 1976, but was defeated, in a bitterly fought election, in 1980, when Mr Edward Seaga (JLP) became prime minister on a platform of private enterprise. Manley and the PLP returned to office in 1989 with a middle-of-the-road programme.

Trinidad and Tobago (administratively associated in 1888) also became independent in August 1962, and a republic within the Commonwealth in 1976. Its political life was shaken in 1970 with 'Black Power' disturbances and the mutiny of part of the army, but the ruling People's National Movement (PNM) was confirmed in power by a handsome majority in 1971. The country's long-serving first prime minister, Dr Eric Williams, a noted historian of the Caribbean, died in 1981. He was succeeded by Mr George Chambers. Elections in 1986 were won by the new National Alliance for Reconstruction under Mr A. N. R. Robinson but the PNM returned to power in December 1991, when Mr Patrick Manning became prime minister.

Barbados became independent in 1966. The Democratic Labour Party (DLP) was ousted in the elections of 1976 by Mr Tom Adams's Barbados Labour Party (BLP), which was re-elected in 1981. The DLP won in 1986 and again in 1991.

The Bahamas became independent in 1973 under the Progressive Liberal Party (PLP) and prime minister Mr (later Sir) Lynden Pindling. The PLP was returned to office in 1977, 1982, and 1987.

Grenada became independent in 1974. Its first prime minister, Sir Eric Gairy, leader of the Grenada United Labour Party (GULP), adopted an increasingly authoritarian style, and was overthrown in a revolution (March 1979) by the New Jewel Movement (NJM) – 'Jewel' being an acronym for Joint Endeavour in Welfare, Education and Liberation – under the popular Mr Maurice Bishop. Dissensions within the NJM leadership led to Mr Bishop's murder by hard-liners (October 1983). A few days later a US invasion force took control of the island. An interim administration under the governor-general, Sir Paul Scoon, led to elections in December 1984 which were won by Herbert Blaize and the New National Party (NNP) coalition. Blaize's death (1989) led to an inconclusive election in 1990, with Mr Nicholas Braithwaite (National Democratic Congress) becoming prime minister.

Dominica became independent, as a republic within the Commonwealth, in 1978. Its first prime minister, Mr Patrick John, was ousted during a political crisis the following year. The elections of 1982 were won by the Dominica Freedom Party (DFP) under Miss Eugenia Charles, who became prime minister. She won elections in 1985 and 1990.

St Vincent became independent in 1979, its first prime minister being Mr Milton Cato of the St Vincent Labour Party (SVLP). The elections of 1984 and 1989 brought victory to Mr James Mitchell and his New Democratic Party (NDP).

St Lucia became independent in 1979, prime minister

Mr John Compton of the United Workers Party (UWP) then being in office. Later that year the St Lucia Labour Party was elected to power, but Mr Compton and his party returned to government after the elections of 1983 and again in 1987.

Antigua became independent in 1981, under the prime ministership of Mr Vere Bird of the Antigua Labour Party (ALP), which won the elections of 1984 and 1989.

St Kitts–Nevis became independent in 1983 under the prime ministership of Dr Kennedy Simmonds (People's Action Movement). He was re-elected in 1984 and 1989.

Montserrat remains a self-governing British colony. *Anguilla* seceded from St Kitts–Nevis in 1967, and its 'unilateral declaration of independence' in 1969 provoked a slightly comic crisis. It is a British colony administered under the Anguilla Constitution Order (1982).

The British Virgin Islands, the *Cayman Islands,* and the *Turks and Caicos Islands,* three small island-groups with very small populations, are British Crown Colonies with varying degrees of internal self-government.

The Netherlands Antilles

Under a Charter issued in 1954 by Queen Juliana, the islands of the so-called 'ABC' group, off Venezuela, *Curaçao, Bonaire* and *Aruba,* and the Leeward Islands of *St Eustatius, St Martin* (Dutch part) and *Saba* were constituted politically as an autonomous part of the Kingdom of the Netherlands. They have a Governor appointed by the Dutch Crown, and an elected legislature, the *Staten.* In 1986 Aruba was removed from this arrangement, becoming an autonomous part of the Kingdom of the Netherlands.

The French Antilles

In 1946 the islands of *Martinique, Guadeloupe, St Barthélemy* and *St Martin* (French part) ceased to be colonies and became two Overseas Departments (*Départements d'Outre-Mer*) of the French Republic, enjoying the same status as the Departments of metropolitan France. In addition to sending senators and deputies to the Senate and Chamber of Deputies in Paris, each of the two Departments – (1) Martinique, (2) Guadeloupe and the other islands – has a locally elected General Council.

The US Virgin Islands

The former Danish islands of *St Thomas, St John* and *St Croix* were sold by Denmark to the United States in 1917 for $25,000,000. They are a self-governing American colony (technically an Unincorporated Territory subject to the Department of the Interior) with a locally elected Governor and legislature. SC

Belize

Though geographically part of Central America, Belize is culturally quite distinctive, as a former British possession, the foundations of which derive from the activities of buccaneers and log-cutters in the early seventeenth century. Britain rejected the claims of both Mexico and Guatemala when they achieved independence from Spain, and in 1871 declared Belize a crown colony. Mexico renounced its claim in 1893 but Guatemala has persisted in its claims. Racially, about 10 per cent of the population of Belize is of European stock, 50 per cent creole (of mixed origin), 20 per cent Mayan Indian and 15 per cent Black Caribs. The economy is based on timber products, sugar (the main export), citrus fruits and bananas.

From 1964, the colony exercised self-government through an elected bi-cameral legislature, with the People's United Party (social democrat) and the United Democratic Party (conservative) as the main contenders. The PUP led by George Price took the country to independence in 1981. Guatemala has consistently refused to recognize this, and Britain retains a substantial military force in Belize and off-shore against Guatemalan pretensions. (Anglo-Guatemalan diplomatic relations were suspended between 1963 and 1986.) With a population of under 200,000 and an economy dependent on primary products, Belize is likely to remain dependent on Great Britain for some time to come, particularly so long as the uncertainty regarding Guatemala persists. But independence for the infant state, as a separate entity with its own cultural identity, is a matter of profound belief for the majority of its people. In the general elections of December 1984, Manuel Esquivel, leader of the UDP, won a landslide victory over George Price's PUP which had dominated the politics of Belize for more than thirty years. Price and the PUP returned to office in the elections of September 1989.   HB/SC

BELIZE

The Guianas

This area, stretching between the Amazon and the Orinoco rivers in northern South America, was once a magnet to European travellers. The Guiana coast was originally discovered by Christopher Columbus on his third voyage to the West Indies. In 1593 Antonio Berrio, governor of Trinidad, sent the first proper description of the region to the king of Spain; Sir Walter Ralegh's famous description was published two years later. During the seventeenth century, the British, Dutch and French made attempts to trade and settle in the Guiana territory, despite clashes with the Spaniards along the coast and in the Orinoco. The common denominators in the Guianas were European imperialism and slavery. Although Spain claimed all the territory, the British, Dutch and French were the first to open it up to commerce. Trading posts and small settlements were established by these nations. Later on European settlers began to concentrate on the production of commercial crops, sugar, cotton, coffee and cocoa, on plantations worked by slaves brought in from the west coast of Africa. This resulted in a society of masters and slaves and, later, indentured immigrants. Though the population in Guyana and Suriname in particular became ethnically mostly African and Indian, the cultural influence was mainly European – whether British, Dutch or French.

In the early centuries the langour and lushness of tropical life, the romantic vision of a land paved with gold, all meant adventure. The march towards the discovery of its identity and common goals still spell adventure to the complex society of the peoples of the Guianas.

GUYANA

Area	214,970 sq km
Population	796,000
GNP per capita (1989)	$340
Capital	Georgetown
Currency	Guyana dollar

When in 1598 the Dutch began to investigate the 'Wild Coast', as the Guiana territory was called, and to establish trading depots or posts, they relied on the Amerindian tribes, especially the Arawaks, Caribs, Warraus, and Akawaios for the trade goods of annatto, dyewoods and tobacco for which they exchanged their axes, knives, cloth, beads, and scissors. Meanwhile the British, Spanish and French

THE GUIANAS

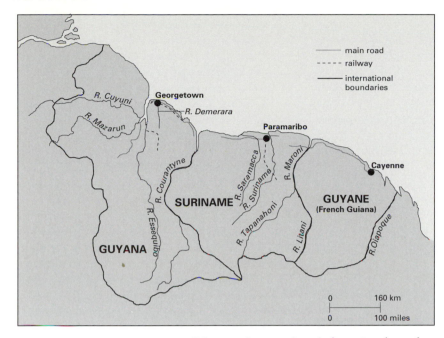

were all laying claim to the whole region from the Amazon to the Orinoco. In 1604 the English under Captain Charles Leigh and in 1609 under Robert Harcourt made unsuccessful attempts to settle small colonies. The Dutch finally established a fort, Kyk-over-al (See-over-all) at the junction of the Essequibo, Cuyuni and Mazaruni rivers and at Nova Zeelandia on the Pomeroon. No formal government was set up until 1621, when the Dutch West India Company was formed. By the 1750s sugar cultivation was on the increase. The Dutch hold on Guiana was greatly enhanced by the administration of the director-general of Essequibo and Demerara, Laurens Storm van's Gravesande (1743–72). By 1775 there were over 300 plantations of sugar, coffee, and cotton, worked by over 100,000 slaves. Van's Gravesande introduced the College of Kiezers (Electors) – a body which was not abolished until 1891.

During the 1781 war with Holland the British captured the settlements in Essequibo, Demerara and Berbice. Between 1781 and 1803 the colonies were tossed back and forth between the British, French and Dutch, falling in 1803 to Great Britain. Finally, at the end of the Napoleonic Wars, Demerara, Essequibo and Berbice were ceded by the Netherlands to Great Britain in the Treaty of London (1814) which ratified the Articles of Capitulation of 1803. By the terms of that Capitulation the former rights and privileges of the people, including the Dutch constitution and Roman–Dutch law, were upheld. The legislature consisted of a Court of Policy and a Combined Court – the latter under its Financial Representatives controlling finance and taxation. This Dutch-style constitution lasted until 1891. In 1831 the three colonies

were united as British Guiana. The Dutch town of Stabroek was renamed Georgetown and served as the capital.

The nineteenth century saw the rise and fall of the sugar industry in the colony, though sugar thereafter remained the key factor in its development. The abolition of the slave trade in 1807 and the later abolition of slavery in 1834 in the British colonies ruined many planters. The loss of their labour force of slaves led to the importation of indentured labourers first from Germany, England, Ireland and Malta, as well as Portuguese from Madeira. The largest number, however, came from India. From 1838 to 1917, 340,962 Indian Immigrants arrived in British Guiana. From 1853 a number of Chinese also came in. Yet from 1838 to 1846 over 100 plantations had to be sold to satisfy debts. At the end of the apprenticeship system in 1838, freed African slaves bought abandoned estates and established villages. By the end of 1848 over 400 estates had been purchased by ex-slaves. The 1850 Commission noted that 47,000 workers had left the estates, which were being run mainly by the East Indian immigrants, the Portuguese having by now branched out into trade. The Sugar Duties Act of 1846, which withdrew the imperial preference to sugar in the British colonies, severely affected the planters. The 1856 Portuguese riots in which Portuguese property was destroyed by the Africans did not augur well for future race relations. The discovery of gold in the 1860s gave a small boost to the economy, while the 1870 discovery of the Kaieteur Falls by Charles Barrington Brown brought fame. Two significant events marked the last decade of the nineteenth century: the new Constitution of 1891, which did not really oust the plantocracy from politico-economic control, and the border dispute with Venezuela. The 1899 settlement awarded the Orinoco to Venezuela but in the 1960s Venezuela revived her claim to 138,000 sq km. The 1970 Protocol of Port of Spain proclaimed a twelve-year moratorium on this dispute but it has been revived in the aftermath of the Falklands conflict.

In 1917, through pressure from the government of India, East Indian immigration was stopped. The East Indians, numbering almost 127,000, became the rice farmers on the coastal areas and later the businessmen and professionals in the city. Agitation for political reform led to crown colony status in 1928 in which the Court of Policy and Combined Court were replaced by a Legislative and Executive Council. The franchise was also extended to women. Throughout 1928–36 there were series of strikes on the plantations. The recommendations of the 1939 Royal West Indian Commission were not put into effect until after the Second World War, in 1945, when the colony received economic aid under the Colonial

Development and Welfare Fund. The 1949 general elections brought the East Indian dentist Dr Cheddi Jagan into the government as spokesman for labour. Later he and his wife formed the People's Progressive Party (PPP) together with Forbes Burnham, a black barrister, as leader. When in 1953 the avowedly Communist PPP won the general elections there were strikes and fear of Communist leanings. Great Britain declared a state of emergency and suspended the Constitution. These events led to a split in the PPP. Burnham left the party and later founded the People's National Congress (PNC). Though in 1957 the PPP again won the elections financial problems as well as racial and ideological issues kept the country in a state of unrest.

The 1963 and 1964 strikes in the city and on the sugar estates crippled the economy and further exacerbated political and racial tensions. In a tense atmosphere general elections were held and won by the PPP. A coalition government was formed under the PNC leader Forbes Burnham and under this government independence was granted on 26 May 1966. The new nation took the name Guyana. On 23 February 1970 it was proclaimed a Co-operative Republic within the Commonwealth. That year also marked the opening of the new University of Guyana (established since 1963) which now offers degrees in arts, social sciences, natural sciences, education, and technology and agriculture.

The 1980s opened depressingly. Prices for and productivity of sugar, rice and bauxite had fallen while oil prices rose. There was a sharp decline in living standards while thousands of Guyanese emigrated to the United States, Great Britain and Canada. In the general elections in December 1980 the PNC gained forty-one of the fifty-three seats in the National Assembly, claiming 'an overwhelming mandate'. Under the new Constitution Prime Minister Burnham was inaugurated president with greatly increased powers. In 1982 exports in the major industries of bauxite, rice and sugar fell by 33 per cent, 14 per cent and 50 per cent respectively, causing severe depletion in foreign currency reserves. Since then shortages of basic food items, raw materials and drugs, among other items, have truncated health, education, and social services. Despite government action, the parallel economy of the huckster trade functions as the vital supply channel.

The start of the 1990s saw the awakening of political consciousness and the growth of new parties, leading to successful demands for free and fair elections, yet the media are still subject to state control. The IMF opened up the country to foreign investment and bolstered support for the government's Economic Recovery Programme (ERP). On its heels came devaluation and inflation which have caused further deterioration in the standard of living. Moreover, the flight of managerial, technical and professional persons from Guyana has posed a major constraint on economic and social development.

City Hall, Georgetown, Guyana

SURINAME

Area	163,000 sq km
Population	422,000
GNP per capita (1989)	$3010
Capital	Paramaribo
Currency	Suriname guilder

The history of Suriname, Guyana's neighbour to the east, was one of early trade, settlement and establishment of plantations, influenced by European rival-

Kaieteur Falls, Guyana. Discovered in 1870, they are nearly five times the height of Niagara.

ries in the seventeenth and eighteenth centuries. In the early seventeenth century several attempts were made to colonize the territory. In 1650 a more permanent settlement was made when Lord Willoughby took possession of the area which is now Suriname and claimed it for England. Willoughby brought in British and French colonizers as well as African slaves, making Suriname a plantation colony. Between 1651 and 1667 about 500 plantations were established under the British. In 1664 wealthy Portuguese Jews fleeing the Inquisition came to Suriname after being unsuccessful in Brazil and Cayenne. The 1665 war which broke out between the Netherlands and England had the usual repercussions in the colonies. In 1667 Abraham Crijnssen with a Zealand fleet captured Suriname. At the Treaty of Breda which marked the end of the Second Dutch War in 1667 England exchanged Suriname for New Amsterdam (New York). However, claiming ignorance of the treaty, an English fleet recaptured the country and sent Crijnssen to Barbados as a prisoner of war. Later in May 1668 Crijnssen was returned to Suriname. With the exception of two British interregnums (1795–1802 and 1804–16), Suriname remained a Dutch possession until independence in 1975. Like their counterparts in Guyana, the Dutch maintained friendly relations with the Arawak and Carib-speaking Amerindians who lived along the rivers and in the hinterland. Many of these Amerindians today live in Christianized villages while others uphold their traditional customs in their jungle habitat.

Throughout the eighteenth and nineteenth centuries Suriname was a typical plantation colony with its two classes: planters and slaves/manual labourers. The plantation economy depended on sugar and slave labour. Imports of slaves into Suriname had been the monopoly of the Dutch West India Company, along with the city of Amsterdam, which supplied over

2500 slaves annually. Although the slave trade was abolished in Dutch territories in 1814, over 1000 slaves were still brought in clandestinely to Suriname every year. These slaves worked the sugar, cotton, and coffee plantations and greatly outnumbered the white population. The colonists, paralysed by fear of this numerical superiority, were especially cruel. Slaves retaliated by not only murdering their masters but running away into the deep jungle surrounding the plantations. These fugitives, known as Bush Negroes or Maroons, remained a threatening force on the edges of the plantations. In 1770 the number of Bush Negroes was estimated to be between 5000 and 6000. Today, this is the largest of Bush Negro populations (six tribes numbering 50,000), now called Bushland Negroes. They play an important role in Suriname's lumber industry yet, like the indigenous Amerindians, live mostly in the interior and exist on hunting, fishing and shifting agriculture.

The causes for the decline of the plantation system in Suriname in the nineteenth century were somewhat similar to those in other plantation regions: abolition of slavery and the development of beet sugar in Europe and the United States, and cotton in the United States. After the abolition of slavery in the Dutch colonies in 1863, when it became obvious that liberated slaves would not remain on the plantations, over 5400 labourers – Portuguese, Javanese, and West Indians, mostly from Barbados – were brought into the colony. Others were imported from China and Hong Kong until 1870 when their emigration was prohibited by the Chinese government. This restriction led to the Dutch concluding a treaty with the British entitling them to recruit labourers from India. The first batch of 'East Indians' arrived from Calcutta in 1873. Between 1873 and 1916 more than 34,000 East Indian immigrants came to Suriname. Immigration ended in 1918, when Great Britain prohibited indentured labour in all its territories and terminated the immigration contract with the Netherlands. The Moslems and Hindus later became independent farmers, educated their children in the Netherlands and became the professional class of teachers, doctors, and lawyers. With the stoppage of East Indian immigration, labourers were recruited from Java. Between 1891 and 1939 over 32,000 Javanese entered Suriname and now form 15 per cent of the population.

Between 1828 and 1845 Suriname shared a Governor-general with the Netherlands Antilles. The European revolution of 1848 influenced the adoption of more liberal policies and caused more attention to be given to the colonies and native populations. In 1865 the government was administered by a *Koloniale Staten* (Colonial Assembly) consisting of thirteen members, nine elected and four nominated by the governor from among the planters and merchants. In 1876 compulsory education for children from seven to twelve was introduced. The 1886 *Koloniale Staten* allowed an increase of elected members from the high-income, educated group. The policy of the *Koloniale Staten* was to establish Suriname as an overseas province similar to the Netherlands in language, culture and religion.

At the turn of the century there was an increasing political awareness among a rising middle class of creoles and Hindustanis. The 1922 Netherlands Constitution Act changed Suriname from a colony to an integrated territory of the Kingdom of the Netherlands. The *Koloniale Staten* became the *Staten van Suriname*. Yet political discontent increased, especially during the Second World War when connections between Suriname and the Netherlands were temporarily suspended. Insistent political demands won universal suffrage in 1949. In 1950 Suriname attained internal autonomy with a governor-appointee and representative of the Queen, a ministerial council, an advisory council and a legislative branch – the *Staten*. On 29 December 1954 Suriname gained an equal partnership in the Tripartite Kingdom of the Netherlands.

With universal suffrage in 1949 racially-orientated political parties mushroomed. The Indians, both Moslem and Hindu, formed one party; the Indonesians, mostly Moslems, formed two others. The National Party of Suriname (NPS), composed mainly of creoles, became the leading party. Its charismatic leader, Johan Pengel, dominated the country's politics from 1958 until his fall in 1969. Though the Hindustani party won the 1969 elections, the president, Jules Sedney, was chosen from the creole NPS as the Hindustanis did not want to emphasize the victory of the Hindu community. The government tried to build up a strong national consciousness over and above racial and ethnic groups. Yet, after Suriname gained independence on 25 November 1975, many Surinamese emigrated to the Netherlands fearing racial upheavals.

Prior to 1937 Suriname was a relatively poor country but after the Second World War the expansion of the bauxite industry boosted the economy. Its main revenue is derived from bauxite and lumber which are exported mainly to the United States and the Netherlands. Its affiliation with the EEC through membership in the Kingdom of the Netherlands brought with it millions of dollars in Development Fund grants. Suriname is also backed financially by loans and grants from the Netherlands.

In the late 1960s relations with Guyana cooled off over a 9600 sq km border dispute regarding the New River triangle in the south-east of the country. How-

ever, in May 1970 the two governments agreed 'to discuss the matter in a civilized manner'.

On 25 February 1980, stimulated by military rather than political grievances, army sergeants seized power from Henck Arron, prime minister since 1977, in a military coup. In December 1982 Commander Desi Bouterse crushed an alleged plot to depose the military government during which period fifteen prominent Surinamese were executed at the military barracks. This resulted in the suspension of $1.5 billion economic assistance by the Dutch government. In the late 1980s the military returned Suriname to civilian rule and a coalition of three parties formed a government. Gradually, however, with Bouterse still commander, the power shifted back to the military, and in December 1990 a coup removed the civilian government. An interim government has promised future elections. The country has been rocked by instability and violence and plagued by unemployment, labour unrest and deteriorating living conditions. There has, however, been a winding down of the civil war with the Maroons, many of whom have fled to Guyane.

GUYANE

Area	90,910 sq km
Population	98,000
GNP per capita (1989)	$ –
Capital	Cayenne
Currency	French franc

Bounded on the east by Brazil and on the south and west by Suriname, Guyane – 'the Cinderella of the French colonial empire' – is the largest of France's overseas departments. Several off-shore islands form part of the colony. Among them, Devil's Island, for years a notorious penal settlement, once gave French Guiana a sinister reputation.

Like the other European nations the French were drawn towards the mythical 'El Dorado'. In 1568 Gaspar de Sostelle with 126 families from Spain attempted a settlement but was driven out by the Indian tribes. Laurence Keymis settled in a bay he called Port Howard in 1596 but the settlement was short-lived. In 1604 under Daniel de la Revardière the French settled on the river where the capital, Cayenne, now stands. Throughout the seventeenth century there were abortive attempts at settlement by the French and the Dutch. These attempts had to be abandoned mainly because of the unfriendliness of the Indians. In 1626 the French erected and garrisoned a fort for protection, the remains of which the

Fish market, Cayenne, Guyane

Dutch found in 1634. Later in the century the Dutch gave permission to David Nassy and other Jews to settle in Cayenne and provide slaves for the Guiana coast. The 1660s saw the return of the French – this time making peace with the Indians. During the Second Dutch War of 1665 the French colony and Sinamary were sacked. In 1667 the fort surrendered to the English who ravaged the country. The French complained against the attack and capture of Cayenne as contrary to the 1667 Peace Treaty. It was again recaptured from the Dutch for France in 1676.

Throughout the eighteenth and nineteenth centuries French attempts to colonize Cayenne proved fruitless and costly. Not only were bad management and an unrealistic approach to conditions responsible for failure but the political refugees who were deported there proved unwilling and unable to cope with the labour situation. Ten thousand out of an estimated 14,000 immigrants died of typhus. In 1794 after the National Convention abolished slavery, freed slaves fled to the hinterland refusing to work on the plantations. In 1808 Cayenne became an Anglo-Portuguese possession for eight years until, by the Treaty of Paris (1816), it became part of the now very small French colonial empire. During the 1820s a flourishing colony was founded at Mana by Mother Ann Marie Javouhay, Superior of the Sisters of St Joseph Cluny, for the freed slaves who had earlier left the plantations. When in 1848 slavery was irrevocably abolished, Cayenne faced severe financial crises. As in British and Dutch Guiana, immigrants were introduced from Asia to fill the labour gap. The discovery of gold in the 1850s brought an influx of immigrants but also lured labour away from agriculture and crippled development. The gold boom was, unfortunately, a brief interlude.

The 1848 decree had also brought the French Guianese full French citizenship and the right to vote. After 1854 Cayenne was governed by a senate decree of Napoleon III and in 1875 all French colonies became French departments with later representation in the French Assembly. A Minister for the Colonies took over the responsibility for the colonies in 1894. The economy, education and culture were modelled on French lines, for French policy was to turn all colonials into Frenchmen. In 1930 the country was divided into two – Guyane and the territory of Inini (the hinterland). Since 1946, Guyane, thoroughly Gallicized, has been an overseas department of France. There was a brief post-Second World War move for local autonomy. The Socialist Party under Justin Catayie urged autonomy in 1960 but was defeated in the 1961 elections.

There have been many attempts to increase the population (only 55,000) and thus fully colonize Guyane. A 1950 project to form a settlement of 'displaced persons' did not succeed – only 150 to 200 people of Czech, Polish and Hungarian origin remain. Another group-colonization scheme in 1961 failed through lack of discipline and finance.

Since 1989 over 10,000 Maroons have fled the civil war in Suriname into Guyane and form 7 per cent of its population. This movement has caused concern over their impact on Guyane's economy and social life. This problem is also linked to security as France has a large satellite (European Ariane) launching centre, at Kourou.   MNM

Further Reading: E. Dew, *The Difficult Flowering of Suriname, Ethnicity and Politics in a Plural Society* (The Hague, 1978); H. Lutchman, *From Colonialism to Co-operative Republic: Aspects of Political Development in Guyana* (Rio Piedras, 1974); W. Rodney, *A History of the Guyanese Working People*, (1881–1905) Baltimore, 1981; T. Spinner, Jr., *A Political and Social History of Guyana, 1945–1983* (Boulder, Colorado, and London, 1984)

Politics and Society

Political traditions of Latin America

The colonial experience has been and still remains the most important single factor in the political tradition of Latin America. With the consolidation of the Spanish and Portuguese colonial empires between 1500 and 1650, it gave a degree of unity to the area unknown in any other part of the world, reinforced by the proselytization of the Catholic Church and (apart from Brazil and Haiti) the dissemination of the Spanish language. The colonies were regarded as co-equal kingdoms, owing direct allegiance to one overlord, the king of Spain, who administered them directly through the Council of the Indies at Seville, through peninsular-born officials, circumscribed in their powers by an elaborated code of law and practice, and subject to the institution of the *residencia* – a final evaluation of their administration – as a check on their activities while in office.

The traditions of this administrative structure were reinforced by its duration. The removal of Spanish royal authority at a stroke, by the forced abdication of Charles IV at Bayonne (1808), removed the keystone. But the empire fell apart only slowly, as conservatives sought to retain their position and privilege, professing their loyalty to his successor, Ferdinand. They distrusted above all the new nation-alistic movement of the 'Liberales' in Spain, who with their new conception of the unity of the state drawn from the writers of the Enlightenment and the experience of the French Revolution, offered the colonies in a sense an inferior status to that to which they had hitherto been accustomed.

Liberalism moreover was associated with anti-clericalism and republicanism. By the early 1820s many conservatives were prepared to accept a republic as the alternative to Liberal interference from Spain, but they fought long and hard against any attempt to erode the traditional rights of the Church. Once independence was achieved, struggles between Conservatives and Liberals became the dominant feature of political life throughout the Spanish-speaking countries and, even in Brazil, where the retention of the monarchy until 1889 prevented its dissolution, Liberals came to be identified with the cause of provincial autonomy, and Conservatives with the goal of a strong state under centralized military–bureaucratic control. In former Spanish America, republican regimes became universal for the lack of possible monarchical candidates, and the mystique of Napoleon lent further support to the emergence of military generalship as the main qualification for political power. Hence the first fifty years of independence are associated above all with the institutionalization of the military caudillo.

Caudillismo – the domination of politics by the caudillo – was thus a creole response to the crisis of decolonization. Being essentially personalist, its impact depended closely on the personalities involved. Simón Bolívar (1783–1830), liberator of Venezuela, Colombia, Ecuador, Peru and Bolivia, was asked to provide a constitution for Bolivia, named in his honour, and sought by his invention of the Areopagus, or board of censors, to reinstate that moral power of supervision which had inadvertently been swept away with the monarchy. His dilemma was that he would not use force to compel his people to be free. Dr José Gaspar Rodríguez de Francia (1766–1840) of Paraguay, an admirer of Benjamin Franklin's practicality, sealed off his country from the outside world to preserve its Rousseauesque, paternalistic society. But this was a solution hardly possible for the coastal South American states, and not at all in Central America, where José Cecilio del Valle (1776–1834) died while the votes electing him to the presidency were still uncounted, his plans for his people, discussed in correspondence with Jeremy Bentham, still unrealized. Bentham's belief in 'the greatest good for the greatest number' and his theories of law had a considerable influence on legal codes in Latin America even in the most dictatorial states, and the prison in Caracas is still called the Panóptico, his 'panopticon'.

The National Assembly of Nicaragua, meeting in Managua, October 1987

Caudillismo

The word *caudillo* simply means chief, or leader. Some historians have, however, sought to give the term a more particularly Spanish American definition, and one that applies specifically to the rulers of the decades immediately after independence. Caudillism is a means for the selection and establishment of political leadership in the absence of a social structure and political groupings adequate to the functioning of representative government. The practice and technique of caudillism, developed during the wars for independence, were based on those of the colonial oligarchies as modified by the regressive effects of irregular civil conflict. The 'typical *caudillo*' is depicted as dictatorial, as basing his power on personal control of informal military force, he himself and his followers being of rural origin. The term *caudillo*, while not necessarily derogatory, carries with it an aura of semi-barbarity. But the term is not a precise one, and on close examination 'typical *caudillos*' do not share many characteristics.

In Argentina today the dominant local figure who controls votes at a provincial or municipal level is denoted a *caudillo*. The term has survived the post-independence years not only in this more humble Argentine use but also as a convenient (often journalistic) label for any politician of stature, national or local.   MD

Most caudillos, however, were military men who had little time for political ideas, such as the ruler of the Argentine Confederation, Juan Manuel de Rosas (1793–1877). Rosas was the real target of Domingo Faustino Sarmiento's *Facundo* (1845), ostensibly a critique of a lesser caudillo of the interior. Sarmiento's contemporary, Juan Bautista Alberdi (1810–84), argued in 1852 that the true ends of government were to populate the national territory. Sarmiento (1811–88) wanted its population to be educated. Ironically, Rosas, who opposed formal unification, was by reaction the creator of the united Argentina of which Sarmiento was to serve as president (1868–74), under the US-influenced Constitution of 1853.

Argentina was distinctive in achieving constitutional shape so late; elsewhere the pattern was one of faction constitutionalism, under which constitutions were rewritten, suspended or simply ignored to suit the convenience of the group currently in power. New constitutions were written to legitimate seizures of power by force, or even the prolongation of a presidential term without resorting to election. Venezuela, the first state to write a constitution (1811), has since had more than twenty. It was assumed throughout the nineteenth century that this was a passing phenomenon that would vanish with 'maturity'. To some extent the establishment of the 'Conservative Republic' in Chile with the Constitution of 1833 and its peaceful political life for over fifty years seemed to confirm this assumption. Only in the 1870s was it realized in Peru by the *civilistas* that Latin American coups and dictatorships were integrally related to the root phenomenon of militarism. While still retaining the constitutional devices to restrain military ambition which had proved persistently useless in the past, they broke new ground in setting up a military academy to professionalize and so tame the military. This proved only a partial success. As time was to prove, an educated officer corps was more skilful in seizing, if not using, political power.

LIBERALISM AND REACTION

By 1857, the year of the Reforma in Mexico, in which the Church lands were confiscated and its privileges demolished, the first impetus of Liberalism was waning. It was soon to be reinforced by the doctrine of positivism originated in France by Auguste Comte, and introduced into Mexican education by Justo Sierra (1848–1912). Positivism, with its theory of stages of human development and in its belief in the certainty of the scientific understanding of society, was, shorn of its mystical origins and reinforced by the prevailing social Darwinism of Herbert Spencer, a strong justification of elite rule. As such it became the official doctrine of the Mexico of the Porfiriato (1876–1911) and, under the influence of Benjamin Constant Botelho de Magelhães (1830–91), found favour among the military leaders who created the Republic in Brazil in 1889 and placed Comte's slogan 'order and progress' on the national flag. Both native vigour and the inevitability of successful struggle was further implanted by Euclides da Cunha (1866–1909) in his quasi-novel of the 'inland sea', *Os Sertões* (1902). In Argentina, Agustín Alvarez (1857–1914) argued more explicitly that the examples of Brazil and Chile showed that stability lay in the forms of the past, and specifically in despotism. In Colombia, where a chair of sociology was established at the University of Bogotá as early as 1862, the Spencerian Rafael Núñez (1823–94), after a brief radical phase, became an evolutionary Conservative. And in Venezuela, after the dictatorship of Antonio Cuzmán Blanco (1829–99) had given way to that of less enlightened successors. Laureano Vallenilla Lanz (1870–1936) in his *Cesarismo Democrático* (1919) not only provided an apt label for the system, but sought to defend it in a way that met with the enthusiastic approval of Mussolini.

The year before, 1918, the 'University reform movement' which began at Córdoba, Argentina, disseminated a new impetus for revolt against despotism throughout the continent. Socialism, in its Saint-Simonian form, had been professed by Alberdi, but not until the last quarter of the nineteenth century did socialist writers find much favour in Latin America. Workers' movements were lacking on which to build, before the growth of the great railway, meat-packing and mining interests in Argentina, Uruguay, Chile, Peru and Mexico. The great organizing ideology for labour prior to 1914 was anarchism, also imported from Europe. Organized unionism was often met with armed intervention, as at Cananea in Mexico in 1906 and in Chile with the strike of 1907 in Iquique. In Mexico, where the reassertion of democratic rights by Francisco I. Madero (1877–1913) brought the onset of the revolution (1910), the Casa del Obrero Mundial was permitted to organize in 1913, and workers, formed by Alvaro Obregón (1880-1928) into the so-called 'Red Battalions', found their spokesmen and won recognition of labour's position in the Constitution of 1917. As Obregón's Secretary of Education, José Vasconcelos (1871–1959) organized Latin America's first attempt at a mass literacy drive and gave state patronage to the arts a new social meaning. Under the presidency of Lázaro Cárdenas (1895–1970), the revolution was consolidated by the assimilation of workers' organizations to the ruling socialist National Revolutionary Party (PNR) and the mass distribution of land, to appease peasant demands for restitution of land, associated with the leadership of the guerrilla leader Emiliano Zapata (1879–1919), grew further in the 1920s.

Indigenismo, the revaluation of the Indian as opposed to the Hispanic contribution to Latin American life, had already had a cultural impact in Mexico and Peru in the 1890s. In part, it was a response to the prevailing dogmas of 'scientific racism' which denigrated all non-whites. In Mexico the young Peruvian student organizer Víctor Raúl Haya de la Torre (1895–1979), influenced by the *indigenista* values expressed in Vasconcelos's *La raza cósmica* (1925), sought to unify the continent on a programme of Indian values by the foundation of the American Popular Revolutionary Alliance (APRA). APRA, implanted in Peru after 1930, dominated Peruvian politics for a generation, though consistently denied the chance to take power by the army. The Marxist, José Carlos Mariátegui (1895–1930), author of the widely read *Siete ensayos de la realidad peruana*, founded in 1928 Peru's first Socialist Party. The views he expressed on the necessity for fundamental change, which in their *indigenista* influence departed noticeably from Marxist tradition, were rediscovered

---

Caciquismo, coronelismo and clientelismo

The term *cacique* derives from the Taino-Arawak word for chief. It is used throughout the Hispanic world for those who exercise local predominance. The Brazilian equivalent is *coronel*, colonel, which derives from the nineteenth-century militia ranks that in Brazil such men often enjoyed. *Cacique* is normally, though not always, used in a pejorative sense, implying one who perverts public institutions for private ends, abuses power and patronage to favour exclusively and excessively his own clientele, manipulates placemen in public office, interferes with justice and policing, controls elections through fraud, etc.

The power of the local cacique or coronel has diverse origins and will vary greatly from region to region. It should be noted that it is frequently false to assume that local power is exercised by landowners, either directly or through dependents, or that *caciquismo* rests either solely or predominantly on force and fraud. The role of local power-brokers has nowhere been rapidly reduced or extinguished by the exertions of central government or by the growth of modern national parties. The term *clientelismo* is now frequently used where *caciquismo* would have been used in the past; it has more modern, urban and bureaucratic overtones. MDD

---

in the 1960s and found expression in the military-guided revolution of 1968 under General Juan Velasco Alvarado which nationalized heavy industries and expropriated the great coastal landholdings. In neighbouring Bolivia, the disaster of the Chaco War had forced a reappraisal earlier, and Bolivia had nationalized its oil (1937) before the revolution of 1952 brought land redistribution and nationalization of the tin mines. Establishing Quechua as an official language in each country in the 1970s was a symbolic step of great importance in practical terms to the millions otherwise pushed outside the national political culture.

Elsewhere, the main influence on the growth of left-wing ideas in this period was the impact of the Great Depression. Chile, after a period of disorder (including a short-lived 'Socialist Republic' in 1931 under Colonel Marmaduque Grove and Carlos Dávila), evolved a 'Popular Front' government on European lines. But the usual outcome, as in Argentina, was a military seizure of power and a series of 'apolitical' rulers suppressing civil liberties for fear of left-wing influence. In El Salvador, Alberto Masferrer (1868–1932) had spoken of a peaceful road to socialism, but when a peasant rising occurred in 1932 thousands were shot down. The influence of the Atlantic Charter and allied wartime propaganda was to topple military governments all over Latin America in 1943–5, but, in the climate of the Cold War, even the 'spiritual socialism' of the Guatemalan Juan José Arévalo (president 1945–51) was suspect, and his successor, Jacobo Arbenz, was overthrown in 1954 trying to carry out a measure of land reform which met with the disapproval of the then government of the United States.

As early as 1900 *anti-yanquismo*, or hostility to the supposedly 'materialist' values represented by the United States, had received eloquent expression from the Uruguayan José Enrique Rodó (1872–1917). In his *Ariel*, Rodó, a positivist, reasserted the idealism which he considered the United States had lost, and which he believed Latin America was destined to preserve. As United States power grew, some, like Vasconcelos, took refuge in traditional Hispanism. Alcides Arguedas (1870–1946) pessimistically argued that the Bolivians were a *pueblo enfermo*, a hopelessly sick people, incapable of development. While he was doing so, however, German military instructors were already implanting the ideas of fascism in his country, and the Chaco War was in part the result of military belief in their mission. Chile remained doubtful about the allied cause in the Second World War, and in Argentina, which remained aloof till 1945, Juan Domingo Perón (1895–1974) was after 1945 to use the inheritance of fascism in the service of a new populistic nationalism which was strongly anti-United States.

REVOLUTIONS AND DICTATORS

The Cuban Revolution, like the Mexican, was to develop an original synthesis of ideas. Unlike its predecessor, however, it was to come to serve as an

Ernesto (Che) Guevara (1928–67), revolutionary hero and martyr who fought beside Castro in the Cuban Revolution

example, not only to a continent, but to much of the emerging Third World, already receptive to the economic doctrine of state-led economic growth (*desarrollismo*) espoused by Raúl Prebisch and his colleagues in ECLA.

Fidel Castro Ruz (b. 1926) and his followers drew their initial inspiration from the liberal nationalist tradition of the Cuban poet–revolutionary, José Marti (1835–95). Their recipe for the capture of political power, embodied by the young Argentine Ernesto 'Che' Guevara (1928–67) in his *La Guerra de Guerrillas* (Guerrilla Warfare), was widely imitated, but proved wildly impractical in most parts of Latin America. The fortuitous timing of the revolution that enabled Castro to ally himself with the Soviet Union enabled his government to survive the hostility of the United States and at the same time to maintain a degree of intellectual independence which it vigorously exploited. In the Second Declaration of Havana (1962) Castro appealed beyond the traditional boundaries of Latin America for a tricontinental alliance of the underdeveloped against the developed world. Later the 1967 death of Guevara himself gave not only Cuba, but the New Left in the United States and Europe, an icon of the revolt of youth against age.

At the same time, Argentine and Brazilian economic theorists were refining traditional Marxist ideas to explain the economic backwardness of Latin America in terms of its subjection to the world capitalist system. Dependency theory, as it became known, originated both from Marxist theory and from Latin American experience, and formed an original contribution to world thought, even though it spread so rapidly its origins were soon forgotten. Rejecting the Keynesian solutions of the *cepalistas*, they argued that the only way to break out of the cycle of dependence was through socialist revolution. But this attempt to cut the Gordian knot was to prove illusory. For with the failure of Cuba's 'Harvest of the Ten Millions' in 1970, the Soviet leadership who had become increasingly impatient with Cuban claims to have evolved a new and independent form of Marxism–Leninism, were able to demand and get a closer adherence to their orthodoxy. By 1979 Cuba had effectively exchanged dependence on the USA for dependence on the USSR.

Meanwhile, the dominant influence in Latin America in the 1970s was that of military dictatorship, seeking to exterminate alien ideas by force. In Argentina, Brazil, Chile and Uruguay, as elsewhere, the military justified their rule by invoking national security; a doctrine largely borrowed from US strategic thought, which, however, Latin American officers applied to domestic rather than international politics. With the revulsion against military atroci-

ties a new move back to democracy began, but the new civilian governments of the early 1980s inherited endemic crisis, and many turned towards a new panacea, that of the libertarian right in the United States from which the 'Chicago Boys' in Pinochet's Chile had drawn their inspiration. By 1990 politicians such as Leon Febres Cordero in Ecuador, Alberto Fujimori in Peru, Carlos Salinas de Gortari in Mexico and – not least – Violeta Chamorro in Nicaragua had been swept to power in a new wave of enthusiasm for free market 'solutions'. Unlike the doctrines of the *cepalistas* and the dependency theorists, however, this new movement failed to generate much of a body of independent Latin American thought and writing.

The enormous enthusiasm that greeted the Papal visits to Latin America of Paul VI and John Paul II demonstrated that the Catholicism implanted by the Spanish and Portuguese remains a vital force. From Brazil in the 1960s came liberation theology, a new synthesis between Catholic and Marxist ideas. Church leaders who felt that this was to go too far, however, in many parts of the continent have nevertheless acted as honest critics of authoritarianism and the abuse of human rights. Though the history of the Latin American political tradition shows so many examples of extreme partisanship, compounded by the frustration engendered by military intervention, the democratic spirit of independence against all comers enjoyed a new flowering in the 1980s, accompanied by grassroots activism from church, neighbourhood and women's movements. and may be expected to continue to display great resilience in the last decade of the century.   PARC

Further Reading: F. H. Cardoso and E. Faletto, *Dependency and Development in Latin America* (Berkeley and Los Angeles, 1977); H. E. Davis, *Latin American Thought: A Historical Introduction* (New York, 1974); T. Di Tella, *Latin American Politics: A Theoretical Framework* (Austin, Texas, 1990); A. Stepan, *Rethinking Military Politics: Brazil and the Southern Cone* (Princeton, 1988); C. Véliz, *The Centralist Tradition of Latin America* (Princeton, 1980)

The military in politics

During the 1980s many Latin American countries emerged from long periods of military government. Although the military continues to exercise a degree of political influence, this would appear to be on the decline if one considers the region as a whole. The military continues to be active where there are insurgencies in progress, and quietly enjoys a number of privileges which are not readily granted to civilians, but at the end of 1990 no general was in any presidential palace in Latin America. Moreover the intellectual swing against populist–nationalist economic strategies has weakened the links between military and state companies.

Until relatively recently, however, military government was a commonplace in Latin America. As in all cases where the military is in power, there was often a conflict between the institutional needs of the military itself and the way in which military presidents sought to exercise political control. At one extreme there was personalism, in which an individual general ran the country as a personal machine. The most notable examples were Batista in Cuba and the Somozas in Nicaragua (both overthrown by revolutionaries), General Manuel Noriega in Panama (overthrown by the United States) and Trujillo in the Dominican Republic (assassinated with some degree of connivance on the part of the CIA). Evidently this is not a stable pattern. At the other extreme there were systems in which the military exerted what amounted to a collective leadership, with little margin for presidential autonomy. Again there are several examples, most notably the Argentine government during 1976–83, but this pattern often leads to unsatisfactory decision-making. It is, however, true that not all military-led governments were purely military affairs; many of them made some provision for civilian politics, and at times offered their opponents some chance of defeating them constitutionally. A good example was the defeat of General Pinochet in the Chilean plebiscite of 1988, and the most recent Brazilian and Uruguayan military regimes came to an end as a result of quasi-constitutional processes.

REASONS UNDERLYING MILITARY INTERVENTIONS

The prominence of the military in politics can be explained in part by historical tradition. The armies that overthrew Spanish rule at the beginning of the nineteenth century were often left without any clear role in the new political order but with the means to compel attention and resources by resorting to force. In Peru, which finally became independent in 1824, the first civilian president did not take power until 1872. In some other countries, however, a civilian tradition was asserted for a time; Chile and Uruguay appeared to have evolved highly stable democratic systems by the end of the Second World War. Even so, the military moved in during the severe social and political crises which these countries faced in the 1970s. Historical explanations are of some value, therefore, but should not be relied upon too exclusively.

Military involvement in politics may be related, at a more general level, to the relative absence of international war in Latin America. There have been a few wars prior to 1945 and a few border skirmishes since; these tended to bring about a return to civilian rule although this did not happen in every case. Military governments are not especially aggressive in foreign policy terms – Argentina's occupation of the Falklands/Malvinas in 1982 being an exception – although it may well be that civilian governments have been forced to take a stronger line on border disputes than they would have wished for fear of military reaction.

Until very recently, all Latin American countries have looked abroad for arms supplies and military training. This has given the supplying power – most recently the United States – considerable opportunity to influence the behaviour of the military. At times (for example in Chile between 1970 and 1973) the United States has tried to encourage military intervention in politics and at others (for example in Venezuela after 1959) it has tried to discourage it, but US influence is rarely a decisive factor except in the small countries of Central America and the Caribbean where it continues to be preponderant. Some groups of army officers have developed strong pro-American views as a result of military collaboration with the United States; the most famous example of this is the position of the so-called 'Sorbonne' group of officers in Brazil. These officers fought alongside the Allies in Italy during the Second World War (the only army unit from Latin America to do so) and went on to form the core of the ESG (Escola Superior de Guerra, or Higher War College), a military–civilian training centre founded in 1949. Since then they have played a major part in Brazilian politics and provided three recent Brazilian presidents (Castello Branco, Ernesto Geisel and João Figueiredo). On the other hand, the United States has at times lost support by intervening too closely in Latin American military affairs. In both Peru and Bolivia anti-US regimes came to power shortly after

Bolivian officer cadets

an insurgency movement was put down ; a part of the reason for this was that the CIA intervened directly in both countries, bypassing the conventional army structure which was antagonized in consequence.

More recently, the larger Latin American countries, notably Brazil, have emerged as important arms manufacturers and Brazil is now a significant arms exporter. Despite this, the Latin American military does not spend on weapons anything like their counterparts in the Middle East or Africa. Military spending is rarely more than 3 per cent of GNP although there has been some recent tendency for this to rise. Military regimes do not necessarily spend more on weapons than civilian governments, although some military presidents have (in the manner of some civilian presidents) sought to strengthen their political positions by a burst of military spending. This has some beneficial impact in the short term, but the long-term importance of military spending for political ends should not be exaggerated.

INSTITUTIONAL AND PERSONALIST RULE

A good basis for comparing different kinds of military rule is the level of institutionalization within the military; here, it must be emphasized, one is speaking only of the military institution and not of the institutionalization of government as such. 'Institutional' military governments are characterized by high overlap between military rank and political office, the existence of an official or semi-official military ideology which serves to legitimize military rule, and relatively stable relationships between the military in government and certain civilian interest groups including economic technocrats, the business sector and the Church. All of this implies (although this is not part of the definition) that institutional military governments can maintain themselves in power despite considerable unpopularity, that they are highly effective in repressing left-wing or trade union opponents.

Personalist military governments, in contrast, tend to be characterized by low overlap between military rank and political office. The original military coup was sometimes led by a relatively junior officer (notwithstanding that he called himself Colonel and later promoted himself General) or alternatively by a senior officer who gradually removed his various rivals from the scene. There are likely to be civilians in the government drawn from a range of interest groups. The regime is likely to seek to legitimize itself through controlled elections or a rigged plebiscite and is, therefore, bound to require a certain degree of popularity since a complete electoral farce may prove politically damaging. Popularity need not amount to majority support but very unpopular personalist regimes may be vulnerable to middle-class discontent expressed through newspaper editorials or student demonstrations (as was Pérez Jiménez in Venezuela in 1957–8 and Odría in Peru in 1956). Personalist regimes will self-consciously present themselves as 'less military' than institutional ones; the president will often wear a suit rather than uniform.

Until around 1960, almost all military regimes in Latin America were of the personalist kind. These had the advantage of permitting close communication between military and civilian elites but were not always perceived as satisfactory by the military itself. For one thing, if the military president acted in an unpopular manner, the military itself would share in the obloquy without being in any position to influence the outcome; for this reason, military officers would at times refuse to defend a military president against popular demonstrations and would instead leave him to his fate. Secondly, the existence of a military caudillo would make it easier for revolutionary opponents of the regime to convert opposition to the ruler into opposition to the political system as a whole. The overthrow of General Batista by Fidel Castro in Cuba in 1956–9 convinced many military officers that something more flexible was needed. Thirdly, as the military institution became larger and its weaponry more sophisticated, it became increasingly difficult in the larger Latin American countries for an individual or a small group of officers to achieve complete personal ascendancy by means of an opportunist military coup; successful coups needed to involve progressively more people, they needed to be more carefully planned and to be more

certain in their execution. This was the lesson drawn by military conspirators in Brazil who failed in 1961 but succeeded in 1964. Increasingly, therefore, coups came to be led by army commanders-in-chief rather than by rebellious colonels. These commanders, once in power, naturally sought to reinforce their positions by retaining control of the key power centres in the military institution. Finally, counter-insurgency experts, including the US government, came to the conclusion that an institutionalized military government would be more effective against revolutionaries than a personalist one because it would become more difficult for the latter to play off particular officers against each other and thereby split the military.

The first institutionalized military regime in Latin America took power briefly in Peru (1962–3). This was followed by regimes in Brazil (1964–85), Argentina (1966–73 and also 1976–83), Peru (1968–80), Ecuador (1972–9) and Uruguay (1973–85). The institutional structure was similar in each case. A senior military figure (often the army commander-in-chief) became president and was supported by a junta made up of the senior military commanders. In most cases, though not all, the junta was directly brought in to the government through the ministries of war, marine and air force. Usually, though not always, civilian technocrats would be brought in to the key economic positions of finance minister and head of the central bank. At all times, however, the military leadership would take soundings from the officer corps as a whole and would lay out the broad lines of policy which civilian technocrats would follow. The military would also retain effective institutional control of a number of matters; security and intelligence-gathering remained exclu-

Chilean soldiers moving into position by the presidential palace, Santiago, on the morning of 11 September 1973, the day of the military seizure of power in Chile

331

sively military preserves. Subsequently, in Brazil and Argentina, a fixed term of office for the president was set.

IDEOLOGIES AND POLICIES

One of the factors which lay behind this transformation was the creation of a distinctive military ideology through the military schools of higher education. Given that the Latin American military has had few opportunities for prolonged armed combat, and that opportunistic coups are now more difficult to execute than formerly, the most important factor determining military seniority has become educational performance. Clearly military evaluations of education include emphasis on discipline as well as if not more than on creative thought. It, nevertheless, remains true that emphasis on education is highly significant. For one thing, the self-confidence which education brings has almost certainly been a key component in sustaining long periods of military rule and reduced the degree of civilian influence on the military outlook. One observer noted that in Peru in the 1930s a general trembled when he met an ambassador; now it is likely to be the other way round. Moreover, education in purely military matters came to be mixed increasingly – among the more senior officers and high-flyers – with education in economic and social questions. The Brazilian ESG, founded in 1949, and the Peruvian CAEM (Centro de Altos Estudios Militares), founded in 1950, were pioneers in this regard. What was created by these institutions, and spread throughout Latin America, was an ideology of military rule. In the post-colonial era, it was asserted, communism was more likely to threaten a country through subversion than invasion. In order to defeat subversion (and, for that matter, to wage successful conventional war), it was necessary for the military to organize systematically and take on a far greater role in civil society than ever before. Subversion could also be weakened by some measure of social reform (as taught at CAEM) or alternatively by a period of rapid economic growth which would turn a weak and underdeveloped country into a developed one (the ESG perspective). In the interim, it was especially necessary to maintain tight political control. In either case, the military was given an agenda for action which might call for a long period of military rule and would certainly have the effect of reinforcing the ideological appeal to the people of an existing military authority. 'Our duty as governors', General (and President) Velasco of Peru once told his men. 'is inseparable from our duty as military officers.'

These various institutional factors which we have considered suggest that the Latin American military can rarely be seen simply as representatives of a particular social class or group. Military officers in fact tend to be recruited from the lower-middle class. Since secondary education is normally a pre-requisite for admission, the lower class is generally excluded. The sons of the upper-middle class find it more agreeable in most cases to make their careers in less disciplined and demanding, and also better paid, occupations mainly in private companies, the law or banks. Social origin is rarely an important factor in military behaviour, particularly since successful officers are, socially speaking, upwardly mobile; indeed, one of the proudest claims of the Latin American military is precisely that it does facilitate such mobility. Moreover, the consciousness of discipline and occasional hardship plays an important part in creating a separate military consciousness and generating contempt for what is seen (often with justification) as the spoiled and cosseted existence of the upper-middle and upper classes. Finally, the hereditary element is an increasingly important factor in the Latin American military. A high proportion of military officers send their sons to follow them and these, in turn, frequently learn political as well as purely military ambition.

If one is to understand the behaviour of the military in politics, therefore, it is best to look directly at how they perceive their institutional interests. One underlying feature is hostility to excessive popular mobilization (often condemned as social indiscipline). Military regimes are sworn enemies of Marxist-led insurgencies and have destroyed these throughout South America with considerable ruthlessness; when engaged in putting down the MIR (a left-wing revolutionary group), Chilean President Pinochet reportedly told a questioner in 1974, 'Of course we torture people; we need the information.' Revolutionaries have had some success against personalist rulers such as Batista in Cuba and Somoza in Nicaragua, but none at all against institutional ones. Military governments are also likely to regard trade unions and critical newspapers with disfavour, but have not generally relied on total suppression. They have preferred to tolerate limited opposition activity on a discretionary basis, cracking down on opponents only if these 'go too far'. Some military governments, notably the Velasco Alvarado regime in Peru (1968–75), have actually encouraged limited popular mobilization, provided that this was kept within the bounds set by the government itself; this government, however, did find it increasingly difficult to channel popular demands in an approved manner and finally clamped down on its own creation. In general, military governments will react against strong popular organizations but may try to co-opt and foster weaker ones in the hope of being able to control them for their own objectives.

It is less easy to generalize about the economic policies pursued by military governments. The military in Brazil (1964), Chile (1973) and Argentina (1976) took power during severe economic crises, with inflation of 100 per cent per annum or more and economic growth falling. Each government responded with a classic IMF-style stabilization package which increased unemployment but also reduced the level of inflation; each government also went some way to dismantling a very high tariff structure. It is, however, hard to see what else they could have done under the circumstances. The Peruvian military, which found a very different situation when it took power in 1968, pursued a mildly expansionist fiscal policy at first, followed by a highly expansionist one which led to crisis in 1976–8. Over the longer term, there are some marked differences between military governments. In Chile after 1973, the Pinochet regime (which began 'institutionally' but later became more 'personalist' in character) pursued classic free market policies very firmly, and aimed to create a market society as well as a market economy. In Brazil, on the other hand, the aim of the military regime has been to develop a kind of state capitalism, with the main public enterprises playing a key role in capital formation. There is something of a military preference for state industry (except in the Chilean

and to a lesser extent Argentine cases) and for the development of heavy industry under national control for security reasons, but this preference sometimes takes second place to the advice of civilian technocrats. The Peruvian military government did undertake some policies of social reform – notably a land reform – but few military governments have been interested in large-scale income redistribution (neither, it is fair to say, have many of the civilian governments).

Military governments are generally durable but not immortal. Until the 1960s it was assumed that a military government would, after a few years, either return directly to barracks and call elections or seek to transform itself into a civilian government by means of elections. One feature of recent military governments is their longevity. The Peruvian military, which took power in 1968, only returned it to civilians in 1980 and the Ecuadorian military returned power after seven years (1972–9); General Pinochet held power until 1990. The Argentine military, after its disastrous war in the Falklands/Malvinas, delivered power to an elected civilian government in 1983. In Brazil, the generals in 1982 allowed direct elections of state governors for the first time since 1965 and allowed indirect presidential elections in 1985. The military in Uruguay, also, allowed elections in 1984, eleven years after seizing power.

One factor making for military rule in the past

Propaganda on display in a Montevideo square prior to the Uruguayan elections of November 1984

was the overconfidence of civilians who believed that they could manipulate military governments to do their own bidding. Ambitious military officers will seek to build civilian support for their own bids for power; they often promise far more than they can deliver and sometimes deliberately mislead civilians about their true intentions. Present-day civilian rulers are much more aware than their predecessors during the 1960s and early 1970s that it is far easier to bring the military into politics than to persuade them back to barracks. Consequently civilian politicians have increasingly sought to build consensus with each other, so as to avert the danger of creating disaffection sufficient to encourage renewed military rule. It also helps that Washington is far more unequivocally opposed to military intervention than it was during the late 1960s and early 1970s; moreover the Communist threat has largely disappeared, in Latin America as elsewhere. For these reasons it is to be hoped that the gradual decline of the military's political power will continue. GP

Further Reading: G. Philip, *The Military in South American Politics* (London, 1985); K. Remmer, *Military Rule in Latin America* (London, 1989); A. Stepan, *Rethinking Military Politics* (Princeton, 1989); T. E. Skidmore, *The Politics of Military Rule in Brazil 1964–85* (New York, 1988)

Social structure and social change in Latin America

INTRODUCTION

It is dangerous to generalize about Latin American social structure. The reasons for this are important. First, although the region has a common cultural identity, stemming from Spanish and Portuguese colonization, some countries display more 'Latin' qualities than others. The countries of the Southern Cone (Argentina, Uruguay, and to a lesser extent Chile) have the most European populations, made up largely of the descendants of European migrants. Other countries, such as those in the Andean zone and much of Central America, have large indigenous populations, or populations of mixed descent. In the Caribbean and Brazil the black population is more numerous, and its influence is also more important culturally.

Second, Latin American countries vary widely in their degree of economic development. This variation accounts not only for the proportion of people to be found in rural and urban areas, but also the kinds of employment and life-styles that different social groups exhibit in both settings. Only Cuba, among Latin American countries, has adopted socialist forms, although the Sandinista government (1979–89) in Nicaragua expressed socialist aspirations.

Some countries, like Argentina and Brazil, have well-established industrial sectors and thus both a relatively large middle class and industrial working class. Other countries have experienced industrialization more recently; mainly since 1940 in the case of Mexico, or since 1970 in the case of some parts of the Andes and Central America. In these cases the internal market is smaller, and the population that makes up the 'market' has only acquired middle- or working-class values within the last couple of decades. It is important to recognize this fact when we look at Latin America from a Western European or North American perspective.

Third, because economic development in Latin America differs from that in the already industrialized countries, the social structure exhibits apparent contradictions that are perplexing to most outside observers. Traditional ways of life co-exist with the 'modern' world to a degree not found in North America, and rarely even in Europe. Poverty and riches live uneasily together. The city streets are given over to donkeys and beggars as well as to Cadillacs and Volkswagens. The modern department store, sometimes part of a multinational chain, shares urban space with countless thousands of street vendors, who form part of what economists term the 'urban informal sector' (meaning that they do not count in official statistics). Even in the countryside the peasant farmer is unlikely to pursue an unchanging, traditional pattern of agriculture, and often rubs shoulders with business farmers employing new agricultural technology, marketing co-operatives and government technicians. The co-existence of a modern capitalist class structure and a 'pre-capitalist' landlord and peasant society should serve to remind us that the former is dependent for its existence on the latter, while the existence of a modern sector in no way implies that the transition to industrial capitalist society will be completed on the European model.

Finally, it is important to emphasize that much that is important in Latin American social structure is not readily observed, and still less readily recorded, in

Dense housing in Rio de Janeiro

the work of social scientists and statisticians. Some groups, especially women and children, are much more 'invisible' to governments and official experts than should ideally be the case. Like much of the Indian and black population, their status is a subordinate one, and what they think and feel is usually unrecorded.

URBANIZATION

Latin America is the most urbanized of Third World continents. Even three decades ago countries such as Chile, Argentina and Venezuela were more 'urban' than 'rural'. Today the picture is of a continent in which the majority live in cities and towns (see table 1). Even areas that are less developed, such as Central America, exhibit the same trend towards urbanization. Census data from 1970 and 1988 suggests that in most of Central America, a region producing export crops such as bananas and coffee, and heavily dependent on important manufactures, the urban population then made up over 40 per cent of the total (table 2).

The increase in size and proportion of the population living in towns is attributable to two processes. First, migration from the countryside has swollen most cities in Latin America and a good many small towns and provincial centres of population. Much of this migration has occurred in stages, as people abandon their rural livelihoods in favour of closer ties with the city. Research in provincial urban centres, such as Huancayo in Peru, suggests that urban links are often longstanding and close relations are maintained with cities hundreds of miles distant. Many of those who arrive in complex urban labour markets, as in the case of Monterrey in Mexico, have acquired training and 'credentials' *en route* to the city. So the image that many people have of the 'peasant' in the city is an inaccurate one; most migrants have long ceased to be peasants when they arrive in the city.

The second process which has contributed to urban growth is the net increase in the urban population itself. People establish themselves in urban environments remarkably quickly, begin to look around for somewhere secure to live and ways of earning a living. Since most of the migrant population is young, it is a relatively short time before their children are born, into urban homes. Cultural adaptation to the city is made easier by the fact that so many other urban residents have only lived there for a decade or less. Latin American cities are literally *being* created, in some cases almost overnight, and urban patterns of behaviour are learned in a pragmatic, highly adaptable way. Contrary to the myth current in the 1960s, when squatter settlements first

TABLE 1
Urban population as percentage of total population

	1960	1980	1988
Argentina	74	82	86
Brazil	46	65	75
Chile	68	81	85
Ecuador	34	45	55
Mexico	51	67	71

Source: International Bank for Reconstruction and Development (IBRD), *World Development Report*, 1980 and 1990 (Washington DC, 1980 and 1990).

TABLE 2
Central America: urban and rural population, percentage distribution patterns, 1970 and 1988

Country	Urban 1970	Urban 1988	Rural 1970	Rural 1988
Costa Rica	41	45	59	55
El Salvador	40	44	60	56
Guatemala	36	33	64	67
Honduras	31	42	69	58
Nicaragua	47	59	53	41
Panama	48	54	52	46

Source: Interamerican Development Bank (IDBN), *Population and Urban Trends in Central America and Panama* (Washington DC, 1977); IBRD, *World Development Report*, 1990 (Washington DC, 1990)

became obvious to casual observers of Latin America, most urban squatters show every sign of knowing what they want and doing what they can to get it. Their 'life chances' may not be good, but this is because of the inequalities that exist in Latin American cities rather than the psychological handicaps imposed by an urban 'culture'.

CLASS STRUCTURE

Most Latin American societies are extremely unequal by the standards of developed countries. The way that an individual is located within his society, in terms of his occupation and income, determines his access to educational opportunities and health provisions as well as his future social mobility. Since land is still an important factor in social status, especially in rural areas, the ownership and control of land is a major variable in the class structure. As we shall see, land ownership, like the ownership of capital, is concentrated in few hands throughout Latin America.

However, factors other than land ownership are of importance in discussing class. The concept of class refers not only to the ownership of the means of production but to the way that this pattern of ownership determines the individual's 'life chances'. The poor are not only materially poor, they also have more limited access to private and public services, worse health and nutrition standards, less educational opportunity and are at greater risk from political violence. Beginning with the occupational structure, table 3 shows the percentage distribution of the labour force in the three economic sectors of agriculture, industry and services. The 'service sector' is a notoriously ill-defined category, and we should recall that most service employment in Latin America is in poorly paid and often casual jobs, on the streets and in slum and squatter housing areas. It is clear from the table that, although industrial employment grew between 1960 and 1988 in Brazil, Ecuador and Mexico, this growth was largely at the expense of agriculture rather than services. Indeed,

TABLE 4
Income distribution: percentage share of household income by percentile groups of households: lowest and highest quintiles

	Lowest 20%	Highest 20%
Costa Rica (1986)	3.3	54.5
Brazil (1983)	2.4	62.6
Peru (1985)	4.4	51.9
United Kingdom (1979)	5.8	39.5

Source: IBRD, *World Development Report*, 1990

TABLE 5
Landholding in north-east Brazil (1975)

Size of property (ha)	Holdings (%)	Area (%)
1–10	70.0	5.4
10–100	24.0	22.8
100–1,000	5.6	41.6
1,000–10,000	.4	23.8
10,000+	negligible	6.9

Source: *Statistical Abstract of Latin America* 1990, Vol. 28, Table 315.

service sector employment grew in each country during this period; in Mexico by thirty-one percentage points. The service sector increased in both Ecuador and Argentina. These figures should serve to remind us that in the more industrially developed societies of Latin America there has been a limit to industrial expansion commensurate with the limited scale of the internal market, and economic recession after 1982.

Estimating the numbers of people outside 'formal' employment is always hazardous but estimates from Brazil show that in industrialized states like São Paulo and Rio de Janeiro under one third of the labour force works in the 'informal economy'. However, in many states, including those of the south as well as the north-east, informal sector employment accounts for about two thirds of the total. Similar figures could be produced for other Latin American countries.

The distribution of income is another indication of a country's class structure, pointing particularly to the different patterns of consumption available to the different social classes. Table 4 shows the percentage of total income received by the poorest 20 per cent of the population, and compares this figure with the share of household income received by the wealthiest 20 per cent. In four of the largest Latin American countries (Brazil, Mexico, Argentina and Chile) the wealthiest fifth of the population received over half

TABLE 3
Labour force: percentage distribution of labour force by economic sectors

| | Agriculture | | Industry | | Services | |
	1960	1988	1960	1988	1960	1988
Argentina	20	13	36	44	44	44
Brazil	52	9	15	43	33	49
Chile	30	n/a	30	n/a	40	n/a
Ecuador	58	15	19	36	23	49
Mexico	55	9	20	35	25	56

Source: IBRD, *World Development Report*, 1980 and 1990.

TABLE 6

Latin America: health and nutrition indicators

Country	Population per doctor		Infant mortality rate (per thousand live births)	
	1965	1984	1965	1984
Argentina	600	370	58	31
Bolivia	3300	1540	160	108
Brazil	2500	1080	104	61
Colombia	2500	1240	86	39
CostaRica	2010	960	72	18
Chile	2120	1230	101	20
Ecuador	3000	820	112	62
El Salvador	n/a	2830	120	57
Mexico	2080	1240	82	46
Peru	1650	1040	130	86
Uruguay	880	520	47	23
Venezuela	1210	700	65	35
United States	670	470	25	10

Source: IBRD, *World Development Report, 1990*.

TABLE 7

Secondary school enrolments as percentage of age group

Country	1965	1987
Argentina	28	74
Brazil	16	39
Chile	34	70
Guatemala	8	21
Mexico	17	53
Peru	25	65

Source: IBRD, *World Development Report, 1990*.

the income in the late 1960s and early 1970s and by the mid-1980s this had changed little. By comparison the poorest fifth of the population received under 5 per cent of total household income.

Particularly in the less industrially developed parts of Latin America landholding is an important element in the class structure. Control over land, usually linked with ownership, is the basis for political power and, inevitably, control over other social classes. Many parts of Latin America – and of Brazil – are less traditional than north-east Brazil, but table 5 illustrates a typical pattern of landholding in an area of large estates and smallholdings (latifundia/minifundia). Much of the land in the large estates is unworked, or given over to extensive cattle-grazing, while the peasant farmers grow crops and raise a few animals on their small, intensively worked plots.

Some indication of the distribution of resources in Latin American societies is provided by data on health and educational provision and nutritional standards. Table 6 illustrates the fact that most Latin Americans are less likely to visit a doctor or nurse than are North Americans. However, some countries, notably post-revolutionary Cuba, have made successful attempts to improve maternal and child health despite a shortage of doctors. This is reflected in the low infant mortality rate. The divergencies within Latin American countries are clearly seen in the figures for access to safe water. In Bolivia only one-third of the population has access to such a supply: in Uruguay almost everybody does.

Access to educational facilities is another indicator of socio-economic development. The figures in Table 7 suggest that, although secondary school enrolments have increased, a significant part of the school-age population does not attend secondary school. In

Latin America the middle and upper classes have privileged access to private universities through private preparatory and secondary schools. Nevertheless, it is important to record the phenomenal growth of the state universities, especially in countries such as Mexico and Peru, which has paralleled the expansion of secondary education.

In many Latin American societies, particularly those experiencing rapid industrial growth, the principal social division is no longer between a landed upper class, a small middle class and the popular masses. The division is between 'accommodated' groups in the middle and working classes and the mass of people, who are often very poor. In Mexico the population covered by a social security programme increased from 9.8 million in 1967 to 22.2 million in 1976. The increase in the proportion of newly insured was no less impressive. In 1967 less than a quarter of the population were covered by social security. By 1976 it had increased to 35 per cent. These figures should give us cause for reflection. Latin American societies are very unequal, and the distribution of 'life chances' is seriously prejudicial to the poor, but in some countries there is an emerging group of relatively secure working- and middle-class people whose principal benefactor, in many cases, is the state.

SOCIAL ORGANIZATION

Quantitative information on Latin American society provides an inadequate picture of the social structure, as it does not represent the important changes in values and behaviour that accompany economic development. It is necessary to look at the way that individuals and groups are organized to appreciate fully the more normative aspects of Latin American society. Perhaps the most ubiquitous social institution in Latin American, as in other societies, is the family.

The role of women, in the family as well as in the labour force, is closely associated with fertility and

TABLE 8
Crude birth rate per thousand population
(selected countries)

Country	Rate	
	1965	1988
Dominican Republic	47	31
Mexico	45	28
El Salvador	46	36
Guatemala	46	40
Ecuador	45	32
Venezuela	42	30
Peru	45	31
Brazil	39	28
Colombia	43	26
Chile	34	23
Argentina	23	21
United States	19	16

Source: IBRD, *World Development Report, 1990.*

family size. Table 8 shows that in 1965 some Latin American countries were experiencing what amounted to a population explosion, as high birth rates were unchecked by natural mortality. In Mexico and the Dominican Republic women were giving birth to three times as many children per thousand as in the United States. In the more 'European' countries of the Southern Cone fertility was much lower than in countries with large Indian and black populations. This is true today, but accumulating evidence from some countries which have provided government backing for family planning, notably Mexico, suggests that the birth rate is coming under control. For the first time women are the major arbiters of their own fertility. The implications of this trend for male/female roles, the part played by the Roman Catholic Church, and the participation of women in the labour force, need to be given closer attention in the coming decades.

At one remove from the domestic unit are those organizations, such as trade unions, which articulate collective interests within the wider society. In some countries, especially those with a weak manufacturing base, trade union membership is low. In other countries it is relatively high, although in these cases trade unions are often virtually an extension of government, and even affiliated to government political parties. In Argentina, Chile, Uruguay and Brazil trade union activity has at times been curtailed by repressive military regimes. In Mexico, on the other hand, state paternalism (not always free from repression, it is true) has played a large part in union growth. The percentage of unionized workers is high in some Mexican economic sectors. In transport and the electricity industry most Mexican workers are members of a trade union, at least nominally, while only 10 per cent are unionized in the service sector, and even fewer in the 'primary sector' (principally agriculture).

For many Latin Americans the organizations to which they are affiliated serve both as instruments of individual self-advancement and the basis for solidarity with others. This movements to occupy land or gain land titles in squatter settlements have gained mass support in countries where such action is tolerated. At the same time cultural identity is important, blacks in Brazil and Cuba participate in Afro-Brazilian and Afro-Cuban religious cults; people of Indian origin join provincial clubs in Lima, Peru. The equivalent associations for the middle classes are similar to those in the industrialized countries: Rotary Clubs, Bar Associations and professional interest groups.

In Mexico again, many more workers are employed in private Mexican-owned firms than in multinationals. Nevertheless, multinational companies play an increasingly important role in the most highly capitalized sectors of many Latin American countries such as Colombia, Brazil and Mexico. One important implication of the growth of multinational companies in Latin America is that their labour force acquires a dynamic which is more closely related to events in Europe or North America than to Latin America. Labour, as well as capital, becomes an international rather than a national commodity. The state in Latin American countries thus emerges as a mediating institution, seeking to legitimize and enforce its actions not only through its relations with national classes, but also with the representatives of international interests, including the multinationals.

SOCIAL CHANGE

We have already suggested various ways in which Latin American societies have changed during the last twenty years or so. The most notable changes have been felt throughout both rural and urban society, and it would be a mistake to attribute social change to urbanization alone. Rural society is no longer characterized by non-market relations. Indeed, it is doubtful whether non-market relations were ever quite as important as some writers on Latin American modernization suggested in the 1960s. Agricultural technologies have shifted the emphasis within rural society from the ownership of land to its control and use. Crop production is increasingly for animal consumption, for livestock and dairy products, many of which are exported, or for the vast masses that have congregated in the cities. Food policy has emerged as a key issue in Latin American society as the consumption habits and nutritional standards of the population are determined more and

King Street, Kingston, Jamaica

more by industrial food processing and sophisticated food distribution and marketing systems. It is a moot question whether these changes will herald an improvement in the diet of most people – indications are that the nutritional standards of the poorest people have actually declined.

Recent decades have witnessed right-wing political repression throughout much of Latin America, making it difficult for opposition left-wing forces to organize politically in defence of living standards. For its part the Latin American left has not always shown a capacity to unite, and political rhetoric has sometimes been a substitute for planning concrete measures aimed at making improvements in living standards. At the same time a now very significant minority of the Latin American population, the middle class and some of the organized working class, has attained living standards comparable with those in Europe and North America. Their ascendancy has been closely related to the increasing intervention of the state in areas of life, such as education and family planning, which were traditionally the preserve of private institutions, notably the Church.   MRR

Further Reading: T. Cubitt, *Latin American Society* (London, 1988); International Bank for Reconstruction and Development (IBRD), *World Development Report* (Washington, DC, 1990); E. Jelin, ed., *Women and Social Change in Latin America* (London, 1990); J. Nash and H. Safa, eds., *Women and Change in Latin America* (South Hadley, Mass., 1985); D. Preston, ed., *Environment, Society and Rural Change in Latin America* (London, 1980); M. R. Redclift, *Agrarian Reform and the Peasant Organization on the Ecuadorian Coast* (London, 1978)

Social structure and social change in the Caribbean

Four features in combination – three historical and one geographical – give the Caribbean its regional coherence and distinguish it from neighbouring Latin America. The historical legacy involves the imprint of colonialism, the sugar plantation and slavery; geography is expressed by insularity. To understand the origin, and diversity, of Caribbean social structure and the developments it has undergone, it is necessary to explore the changing interrelationships between these key factors. Yet by no means all Caribbean societies have experienced insularity or the same chronology, nor have they all equally and completely evolved out of the mould of political dependence, sugar monoculture and social inequality in which they were set by the early nineteenth century.

INSULARITY, COLONIALISM AND DECOLONIZATION

The Caribbean region embraces fifty-odd societies strung out in an archipelago which stretches for more than 2000 km from Cuba to Trinidad; it also includes the three Guianas on the shoulder of South America and Belize in Central America. The political, social and economic histories of these four mainland territories link them to the Caribbean rather than to Latin America. Moreover, although they are continental in location, their settlement pattern is coastal, and sandwiched, island-like, between the sea and an empty interior.

Social and political boundaries in the archipelago coincide with islands, each of which is clearly demarcated living space, isolated from its neighbours by the sea. Only Hispaniola – occupied by Haiti and the Dominican Republic – and St Martin – partitioned between France and the Netherlands – are shared by two polities. Insularity implies smallness. Caribbean territories range in size from Cuba with 110,000 sq km and more than 10 million inhabitants down to the Grenadines, each with a few hundred hectares and several score cultivators and fishermen. Most islands are smaller than Barbados, which is approximately the same size as the Isle of Wight. Even the mainland territories, even though large in area, record small populations.

Territorial fragmentation and small size – or small population – ensured that the most outstanding historical features of Caribbean societies would be their political dependence. The partitioning of the region by the Spanish, French, British, Dutch and Danish during the seventeenth and eighteenth centuries and United States intervention in the Greater Antilles since the nineteenth century, culminating in the annexation of Puerto Rico in 1898 and the purchase of the Danish Virgin Islands in 1917, have ensured that each territory's connections – political, economic and intellectual – have been forged almost exclusively with metropolitan countries in Western Europe or North America. Soviet Russian involvement in post-revolutionary Cuba has perpetuated this pattern.

Thirty years ago, only the three largest Caribbean units were independent, and two of them, Haiti and Cuba, have special symbolic significance for the others. Haiti's independence from France in 1804 was achieved in the aftermath of the area's only successful slave rebellion. Cuba, too, is a Caribbean anomaly. It is big and sophisticated by regional standards; and it fought two wars of independence in the nineteenth century before securing its freedom (although under *de facto* US control) from Spain in 1898.

Since the Second World War, however, metropolitan countries in Western Europe have been as anxious to decolonize as the islands have been to secure self-government and independence. Setting economic viability above political sovereignty, the French and Dutch West Indies have been decolonized by incorporation. Guadeloupe, Martinique and Guyane have become separate *départements* of France and send representatives to the Chamber of Deputies in Paris. Holland combined with its Caribbean possessions to form the Tripartite Kingdom of the Netherlands, but Suriname became independent in 1975 and the Dutch Antilles may also eventually secede, possibly atomizing into separate island states. Aruba gained separate status in 1986 and is scheduled for independence in 1996.

Fragmentation has already created a myriad political entities in the Commonwealth Caribbean. British post-war policy aimed to launch all the Commonwealth units into independence through the West Indies Federation, but insular rivalries and fears of either subordination or financial burden led to its collapse in 1962. Jamaica, Trinidad, Barbados and Guyana became independent in the 1960s, the Windwards in the 1970s and Antigua and Belize and St Kitts–Nevis in the early 1980s. Yet Montserrat, the British Virgin Islands, the Caymans, the Turks and Caicos Islands and Anguilla remain self-governing British territories – indeed, the majority are colonies, and even in an era of independence many other small islands are still dependencies. Carriacou, subordinate to Grenada, boasts its own fief, Petite Martinique; and Barbuda, with 1200 inhabitants, would have preferred the perpetuation of British colonialism to the perils of mismanagement and exploitation by recently independent Antigua, to which it is constitutionally tied.

PLANTATIONS, SLAVERY AND EMANCIPATION

Colonialism determined not only the historical subordination of Caribbean societies and their orientation towards distant metropoles, but their economic development as sugar plantations within the mercantilist systems of the north-west European powers. By the second half of the eighteenth century, when the West Indian sugar industry was at its peak, plantation cultivation had spread to virtually all the British, French, Dutch and Danish possessions, though the Spanish colonies remained either undeveloped – as in the case of Trinidad – or as revictualling stations on the route from the peninsula to the main.

Colonial plantations in the Caribbean created a grossly inegalitarian social hierarchy based upon legal estate. During the seventeenth century the major strata of Caribbean society were differentially incorporated as white free men and black slaves; and, when miscegenation became more prevalent in the mid-eighteenth century, an intermediate coloured element was formed through the manumission of the illegitimate offspring of the white elite. These legal estates determined that whites alone were fully fledged citizens: the brown emancipated population enjoyed only limited civil rights, as did the increasing body of free blacks; slaves, whether black or the illegitimate, coloured offspring of poor whites, were non-persons, chattels to be bought and sold. Status and power were inversely related to group size. In Jamaica in 1825, for example, 25,000 whites legislated for a colony with 40,000 coloureds and 340,000 blacks.

A 'white bias' permeated all levels of the creole pigmentocracy. Possession of a white skin, aquiline nose, straight hair and thin lips became a badge of status, and gradations from the 'bad' features of the black to the 'good' features of the European, exemplified by mulattoes, quadroons, mustees and mustifinos (who were generally treated as white), formed stages on the road to whiteness and high rank. Moreover, the white bias carried cultural connotations: everything European was desirable; Africa was to be denigrated.

Caribbean legal estates during slavery determined not only the status of the constituent corporate categories – slaves, freemen, citizens – but the cultures they practised. African traits were largely eroded under the system of plantation slavery; the free people of colour (and the free blacks), while orientating themselves towards Europe, combined the behaviour of masters and slaves; and the whites practised a creole version of eighteenth-century European culture. Slaves were a pre-literate group and communicated in a creole version of English or French; their household structure was liable to continual disruption through sale or redeployment of individuals, and serial polygamy was the norm, with mothers rearing half-siblings; and their religious activity ran the gamut from witchcraft and African beliefs, through cults such as Vodún and Shango, to conversion to Catholicism or Protestant non-conformism – depending upon the norms of the colony's mother country.

Slave opposition to servitude took many forms – malingering, magico-religious activities, suicide, abortion – and rebellion. In Jamaica alone, twenty-nine rebellions took place over a period of 150 years, but only in Haiti did slave revolt generate revolution and independence. For, in the final analysis, the cohesion of these potentially unstable creole, slave societies in the Caribbean depended on force or the threat of force. The political and legal supremacy of the minority group of whites was reinforced by the whip, by metropolitan military detachments and by local militias, usually under white control and with free coloured non-commissioned officers.

Notwithstanding adamant elite opposition to change, the legal framework of the Caribbean creole societies was slowly dismantled in the nineteenth century. Slaves were emancipated in the British colonies in 1834, in the French and Dutch territories in 1845 and 1863 respectively, in Puerto Rico in 1873 and in Cuba as recently as 1886. The contrast between early British and French emancipation and late Spanish slave abolition was largely a reflection of economic differences: the sugar colonies of the north-west Europeans reached their apogee in the eighteenth century but were in decline by the early 1800s; the Spanish colonies developed as sugar monocultures only in the nineteenth century, and experienced their peak in the early twentieth century under US capitalism. Nevertheless, all Caribbean territories entered the twentieth century with a heritage of plantation slavery.

Nineteenth-century emancipation set in motion fewer changes than the planters had feared, largely because the landholding systems and property-restricted franchises – Haiti excepted – favoured the established order. Nonetheless, emancipated slaves were free to sell their labour, migrate, squat or purchase land. A substantial 'reconstituted' peasantry emerged in Haiti, Jamaica and the Windward Islands, though in the larger Leewards, Barbados and the Spanish-speaking islands the ex-slaves were unable to acquire land of their own and remained as plantation workers. In Trinidad, annexed by Britain from Spain in 1815, the small ex-slave population gravitated into farming or, more significantly, into urban occupations, notably in Port of Spain, the capital.

At the mid-point of the Caribbean's experiment with slave emancipation, the peasant-inspired Morant Bay Rebellion broke out in Jamaica in 1865. The white elite and its brown allies abandoned the old Assembly system in favour of Crown Colony Government, which had already been instituted in Trinidad. The Leeward Islands followed suit, and by the end of the nineteenth century virtually all the British colonies were under direct rule. The main effect was to place control of each island's destiny in the hands of white expatriate officials – and white creole planters and professionals. The rapid advance to power of the brown and black middle stratum after 1834 was halted, and the potential voting strength of the burgeoning group of black peasant freeholders was neutralized.

The complexity of many societies was increased by immigration of East Indian and Chinese indentured labourers, and the arrival of free Chinese, Syrians, Lebanese and Spaniards; some islands, however, experienced a simplification of their creole stratification through racial extermination or outmigration.

By the end of the depression of the 1930s, it was possible to distinguish a number of distinct types of Caribbean society that had emerged out of the creole model based on plantation slavery. Jamaica perhaps most closely resembled that model, in that it then

House of beaten metal, Belize

consisted of three ranked cultural segments, correlated with colour, each with differential access to resources. Small, homogeneous folk societies, such as Barbuda and Anguilla, were culturally similar to black Jamaican peasant communities. Haiti and the Windward Islands resembled Jamaica, but had lost their whites through genocide and emigration, respectively, and had brown elites instead. In Cuba massive white immigration over the previous fifty years for work on the sugar plantations had swamped the creole stratification and reduced the non-whites to enclaves in a class-based hierarchy. Puerto Rico was similar, though with lower slave imports and much smaller-scale Spanish immigration.

Another example of late immigration disrupting the creole stratification – in contradiction to Jamaica, where the Chinese and Syrians occupied status gaps within the social hierarchy – is provided by Trinidad and British Guiana (now Guyana). Between 1845 and 1919 tens of thousands of Indian indentured labourers were brought in to work on the nascent sugar estates. In Trinidad they accounted for over one-third of the population; in British Guiana they threatened soon to form the majority. Yet in both colonies the East Indians constituted an endogamous, spatially segregated and culturally distinct segment external to the creole stratification.

During the first four decades of the twentieth century adult (often only male) suffrage existed in Haiti,

Cuba and Puerto Rico, though none was considered a democracy. In the Commonwealth Caribbean, property restrictions meant that less than 10 per cent had the vote; politics remained an elite pastime, and the reins of government were held in expatriate hands. The conjunction of a restricted franchise with the international economic depression created severe labour disturbances in many Commonwealth islands, notably Jamaica and Trinidad. Pressure was mounted for universal adult suffrage and independence; political parties and trade unions were formed. Universal adult suffrage was gradually introduced into the British colonies after 1944, and a long period of constitutional decolonization began which lasted, in most cases, for almost twenty years before independence was finally granted.

NEO-COLONIALISM

Despite adult suffrage and sovereignty, Caribbean societies remain culturally and racially stratified and economically dependent. Whites and mobile minority groups – the architects and beneficiaries of the old order – are everywhere under attack. Their residual identities, however strong, provide no basis for expressions of national solidarity. But black and East Indian electorates have been outmanoeuvred by 'brown' politicians, who have not hesitated to project overseas an Anglo-Saxon image of their island realms. Within the Caribbean, coloured political elites, supported by white commercial interests, have promoted a multi-racial ethic. Racial and cultural variations rarely receive public mention, and the official line everywhere emphasizes racial harmony.

The brown and black middle stratum which has filled the political and administrative vacuum left by the whites, has carefully created symbols of national unity. Local heads of state are usually black, local art forms receive government patronage, and annual celebrations of independence provide a holiday from the poverty which engulfs the lower stratum. In Jamaica, the British honours system, which co-opted local leaders, has been replaced by a new set of national awards. Trinidad's pre-lenten Carnival is promoted by the government to cast the national image in the mould of black creoles – as distinct from that of East Indians, who have traditionally formed the backbone of the political opposition.

Important though these changes have been, West Indian youth dismisses them as mere tokens. During the late 1960s and early 1970s black power became a vehicle for protest throughout the islands and its practitioners advocated a break with economic imperialism and white racism. West Indian intellectuals, in particular, have protested at the penetration of each Caribbean economy by foreign enterprise. In their view, 'neo-colonialism' prevails, and each island remains dependent on overseas capital, decision-makers and technologies – and not solely in the traditional agricultural sector.

At the end of the growth decade of the 1960s, North American companies were pre-eminent in the Jamaican, Haitian, Dominican Republican and Guyanese bauxite industries; Texaco and Shell dom-

Sugar factory, Jamaica

inated Trinidad's oil economy; Tate and Lyle and Bookers were the giants of Commonwealth Caribbean sugar production; and Fyffes and Geest held a near monopoly in the marketing of West Indian bananas in Britain. But Caribbean nationalism during the 1970s, in the wake of Cuba's socialist revolution, created pressures to change the role of multinational corporations in the larger islands. The West Indies Sugar Corporation, a subsidiary of Tate and Lyle, divested itself of cane land in Jamaica and Trinidad; Jamaicans and Trinidadians, it was agreed, would eventually hold a 51 per cent share in foreign banks; Jamaica in 1974 extracted a tenfold rise in its bauxite revenues from the North American companies and contracted with Kaiser to purchase 51 per cent control of the local company together with all its holdings in land; Trinidad has purchased Shell's assets in the island. The cleanest sweep through state ownership occurred in Guyana, where the Co-operative Republic nationalized the bauxite and sugar companies and now controls 80 per cent of the economy. Nevertheless, vital economic decisions are still made overseas, and the Lesser Antilles lack even these concessions to national ownership or popular involvement.

Special problems of economic development and diversification attach to islands with less than 100,000 inhabitants. In the Windwards and Leewards tourism has been embraced as a panacea, but it remains an enclave in the economic and spatial structure of the islands – as it does in larger Puerto Rico, Jamaica and Barbados – funded largely from overseas, imposing high infrastructural costs on island governments, employing few local workers, and consuming imported, rather than peasant-produced food.

Even more damaging than dependence has been the inability of the peripheral capitalist economies in the Caribbean to generate the economic growth and employment opportunities on which gradual social change has been predicated. Sugar and banana output have faltered; tourism is vulnerable to economic depressions, and, like bauxite mining and tax-incentive manufacturing, employs thousands where tens of thousands look for work. From oil-rich Trinidad to the Americanized Commonwealth of Puerto Rico, massive and increasing unemployment, underemployment and marginality characterize urban and rural dwellers alike. With the population doubling every forty years in many islands, it is not surprising that most Caribbean peoples are latent emigrants – and not a few are radicals.

Emigration and protest are linked in the cult of Rastafari which has diffused from Jamaica to most of the Commonwealth Caribbean. For Jamaican cultists, Rastafari – or Haile Selassie – is God. Not only is God black, but blacks are the true children of Israel, God's elect, who were carried into captivity in the Caribbean and placed under the yoke of white and brown Babylonians. Redemption depends on repatriation to Africa or, more specifically, to Ethiopia.

For many black power advocates of the 1970s West African tribal costume, Afro haircuts, American black power terminology and slogans such as 'black is beautiful' and 'Castro is the blackest man in the Caribbean' were adequate expressions of a new, post-colonial identity. But for socialists looking for structural change, it was Cuba's break with United States capitalism in the aftermath of Fidel Castro's revolution that was most appealing. Moreover, the 'New Man' and 'New Society', based not on material inducements but moral incentives, to which Cuba temporarily aspired in the 1960s, not surprisingly still appeals to Caribbean idealists, surrounded as they are on their own islands by materialism, poverty and racial disadvantage.

But most Caribbean societies have either not tried or have failed to make their social structures more radically egalitarian in the last twenty years, and the economic recession (from 1981 onwards) undoubtedly widened the gap between rich and poor. Paradoxically, those islands that are most politically dependent – Puerto Rico and the French Antilles – have the highest standard of state welfare. And comparison between Cuba and the Commonwealth Caribbean shows that residents of the latter enjoy more personal freedom if less social equality. The only Commonwealth islands to emphasize social equality have been Jamaica under Michael Manley's People's National Movement and Grenada under Maurice Bishop's short-lived People's Revolutionary Government. Manley's programme of democratic socialism was overwhelmed by economic forces and the ballot box in 1980; his return to power in 1989 was followed by a more orthodox policy. Bishop's government came to an end in 1983 with his murder, followed in short order by an American invasion.

CONCLUSION

A view of Caribbean society through time shows how the eighteenth-century colonial distinction between slaves, freemen and citizens subsequently became a temporal sequence of change experienced by blacks and browns. In Haiti, slave rebellion created black freemen who were simultaneously citizens; in Cuba, Puerto Rico and the British West Indies, the time lapse between emancipation and citizenship was wider and wider. Only in the last forty years have Commonwealth Caribbean blacks – and East Indians

– enjoyed the political status of the eighteenth-century white elite. However, this tardy change from freemen to colonial citizens was closely followed by a change in the status of the societies as well – from island colonies to self-governing dependencies or independent states.

If most Caribbean units are no longer colonial, few Caribbean economies – Cuba and St Kitts excepted – are reliant on sugar plantations. Yet dependence on one or two primary products remains a hallmark of Caribbean societies, and under these conditions economic growth and related social change have been difficult to achieve, especially in the context of rapid population growth. Politics and awards for secondary and higher education have created non-white occupational mobility on a scale without parallel in the past. But the majority of West Indians find their social status and material standards remain disappointing and unacceptable. Nevertheless, the prospect of radical change along Cuban lines is no more appealing to most islanders than to the region's largest neighbour and self-appointed guardian, the United States.

Independence, so long awaited, ought to mean more than stuttering economic development based on dependence on external forces and the enactment of Westminster-style democracy under circumstances which encourage domination by conservative political elites. But, in view of the small-scale insularity of Caribbean societies and the long record of oppression and impoverishment in the black republic of Haiti, even these modest achievements could easily be undermined.   CC

Further Reading: C. Clarke, ed., *Society and Politics in the Caribbean* (London, 1991); F. W. Knight, *The Caribbean: the Genesis of a Fragmented Nationalism,* 2nd edition (New York, 1990); D. Lowenthal, *West Indian Societies* (New York, London, Toronto, 1972); S. Mintz and S. Price, eds., *Caribbean Contours* (Baltimore and London, 1985); A. Payne and P. Sutton, eds., *Dependency under Challenge: the Political Economy of the Commonwealth Caribbean* (Manchester, 1984)

Political parties in Latin America

On the face of it the variety of party types in Latin America is considerable. Some parties are mass parties with long traditions and deep popular roots. Others are no more than cliques with only an episodic existence. Structurally, some are highly centralized, while others take decisions in an open and democratic fashion. And their ideological range is equally wide, from neo-fascist Catholic nationalism to extreme-left voluntarism.

A convenient way of organizing this diversity is to link party types to the evolution of their national political systems. Five stages can be identified: traditional party systems in the period of political reconstruction that followed independence; the rise of 'protest' and 'access' parties during the period of growth that followed reconstruction; the 'national popular' phase linked to the reorientation of the international trading system after 1929; the partial eclipse of civilian rule during the last few decades; and the return to democracy since 1980.

LATE-NINETEENTH-CENTURY DEMOCRACY

By the end of the nineteenth century a relatively uniform party configuration had emerged in Latin America. Politics in most states had ceased to be a matter of armed violence between regions and had come to be dominated by the conflict between Liberal and Conservative parties, each armed with a borrowed doctrine. Liberals sought to promote national development (by which they meant the development of primary exports along with the infrastructure this required) through the promotion of open trade, a loose form of government, and the lessening of Church influence. Conservatives, reflecting a more specifically colonial heritage, sometimes argued for the protection of domestic industry, for a powerful unitary state, and for a privileged position for the Church and other corporate groups. In some cases (for example, in Mexico under Porfírio Díaz) the struggle was resolved through dictatorial rule, and this had important consequences since it meant that neither access nor protest parties had the freedom to develop which they enjoyed elsewhere. But, even where party politics was competitive, it remained thoroughly oligarchic, thanks to a restricted franchise and (in many countries) the stifling of opposition.

Oligarchic politics has since collapsed but the practice of borrowing ideology has not. The development in this century of Socialist, Communist and reformist parties elsewhere has been mirrored throughout Latin America. Partly this reflects the political space created by the collapse of the old two-party system (where it existed) but also the fact that money as well as intellectual and moral support has been forthcoming from outside. But this is less important than has sometimes been claimed, and the charge that many parties – especially those of the centre and left – are merely imitative is hard to sustain. Only the most orthodox of the Communist parties have been willing to subordinate themselves to external direction, and even they have suffered repeated splits in consequence. Whatever their doctrinal debts and however venal (as when accepting external help for electoral purposes), most remain stubbornly idiosyncratic.

Parties of protest

Along with the economic growth that accompanied political reconstruction towards the end of the nineteenth century there emerged working-class and petty-bourgeois political interests that the old system could not satisfy. Some of these interests initially attempted to work through the system while others (notably the anarchists and syndicalists) rejected the parliamentary road altogether. But, in the face of continued intransigence from the elite, most turned either to the new parties that sought a wide distribution of power within the prevailing system or to the parties of protest, first Socialist and, after 1917, Communist.

Most of the Communist parties of Latin America developed as splinter groups from existing Socialist parties or anarchist movements, and from that time on relations between Communists and Socialists have rarely been harmonious. Divided by history, by real policy differences and by their struggle for the loyalties of the intelligentsia and workers, they, nevertheless, have more in common than either would want to admit. Both accept the necessity of a capitalist stage of development, the parliamentary road, and the convenience of co-operation with other progressive parties. As a result, both have suffered from splits by radicals tired of a policy of gradualism that has, so far, brought few results. In the case of Cuba, state power was won by military means and the dominance of state over party has been maintained.

These parties of the left have been vigorously attacked, more from the ultra-left than from the right, as elitist, academic and anti-nationalist, though they are less internationalist in practice than in rhetoric. There is some truth in these charges, but

President Víctor Paz Estenssoro of Bolivia (fourth from left on balcony) above a stylized depiction of himself and other revolutionary heroes, La Paz, 1963

it is hard to see how it could be otherwise. Both have had to work under conditions where the working-class voice is poorly articulated and the class badly or paternalistically organized, and where the state seems ever ready to step in on behalf of those whom the left would seek to threaten. The experience of Chile indicates the difficulties involved. There, with the aid of a centre-right alternative and an electoral system that encouraged broad polarization, the Socialist and Communist parties were able to attract mass support and elect their Popular Unity (UP) coalition into power in 1970. But their very success along with their insistence upon a parliamentary and legal road to socialism when the opposition was not so constrained led to their overthrow and proscription. It seems that the more success such parties have, the more they are likely to fail, and conversely, that continued impotence is the price of their survival.

ACCESS PARTIES

Access parties are more difficult to categorize. Some, like the Radical parties of Argentina and Chile, developed towards the end of the last century. Others, like Democratic Action (AD) in Venezuela or APRA in Peru, evolved during the inter-war years as anti-

dictatorial nationalist movements, but their early radicalism has since become much attenuated. Yet others, like Popular Action (AP) in Peru or the Christian Democrats (PDC) in Chile, were post-war developments. In states where they have failed to develop (such as Mexico) many of their characteristics are found within the national popular parties.

The first of these characteristics is their lower-middle-class base. Though they also get support from the working class and, at the level of leadership, from upper-middle-class strata, they have a special appeal for those with something to lose but even more to gain from political mobilization. This accounts for their deliberately opaque but loosely reformist ideology which typically consists of support for increased expenditure on education and selective welfare and for high levels of public employment, but does not contemplate any serious alteration in the existing distribution of wealth and power. Above all – and this is why their attachment to civil institutions is so strong – they are dedicated to the provision of spoils for their supporters in the form of jobs, subsidies, entitlements and exemptions. This is often a matter of exchange between individuals, but it can also involve obligation between the party and some work-specific group as was the case in the relationship between landless labourers and the Democratic

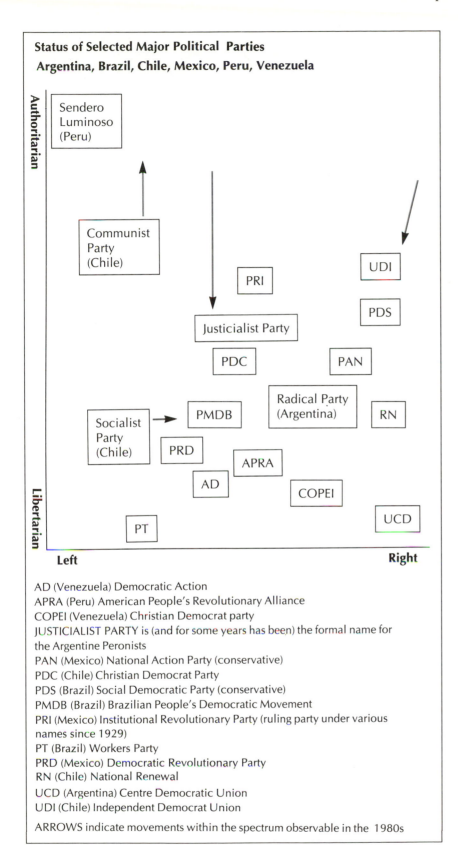

Status of Selected Major Political Parties
Argentina, Brazil, Chile, Mexico, Peru, Venezuela

AD (Venezuela) Democratic Action
APRA (Peru) American People's Revolutionary Alliance
COPEI (Venezuela) Christian Democrat party
JUSTICIALIST PARTY is (and for some years has been) the formal name for
the Argentine Peronists
PAN (Mexico) National Action Party (conservative)
PDC (Chile) Christian Democrat Party
PDS (Brazil) Social Democratic Party (conservative)
PMDB (Brazil) Brazilian People's Democratic Movement
PRI (Mexico) Institutional Revolutionary Party (ruling party under various
names since 1929)
PT (Brazil) Workers Party
PRD (Mexico) Democratic Revolutionary Party
RN (Chile) National Renewal
UCD (Argentina) Centre Democratic Union
UDI (Chile) Independent Democrat Union

ARROWS indicate movements within the spectrum observable in the 1980s

The interest of access parties in spoils is not unique, but is a persistent theme of almost all party life outside the left. Its roots lie in the overall scarcity, compounded by maldistribution, of desirable public and semi-public goods. Since only the state can supply these goods to those who have no access to them through the private sector (the lower-middle and working class), the struggle to control the state and its powers of patronage becomes highly competitive. The exchange of influence-peddling in return for votes or other kinds of political support is a major factor in the ability of these otherwise ill-defined parties to attract popular support. But it also has vicious consequences, namely high levels of partisan violence (which in Colombia reached civil war proportions in the 1950s), the erosion of public confidence in political institutions, and wasteful and corrupt administration. Moreover, however well developed and sensitive, spoils systems by their nature rest on reciprocity, and so, for the most part, exclude the powerless and disorganized who have little with which to bargain.

NATIONAL POPULAR MOVEMENTS

It was to the needs of this last group that the national popular movements of the 1930s and 1940s addressed themselves. Power was seized by a déclassé military in Argentina, and elsewhere through civilian protest (though in Peru APRA never succeeded), but the crisis of the old order was much the same everywhere: the collapse of export-led growth after 1929, the development in the more advanced economies of an industrial base and with it a better articulated working class, and the growing belief that the state could and should intervene more aggressively in the economy in order better to promote national development. Though rather too much has been made of it, structurally these movements inclined towards charismatic leadership (Perón in Argentina, Lázaro Cárdenas in Mexico, Getúlio Vargas in Brazil, Víctor Paz Estenssoro in Bolivia, Víctor Raúl Haya de la Torre in Peru, for example), towards an ideology of national redemption, and towards a corporate form of organization. Though their specific policies varied (for example, substantial agrarian reforms that took place in Bolivia and Mexico were not matched in Brazil or Argentina), they generally involved the expropriation of foreign-owned infrastructure, the mobilization by the state of capital and labour organizations, the erection of tariff barriers and the introduction of large-scale consumption subsidies.

In most cases this not only led to significant growth and to a redistribution of income towards the

Action party of Venezuela. Whichever characteristic predominates, it accentuates the tendency within such parties towards 'familistic' recruitment and informal decision-making.

working class and on occasion the peasantry, but also to an inflated public sector, uncompetitive domestic industry and persistent inflationary and balance-of-payments crises. This might not have mattered had there been a transfer of power to the working class instead of to the state, but the alliance between the working class and national capital that had been orchestrated from the executive branch required continued growth if its contradictions were to be resolved. When this stopped and class polarization emerged in its place, none of the national popular regimes were able to withstand intervention by the military.

In Mexico the regime did survive, but this was largely because the radical stance taken by Cárdenas was abandoned in the 1940s by his successors. The Institutional Revolutionary Party (PRI) held on to power precisely because of its contradictory attributes. It claimed to be a creation of the people but was in reality organized by the state and remained part of it. Though highly centralized, it allowed for modest dissent and the expression of regional peculiarities. Its nationalist and redistributive rhetoric gave it a popular legitimacy of sorts, but it took care not to endanger seriously the interests of the established and powerful. And, when threatened, it did not hesitate to join with the state in using violence.

MILITARY GOVERNMENTS

Throughout the 1960s and 1970s much of Latin America fell under military rule. Though party politics survived in Costa Rica, Mexico, Venezuela and Colombia, elsewhere the coup replaced the ballot box. Even Uruguay and Chile – traditionally hailed as bastions of democracy – were unable to resist this general trend.

Some of the responsibility lay with the civilian political system itself. The parties chose not to offend the economically powerful by serious and much needed reform of the tax, tariff and credit systems, but they could not ignore the demands of ordinary voters either, and bought their support (and bought off their dissent) by padding the state payroll and subsidizing consumption goods. If this were not enough they also underwrote pork-barrel investment projects of dubious worth. Driven by 'short-termism' and locked into outmoded populist development strategies, they increasingly solved their difficulties by printing money. The result was uneven growth, high inflation and low confidence which led, in turn, to strikes, riots, capital flight and the use of violence by extremists on the left and right. When the military overthrew rule by party (as they did in Bolivia and Brazil in 1964, Peru in 1968,

Argentina in 1966 and 1976, and Chile and Uruguay in 1973) few were surprised.

The interlude of military rule was everywhere authoritarian, and in Argentina and Chile it was terroristic. Many officers believed they had entered office to take the politics out of government. Civilian politicians, they believed, had proved to be not only corrupt but also incompetent. They would do better, in part, by abolishing politics. This goal of depoliticizing society was never achieved. Even in Chile and Peru where the anti-politics mood was especially acute, the old parties survived substantially intact. This was partly because military efforts to create alternative party structures (such as ARENA in Brazil) were incompatible with authoritarianism, but it was also because the coups that had brought them to power had enjoyed the support of some civilian politicians, as with the Christian Democrats in Chile. Though parliaments were closed and public campaigning prohibited, privately the military continued to talk to civilian leaders, leading some to conclude that the military were themselves a kind of 'political party'. Certainly, if civilian politics had never really been as democratic as is claimed, neither were the armed forces as 'militaristic' as they looked.

THE RETURN OF DEMOCRACY

By the early 1980s military rule was drawing to a close. Some economic success had been recorded in Chile and Brazil but in most cases the generals proved to be no more competent (or indeed honest) than the politicians they had ousted. The process of democratic 'opening' was slow in Brazil and Chile but fairly rapid elsewhere. Most striking was the way in which old parties such as the Colorados in Uruguay, APRA in Peru and the UCR in Argentina managed to return largely intact to the political fray.

But the circumstances in which they returned could hardly have been worse. The second oil shock, the debt crisis and sagging commodity prices meant that everywhere political leaders faced difficult choices. On the one hand they were hard pressed by their creditors to introduce orthodox austerity packages, but on the other they had to confront the pent-up demand of voters for jobs, health care, housing and land. Initially their response was to compromise these pressures by heterodox stabilization plans (as in Argentina and Brazil), and in Peru they even returned to old populist strategies. But the stagflation of the 1980s gradually pushed all of them towards orthodox macro-economic management. By 1990 political parties throughout the region had (albeit reluctantly) embraced the new varieties of privatization, sound money, foreign investment, and

Poster upholding the ideas of a recently killed Liberal presidential candidate, assassinated in 1990 by the Medellín drug cartel. The street is in Cali, Colombia.

The survival of competitive politics cannot be assured, but there are some hopeful signs. One is the spirit of cross-national co-operation in the region. Presidents have come to believe that rivalry between countries only encourages the military, and, further, that the democratic experience is a continental-wide and hopefully indivisible one. Party professionals now accept that partisan competition has limits, that legal opposition has a role, and that knocking on the barracks doors is in no-one's long-term interest. Major problems remain, among them widespread corruption, but the political classes of Latin America seem to be learning that democracy has rules, and may in the future respect them more than they have in the past.

WL

Further Reading: R. Alexander, ed., *Political Parties of the Americas*, 2 vols. (Westport, Conn., 1982); M. Conniff, ed., *Latin American Populism in Comparative Perspective* (Albuquerque, New Mexico, 1982); P. Drake and E. Silva, eds., *Elections and Democratization in Latin America 1980–85* (San Diego, 1986); S. Eckstein, ed., *Power and Popular Protest: Latin American Social Movements* (Berkeley and London, 1989); J. Linz and A. Stepan, eds., *The Breakdown of Democratic Regimes: Latin America* (Baltimore, 1978); C. O'Maoláin, ed., *Latin American Political Movements* (London, 1985)

reduced public expenditure. Erstwhile populist parties such as the Peronists in Argentina, the PRI in Mexico, and Christian Democracy in Chile have thus abandoned their old constituencies.

Naturally this has led to protest. In Colombia and especially Peru guerrilla movements continue to interrupt public order. In Brazil, Argentina, Venezuela and Mexico the ruling parties have suffered internal splits and popular protest in the form of street riots, wild-cat strikes and looting. But protest has still been relatively muted given that, under democracy, the people have the freedom to organize that was denied them under the military. It seems that voters have learned that inflation is also their enemy and that painful structural change may have to be accepted if their economies are to recover.

Party activists also seem to have learned that democracy in an economically dependent region has its limits. Almost everywhere they have declined to punish the military for their transgressions, have sought to limit trade union rights, and (Peru and Chile aside) have managed to marginalize the left. The lessons from Venezuela, Mexico and Colombia where democracy was not overthrown seem to have been learned: democracy cannot frighten foreign and local capital if it is to survive. Even those who are most critical of this pragmatism have reluctantly accepted the lack of an alternative.

Trade unions

Although there are examples of trade unions forming in the mid-nineteenth century, and even instances of strikes not much later, it is in the last decade of that century that we must date the rise of modern labour movements in Latin America. Of course, there are wide differences between countries, but, in general, labour movements developed when industrial development had created a substantial urban labour force, when immigrant workers from Europe brought with them ideologies and models of union development (mostly anarchist and anarcho-syndicalist), when political elites realized that they had to come to terms with such movements if only to tame them, and when, in several countries at least, miners (in copper, nitrate and tin) provided a focus for working-class protest.

One must not exaggerate the militancy or ideological commitment of early labour movements. Conservative Catholicism was more important as an influence than militant anarchism. For every radical migrant from Europe, there were many more whose major aims had very little to do with politics and much more to do with self-advancement. Trade unions were influenced by, rather than influences on, the economic and political cycle. Unions could do little to arrest the decline of real wages during depression, or to protect their members at times of political authoritarianism.

The growth of trade unions reflected the overall development of Latin America in the twentieth century. Industrial development allowed the formation of stronger unions. The growth of the political left introduced new ideologies to the labour movement – Communism replaced anarchism in importance, only to be challenged by the growth of socialist movements, of Christian democracy, and of other left-wing groups such as (in the 1960s) the Maoists, Trotskyists and Castroists. But the pattern of development was far from uniform – it could hardly have been so where some countries had a labour shortage and others a huge surplus. In some countries, Chile or Argentina for example, labour came to play a crucial political role; in others, such as Colombia or Venezuela, it remained subordinate to the major political parties; and in others, such as Paraguay, labour remained firmly controlled. In order to try to understand these developments we cannot simply describe the trade unions as such. We must look at the social structure of Latin American countries and at their political systems.

THE NATURE OF THE WORKING CLASS

Women workers at a Volkswagen factory, São Paulo, Brazil

What *is* the working class in Latin American countries? Where does it end and the middle class begin? What is the relationship between a factory worker in

a settled occupation, earning a reasonable income, and a street vendor, living in a shanty town and perhaps only recently arrived from the countryside? These questions are not merely statistical ones. They have great implications for the analysis of social class, and for political behaviour.

One immediate problem in trying to define the working class is the very small size of most industrial or manufacturing enterprises and consequently the relatively small number of industrial workers employed in what is regarded as the 'modern sector'. In Chile close on half of all manufacturing workers are employed in firms of five workers or fewer; in Peru the average size of unions in manufacturing industry is about sixty members; and even in Brazil in the 1960s firms of fewer than five employees represented about 70 per cent of the total number of industrial firms. It is true that in some countries, such as Brazil, the manufacturing boom of the late 1960s and 1970s has increased very substantially the number of workers in large modern factories. But the economic collapse of the 1980s reversed this trend in all countries, and saw the growth of employment in the so-called informal sector of the economy. This was a response to increasing unemployment, and clearly weakened the power of trade unions: not only did they have fewer members, but the threat of unemployment curbed labour militancy.

But it is a mistake to think of small or artisanal enterprises as residual or marginal, destined to disappear with economic progress. On the contrary, in many countries the number of artisanal firms is growing, often in a dependent relationship with large, often foreign-owned, capital-intensive plants. What is the class and political position of workers in these small enterprises? Their close relationship with an employer makes it easier for them to be controlled and obviously far more difficult for them to organize a trade union. The size of this group and its economic importance mean that any trade union movement with claims to represent the working class as a whole would need to incorporate it; but there are few examples of any successful attempts to join together workers in large-scale enterprises with those at the other end of the scale.

Even more difficult to classify are workers who are self-employed, and who do not employ anyone else (apart from unpaid family labour). These people, neatly categorized as in the 'service' sector, lack stable employment and organizational structures, and often work immensely long hours for very little. Nor are their numbers insignificant. In Chile about 20 per cent of the urban labour force is classed as self-employed; in Brazil it is nearer 30 per cent. Yet their lack of involvement in trade unions does not mean that they cannot act with organized labour. On the

Banners of traders' organizations, La Paz, Bolivia: associations of the self-employed are often important in Latin America.

contrary, as so much of union activity, as we shall see, has to be political, rather than industrial, these self-employed workers can often (though not always) act as the allies of the unions in a common struggle against government austerity policies that affect the whole community, or against miserable living conditions that affect all the urban poor. But their association with organized labour tends to be an activity of crisis, born out of desperation, as in the general strike in Peru in 1977 against an increasingly repressive government, or in the *cordones industriales* ('industrial belts' of worker-occupied factories) that developed in Chile in 1972-3 in order to defend the beleaguered Allende government.

A third related difficulty is the often tense relationship between blue-collar and white-collar workers, between wage earners and salaried employees. Social status is important in Latin America. A white-collar worker feels superior to manual labourers; he enjoys a different and better social security system; he operates under a different labour code; and, though he can often act in a militant way, he does not necessarily support the political left. White-collar workers are numerically important, rarely less than a third of the urban labour force, and many of them will be employed by the government. Very often they will seek political distance from the working class by associating themselves with a distinct political party. In Chile, for example, while most manual workers were organized in the Socialist or Communist parties, the white-collar workers were associated with the Radical Party and later the Christian Democratic Party, and, of course, they played an important role in the middle-class opposition that did so much to bring down the Popular Unity government of President Allende. In Peru for a long time they provided a strong element in the APRA party, a party that started on the left in the 1930s but became more right-wing and opportunistic in later decades. But one important group, the schoolteachers, who constitute the single largest (and perhaps most militant) union in Peru are now largely dominated by Maoist leaders. The political allegiance of white-collar workers is difficult to predict in advance; their militancy is often intense but their political sympathies show considerable inconsistency. The problem that this underlines is once again that of constructing a solid and unified labour movement with a clear strategy and a common political allegiance.

Two other points must be mentioned because they are crucial in affecting the labour market and in determining the political influence of the working class. There is, firstly, the very low rate of participation of women in the paid work force. Generally

351

women constitute around 20 per cent of the active labour force and those who do work generally do so in domestic occupations or in agriculture or in the so-called service sector, which employs two thirds of female labour, usually in low-paid, menial occupations. Wages for women are two or three times lower than those for men. Female participation in the rural labour force has increased partly because men migrate to better-paid jobs in the towns. Women, therefore, work in occupations that are normally not unionized, and their level of political participation is generally lower or more conservative than that of men.

Secondly, trade unions are not confined to urban and mining areas; they also exist in the countryside along with a whole host of other organizations such as leagues, movements, co-operatives, communal and ethnic associations. And in many Latin American countries the largest single occupational group is rural workers, and they are often the majority. There are, however, many different types of rural worker. Plantation workers such as sugar workers in Peru, or banana workers in Central America, are best seen as a rural proletariat working for a wage. These workers often form unions similar in nature and function to those of urban workers, whereas peasants mostly grow subsistence and sometimes cash crops on their own plots of land, tend to organize on the basis of locality and, if politically mobilized, are more likely to unite in a mass movement and engage in direct action rather than collective bargaining. Generally speaking, their contact with urban labour is slight, even in countries which had an advanced labour movement such as Chile. Their aims are different, their work styles and communities often have little in common with urban labour. Sometimes they can be united through common association with a political party, but that is nowadays rarer, given the widespread restrictions on party activity. A worker–peasant alliance may be theoretically necessary to make a successful revolution or even to construct a majority political party, but the practice of such an alliance looks remote for most of Latin America.

NATIONAL DIFFERENCES

The general point that will have emerged so far is the marked differentiation between the various groups that compose the working class in Latin America. But it would be superficial and misleading not to emphasize that there are also great differences between the various countries.

For example, in spite of repression of union activities during the military regime of 1976 to 1983, and in spite of economic recession thereafter, Argentina still has an occupational structure that resembles many European countries, with a large proportion of its work force employed in modern factories, and only a small proportion employed in agriculture. Argentine unions are much reduced in influence, but they still have centralized bureaucratic structures and organize whole industries. Chile is exceptional, not because of the size or strength of its union movement, but because of the high degree of political affiliation and commitment which survived even the onslaught of the extreme anti-union policies of the Pinochet government. Cuban unions have been an exception since the revolution and are more typical of the state-controlled unions of the Soviet Union in the era before perestroika.

Although any generalization needs to be hedged around with many qualifications, it is possible to make the following points.

Only in Argentina are the majority of urban workers organized in industry-wide unions with a powerful bureaucracy that engages in national collective bargaining. But even Argentine unions have lost much power because of economic recession, increasing unemployment, and their loss of influence in the Peronist movement.

Most other countries do have a number of powerful industry-wide federations but they organize only a small, sometimes privileged sector of the workforce, and can be rather detached from the general politics of labour (though that does not mean lagging behind; they can, in fact, be in advance). Petroleum workers or miners are, by the nature of their occupations, often isolated from the main urban centres. In Bolivia the tin miners played a leading role in the country's politics, and miners embraced a number of left-wing parties, including the only influential Trotskyist party in Latin America. But the collapse of the tin industry has reduced the once powerful miners' federation to a shadow of its former influence.

In Mexico and Brazil, economic development has recently seen the emergence of large and powerful unions – above all in the motor vehicle industry – but in these countries, until very recently, the structure of trade unionism was imposed by the government, and controlled by it, though not always easily, and with periods when unions threatened to break away from domination by the government.

Generally in Latin America trade unions are small, weak, poor and hamstrung with all sorts of regulations, legal and political, imposed by governments, and intended to inhibit the development of a free and independent labour movement. The bargaining agent is the small local plant union, more often than not engaged in a long process of trying to stop real wages falling even more behind the rate of inflation. Most workers, however, are employed in firms too small even to have a union, and so are not covered by the minimal guarantees that an active plant union can bring. Labour relations inside many factories or in many firms are, therefore, often paternalistic and the union, should one exist, is something of a company union. Unions fight to keep job turnover low, and in some countries it is much lower than in Europe, for example. The interest of employers, however, is in rapid turnover and this is often the case in sectors where unions are weak.

A general exception to this description is the state employees. The state in Latin America is often a very important source of employment and, although in most countries there are prohibitions against state workers forming unions, in practice this is ignored. State employees also have the advantage of being organized in large numbers and facing one employer – the government, which has power in theory to alter wage rates. But the process of privatization of state assets has inevitably reduced the numbers and influence of state employees in those countries where state enterprises have been sold to the private sector, as in Chile.

UNIONS, POLITICS AND THE STATE

It has been a persistent intention of governments in Latin America to curb the interests of the working class. Hence most countries have complex and elaborate labour codes, often promulgated before organized labour was in any sense a political threat. As labour has become a political threat, so the state has intensified its attempts to control or coerce labour movements.

Labour law regulates almost every aspect of union activity from collective bargaining to the way of selecting leaders. And, if there is legal conflict, Latin American judiciaries have shown themselves more likely to favour the government than the workers. But, apart from control over the activities of labour, some governments have even determined the structure of union organization, aiming particularly to prevent the emergence of a central national labour organization. The Brazilian labour code, for example, with the Ministry of Labour at the apex, lays down a very precise system of confederations, federations and local unions. Virtually all labour codes establish the difference between white- and blue-collar labour.

Apart from such open attempts to regulate labour, governments do not hesitate to employ other methods. The most notorious is that of repression, and instances are sadly too frequent of labour leaders removed from office, deported or even assassinated in the interests of 'national security'. However, it may be questioned whether this is as effective a method of control as co-option of labour leaders by a system of patronage and corruption and of unionists by an extensive system of government social welfare schemes. For many years Mexican labour was led by men bought off by the government and notorious for their corruption (though this did not mean that they were inactive as union leaders, especially if confronting an employer unpopular with the government). Labour can co-operate with progressive or well-inclined governments as it did with President Cárdenas in Mexico in the 1930s. But the reality is that progressive governments of this type are rare in Latin America, and that what may start out as co-operation can end as manipulation.

Demonstration, Mexico City

The intention of such detailed regulation of unions was to remove labour from politics and to control their operations. Yet the consequences have been exactly the opposite. Because governments regulate so closely matters crucial to trade unions (incomes policies are an obvious example), unions must confront or try to influence governments if they are to achieve any of their basic objectives. Because legal regulation has made unions weak, they are forced to seek political allies to attempt to influence government policy. So in most countries in Latin America trade unions are associated with one or another political party – Socialists, Communists, or Christian Democrats in Chile; Peruvian sugar workers with the APRA, Peruvian schoolteachers with the Maoist left; Venezuelan peasant unions with AD (Democratic Action); the Mexican labour movement with the PRI (Institutional Revolutionary Party), and so on. The major exception, as always, is Argentina, where a political movement, Peronism, was dominated by the power of the trade unions, especially after 1955.

This close association with political parties brings advantages and disadvantages. The connection with a party can help to unify disparate occupational groups; it can articulate diffuse interests into a coherent strategy; it can aid and defend labour in crisis; and it can act as a source of funds and of legal advice. But there are disadvantages too. Because more than one party competes for the support of labour, there is the danger of sectarianism and the subsuming of the interests of the unions in those of the party (the best-known example of this is probably that of APRA in Peru). When a weak union movement needs an impetus towards unity, political differences can be a further dividing factor. And, when political parties are suppressed, then labour movements associated with such parties suffer as well. However, the North American model of apolitical unionism is totally misplaced in Latin America. Even the most basic expression of union activity is likely to be defined by the government as 'political'; and any attempt at collective action on behalf of the welfare of the poor is likely to be seen as subversive too.

An additional complication should be mentioned (though to explore its ramifications would be very complex) and that is the activities of international bodies. By this one means mostly North American influences whether directly through mutual involvement in the ORIT (Inter-American Regional Organization of Labour), or indirectly through American-based training institutes such as the AIFLD (American Institute for Free Labour Development), or more clandestinely through the CIA. A great deal of money is spent by these groups in Latin America; rather less, though still a great deal, is spent by various Christian groups channelled through CLAT (Latin American Confederation of Workers). How effective it is, is another matter. One should not underestimate the capacity of local labour movements to manipulate their much wealthier counterparts. But such activities are usually an intrusion into local politics and a force for division.

CONCLUSION

Popular protest, involving though not confined to trade unions, has been crucial in bringing about the demise of military regimes in a number of Latin American countries. After ten years of industrial peace, 1978 saw massive and impressive strikes in Brazil. A successful general strike in Peru hastened the military's decision to return the government to civilian hands. Popular protest in Chile, organized by the copper workers in May 1983, put the all-powerful Pinochet regime on the defensive, and set in motion a process of political liberalization that led to Pinochet's defeat in a plebiscite in 1988.

As the most organized sector of the majority of the urban and rural poor, trade unions have been forced to speak for and defend those sectors. Trade unions transcended their specific functions in authoritarian regimes because those regimes made it impossible for them to perform their normal role. Unions therefore had little alternative in dictatorships other than to demand political liberty as a condition for union freedom.

The challenge that faces unions in the recently established democracies is altogether more delicate. Unions have simultaneously to defend their members' interests and play a positive role in the process of democratic consolidation, which can mean curbing rank and file demands. Moreover, they have to perform this dual role at a time when recession has brought widespread suffering to their members. This challenge underlines the point previously stressed: the close relationship between the labour movement and the national political and economic system. The political context may have changed from dictatorship to democracy, but the role of labour remains one that inextricably mixes economic with political demands.

AEA

Further Reading: A. Angell, *Politics and the Labour Movement in Chile* (London, 1972); E. Epstein, ed., *Labor Autonomy and the State in Latin America* (Boston, 1989); K. Erickson, *The Brazilian Corporative State and Working Class Politics* (California, 1977); Latin American Bureau, *Unity is Strength: Trade Unions in Latin America* (London, 1980); I. Roxborough, *Unions and Politics in Mexico: The Case of the Automobile Industry* (Cambridge, 1984); H. Spalding, *Organised Labour in Latin America* (New York, 1977)

Insurgency and terrorism

Social and political change has often been secured violently in Latin America, whose very independence owed much to the use of guerrilla warfare against the Spanish. The leading role played by the military in politics often meant that changes of government came about through resort to arms by civil violence throughout the nineteenth and early twentieth centuries. Terror was used by those seeking to maintain power and by those aiming to acquire it, all of this against a varying a back-drop of rural banditry and urban crime. This century, most Latin American countries have experienced significant insurgencies. The majority have been inspired by leftist ideologies, which offered attractive visions of juster and more equal societies; spontaneous revolts such as the one which countered electoral fraud in Costa Rica in 1948 are rarer. But two successful contemporary insurgencies stand out – Cuba in 1959 and Nicaragua in 1979.

THE INSPIRATION OF CUBA

The Cuban revolution of 1959 was especially notable, suggesting that the corrupt dictatorships of old could be overthrown by popular revolt if guided by a revolutionary vanguard. As the first Marxist-Leninist state in the Americas, under Fidel Castro Cuba became an inspiration to would-be insurgents elsewhere. It was also able to supply safe havens, bases

Régis Debray, publicist of revolution in the 1960s

and arms to potential leftist insurgents, as well as moral and political support.

Ernesto 'Che' Guevara (1928–67), one of Castro's chief lieutenants, drew on the Cuban experience to develop a blueprint for rural guerrilla warfare throughout Latin America, theories also articulated by French Marxist writer Régis Debray (1940-91). This had been sorely lacking – orthodox Marxist-Leninist prescriptions for revolution imported from Europe were palpably inappropriate to Latin America. Guevara and Debray played down the role of the mass party, arguing instead that a small band of rural guerrillas could hasten the revolutionary process by creating a revolutionary nucleus (or focus). The theory caused divisions between the sceptical old guard happy to toe the Moscow line and the younger activists eager for immediate action and change. The eagerness of the latter, usually educated middle-class idealists, led to insurgencies in Paraguay, Argentina and the Dominican Republic (1959), in Venezuela and Colombia (1961), in Guatemala and Ecuador (1962), in Peru (1963), in Bolivia (1967) and in Brazil (1968). Hopelessly inadequate preparation, and the strength of the respective armed forces, who were benefiting from US provision of counter-insurgency training in the aftermath of the Cuban revolution, ensured their abject failure. Only in Colombia and Venezuela did the insurgencies linger on. Guevara's own abortive venture in Bolivia, which resulted in the death of nearly all his group, symbolized the inadequacy of this first wave.

A second generation of Marxist revolutionaries nonetheless emerged soon after, sharing Guevara's belief in armed struggle by dedicated guerrillas. But rather than fight in the countryside they sought to wage their war in the cities. Campaigns of terrorism were launched against military regimes and business in Brazil (1964–70), Uruguay (1968–72) and Argentina (1969–76), involving assassination, kidnap, bombings and sabotage. Urban terrorism proved more destabilizing that rural insurgency because it struck at the heart of the ruling elite, but it was equally ineffectual in arousing the masses. The savagery of the urban guerrillas was to be matched by the brutality of the security forces, who set out to solve through murder and torture what the politicians could not solve legally. Paramilitary 'death squads' arose which attempted to purge society of anyone suspected of leftist subversion, and at least 10,000 'disappeared' in Argentina alone.

THE REACTION TO NICARAGUA

By the late 1970s most Latin American countries laboured under military rule. The 1979 Nicaraguan

'Sandino lives' – wall painting, Matagalpa, Nicaragua

and conduct only a rural campaign – at the cost to the regime of US military aid, withdrawn in protest at the level of officially sponsored violence. In El Salvador, US military aid was maintained in spite of the equally high level of human rights abuses because the rebels here appeared more likely to overthrow the government. This aid, added to the rebels' own lack of military preparedness, helped prevent a rebel victory. Over the next decade the guerrillas, grouped together as the Farabundo Martí National Liberation Front (FMLN), conducted an effective guerrilla campaign against the armed forces which gave them control over large swathes of Salvadorean territory. Terrorist activities in the capital San Salvador were assisted by strong urban networks. But the most the rebels achieved was a stalemate, massive US military and economic help having allowed a rapid expansion and upgrading of the Salvadorean armed forces.

The role of the USA in countering leftist insurgency in Latin America has proved crucial, and is a logical extension of the Monroe Doctrine whereby the United States appointed itself regional policeman in this, its 'backyard'. The struggle against communism which underpinned much of post-war US foreign policy has also provided a rationale for direct or indirect intervention. But the common theme is that the United States has seen fit to ensure that, as far as possible, political developments in Latin America serve its own interests. The gunboat diplomacy of old having become politically problematic (although the US invasion of Panama in December 1989 suggests not altogether impossible), greater emphasis has been laid on support of local anti-communist forces.

The Reagan administration (1981–89) sought not only to prevent 'another Nicaragua', but to reverse the gains of the Sandinista revolution by backing a counter-revolution – covertly recruiting, training and funding a guerrilla army dedicated to overthrowing the Sandinistas. This insurgent force, or 'Contras', contained fighters with genuine grievances against the Sandinistas, and had a constituency among disaffected sectors of the population. Some were former Sandinistas disillusioned by their government's more authoritarian behaviour, others their former enemies in Somoza's National Guard. But their very diversity, along with the inevitable tag of being a mercenary outfit, made theirs a flawed organization. The Contras were never able to gain the upper hand militarily, being poorly motivated and facing a larger army led by experienced former guerrillas. The insurgency did, however, beggar the country economically before an increasingly uneasy US Congress defied the President and suspended military aid, effectively finishing the Contras off as a military force and throwing them into the emergent Central American peace process.

revolution was therefore a breath of fresh air to the revolutionary left, much as Cuba had been twenty years earlier. A small but dedicated revolutionary vanguard had again been seen to mobilize massive popular support for overthrowing the old order. Capitalizing on popular outrage at the presumed government assassination of opposition leader Joaquin Chamorro, the National Sandinista Liberation Front (FSLN), leftist-led but representing a diversity of centre-leftist political tendencies, left the mountains to lead an all-out assault on the cities which scared the Somoza dictatorship into flight. Crucial to the success of the revolution were Somoza's international isolation and the role played in the fighting by urban support groups, some of them based on church groups. For the first time, the left-leaning liberation theology was seen to be politicially effective: the first government involved three priests in cabinet posts, including Foreign Minister Miguel D'Escoto. This showed just how influential the Catholic Church's new stance against poverty and unjust government could be in a continent where traditionally it had acted as a conservative force.

The Nicaraguan revolution was expected to have a knock-on effect throughout Central America and possibly further south. Insurgencies were gaining ground in Guatemala and El Salvador in the early 1980s because of anger at the brutal response of the ruling elites to calls for reform. But vicious counter-insurgency operations in Guatemala in the early 1980s eventually forced the National Revolutionary Guerrilla Unity (URNG) to withdraw from the cities

Changes in the international political order, most especially the retreat of communism in Eastern Europe and the end of the Cold War, now had an effect on superpower behaviour. The mood was for resolution of third world conflicts, rather than support of client protagonists. Hence the Soviets pressured Nicaragua to accept free elections in 1989 (and to respect their subsequent defeat) in return for the demobilization of the Contras, and the United States under President Bush began persuading the Salvadorean government to begin peace negotiations with the FMLN. This represented a sea-change in Central America. Governments and insurgent forces in Nicaragua, El Salvador and Guatemala realized that there existed a rare opportunity for trading social and political reforms for disarmament. With populations hungry for peace, and the United States, Soviet Union and neutral regional governments pressing for negotiated settlements, this path was also to some extent becoming a tactical necessity. Against the back-drop of the continent-wide reversion to democratic rule by 1990, insurgency and terrorism were becoming still harder to justify, as witnessed by divisions within the Chilean armed left after the end of military rule in 1990. Many left-wing groups split into reformers and hard-liners.

In Colombia the leftist insurgency begun by the peasant-based Armed Revolutionary Forces of Colombia (FARC) in the 1950s gained strength over the next four decades, especially when five other leftist groups joined the struggle in the second half of the period. Guerrillas supplemented their operations against the government with highly effective campaigns of kidnapping and extortion, thereby terrorizing the land-owning and business class throughout wide areas of the country. Opposition to foreign involvement in extractive industries, notably the oil sector, made foreign business a target as well. But here again, political reforms designed to make the democratic system more widely accessible undercut support for the guerrillas, who were in any case unable to increase their urban strength. Peace negotiations with successive Liberal governments in 1990–91 resulted in the majority of insurgent groups abandoning the armed struggle, with the remainder grudgingly committed to the process. Crucially, the M-19 guerrilla movement gained immediate electoral success following its surrender of weapons, in spite of the assassination of its leader and first presidential candidate Carlos Pizzaro.

INSURGENCY AND DRUGS

External change has had no impact on the xenophobic neo-Maoist Peruvian Sendero Luminoso (Shining Path) guerrilla movement, which despises all deviation from the radical neo-Maoist ideology of its founder and leader Abimael Guzmán. In seeking to overthrow the established order, Sendero has crippled the economy, causing some $22 billion damage, and set off a vicious war in which over 20,000 have died since the group's first armed action in May 1980. Guzmán and his followers sowed the seeds of rebellion in the isolated and neglected Andean trapezium, playing on some traditional Indian beliefs to gain support for an attack on the (white) Lima-based government. More influential still was the extreme violence meted out to dissenters. The Sendero insurgency has since re-focused on other areas, aiming to cut Lima off from its agricultural and mining hinterland, and developing an urban terrorist campaign in the capital following infiltration of the labour movements. Sendero and the smaller, more orthodox Guevara-inspired Tupac Amaru Revolutionary Movement (MRTA) have developed strongholds in the coca-growing regions of northern Peru, securing local support by ensuring that local farmers gained a fair price from drug-traffickers for their coca crops, and providing protection from anti-narcotics operations. Sendero's cut was in 1991 estimated to be larger than the official defence budget.

The vast fortune gained by criminal organizations trafficking cocaine to the US markets has in certain countries given them virtual immunity from the law. In Colombia, the Medellín-based cartel from the late 1970s onwards built up powerful private armies to protect its interests, routinely assassinating policemen, judges and even politicians who opposed it. Bribery gained further protection. An eventual government crack-down in 1989 was met with a declaration of 'all-out war' by the drug mafia, who then launched the most intense campaign of terrorism witnessed in modern Latin America. The country endured hundreds of bomb explosions in the main cities, the downing of an airliner, the assassination of several hundred policemen, and incalculable damage to its image abroad before the cartel leaders tired of the fight and began to seek an accommodation with the government. Although that government overcame the security threat, it had repeatedly made it plain that it cannot by itself halt the flow of drugs while demand remains high in the industrialized northern 'user' countries. Until then, there is the possibility in all countries that well-armed drug mafias may use terrorism to ward off the authorities.

In choosing to tackle the problem of drugs at source, pressurizing all countries to eradicate drug crops where they exist and clamp down on trafficking at every opportunity, the United States may be fuelling the conditions for further rebellion. Agreement in 1991 to provide US military training and aid for anti-drug programmes in Peru and Bolivia, where the majority of cocaine is produced, has stirred nationalist resentments to the extent of provoking a violent backlash. In the emerging conflict over drugs, the claims of indigenous communities in the region, and continued poverty and social inequality are possibly the bases for future insurgency.　　　DB

Further Reading: O. Cabezas, *Fire from the Mountain: The Making of a Sandinista* (New York, 1985); R. Debray, *A Critique of Arms* (London, 1977); J. Dunkerley, *The Long War – Dictatorship and Revolution in El Salvador* (London, 1982); R. Gillespie, *Soldiers of Peron: Argentina's Montoneros* (Oxford, 1982); R. Gott, *Guerrilla Movements in Latin America* (London, 1970); C. Marighela, *For the Liberation of Brazil* (London, 1971); M. Radu and V. Tismaneanu, *Latin American Revolutionaries. Goals and Methods* (Washington, DC. 1990)

The Church in Latin America

From the earliest colonial times Roman Catholic values and practices have been an integral feature of Latin American society and culture. In large measure the region's religious history has been the history of Roman Catholicism. That Church's representatives entered the area, along with the earliest colonizers, as the ally and legitimator of Spanish and Portuguese colonial authorities. The latter effectively guaranteed the Church against ideological competition whilst the Church itself engaged in a mass conversion. The Church and colonial society were therefore viewed as essentially co-terminous communities.

By special Papal concession imperial authorities exercised unprecedented controls over the Church in the New World. The Spanish and Portuguese crowns controlled senior ecclesiastical appointments and co-opted churchmen into the imperial administration. The Church's spiritual authority was similarly exercised in defence of the status quo. In return the Church received such privileges as extensive land-holdings and control over education. There were limited 'Church-state' conflicts over, for example, the rights of Indians, and the Jesuits even established paternalistically-run Indian communities largely free of secular control. The general picture, however, was of a Church wedded to the secular power and upholding the existing hierarchically structured social order. An orthodox Thomist theology, which perceived society in necessarily hierarchical terms, provided no basis for extensive social criticism; equally, the Church was conceived in clerical terms with the laity being accorded an essentially subordinate and passive role.

THE CHURCH'S ROLE IN THE POST COLONIAL ERA

Given the Church's links with the imperial powers, only a handful of clergy, notably in Mexico, were actively associated with the independence struggle. After independence the new republics sought to maintain those controls over the Church once exercised by imperial authorities, whilst the Papacy sought to recover lost authority. Divisions within the governing elites of the new states further complicated the situation. Some, associated with Liberal parties and influenced by contemporary rationalism, liberalism or positivism, sought to curb clerical influence. In response the Church formed alliances with traditional upper-class interests generally associated with Conservative parties. In Chile and Colombia, for example, Liberal versus Conservative confrontations over the Church were a major source of ideological division.

Conflicts over the Church's social and political position had differing outcomes. At one extreme was Colombia where, in 1887, Church and state concluded a (still existing) Concordat that guaranteed to the Church a privileged and officially established position. At the other extreme was Mexico which, during the revolution, experienced a period of militant anti-clerical activity aimed at the definitive eradication of ecclesiastical influence. This gave way to a largely peaceful *modus vivendi* but one that still left the Church without much direct political influence. More striking, the Cuban Church, which had always lacked deep social roots, was driven to the margins of society as a consequence of revolution.

Elsewhere, in Chile for example (1925), the Church was ultimately disestablished but retained a

Corpus Christi procession, Cuzco, Peru

de facto position of considerable significance. Throughout the region, however, the Church retained the hallmarks of its origins by remaining a more or less uniformly conservative institution generally united in support of established social structures.

The often seemingly secure nature of the Church's position tended to obscure the limited nature of its impact upon popular religious practice. The apparently successful mass conversion policy frequently left the indigenous population with a syncretic religion in which Catholic practices or values co-existed with beliefs and rites of pre-colonial origins. The later importation of slaves also, in reality, meant the introduction of African religious practices. The net result was a frequently tenuous link with official ecclesiastical structures. Equally, many apparently more orthodox Catholics shared in a popular 'cultural' religion which accepted Catholic symbolism and ritual as part of the prevailing culture but without high levels of religious understanding or explicit commitment. The higher levels of commitment tended to be disproportionately associated with middle- and, more especially, upper-class groups for whom formal religious practice was one part of a general upper-class life style. The commitment was generally individualistic and pietistic in character. Just as popular religion tended to promote passivity in face of prevailing inequalities, so more orthodox expressions of Catholicism continued to lack a socially critical component.

Socioeconomic and political changes in the area eventually exposed underlying weakness in the Church's position and, albeit gradually, constrained the institution to re-evaluate its relationship with the surrounding society. To some extent changes reflected fresh theological thinking percolating through from Europe but they also signified a response to changing realities. Thus, processes of economic development, some industrialization and, above all, urbanization in the late nineteenth and early twentieth centuries eroded the basis of the relatively static and largely rural society within which the Church had first developed and had cultivated its upper-class alliances. New middle- and lower-strata groups emerged, of a potentially more secularized kind. Equally, massive emigration from Europe to such countries as Argentina, Brazil and Uruguay meant the emergence of significant Protestant groups as well as of new secular ideologies.

Initial Church responses were of a generally defensive nature. They first took the form of working-class groups, run on paternalistic lines, for the promotion, for example, of mutual aid societies.

Later, particularly from the 1920s onwards, serious efforts were made to mobilize Catholic laity, under clerical auspices, through such bodies as Catholic Action. Some union movements of Catholic inspiration were also created. For example, what is still the largest union confederation in Colombia, the UTC (Colombia Workers' Union) was established in 1946 at the instigation of Jesuits. In Argentina and Brazil initial clerical reactions to fresh challenges sometimes took the form of alliances with ultra-nationalist or even fascist-type movements. In nearly all cases, however, the accent was on defending ecclesiastical institutions against perceived threats and on the possibility of pre-empting more radical change. The underlying presupposition was generally of a clerical triumphalism that envisaged an eventual return to the earlier 'neo-Christendom' position.

The difficulties and possible dangers inherent in such responses were indicated, for example, in Argentina where the hierarchy initially saw alliance with Perón's nationalist populist regime (1946–55) as an appropriate means of underwriting clerical influence within a menacing environment. At the outset Perón accepted such support as a useful source of legitimacy. Ultimately, however, he was constrained by political and economic crises to appeal to anti-clericalism, evidently widespread amongst his urban lower-strata following, as one means of rallying the latter's support. This tended, in practice, to reinforce the Argentine hierarchy's prevailing conservatism which later expressed itself in a generally uncritical attitude to the military dictatorship of 1976–1983.

THE CHURCH AND RADICAL POLITICS

During the 1950s support grew for less obviously defensive initiatives. Revised understandings, derived from such European theologians as Jacques Maritain, contributed to more positive evaluations of secular demands for greater political participation and the more equitable distribution of resources. Significantly enough, the Chilean Church was in the vanguard. It had felt particularly keenly the competition of secular left-wing parties and of Protestant groups and so had particularly strong incentives to revise traditional strategies. Thus, efforts were made to mobilize peasants and support was given to the cause of land reform. Of particular significance was the emergence of a reformist Christian Democratic Party committed to significant structural changes. The party (which had less successful counterparts elsewhere in Latin America) was not directly linked with the hierarchy and accepted Chilean society's pluralistic nature to the extent of deliberately appealing beyond the Catholic community's confines. It was, however, of avowedly Christian inspiration and ultimately aimed, in principle, at the construction of a society constituted in accordance with revised understandings of Catholic social doctrine.

Latin America's Christian Democrats have had difficulty in relating general principles to the exigencies of mundane conflicts. In the case of the Chilean government of Eduardo Frei (1964–70) there were particular difficulties in maintaining an alliance between those who saw Christian Democracy as the best available defence against unwelcome changes and those positively committed to reform.

During the 1960s the terms of Latin American religious debate were significantly transformed by the emergence of more radical and politicized understandings of Catholicism. This was partly the consequence of long-germinating changes in the local Church and of the latter's response to an increasing sense of crisis in the region's economic, social and political life. Not least, the Cuban revolution led to a heightening of political expectations and tension. Notably in Brazil, this was reflected in some Catholic participation in attempts to mobilize previously quiescent groups, especially amongst the peasantry. The radical Catholic 'Movement for Basic Education' contributed to the general if limited radicalization process that preceded the 1964 military coup. Above all, the Brazilian, Paulo Freire, developed the influential concept of '*conscientização*' signifying the effort to raise the political consciousness of lower-strata groups in order to equip them for their own eventual political emancipation. Such developments had some support from the Brazilian hierarchy and, particularly, from the famous Archbishop Helder Câmara of Recife who played a major part in creating ecclesiastical bureaucratic structures capable of guiding the processes of change. Other parts of the hierarchy, however, were ambivalent or hostile. Nevertheless, precedents for further forms of radical Catholic political engagement had been established.

In the next two decades such forms of engagement became increasingly common. These developments often arose out of currents of Catholic thought associated with the Second Conference and even violent struggles with established military-backed regimes.

Some Nicaraguan priests participated in the revolutionary Sandinista government. A Chilean 'Christians for Socialism' group, which played a prominent part in debate during Allende's regime (1970–3), acted as a model for similar radical groups committed to a peaceful evolutionary route to socialism. More common has been the espousal of reformist positions, though their advocates have been divided over the depth or speed of change. Portions of the Brazilian hierarchy, for example, have been bitterly critical of the general effects of capitalism on Brazilian society whilst others have tended to focus on specific injustices or violations of human rights. There are other, more traditional elements, whose chief priority is pastoral work conceived in conventional terms, who seek to limit political involvement to the enunciation of general principles. They fear that the importation of political divisions into the Church will damage the institution's cohesion and credibility. They also fear that politicization will ultimately lead to the loss of a distinctive Christian identity. Major concerns for them are the decline in priestly vocations, wavering on such issues as birth control and other symptoms of the crisis of authority, through which Roman Catholicism, in general, is passing.

Finally, a vociferous minority of influential ultra-conservatives has sought to co-opt the Church into the service of authoritarian regimes on the grounds that they are upholders of national security against a perceived Marxist threat. The 'Tradition, Family and Property' group is an example of such 'Integralist' pre-Vatican II Catholics.

For most Catholic spokesmen, experience of military government had some radicalizing effects. In both Brazil and Chile, for example, much of the hierarchy initially acquiesced in or welcomed military intervention. Subsequent experience of repression generally solidified Church opposition. Churchmen were among the most articulate critics of systematic violations of human rights and Church organizations provided support for victims as well as for lower-strata victims of official economic policies. Within these contexts grass-roots 'Basic Christian Communities' have proliferated. These localized flexible structures have offered unprecedented opportunities for lay participation and have helped disadvantaged groups to acquire political consciousness and skills. In Brazil recruits from such quarters played a significant part in launching the Partido dos Trabalhadores (PT) – a political party created in 1979 under the auspices of labour leaders who have received considerable official Church support. Conversely, many opposition groups turned to the Church as the most credible source of assistance and protection. It underlines the fact that no Latin American organization, apart from the state, has such a developed and extensive organizational network. The Basic Communities give added depth and flexibility to already established parochial and diocesan structures. Equally, the Church can call on the pastoral, intellectual and political skills of international religious orders. The institution, thus motivated and constituted, played a major role in mobilizing opposition to the erstwhile military dictatorships of such countries as Brazil and Chile, so undermining their credibility.

The above-mentioned divisions cut right across the once firm boundary dividing Catholics from

Protestants. The latter have grown dramatically in number in the past three decades (in Brazil and Chile, for example, from 15 to 20 per cent of the population are now Protestants) and have divided along lines that, to some extent, mirror divisions in the Catholic Church. Thus, such long-established and mainly conservative middle-class groups as the Lutherans have seen the emergence of activists sharing many of the preoccupations of Catholic 'theologians of liberation'. Latin American Protestantism's numerical growth, however, is much more due to charismatic Pentecostal groups, with particularly extensive followings among the urban poor, who generally eschew political involvement. Equally, ultra-conservative biblically fundamentalist groups, frequently of United States' origin, remain largely uncritical of the established order. In this connection it seems significant that, during the years of the Pinochet regime in Chile an estimated 15 per cent of army officers became Protestants.

More traditional Roman Catholic elements, concerned about the general direction of post-Medellin changes, have actively sought to halt radicalizing tendencies. Led by Cardinal Trujillo of Colombia, such groups acquired control of CELAM's official apparatus, and at the third conference of Latin American bishops, held in Puebla (Mexico) in 1979, sought to re-emphasize the centrality of the Church's traditional evangelical or missionary task. Puebla's eventual findings, however, appeared to be a compromise which testified to the continuing influence of more radical groups. Renewed stress was placed upon the Church's traditional pastoral responsibilities, but adherence to the cause of justice was also proclaimed. During the 1980s Pope John Paul II has personally witnessed to this tension. Thus the Vatican has pursued an appointments policy clearly designed to produce more conservative Latin American episcopates. Equally, papal visits to Latin American countries have been used to proclaim the importance of human rights and social justice. Debates about the appropriate religious responses to Latin America's problems seem, therefore, bound to continue.   KM

Further Reading: D. Keogh, ed., *Church and Politics in Latin America* (London, 1990); D. H. Levine, ed., *Churches and Politics in Latin America* (Beverly Hills, 1980); D. Martin, *Tongues of Fire: The Explosion of Protestantism in Latin America* (Oxford, 1990); S. Mainwaring, *The Catholic Church and Politics in Brazil 1916–1985* (Stanford, 1986); S. Mainwaring and A. Wilde, eds., *The Progressive Church in Latin America* (Notre Dame, Indiana, 1989); S. Mews, ed., *Religion in Politics, a World Guide* (London, 1989)

The Church and the poor

from *Evangelization in Latin America's Present and Future*

Final Document of the Third General Conference of the Latin American Episcopate, Puebla, Mexico, January–February 1979

On wealth

Turned into an absolute, wealth is an obstacle to authentic freedom. The cruel contrast between luxurious wealth and extreme poverty, which is so visible throughout our continent and which is further aggravated by the corruption that often invades public and professional life, shows the great extent to which our nations are dominated by the idol of wealth. These forms of idolatry are concretized in two opposed forms that have a common root. One is liberal capitalism. The other . . . is Marxist collectivism. Both are forms of what can be called 'institutionalized injustice'. Finally we must take cognizance of the devastating effects of an uncontrolled process of industrialization and a process of urbanization that is taking on alarming proportions. The depletion of our natural resources . . . will become a critical problem. Once again we affirm that the consumptionist tendencies of the more developed nations must undergo a thorough revision.

On the 'preferential option for the poor'

As the Pope has told us, the evangelical commitment of the church, like that of Christ, should be a commitment to those most in need . . . The Son of God demonstrated the grandeur of this commitment when he became a human being. For he identified himself with human beings by becoming one of them. He established solidarity with them and took up the situation in which they find themselves – in his birth and in his life, and particularly in his passion and death, where poverty found its maximum expression. For this reason alone, the poor merit preferential attention . . . In her Magnificat (*Luke* 1:46–55) Mary proclaims that God's salvation has to do with justice for the poor . . . When we draw near to the poor in order to accompany them and serve them, we are doing what Christ taught us to do when he became our brother, poor like us. Hence service to the poor is the privilege, though not the exclusive gauge, of our following of Christ.

CULTURE

Literacy and education

Latin American educational systems vary considerably, reflecting differences in history, political institutions, national priorities, levels of social and economic development, patterns of urbanization, and industrialization. Yet a number of major issues, trends, and problems can be identified as common in the the region. Education systems, despite remarkable growth since the 1970s, have been constrained by economic and political factors in effecting social change and promoting equity, and generally have failed to promote a more equitable distribution of income and social services. Despite significant improvement in enrolment rates, the provision of educational opportunities continues to be closely related to the social and economic status of the people involved, and the degree of individual advancement within the formal education systems is related to his or her parents' socioeconomic background, place of residence, and educational history.

Noteworthy achievements have occurred in recent years in the quantitive expansion of systems and in the improvement of educational content and processes. The value of such achievements should not be underestimated, given the rapidly increasing school-age population, the costs involved, and competing demands on national budgets. Between 1980 and 1988, the total number of children enrolled in school in the region grew from 87.2 to 103.1 million, an increase of 18.2 per cent, being 12 per cent in primary, 32 per cent in secondary, and 43 per cent in higher education. In 1988, there were 72.7 million children in primary, 23.4 million in secondary, and 6.9 million in higher education.

All the countries in the region have compulsory education, ranging from five to twelve years in length. The entrance age ranges from five to seven years. In 1985 in eight out of twenty-three countries (Argentina, Barbados, Chile, Costa Rica, Guyana, Jamaica, Mexico and Panama) 95 per cent or more of six-through-eleven year olds were said to be in school. By 1985, approximately 92 per cent of primary school age children were enrolled, and 60 per cent of those who enrolled completed the course of study. However, the goal of universal education remains unmet, largely due to drop-outs and lower rural enrolment. The average annual growth rate of enrolment in primary education between 1950 and 1980 was 3.3 per cent. Between 1980 and 1986, it fell to 1.6 per cent, although in Costa Rica and El Salvador it was 5 per cent.

DROP-OUT

High rates of drop-out and repetition remain a problem in several countries. Studies suggest that the major reasons are related to poverty, particularly in the rural areas. In North-eastern Brazil, for example, repetition and drop-out rates in some primary schools in 1988 reached 66 per cent. In rural places distance from school and financial constraints continue to prevent parents from sending their children to school, as they need them for work for which formal education appears irrelevant. Also, poorer children from culturally deprived backgrounds may fail to adapt to the formal learning situation or the rigid exam system, they may be obliged to travel with parents who are migrant labourers, or they may miss school during the planting and harvest seasons. Schools in many cases consist of only one room and do not offer a full primary curriculum.

The trend of declining mortality rates amongst the under-fives that began in the previous decade continued into the 1980s. Even so, in some of the countries and in rural areas, malnutrition and related illnesses continue to cause children to drop out of school, or affect their achievement by reducing their ability to concentrate and learn.

NON-ENROLMENT

Problems of non-enrolment are more acute in rural areas than in towns. In Guatemala in 1982, 56 per cent of urban seven-year-olds were enrolled in school, compared with 25 per cent of their rural contemporaries. In 1986 farmers' children constituted 36 per cent of the school age population of Latin America but only 31 per cent of the primary and 12 per cent of the secondary level enrolments. Table 1 gives enrolment percentages for primary, secondary, and higher levels of education for twenty countries in the region for school years beginning in 1983, 1984 and 1985. (Seventeen countries show gross rates for primary school enrolment of over 100. This is because the rates express the enrolment of all ages in primary school as a percentage of the population of primary school age, but some older children are still in primary school due to late entrance or repetition.)

REPETITION

Repetition continues to be a problem in Latin America. In one third of the countries over 20 per cent of the pupils repeat their first year of education, although this is an improvement over a decade ago when this level applied in over half of the countries.

TABLE 1
Gross Enrolment Ratios for the first, second, and third levels of education

Country	School year beginning	First level	Second level	First and second levels	Third level
Argentina	1985	108	70	94	36.4
Bolivia	1984	91	37	75	19.5
Brazil	1983	102	42	87	–
Chile	1985	109	69	95	15.8
Colombia	1985	117	50	82	13.0
Costa Rica	1985	101	41	75	23.0
Cuba	1985	105	85	94	21.4
Dominican Republic	1985	124	50	88	–
Ecuador	1984	114	55	86	33.4
El Salvador	1984	70	24	60	12.8
Guatemala	1984	76	17	50	8.2
Haiti	1984	78	18	50	1.1
Honduras	1984	102	33	74	9.6
Mexico	1985	115	55	87	16.0
Nicaragua	1985	101	39	76	9.8
Panama	1985	105	59	83	25.9
Paraguay	1985	101	31	68	–
Peru	1985	122	65	98	24.0
Uruguay	1984	108	70	90	26.1
Venezuela	1985	108	45	79	26.4

Source: *Statistical Abstract of Latin America*, vol. 27.

In many countries students have to sit an exam at the end of every year, and promotion tends to be based entirely on the result, regardless of class performance. Moreover, there is a distinct urban bias in many primary education systems, with few primary curricula including agriculture, even though it is still the basic activity of many of the countries in the region, and most schooling not being flexible enough to accommodate the other demands on rural children's time. Added to this is a shortage of instructional materials, particularly books – 80 per cent of the students lack maths books in the Dominican Republic, 75 per cent are without texts in Haiti and 67 per cent of the students are without them in Peru. Repetition is more prevalent among rural pupils, especially girls, from low socioeconomic backgrounds.

Another explanation for poor performance and resulting drop-out or repetition by children of low-income families can be found in the limited availability of preschool education in the region. Although the number of preschools increased almost everywhere into the 1980s and doubled in thirteen countries, the total enrolment for the region was only 9.1 per cent. The trend has been towards government support for pre-schools, so that by 1989 in eighteen of twenty-four countries more than one half of the preschools were public. Nevertheless, funding levels have remained low. In 1988 only four countries invested more than 0.5 per cent of their education budget in preschools: Cuba, Mexico, Chile, and Guyana.

PRIMARY EDUCATION REFORM

Measures are being adopted to improve the quality and delivery of primary education and reduce the high rates of drop-out and repetition, not least of which are attempts to make the primary school curricula more interesting and relevant for the students. For example, some vocational and technical training courses are being offered to students who expect to join the work force directly following primary school. Some nutrition and hygiene classes are being introduced in order to improve health conditions. Indigenous materials are being developed, and radio and television are being used to reach children in remote areas. Interactive radio has been used in Nicaragua for maths, and in Mexico and the Dominican Republic for a number of subjects. Radiovision (tape-slide) and teleconferencing (audio-visual) presentations are being used in Peru.

Criticism of formal education systems in the region on the grounds that they exclude the participation of the population in the design and provision of educational services and that they are unnecessarily costly has prompted some governments to decentralize and privatize their systems. In a 1980–81 reform Chile transferred responsibility for its schools to municipalities and placed vocational schools under private sector management. Subsequently, promotion rates increased and drop-outs declined, but problems arose because of teacher and

Guambiano Indian schoolchildren, southern Colombia

importance. For example, government representatives met in Mexico City in 1984 to inaugurate the Major Project in the Field of Education in the Latin American and Caribbean Region, a comprehensive intraregional education reform and development strategy designed to meet basic educational needs by the year 2000.

SECONDARY EDUCATION

Between 1980 and 1988 the number of countries with more than a 50 per cent enrolment rate in secondary education increased from eleven to fifteen, and as many females as males were enrolled. In fact, secondary education has expanded more rapidly than primary education since 1980, and from 1980 to 1988 enrolments in secondary education rose by 2.5 per cent.

While states continue to be the major providers of secondary education, between 1980 and 1987 on average private secondary schools increased in relative importance (see Table 2). Of the seven countries surveyed, none had more than 28 per cent of its secondary school students in private schools in 1980, but by 1987, three had enrolments of over 40 per cent.

The number of fifteen to twenty-four year olds in several countries is expected to have increased annually between 1990 and 2000 at over 3 per cent. Consequently, there have been attempts to relate secondary education to the job market through the introduction of more vocational and technical training at secondary school level. In addition, most Latin American countries have established national vocational training institutes to train young people and unskilled workers already in the labour force.

HIGHER EDUCATION

Higher education enrolment increased more rapidly than primary and secondary education between 1980

union opposition and municipal inexperience. Although other countries, including Argentina, have found local management of education more complicated and expensive than anticipated, the trend toward decentralization is clearly continuing. In Mexico and Brazil, primary and most secondary education has been delegated to state and local governments.

Such reform measures appear to have met with only limited success. Emphasis within the formal education systems continues to be too oriented to rote learning, too geared to exams rather than student ability, impractical, and with little attention to the discussion of local and national resource and environmental problems, or national and international social, economic and political questions.

Reform measures which attempt to develop education systems and programmes suited to the problems, needs, and the sociocultural and economic characteristics of countries are growing in scope and

TABLE 2

Percentage of pupils in the private sector at the secondary level

Country	Year	Per cent	Year	Per cent
Argentina	1981	30.7	1986	29.3
Bolivia	1980	27.4	1988	21.2
Chile, humanities & science	1980	23.5	1987	40.1
Chile, vocational & technical	1980	28.2	1987	56.3
Costa Rica	1981	6.7	1988	7.4
El Salvador	1984	46.9	1988	50.4
Venezuela	1980	19.1	1987	18.9

Source: Grosh, Margaret E., *Social Spending in Latin America: The Story of the 1980s*, World Bank Discussion Papers, 1990

TABLE 3
Public expenditure on higher education: the percentage of the education budget devoted to higher education in various countries

Country	Year	Per cent	Country	Year	Per cent
Argentina	1987	43.5	Honduras	1987	1.7
Barbados	1988	14.9	Jamaica	1988	20.7
Bolivia	1988	23.2	Mexico	1988	31.7
Brazil	1986	17.6	Nicaragua	1987	16.0
Chile	1987	21.6	Panama	1988	22.4
Colombia	1987	20.3	Paraguay	1985	23.8
Costa Rica	1988	39.9	Peru	1987	2.6
Cuba	1988	14.0	Suriname	1988	7.7
Dominican Republic	1988	2.7	Trinidad & Tobago	1986	2.8
Ecuador	1988	18.4	Uruguay	1988	21.8
Guyana	1985	17.8	Venezuela	1988	35.0
Haiti	1987	9.3			

Source: *Statistical Yearbook 1990*, UNESCO.

and 1985, from 4.8 to 6.4 million, an annual growth of 6.4 per cent. By 1985 the tertiary enrolment rate in all but two countries in the region had reached over 10 per cent, and in six it exceeded 25 per cent, for the eighteen to twenty-three age group. In 1970 only four countries had enrolment rates exceeding 10 per cent. The region already has the highest university enrolment rate in the developing world, and by 2000 this is expected to rise to 18 per cent. Several countries already exceed that figure: in Argentina it is 36.4 per cent, Uruguay 31.7 per cent and Ecuador 33.1 per cent of all twenty- to twenty-four-year-olds. The rapid increase in higher education in these countries has been achieved largely as a result of greater public expenditure and at the expense of investment in primary education. In the region as a whole, over 18 per cent of total government education expenditure since 1985 has been for higher education, and five countries – Costa Rica, Jamaica, Panama, Argentina, and

Mexican secondary schoolchildren with computer

Venezuela – have directed 30 per cent of their education budgets to higher education, as seen in Table 3.

Mexico provides a good example. In 1980, 817,558 students were enrolled in Mexican universities. In 1988, the figure was 1,256,942, an increase of almost 54 per cent. Moreover, the number of graduate students had reached 39,675 in 1985, an annual percentage increase from 1975 of 7.67 per cent.

Another feature of this growth has been the expansion and proliferation of private universities, many publicly supported by grants or student scholarships. In 1985 private universities accounted for 35.2 per cent of the Latin American student population, up from 34.4 per cent in 1980. In Brazil, on the other hand, the government has traditionally supported a few top-quality public universities, leading to a profusion of private tertiary institutions of varying quality; the government has recently increased its support for public institutions. In 1985 over 59.3 per cent of Brazilian university students were in private universities as against 64.3 per cent in 1980.

In recent years many countries have introduced polytechnic institutes specializing in single subject areas such as engineering, agricultural sciences, nursing, and education as an alternative to universities in an attempt to relate higher education to specific employment opportunities.

This rapid expansion in the number of students in higher education has not been accompanied by an equivalent expansion of appropriate job opportunities at the level of education received. There are an increasing number of higher education graduates in low-status occupations in the tertiary sector, semi-employed, or unemployed. Taking an extreme example, in Venezuela, the number of the unemployed without university education increased by 143 per cent between 1980 and 1990, whereas the

TABLE 4
Illiteracy rates, 1990 estimates

Country	Total adult illiterates (over 15)	Per cent male	Per cent female	Total	1980 rates for comparison
Argentina	1,064,600	4.5	4.9	4.7	6.1
Brazil	18,406,700	17.5	18.9	18.9	25.5
Chile	603,200	6.5	6.8	6.6	8.9
Colombia	2,701,700	12.5	14.1	13.3	14.8
Costa Rica	138,500	7.4	6.9	7.2	7.4
Cuba	30,434	5.0	7.0	6.0	2.2
Dominican Republc	743,700	15.2	18.2	16.7	31.4
Ecuador	909,100	12.2	16.2	14.2	16.1
El Salvador	786,800	23.8	30.0	27.0	32.7
Haiti	1,857,900	40.9	52.6	47.0	65.2
Mexico	7,065,700	10.5	14.9	12.7	17.0
Panama	187,100	11.9	11.8	11.9	14.4
Paraguay	252,400	7.9	11.9	9.9	12.5
Peru	2,024,500	8.5	21.3	14.9	18.1
Uruguay	87,700	3.4	4.1	3.8	5.0
Venezuela	1,450,000	13.3	10.4	11.9	15.3
Total	38,310,034	13.1%	15.8%	14.3%	–

Source: Drawn from *Statistical Yearbook 1990*, UNESCO.

number of university-trained unemployed increased by 264.7 per cent. In Chile in 1984 general unemployment had increased by 72 per cent from its 1980 figure, but the university-educated unemployed increased by 131.8 per cent over the same period of time.

LITERACY

Many governments have conducted literacy campaigns during the past decade, and illiteracy rates have decreased sharply, as shown in Table 4. There continue to be wide differences in literacy rates among countries in the region. In 1990 Argentina, Chile, Costa Rica, Cuba, and Uruguay had illiteracy rates of less than 10 per cent, while 44.9 per cent of the adult population of Guatemala and 47 per cent in Haiti were illiterate. In all countries, except Panama and Venezuela, a larger percentage of women than men are affected, with the rate for men over fifteen years of age being estimated at 13.1 per cent, and for women 15.8 per cent across the region as a whole in 1990.

Though illiteracy rates have declined, the overall number of illiterates, because of the growth of the population, has increased. In 1990, there were 38 million illiterates in the region, 17 million more than in the early 1980s. In the past ten years the *absolute* number of illiterates has increased in seven countries, namely Costa Rica, Mexico, Panama, Colombia, Ecuador, Paraguay and Peru. In seven other countries (Argentina, Brazil, Chile, Ecuador, El Salvador, Haiti, and Uruguay) the number of illiterates has not decreased significantly.

Persistent high rates of illiteracy in some countries can be attributed to the highly dispersed nature of the rural population. Many Latin Americans continue to live in small communities. The consequences are evident. Illiteracy rates among rural youths are high in most countries, whereas illiteracy among people over fifteen years of age living in urban centres has almost been eliminated. Commonly, the rural illiteracy rate for people over fifteen is double or triple the urban figure.

Literacy for the elderly: poster advertising a United Nations-sponsored campaign in Bolivia

Another explanation for high illiteracy rates in some countries, such as Guatemala, Bolivia, Mexico, Peru, and Ecuador, can be found in the high proportion of indigenous population. Discrimination against the indigenous populations and their languages has existed since the European conquest and has had its effects on the illiteracy rates. Indigenous languages in some countries have been ignored, pushed aside or banned by the official education systems. The emphasis has been on teaching the official languages as a means of incorporating minorities into the national society.

Finally, other contributory factors are the lack of organized pressure for literacy from the rural population, insufficient political will to change, or motivation and stimulation to acquire literacy skills.

The 1980s have been called the 'lost decade' in Latin America. Two world recessions in the first years of the decade produced widespread economic repercussions many countries experiencing decline and stagnation.

But the region made significant progress in education in the decade despite such severe constraints. Continuing success will require economic recovery and imaginative use of resources by governments and educators. DW/AG

Further Reading: O. Corvalán–Vásquez, 'Trends in Technical-Vocational and Secondary Education in Latin America', *La Educación: Revista Interamericana de Desarrollo Educativo, No.* 104, (Washington, DC, 1989); M. E. Grosh, *Social Spending in Latin America* (Washington DC, 1990); L. O. Roggi, 'La Educación en America Latina y el Caribe durante los Próximos 25 Años', *La Educación: Revista Interamericana de Desarrollo Educativo,* No. 101, (Washington, DC, 1987); D. R. Winkler, *Higher Education in Latin America: Issues of Efficiency and Equity* World Bank Discussion Papers, (Washington, DC, 1990)

The Spanish of Latin America

The speech of the Iberian peninsula came to the Americas through conquest: its carriers were conquistadors and missionaries, sailors and adventurers. Aft first, they came mainly from the south of Spain: a random sample of immigrants to what is now Panama tells us that before 1530 there came thirty-eight men from Castile, twenty-two from Extremadura, forty-four from Andalusia, seventeen from León and Asturias, one from Aragón, eleven from the Basque provinces and one from Galicia.

Later the patterns changed, and the percentage of Galicians and Basques increased substantially. With the growth of townships, the rounding up of Indians on the plains into settlements, the establishment of missions and *encomiendas*, a very great number of indigenous people gave up their language in order to learn the speech of a new administration, a new law and a new culture. In parts of the new empire, too, the decline in numbers of population indicates that resistance was at an end by the seventeenth century. By 1570, the indigenous population in Peru had fallen possibly by as much as 80 per cent and that of Mexico perhaps by even more.

The variants of Spanish introduced by the new overlords may well have indicated their points of origin in Spain, but they were modified later under the influence of indigenous languages where these survived and, above all, by geographical and ecological factors, such as altitude. The most important division in American Spanish has been pointed out by the Argentine scholar Angel Rosenblat: it is the division between highland and lowland speech.

HIGHLAND SPANISH

Highland Spanish, or *serrano*, as heard in the Mexican uplands or the plateaus of the Andes tends to sound 'clipped', with vowels closing or being lost, and with certain consonants being more forcefully articulated than in lowland or coastal areas. Vowels, especially unstressed vowels, close or disappear particularly before a sibilant: *trátse, croksí (trátase, creo que sí)*. Added to this is the confusion between /e/ and /i/ and between /o/ and /u/ where indigenous languages are spoken and bilingualism is common: *Pidro, comir (Pedro, comer)* and *decen, asé (dicen, así); ahura, culiflor (ahora, coliflor)* and *jogo, borro (jugo, burro)*. Such confusion occurs in peninsular Spanish dialects as well, though to a much lesser extent. It may be due in part to the fact that indigenous languages such as Quechua have no /e/ or /o/ among their phonemes.

Amongst consonants, the devoicing of /b/, /d/ etc. seems to have been a feature of both highland and lowland Spanish where indigenous languages were spoken: thus *poscando, alcón (buscando, algún)* in a sixteenth-century Mexican text, *curato, vifs, ustets, (curado, vivos, ustedes)* in modern Peruvian but *nata, lloper (nada, llover)* in jungle Spanish, also from Peru. Final /n/ will velarize to [ng]: *bieng, imáng (bien, imán)*; /r/ in initial, final or trilled pronunciation will become assibilated, giving a sound like *sh*, or *j* in French *je: ropa, amar, arriba* will sound *žopa, amarsh, a žiba*. Plosives /p/, /t/ and /k/, sibilant /s/ (or /z/), sibilant /s/ (or /z/), fricatives /f/, /v/

369

Andres Bello on the Spanish Language in America

Andrés Bellow (born in Caracas, Venezuela in 1781; died in Santiago, Chile, in 1865) was Latin America's most remarkable nineteenth-century intellectual, a polymath who published writings in a great variety of fields. His Gramática de la lengua castellana destinada al uso de los americanos *(Santiago, Chile, 1847) is commonly considered to be one of the greatest grammars of the Spanish language.*

[from the Preface]

I do not have the pretension to write for Spaniards. My lessons are directed at my brothers, the inhabitants of Spanish America. I judge to be very important the preservation of the language of our forbears in all its possible purity, as a providential means of communication and a link of brotherhood between the various nations of Spanish origin across the two continents. But I will not go so far as to recommend a superstitious purism. The prodigious advancement of the arts and sciences, the diffusion of intellectual culture, and political revolutions, demand new signs to express new ideas; and the introduction of new words, taken from ancient and modern languages, has ceased to offend us except when it is manifestly unnecessary. . . The greatest ill of all which, if it is not stopped, will deprive us of a common language, is the flood of new constructions which are invading and muddying much of what is written in America, and which, by altering the structure of the language, tends to convert it into a multitude of irregular, licentious and barbarous dialects, embryos of future languages, which would reproduce in America what occurred in Europe with the corruption of Latin. Chile, Peru, Buenos Aires, Mexico would all end up speaking their own languages. . . as happens in Spain, Italy and France, where certain provincial dialects dominate alongside various others – hampering the spread of education, the education, the execution of law, the administration of the State, and national unity. A language is like a living body: its vitality does not consist of the constant identity of its elements, but in the regular uniformity of the functions these exercise, from which comes the form and nature that distinguishes the whole. Whether or not I exaggerate the danger, this has been the principal reason that has induced me to compose this book . . .

africates /ch/ are all pronounced with more force than in the lowlands or coastal areas.

In the matter of verbs, one of the most distinctive features of Andean highland Spanish is the influence of indigenous languages, e.g. the use of the gerundive in Spanish, *dice que va venir diciendo* ('he says he's coming') is a direct translation of Quechua *hamunqa nin, nispa,* literally, 'he says he's coming, saying'. Other examples are *los ninos eran jugándose* ('the children were playing') or even the Argentine *¿cómo le va yendo?* 'how are you?' The extended use of the gerund can also be found in fifteenth- and sixteenth-century Spanish, however, and some maintain that it also owes a lot to the influence of English, e.g. 'I am sending you a cheque' = *le estoy enviando un cheque,* heard in Colombia and elsewhere. But all three sources of influence are valid. Another trait of mountain speech or *serrano* is the use of diminutives: *así ahorito no más, todito molidito bonito, estito, agüita,* which is again due to indigenous influence but also a feature of mountain dialects in Spain, e.g. Asturian.

LOWLAND SPANISH

Here one finds most of the characteristics of Andalusian Spanish: the relaxation of consonants, often so extreme that the sound disappears altogether *(ecir* for *decir)* as well as a tendency to confuse: *ábrelo/áurelo, boñiga/moñiga, periódico/periólico, madre/magre, está observando/ehtá okservando, difunto/dihunto.* As in Andalusian, *bue-* often emerges as *güe-: güeno,* with its unvoiced version behaving similarly: *fue* pronounced *hue* or *jue: afuera = ajuera.* in general, then, plosives relax to fricatives *(b, d* give /b/, /u/, and /d/, and the point of articulation in the mouth goes back *(d* to r/l, *b* to *g, f* to *jota* or *h).* /r/ in initial or trilled use is pronounced as a uvular (i.e. as a French /r/), especially in Panama. This is thought to have originated in Puerto Rico. The major contrast with highland Spanish consonants occurs in the lowland aspiration or disappearance of /s/ at the end of a syllable or word (again an Andalusian characteristic): *ehtá, loh hombreh; la ciudade, la mamá (está, los hombres; las ciudades, las mamás).* The aspiration of /s/ to /h/ is typical of Chilean Spanish, and the complete disappearance of /s/ of Argentine, but it will not be long before all aspiration disappears, and all Latin American lowland Spanish will have followed the example of French in eliminating /s/ in these positions (cf. *tête* for old French *teste, forêt* for *forest,* etc.). The question often asked of how the plural is distinguished from the singular in e.g. *las mamás* and *la mamá* when the /s/ has disappeared is answered simply: often the quality of the final vowel is more open in the plural than in the singular. Otherwise the context will provide the clue.

The only other point to make about the sibilant is that in Latin America the Andalusian practice of *seseo* (substitution of the /s/ sound for /th/ common elsewhere in Spain) is followed in both lowland and highland Spanish, that is /s/ and /c/ are both pronounced as /s/, e.g. *cocer* (cook) and *coser* (sew) will both sound identical (like Castilian Spanish *coser*).

Of vowels in lowland Spanish there is less to say: in Colombian coastal areas as in Panama and other places one can sometimes detect a lengthening of a: *graande, yo las lleevo, bastaante*. There is also confusion of /e/ and /i/ and /u/ (e.g., *térmeno* for *término*) as in peninsular dialects, but not as pronounced as in highland speech.

CAUSES OF THE HIGHLAND/LOWLAND DIFFERENCE

Although factors such as the regional provenance of peninsular Spanish migrants as well as the influence of indigenous languages do affect types of Latin American Spanish (as for instance in the Yucatán peninsula of Mexico, where the Spanish is influenced by Mayan), the chief cause of divergence and differentiation is ecological. The effects of altitude on speech have, over the centuries, been profound. At 4000 metres there is 30 per cent less oxygen in the air than at sea level, and mountain dwellers have lung-capacities of 1600 cc more volume than have coastal peoples. Pulmonary ventilation (or the amount of air expelled and inhaled in breathing or speaking) is correspondingly greater. This affects the pronunciation of certain consonants. Medical Aerospace experiments made in altitude speech have shown that at 10,700 metres these consonants are articulated with no less than ten times more force than they are at coastal level, where vowels show no increase at all. At 6100 metres the force has only decreased to nine times, and at 3–4000 metres is still substantial. Indigenous mountain languages such as Quechua or Aymara (and elsewhere in the world Tibetan and Caucasian languages) have a richness of consonants which result from this increased ventilation. Thus Quechua has fifteen different phonemes where standard Spanish has four: /p/, /t/, hard /c/ (or q), /ch/. Furthermore, the 'strong' pronunciation of consonants at the expense of vowels stays with highland speakers long after they may have migrated to lowland or coastal areas: inhabitants of Guayaquil or Lima may keep their *serrano* speech for generations after coming from the mountains.

STANDARD AND NON-STANDARD USAGE

As in every linguistic domain, both 'correct' and not-so-correct usage in Latin American Spanish can be heard. Colombia has long claimed to possess the purest form of Spanish, and its Academy has been called *El santuario de la lengua española* ('the sanctuary of the Spanish language'). But as time passes, there is doubt as to whether standard Spanish will survive much longer. This is not to say that a speech called Spanish will not continue for centuries, even as the hoariest pidgin English will still be called English. But there are signs of change: many are understandable slips common to all colloquial usage: *el radio* for *la radio, la idioma* for *el idioma*. But the breakdown of grammar goes hand in hand with the lessening of authority in schools and the growing of the prestige of the media, particularly of television programmes. *El conejo* gives *la coneja, el ratón, la ratona; el tigre, la tigra; el estudiante, la estudianta; Jesus, Jesusa*. Verbs, following the evolution of Vulgar Latin, simplify: *andó, andaron* for *anduvo, anduvieron*; the construction of *ir a* + infinitive: *voy a andar, vamos a ser*. These are forms that often occur in dialects of peninsular Spanish, but here they seem to have come to stay for good in the standard speech itself.

Voseo is another feature of Spanish in many parts of Latin America, and in particularly wide use in Argentina: it concerns the use of *vos* for the second-person singular, normally rendered by *tu: vos cantás, vos comés, vos sos*, with varients *(vos cantáis, vos coméis, vos sois* etc.). This extends to other tenses: *vos cantabas, vos has cantado, vos cantaste* or *cantastes, vos contarás*.

Other phenomena are also shared with Andalasian: in addition to *seseo*, /ll/as in *calle* emerges as [z], *ca že (ž as j* in French *je*). This is typical of Argentine Spanish; in the highlands of, say, Colombia or Ecuador, /ll/ is pronounced as it is written, whereas in other parts of the same countries it may be pronounced as [y]. Finally, archaisms still remain, e.g. *vido* for *vio* (Mexico), from colonial days.

The most recognizable types of Latin American Spanish come from Mexico, Panama, Colombia, Chile and Argentina, though highland speech is also easily distinguishable from lowland or coastal. Many countries, such as Peru or Ecuador, vary greatly within their own boundaries, and the same could be said of Bolivia and Venezuela. So-called Andalusian patterns of speech are noticeable in the Central American republics, though less so in Costa Rica. Uruguayan Spanish is much like Argentine or *platense* (River Plate), and Paraguayan more like Chilean, and with an intriguing Guaraní influence.

THE EFFECTS OF BILINGUALISM

One of the most interesting questions to be asked in the sphere of Latin American Spanish is that which

371

concerns the influence of the United States. Chicano, the Spanish of former Mexican provinces incorporated by the United States, as also the speech of imigrants from Mexico, may point the way in which the whole drift of the language is moving. Phenomena in Chicano such as code-switching (*se está brushing his teeth, tu miras funny*) reflect a facility of speech register manipulation that is apparent too in *engañol* or *spanglish* (as spoken in Puerto Rico).

Creole and pidgin dialects based on Spanish should also be mentioned: two examples are *papiamentu* (the Spanish–Dutch speech of Curaçao) and *palenque*, an African-influenced dialect of the descendants of slaves in Colombia. Different criminal jargons and slangs also add to the sociolinguistic riches of Latin American Spanish: *lunfardo* (urban argot of Buenos Aires which had a strong influence on tango-songs in the 1920s), *replana* (Lima), *coa* (Chile) and *caliche* (Mexico). An interesting though short-lived Spanish-Italian hybrid was *cocoliche* (Argentina).

The future of American Spanish is anybody's guess: the severe simplifications in grammar which have already been touched on, the lessening authority of normative grammar, the colloquial and frequently very sub-standard language pouring through the media, the ubiquitous North American television programmes and cartoons – all these would suggest that as we move into a less literate society, where the schoolroom has less authority, so Spanish as we have known it may well change, simplifying its grammar on one hand, and indulging in the wholesale importations of vocabulary on the other. However, another case can be made: the necessity of maintaining a commercial and cultural universal language in Latin America, the establishment's determined efforts to keep Spanish in its traditional state, the fact that Spanish is one of the great world languages of today with an immensely powerful status – all these give one pause for thought. Out of every ten people speaking Spanish today, eight will be from Latin America. Above all, the very likely emergence of a classical norm through the written word and the almost dizzy ascent of Latin American literature itself into being one of the most notable in the world, makes the eclipse of Spanish as we have known it far less certain than might be supposed from some of the examples mentioned earlier.

DG

Further Reading: I. Amastae and L. Elias-Olivares, eds., *Spanish in the United States: Sociolinguistic Aspects* (Cambridge, 1982); J. E. Davis, *The Spanish of Argentina and Uruguay* (Berlin, 1982); C. E. Kany, *American-Spanish Syntax* (Chicago, 1945); *American-Spanish Euphemisms* (California, 1960); *American-Spanish Semantics* (California, 1960)

Brazilian Portuguese

Portuguese ranks second only to Spanish among the Romance or neo-Latin languages spoken today, and over 90 per cent of its speakers are Brazilian. Interestingly, this New World Portuguese is perhaps more uniform, in spite of Brazil's geographical vastness, than the modes of speech frequently found in neighbouring valleys of northern Portugal, the very cradle of the Portuguese tongue.

PORTUGUESE IN THE NEW WORLD

Brazil was settled quite slowly during most of the sixteenth century. Certain language characteristics shared by Brazilian Portuguese with that of southern Portugal have led some linguists to conclude that early colonization of Brazil was accomplished predominantly by Portuguese from the south, although surviving evidence seems to refute that conclusion, and to show that the early settlers came from all corners of Portugal. As a possible explanation for this linguistic similarity, it has been suggested that a levelling of speech habits, akin to that which occurred in southern Portugal during the Reconquest, took place among colonists of varied dialectal backgrounds.

Additionally, despite innovations introduced by intense and prolonged contact with Amerindian tongues and those of African slaves brought to work in Brazil, modern Brazilian Portuguese preserves many archaic features of the pre-eighteenth century metropolitan language. Indeed, many of the more obvious current differences between European and American Portuguese appear to be the result of changes in Lisbon speech of the eighteenth and nineteenth centuries which were not adopted in Brazil.

The history of Brazilian Portuguese may be broadly divided into three periods. The first extends from the beginning of colonization up until the expulsion of the Dutch in 1654. Early communication among Portuguese colonists and the coastal indigenous tribes, because of the minuscule number of white settlers, often relied on the *língua geral*, a Tupi–based lingua franca the use of which the Portuguese crown forbade in 1727. Today, Tupi is spoken only in isolated areas of the Amazon valley and along the border with Paraguay. Even though the influence of Tupi on the Portuguese of Brazil has been overestimated by some, its contribution to the lexicon is undeniable. The vocabulary of flora and fauna abounds in Tupi words, and if toponymics and

MAJOR DIALECT DIVISIONS OF BRAZILIAN PORTUGUESE

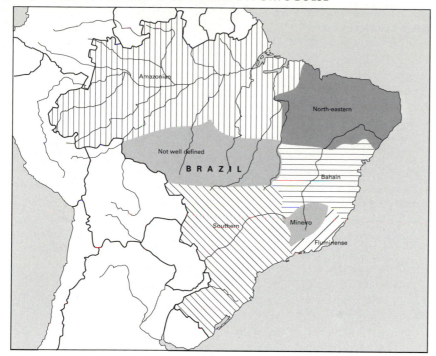

personal names of indigenous origins are counted in, the list swells to over 10,000 words.

During the second period (roughly 1654-1808), the *língua geral* receded into the interior, losing ground to the creolized Portuguese arising from the interaction of mestizo, Indian, and African elements. While African influence on Brazilian Portuguese is lexically less significant than that of Tupi, Brazilian speech may well owe its musical cadence to its earlier black-slave population. Of the two most important African languages brought to Brazil, that of the Yorubas was concentrated predominantly in the Bahian territory, while the Kimbundu tongue operated over a broader geographic area. It is believed that a Tupi–Kimbundu creole speech was the basis for the *caipira* dialect of Brazil, which at one time dominated all of old São Paulo province, reaching even to the hinterland of the north-east, and which, in the eyes of some linguists, explains the relative consistency of popular speech in the backlands today. Although the lexical presence of the Tupi and African languages is felt throughout the sociolinguistic gamut of modern Brazilian speech, its impact is clearly more pervasive among uneducated or rural speakers, in whose speech the elimination of the final plural *-s* of nouns and adjectives, as well as the massive reduction of conjugated forms in the verb, is in marked contrast with the educated or literary tongues of the language.

The third period began with the transfer to Rio de Janeiro of the Portuguese court in 1808, after which urban Brazilian speakers came under renewed intense exposure to continental speech patterns, in turn causing city speech, even among the more modest social classes, to draw closer to the literary standard, while differences between urban and rural usage became more accentuated. After achieving political independence from Portugal, and especially with the advent of Romanticism, Brazilian writers, notably José de Alencar, strove to demonstrate Brazil's literary and *linguistic* independence from Lisbon through the artificial use of Indian themes and terms. During this period a number of Brazilian intellectuals even proclaimed the language of their nation to be separate from Portugal's. Only after the initiation in 1922 of the movement known as modernism did Brazilian authors try to depict the linguistic realities of their homeland, without denying the common bases of the Portuguese idiom.

DIALECTS IN BRAZIL

In the absence of a complete linguistic atlas of Brazil, the most acceptable dialectal partitioning yet proposed is that by Antenor Nascentes. According to his scheme (see map), Brazilian speech divides geographically into two major groups: north and south, the two being separated by a zone stretching from the mouth of the Mucuri River, between Espírito Santo and Bahia, to the city of Mato Grosso in the state of the same name, and passing through Minas Novas, Pirapora and Cuiabá. The north is further subdivided into two sub-dialects; *Amazonian*, which embraces the states of Acre, Amazonas, Pará, and north-western Goiás; and *north-eastern*, including the states of Maranhão, Piauí, Ceará, Rio Grande do Norte, Paraíba, Pernambuco, Alagoas, and north-eastern Goiás. There are in addition four southern sub-dialects: *Bahian*, which encompasses the states of Sergipe, Bahia, northern Minas Gerais, and east-central Goiás; *fluminense*, which includes the state of Rio, Espírito Santo, the Distrito Federal, and part of eastern Minas Gerais; *mineiro*, covering central, western, and part of eastern Minas Gerais; *southern*, bounding the states of São Paulo, Paraná, Santa Caterina, Rio Grande do Sul, southern Minas Gerais and its western triangle, southern Goiás and the southern half of Mato Grosso. The area from the Bolivian border extending across the northern half of Mato Grosso and including west-central Goiás, being sparsely populated, reveals no truly characteristic dialect traits, in the opinion of Nascentes.

STANDARD BRAZILIAN PORTUGUESE

Given its long-standing historical and cultural importance it is not surprising that Rio de Janeiro should set the modern standard for educated speakers of Brazilian Portuguese. The pronunciation of Rio, known as *carioca*, constitutes a sub-dialect of *fluminense* speech, and its status as the preferred linguistic model for the country has been confirmed officially by two norm-establishing congresses: that of the *Língua Nacional Cantada,* in 1937, and that of the *Língua Falada no Teatro* of 1956. The *carioca* accent, therefore, serves as the norm for theatre, radio, television, and instruction, and is currently gaining in extension, both geographically and socially.

Some of the more striking features of educated speech in Rio as compared with that of Lisbon, besides those of a lexical sort, include: the preservation of a slower and softer mode of intonation, with more evenly distributed stress patterns, once characteristic of Lisbon speech as well; the retention of vowel clarity in unstressed syllables in contradistinction to the muting or discoloration of such vowels in Portugal as the result of an intensification of stressed syllables; stronger nasalization in Brazil of accented vowels occurring before nasal consonants; the occlusive pronunciation of inter-vocalic *b, d,* and *g,* which are fricatives in Lisbon; the unvoiced aspiration and even loss of final *r,* especially of infinitives, in Rio; the preservation in Brazil of the *close* articulation of stressed *e* before a palatal consonant, which has *opened* to *a* in Lisbon; vocalization of word-final *l* [Braziu], where it is velar in Portugal [Braził]: though the palatalization of syllable-final *s, z,* and *x* is shared by both *carioca* and Lisbon speech, the more archaic, sibilated variety of these consonants is still prevalent throughout Brazil; perhaps the most obvious phonetic characteristic of Rio speech, however, is the palatization of *d* and *t* before an *i* or unstressed *e,* where the *d* is pronounced as the voice affricate [ǰ] and the *t* as its voiceless counterpart [č].

While there have been several orthographic reforms and accords between Brazil and Portugal during the course of the twentieth century, certain phonetic differences between Old and New World Portuguese make total standardization impossible. Current Brazilian orthographic practices are regulated by a 1971 law, set out in *A nova ortografia oficial* (Rio de Janeiro, 1972).   JJN

Further Reading: J. Mattoso Câmara, *The Portuguese Language,* trans. Anthony Naro (Chicago, 1972); B. J. Chamberlain and R. M. Harmon *A Dictionary of Informal Brazilian Portuguese* (Washington, DC, 1983); H. W. Hoge and P. J. Lunardini, *Oral Brazilian Portuguese* (Wisconsin, 1965); E. Thomas, 'Emerging Patterns of the Brazilian Language', in *New Perspectives of Brazil,* ed. Eric N. Baklanoff (Nashville, 1966); E. Thomas, *A Grammar of Spoken Brazilian Portuguese* (Nashville, 1974)

Caribbean English

'Caribbean English' must be interpreted as applying to a number of different situations. The United States uses English as its vernacular and as its standard language, although the linguistic frontier between Spanish and English in the southern states is creeping northwards because of immigration from the Caribbean and Mexico, and varieties of both black English and of creole English (e.g. that of the Seminoles of Bracketville, Texas) are regarded by some as vernaculars distinct from Standard American. Around the western seaboard of the Caribbean there are creole English-speaking communities from Belize to Panama (e.g. in Bluefields, Limón, the Canal Zone) and in the islands off the coast (e.g. San Andrés and Providencia). In the case of Belize, the language of education is officially Standard English but a good deal of vernacular 'explanation' in fact takes place in classrooms, in creole English, Spanish, Maya or Carib for example; in the other countries of the isthmus Spanish is the official language. At the southeastern boundary of the Caribbean three creole-speaking countries intrude into the officially Portuguese and Spanish-speaking enclaves of Brazil and Venezuela: the Guianas; with Standard English being the official language and creole English the most widely-used vernacular in Guyana, Dutch the official language and three English-related creoles the common vernaculars in Suriname (Sranan, Saramaccan and Djuka), and French and creole French the languages of Guyane or French Guiana.

In the Antilles, the former British West Indian islands all have Standard English as their official language, though the Standard in use is being modified by recognition – both tacit and explicit – of accepted differences between educated West Indian and educated British or American usage. In some of the islands the vernacular usage is a creole or modified creole English (e.g. the Bahamas, the Leewards, Jamaica, St Vincent, Barbados, Trinidad, Tobago) while in others the effect of French planter colonization is still evident in widespread or partial use also of a creole French vernacular, as in Dominica, St Lucia and – now dying out – in Grenada and in a very fragmentary way in Trinidad. English is also very commonly used in the Dutch Antilles, particularly the northern group of St Martin, St Eustatius and Saba, as it is in the Virgin Islands.

The differences between the creole vernaculars and more standard English are at all levels of linguistic organization: phonology, syntax, the lexicon and semantics. The precise processes by which creole (or 'locally-born') languages evolve are in dispute, but certainly in the Caribbean owe something to the regional and social provenance of British settlers in the seventeenth and eighteenth centuries, something to the systematic features of the languages of the West African slaves taken to the Caribbean, something to possibly universal processes which give rise to patterns of linguistic behaviour in contact situations, and something to the various models towards which different groups within the Caribbean have converged from time to time, whether those models were provided by Maroon (runaway slave) settlements dominated by West African speakers, or by urban free black and coloured creole society, or by the official language of the colonial power, e.g. Dutch, or English, or Spanish. Today, indigenous models are of growing importance in both speech and writing.

RBLeP

Further Reading: F. G. Cassidy and R. B. Le Page, *Dictionary of Jamaican English*, 2nd edition (Cambridge, 1980); J. Holm, *Pidgins and creoles* 2 vols. (Cambridge, 1988, 1990); R. B. Le Page and D. DeCamp, *Jamaican Creole* (London, 1960); P. A. Roberts *West Indians and Their Language* (Cambridge, 1988); J. Voorhoeve and U. M. Lichtveld, *Creole Drum* (Newhaven, Conn., 1975)

Caribbean French

The French linguistic presence in the Caribbean is manifold. Standard French is the official language of Haiti and the French Overseas Departments (Martinique, Guadeloupe with its dependencies, and Guyane). Only minor features of pronunciation (such as the quality of the nasal vowels or *r*) and some items of vocabulary (e.g. *morne* 'hill', *driver* 'to loiter', *béké* 'locally born white person', *figue* 'banana'), many of them derived from creole (cf. below), distinguish the local variety. It lacks certain of the stylistic registers of metropolitan French, their function being carried out by creole.

A French dialect, heavily influenced by that of Normandy, is used in daily conversation by the white inhabitants of St Barthélemy (a dependency of Guadeloupe), and by a small enclave of older speakers in St Thomas (US Virgin Islands). The most widespread French-based language in the region, however, is creole (French *créole*, in the English-speaking islands *patois*), which is the mother tongue of the majority of the population in the French territories (except for St Martin), Haiti, St Lucia and Dominica, as well as some older inhabitants of Grenada and Trinidad. French and its northern and western dialects, as spoken by the early settlers, provided creole with most of its vocabulary, but little of its grammar: e.g. creole has no grammatical gender distinctions, and the verb does not change for person or tense (the latter being expressed by separate particles) – features which it shares not only with French-based pidgins and creoles elsewhere in the world, but also with lexically unrelated creole languages. (Such similarities have been variously explained, the theories currently most widely held being those which either draw parallels with the African languages spoken by the slaves, or point out the universality of such features in language contact situations.) The Caribbean French creoles are mutually intelligible, but not identical, that of Guyane being the most conservative, and that of Haiti distinguished from the others by numerous items of vocabulary and some major grammatical features. Nor are they uniform within themselves: Haitian presents three distinct regional varieties, and all the creoles living in contact with French are undergoing its influences, to a greater or lesser extent depending on socioeconomic factors, in a process of decreolization.

In Haiti and the French territories, French has traditionally been used for official and written communications, education, church services, newspapers and broadcasting, and has been the medium for writers such as Jacques Roumain, Aimé Césaire, Léon Damas and Edouard Glissant; whereas creole has been the spoken language of the masses, indispensable for intimate conversation and jokes for all classes, and the vehicle for a rich oral literature of stories, songs and proverbs. Sporadically written since the eighteenth century (poems, a Napoleonic proclamation, catechisms), creole now increasingly appears in the media and in written literature (F. Morisseau-Leroy's play *Antigone en créole*, 1953; Frankétienne's full-length novel *Dézafi*, 1975). In Haiti, creole (sometimes locally spelled *kréyol*) has been the language for literacy campaigns, and is used as a medium of instruction in primary schools; in the French West Indies, it has been allowed in the classroom since 1983.

GA-B

Further Reading: M. F. Goodman, *A Comparative Study of Creole French Dialects* (The Hague, 1964); A. R. Highfield, *The French Dialect of St Thomas, US Virgin Islands* (Ann Arbor, 1979); D. R. Taylor, *Languages of the West Indies* (Baltimore, 1977); J. J. Thomas, *The Theory and Practice of Creole Grammar* (Port of Spain, 1869; repr. London and Port of Spain, 1969)

Amerindian languages

It has long been assumed that the indigenous peoples of the Americas originate from nomadic stock that crossed the Bering Straits from north-east Asia tens of thousands of years ago. These brought to the American continents an Asiatic type of man who formed the human core of waves of tribes. The languages they brought with them belonged to some 250 linguistic groups and have been estimated at well over 2000. Today, barely 100 groups remain covering some 800 languages. The condition of their speakers might suggest that their native speech will eventually disappear as the long fingers of technology and western civilization close over their cultures and their ways of life. Whether in mountain valleys or in the great jungle areas of the Amazon, the inroads made by mining companies, road builders and other 'developing' or 'acculturating' interests continue implacably the mopping-up operations started by the exploiters of the sixteenth century.

Even by 1600 Indians such as those on the plains and savanna land of modern Panama had been rounded up into manageable compounds and de-tribalized settlements, or had instead fled to outlawry in the mountains to the north. Places more difficult of access kept their indigenous cultures, for neither the high valleys of the Andes nor the steaming jungles of the Amazon basin have proved attractive for permanent European settlement. Either altitude or intense heat have been the salvation for many a native culture. Time alone will tell whether the contempt traditionally accorded the Indian by the majority of settlers, the creoles and the mestizos (those of mixed Indian and European blood) will work towards turning everyone into 'good' Peruvians or Mexicans, i.e. those speaking only Spanish, or whether the dogged adherence to their identity will in the end ensure their survival. Quechua was declared an official language of Peru in 1975 (with what effect remains to be seen), and Guaraní has long been spoken by over 90 per cent of Paraguayans. Yet it depends, as in so much language behaviour, on prestige factors, on the concept of 'getting on' in the mind of the migrant to the city and above all on being able to talk the language of commerce and technology. As urbanization increases and the countryside loses more and more of its population, one may well question the outcome.

Only the missionaries have been instrumental in actually encouraging the expansion of indigenous languages in the past. In a similar way evangelizing bodies such as the Summer Institute of Linguistics encourage them today through their work in translating the Bible.

It will be best at this juncture to indicate the areas where indigenous languages are still spoken.

MEXICO AND GUATEMALA

The language of the Aztecs, belonging to the Uto-Aztecan group, remains spoken for the most part on the great central plateau of Mexico. It has some 1 million speakers, nearly a quarter of whom are monolingual. Words such as *tomato*, *avocado* and *chocolate* are taken from their speech, today called Nahua or Nahuatl. The other great language of Mexico is Maya, which with the other thirty or so members of its family spreads from the Yucatán peninsula to the whole of highland Guatemala. It is thought that some 2 million speak one or another of the Maya languages. The principal variants are Yucatecan, Quiche (in Guatemala), Cakchiquel, Mam and Kekchi. Of these last Quiche is an important cultural medium: it has as literary monument the *Popol vuh*. Another Maya language is Huastec, spoken in Veracruz, but it lies some 2000 kilometres away from the main Maya area.

Apart from the two language areas of Aztec and Maya, Mixtec and Zapotec (south-east Mexico), as well as Otomi and Totonac all command over 100,000 speakers each. Sixty per cent of others such as Chatino, Mazatec and Tlapeneco were monolingual as late as the 1940s. The percentage is much lower now.

All in all, Mexico has some 2-3 million indigenous speakers among its inhabitants. Guatemala has a far higher proportion.

CENTRAL AMERICA

El Salvador has speakers from the Mísquito (or Mósquito) family as well as from the Lenca (Cacaopera and Chilanga respectively), but numbers are not more than a few hundred. The Lenca family is also represented in northern Honduras. Honduras itself in the mid-twentieth century had some 80,500 native speakers using Jicaque, Paya, Sumo, Zambo and Mísquito – these out of a total popupation of some 2.5 million. The area also includes black Carib speakers, as does also Belize. Mid-twentieth-century Nicaragua had some 21,500 indigenous speakers, Mísquito being the principal native language with 20,000. Costa Rica's total is some 20,000 (around 1 per cent of the country's population). Some half dozen languages are spoken in north and south: one of these is Guaymí, which straddles the border with

THE TUPI-GUARANI LANGUAGE FAMILY

northern Brazil) and at one time is said to have covered an area reaching as far north as Florida. *Canoe*, *tobacco* and *hammock* are Arawak words. It is spoken, in one or other of its sixty variant family members, in the Amazon basin towards the west and nearer the Andes.

Another important linguistic family is Gê, spoken at one time over most of the southern half of Brazil and especially on the table lands of the Mato Grosso and Goiás. There are three main groups of Gê speakers with at least eight major sublanguages.

The most extensive of all lowland family groups today is Tupi–Guaraní, spoken in one or other of its forty-nine variants from the Guianas down to northern Argentina. Because of the efforts of Jesuit missionaries in the seventeenth and eighteenth centuries, Guaraní was accorded a respect which – at least in Paraguay, where it is an official state language – has never diminished. (The Jesuits have been criticized for not preparing the Indians for the 'modern world' but one would be hard put to pretend that what came after the Jesuit expulsion from Paraguay at the end of the eighteenth century was from any point of view an improvement on what they had already achieved in the way of co-operation and productiveness.) In the Paraguayan capital, Asunción, today, the Guaraní spoken is strongly influenced by Spanish and is known as Yopará.

Other families of languages spoken by Brazilian Indians are Tucano, Catukina and Puinave. To the south and in the Argentine Chaco, a few languages still survive: Mataco, Chunupí, Chorote and Toba. And in Paraguay, Lengua still flourishes in the Chaco missions.

SOUTH AMERICA: THE HIGHLANDS

The most powerful and extended language unit in highland South America is Quechua or Inca, a heritage of the vast empire which in the early fifteenth century had two capitals, in Cuzco (now south-east Peru) and Quito (now capital of Ecuador). Today, Quechua is spoken by at least 8 million people, with dialect groups running the length of over 3000 kilometres of mountain ranges north to south, from southern Colombia to northern Chile and Santiago del Estero in central Argentina. Quechua is usually classified under eight dialects: Ecuadorian (in Ecuador, as in Argentina, it is called Quichua), Lamas, Ancash, Huancayo, Huanca or Ayacucho, Cuzco, Bolivian and Santiago del Estero. Of these, the Cuzco dialect has long been considered as 'classical' Quechua. The language in general has expanded since the conquest, as already mentioned, but immigrants to cities like Lima are often very eager to

Panama, itself with native speakers in the mountainous west and also in the extreme east: the Cuna of the St Blas islands and the Darién mainland, and the Chocó.

SOUTH AMERICA: THE LOWLANDS AND COASTAL AREAS

In the north of the subcontinent, the Carib family is represented in lowland Colombia, but above all in the Guianas, Venezuela and north-east Brazil. Its centre of dispersal, however, would seem to have been between the upper Xingú and Tapajoz rivers. An interesting feature of Carib is that it has actually been extended in the last few centuries, as has Quechua. Black Carib, started by the fusion of Carib Indians with blacks when they were deported by the British after a rebellion in 1795, is spoken in Belize and Honduras, as already mentioned, but also in Nicaragua and Costa Rica.

Arawak, the first native language encountered by Columbus, had its centre of dispersal between the rivers Orinoco and Negro (i.e. in Venezuela and

pretend they know nothing of it. On the other hand, one of the most identity-conscious groups within the Quechua linguistic empire are the Otavalo of northern Ecuador, who possess, furthermore, an enviable reputation as a commercially successful and industrious people. Other tribes in Ecuador with a comparable sense of pride in their identity are the Colorado of the north and the Jívaro, who live in the south-east of the country and continue over into Peru. These last two named are technically lowland peoples.

In Colombia, and north of the Quechua area, the Chibcha civilization is hardly represented any more by its language, though members of the family itself, like Guaymí and Cuna, are still spoken in Costa Rica and Panama. In Colombia the largest indigenous group is that on the Guajira peninsula (the very northernmost tip of the subcontinent, on the Colombian-Venezuelan border) where the inhabitants speak one of the Arawak languages. Another interesting linguistic island is that of the Guambionos and Páez in southern Colombia.

Around Lake Titicaca, on the border of Peru with Bolivia, the Aymara language has well over half a million speakers. It is thought to be the speech of the builders of the great centre of Tiahuanaco, a short distance to the south of the lake itself. Another group in this area are the Uru–Chipaya. The Uru islands are on Lake Titicaca, and though no islanders now speak the language, it still survives among the Chipaya villages to the west of Oruro. That there may be an interesting link between them and the Mayan language culture of Mexico and Guatemala has been suggested.

Further south, in what is now southern Chile, the Araucanian or Mapuche Indians still speak their language, though since the 1880s they have been confined to the reserves near Temuco and Nueva Imperial. In the north the Araucanians' language was known as Picunche, in the centre Mapuche and the south Huilliche. It is Mapuche that survives. At least a quarter million of these speakers survive, out of a total Chilean population of 13 million. In Argentina the problem of Indians wanting to keep their traditional lands was solved simply by massacring many of them in the late nineteenth century. There still remain numbers of Aracuanians on the reserves in, for instance, the province of Neuquén. The northern Chaco has a few tribes such as the Mataco, to whom we have already referred. It has to be stressed that statistics in this area are extremely unreliable; even the definition of an indigenous inhabitant varies from country to country and one census authority to another. Mestizos, who may speak an indigenous language (as very many do in Peru), may not qualify as Indians on the ground that they do not inhabit a specifically Indian community, or live in towns.

QUECHUA AND AYMARA LANGUAGE FAMILIES

QUECHUA

A short article cannot easily give an adequate idea of some eighty to a hundred language families. A very brief description of the salient features of the largest and most widely spoken language, Quechua, may nevertheless be of interest as an introduction to the subject.

Quechua, or Inca, has a very rich consonantal phoneme-range. Thus, where Spanish or English have as phonemes /p/, /t/ and /k/ (or /q/), and Spanish has /ch/ – in other words four phonemes in all, Quechua has fifteen. In addition to the simple occlusive (p,t,k,ch) it has an aspirated version (ph,th,kh,ch) and a glottalized one (p',t',k',ch') and in addition /q/ is distinct from /k/ in pronunciation and forms distinct phonemes /q/, /qh/ and /q'/. There are, however, no voiced occlusives in Quechua, no /b/, /d/ or /g/. Vowels are limited to three, /a/, /i/ and /u/. Next to a /q/, however, /i/ will sound as /e/ and /u/ will sound as /o/. Thus what is in reality *Quichua* is pronounced more like *Quechua*.

There is no article as we know it, and no gender marker. The plural is marked by the suffix -*kuna*: *warmikuna* 'women', *wasikuna* 'houses'. Prepositions are also suffixed to the noun: *runa* 'man', *runapaq* 'for the man'; *wasi* 'house', *wasipa* 'of the house'. In verbs, the subject is indicated by suffixing a personal pronoun into the verbal root: *munay* 'to love' gives *munani* 'I love', *munanki* 'you love', *munan* 'he loves', *munanchis* 'we – that is, both you

The Lord's Prayer in Quechua

with literal translation into English

Yayayku,
Our Father,
Hanaq pachakunapi kaq,
Who is in the upper heavens,
Sutiyki munasqa kachun.
May your name be beloved.
Qhapaq kayniyki ñoqaykuman hamuchan;
May your power-being come to us;
Munayniyki rurasqa kachun,
May your wish be done,
Imahinam hanaq pachapi, hinataq kay pachapipas.
As in the upper world, so in this world too.
Punchawnin kuna tantaykuta qowayku;
Give us now our day's bread;
Huchaykutari pampachapuwayku,
And bury our sins for us,
*Imahinam ñoqaykuman huchallikuqkunata
pampachayku hina.*
As we too bury those sins which have been
committed against us.
*Amataq kachariwaykuchu wateqayman
urmanaykupaq,*
And please do not send us (for us) to fall into
temptation,
Yallinraq mana allinmanta qespichiwayku.
Rather keep us away from the not-good.
Hinataq kachun.
Amen.

communities which sometimes find it difficult to communicate with one another even when they belong to the same linguistic family. In the mountains, on the other hand, lines of communication are far easier and languages can travel more quickly either in the wake of a conquering army or through commerce and trade. There are thus fewer languages on the highland plateaus, and more assimilation of one language by another. Quechua absorbed many Indian languages less powerful than itself (and is still doing so). Thirdly, that the valleys leading down from the plateaus have as often as not been conquered from above, and not laboriously from down below. This gave the Incas, for example, a kind of herringbone pattern of conquest attacking valleys below as they moved along an axis at some 3000 metres. This again favoured linguistic expansion. As a result, the Inca system of communication and their highways often meant that their language would face little opposition. Their runner-team organization in particular was efficient, and it is said that a fish caught in the ocean could be served on the emperor's table in Cuzco the next day. What a fish can do a word might do as well, though it be from the emperor's table back to the coast.   DG

Further Reading: D. J. Gifford and P. F. Hoggarth, *Carnival and Coca–Leaf* (Edinburgh, 1976); M. J. Hardman, ed., *The Aymara Language in its Social and Cultural Context* (Florida, 1981); Y. Lastra, *Cochabamba Quechua Syntax* (The Hague, 1968); J. H. Steward and L. C. Faron, *The Native Peoples of South America* (New York, 1959); J. A. Suárez, *The Mesoamerican Indian Languages* (Cambridge, 1983)

and I or we – love', *manaiku* 'we – that is *not* you, but I or we – love', *munankichis* 'you (plural) love', *munanku* 'they love'. Much Quechua is influenced by Spanish, and some estimates put Spanish in Quechua vocabulary at as much as 50 per cent. Still, most of the simple greetings or commonly used words are indigenous: *ari* 'yes', *manan* 'no', *paqarinkama* 'until tomorrow'.

CONCLUSIONS

Such a cursory glance at the indigenous languages spoken in what is now Latin America would be incomplete without certain conclusions: firstly, that the survival of indigenous languages has been greatest in the mountains or in the jungle. Coastal plains were 'civilized' or cleared almost completely by the Spanish, the Portuguese or other colonizers. Secondly, that two patterns of survival can be discerned: jungle languages tend to be many and varied because so many of the communities are insulated one from another by forest. Consequently, they grow apart from one another both socially and culturally. Rivers have along their banks a succession of indigenous

Native American literature

A great hidden chapter of world literature is that which belongs to the native peoples of the New World, especially those of present-day Latin America. It has stayed hidden for practical and ideological reasons. First there is the question of the recording systems used by native Americans, the matrix of their literature, which like the Inca quipu, appear alien and incompatible with the alphabet and are therefore dismissed as 'non-literary'. Then there is the question of deciphering these scripts, a task that scholars still have to complete. Then again there is the question of the sheer availability of texts. Until recently classics in native script, like the precious screenfold books of Mesoamerica, could only be examined in inadequate reproductions; and only now are attempts being made even to catalogue the great corpus of pre-Columbian inscriptions in stone and wood, notably the hieroglyphic texts of the lowland Maya, several of which are of considerable length and literary interest. As for the alphabetic texts in major native languages recorded by native scribes after the European conquests, few have been adequately edited and translated into English, and the same is true of the major oral traditions subsequently collected in South America. In this respect such key works as the Nahua Cuauhtitlan Annals, the Quechua Huarochiri Narrative and the Guaraní *Ayvu Rapyta* have been scandalously neglected (especially since good versions exist in German and Spanish).

This state of affairs can be partly explained by an inherited reluctance to admit that the New World ever possessed anything equivalent to the script and scripture which in Christendom, as in Islam, have served as a chief ideological defence of empire. An allied difficulty has arisen from the fact that such accounts of its native literature as exist tend not to be literary but to obey anthropological and other criteria; and therefore the texts have often been turned to some ulterior purpose rather than being respected for themselves, as specific and unique arrangements of symbols and words. This tendency began in the sixteenth century in the great ethnographic work of Friar Bernardino de Sahagún who, in gathering Nahua texts in Mexico, increasingly moulded them to his own Renaissance philosophy. And in our day it is typified in the work of Claude Lévi-Strauss who, in reporting on American cosmogonies in the four volumes of his *Mythologiques*, relies on French summaries of original texts in order to fit them into his 'structuralist' frame. Nonetheless, enough has been published to make feasible a survey of at least the classics in the major scripts and languages of the Latin American area, whose origins long antedate Columbus and whose grand themes point to a common ancestry.

THE QUESTION OF SCRIPT

Before the Christians arrived with their alphabet, America possessed recording systems of its own, integral by origin with the calendars and tribute economics, the religions and social practices peculiar to that part of the world. Only one of these systems may be readily compared with the alphabet, insofar as it is

phonetic and records speech graphically. This is the hieroglyphic writing sumptuously cut in panels and stelae at lowland Maya cities like Palenque, Tikal and Copan from about AD 300 to 900; especially noteworthy are the two triolgies of low-relief panels at Palenque, carved in the late seventh century. The one in the Temple of Inscriptions gives a biography of the king Pacal, buried there, and ranges far back into prehistory; the other deals more with the city itself, the ancestry of its rulers in the aristocratic 'tree-birth' that occurred at about the time of Christ, the tribute ensured by its warriors and the maize cultivated by its farmers. After the 'collapse' of the lowland cities hieroglyphic continued to be used in screenfold books, of which three examples survive, named after the cities that now house them: Dresden, Paris and Madrid ('Grolier' is a fourth). Ritual histories intricately bound up with astronomy and cosmogony, they bear dates which like those in the inscriptions go back millions of years. Furthering this long tradition, in the sixteenth century many lowland Maya authors adopted the alphabet, and used it to transcribe the hieroglypic heritage. In the alphabetic Maya books particular to the towns of Yucatán and named collectively after Chilam Balam or Priest Jaguar, calendrical history and ritual chants follow the patterns established in the hieroglyphic texts. At the core of the Chilam Balam group is the Katun Count (*u kahlay katunob*) found at Tikal and in the Paris screenfold and transcribed in the Books of Tizimin, Chumayel, Mani, Oxcutzcab and Kaua. A time cycle of thirteen *katuns* (each of which lasts twenty years of 360 days) and the wheel of rotating government, this Count prompted an elaborate rhetoric of forecast and résumé in public affairs; it served as the basis, on the one hand, for personal prophecies (like those of Chilam Balam himself), and on the other for historical chronicles ranging back towards the beginning of this era, Katun 4 Ahau or 3113 BC.

Within the same cultural region of New Spain or Mesoamerica, which in literary terms extends from Nicaragua in the east to Michoacán in the west, hieroglyphic co-existed with the closely related script often called 'Mixtec-Aztec' and here referred to as iconic. Like hieroglyphic, it employs ritual sets of numbers and signs (9, 13, 20) and appears in inscriptions, which in this case date back well into the first millennium BC and survive the Spanish invasion. And it appears likewise in screenfold books, of skin as well as paper, and in scrolls, of which several dozen survive in all, and was also extensively used in books of European paper and binding. Very variously named, these iconic texts may in the first instance be usefully grouped by genre: poetic and highly structured ritual histories to which cosmogony and esoteric dating are indispensable; political and migration histories, like that of Cuauhtinchan which traces over millennia the fortunes of the Toltecs and their Chichimec allies; year-by-year annals, with a more open boustrophedon or linear format, stemming from major centres like Tilantongo and Tepexic, and from lesser towns like Tlapa and Huichapan; genealogies; biographies like that of Tilantongo's great hero Eight Deer; synoptic time-maps and *lienzos*; and tribute records like the gorgeous example from the Aztec capital Tenochtitlan, prepared for viceroy Mendoza.

Time map, title page from the Fejérváry screenfold

Unlike hieroglyphic, iconic script was not bound exclusively to the phonetics of any one Mesoamerican language and, outside the hieroglyphic zone, it was used internationally by speakers of Nahua like the Toltecs and Aztecs, Otomanguans like the Mixtec, Zapotec and Otomí, and highland Maya like the Quiche who describe the script of their forefathers as 'Toltec'. To convey meaning, iconic script may rely on such pictorial factors as colour, precision of outline, and layout, as in complex page-designs that resemble modern Navajo sandpaintings and which in the ritual screenfolds may serve to give title-dates (for example, page one of the Fejérváry screenfold). And because of this pictorial quality iconic texts have sometimes been assigned in the realm of fine art rather than literature. Nonetheless, they remain the classic antecedent to the many alphabetic texts written in Nahua and other Mesoamerican languages. This is obviously so with genre documents relating, say, to genealogy or tribute, and with annals like those of Cuauhtitlan and those incorporated into the work of such native historians as Chimalpahin, Tezozomoc, Castillo and Ixtlilxochitl. More intricate is the case of the ritual genre, for here iconic script relies most on the techniques, peculiar to it, of multiple reading and of shifting between dimensions of time by means of ciphers and signs. In fact it is the key to alphabetic accounts of cosmogony, where the 'Suns' of creation encapsulate the past in the present, and of ceremonial esoterism. For example, in the *Twenty Sacred Hymns* collected by Sahagún in alphabetic Nahua, the rain god's persona is termed the 'Jaguar-Snake'. What is meant remains opaque without the help of the Laud screenfold, where the rain god's Jaguar is revealed as his thunder-roar and his Snake as his lightning; moreover, in the ritual set of Twenty Signs, Jaguar is XIV and Snake is V, which together make XIX, the number of the rain god's mask (or persona) in the same set of Signs.

Turning from New Spain to Peru and the Inca empire, Tawantinsuyu, we encounter another sort of recording system altogether, which in sheer physical and etymological terms bears little relation to usual European definitions of literature or letters. For the components of the Inca system are not marks on a page but knots made in the coloured cords of the object known by the Inca or Quechua term 'quipu'. With the Spanish invasion of the sixteenth century, quipus were burnt and scattered just like the paper and parchment books of Mexico, so that only 400 or so have survived; and they were long deemed mere 'mnemonic' devices, theoretically little more complex than knots in a handkerchief. Nowadays much more is understood of the quipu's pure and mathematical logic and of how in the actual working of the Inca state it could have had the function enjoyed by

A quipu as depicted by Guamán Poma

hieroglyphic and iconic script in Mesoamerica. Hence in its turn the quipu may now be properly acknowledged as the literary antecedent to alphabetic texts written by Quechua- and Spanish-speaking authors, who indeed in several instances asserted that they were transcribing from quipu originals. A well-known case is Guamán Poma's *Nueva corónica* (a pun on 'crown' and 'chronicle') of pre-Hispanic Peru, whose chapters, each with its set of formulaic illustrations, reproduce the bureaucratic structure of the Inca state. Other examples can be found in the *Zithuwa Liturgy* with its patterns of set phrases and epithets, and in the kingship drama *Apu Ollantay* where the quipu both serves as a means of communication and reflexively confirms the structure of the play itself, with its thrice five scenes.

Beyond the urban focuses of Mesoamerica and Tawantinsuyu yet other recording conventions exist or have existed; but they have not been systematically related in this way or at any length to literary compositions in alphabetic script. Nonetheless, the *timehri* incised and painted by the Carib and Arawak, and once adapted by the ancient Chibcha to their ends, encapsulate the cosmogony of northern South America; indeed they relate conceptually to the ritual sets of Mesoamerica like the Twenty Signs, the Thirteen Birds or Fliers, and the Nine Causes or Mothers of Creation. And among the Cuna of Panama a similar sort of pictograph, written in boustrophedon, serves to record the Ikala or therapeutic epic chants of

their shamans. In all, the part of native Latin America where graphic and other recording conventions appear least essential to literature is precisely that which prompted Montaigne to pronounce that the New World was so young that it had 'yet to learn its ABC': the Tupi–Guaraní territories which stretch from the Amazon to Paraguay, to which may be added groups further south like the Mapuche or Araucanians of Chile.

LITERARY THEMES AND GENRES

Among the great unifying themes of native American literature, the genesis story is paramount. For the same basic account recurs from southern Peru to northern Mexico and the Navajo; in Tawantinsuyu it is set out by Guamán Poma and the Quechua Huarochiri Narrative, and in Mesoamerica by such texts as the *Popol vuh* of the highland Maya, the Nahua Cuauhtitlan Annals, and the heavily glossed iconic history from Tenochtitlán named after Huitzilopochtli. In this scheme the time we inhabit, far from existing independently, incorporates the four suns, 'sproutings' or lives of the past, in a way that recalls Hesiod's *Works and Days*. Some of the detail of what these lives were like and how they ended vary, but overall the structure remains the same. The first two lives end respectively in the Flood and the Eclipse, both catastrophes resulting from malfunction in the sky or upper regions. In the Flood, also reported in the creation cycles of the Tupi–Guaraní (the *Avyu Rapyta*; cf. the Makiritare *Watunna* and the Huitoto *Nainu-Ema*), the first race of men reverts to fish, while during the Eclipse the second race is set upon by its domestic creatures, dog and turkey in Mesoamerica, llamas in Peru. Higher up the evolutionary scale, the third life focuses on the struggle between scale-covered reptile and feathered bird on the one hand and the hairy mammals on the other. The fourth life is the epic story of man's ascent, of his difference from monkey and his capacity to inherit memory and to deceive. All this issues into the creation of contemporary humans from maize, which is known archaeologically to have become a staple in Mesoamerica and elsewhere around 3000 BC, the date taken as the start of the present era in hieroglyphic dating and in iconic annals like those of Tepexic.

Chronologically, this whole creation story lasts for a period commensurate with the millions of years spoken of by Guamán Poma and recorded hieroglyphically at Quirigua (Stela D, 400 million years) and in the Madrid screenfold (p. 57, 780 million years). Moreover, the iconic screenfolds show us that the transition from one life to the next is equivalent to a shift between orders of time, the smallest of which is the astronomically derived precessional cycle of 26,000 years; as the fifth life or sun, our era conventionally equals a fifth of this period (5200 years). Recounting the development of maize from lesser cereals, the Huitzilopochtli History spells out the pre-era and era spans in lots of 400 years (52 plus 13 feathered turquoise in iconic script, or 65 x 400 years).

When it comes to linking this genesis to the modern world a commonly used device is that of the culture hero and patron deity who champions the interests of a particular town or tribe. The thematic similarities between heroes of this kind from various parts of North and South America – Nanabush, Huitzilopochtli, Quetzal-Snake, the Twins, Bochica, Viracocha, Zume – attracted much attention in the late nineteenth century, as 'American Hero Myths', to quote D. G. Brinton's title. The motifs that recur in their respective life-stories invite close comparison, above all their pathenogenesis or miraculous conception. According to Cristóbal de Castillo, when the mother of Huitzilopochtli, who led the Aztecs to glory, conceived him ostensibly from a ball of down, her brothers grew angry and suspicious and they plotted to kill her only to be slain by the new-born hero who leapt from the womb fully armed. By contrast, the miraculously conceived Quetzal-Snake of Tula lived in obscurity until the age of nine, when he searched disconsolately for the bones of his father; the intellectual influence of his namesake on the early states of Mesoamerican civilization is reported in the Tepexic Annals and at Palenque. A different answer again to the social embarrassment of parthenogenesis is proposed by the highland Maya in the Popol vuh. For there the hero Twins engendered from their father's spittle after his death are brought into his first wife's family against the wishes of the grandmother; and they are fully accepted only when this matriarch involuntarily disowns her legitimate and first-born grandsons, the Twins' elder half-brothers, by laughing at the antics which the Twins make them perform with their music. In the Inca story of Viracocha told in the Huarochiri Narrative, it is he, the hero, who magically engenders; and the moral problem of fatherhood arises only when the child is weaned and the mother needs support. Then the young men of the village line up across the street and the one towards whom the child crawls is adjudged the father. In these four particular versions of the same literary motif, with their emphases on alacrity, inner searching, wit and paternalism, we may detect traces of the social ideologies which the texts in question defend.

Because of the different functions of literature within the various native societies of Latin America, it is mostly unhelpful to classify texts overall by genre. Yet in the case of performed literature, poetry and drama, some parallels can be drawn. In certain key respects the lyric poetry composed at Cuzco, the capital of Tawantinsuyu, has much in common with that of the Aztec capital Tenochtitlan. For in both places poetry became something acknowledged and produced in its own right, no longer closely tied to social function as a chant, say, for making rain, arousing warriors, consoling mourners or encouraging planters of maize. In Cuzco the haravek or court poets cultivated for their own sake the songs of warriors, planters and shepherds, with a skill that has left an enduring mark on Quechua, as the collection Tarmap Pacha Huaray (1905) testifies, and which survives in lyrics today, especially the pastoral yaravi (a term derived from haravek which has passed into the repertoire of Spanish American literature). At Tenochtitlan similar practices were followed among the brotherhood of court poets, which included King Nezahualcoyotl of Texcoco; many of their Nahua lyrics, preserved in the Cantares mexicanos and Ballads of the Lords of New Spain manuscripts are divided into modes, according to the social function they once had.

In addition to this, as imperial courts and centres of four-part empires (which is what Tawantinsuyu means) Cuzco and Tenochtitlan received the songs of their subjects literally as items of tribute, captured voices, according to a widespread American custom reported in the Cakchiquel History. Hence, from their privileged position the court poets came to appreciate the particular styles of the provinces around them, savouring them as something different from the metropolitan norm, with touches of the exotic. Guamán Poma defines the very geography of Tawantinsuyu through the songs and 'flowery music' typical of each of its four parts, all contributing to the wealth of the centre: large drums and quena flutes from Collasuyu; deer-horns and tambourines from Chinchasuyu; wild topless dancers and pan-pipes from Antisuyu; and satirical singers with death-masks from Condesuyu. In the Tenochtitlan collections, certain poems strive to capture the rough style of the Otomi to the north-west while others imitate the aesthetic of the Gulf Coast and Cuextlan, renowned for its exquisite etching in shell.

A similar example of literary sophistication occurs in the highland Maya play Rabinal Achi, from the same Quiche region as the Popol vuh. The main speech in this work conveys, with huge rhetorical power, the defiance of a captured warrior facing death: as such it recalls the set speeches which captives were obliged to make by the code of war observed by the Tupi and neighbouring South Americans, the point being, the greater the defiance, the greater the victor's satisfaction. Known by the term *carbet*, these speeches attracted the attention of early European visitors to Brazil, who copied some out in their travel diaries, along with love-charms and other set pieces. This warrior defiance also forms an important part of the Inca play *Apu Ollantay*, which as a kingship drama belongs to a whole cycle of plays extending from the first Inca *Manco Capac* to the last, *Atahuallpa*, whose tragedy is still performed annually in the Bolivian Andes. The speech in which the eponymous Ollantay defies the Inca Pachacuti (scene 4) resembles the *carbet*, it being the case that this hero stems from the Amazonian or north-eastern quarter of Tawantinsuyu, known as Anti-suyu (whence Andes). Historically, the Anti 'savages' bewildered the Inca with their knowledge of just the poisons and drugs used by Ollantay and his men in the play, and were reckoned especially wild and therefore satisfying to the metropolitan Cuzco audience. In an earlier scene (2), the same play provides a striking example of the framing of songs proper to the work-a-day world of Tawantinsuyu, when the song to scare birds from the crops ('Don't eat now, little bird, dove, dove of mine, in the lady's field') serves to warn Ollantay to keep away from the royal heroine; in fact the song is doubly framed, being performed before Pachacuti at his court, a small play within the play.

NATIVE AND WESTERN LITERATURE

In invading America, Europeans imported not just the alphabet but a literary tradition, Christian and secular. Indeed they and their heirs on occasion went so far as to transpose this tradition directly into the major American languages, cases in point being the

'Inca pageant' at Inti-Raimi (Festival of the Sun), Sacsahuaman – staged every 24 June at 1 pm.

hymns composed in Tupi by Anchieta and in Nahua by Sor Juana, and the sermons in 'literary' Quechua composed by Spanish priests in Peru and quoted (with derision) by Guamán Poma. From their side, Indian converts helped in this task while others worked independently, adapting imported texts to their own ends. In Cuzco successors to the *haravek* like Medrano imitated the poetry of Góngora while the cycle of kingship plays was enriched with characters like the *gracioso* or buffoon typical of Spanish Golden Age drama, and the eponymous Faustian heroes of the plays *Yauri Tito Inca* and *Usca Pauccar*, who sell their souls in an effort to regain the lost royal power of the Inca.

In Mexico the lyric collection of Nahua *Cantares mexicanos* came to embrace Christian songs (and in turn began a line in Spanish Mexican poetry that extends through the Romantics to modern writers like José Emilio Pacheco). Also in Mesoamerica, the ritual bird and animal numbers and signs of iconic script served as a rich local resource for the Nahua translators of Aesop's *Fables*. A yet more radical kind of translation can be found in the ritual screenfold histories, produced today in Mexico, of native paper, whose shamanist iconography now includes animals of European origin and number sets like the twelve hours of night and day. To the north, when taking over a Spanish version of *Cinderella*, the Zuni respected the same shamanist priorities, focusing on the relationship between the heroine and her flock of turkeys who, neglected while she is at the dance, revert to the wild and recover their own song and voice.

Fully aware of their role as transcribers of hieroglyphic texts, the lowland Maya authors of the Chilam Balam Books went to great lengths in reconciling this heritage with literature imported by the Spanish. The Books of Chumayel, Ixil and Kaua, for example, focus on the Biblical Genesis and commentaries by Christian scholars such as St John of Damascus and Alfonso X, which are integrated with Maya cosmogony to produce wholly ingenious accounts of the 'beginning of time'. The Book of Tuisk contains hagiographical and apocryphal tales, while the Books of Kaua, Mani and Chan Kan translate into Maya the *Thousand and One Nights* story of the maid Tawaddud or Teodora. It was chosen because it concords so well with the chapter of riddles included in the Chilam Balam Books and used to examine candidates under the *katun* system of government in Yucatán.

Going in the opposite direction, the influence of native upon Latin American literature has been enormous, and forms but a recent chapter in a story that in Europe includes Montaigne, Vico's disciple Boturini, Herder, the Romantics Schiller, Lenau and Southey, as well as Antonin Artuad and D. H. Lawrence. As in English-speaking America, whose

'Indianist' writers extend from Longfellow to Charles Olson and Ed Dorn in the United States and include Wilson Harris in Guyana, the criterion here is not simply attention to native Americans as such but attention to their literature. It is this distinction which in the Andean area separates the novelist José María Arguedas, whose *Fox from Above* draws constantly on the Huarochiri Narrative, from predecessors like his Bolivian namesake Alcides Arguedas. In the case of the Guatemalan Miguel Angel Asturias it was the experience of reading and translating the *Popol vuh* and the Cakchiquel History which first helped him to understand his contemporary Maya compatriots and therefore to produce his masterpiece *Maize Men.* Then, in consciously updating Rubén Darío's ambition to be 'the poet of America', the Nicaraguan Ernesto Cardenal, at the crossroad of the continent, has composed his *Homage to the American Indians* through repeated quotation and reference to their literature (the Iroquois Book of Rites, *Cantares mexicanos*, Borgia screenfold, *Popol vuh*, Chilam Balam Books, hieroglyphic stelae at Quirigua and Uaxactun, etc.). Lastly, it should be noted that American Indian texts may play a crucial role even in works not normally associated with them at all. For example, in Carpentier's novel *The Lost Steps* the answer to the hero's quest is provided by the *Popol vuh* and its account of the domestic revolt during the Eclipse, the Quiche text being singled out as 'the only cosmogony ever to have intuited the threat of the machine and the tragedy of the Sorcerer's Apprentice'. In 'The handwriting of the god' by Jorge Luis Borges (whose sympathies are hardly known to be Indianist), this same passage from the *Popol vuh* informs the climactic vision of a Maya priest condemned by Alvarado to a hemispherical prison, which, the reader soon discovers, contains the hidden Indian mind of Latin America.   GB

Further Reading: M. Ascher and R. Ascher, *Code of the Quipu: A Study in Media, Mathematics and Culture* (Ann Arbor, Michigan, 1981); J. Bierhorst, *the Mythology of South America* (New York 1988); G. Brotherston, *Image of the New World: The American Continent Portrayed in Native Texts* (London and New York, 1979); G. Brotherston, *Book of the Fourth World: Reading the Native Americas through Their Literature* (London and New York, forthcoming); M. de Civrieux, *Watunna: An Orinoco Creation Cycle* (edited and translated by David M. Guss, San Francisco, (1980); M. S. Edmonson ed., *Literatures, Supplement to the Handbook of Middle American Indians* (vol. 3, Austin, Texas, 1985); M. León-Portilla, *PreColumbian Literatures of Mexico* (Norman, Oklahoma, 1969); A. G. Miller ed., *The Codex Nuttall. A Picture Manuscript from Ancient Mexico* (New York, 1975); L. Schele and D. Freidel, *A Forest of Kings. The untold story of the ancient Maya* (New York, 1990); J. Sherzer, *Kuna Ways of Speaking: An Ethnographic Perspective* (Austin, Texas, 1983); D. Tedlock, ed., *Popol vuh* (New York, 1985)

Spanish American literature

COLONIAL LITERATURE

Spanish American colonial literature (1492–1810) was an extension of Spanish literature of the same period, its variations explicable precisely in terms of the imperial relationship between America and Spain. Many of the best-known works are not formally literature at all, but are historical chronicles written by priests, soldiers and explorers about the geography of the newly discovered region and the nature of its inhabitants. Of the Indian literatures of the continent there is only a faint trace in the imaginative poetry and prose of the colonial period.

In the Mexican ambit the best-known chronicles are those of Columbus, Cortés, Sahagún, Durán, Landa and Bernal Díaz del Castillo's *True History of the Conquest of New Spain* (1580), in an age when historical writing was still a branch of literature on the classical model. In Peru the foremost history was the *Comentarios reales* (1609; *Royal Commentaries of the Inca*, Texas, 1966) of the Inca Garcilaso de la Vega (1539–1616). A purely literary reaction to the experience of the conquest is found in poems such as *La Araucana* (1569) of Alonso de Ercilla (1534–94). The demands of the epic form made this account of the wars in Chile the first truly humane response in American literature to contact with the aboriginal population. Ercilla communicates the outlook of the Spanish ruling elite, a value system based upon honour and courage, which represents the dominant but ultimately less significant line of colonial literary production: military and aristocratic during the epic period of discovery and conquest, aridly ecclesiastical in the more sedentary age of the seventeenth and eighteenth centuries, a time of settlement and consolidation. The writers now remembered, therefore, are notable for their departure from these norms and for the elements of Americanist originality and protest in their works.

Note: The titles of literary works referred to in this and subsequent articles are followed by the date of first publication and a translation of the title into English, where appropriate. Where an English translation has been *published*, the title is italicized and followed by the place and date of publication.

Bernal Díaz conveys traces of class conflict, the resentment of the lower ranks against their seigneurial commanders. 'Inca' Carcilaso is the first great mestizo writer, son of a Spanish hidalgo and an Inca Princess. The taint of the illegitimate half-caste produces striking contradictions: a longing to be accepted, his elegant and noble style, bitter resentment at rejection, and a retrospective exaltation and vindication of the values and achievements of the Incas whom the Spaniards had subjugated. A century later, in the age of the baroque, dominated by the influence of the Spanish poet Góngora, colonial Latin America's greatest poet was a woman, Sor Juana Inés de la Cruz (1651–95), whose life and poetry were shaped by her implicit struggle against subservience, in a society now largely static. (It is also worth mentioning that the great Golden Age dramatist Juan Ruiz de Alarcón (1581–1639) was born and brought up in Mexico, and some critics see Mexican influences in his work.) The eighteenth century was equally barren in literary terms, reflecting the inquisitorial desolation of a still unenlightened mother country. But the continent was beginning to stir with Creole resentment of colonial rule, though the best-known literary work of the era, in an age of travellers (from La Condamine to Humboldt), is Concolorcorvo's *El lazarillo de ciegos caminantes* (1776; *El Lazarillo: a guide for Inexperienced Travelers*, Indiana, 1966), the semi-picaresque record of a journey from Montevideo to Lima by a disenchanted official of the Spanish colonial administration

Increasingly the fundamental problem of the divorce between American contents and European forms becomes apparent, and conventional labels – the Baroque, the Enlightenment, etc. – should not be taken too literally in evaluating colonial literature.

THE NINETEENTH CENTURY

Fittingly, the first famous work of the independence period in Spanish America (1810–30) was a picaresque novel, *El periquillo sarniento* (1816; The Itching Parrot), by the Mexican Fernández de Lizardi (1776–1827), a satirical look by a political journalist at opportunism and corruption in a society whose structures no longer conformed to the reality bursting out from below. This fascinating and contradictory era of enlightenment (whose essential antecedents are the American Revolution of 1776 and the French Revolution of 1789), later to be recalled in Alejo Carpentier's magnificent novel *El siglo de las luces* (1962; *Explosion in a Cathedral*, New York, 1963), is reflected in the transition between a neo-classical style founded on order, harmony and reason, and a romantic movement of polit-

Domingo Faustino Sarmiento, Argentine writer and president (1868–74)

ical passion and private sentimentality which would make a particularly lasting imprint upon Spanish American literature precisely because it corresponds to the early decades in the history of the new nations. Even in the works of poets still constrained by the neo-classical mode, American themes revealed the direction of Creole thought. Examples are the *Silva a la agricultura de la zona tórrida* (1826; Ode to the Agriulture of the Torrid Zone), by Andrés Bello (Venezuela, 1781–1865), a towering figure in nineteenth-century cultural history; *La victoria de Junín. Canto a Bolívar (1825;* The Victory at Junín. Song to Bolívar) and *Al general Flores, vencedor en Miñarica* (1833; To General Flores, Victor at Miñarica), by the Ecuadorean José Joaquín Olmedo (1780–1847), hymns respectively to the independence struggles and the period of anarchy and civil war which followed; and the celebrated romantic Americanist poems, *En el teocalli de Cholula* (1820; In the Temple of Cholula) and *El Niágara* (1824; Niagara), by the Cuban José María Heredia (1803–39).

Direct Spanish influences now disappeared with astonishing rapidity; that of France, underground in the eighteenth century, became overt and took on an almost official status. The nineteenth century was to be dominated by three essential themes; America and its landscapes (its history would take longer to assimilate); national politics, especially *caudillismo* and dictatorship; and later the Indian question. Many personalities at this time were notable simultaneously in politics, thought and letters.

An archetypal example is Esteban Echeverría (Argentina: 1805–51), a romantic by temperament and formation, who met Victor Hugo and others in Europe, and imported their themes and mannerisms into Latin America through Buenos Aires. He wrote the first true romantic poems of America, *Elvira o la novia del Plata* (1832; Elvira, or the Argentine Bride) and *La cautiva* (1837; The Captive) – hardly entertaining reading today – the first brief anticipation of the naturalist genre, *El matadero* (1838; *The Slaughter House*, New York, 1959), many years before Zola; was a leader in the intellectual opposition to the Argentine dictator Rosas; and produced the influential *El dogma socialista* (1845). Rosas inspired other famous works. One, profoundly Latin American in its electicism and contradictory originality, was Domingo F. Sarmiento's *Facundo: civilización y barbarie* (1845; *Life in the Argentine Republic in the Days of the Tyrants*, New York, 1868), written, like much of Echeverría's work and so much literature of the continent from that time to this, in exile. Sociological tract, political manifesto, dramatic investigation into the nature of Argentine man in a romantic Americanist perspective, *Facundo* is one of the vertebral books of Latin American history. Less impressive an achievement, but still important as the first true 'dictator novel', is *Amalia* (1851), the work of another Argentine, José Mármol (1818–71). Elephantine, superficial, overblown, it is nonetheless essential for an understanding of Spanish American romanticism. A different example is *Maria* (1867), a tearful melodramatic novel by the Colombian Jorge Isaacs (1837–95), still much read today and filmed on several occasions.

A major nineteenth-century contribution of Argentina and Uruguay to Spanish American literature was 'gauchesque' poetry. It was written not by gauchos, but by poets, sometimes rural but more usually city-reared admirers of the 'men on horseback', the most famous being Bartolomé Hidalgo (1788–1822), Hilario Ascasubi (1807–75), Estanislao del Campo (1834–80), and the great José Hernández (1834–86), whose long narrative poem *Martín Fierro* (1872), genuinely popular in inspiration and appeal, is another of the foundation works of Latin American literature. Hernández' gaucho is no amusing rustic, but an outsider, like Lorca's later Spanish gypsy; and whereas Sarmiento had seen him as an atavistic threat to developing civilization Hernández defends him as the soul of Argentine nationhood. The pampa Indians, however, are seen as unredeemably barbarous, in characteristic Argentine tradition.

In regions with different historical experiences, it was necessary to come to terms with Indian culture instead of suppressing it, and the last quarter of the nineteenth century sees the development of a dual treatment of the Indian: the exaltation of his past through 'Indianism', as in the long romantic poem *Tabaré (1879)* by the Uruguayan Juan Zorrilla de San Martín (1855–1931), or in *Cumandá* (1879), by Juan León Mera (Ecuador, 1832–94); and the 'indigenist' movement's condemnation of his unending subjugation and exploitation: *Enriquillo* (1879; *The Cross and the Sword*, London, 1956), by the Dominican Manuel de Jesús Galván (1834–1910), or, especially, *Aves sin nido* (1889; *Birds without a Nest*, London, 1904), by the redoubtable Peruvian authoress Clorinda Matto de Turner (1854–1909). The most important force behind the indigenist movement, however, was the formidable essayist and poet, Manuel González Prada (Peru, 1848–1918).

Many nineteenth-century novels from Spanish America seem indigestible today. There is no equivalent to a Galdós in Spain, an Eça de Queirós in Portugal, or a Machado de Assis in Brazil. If the novel is essentially a realist form tinged with all the 'impurities' that reality imposes upon art, the nineteenth–century Spanish American version is best understood as a transition from romantic-costumbrist elements ('creolism' or 'regionalism') to naturalism by the end of the century. For classical bourgeois realism in the mould of Stendhal, Balzac, Flaubert, or the mature Zola, we shall search in vain. The most representative novels of the period, after those mentioned, are *El fistol del diablo* (1845; The Devil's Tiepin), by the Mexican Manuel Payno (1810–94); *Martín Rivas* (1862; New York, 1918), by the Chilean Alberto Blest Gana (1830–1920); *Cecilia Valdés* (1882; New York, 1962), by the Cuban Cirilo Villaverde (1812–94); *Juan de la Rosa* (1885), by the Bolivian Nataniel Aguirre (1843–88); *El zarco* (1888; *El Zarco, the Bandit*, London, 1957), by the Mexican Ignacio Manuel Altamirano (1834–93); and, in a mould at once more traditional and more original, the innumerable *Tradiciones peruanas* (*The Knights of the Cape*, New York, 1945) of Ricardo Palma (Peru, 1833–1919). The naturalist movement was well under way by the end of the century, and the legacy of *El matadero* was assumed by Eugenio Cambaceres (Argentina, 1843–88) with *Sin rumbo* (1885; Aimless), and extended by the best-known representative of the current, Federico Gamboa (Mexico, 1864–1939), with novels such as *Santa* (1903).

MODERNISMO

But the crucial development at the end of the nineteenth century, in a remarkable shift of the centre of gravity away from the Southern Cone, was *modernismo*, which has sometimes unkindly been called

Rubén Darío (1867–1916)

French poetry written in Spanish. It continued the assimilation of European romanticism whilst absorbing the formalist lessons of parnassianism and symbolism. This came at a time when Latin America was being rapidly incorporated into the international economic system, its ruling elites were exporting raw materials in exchange for luxury consumer commodities, and a gradually emerging middle class was searching for its political and cultural expression. Despite the modernists' cry of art for art's sake and their lack of interest in politics, these realities were transparently encoded in their poetry.

The two giants of this period – both from small countries – are the Nicaraguan Rubén Darío (1867–1916), the more characteristic of the movement as a whole, and the Cuban José Martí (1853–95), whose life and work anticipated directions which Spanish American poets were to take once modernism was at an end. Darío, though less admired nowadays, was the most influential poet since Góngora, and the most effortless versifier in Spanish

poetic history. Martí is the model of the committed poet and universal man: patriot and martyr, convinced Americanist, brilliant journalist and publicist, at once spontaneous and profound. He spent some time in Spain and more in North America. Darío lived in Chile and Argentina, where his influence was considerable, and then in France and Spain where, for the first time but not the last, disbelieving Spaniards had to accept the idea of their literature being revolutionized by the 'Americans'. *Modernismo* was characterized by cosmopolitanism, eclecticism, frequent references to other artistic modes, and a systematic juxtaposition and interweaving of the five senses in poetry which was skilful, supple and musical, though rarely profound. In prose it left little enduring work: typical were the *crónicas*, short pieces evoking people, places and 'sensations', of which the foremost exponent was the facile Guatemalan expatriate Enrique Gómez Carrillo (1873–1927).

Modernismo began 'officially' in 1888 with Darío's book *Azul*, and faded during the First World War when the *belle époque*, of which it was a peripheral reflection, came to an end. The outstanding writers of the dominant northern group were Darío himself, the Cuban Julián del Casal (1863–93), the Mexicans Manuel Gutiérrez Nájera (1859–95), Salvador Díaz Mirón (1853–1928), Amado Nervo (1870–1919), and Juan José Tablada (1871–1945); and the Colombians José Asunción Silva (1865–96), Guillermo Valencia (1873–1943), and Porfirio Barba Jacob (1883–1942); along with José Martí. Important poets from further south were José Santos Chocano (Peru, 1875–1934), another who pushed the movement in the direction of Americanism (or *mondonovismo*); the Bolivian Ricardo Jaimes Freyre (1868–1933), the Uruguayan Julio Herrera y Reissig (1875–1910); and the Argentine Leopoldo Lugones (1874–1938). From that day to this *modernismo*, obsessed with the rare and exotic, has been considered elitist, aestheticist and evasive, a not unfounded charge; but it undeniably transformed literary Spanish and prepared the assimilation of the European 1920s avant-garde and the transition from a regional to a universal literature. By 1920, however, only Hernández and Martí had approached solutions to the harmonization of form and content in Spanish American literature. Only in the 1920s would this be regularly achieved by poets, and not until much later, with one or two exceptions, by novelists.

THE IMPACT OF THE MEXICAN REVOLUTION

The post-war period saw two distinct currents in Spanish American literature: in the novel, the further development of a vigorous regional strain focusing on the inhabitants of the rural interior and their struggle with natural and social forces; and in poetry, the full integration of many poets into the international avant-garde, especially through the filter of Paris, where so many were in residence between the wars. The biggest single influence on art was the Mexican revolution (1910–20) which, through the cultural policies of José Vasconcelos, transformed the conception of America's historical identity and mission with its aggressive recuperation of the pre-Columbian heritage and rejection of the Hispanic legacy. If *modernismo* corresponds broadly to the integration of Spanish America into the world economy, the regionalist novel of the 1920s reflects the ensuing incorporation of the interior, a bifurcation once again of European form and American content; but the Mexican revolution offered the alluring image of a nation in search of American forms to express American realities.

One immediate result was the novel of the Mexican revolution itself, usually dated 1910–40, though of course authors have continued to write about the revolution to the present time. It is a regional subgenre, like the 'gauchesque'. The best-known example is *Los de abajo* (1915; *The Underdogs*, New York, 1963), by Mariano Azuela (1873–1952), which went unread until 1924: terse, cinematographic, sceptical, but exceptionally vivid, its most striking contribution to Latin American fiction is its remarkable grasp of popular speech. Other important works are Martín Luis Guzmán's *El águila y la serpiente* (1928; *The Eagle and the Serpent*, New York, 1930) and *La sombra del caudillo* (1929; *The Shadow of the Caudillo*), Gregorio López y Fuentes's *Mi general* (1934; *My General*), Rafael F. Muñoz's *!Vámonos con Pancho Villa!* (1931; Ride with Pancho Villa!), and Mauricio Magdaleno's *El resplandor* (1937; Ablaze). Mexico's official indigenist policies also encouraged a vigorous committed current in other countries, such as *Raza de bronce* (1919; Race of Bronze) by the Bolivian Alcides Arguedas (1879–1946). The Peruvian Ciro Alegría (1909–67), became the most successful indigenist novelist of the period to 1960.

If poets after independence had vacillated between a neo-classical celebration of America's agricultural promise and a more spiritualistic romantic exaltation of its stupendous landscapes, the emphasis now was on the relation between men and the earth, with implicit contrasts in many writers between Indian collectivism and European individualism, or between materialist peasants and workers and a corrupt idealist oligarchy. *Los de abajo* had indicated this theme; other notable novels of the land were *La vorágine* (1924; *The Vortex*, New York, 1935), by the Colombian José Eustasio Rivera (1888–1928), who used his experiences on an Amazon boundary commission to create a narrative about the jungle and the capitalist exploitation of man and nature, with a fascinating blend of romantic and naturalist elements; *Don Segundo Sombra* (1926; New York, 1935), by Ricardo Güiraldes (1886–1927), a nostalgic and impressionistic view of the gaucho from the standpoint of a cosmopolitan Argentine landowner; and *Doña Bárbara* (1926; New York, 1931), by the Venezuelan Rómulo Gallegos (1884–1969), later briefly president of his country, who took his theme – the struggle between civilization and barbarism – from Sarmiento, to produce one of the most influential symbolic works of Spanish American fiction. Few novels have dated as badly; yet Gallegos's true objective was, as Alejo Carpentier has said, that of defining Latin American reality as a whole, pointing a finger and 'naming' things like Adam. Finally, no history, however brief, can overlook the unique short stories of the tortured Uruguayan writer, Horacio Quiroga (1878–1937), which relate men's struggles against the horrors of the American jungle.

MODERN SPANISH AMERICAN POETRY

In poetry the 1920s were the age of the avante-garde, continuing the cosmoplitan thrust of *modernismo*, but with an increasingly American perspective. The Mexican revolution had made the Spanish American

Pablo Neruda (1904–73)

republics less inclined to accept unconditionally the moral and cultural superiority of European civilization. The 1918 Córdoba (Argentina) student movement showed artists and intellectuals, for the first time, the possibility of an alliance between intellectual petty-bourgeoisie and workers; and the dizzying speed of the North American penetration of the Latin American economies, with dollar diplomacy, the Big Stick and the invasion of urban mass culture – jazz, the movies, radio, US-style journalism – made the defence of Spanish American culture an urgent and overtly political imperative. In Cuba, a logical development was black poetry, with Emilio Ballagas (1908–54) and the great mulatto poet Nicolás Guillén (b. 1902), whose work was vivid, straight-forward, profoundly popular and politically aggressive; as well as black. Luis Palés Matos (1898–1959), a white Puerto Rican, was another inspired creator of Afro-American poetry.

In Paris the Chilean Vicente Huidobro (1893–1948), friend of Apollinaire and so well integrated in the milieu that much of his work was written in French, originated a movement called creationism; while in Argentina, the Spanish 'ultraist' movement briefly captured a writer who had also lived in Europe and would later be more famous for his fiction, Jorge Luis Borges (1899–1986). But the two greatest names of the period, and of the century, are the haunted Peruvian, César Vallejo (1892–1938), poet of twentieth-century orphanhood, and Pablo Neruda (1904–73), a man by contrast always at home in the world, one of many outstanding Chilean poets and, in 1971, the second, after Gabriela Mistral (1945), to win the Nobel Prize. Both men became Communists, like Nicolás Guillén, working their different ways from an early post-*modernista* phase through avant-garde experimentalism – Surrealism is a fundamental influence in modern Spanish American poetry – and on to more openly defined political attitudes. Vallejo's best-known works are *Trilce* (1922), painful, disconcerting, unique, and the heart-rending *Poemas humanos* (1939; *Human Poems*, London, 1969); Neruda's the *Primera residencia en la tierra* (1933; *Residence on Earth*, New York, 1946), and the immense if uneven *Canto general* (1950; General Song), including the magnificent 'Heights of Macchu Picchu'. Both can be compared with the great Spanish poets of the 1920s renaissance – Alberti, Lorca, J. Guillén, Aleixandre, then Hernández – all influenced by Darío and two other great peninsular poets, Machado and Jiménez. A further crucial factor was the rehabilitation of Góngora. In 1936 most of these men experienced the Spanish Civil War as spectators or combatants, mainly with the Republicans. A somewhat younger participant was Octavio Paz (Mexico, b. 1914), whose best-known work is *Piedra de Sol* (1958; *Sun-Stone*, New York, 1963) and whose genius extends to essays and criticism. (Paz won the Nobel Prize for Literature in 1990.) Whereas the Spanish American novel was by no means free of nineteenth-century regionalist and costumbrist elements, and still rudimentary in technique – a partial exception was *Don Segundo Sombra* – Latin American poets, though not yet widely appreciated, were now fully up to date and able to compete on the world stage. The Spanish experience ensured that they would be committed.

In fact Latin American thought had been influenced since the early years of the century by the growing menace of the United States, and it was virtually impossible by the 1920s for a major thinker to admire that nation as Sarmiento had in the previous century. The best-known *pensador* was José Enrique Rodó (1871–1917), an Uruguayan essayist who counterposed Latin America's 'Arielist' inclinations to the barbarism of the North American 'Caliban'. Yet despite its immense influence, supported by the works of other ideologists like the Peruvian Francisco García Calderón (1883–1953) or the Argentine Manuel Ugarte (1878–1951), Rodó's spiritual message was at bottom no less elitist than the stance of the modernists. By the 1920s the undertaking was to redeem the Calibans – the masses – in Latin America itself, and it was now the often contradictory ideas of thinkers like José Vasconcelos (1882–1959), José Ingenieros (1877–1925), Haya and Mariátegui, which set the new tone. It was also an era of important cultural magazines: *Repertorio Americano* in Costa Rica (1920–58); *Martín Fierro* (1925–8) and *Sur* (1930–70) in Argentina; *Amauta* in Peru (1925–30); *Revista de Avance* in Cuba (1927–30); and *Contemporáneos* in Mexico (1928–31); followed later by *Marcha* in Uruguay (1938–74) and *Cuadernos Americanos* in Mexico (1942–).

THE RISE OF THE NOVEL

The 1930s in Latin America, as elsewhere, appears a grim and even desolate period in literary production. Only one classic novel appeared, *Huasipungo* (1934; London, 1962), by Jorge Icaza (1906–78), one of a generation of radical Ecuadorean writers. This work gave a brutal 'socialist realist' slant to the treatment of Indians in highland Ecuador. Amidst other anti-feudal and anti-imperialist works, Ciro Alegría produced a short novel *Los perros hambrientos* (1939; The Hungry Dogs), and a very famous long one, *El mundo es ancho y ajeno* (1941; *Broad and Alien is the World*, New York, 1941), which are among the last classics of the regionalist genre. Later fiction

Jorge Luis Borges

Jorge Luis Borges (1899–1986) grew up in the Palermo district of Buenos Aires. His paternal grandmother was English, as was his first teacher, and Borges himself later acquired a comprehensive knowledge of (and affection for) English literature – not without effect on his own work.

Just before the First World War Borges was taken by his family to Europe, and was forced to stay there by the war, so completing his secondary education in Geneva. On his return to Argentina in 1921 he joined forces with other writers to create a new literary magazine, *Proa*. His first collection of poems (1923) was a beautiful evocation of his native city. Soon noticed as a poet and essayist, he turned in the 1930s to the short story. This was to be his classic form; he did not write novels. The stories revealed a complex mind and a clear, limpid prose-style strikingly at variance with the recent Spanish American literary tradition.

With the overthrow of Perón in 1955, Borges became director of Argentina's National Library, a post he held until Perón's return in 1973. Now firmly established as a major figure in Argentine and Latin American letters, he became more widely known abroad in 1961 when he shared the Formentor Prize with Samuel Beckett. Translations of his works soon appeared in English (translations in French had been published during the 1950s). Despite the onset of blindness, Borges relished his new-found international fame, frequently travelling and lecturing in Europe and the United States. In 1967 he gave the Charles Eliot Norton Lectures at Harvard. He received honorary degrees from many universities, including Oxford and Cambridge. International prestige brought about something of a diminution in his literary output, but in the 1970s he pleased his admirers with several new collections of short stories and poems.

Borges's marriage in 1967 to Elsa Astete Millán was a failure. In 1986, shortly before his death in Geneva, he married María Kodama, a former student and the devoted companion of his old age.

English translations of Borges's writings include (with dates of translation) *The Aleph and Other Stories* (1970), *The Book of Sand* (1977), *Doctor Brodie's Report* (1972), *Dreamtigers* (1964), *Ficciones* (1962), *The Gold of the Tigers* (1977), *Labyrinths* (1962), and *A Universal History of Infamy* (1972).

beat *Tierra de nadie* (No-man's-land) by Juan Carlos Onetti (Uruguay, b. 1909) to a major prize in New York as a dividing of the waters. Onetti's grey, disenchanted urban novels, such as *El astillero* (1961; *The Shipyard*, New York, 1968), with overtones of Céline, Camus or Sartre and unostentatious but subtle mastery of techniques which communicate complex states of consciousness and moral ambiguity, were interpreted by many as a sign that Latin American fiction was moving at last from the country to the city and coming up to date. Gloomy metaphysics, relieved only by a somewhat desperate line in fantasy, remained a hallmark of River Plate fiction in such works as *Todo verdor perecerá* (1941; *All Green Shall Perish*, London, 1967), by Eduardo Mallea (Argentina, b. 1903); the vast *Adán Buenosayres* (1948; Adam Buenosayres) by Leopoldo Marechal (Argentina, 1900–70); the obsessive *Sobre héroes y tumbas* (1961; On Heroes and Tombs), by Ernesto Sábato (Argentina, b. 1911); and the tales of bureaucratic alienation penned by Mario Benedetti (Uruguay, b. 1920). Meanwhile in Mexico, Agustín Yáñez (1904–80), with *Al filo del agua* (1945; *The Edge of the Storm*, Texas, 1963), introduced certain Freudian insights and techniques into a novel which thus became the last work about the Mexican revolution from the period of consolidation and the first to apply new literary methods at a time when the revolution itself was perhaps 'dead'.

would require something more than exoticism or outrage to be accepted. It has become a critical cliché to see the moment in 1941 when Alegría's latter work

Jorge Luis Borges (1899–1986)

In reality, however, more had been happening in the 1930s than meets the eye, and a revision of the history of twentieth–century Latin American narrative is perhaps overdue. Three major writers, Miguel Angel Asturias (Guatemala, 1899–1974), Jorge Luis Borges and Alejo Carpentier (Cuba, 1906–80) – the 'ABC' of twentieth-century Spanish American fiction – had begun in the late 1920s ad 1930s to write works different from anything seen in the continent before. This is particularly true of Asturias and Borges, the first of whom would turn to the pre-Columbian tradition and the relation between language, myth and consciousness among the popular masses, while the second would effect the same operation with regard to the structural connections between Latin American high culture and the masterworks of universal civilisation. Asturias's best-known novel, *El señor Presidente*, completed by 1933, remained unpublished until 1946 (*The President*, London, 1963). Borges's stories – revolutionary in form – and essays appeared regularly from the 1930s, but were not influential until the 1960s (*Labyrinths*, New York, 1962; *A Personal Anthology*, London, 1968). The result, which has a lot to do with the sociology of readership, the economics of publishing and, in Asturias's case, problems of censorship, is that even when the Guatemalan launched *El señor Presidente in* 1946, followed in 1949 by his greatest work, *Hombres de maíz* (*Men of Maize*, New York, 1975), an interpretation of the entire span of Latin American history from the standpoint of the Indian, in the same year as Carpentier's 'magical realist' novel, *El reino de este mundo (The Kingdom of this World*, London, 1956), few critics realized that a new era was upon them. Yet it had even then been under way for many years, since in terms of composition *El señorPresidente*, Asturias's weird surrealist horror-movie, was virtually contemporaneous with *Doña Bárbara*, and Borges had begun writing his remarkable fictions not long after *Huasipungo* first appeared. Such are the vagaries of an uneven development.

From about 1945, then, most Spanish American writers could begin to incorporate in their works the lessons of post-1914 Euro-American fiction – Proust, Kafka, Joyce, Woolf, Faulkner, Dos Passos – in a way that only a few, thanks to their acquaintance with Europe, had been able from the 1920s onwards. Yet when the Latin American novel finally 'boomed' in the early 1960s, critics claimed that only now had writers fully absorbed the innovations of their great European precursors. The same criticism has tended to see the 1950s as a kind of no-man's-land, yet a succession of books was written then as important as anything to be produced in the 1960s: Carpentier's *Los pasos perdidos* (1953; *The Lost Steps*, London,

1956), the baroque account of a modern city-dweller's confrontation with nature and the past; *Pedro Páramo* (1955; New York, 1959), a subtle Faulknerian evocation of the anonymous nightmares of rural Mexico by Juan Rulfo (1918–86); *Los ríos profundos* (1958; *Deep Rivers*, Texas, 1978) followed later by *Todas las sangres* (1964; Everyone's Blood), a brilliant 'neo-indigenist' blend of native myth and contemporary class struggle by the half–Quechuan writer José María Arguedas (Peru, 1911–69); *Hijo de hombre* (1959; *Son of Man*, London, 1965), a moving epic of the Chaco War by another bilingual writer, Augusto Roa Bastos (Paraguay, b. 1918); and *La región más transparente* (1958; *Where the Air is Clear*, New York, 1960) by Carlos Fuentes (b. 1928), an X-ray of Mexico City reminiscent of Dos Passos; while Onetti continued to write prolifically and Julio Cortázar (Argentina, 1914–84) was becoming the continent's most original short-story writer after Borges.

THE 'BOOM' AND AFTER

The event which brought Latin America's image into sudden focus was the Cuban revolution of 1959. In literature this confirmed the long swing to a militantly committed poetic current, conversational in tone, which continues today; and initially catalysed a succession of politically and morally ambiguous novels which, since ambiguity is an element on which the novel thrives, met with unprecedented critical and commercial success. A numerically and economically significant middle class now existed in several republics, and was prepared for the first time to read novels by its own writers. It seemed there was an inexhaustible supply of talented authors bursting to express the fertile promise of that historical conjuncture. And yet, it we exclude novelists already established and now rejuvenated – Asturias (Nobel Prize, 1967), Borges, Carpentier – those who had been writing steadily before but were now more noticed – Onetti, Arguedas, Rulfo, Roa Bastos, José Donoso (Chile, b. 1924), author of *El obsceno pájaro de la noche* (1970; *The Obscene Bird of Night*, New York, 1974) – and a number of one-novel writers like Cuba's José Lezama Lima (1910–76) with his astonishing erotic symphony *Paradiso* (1966; New York, 1974), we can see that the centre of this whirlwind was really four major talents: Julio Cortázar, himself really a member of an earlier generation, who had now started writing novels like *Los premios* (1960; *The Winners*, London, 1965), *Rayuela* (1963; *Hopscotch*, New York, 1966), a playful avant-garde tour-de-force on the relation between language, literature and reality, and *Libro de Manuel* (1973; Manuel's

realities and illusions of Latin America's inhabitants. (García Márquez was awarded the Nobel Prize in 1982.) After these, and particularly after the hardening of the Cuban line on freedom of expression, successive novelists quickly narrowed their focus, renounced general interpretations of Latin American reality, and turned to another 'new novel', the postwar French version, forcing critics to coin expressions like 'post-boom' or 'post-Modernist', to define it.

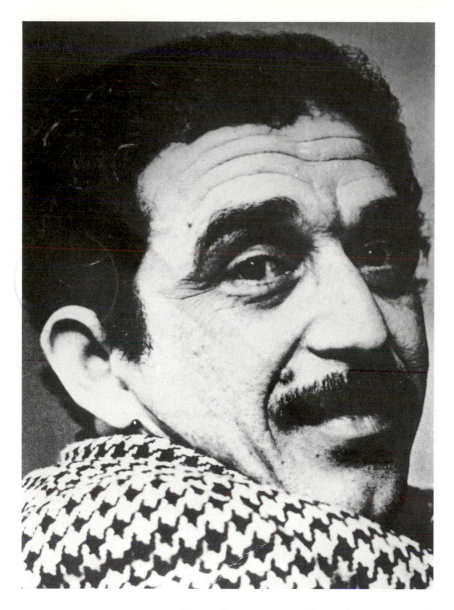

Gabriel García Márquez (b.1928)

Book); Carlos Fuentes, author of *La muerte de Artemio Cruz* (1962; *The Death of Artemio Cruz*, New York, 1964), *Cambio de piel* (1966; *Change of Skin*, New York, 1968), and the blockbusting *Terra nostra* (1975; *New York*, 1976); Mario Vargas Llosa (Peru, b. 1936), phenomenally successful architect of *La ciudad y los perros* (1963; *The Time of the Hero*, New York, 1966), *La Casa Verde* (1966; *The Green House*, New York, 1969), an interpretation of Latin American history as ambitious as Asturias's *Hombres de maíz*, the obsessive, labyrinthine *Conversación en la Catedral* (1971; *Conversation in the Cathedral*, New York, 1974); and the majestic *La guerra del fin del mundo* (1918); and also of course, Gabriel García Márquez (Colombia, b. 1928), author of the most famous novel of all, the magical *Cien años de soledad* (1967; *One Hundred Years of Solitude*, New York, 1970), which some critics compared with *Don Quixote* for the breadth of its perspective on the

---

Gabriel García Márquez

Gabriel García Márquez, one of the most brilliant writers of the brilliant Latin American group that came to prominence in the 1960s (during the so-called 'boom'), achieved instant international recognition with the appearance of *One Hundred Years of Solitude* (1967). The novel was translated into upwards of thirty languages and sold around 30 million copies in the first two decades after publication.

García Márquez was born in 1928 in the small town of Aracataca (La Guajira) near the Caribbean coast of Colombia. He was the eldest of sixteen children. In the 1940s he studied law at the National University, Bogotá, but never qualified, turning instead to journalism. He worked for the Bogotá newspaper *El Espectador*, which also printed his first fiction. The newspaper sent him to Europe, but was itself closed down in 1955 by the dictator Gustavo Rojas Pinilla, leaving García Márquez stranded in poverty in Paris. He visited both Italy and Eastern Europe after this event and 1958 moved to Venezuela. Shortly afterwards, as a convinced supporter of the Cuban Revolution, he took a job with the Cuban news agency Prensa Latina, but resigned the post in 1961. Thereafter he settled in Mexico – but first, out of admiration for William Faulkner, took a bus trip with his wife and small son through the American South. He has also lived at intervals in Spain.

In 1978 the Panamanian dictator Omar Torrijos invited García Márquez (together with the English writer Graham Greene) to accompany him to Washington to witness the signing of the Panama Canal Treaty. In 1982 he became the fourth Latin American to win the Nobel Prize for Literature; he attended the Stockholm ceremony dressed in casual attire.

Many of García Márquez's books have been translated into English, including (with dates of translation): *The Autumn of the Patriarch* (1975), *Chronicle of a Death Foretold* (1983), *The General in his Labyrinth* (1990), *Leaf Storm and Other Stories* (1978), *Love in the Time of Cholera* (1988), *No One Writes to the Colonel and Other Stories* (1968), and *One Hundred Years of Solitude* (1970).

One symbol of that era is the confrontation between the Cuban cultural review *Casa de las Américas*, edited by the poet Roberto Fernández Retamar, with its Marxist stance and inexorable espousal of 'socialist realism' and a Third World perspective, and the cosompolitan *Mundo Nuevo*, directed from Paris by the liberal Uruguayan critic, Emir Rodríguez Monegal, which eventually turned out to have been financed by the CIA. The Cuban revolution recalled the tradition of José Martí, turned Nicolás Guillén into a living symbol of its identity, and awaited the birth of Che Guevara's socialist 'new man'. The difficulties of this for some intellectuals are gloomily conveyed in Edmundo Desnoes's novel *Memorias del subdesarrollo* (1967; *Memories of Underdevelopment*, New York, 1968). The 'boom' novelists meanwhile found themselves increasingly subject to the pressures of commercialism and the lure of an almost Hollywood-style adulation combined with a propaganda campaign that turned them into public figures on an international scale. The final parting of the ways came in 1971 with the celebrated 'Padilla affair', when Latin American writers and intellectuals were forced to choose sides. Interestingly and ironically, three of the most successful novelists typifying the era are Cuban exiles, Guillermo Cabrera Infante (b. 1929), whose *Tres tristes tigres* (1963; *Three Trapped Tigers*, New York, 1971) and *La Habana para un infante difunto* (1980; *Havana for a Dead Prince*) are brilliant exercises in linguistic pyrotechnics, humour and eroticism, all characteristic expressions of the 'post-boom'; Severo Sarduy (b. 1937), whose critical postures and fictional productions, like *De dónde son los cantantes* (1967; *From Cuba with a Song*, New York, 1973) and *Cobra* (1972), have made him a doyen of the French structuralists, especially the *Tel Quel* group; and Reinaldo Arenas (1943–90), whose best-known work is the glittering *El mundo alucinante* (1969; *Hallucinations*, London, 1971).

RECENT TENDENCIES

The 1960s had been not only an age of – ultimately abortive – political ferment in the West, but also of pop culture and playfulness. This is reflected in the works of other young writers like the 'new-wave' Mexicans Salvador Elizondo (b. 1932), Fernando del Paso (b. 1935), Gustavo Saínz (b. 1940) and José Agustín (b. 1944), the Peruvian Alfredo Bryce Echeñique (b. 1939), and the Argentines Néstor Sánchez (b. 1935) and Manuel Puig (1932–90). Puig is particularly interesting since his novels, such as *La tración de Rita Hayworth* (1968; *Betrayed by Rita Hayworth*, New York, 1971), tend not so much to celebrate pop culture as to reveal its alienating effect on the lives of ordinary people. *El beso de la mujer araña* (1976; *Kiss of the Spider Woman*, 1979) inspired an Oscar-winning Hollywood movie. The 1970s saw dictatorship return to much of the continent, and three established writers produced a now famous trio of novels on the phenomenon to add to Asturias's classic *El señor Presidente*: Carpentier, *El recurso del método* (1974; *Reasons of State*, London, 1976); García Márquez, *El otoño del patriarca* (1975; *The Autumn of the Patriarch*, New York, 1976); and Augusto Roa Bastos, *Yo el Supremo* (1974; *I the Supreme*, New York, 1986), undoubtedly one of the most original and important recent works of Latin American literature. Undoubtedly, however, the rise of women writers to prominence is particularly noteworthy. The Argentine Luisa Valenzuela (b. 1938) found success with *Cola de lagartija* (1983; *The Lizard's Tail*, 1983), and real literary stardom awaited Chile's Isabel Allende (b. 1942), with her bestsellers *La casa de los espíritus* (1982; *The House of the Spirits*, 1985) and *Eva Luna* (1987; New York, 1988).

If the novel has recently been influenced by the cinema and other forms of urban mass culture, poetry is increasingly shaped by oral forms, popular verse and the protest song movements of the late 1960s and 1970s, led by Cuba and Chile. As elsewhere, the quelling of old-style 'inspiration' has meant a dearth of labels for new trends; but one sees a diminution of traditional concepts of imagination and rhetoric and a concentration on less ambitious forms and everyday language (*sencillismo*). While there are positive reasons for this, one factor must be a simple loss of poetic insight into daily life characteristic of western poetry as a whole. Neruda and Paz remained the dominant poets long after the Second World War. Now the main influences are Nicanor Parra (b. 1914), the Chilean originator of the 'anti-poem', and the Nicaraguan revolutionary priest Ernesto Cardenal (b. 1925), who in 1980 became minister of culture in the Sandinista government, symbolizing the goal of those various young Spanish American poets of recent times – like Javier Heraud (Peru, 1942–63), Otto René Castillo (Guatemala, 1936–67), Roque Dalton (El Salvador, 1935–75), Francisco Urondo (Argentina, 1930–76) – who have lost their lives in guerrilla struggles. Parra and Cardenal owe much to Vallejo's path-breaking use of popular idiom decades before. Curiously, though, Cardenal is also indebted to Ezra Pound's collage technique, juxtaposing the vulgarities of contemporary pop culture and ad-language with quotations from the classics, especially, in this case, those of pre-Columbian cultures.

When Octavio Paz optimistically declared in the

1950s that Latin Americans were 'now the contemporaries of all men', he was still speaking for only a select few. Today, however, when almost all the republics have a well-educated middle class subject to the daily barrage of international TV, radio and cinema, and when many Latin American writers of both left and right appear regularly in the pages of even British magazines, the statement appears to have more meaning. With fiction becoming increasingly hermetic, convoluted and even narcissitic, and poetry every more prosaic and matter-of-fact, the future is unusually difficult to predict. As 1992 and the end of the century approached, writers began to succumb to apocalyptic temptations: notable examples are Fuentes's *Cristóbal Nonato* (1987; *Christopher Unborn*, 1988), and García Márquez's *El amor en los tiempos del cólera* (1985; *Love in the Time of Cholera*, 1988) and *El general en su laberinto* (1989; *The General in His Labyrinth*, 1991). No doubt the Latin American literary New World has further surprises in store.   GM

Further Reading: S. Basnett, *Knives and Angels: Women Writers in Latin America* (London, 1990); E. Caracciolo Trejo, ed., *The Penguin Book of Latin American Verse* (London, 1971); B. G. Chevigny and G. Laguardia, *Reinventing the Americas* (Cambridge, 1986); A. J. MacAdam, *Modern Latin American Narratives: The Dreams of Reason* (Chicago, 1977); G. Martin, *Journeys through the Labyrinth: Latin American Fiction in the Twentieth Century* (London, 1989); J. Wilson, *An A to Z of Modern Latin American Literature in English Translation* (London, 1989)

Brazilian literature

In the colonial period, the social and cultural characteristics that distinguished the five regions of Brazil – Bahia, Pernambuco, Minas Gerais, Rio de Janeiro and São Paulo – were reflected in the work of writers from those areas, thus creating definite regional trends and certain sets of values which added to the variety of Brazilian literature. Some Brazilian critics argue that Brazil did not possess a national literature 'in a general and specific sense before the end of the eighteenth century'. But the early works of the colonial period show an identifiable character of their own that cannot easily be dissociated from the Brazilian scene. The themes which have dominated Brazilian literature throughout – the Indian, the black, the sugar-cane, the drought, the *sertão* or backlands, the

Amazon, Bahia, the sky-scraper – are the hallmarks of an original literary production. It has grown along consistent lines of development, even though the critical divisions adopted for changes in style may follow broadly European categories: the baroque era (1601–c.1770), neo-classicism (c.1760–1836), romanticism (1836–c.75), realism (c.1870–1922), and modernism (1922). These divisions are justified to a large extent by the fact that the main cultural currents that influenced the Brazilian intelligentsia come from Europe and were originally received through Portugal. Direct contacts with the wider world from the mid–nineteenth century onwards rendered this relationship far more diversified and led in our own time to a growing attachment to Brazilian oral literature.

THE COLONIAL ERA

The *Carta* (Letter) of Pero Vaz de Caminha on the discovery of Brazil, addressed to King Manuel and written between 22 April and 1 May 1500, is the first piece of literary merit to describe the new land. Caminha had sailed in the fleet of Pedro Alvares Cabral and in the *Carta* was informing the king about the results of the expedition. His description of the Amerindian reveals the illusions and dreams of the western mind in its search for an earthly paradise, but it also shows sound common sense. All the aspects described by Caminha, such as the apparent docility of the Indians, are those most suited to the convenience of the Portuguese explorers and project their image of themselves rather than that of the peoples they found. But there is also in this text a freshness of detail in the observation of the early contacts of the Portuguese with the Indians that reveals a spontaneous and immediate realism. This remains a characteristic of the literature of the colonial era, which often has a tone of praise for the land and its resources. Pero de Magalhães Gândavo, a Portuguese of Flemish origin whose dates of birth and death are unknown, produced around 1570 a *Tratado da Terra do Brasil* (published in 1826; Treatise on the Land of Brazil) and the *História da Província de Santa Cruz* (1576; History of the Province of Santa Cruz). But, while striking a laudatory note, he shows clearly some aspects of Amerindian society, such as polygamy, inter-tribal wars and ritual revenges and anthropophagy, which detract from the paradisiacal vision given by Caminha. This kind of work of reportage constitutes a genre of its own; it was enriched by the experience and the missionary activity of the Jesuits in the new land.

Fr. Manoel de Nóbrega (1517–70) presents a balanced picture of Indian society, being less racially biased, though not free from prejudice, than his contempories in his *Diálogo sobre a conversão do gentio* (1577–9; Dialogue on the Conversion of the Heathen). Gabriel Soares de Sousa (1540?–91) provides in his *Tratado descritivo do Brasil em 1587* (Descriptive Treatise on Brazil in 1587) the most comprehensive description of the peoples, flora and fauna of the territory known to the Portuguese in the sixteenth century. But José de Anchieta, SJ (1534–97) was the first to combine the needs of religious indoctrination with literary quality, both in his religious poems and in his *autos* or morality plays. In these he followed the Iberian tradition in a rather innovatory way, by combining Portuguese and the native languages. Less successful was the attempt by Bento Teixeira (*c.* 1560–?) to produce an epic poem, *A Prosopopéia* (1601), in praise of the Pernambuco ruler, Jorge de Albuquerque Coelho. His preoccupation with the form of poetic diction used by Camões in *The Lusiads,* whose pattern he tried to imitate, makes him a minor precursor of the new baroque style.

The logical and ordered syntax of the Renaissance was now giving way to sentences of conflicting meaning, to contradictory and problematic statements. The north-eastern intelligentsia of Brazil, where the prosperity of the sugar-cane planters had created by 1600 an urban civilization, expressed its own complexity of thought, couched in the stylistic subtleties of Europe. The towering figure of this period is Fr. Antônio Vieira, SJ (1608–97). His numerous sermons (published in Lisbon, 1679–1748, 16 vols.), are inextricably linked to his political and social crusades. Vieira attacks the Inquisition, defends the Indians from slavery, criticizes the presence in Brazil (1524–54) and the religious ideas of the Dutch, and urges the people of Brazil to expel them (sermon preached in Salvador, 11 May 1640). His sermons are magnificent pieces of mannerist prose in which the power of his imagery is matched by flawless argument. These qualities of Vieira's style are present in all his writings, even in his voluminous correspondence, addressed to the king and to other influential people. Vieira was born in Lisbon and spent most of his life in Brazil. But the poet Gregório de Matos (1633–96) went from Bahia to Portugal, where he graduated in law at the university of Coimbra, and was made a judge before returning to his native town (1681), preceded by the fame of being a caustic satirical poet. Matos spares no one, nor any institution, in his satires. The Church, the colonial authorities, the new aristocracy of Indian blood, the menial classes, or whoever incurred his displeasure, was brutally, and often unfairly, castigated. His craftsmanship as a poet, where he introduced many indigenous words into his speech, is better shown in his religious and metaphysical verse. He exhibits here an outstanding mastery in the handling of conceits which serve the mood of his meditations on time and the human condition.

Between 1760 and 1840, Brazilian literature gradually adopted the neo-classical style. The most important writers of this tendency came from Minas Gerais. Cláudio Manuel da Costa (1729–80) in his *Obras* (1768; Works) praises his native land, which he says can vie in the excellence of its streams and hills with the Portuguese rivers and plains hallowed by literary tradition. Antônio Gonzaga (1744–1810) produced a fine collection of lyric poems, *Marília de Dirceu* (1792–99/1812), and published anonymously his *Cartas chilenas* (1789; Chilean Letters), a vigorous satire against the governor of Minas. The stand of Gonzaga and other Minas writers against the Portuguese authorities led to their arrest in 1789 under the accusation of being involved in a plot to overthrow the colonial government.

INDEPENDENCE AND THE NINETEENTH CENTURY

This dissatisfaction culminated in the proclamation of independence on 7 September 1822. The opening up of Brazilian ports to international navigation, after the Portuguese court settled in Rio in 1808, favoured the growth of a national elite and created the economic and cultural conditions for the flowering of romanticism. The search for national origins, the expansion of imagination and individual freedom were the main characteristics of this complex movement. Goncalves de Magalhães (1811–82) deals rather diffidently with romantic motives and moods in his *Suspiros poéticos e saudades* (1836; Poetic Sighs and Nostalgia). But he soon turns his attention to typical Brazilian themes, becoming one of the first *americanista* poets of the period. His impressive epic poem on the great Indian rebellion of 1506 against the Portuguese, *A confederação dos Tamoios* (1856; The Confederation of the Tamoyos), shows the Indian leader, Ambiré, and his wife, Iguaçu, giving their lives in the struggle for freedom. An artist far superior to Magalhães, however, is Gonçalves Dias (1823–64). His *Primeiros cantos* (1846; First Songs), *Segundos cantos* (1848; Second Songs) and *Últimos cantos* (1851; Last Songs) express in highly polished verse not only the beauty of Brazilian nature and the poet's nostalgia for the beloved country, but also the Indian protest against the occupation of the land by the Portuguese (*O canto do Indio*, Song of the Indian). Dias tries also to see the inner conflicts that rend Indian society. In his poem, *Marabá,* he voices the anguish of a half-caste woman repudiated by her own tribe.

The epic and lyric tone so common in this Indianist poetry dominates also most of the fiction produced by José de Alencar (1829–77). He depicts magnificent frescoes of Indian life in *O Guarani* (1857; The Guarani), and *Iracema* (1865; *Iracema, the Honey-Lips,* London, 1886), two masterpieces of Indianist romantic literature. In *Iracema* he tries to create a new idiom, different from European Portuguese, by introducing a large number of Tupi expressions. But Alencar shows also in his novels the motley variety of Brazilian society, and is a definite precursor of realism. His novels of city life – *Viuvinha* (1860; Little Widow) *Lucíola* (1862), *Senhora* (1875; Lady) – are focused on the conflict between passion and the aspiration for social advancement. There is a remarkable shift in the tone and content of Brazilian Romanticism with Antônio de Castro Alves (1847–71), for the wide range of emotions he explores in his work and for the daunting vigour of his cosmic imagery. In his love poems he expresses an uninhibited sensuality that is only equalled by the majestic dignity of his social protest. In *Espumas flutuantes* (1870; Floating Foam) and *A cachoeira de Paulo Afonso* (1876; Paulo Afonso Falls) he lends a new and universal appeal to Indian themes. His condemnation of slavery, *Os escravos* (1883; The Slaves), still remains an unsurpassed piece of genuine poetic invective and human sympathy.

In the search for national inspiration with the *indianista* authors, Brazilian literature discovered the conflicts of subjectivity and attained a social awareness in the poetry of Castro Alves and his followers, that was soon to be strengthened by the abolitionist campaign coming from Recife and Rio de Janeiro. These conditions were favourable to the emergence of realism around 1880, a movement that was also shaped to some extent by Manuel Antônio de Almeida (1831–61) in his picaresque novel, *Memórias de um sargento de milícias* (1854–5; Memoirs of a Militia Sargeant).

The greatest realist novelist of Brazil, and one of its best short-story tellers, was J. Machado de Assis (1839–1908). His *Memórias póstumas de Brás Cubas* (1881; *Epitaph of a Small Winner,* New York, 1952) firmly established the new movement. The narrator of this book tells his own story after his death. In a detached and ironical vein, and after many philosophical digressions, he shows up the shallowness of a great love affair. In *Quincas Borba* (1891; *Philosopher or Dog?* New York, 1954; *The Heritage of Quincas Borba,* London, 1954) he deals with a similar theme. But by revealing the growing madness of his main character, Machado exposes the assumptions of the romantic mind and the harsh materialism of society. He excels in this analysis of contrast and centres his observation on the development and ambiguity of social relations and their effect on his characters. Thus *Dom Casmurro* (1900; New York, 1953) explores the elusiveness of memory. And *Esaú e Jacó* (1904; *Esau and Jacob,* London, 1966) stands as an allegory of Brazilian society seen through the eyes of a young woman divided and confused in her love for twin brothers.

TWENTIETH-CENTURY TRENDS AND WRITERS

In 1897 the republican government violently crushed a religious movement in the backlands of Bahia led by the messianic figure of Antônio Conselherio. The heroic resistance of the poor people of Canudos against the army made the problems of regionalism better known to the nation. And Euclides da Cunha (1866–1909) produced in *Os sertões* (1902; *Rebellion in the Backlands,* Chicago, 1944) an epic assessment of the rebellion that reveals a painful consciousness of the reality of the country.

The rebellion was a decisive factor in the minds of the São Paulo intelligentsia, now particularly receptive to new European ideas, and beginning to recognize the character of their own industrial society. The

Joaquim Machado de Assis, (1839–1908), at the age of 25

Jorge Amado (b.1912)

do Rêgo (1901–57) produced a moving picture of the decline of a great estate in his sugar-cane cycle of novels, from *Menino do engenho* (1932; *Plantation Boy*, New York, 1966) to *Fogo morto* (1943; Dead Fire). The greatest writer of this group, however, is Graciliano Ramos (1892–1953), who shows perceptively in *Vidas sêcas* (1930; *Barren Lives*, Austin, 1965) the social roots of a natural calamity. He is also a shrewd analyst of personal disintegration (*Angústia*, 1936; *Anguish*, New York, 1946) and of the complex position of women in society. In João Cabral de Melo Neto (b. 1920), the north-east finds a demanding poet who treats the word with loving austerity (*Poesias completas*, 1968; Complete Poems), following the lesson of Carlos Drummond de Andrade (1902–88), the greatest contemporary poet of Brazil. Drummond's search into the dialectic of reason and perception of the object has given superlative quality to his poetical work. And this quest is still at the root of all the experimental ventures of the *concretistas*, who have their main figure in Haroldo de Campos (b. 1929).

Brazilian literature was now to move into a deep exploration of language and ideas. Jorge Amado (b. 1912) began by writing populist novels on the cocoa planters and workers (*Cacau*, 1933; Cacao; *Suor*, 1934; Sweat), evolved to neo-realism (*Seara Vermelha*, 1946; Red Cornfield) and adopted in the 1950s the picaresque genre for his stories on Bahia. Yet, throughout all these changes, Jorge Amado remained the same inimitable story teller of his region, who has given us some admirable portraits of women (*Gabriela, Cravo e Canela*, 1958; *Gabriela, Clove and Cinnamon*, New York, 1962), making him the most popular Brazilian author at home and abroad. Erico Veríssimo (1905–75) introduced the *gaúcho* novel into Brazilian fiction and showed a remarkable psychological insight into his characters (*Clarissa*, 1933; *Música ao longe*, 1935; Faraway Music; and in the trilogy, *O tempo e o vento*, 1954–62; Time and the Wind). But the real change in Brazilian fiction dates from 1956, when J. Guimarães Rosa (1908–67) published an original novel, *Grande sertão: veredas* (*The devil to Pay in the Backlands*, New York, 1963), in which the *sertão* becomes a metaphor for the whole world. The power of linguistic creation transcends geographic and national boundaries to make it a work of universal appeal and a true literary masterpiece. It is an extremely complex fable on the destiny of man and the essence of evil set against the symbolic background of the Minas *sertões*. This capacity to question the self and the sense of existence at all cultural levels is one of the most fascinating features of contemporary Brazilian literature. In *Quarup* (1967) by Antônio Callado (b. 1917) and *A pedra do reino* (1971; Stone of the King-

Modern Art Week, held in São Paulo between 11 and 18 February 1922, introduced *modernismo* (not to be confused with the very different movement of the same name in Spanish America) in Brazil. By creating their own brand of futurism and by engaging a constant dialogue between literature and the plastic arts, by producing multiple styles and including oral language in the literary discourse, the modernists radically changed the character of Brazilian literature. Mário de Andrade (1893–1945) gives a critical vision of São Paulo in his poem *Paulicéia desvairada* (1922; *Hallucinated City*, Nashville, 1966), and deals with the question of a hero with a composite national character in his novel, *Macunaíma* (1928). Manuel Bandeira (1886–1968), in contrast, discovers modernism in the continuity of tradition. His poetic diction combines easily the colloquial and the ironical and succeeds admirably in turning personal fantasy into collective myth.

Bandeira was quite receptive to the *Manifesto regionalista* (1926; Regionalist Manifesto) issued by Gilberto Freyre (1900–87), a sociologist who drew attention to the importance of the north-east, where recurrent drought emerges as an inescapable fate. But it is on the authors who chose that region as the background to their work that Freyre's influence was most enduring. After *A bagaceira* (1928; *Trash*, London, 1978) by J. Américo de Almeida (1887–1980), an old-fashioned novel on the sugar-cane theme, J. Lins

dom) by A. Suassuna (b. 1927) the quest for the self and national identity is pursued as being one and the same through folklore and popular literature. A quest for identity through the myth can be seen in *O centauro no jardim* (1980; *The Centaur in the Garden*, 1984) by Moacyr Scliar (b. 1937), a leading Judeo-Brazilian novelist. Clarice Lispector (1917–77), known as a highly philosophical writer, as in *A maçã no escuro* (1961; *The Apple in the Dark*, 1967), has gained a growing world reputation.

New directions in fiction are noticeable in the work of Osman Lins (1924–78), a demanding author who questions the limits of the narrative and the novel as a genre (*Nove novena*, 1966; *Avalovara*, 1973), and in the atmospheric novels of Autran Dourado (b. 1926), who evokes the decadence of Minas society. Dalton Trevisan (b. 1925) is a tormented observer in *A guerra conjugal* (1969; Conjugal Warfare) and *O vampiro de Curitiba* (1970; The Vampire of Curitiba) of erotic fantasies and domestic attrition. Perhaps the most important novel of the 1980s was *Viva o povo brasileiro* (1984; *Invincible Memory*, New York, 1989) by João Ubaldo Riveiro, an anti–epic of Brazilian history covering four centuries of real and imaginary events – a truly modern classic.   LSR

Further Reading: A. Coutinho, *An Introduction to Literature in Brazil* (New York, 1969); R. E. DiAntonio, *Brazilian Fiction* (Fayetteville and London, 1989); D. Haberly, *Three Sad Races: Racial Identity and National Consciousness in Brazilian Literature* (Cambridge, 1983); J. G. Merquior, 'Pattern and process in Brazilian Literature: Notes on the Evolution of Genre', *Portuguese Studies*, Vol. 3 (London, 1987); D. Patai, *Myth and Ideology in Contemporary Brazilian Fiction* (London, 1983)

English Caribbean literature

In his novel *The Mimic Men* (1972) the Trinidadian V.S. Naipaul (b. 1932) writes: 'The empires of our time were short-lived, but they have altered the world for ever; passing away is their least significant feature.' The literature of the English-speaking Caribbean (i.e. the West Indies) has flourished only since 1950, but it is constantly and searingly marked by its awareness of a colonial history stretching back to the seventeenth century. Remarkably, thirteen years before the establishment of the first English colony in the West Indies, William Shakespeare's *The Tempest* (1611) put on stage a character called Caliban who in retrospect has provided one of the most potent self-images for the writers and intellectuals of the post-colonial Caribbean. Prospero, the European nobleman exiled on an unnamed island, had originally made much of the island's native inhabitant, but by the beginning of the play has reduced him to slavery. Caliban, forced into obedience by Prospero's magic art, can only rail against him:

> You taught me language; and my profit on't
> Is, I know how to curse. The red plague rid you
> For learning me your language! (I.ii.365–7)

The paradox is acute. The quest that has been at the centre of modern Caribbean writing – the search to formulate a racial and cultural identity – takes place in the language of the colonizer and often involves a journey to or exile in the colonial metropolis. C. L. R. James (Trinidad, 1901–89) prefaces his extraordinary book on cricket (*Beyond a Boundary*, 1963) by speaking of the need to track down his ideas in England: 'To establish his own identity, Caliban, after three centuries, must himself pioneer into regions Caesar never knew.'

Unlike other post-colonial societies, the islands of the Caribbean have no indigenous culture to provide any ready-made locus of authentic (because non-colonial) values. Caliban is in fact an anagram of 'Canibal', Columbus's version of the name of the inhabitants of the eastern West Indies: it is the origin therefore both of the geographical term 'Caribbean' and that byword for the ultimate in savage behaviour: 'cannibalism'. The Caribs, as they are now referred to, had no writing and, though they survived longer than the neighbouring Arawaks – exterminated before English colonization began in the area – they left little cultural legacy and make only marginal appearances in Caribbean literature. Caribs and Arawaks still live in Guyana where Wilson Harris (b. 1921) has explored and elaborated their oral narratives in *The Sleepers of Roraima* (1970) and *The Age of the Rainmakers* (1971).

During the early colonial period little writing was done in the English Caribbean itself. The most significant literary form was the diary or journal of the English planter or visitor, a mode that begins with Sir Henry Colt's remarkable journal of 1631 and includes works such as 'Monk' Lewis's *Journal of a West Indian Proprietor* (1834) and Lady Nugent's *Journal* (1839). The other book, set largely in the Caribbean, that has provided almost as powerful a set of literary references as *The Tempest*, is Daniel Defoe's *Robinson Crusoe* (1719).

The attempt to create a West Indian literature in English can be dated from the beginning of this century with the significant, if short-lived, *All Jamaica Library* whose first volume was *Becka's Buckra Baby* (1903) by Tom Redcam (pseudonym of T. H. Mac-Dermot, 1870–1933). Exceptionally, the five volumes of this venture were published in Kingston. Most subsequent West Indian literature has been published in England, increasingly so in the last thirty years. The frequent pattern of literary and political involvement, emigration and writing from and about exile, was early established. The Trinidadians Alfred H. Mendes (b. 1897) and C. L. R. James were instrumental in the establishment of a native cultural life in the late 1920s and early 1930s but their influential realist novels (Mendes's *Pitch Lake*, 1934, and James's *Minty Alley*, 1936) were published after they had emigrated. The pressure towards emigration has been described more recently by the novelist George Lamming (Barbados, b. 1927):

This was the kind of atmosphere in which all of us grew up. On the one hand a mass of people who were either illiterate or if not, had no connection whatever to literature since they were too poor or too tired to read; and on the other hand a colonial middle class educated it seemed, for the specific purpose of sneering at anything which grew or was made in native soil.

James, like so many others after him, came to London (in 1932) as a necessary step in his literary career. He became instead a political theorist and commentator, and author (in 1938) of *The Black Jacobins*, the story of the Haitian revolution. Lamming himself came to London in 1950, in the footsteps of the Guyanan novelist Edgar Mittelholzer (1909–65)who had achieved rapid success with his *A Morning at the Office* (1950). He was followed shortly by almost a whole generation of the best West Indian writers, amongst them Roger Mais and Andrew Salkey, from Jamaica, Samuel Selvon and V. S. Naipaul from Trinidad, and Wilson Harris from Guyana.

EXPLORATIONS OF IDENTITY

If Caribbean literature is unified by the felt absence of a single cultural tradition, the breadth of responses to this absence has been enormously varied and has recently produced in English a tremendously vigorous and exciting literature. Only the main outlines can be indicated here.

Derek Walcott (St Lucia, b. 1930), the poet and playwright, restates Caliban's dilemma by naming its horns Africa and the English language:

I who am poisoned with the blood of both,
Where shall I turn, divided to the vein?
I who have cursed
The drunken officer of British rule, how choose
Between this Africa and the English tongue I love?
Betray them both, or give back what they give?
How can I face such slaughter and be cool?
How can I turn from Africa and live?
('A Far Cry from Africa' in *Selected Poems*, 1964)

It is difficult to overestimate the importance of Africa for modern Caribbean writing as a whole. The sense that Caribbean culture can find its authentic voice as part of African tradition has always been strongest in French-speaking Haiti, but the shared awareness of a common past in slavery and a common origin in Africa led to early links between English-speaking West Indians and North American blacks. The Jamaican Claude McKay (1890–1948), author of one of the classic novels of Caribbean peasant life, *Banana Bottom* (1933), went to the United States in 1912 and was closely associated with the black literary movement known as the Harlem Renaissance. More recently West Indians have tested the potent ideal of 'Africa' against its contemporary reality by visiting and often living there. *The Leopard* (1958) by V. S. Reid (Jamaica, b. 1913) and *Other Leopards* (1963) by Denis Williams (Guyana, b. 1923) are just two of a series of fine and complex novels to come out of this encounter. Africa also figures prominently in the trilogy of long poems by the Barbadian Edward Kaman Brathwaite (b. 1930), *The Arrivants* (1973), perhaps the only West Indian poem comparable in scope and ambition to Aimé Césaire's magisterial *Cahier d'un retour au pays natal*.

English language and literature have been dominant influences, albeit ones handled with the ambivalence due to the culture of the colonizer. Caribbean speech patterns have been increasingly employed in much West Indian literature, and systematically in works like V.S. Reid's novel *New Day* (1949) and *Jamaica Labrish: Jamaica Dialect Poems* (1967) by Louise Bennett (b. 1919). Some of the finest West Indian writing has set out to rework English versions of colonial history. George Lamming uses *The Tempest* for his novel set in contemporary London, *Water with Berries* (1971). *Wide Sargasso Sea* (1966) by Jean Rhys (Dominica, 1890–1979) tells the story of Antoinette, the mad Mrs Rochester in Charlotte Bronte's *Jane Eyre* (1847). And Derek Walcott's poems in *The Castaway* (1965) draw imaginatively on the figures of Robinson Crusoe and Friday. Walcott is in fact notable for his superb command of the resources of the English poetic tradition, but, typically, makes that command, his relationship with

V.S. Naipaul (b.1932)

that tradition, into the subject-matter of his poetry, which often becomes a fraught and ambiguous meditation on the fragmented heritage of English culture.

As the earlier quotation from Naipaul suggests, the European colonial empires altered the world forever, and Walcott is by no means alone in his close inquiry into the enduring significance of the colonial past. Something of the varied unity of contemporary West Indian literature is suggested by the fact that four such different writers as George Lamming in *Natives of My Person* (1972), Wilson Harris in *Palace of the Peacock* (1960), Milton McFarlane (Jamaica, b. 1927) in *Cudjoe the Maroon* (1977) and V. S. Naipaul in *The Loss of El Dorado* (1969), should recently have written such accomplished works set in the colonial period. All of them in different ways concern quests. *Natives of My Person* is a remakable novel about a seventeeth–century vogage of colonization from strife-torn Lime Stone (Europe) to the Caribbean island of San Cristobal, written in Lamming's extraordinary heightened prose. *Palace of the Peacock* (part of Harris's ambitious 'Guyana Quartet') moves between the sixteenth century and the twentieth as it tells of two related voyages into the interior, journeys of self-discovery, the 'deepening cycle of exploration' (the phrase is Harris's) with which he attempts a reconstitution of the fragmented Caribbean psyche. Cudjoe was the Maroon guerrilla leader who led the resistance against a whole series of unsuccessful English attempts between 1655 and 1739 to destroy the towns established by runaway slaves in central Jamaica. McFarlane's quest is the recovery and dissemination of this history, passed down in secret oral traditions amongst the still largely autonomous Maroon communities, and part of the important process of rewriting Caribbean history from the perspective of the oppressed classes. Naipaul's *The Loss of El Dorado* similarly tells what he calls 'two forgotten stories', two moments when 'history' touched Trinidad: its part in Sir Walter Ralegh's search for El Dorado, and the later British attempt to foment revolution in Spain's American empire. Naipaul's is a carefully researched history but, like McFarlane's, consists in a powerful and imaginative recreation of crucial events in Caribbean history. In their different ways these four books all exemplify the remark made by the Martiniquan writer Aimé Césaire that the quickest way to the future is through the past.

Naipaul's career is almost a parody of West Indian exile in his complex trajectory through Trinidad, London, India, Africa and South America. Most of his work has been signally autobiographical, the major novels such as *A House for Mr Biswas* (1961) and *The Mimic Men* (1967) often following his initial exploration of these territories in journalism and travel-writing. Naipaul's quest in other words has been an acutely personal one which has taken him, his critics say, away from West Indian society as he becomes a universal traveller, ironically dissecting the decaying carcass of the modern world *(The Middle Passage,* 1962; *The Return of Eva Peron,* 1980).

Naipaul is, however, exemplary in the honesty with which he has confronted the problems of form. The West Indies has produced a whole series of classic novels since *A Brighter Sun* (1952) by Samuel Selvon (Trinidad, b. 1923) and George Lamming's autobiographical *In the Castle of My Skin* (1953), but the pressure to speak urgently and directly has tended (perhaps increasingly) to fissure the formal conventions of the European novel. Naipaul would here be in the company of his political opponents, *The Loss of El Dorado* resembling C. L. R. James's *The Black Jacobins* in its careful historical research presented with a novelist's imagination and narrative drive; *The Middle Passage* resembling the telling political diaries, *Havana Journal* (1971) and *Georgetown Journal* (1972) of the Jamaican Andrew Salkey (b. 1928) in their attempt to make personal sense out of the complexities of political and intellectual life in the contemporary Caribbean.　　　　PH

Further Reading: E. Baugh, ed., *Critics on Caribbean Literature* (London, 1978); P. Burnett, ed., *The Penguin Book of Caribbean Verse in English* (Harmondsworth, 1986); D. Dabydeen and N. Wilson–Tagoe, *A Reader's Guide to West Indian and Black British Literature* (London, 1988); B. King, ed., *West Indian Literature* (London, 1979); M. Morris, ed., *The Faber Book of Contemporary Caribbean Short Stories* (London, 1990); G. Lamming, *The Pleasures of Exile,* 2nd edition (London, 1984); A. Saakana, *The Colonial Legacy in Caribbean Literature* (London, 1987)

French Caribbean literature

The native inhabitants of the Caribbean are as absent from the modern literature in French as from that in English. This was not always so. By far the most important Caribbean genre of the seventeenth and eighteenth centuries was the series of historical and anthropological works written by the Dominican and Jesuit missionaries. Phenomenally unsuccessful in their missionary activities, the fathers, often resident in the Caribbean for a large part of their lives, produced a series of valuable and influential books, none more so than *Histoire génerale des Antilles habités par les Français* (1667–71; General History of the French Antilles) by Jean-Baptiste du Tertre, which contains this classic description of the native inhabitants.

> The Savages of these islands are the most contented, happiest, least vicious, most friendly, least false, and the least tormented by sickness, of all the nations in the world. For they are still just as nature made them, that is to say living in great simplicity and natural naivety: they are all equal, with almost no form of superiority or servitude.

These Caribs, difficult to recognize in the cannibals that were later to horrify Robinson Crusoe, reappear nearly a hundred years later as living in what Rousseau called mankind's happiest and most stable epoch, the true youth of the world. By then (1754) the Caribs were fighting a desperate and soon-to-be-lost battle against the English and French colonists. But in Aimé Césaire's powerful rewriting of Shakespeare's play, *Une Tempête* (1969; *A Tempest*, New York, 1974) Caliban is, despite his name, a black; and it is the black experience that forms the heart of modern Caribbean literature in French.

However, although properly belonging to the mainstream of French poetry, mention should first be made of the long tradition of poems of exile by French Caribbean writers, linking Nicolas-Germain Leonard (1744–93), who when in France wrote nostalgically about Guadeloupe and *vice versa*, with Saint-John Perse (pseudonym of Alexis Léger) whose eleven years in Guadeloupe (from his birth in 1887 to 1908) produced the stunning *Images à Crusoé* (1904; 'Pictures for Crusoe' in *Collected Poems*, trans. W. H. Auden *et al.*, Princeton, 1971).

Haiti, independent since 1804, has clear precedence in the development of a literature of its own, the first signs of this becoming apparent in the late nineteenth century with the publication of *De l'égalité des races humaines* (1885; On the Equality of Human Races) by Anténor Firmin (1850–1911). This riposte to the deepening racial prejudice of high imperialism affirmed the achievements of African civilizations and the place of blacks as the cultural equals of their oppressors. It is thus closely tied to the current that only later became known as *négritude*. The US military occupation of Haiti from 1915 to 1930 – described in *Le choc* (1932), a novel by Léon Laleau (b. 1892) – led to a general cultural reassessment of which *Ainsi parla l'oncle* (1928; So the Uncle Said) by Jean Price-Mars (1876–1970) is the main document. Price-Mars urged the study of popular culture, the folklore, music, proverbs and religious practices of the Haitian people, ignored by the nineteenth-century intellectual elite: 'We have no chance of being ourselves unless we repudiate no part of our ancestral heritage. And indeed this heritage for eight-tenths of us is a gift from Africa.' Most contemporary Caribbean literature in French has been written under the influence of such formulations. In Haiti itself *La Revue indigène* (founded 1927) was a significant forum for such work, and it was the novelist and poet Jacques Roumain (1907–44) who founded the *Bureau d'ethnologie* in 1941.

In 1931 Léon Laleau wrote a poem, 'Trahison', which contained these lines:

> And this despair, equal to no other,
> for taming with words from France
> this heart which came to me from Senegal.

The dilemma – Africa with the words of France – is analogous to that faced by English-speaking West Indian writers, but Laleau's despair quickly gave way to an anger and assertion which have generally had little time for the meditative ironies of Naipaul or Walcott; whether in the famous collection *Pigments* (1937) by Léon-Gontran Damas (Guyane, 1912–78) with its absolute rejection of everything European; or in Carl Brouard (Haiti, 1902–65) already (in 'Nostalgie', 1927) writing of Africa as home. These works contain the language and sentiments of *négritude*. Although the word itself was only coined in 1939 by Césaire, the ideas themselves came to fruition in Paris in the early 1930s, stimulated by the meetings of French Caribbean and French African writers. The three great monuments to this collaboration are Leopold Senghor's influential anthology of black Caribbean and African poetry, *La nouvelle poésie nègre et malgache de langue française* (1948; The New Black and Malagasy Poetry in the French Language), the periodical *Présence Africaine* (founded 1947), and the extraordinary essays on the politics and psychology of colonialism and decolonization,

Peau noir, masques blancs (1952; *Black Skin, White Masks*, New York, 1967) and *Les damnés de la terre* (1961; *The Wretched of the Earth,* London, 1967) by the Martiniquan Frantz Fanon (1925–61).

But the great poem of *négritude* is *Cahier d'un retour au pays natal* (1939; *Return to my Native Land,* London, 1969) by Aimé Césaire (Martinique, b. 1913). In 1942 Suzanne Césaire wrote: 'Martiniquan poetry will be cannabalistic or it will be nothing.' *Cahier* is fully cannibalistic: savage in its anger at imperialism, violent in its wrenching of French verse form and syntax. The poem begins by invoking in blistering prose poetry the poverty and despair of colonial Martinique. Soon the poet finds his voice

> We shall speak. We shall sing. We shall shout. Full voice, great voice, you shall be our good and our guide

and begins his hymn to blackness:

> my negritude is not a stone,
> nor deafness flung out against the clamour of the day
> my negritude is not a white speck of dead water on the dead eye of the earth
> my negritude is neither tower nor cathedral

Négritude is the dialectical opposite of white racialism; not a black racialism by rather an acceptance and affirmation of the identity of blacks as colonized peoples. Fanon puts it well:

> The white man… desires the world and wants it for himself alone. He considers himself predestined to rule the world. He has made it useful to himself. But there are values which do not submit to his rule. Like a sorcerer I steal from the white man a certain world which he cannot identify.

So, in direct opposition to the colonial impulse, Césaire celebrates:

> … those who have never invented anything
> those who never explored anything
> those who never tamed anything
> those who gave themselves up to the essence of all things
> ignorant of surfaces but struck by the movement of all things
> free of the desire to tame but familiar with the play of the world.

The doctrines of *négritude* have been elaborated most extensively by the Senegalese poet Leopold Senghor. Césaire, meanwhile, has continued writing against colonialism in his poetry and plays, and in his lyrical essay *Discours sur le colonialisme* (1955; *Discourse on Colonialism*, New York, 1972).

While the poets of the 1930s were speaking with power and grandiloquence, the novelists were involved in the sort of documentary investigations that have their equivalents at this time in most parts of the continent. René Maran (Martinique, 1887–1960) had already written what has been called the first novel of *négritude*, *Batouala* (1921: *Batouala*, New York, 1972); but Jacques Roumain initiated a tradition of writing about the realities of Haitian proletariat and peasant life that culminated in the work of Jacques Stéphen Alexis (1922–61), killed leading an unsuccessful invasion of Duvalier's Haiti. Roumain's most important novels are *La montagne ensorcelée* (1931; The Enchanted Mountain) and *Gouverneurs de la rosée* (1944; *Masters of the Dew*, London, 1978). Alexis's masterpiece is *Compère Général Soleil* (1955; Old General Sun). Other prose writers within this tradition include the Haitian Philippe Thoby-Marcelin (1904–75) (*Canapé Vert*, 1944; *Canapé Vert*, New York, 1944; *le Crayon de dieu*, 1951; *The Pencil of God*, London, 1952), the Martiniquan Joseph Zobel (b. 1915) (*La rue cases-nègres*, 1950; *Black Shack Alley*, New York, 1980), and the Guadeloupian Simone Schwartz-Bart (b. 1938) (*Pluie et vent sur télumée miracle*, 1972; *The Bridge of Beyond*, London, 1975).

The connection between politics and literature, always close in the Caribbean, has been especially so in the French-speaking areas. Roumain founded the Haitian Communist Party in 1934 and Césaire has for many years been a Deputy for Martinique to the French National Assembly – first as a Communist and then (after 1956) as a member of an independent revolutionary party. More recently, the exiled Haitian poet René Depestre (b. 1927) has, like the Uruguayan Mario Benedetti, expressed his support for the Cuban revolution by living and working in Cuba, and is now writing in Spanish as well as French. His early work in French remains notable; his recent *Poète à Cuba* (1976; Poet in Cuba) could prove to be one of the central intellectual and poetic works of the contemporary Caribbean.   PH

Further Reading: A.J. Arnold, *Modernism and Negritude; The Poetry and Poetics of Aimé Césaire* (Cambridge, Mass., 1981); G. R. Coulthard, *Race and Colour in Caribbean Literature* (Oxford, 1962); J. Dash, *Haiti and the United States: National Stereotypes and the Literary Imagination* (London, 1988); N. Garrett, *The Renaissance of Haitian Poetry* (Paris, 1963)

Amerindian music

In the high civilization areas of both Mexico and Peru, much more complex instruments were in vogue before AD 1000 than in 1500. Among archaeological instruments excavated at *c*. AD 1000 sites in Tabasco and Veracruz (east coastal Mexico), clay multiple flutes of three or four pipes document harmonies not yet known by contemporary Europeans; the pipes blown from a single mouthpiece sounded chords such as f#–a–c^1–e^1, f#–a–c^1–d^1, and f#–a–bb–e^1. Tabasco archaeological instruments included also 'goiter' flutes, the protuberance at the neck of the single vertical tube serving as an oscillating air chamber that changed the sound to a reedy quality. The most complex archaeological instruments excavated at Peruvian coastal sites are Nazca clay pan pipes of as many as thirteen tubes. The adjacent tubes often sound microtone intervals. The cane panpipes still played in highland Peru require large breath supplies. Fortunately dwellers in the high altitudes of the Lake Titicaca area have long been adapted physically to their conditions, and have large lung capacity.

Vast cultural differences separated the less privileged Taino islanders met in the West Indies by Columbus during his four voyages (1492–3, 1498, 1502) from the more sophisticated mainlanders subdued by Cortés (Aztecs, 1521) and Pizarro (Incas, 1533). Nonetheless, all but a few Amerindians met by first-generation European explorers resembled each other in possessing drums, rattles, and other instruments to which they sang and danced.

The Aztecs' favourite pair of percussion instruments, each emitting two pitches, were the *huehuetl*, an upright barrel-shaped wooden drum covered at the top with animal skin and played with the bare hands; and the *teponaztli*, a horizontal cylinder wooden slit-drum, the two slabs of which (emitting pitches a third or fourth apart) were struck with rubber-tipped mallets. To enhance power, the blood of sacrificial human victims was poured into *teponaztli* interiors on important state occasions.

In addition to drums, the Incas favoured sexually significant vertical flutes and cane or clay panpipes joined in vertical rows. Although not addicted to human sacrifice as were the Aztecs, the Incas painted their drums vermilion to enhance their power. Because eight was the most powerful number and size mattered, Inca men played eight large drums at accessions or at victory celebrations. Women played small concave hand drums for less imposing calendar observances.

Musical perfection counted so heavily in Aztec rituals that a drummer who missed a beat was summarily withdrawn from the ensemble and sacrificed to the offended deity. Training of the harshest kind forced Aztec youth in the *calmécac* ('seminary') to memorize lengthy sung narratives recounting Aztec cosmology and history. Men dominated bloody Aztec rituals. But at the Inca capital of Cuzco, maidens under eighteen years old provided musically high-pitched solace for warriors returning from battle in the four corners of the New World's largest pre-Columbian empire.

The earliest Amerindian melodies published anywhere were five Tupinambá chants included in Jean de Léry's *Histoire d'un voyage faict en la Terre dv Bresil* (Geneva, 1585). A Calvinist visitor to the area of Rio de Janeiro in 1557–8, Léry, long after returning to Europe, certified having heard one of the five melodies sung to texts praising a beautiful bird of yellow plumage (*Canidé-iouue*), another in praise of a large succulent fish. The remaining three enter Léry's chapter 16 ('What can be called religion among the Brazilian Savages'). He heard them at a ceremony gathering 500 or 600 Tupinambá every third or fourth year. They repeated one chant of ten notes in a gradual crescendo lasting more than fifteen minutes. The next melody of fourteen notes covering a range of a fifth served as a refrain repeated intermittently during a three hour men's circle dance. Women never joined this dance. To instill valour wizards leaped about blowing tobacco smoke into the dancers' nostrils. All Amerindians, wherever met by the first Europeans, used music and dancing in religious rituals designed to serve not as a mere entertainment but as appeasement of supernatural powers.

Tupinambás in Brazil, Caribs in the Antilles, Aztecs and Mixtecs in central Mexico, all mixed their sanguinary rites with music that terrorized such early European arrivals as Hans Staden, Jean de Léry, and Bernal Díaz del Castillo and his companions. On the other hand, Spanish writers such as Toribio Motolonía and Diego Durán greatly lauded ceremonial dances in Aztec courtyards performed in perfect time by scores of feather-adorned workers to the beat of *huehuetl* and *teponaztli*. *Canteres en idioma mexicano*, a Mexican National Libarary manuscript dating from 1551 to 1563 that contains Aztec language songs with interspersed *teponaztli* patterns, gives valuable clues to the drumming sequences that were in vogue as late as a generation after the fall of the Aztec capital.

What typified high culture expressions both before and after European contact differs considerably from Venezuelan and Brazilian tribal traits documented by 1911–13 sound recordings analysed by

Bolivian Indians playing traditional instruments: pututu horn, panpipes and drum

together equal-sized elements as if in a long necklace of equal-sized beads.

More recently (1975), the Hungarian Academy of Sciences has published a large collection of Nambicuara Indian melodies collected in the Brazilian Mato Grosso by Lajos Boglár and analyzed by István Halmos that opens new vistas with its mention of globular nose flutes and intervallic series not known among the tribes familiar to Hornbostel. They rightly concluded that South American Indian music studies of the type concluded by them and by Isabel Aretz, Luis Felipe Ramón y Rivera and their disciples at the Instituto de Investigación Etnomusicológica y Folklórica at Caracas continue offering ever new insights into huge neglected areas.   RMS

Further Reading: *Cantares en idioma mexicano. Songs of the Aztecs,* translated from Nahuatl with an introduction and commentary by John Bierhorst (Stanford, 1985); R. Stevenson, *Music in Mexico: a Historical Survey* (New York, 1952 and 1971); *The Music of Peru: Aboriginal and Viceroyal Epochs* (Washington, DC, 1960); *Music in Aztec and Inca Territory* (Berkeley and Los Angeles, 1968 and 1976); 'Aztec Music', 'Maya Music', 'Inca Music' in *The New Grove Dictionary of Music and Musicians,* 20 vols. (London, 1980), I, 760–1; IX, 56–7; XI, 852–4; 'Aztec organography', *Inter-American Music Review,* vol. 9, no. 2 (1988), pp. 1–19.

Folk, popular and dance music

the ethnomusicological pioneer, Erich M. von Hornbostel. These twentieth-century recorded examples permitted his making the following oft-quoted generalizations concerning Venezuelan and Brazilian Indian style: so far as vocal timbre goes, singing gives the impression of the emphatic, entries are strongly accentuated, phrase beginnings are punctuated by strong exhaling, strong dynamic accents herald the first tone of each motive. A brief motive forms all the melody, its constant repetition the chant. Something severe and transcendental pervades all Indian chants. In the melodies, small descending intervals the approximate size of a minor third or major second abound. In dances, each quarter note is heavily accented, drumming never includes complex patterns but is always a steady uniform series of strikes sometimes not coordinated with the rhythm of the singing. Their music characteristically strings

Latin American folk music derives from three major sources: the indigenous Indian, the colonizing Hispanic, and the transported African. Elements from all three are found in many combinations within musical form, structure, genre, instrumentation, vocal and performing style and practice, melody, rhythm, metre, scale (i.e. all musical and extra-musical parameters). In most places there is fusion into culturally mixed forms. Areas where archaic features, traced to a particular source, have been retained, reveal the crucial role of the type of contact between peoples, local and national political and cultural history, the use and function of music and the people's aesthetic.

The Spanish used music in their efforts to Christainize the indigenous population and the result was far from uniform. According to the musicologist Gérard Béhague, Inca culture seems to have resisted

Quechua Indians, Cuzco area, Peru, playing violin, harp and quena

erosion rather better than Aztec culture: the former being influenced by the Hispanic, the latter mostly displaced. The result is a whole cycle of religious festivals, ostensibly Catholic, but with many native elements in music, dance and instrumentation accompanying the liturgical calendar of the Catholic Church. The most notable are the Carnival festivals which take place to mark the beginning of Lent in Brazil, Bolivia, the Caribbean area, northern Argentina and many other places. A whole body of folk song and dance is associated with such occasions, as are elaborate, ornate, highly decorated costumes (each of which have historical meaning).

While the structure of annual religious festivals may remain constant, the actual songs and dances performed within them show the changing taste of the participants in terms of genre, instrumentation and musical arrangement. The origin of such change is the city, for many participants will have returned to the country from urban areas bringing new popular songs with them, or will have migrated to the city taking their tradition with them. The Brazilian samba is most commonly associated with the annual Carnival in Rio de Janeiro for which working-class neighbourhood samba schools will prepare all year. It is also performed in the Capoeira (ritualized martial art) cult in Bahia and in other cults and rituals in north-eastern Brazil. Its specific local identity can be traced to distinctive drum patterns which reveal the different African ancestry of those involved, as do other aspects of performing practice. Many dramatic dances with a religious central subject involve the bringing together of Catholic saints with deities brought from West Africa as do 'Voodoo' in Haiti and Sawena possession cults in Cuba, Haiti, Jamaica, Trinidad and Brazil.

The development of many secular forms of music is traced back to the instrumentalists who accompa-

nied Cortés on his first expedition. They brought with them the first string instruments (lute, harp, violin, guitar) and the Indians made their own variants: the Andean *charango*, a hybrid lute–small guitar, with five pairs of strings which uses an armadillo shell as a resonating case; the *tres* and *cuatro* (small three- and four-stringed guitars); the *guitarrón*, a twenty-five-string guitar found in Mexico today, used originally as accompanying instrument to traditional sung poetry in Chile, *Canto a lo poeta* (Song in the manner of the poet), based on the Spanish *décima*. The verse structure of the *décima*, *glosa* and *copla* (with their prevailing syllabic line and stanza length and classic rhyme scheme – usually abbaac-cddc) is found in many countries, not only in folk forms accompanying events of the cycle of life (birth, courting, marriage, death) but also, for example, in the *canción mexicana*. Song forms derived from the early Renaissance *romance* are wide-spread, most purely in Colombia and Chile, with structural traces in Argentina and Ecuador, and most notably in the *corrido*, the typical ballad of the Mexican revolution, which was revived in the 1940s. Other folk songs such as *tonadas* (Chile and Argentina) and *estilos* (Argentina and Uruguay) have maintained Spanish literary forms as have many children's rhymes and songs, and Christmas songs which also show mestizo characteristics. The sung 'duel' using a variety of intricate forms is still found in Cuba, north-east Brazil, Chile, Argentina and Venezuela. Such forms have significant specific identifying traits generated by the particular cultural and political history of the area.

DANCES

Apart from dances associated with religious occasions, secular circle and couple dances are also found today, the former more often in collective, peasant, communal areas (reminding us that the sung text was originally inseparable from dance movement), the latter in villages, towns, and urban areas: the structure and forms relating to urban organization. Almost all important folk dances have their urban counterpart, for example the *huayno*, *yaraví* and *taquirari* in the Andean area: the major distinguishing features of the urban forms are to be found in details of performing practice and instrumentation foreign to rural tradition.

From the Peruvian colonial dance of the first half of the nineteenth century, the *zamacueca*, have evolved the *zamba* and the *cueca* which through usage have developed as separate dances. The *cueca* is a couple dance in which both partners hold and use a handkerchief: imitative of the courtship of cock and hen, it is performed with much regional variation in such features as movement of the handkerchief, fingersnapping and footwork. In Chile the *cueca* is the national dance, in Argentina it is known as the *chilena*, while in Peru the name was changed from *chilena* to *marinera* at the time of the War of the Pacific. A rhythmic feature of this dance and many others (such as the Venezuelan *joropo*, the Mexican *son* and *huapango*, for example, 'La Bamba') is what is termed the 'hemiola' effect when bars of 6/8 and 3/4 are either in simultaneous use by singer and in the accompaniment or alternating; this rhythmic pattern is not only found in Spanish music where it is thought to have originated, but also in African music in cross-rhythmic patterns of the drum.

Nineteenth-century salon dances (waltz, mazurka, contredanse, polka) were brought to Latin America, influencing and fusing with folk and popular forms, for example the Mexican *jarabe*, most pop-

ular at the time of the War of Independence, and later on typically performed by Mariachi ensembles. European and North American twentieth-century dances have appeared in hybrid forms in local dance halls, for example, the *samba-fox* , and *rumba-fox*. Cuba, of all Latin American countries, has been the source of many influential popular genres: the *habanera, danza cubana*, bolero, mambo, conga, cha-cha-cha, all of which have strong Afro-Cuban features in rhythm, syncopation, metre and dance movements. The Colombian *cumbia* is today danced all over the continent and it too exhibits many African features in its choreography, and its frequent call and response structure.

Most song texts reveal the cultural attitudes and beliefs of the people amongst whom they originated, and many are spontaneously or consciously, directly or indirectly vehicles for political and social comment: for example, the Peruvian *vals*, the Argentine tango, the Brazilian *samba-canção*, the pre- and post-revolutionary Cuban *son* and *guaracha* of Carlos Puebla.

One of the most renowned of all Latin American popular dances is the Argentine tango. Scholars debate the origin of the name *tango* , which may have been the name for a drum used by black slaves, and was perhaps later used to refer to locale, accompaniment and then the dance itself. Three types of tango are usually differentiated: the mainly instrumental *tango-milonga* played by orchestras in the 1920s; the romantic, melodic, vocalized *tango-romanza* of the same era; and the *tango-canción*. It is the latter which, like the singer who popularized it internationally, the authentic superstar Carlos Gardel (1890–1935), has come to symbolize the tango. The music of the dance brought together elements of folk and popular dances traced over the whole continent and beyond: the Andalusian tango, the Cuban *habanera*, the *milonga* of the River Plate area. Those who listened to its essentially sentimental and often pessimistic lyrics were the new immigrant population from all parts of Europe as well as the interior of Argentina. The tight choreographic structure, the mannerisms and movements of the dancing couple, the relationship between man and woman in the text have been related to the *compadrito* underworld culture of Buenos Aires and the stereotyped sex roles of that subculture – a subculture often evoked by tango lyrics.

The economic boom in the United States after 1945 stimulated much technological innovation (45 rpm and long-playing records, record players, radios); and the growth of the recording industry with its network of promoters and distributors, and the subsequent increase in the number of radio stations, had repercussions throughout the world which

The Beija Flor samba school taking part in the Rio de Janeiro Carnival. The samba schools mount floats for the procession, often spending a whole year in preparation.

407

Dancers at the Oruro carnival, Bolivia

were no less significant in Latin America than elsewhere. Latterly, there has been an increasing reliance on cassettes. From the beginning, popular musical forms have been produced locally in all countries: originally rock-and-roll had its own local imitators; today Argentina has its own 'rock nacional'. This, with the independent example of British punk, has also inspired original rock groups in Chile and Peru. Brazil has a strong rock tradition with an annual festival.

MUSIC AND POLITICS

Continental and national responses to the Cuban revolution and the activities of liberalizing governments promising much needed reforms in the 1960s influenced many musicians, who, because of their musical interests and political philosophy, were already involved in national folkloric movements, which were themselves sometimes encouraged by government economic and political policy, for example, the neo-folklore boom in Argentina in the 1950s and 1960s. The case of Chile is the most notable: here Violeta Parra (1917–67) and others travelled and collected rural folk songs and dances in the late 1950s, performing and teaching the material to urban audiences and, in the case of Parra, going on to write her own material in the folk idiom. This practical research influenced the next generation of musicians which included Violeta Parra's own children, Angel

Carlos Gardel, Argentina's most successful tango singer

The irresistible rise of the tango

The tango, Argentina's most celebrated export, won worldwide fame (and notoriety) in 1913–14. It had originated some time around 1880 in the *arrabales* (poor outer districts) of Buenos Aires – a spontaneous popular fusion of the Spanish-Cuban *habanera*, the local Argentina *milonga*, and the dance traditions of Buenos Aires' then dwindling black community. From 1900 its musical forms developed fast, with the bandoneon (a German-made relative of the accordion) becoming the key instrument in most tango bands.

Given its definitely low-life origins, the dance was at first rejected by the upper and middle classes in Argentina, but this snobbish attitude did not survive the tango's sudden blaze of international glory. In 1913 (later labelled 'the tango year' by H.G. Wells) the dance became immensely popular in Europe, from where it soon spread to North America. (It later came to have a considerable following in Japan.) By this time the originally somewhat fierce steps favoured in the Buenos Aires *arrabales* had been tamed into an aceptable dance-floor form – although this should not be confused with the thoroughly distorted version danced by Rudolph Valentino in the film *The Four Horsemen of the Apocalypse* (1921).

In Argentina the international triumph of the tango paved the way for its 'golden age' (roughly 1920 to 1950), a period which saw the proliferation of highly professional bands and distinguished singers. Around 1920 the tango developed into a form of popular song, brilliantly perfected by the baritone Carlos Gardel (1890–1935), now considered the supreme figure in the entire tango story. Tango moved into the cinema, with both musicals and comedies. Gardel himself was taken up by Hollywood, becoming a star in Hollywood and France in films made by Paramount between 1931 and 1935. For a while the dance was overshadowed by the song, but it revived once more in the mid-1930s, a factor that ensured it a further lease of life as the dominant component in Argentine popular taste. Only in the 1950s, in the face of challenges from Argentine folk music and international pop music, did its hold on public affection significantly weaken.

Then the 1980s saw a moderate revival of international interest, accounted for in part by the European popularity of the 'avant-garde' musician Astor Piazzolla and by the spectacular triumph of the music-and-dance show *Tango Argentino* in New York (1985–6), in many North American and European cities, and in London (1991). It is unlikely that there will ever be a last tango in Buenos Aires.

and Isabel; it was a bridge between the older generation of popular poets and the new generation of what became known as *nueva canción* ('new song'). Student groups started, many of them involved in the struggle for university reform, and their continental political philosophy resulted in their choosing Indian names (as, for example, Inti-Illimani) and drawing on the music of the whole continent. Their use of indigenous instruments (the bamboo *quena* or flute, panpipes, drums, guitar variants such as the *charango, tres* and *cuatro*), African percussion instruments (güiro, maracas, claves), their professional concern with performance, their smooth singing style and harmonization, exhibit a new fusion of folk and popular and some of their music (especially the longer pieces, the *cantatas*) is influenced by classical form.

Chile is a prominent case as much for the variety of music, the evidence of supportive festivals and a distribution network, as for the large number of musicians involved, who saw themselves as following a historical tradition, and who, as musicians, actively supported the election of Salvador Allende as president and his Popular Unity coalition as government. Following the military coup of 11 September 1973, Víctor Jara, the singer and theatre director, was brutally tortured and murdered, and other cultural activists tortured and imprisoned, and forced into exile. Their music, until the late 1980s, was one of exile, solidarity and resistance. Similar music and musicians have existed in Uruguay and Argentina (with most of them forced into exile by military governments) and do exist in other countries (Mexico, Brazil); occasionally International Festivals are organized, as in Cuba in 1967 and Mexico in 1982. In Brazil, the *Bossa Nova* of the 1950s was later linked to the Jovem Guarda movement which re-vitalized

Capoeira dancing, Bahia, Brazil

popular music with its new style of fluid subdued singing, integrating with harmonic, melodic and rhythmic elements. *Salsa*, rooted in Cuban *son*, Dominican *merengue* and Puerto Rican *plena*, filtered and fused with the ever-evolving Latin bigband traditions of North and South America, and is now popular all over the continent – mostly as a dance, though with topical comment in Cuba (through Los Van Van and Orchestra Reve) and with a political input in the case of the Panamanian star Ruben Blades.

JF

Further Reading: Entries in the *New Grove Dictionary of Music and Musicians,* 20 vols. (London, 1980) by continent, ethnic group, country, song, dance and instrument; S. Collier, *The Life, Music and Times of Carlos Gardel* (Pittsburgh, 1986); A. Guillermoprieto, *Samba* (London, 1990); J. Jara, *Victor, an Unfinished Song* (London, 1983); C. A. Perrone, *Masters of Contemporary Brazilian Song, MPB 1965–1985* (Austin, Texas, 1989). *See also* the following journals: *Latin American Music Review* (Austin, Texas, 1980–), and *Popular Music Journal* (Cambridge), Vol. 6, No. 2 (May 1987), Vol. 7, No. 1 (January 1988), Vol. 8, No. 1 (January 1989), Vol. 9, No. 3 (October 1990).

Caribbean music

The musical life of the Caribbean islands is immensely rich and varied and much of it is similar to that found on the main continent of Latin America. The traditions of the African peoples who were brought in slavery to the sugar plantations have mixed with those of the colonizing groups from Spain, France and Britain and the result is a complex cultural spectrum. None of the aboriginal peoples survive and their cultures have been preserved only in archaeological remains and in certain elements of folklore.

African and Christian rituals have blended to produce cults such as Vodún (Voodoo) in Haiti, Santeria, Abakué, Congó and Lucumí in Cuba, Kumina in Jamaica, and Shango in Trinidad: Shango, for example, combines Nigerian Yoruba with Catholic and Baptist beliefs. Such cults are of particular importance in rural areas but are not only found there. They have evolved by combining similar or compatible elements from different belief systems: cult leaders, animal sacrifice, trance and spirit possession (of people or of one of the drums which play a fundamental role in the ritual), and worship of saints (which are typically an amalgamation of African deities with Christian saints) may be found alongside baptismal rites, Bibles, candles and crosses. African

Bob Marley

identity, wear their hair in dreadlocks (tiny plaits) and smoke *ganja* (marijuana) as part of their religious practice, serving Jah (God), his representative on earth (Emperor Haile Selassie of Ethiopia) and closely reading the Bible. Their music, *reggae*, whose song texts transmit their philosophy, combines Afro-American and European elements and uses equipment familiar to modern rock groups. Their social significance was underlined by the musical intervention of its late representative, the internationally famous Bob Marley, in the political life of the island, and his state funeral in May 1981. *Soca* has emerged from a fusion of reggae and other Caribbean traditions with rock. In the French Antilles *zouk*, derived from *biguine*, *compas* and *cadence-lypso*, has had considerable influence, extending to the rest of the Caribbean, Europe and Africa.

A whole multitude of continentally influential dances have orginated in Cuba, including the rumba, the bolero, the cha-cha-cha, as have the *son* with its distinctive syncopated form, and the ironically humorous and lively *guarachas* and *guajiras* (especially those of Carlos Puebla whose four-man groups include a *marímbula* player). A host of other forms are performed by members of the *Trova*, the *Nueva Trova* (the self-critical song of the revolution) and by jazz and other bands. Their music embraces internationally contemporary trends in sound as well as the whole Cuban tradition.   JF

features which permeate this and many other forms of music-making are leader-chorus alternation, body gestures, the movements and choreography of dances and the rhythms played by the various percussion instruments, such as drums (in various sizes and shapes), shakers and scrapers (these instruments vary in shape, size and materials, and are known by local names on different islands). The popular European misconception conveyed by the term 'black-magic' persists because many cult leaders practise folk-medicine and healing rites that outsiders are rarely permitted to observe.

The Spanish origin of music in rural areas (identified through elements of structure, form, scale, harmony) can be found in funeral songs, music for such festivals as Cruz de Mayo, and in forms of *décima* singing (such as *punto* in Cuba). The Spanish also brought string instruments and local variants have evolved; for example, the *tres* and *cuatro* (small three- and four-string guitars), or the three-stringed bamboo violin in Jamaica. The *tres* is used with the *tambora* drum to accompany the national dance of the Dominican Republic, the *merengue*.

The Trinidadian calypso (as sung, for example, by the Mighty Sparrow), popular throughout the Caribbean, forms part of the repertory of steel bands. New texts, which are typically social commentaries, are constantly re-set to established melodies and rhythmic forms. In Trinidad and Jamaica there also exists a separate musical tradition of the East Indian community (Hindu and Muslim).

In Jamaica, the Rastafarians are a significant religious group who foster black consciousness, African

Classical music and major composers

THE COLONIAL PERIOD

The cultivation of classical or 'serious' music, as opposed to folk or popular music, in Latin America began in the sixteenth century. European composers were appointed at that time to serve as chapel-masters in the churches that proliferated throughout the newly founded colonial cities. They produced sacred music, which followed the styles of the European masters, to accompany the celebration of the divine offices of the Church. It remained attached to European styles and methods of composition until long after the Spanish and Portuguese colonial period, unlike folk song which slowly revealed traces of a mestizo idiom as the colonial period progressed.

The founding of the first centre for music education by the Franciscan, Pedro de Gante, in Mexico, only five years after Cortés's conquest in 1519, set in motion an uninterrupted stream of developments. Significant achievements soon followed in the fields of composition, performance, and the manufacture of European instruments. Manuscript copies of the most outstanding examples of European music and the works of New World composers were made permanently available to the main cathedrals. Simultaneously, distinguished choir-masters, who were committed to the development of vocal and instrumental ensembles and qualified to perform with a repertoire, were appointed to the cathedrals. Music-printing quickly followed in 1556, when an Ordinary of the Mass containing chants in Gregorian notation was published in Mexico. The Spanish crown conferred a variety of musical privileges upon cities throughout its colonies, while Portugal provided for the early establishment of music instruction through the Conservatório dos Negros, a school run by the Jesuits in the sugar plantations of Santa Cruz, near Rio de Janeiro.

The twentieth-century Brazilian composer, Heitor Villa-Lobos

Among the treasures of early Church music in Mexico, the works of Hernando Franco (1532–85) certainly bespeak a composer of indisputable technical competence. His music partakes of the styles of his outstanding European contemporaries: Palestrina, Lassus, and Victoria. Franco was born in Europe, like most of the early composers appointed to the chapel-masterships of colonial churches. His career developed in Mexico City and Guatemala. From his works, as from those of his contemporaries such as Juan de Lienas (dates unknown) also active in Mexico, many traditions evolved that became significant for a host of native masters who succeeded them in the musical posts available in Hispanic America.

One of these masters was Gutierrez Fernández-Hidalgo (c.1553–1620) who held posts at cathedrals in Bogotá, Colombia, and Chuquisaca (now Sucre, Bolivia). Fernández-Hidalgo was one of the most outstanding Spanish Church composers of the late sixteenth-century.

Composers following Fernández-Hildalgo in the seventeenth and eighteenth centuries included Francisco López Capillas (c.1615–74) in Puebla and Mexico City; Juan de Araujo (c.1646–1712), José de Orejón (c.1705–65), Tomás Torrejón y Velasco (1644–1728) in Peru; Esteban Salas (1725–1803) in Cuba; and José Mauricio Nunes Garcia (1767–1830) in Brazil. These composers were landmarks in the development of Church music. Their achievements were also supported by the active participation of many other skilful composers and by a musical life that, in many of the colonies, remained at all times open to the latest influences and achievements of Europe.

This period, sometimes known as the 'American baroque', is recognized for its splendid contributions in the fields of architecture, sculpture and poetry, as well as for its music. Along with the literary achievements of Sor Juana Inés de la Cruz, Mexico saw the development of a composer, Antonio de Salazar (Mexico City cathedral chapel-master, 1688–1715), who set some of her poems to music. While Aleijandinho (Antônio Francisco Lisboa) accomplished impressive sculptures in Minas Gerais, Brazil, Joaquin Emerico Lobo de Mesquita (c.1740–1805), one of a host of musicians who were affiliated to religious brotherhoods in that province, produced outstanding sacred compositions.

This predominance of sacred music was due to the centralization of musical activities around the Spanish and Portuguese Church, but towards the end of the colonial period, secular forms developed. Tomás Torrejón y Velasco contributed the oldest surviving example of an opera in Latin America, *La Púrpura de la Rosa*. This opera utilized a text of the Spanish dramatist Calderón de la Barca, and was produced in

Lima in 1701 to celebrate the eighteenth birthday of King Philip V of Spain.

The *villancico* was another form of secular music that became increasingly cultivated by professional composers of the colonial period. This particular form, introduced by the Spaniards in the early stages of colonization, found its first fertile soil for New World development in the sphere of folk music. Soon musical examples showing traces of Indian and African influences were being sung by the populace. Shortly thereafter, the *villancico* reached the level of serious music. Settings were for two, three and four voices, as well as for solo voice with instrumental accompaniment. These compositions were similar in their technical approach to those of the Spanish composers of the period. Yet, at times, the use of certain rhythmic and melodic devices and the use of texts in local dialects linked them to either Indian or Afro-American traditions in music.

Other forms of secular music found their way into the repertory of serious composition by the end of the eighteenth century. One was the *contradanza* which, in Cuba, was the source for the development of forms such as the *habanera* and the *danzón*. Another was the *modinha*, a love song in two parts with a repetition of the first section at the end, popular in Brazil and Portugal alike. During the nineteenth century, the *modinha* was strongly influenced by Italian opera, especially when it was cultivated by composers as an art form.

ROMANTICISM

Musical Romanticism in Latin America developed side by side with political independence. The stage of music development at this particular moment in Latin America was uneven. Some countries were at a pinnacle of their musical lives. Others had entered a phase of depression in which standards of performance had declined notoriously and composition appeared to be confined to weak imitations of Italian opera, to patriotic hymns, and to salon dances. As the New World disengaged itself from Spanish and Portuguese hegemony, other foreign influences entered the picture. For example, the Parisian tastes that ruled fashion, architecture, and home furnishings were matched by a wide repertoire of French dances found in upper-class households. By the end of the century, these dances had been assimilated by the mass of the people. Thus, local replicas of the mazurka, minuet, polka, waltz, tarantella, and contredanse became a part of the popular heritage.

Many of these European dances also reached the repertoire of concert music in the form of short virtuoso pieces. Such pieces were written especially for the piano, by composers who seemed strongly influenced by Chopin, Liszt, and European Romantics of lesser stature. Outstanding among these were Ricardo Castro (1864–1907) and Filipe Villanueva (1862–93) in Mexico; Ignacio Cervantes (1847–1905) and Nicolás Ruiz Espadero (1832–90) in Cuba; Leopoldo Miguez (1850–1902) and Henrique Oswald (1852–1931) in Brazil; José Maria Ponce de León (1846–82) in Colombia; Felipe Larrázabal (1816–73) in Venezuela; Amancio Alcorta (1805–62) and Juan Bautista Alberdi (1810–84) in Argentina; and Federico Guzmán (1837–85) in Chile.

Yet, in spite of the abundance of virtuoso instrumental music usually derived from the salon dances of the period, opera in the Italian style dominated art music throughout Latin America in the decades after independence. Elegant opera houses were built in the capital cities. The aristocracy gathered to hear the works of Paisiello, Pergolesi, Rossini and other Italian masters, or those of native composers who imitated the styles of their European counterparts – sometimes to the extent of setting their librettos in Italian. Carlos Gomes (1836–96) was Latin America's foremost opera composer of the Romantic period. Born in Brazil, he belonged to a host of over fifty more or less serious composers active in that country between 1830 and the end of the century.

Together with the production of opera and instrumental music by the composers of this period, nineteenth-century Latin America saw the rise to stardom of many of its first vocalists and virtuoso instrumental performers. Opera theatres in the New World received with frenzied enthusiasm the performances of such outstanding Italian prima donnas as Patti and Tetrazzini. Local examples included Luisa Pujol (1857–1907), the first Argentine soprano to sing at La Scala; Rosa Negri (1862–92), the aristocratic Chilean soprano; and Angela Peralta (1845–83) who starred in the first performance of numerous Mexican operas. String virtuosity was also carried to a high level of prestige by two Cuban mulattoes, Brinidis de Salas (1852–1911) and José White (1836–1918). Pianists were represented by virtuosos of high calibre in various countries, as exemplified by the internationally recognized pianist/composer, Louis Moreau Gottschalk, from New Orleans, who frequently toured and even lived in Latin America. In Cuba, the composer Ignacio Cervantes was also a concert pianist and was considered a rival to von Bülow and the young Paderewsky. No less prestigious were Honorio Alarcón (1859–1920), the Colombian winner of international piano contests in Leipzig and Paris; Tomás León (1826–93) from Mexico; or the world-famous Teresa Carreño (1853–1917) from Venezuela, who was praised by Brahms, Liszt, and Grieg.

NATIONALISM

Before the nineteenth century was over, Latin America started developing musical styles that were more concerned with local and national traditions. Composers began to search in their own folk music for self-assertion and identification. They started drawing from traditional songs, dances, rhythmic and melodic materials. They applied these folk elements to the diverse forms and aesthetics of European music current at the time. The incorporation of folk and popular arts into the serious musical life of each country was accelerated by the rapid rise of the middle class and increased participation by the native sectors of the society.

Nationalism in music developed before the turn of the century in works by Ignacio Cervantes, whose twenty *danzas* represent a parallel in Cuban music to Greig's Norwegian Dances, and in works by Alberto Nepomuceno (1864–1920), author of a *Serie Brasileira* based on folk themes and rhythms from his native Brazil, completed in 1871. Such pioneering works were soon to influence other composers. One of them was the Mexican, Manuel Ponce (1886–1948), who received international recognition with his early popular song, *Estrellita*. He later became involved in developing a national idiom in composition, thus leading the way for his compatriots, Silvestre Revueltas (1899–1940) and Carlos Chávez (1899–1978).

These composers were only matched in their prestige in the years following the First World War by Heitor Villa-Lobos (1887–1959), a Brazilian who achieved a position of equality with the most outstanding European masters of his time.

Many Latin American composers participated in the early development of musical nationalism. Two composers from Cuba, Amadeo Roldán (1900–39) and Alejandro García Caturla (1906–40) depicted characteristic features of Caribbean-evolved Afro-American traditions. Other composers' works were nourished by both French Impressionism and the folk traditions of their own countries, as was evidenced in the music of Vicente E. Sojo (1887–1974) from Venezuela, Alberto Williams (1862–1952) from Argentina, Eduardo Fabini (1882–1950) from Uruguay, Pedro Humberto Allende (1885–1959) from Chile, and Guillermo Uribe–Holguín (1880–1971) from Colombia.

Until the time of the Second World War, composers in Latin America remained largely attached to the resources embodied in their folk music. Following in the steps of Villa–Lobos, Brazil produced such outstanding examples as Oscar Lorenzo Fernandez (1897–1948), Francisco Mignone (b. 1897), and Camargo Guarnieri (b. 1907). The disciples of Carlos Chávez in Mexico followed the nationalistic approach of their master in their early compositions. Outstanding among them is Blas Galindo (b. 1910). Outside Brazil and Mexico, national trends in serious music were perpetuated by many Latin American composers. Most of them were simultaneously open to the latest methods of composition developed in Europe, and allowed the traditions of their own countries to permeate their styles, for example, Juan José Castro (1895–1968) and Carlos López Buchardo (1881–1948) in Argentina; Carlos Isamitt (1887–1974) in Chile; Juan Bautista Plaza (1898–1965) in Venezuela; Antonio Maria Valencia (1902–52) in Colombia; José Ardévol (1908–81) and Harold Gramatges (b. 1918) in Cuba.

CONTEMPORARY STYLES

Nevertheless, exceptions to such nationalistic trends also existed. Some were sustained by the prevailing cosmopolitan cultural environments surrounding them, and others, by their deliberate opposition to the use of folk materials because of the limitations that these allegedly imposed on their styles. These

Alberto Ginastera

composers felt that their work could be strengthened by a freer handling of the aesthetics and methods of composition originating in Europe, which they considered as representative of their own heritage as classical composers, as folk music was of the ethnic sectors. One of these composers was the Mexican Julián Carrillo (1875–1965), author and practitioner of a theory called *Sonido Trece*, involvling the use of quarter, eighth and even smaller fractions of a tone. Another was Juan Carlos Paz (1897–1972) in Argentina, who pioneered the development of Schoenberg's twelve-tone serialism in Latin America. Domingo Santa Cruz (1899–1987) from Chile was yet another composer of music which was aloof from any folkloristic influences.

By the late 1940s, a number of composers who had either sponsored a type of self-imposed nationalism, or had been strongly influenced by the folk traditions of their countries, began gradually moving away from such tendencies. Simultaneously, a new generation emerged of musicians free from any need of deliberate borrowing from native music. They were plainly aware of their belonging to cultures that owed as much to Europe as to their own native environments. Musically, this trend is reflected in the works of a host of composers throughout Latin America, who come from areas either rich or poor in indigenous traditions, and who are all committed to a wide range of methods of composition. The work of the outstanding Argentine composer, Alberto Ginastera (1916–83), eloquently exemplifies the case of a composer who, after an early period of deliberate nationalism, moved to a position more concerned with the universal values of music than with forcing folk devices into classical composition.

The same historical forces that led Ginastera away from nationalism also stimulated similar developments in other composers of the same generation: Roque Cordero (b. 1917) from Panama, Claudio Santoro (1919–89) from Brazil, Alfonso Letelier (b. 1912) from Chile, Blas Galindo (b. 1910) from Mexico and Jorge Sarmientos (b. 1933) from Guatemala. Others of this generation of composers were only slightly touched by the spell of nationalism, for example, Juan Orrego-Salas (b. 1919) from Chile and Hector Tosar (b. 1923) from Uruguay.

The stylisic developments of a sequence of such musicians succeeded in putting Latin America on the map of world contemporary music by the early 1960s. Competent use of the most advanced techniques and methods of composition characterized this generation of Latin American composers. Atonality, serialism, aleatoric and electronic methods are used together with advances originating in composers' lack of dogmatism regarding the techniques employed.

These advances were employed by a group of Mexican composers who were stimulated by the cosmopolitan approach of the Spanish-born (and later naturalized-Mexican) composer, Rodolfo Halffter (1900–87). Manuel Enríquez (b. 1926), Jorge de Elias (b. 1939), Hector Quintanar (b. 1936), and Mario Lavista (b.1943) share in redirecting their country's music away from the nationalistic trends that had prevailed until the early 1960s. Their use of improvization as a tool of composition, of electronic sounds, and of new performance techniques employing traditional instruments, results in replacement of conventional notation methods by a variety of 'graphisms' involving unprecendented symbols.

A number of other Latin American composers also utilize these techniques. In Chile, Gustavo Becerra (b. 1925), León Schidlowsky (b. 1931) and Alejandro Guarello (b. 1951) follow paths of evolution similar to those of the aforementioned Mexicans, while Juan Amenábar (b. 1922) and José V. Asuar (b. 1933) engage in creating electronic music. In Brazil, Edino Krieger (b. 1928), Marlos Nobre (b. 1939), Willi Correa de Oliveira (b. 1938), and Jorge Antunes (b. 1942) support similar advanced positions in music – especially when compared to that of Oswaldo Lacerda (b. 1928) who remains attached to a very subtle nationalism applied to a modern idiom. In Argentina, Ginastera's progressive stand in composition is emulated by a few of his contemporaries, for example, Roberto García-Morillo (b. 1911) and Roberto Caamaño (b. 1923), and a host of younger composers. Notable among these are Mario Davidowsky (b. 1934), Mauricio Kagel (b. 1931), Antonio Tauriello (b. 1931), Alcides Lanza (b. 1929), Gerardo Gandini (b. 1936), Armando Krieger (b. 1940); in the field of electronic composition, Francisco Kröpfl (b. 1928); and Astor Piazzolla (b. 1921), who has succeeded in incorporating the tango on to the most sophisticated level of art music. In Uruguay, the Italian-born Guido Santórsola (b. 1919) and Hector Tosar give a forward impluse to their compatriots León Biriotti (b. 1929), Antonio Mastrogiovanni (b. 1936) and Sergio Cervetti (b. 1941), conquering unprecedented international recognition for Uruguayan music.

Beyond Mexico, Chile, Brazil, Argentina, and Uruguay, other Latin American countries are also making a name for themselves in modern music. These countries are characterized by either individual exponents, for example, Ecuador by Mesías Maiguaschca (b. 1938) and Bolivia by Alberto Villalpando (b. 1940), or by cohesive groups of composers sharing the same progressive views within a variety of approaches. The latter is the case for Peru if we consider the nature and quality of the achievements of a host of composers trained by the German-born

Rodolfo Holzmann (b. 1910), for example, Enrique Iturriaga (b. 1918), Celso Garrido-Lecca (b. 1926), Enrique Pinilla (b. 1927), Cesar Bolaños (b. 1931) and Edgar Valcarcel (b. 1932). It also applies in Colombia and Venezuela. In the former, a very subtle concern for musical nationalism still persists in the works of Luis Antonio Escobar (b. 1925), while Fabio González Zuleta (b. 1920) adheres to serialism, Jesus Pinzón (b. 1928) and Blas Emilio Atehortua (b. 1933) represent the avant-garde. A similar pattern is encountered in Venezuela where the leading figure up until his death was Antonio Estevez (1916–88), who, after an evolution that took him from an early nationalism to electronic music, worked side by side with some who perpetuate musical folklorism and some representing more cosmopolitan approaches – composers such as Rhazes Hernández López (b. 1918), Alfredo del Mónaco (b. 1938), and Ricardo Lorenz (b. 1961).

In the Caribbean area, both Cuba and Puerto Rico are contributors to the mainstream of recent developments with a variety of creative achievements as important as those of the rest of Latin America. Three outstanding Cubans living in the United States, Aurelio de la Vega (b. 1925) Julian Orbón (1925–91), and Tania León (b. 1944) share international recognition along with their compatriots active in Cuba itself, Juan Blanco (b. 1920), Carlos Fariñas (b. 1934), and Leo Brouwer (b. 1939). In Puerto Rico, the achievements of Hector Campos-Parsi (b. 1922) within aesthetics progressing from neo-classicism to atonality have been followed by those of the progressive Rafael Aponte-Ledée (b. 1938) and Roberto Sierra (b. 1953).

From this overview of Latin American music, we may conclude that countries which had remained creatively inactive until the 1950s were brought to the forefront of music by many qualified individuals or groups of composers. Simultaneously, the recent development of concert life has opened the doors to a considerably wider exchange of conductors, instrumentalists and singers, both within Latin American countries and with the rest of the world. Cities like Mexico, Caracas, Rio de Janeiro, Buenos Aires and Santiago compete nowadays with important urban centres in the United States and Europe, both in the length and quality of their concert seasons. Each of these cities has at least one permanent orchestra. There are opera houses of world-wide prestige (such as the Teatro Colón of Buenos Aires) and chamber music ensembles of recognized competence scattered throughout Latin America.   JO-S

Further Reading: G. Béhague, *Music in Latin America: An Introduction* (Englewood Cliffs, NJ, 1979); G. A. Chase, *A Guide to the Music of Latin America*, 2nd edition (Washington, DC, 1962); N. Slonimsky, *Music of Latin America* (New York, 1945); *The New Grove Dictionary of Music and Musicians*, 20 vols. (London, 1980)

Pre-Columbian painting, sculpture and architecture

For it is one thing to read a description like mine of a city such as this and quite another to see it with one's own eyes, in all its strength and grandeur…
(Bernal Díaz del Castillo, 1568)

When the Spanish arrived in the New World they encountered its two greatest empires, the Mexican Aztec in 1519 and then the Inca in 1531. Some, like Bernal Díaz, who described his wonder at the Aztec capital growing from the lake of Texcoco, appreciated their achievements. Yet most of the conquerors sought pure riches and thought nothing of melting down exquisite gold and silver craftsmanship, so that now little is left of the treasures adorning Incan cities. This confrontation between Old and New World pinpoints a central difficulty in understanding the art of native America; despite its glamour, the images express ideas and traditions which had evolved independently through successive cultures over more than two thousand years. Often they were, and still are, alien to outsiders' eyes.

Teatro Colón, Buenos Aires. The world's largest opera house, it was completed in 1908.

The two great centres of civilization developed in Mesoamerica, including the highland and tropical forest zones of Mexico and Guatemala; and to the south along the narrow shelf of land between the Andes and the Pacific coast, especially in Peru. It has been shown that some goods filtered through Central America but direct contact between these two regions is not documented. Nonetheless, there are similarities in the art produced in these regions at a most fundamental level. In the quality of their workmanship the native craftsmen excelled in manipulating materials such as stone, clay and metals using the simplest of tools. Only the grandest schemes could have stimulated the technical invention and organized the labour necessary to erect massive stone buildings without use of the wheel, so it is no surprise to find that this work was overwhelmingly dedicated to the gods. In a sense this was a very practical objective since their dieties were not abstract but the characterization of elements man depended on and were propitiated exclusively by ritual specialists. Over time the power of the elites who directed this work grew and they became akin to gods. Thus craftsmen were not free to vary the content or style of their work; locally this gave a firm pattern to building and craft, yet the variations over time and in diverse areas show how inventively different materials were used to express these relationships. The growing archaeological records help us to understand such qualities.

MESOAMERICA

Cities and architecture

After 1000 BC society became increasingly centred on cities dominated by grand ceremonial building and two distinct types of architecture emerged in Mexico

and among the Maya of modern Guatemala.

Among early societies, remains of the Olmec culture on the Gulf coast have caused avid speculation as they seem to anticipate major developments in Mexican civilization; in architecture the ceremonial centre of La Venta, dated 900–400 BC, was built up around two great pyramidal mounds setting the pattern of Mexican urban centres. This is seen at Teotihuacán in the Valley of Mexico where a powerful religious cult developed; at its greatest expansion (250–150 BC) the city covered more than 20 km with a population estimated at over 100,000 people; it was even rebuilt three times before meeting ruin around AD 900. Districts for traders, craftsmen and farmers were laid out on a grid plan and the courts of the elite flanked a ceremonial complex with the Pyramid of the Sun towering 61 m above. Each of its sides rose in four tiers encased in a type of stone façade known as *talud-tablero*. This gave the effect of distancing observers on the ground from ritual performed in a temple on the summit. The main stairway, cut through the tiers of the pyramid, faces onto the Avenue of the Dead which links further temples and ornamented palaces.

Some of the finest lowland Maya architecture built in the Petén region of Guatemala shows the classic features preferred by this sophisticated people, although they experimented with refinements throughout their long history (400 BC–AD 1250). Unlike Mexican cities there is little evidence of rigid planning and the houses of lower classes must have clustered round the impressive complexes of palaces, courtyards and pyramids. Mayan temple-pyramids are tall and steep, rising to as much as 65 m, and embellished with masonry roof combs to emphasize the height. Rooms in the apical temple were roofed with overlapping stones forming a corbelled vault;

the true arch does not appear in pre-Columbian building. The temple of the Giant Jaguar at Tikal is a good example of the type; it was built around AD 700 over an immensely rich tomb with the entire surface painted in vigorous colours, but it was used for ritual purposes rather than as a mausoleum.

Throughout Mesoamerica ball courts are found as a peculiar architectural feature. The game had a ritual significance; the object was to win by shooting the rubber ball through stone rings projecting from the walls of the 'I' shaped court. Spectators watched from lateral benches and in areas like El Tajín, Veracruz (AD 600–900), where the cult was most influential, they would also witness the sacrifice of the hapless loser's life.

Sculpture and building decoration

Great skill was dedicated to stone sculpted into friezes or three-dimensional figures on a monumental or miniature scale. The Olmec sculpted free-standing heads from blocks of stone weighing up to 20 tons; by using dense jade the same proportions were transferred to miniature figures of 'baby-faced men' with 'jaguar mouths' beautifully carved without metal tools. Sculptural styles varied over time in different regions but a general idea was to portray the gods; they changed too, the most persistent being the rain god whose ringed eyes and fangs appear in many forms. At Teotihuacán each being in the pantheon took a conventional form, as in friezes on the Temple of Quetzalcoatl of realistic snakes' heads alternating with the stylized rain god. Important cult objects were also sculpted; all the paraphernalia of the ball game was found in stone at El Tajín. Later, the warlike Toltec introduced warriors as columns for altar

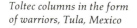
*Toltec columns in the form
of warriors, Tula, Mexico*

stones at Tula around AD 900–1200, and their *chacmool* portray other warriors reclining with a sacrificial bowl held on the stomach. At the height of the sacrificial cult (from AD 1345 to the Spanish conquest), an Aztec sculpture of the goddess Coatlique decked in human skulls, hands and hearts is a potent example of their obsession with death.

The Maya covered their buildings with façades in a profusion of stylized ornaments and deities, but they also took special care to record the prowess of their dignitaries in life-like scenes on relief panels and stelae. The graceful yet detailed figures are among the most beautiful pieces of pre-Columbian sculpture and carved hieroglyphs document the celebrations, justly commemorating their patrons. There is even a record of the colour of such occasions surviving in frescoes painted in a similar style at Bonampak about AD 800.

Ceramics

Pottery shows the inventive imagination of Mesoamerica better than any other medium. Work in clay served as an apprenticeship for sculpting stone; peculiar to the region are countless figurines of men, animals and deities sometimes doubling as jars or whistles. In the Tlatilco tradition, dated 1000–800 BC, little household talismans are energetically portrayed as humans with slanting eyes. They contrast with the laughing men of the later Las Remojadas, Veracruz style which, together with the quite inde-

pendent dogs and men of west-coast ceramic styles, provide a uniquely light touch in Mesoamerican art.

Like the figurines, vessels were moulded or modelled by hand without use of the potters' wheel. The range of forms seems infinite, with curious variations on basic shapes of plates, bowls, bottles and jars; there are even 'teapot' forms and vessels with tripod legs were a particular favourite. Decoration is equally varied with a range of stamped, incised or applied designs; glazing was unknown but sheen was produced by burnishing or from the iridescence of metal in the clay-body. Exceptionally refined ceramics described as 'Thin Orange' were traded widely from Teotihuacán; the contemporary Monte Albán culture left more elaborate, increasingly baroque, ceramics. Within the Maya area grotesque urns were made with the same skill as fine Nebaj vessels of AD 700 decorated with polychrome painted figures similar to those in relief carving.

Jade, turquoise, feathers…

Jade was a prized material; nowhere are native and Spanish values better contrasted. Díaz saw his companions sink into Lake Texcoco with pillaged Aztec gold while he carried away four jade pieces which he exchanged for food and help among the Aztec. Jade and stones of similar quality had been traded since 900 BC. Both the Olmec and Maya excelled in lapidary work, producing calmly sophisticated masks, vessels, figures, ear-flares and belts smoothly polished with sand; sometimes these were buried unused in prestigious caches, a practice which increased the value of jade still further. The Mixtec-Puebla culture shows inspired craftsmanship from the tenth century, excelling in bone and wood carving, feather mosaics and painted screenfold books (the so-called 'codices'). Among the contents of native codices are records of all the luxurious materials, jewellery and costume sent in tribute from designated areas to the great city centres. In this way the Aztec collected Mixtec craft and learnt from their skill, but in Aztec hands delicate craftsmanship became tinged with a dread and gloom especially evident in skulls and masks inlaid with turquoise or in obsidian knives flaked to a sharp edge for cutting out human hearts.

…and gold

Since techniques of metalwork were introduced to the west coast from Peru and Ecuador around AD 800–900, they were used almost exclusively for ornament, rarely for tools. The Mixtec perfected the art in golden filigree rings, necklaces dangling with pendants, masks and bells; and it is a curious tribute to their skill that the finest native jewels sent to the Emperor Charles V were made by them.

Chimu pot from the Peruvian coast, c.1200–1400

THE ANDES

Architecture and stone-carving

The most complete archaeological record in South America falls within the boundaries of Peru. Monumental building in the valleys of the arid coastal belt and in the high Andes shows a distinctive split in cultural tradition. Stone was a primary building material in the highlands, while sun-baked mud adobes were used on the coast. In comparison with Mesoamerica, sculpture was not as developed an art form though its content, often religious, was important.

In the site of Chavín de Huántar built about 600 BC in the northern highlands, the influence of earlier grand building projects like Cerro Sechín on the coast can be seen. Chavín was primarily a religious site and the spreading temple complex consists of vast rectangular pyramids of two or three levels enclosing a central court. The plan is complicated by subterranean passages and stairways. These elements did not form an architectural type and the importance of Chavín culture, evident between 1100 and 300 BC, lies in relief designs sculpted in the stone façades and friezes which covered the building. One free-standing stele called the Raimondi Stone incorporates some important motifs. A fanged being is portrayed with a staff in each hand and a headdress embellished with serpents and feline heads; in other friezes they appear alongside condors or eagles. Essentially Chavinoid, these stylized emblems recur throughout Peru; at

Inca gold mask

times the study of Peruvian iconography seems like 'hunt the cat' because the motifs have been identified in other areas as evidence of the cult's spread.

At the southern highland site of Tiahuanaco on the shores of Lake Titicaca in Bolivia, a similar figure holding two staffs and wearing a headress (now very damaged) forms the centrepiece of a monolithic 'Gateway of the Sun'. This mysterious civilization is not well understood; even the site reconstruction is disputed; but between 800 BC and AD 1200 a cult in which feline motifs appear spread into the Bolivian highlands and through a sister-site at Pucara in Peru to the southern coast.

On the coast, independent cultures flourished in productive river valleys, with the working population segregated from the secular or religious centre to live on the land above the level of irrigation. At the site of Moche on the northern coast, flourishing between AD 150 and 800, only the ruling dynasty and their civil and religious administrators lived in a complex dominated by two flat-topped pyramidal mounds of adobe. The larger Pyramid of the Sun must have reached almost 100 m in height and required the organization of a massive workforce to build it. The successor to Moche, in AD 900, was the Chimú site of Chan Chan where there are ten high-walled enclosures with an average span of 390 by 200 m. Each became a mausoleum in which a deified ruler was buried with his property. As the power of

Pre-Columbian Chimu pot, Peru

*Drawing from the
'Raimondi Stone', Chavín,
Peru*

blocks of stone weighing up to 60 tons. Temples, palaces, storehouses and roads with posthouses were built with skilled speed by thousands of workers throughout the vast empire, which stretched from Colombia to Argentina by the time of the Spanish conquest. Pure engineering in stone is balanced by a sensitive use of natural rock to sculpt haunting abstract forms.

Ceramics

From their appearance in 1500 BC, Peruvian ceramics document the shift of successive cultures. Known techniques were similar to those of Mesoamerica although there was less variation in form; but in the inventive vitality of painted or moulded decoration their ceremonial ware excels. Among north-coast cultures a favoured form used a bridge or stirrup-handle and the Moche moulded them perfectly with portraits of dignitaries and scenes of daily life such as weavers, curing practices, musicians and even explicit copulation. Ceremonial events are painted with black line cartoon-like characters on a white ground. The snakes and condors of Tiahuanaco and Pucara pottery are defined in colours like designs taken from weavings; often the most realistic element is a moulded puma head. The early polychrome motifs of south-coast Nazca potters during the first centuries AD show birds and fish in the most lyrical of all Peruvian designs; later, about AD 600, they adopted Tiahuanacoid designs. White slipped figurines with black line adornment were made by the central-coast Chancay around AD 1200; their crude homeliness indicates the relative isolation of this culture. Incan pottery was mass-produced; the classic forms, like a water jar with pointed base, lugs and long neck with flaring lip, are elegant but the geometric designs are restrictive.

Metalwork

The myth of Incan silver and gold reached the Spanish in the Caribbean, giving a powerful incentive to explore southwards. Years after the event the Inca Garcilaso de la Vega wrote about the Spaniards' impressions of Cuzco; they saw gardens in the Inca's palace where all manner of birds and animals were set in their natural landscape. The scene was made entirely of gold and silver; for once the explorers' dreams were overwhelmed. The craft, which the Inca inherited, had been developed since 900 BC; by the first century AD various metals and alloys could be worked in many techniques, including some unknown to the Old World. The Moche used them to make tools and jewellery of quality, but the first real excess of wealth and status displayed in metal can be attributed to the Chimu who were integrated into the Incan empire in the late fifteenth century.

living kings increased, they continued to be worshipped after death as gods.

The extent of Incan architecture and engineering was unprecedented in the Andes and was designed by the Inca, a living god in charge of a massive military and political organization. Cuzco, the capital, was planned in the shape of a puma with the great fortress of Saccshuamán at its head. The style of their monolithic building is well appreciated in the three zig-zag terraces of Saccshuamán with perfectly matched

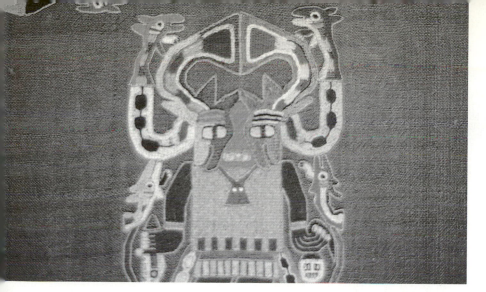

Detail of embroidered Paracas mantle, c.350 BC

Latin American painting, sculpture and architecture to 1830

AFTERMATH OF CONQUEST

Textiles

One of Peru's greatest treasures lay buried in subterranean tombs on the south coast until 1925. Hundreds of mummies interred by the people of the Paracas culture, between 500 and 100 BC, had been wrapped in layers of the most exquisite cloth perfectly preserved by the arid desert. The finest handspun threads of cotton and wool of native camelids were woven in a variety of techniques including weft and warp-stripe, brocade, embroidery and lace. But it is the colours defining figures of fantastic monsters, birds, serpents and animals that are truly astounding. Natural dyeing had obviously been perfected with hundreds of colour gradations. It is likely that the south coast particularly excelled in weaving; but superb textiles of pile and tapestry from Tiahuanaco and the most delicate guaze and painted cloth from Chancay have also survived, suggesting that humid conditions in the highlands have destroyed many other examples. Cloth is easily transported and the cross-currents in iconography of distinct cultures may partly be attributed to textile designs. Examples of Incan weaving have survived and from discussions in early Spanish chronicles their importance is known quite precisely. Cloth was classified and the finest was specially woven and reserved for the Inca himself; it was piled high in storehouses which were a wonder to the Spanish. Religious and secular symbols were woven into cloth and no gift between dignitaries was complete without it. Small wonder, then, that this most versatile of all pre-Columbian arts has actively survived to the present. FN

Further Reading: G. Bawden and G. W. Conrad, *The Andean Heritage* (Cambridge, Mass., 1982); N. Hammond *Ancient Maya Civilisation* (Cambridge, 1982); A. Kendall, *Everyday Life of the Incas* (London, 1973); L.G. Lumbreras, *The peoples and Cultures of Ancient Peru* (Wasington, DC, 1974); M. Porter-Weaver, *The Aztecs, Maya and their Predecessors: Archaeology of Mesoamerica,* 2nd edition (London, 1981); G. C. Vaillant, *The Aztecs of Mexico* (Harmondsworth, 1965)

Within a few years of the conquest the Spaniards had effected in their American territories an artistic revolution the scale and speed of which is probably unique in the history of art. Construction of the massive stone temples and palaces of the Aztecs and Incas ceased immediately; objects with ritual connotations were destroyed, and many traditions of exquisite craftsmanship disappeared almost overnight. There were, of course, survivals, even revivals, but these were restriced to the minor arts, or, in the major arts, to decorative details and occasionally to technical innovations. The entirely new range of art and architecture required by the conquerors left little room for anything but stylistic influence to spread across from native traditions. This influence certainly played a part in producing a distinctive colonial style, but it should not be confused with a true survival.

It is also important to be aware that, while differing profoundly from indigenous art, colonial art also differs from that of the Iberian metropolis. Some differences were deliberate, others not, but they were all products of the new situation. The lack of European-trained craftsmen and of traditional European materials, or different climatic and geographical features – frequent earthquakes, for example – necessitated modifications from European norms. Crucial too is the fact that, throughout the colonial period, art's primary role was as a servant of the Church: in the early years this was not an established Church, as in Europe, whose members had been familiar with Christian images and symbolism for centuries, but a Church involved above all in a massive missionary enterprise. It was recognized by churchmen that there was much in Christian doctrine that could confuse the neophyte, and so they enforced, principally through the medium of the Inquisition, a restricted range of subject matter: only Christ, the Virgin, the more respectable saints and stories from the New Testament are commonly represented. Another change was that new architectural forms had to be devised to cope with the huge Indian congregations.

As well as such modifications in subject matter and type, there were considerable modifications in style. An often miscellaneous selection of European examples served as models, not exclusively nor even predominantly Iberian. From Seville came large numbers of paintings and sculptures hurriedly and often shoddily made specifically for the American market; from Italy, France, Germany and especially the Low Countries came engravings and popular prints, and even a few architectural plans. The copying and recopying of such models – often copies themselves – resulted in simplifications, misinterpretations and a flattening of the forms in architectural decoration as well as in painting and sculpture. This last was particularly true of those areas where the most developed indigenous cultures had flourished: Central America and the Andean region. The convincing representation of the three-dimensional world on a two-dimensional plane played little or no part in native artistic traditions, and in these areas, where to begin with the art and architecture were largely produced by retained native craftsmen, this loss of contour resulted in a distinctive decorative style. Those areas where there were smaller, less culturally sophisticated populations tended to remain more closely dependent on European models.

In the areas of greater density of native population it is useful to recognize, at least during the first 150 years or so after the conquest, a distinction between art produced for the native population, largely by anonymous native craftsmen, and art produced for the colonists. The latter lived in the newly founded towns, where the cultural orientation remained firmly European; European artists and craftsmen who emigrated to America settled in these towns, and tended to form themselves into guilds whose membership was restricted to those of European blood. Not surprisingly, the art produced in this context consciously emulated European models. One of the functions of such art was to reinforce the colonists' sense of their own European identity, whereas the primary function of the art produced for the Indians, was, at least to begin with, to encourage their conversion to Christianity, for which the adherence to current European artistic styles was irrelevant.

ARCHITECTURE

Christian churches were usually the first permanent signs of the European colonization of America: for the colonists their churches, situated prominently at the centre of their newly laid-out grid-plan towns, were symbols of their secure foundations in the New World; for the Indians, the missionary churches which they were required to build in their own towns and villages were the material manifestations of the new order.

It was decreed that the construction of churches should be financed by the settlers, the crown and the native population in equal proportions; in practice what tended to happen was that the settlers, and often the crown representatives too, paid their shares from profits from the various tributes collected from the Indians, while the Indians contributed their own share in the form of labour. The native involvement in these buildings was therefore considerable, but in the sixteenth century at least this was rarely evident. The tens of thousands of Christian missionary churches built during the sixteenth century were immediately recognizable as such, however simple their construction. The essential elements which turned a barn-like structure into a church were a bell-tower, and a definition of the entrance or entrances by some reference to the architectural system known in Europe as 'classical': columns or pilasters surmounted by an entablature and perhaps a triangular pediment. Churches in this plain but unmistakably European style continued to be built throughout the colonial period, and examples survive in many places.

Not all the early churches were so rudimentary. In Mexico in particular the three mendicant orders initially authorized to work in the New World – the Franciscans, the Dominicans and the Augustinians – were quick to establish a series of substantial monastic houses with imposing vaulted churches alongside. These buildings were not designed by architects but by the friars themselves, and executed almost entirely by the Indians. It is interesting that although the true arch and therefore also roofing by means of stone vaults were unknown in America before the conquest, the Indian masons, under the guidance of the friars, grasped the principle almost immediately. Good examples of sixteenth-century Franciscan monastery churches survive at Huejotzingo and Tepeaca, and of Augustinian churches at Acolman and Ixmiquilpan, all in Mexico.

As well as these churches and monasteries, in areas of great missionary activity a new architectural form appeared during the early colonial years: the open chapel, or *capilla de indios*. This, a simple vaulted structure, open on one or more sides, and facing on to a large open space, was probably developed to cope with the huge Indian congregations. Crowds could gather in front to hear the prayers and teachings of the priests within, who were thus afforded both shelter and distinction. Several examples survive, as at Teposcolula and Tlahuelilpa in Mexico. The space in front of both churches and open chapels was often enclosed by a wall to form an atrium, so in effect extending the jurisdiction of the church, and in the corners of these atria small oratories called *posas*

Cathedral, Mexico City, constructed between the 1560s and the early nineteenth century, and the largest of all Latin America's many cathedrals.

were often built, where temporary altars were erected during religious festivals. This emphasis on exterior ritual may have been a concession to indigenous practices: Indian worship had traditionally taken place in the open air.

The sixteenth and seventeenth centuries

In Central America during the sixteenth century the favoured style of architectural decoration, resources permitting, was that of the plateresque, the Spanish version of the architectural style of the Italian Renaissance. The first American cathedral, Santo Domingo on the island of Hispaniola, built between 1512 and 1541, boasts a splendid double-arched west portal in this style, which must have been executed by Spanish masons. So too must have been the façade of the Augustinian church at Acolman (1560) which served as the prototype for other Augustinian façades including that at Yuririapúndaro (1566). These two make an interesting comparison as in the latter, while clearly a copy of that at Acolman, the architectural members are subordinated to the flat, decorative carving, betokening Indian craftsmanship. In South America the substantial churches which survive from the sixteenth century are more austere in appearance, the Colombian cathedrals of Cartegena (1585) and Tunja (1600) being closer to the Italian Renaissance pattern, while San Francisco

in Quito, Ecuador (1580s?), echoes the severe style of the Escorial in Spain.

Most of the major American cathedrals, although founded in the sixteenth century, were built during the seventeenth and eighteenth centuries, when the then secure and increasingly prosperous settlers could turn their attention to the adornment of their cities. The history of these cathedrals is long and complicated, often stretching from the late sixteenth century when ambitious (often over-ambitious) plans were drawn up, through various stages of construction during the seventeenth century, to final completion sometimes in the eighteenth or even nineteenth century. Mexico City cathedral is an extreme case: begun in 1563, by 1615 the main walls were only half built; it was dedicated in 1656 although the interior was not completed until 1667, the bell-towers not until 1791, and some other details not until 1813. Several cathedrals suffered badly from earthquakes both during and after their construction, as for example those of Antigua (Guatemala), Lima (Peru), and Santiago de Chile (this last was also burnt down in 1769, shortly after having been rebuilt to new designs after repeated earthquake damage); others, for example at Bogotá (Colombia) and Córdoba (Argentina), fell down as a result of the inexperience or lack of training of the builders in charge.

*Church of La Compañía
(Jesuit Church), Quito,
Ecuador (1765). Elaborate
façades became more
common in colonial
architecture in the
eighteenth century.*

*Church of La Compañía
(Jesuit Church), Cuzco,
Peru. The façade was built in
the 1650s and 1660s.*

Nevertheless, the majority of cathedrals surviving today whose foundation dates back to the sixteenth century present an internal arrangement which is closely related to the original design. Most are large, gothic-vaulted structures in the hall-church mode of three or more aisles of equal height. The massive gothic-vaulted cathedral of Seville (completed 1506) was often the model, but the old-fashioned gothic vaults were also popular because they were simpler and cheaper to construct than domical or barrel vaults, and also, being lighter, they were more resistant to damage by earthquakes.

It is with the façades that designers had the greatest chance to experiment. The predominant type in larger Spanish American churches is the retable-façade, similar in format to a retable, the elaborate sculptural altarpiece so common in Spain and Latin America. A basic architectural framework surrounds the main portal, and a series of niches is filled with statues and/or relief panels depicting saints or scenes from the life of Christ. In the seventeenth century some of the most imaginative retable-façades were produced in Peru. Cuzco cathedral was planned in 1582 by Francisco Becerra (who also designed Lima and Puebla cathedrals), but the façade design dates from about 1650. The clusters of columns and sweeping segments of pediment suggest a strong upward movement towards the delicate pinnacles and scrolls at the top. The façade of the Jesuit Church in Cuzco was built at the same time (1651-68) and in deliberate rivalry with the cathedral across the square. Here the lateral portals are dispensed with, and the bell towers appear to be squeezing the façade into an even more pronounced vertical thrust. The upward curvings of the broken pediments are emphasized by those of the entablature which bulges up into a tri-lobed arch above the whole façade, an extraordinarily imaginative device which prefigures similar developments in Europe. The influence of these two designs can be found over a wide area; good examples are San Francisco, Lima (pre-1664), Lampa near Lake Titicaca (1685), and Sucre cathedral side portal (1693).

The eighteenth century

During the eighteenth century façades became increasingly elaborate: the twisted Salomonic column seems almost obligatory, and all the architectural members are encased in a riot of shallow-relief carving of a generally organic nature. Influential examples include La Merced in Antigua, Guatemala (1760), the Compañía, Quito (1765) and San Agustín, Lima (1720). The carving of the façade of the Compañía in Arequipa (1698) was the prototype of the sculptural style known as 'mestizo' which spread through southern Peru, Bolivia and nothern Argentina, and which is characterized by a *horror vacui* and by the inclusion of indigenous plants and animals. In the mid-eighteenth century, in Mexico in particular, the sculptural forms tended to become three-dimensional, sometimes actually replacing the traditional architectural members. An excellent example that combines both two- and three-dimensional sculpture is the facade of the cathedral of Zacatecas in Mexico (1752): the columns of the first storey are wreathed in leaves and fruit, while in the upper storeys the columns are replaced by shells, bunches of grapes, masks and scrolls arranged in vertical bands. When this sculptured column-substitute has anthropomorphic features it is called an *estípite*, and as such becomes one of the hall-marks of the baroque in Latin America. The *Sagrario*, Mexico City, with facades completed in 1768 by Lorenzo Rodríguez (*c.*1704-74), may perhaps been seen as the *estípite*'s most outstanding victory.

Church of Santa Prisca, Taxco, Mexico, built in the eighteenth century with fortunes made from silvermining

The use of colour was another common feature of Latin American baroque architecture. Brightly coloured glazed tiles were often used with striking effects in Mexico, as at San Francisco, Acatepec (*c.* 1730), and in the Sanctuary, Ocotlán (*c.*1750), where the frothy white sculpture of the portal (which includes *estípites*) is set off to advantage by the red-tiled bases of the flanking bell-towers. In Peru the carved church façades were sometimes painted in bright colours.

Ecclesiastical architecture dominates the Spanish colonial record in America. Secular architecture, whether public or domestic, was always less important. Despite this, many examples of colonial houses and larger buildings survive in all the cities which in their day were focal points of the Spanish empire. Among the finest civic buildings still to be seen are the School of Mines in Mexico City, designed by the architect and sculptor Manuel Tolsá; the Torre-Tagle mansion in Lima, Peru, which now houses the Peruvian foreign ministry; and the austere neo-classical Royal Mint (Casa de la Moneda) in Santiago, Chile, designed by the Italian architect Joaquín Toesca and used after 1846 as the Chilean presidential palace.

Brazilian architecture only came into its own in the eighteenth century, notably in the rich mining province of Minas Gerais. In contrast with the architecture of the Spanish colonies, it demonstrates less concern for external ornament (an important exception is the façade of São Francisco, Salvador, of 1703) and concentrates on internal spatial arrangements. The aisled hall-church form, so popular elsewhere, is rejected in favour of the inventive use of a single spatial unit, often oval or octagonal in plan. Good examples are N. S. do Pilar (1720–33) and the Rosario (completed by 1785) both in Ouro Preto, and São Pedro in Recife (1728–82). One such church, São Francisco, Ouro Preto, was designed and executed between 1766 and 1794 by the remarkable Aleijadinho (Antônio Francisco de Lisboa), better known as a sculptor.

The political tensions of the late eighteenth and early nineteenth centuries were paralled in America, as in Europe, by a reaction against the artistic styles of the previous two centuries. For the intellectual elite the fantastic elaborations of Latin American baroque became equated with the corruption and decadence of the old colonial order, but the neo-classical movement in America was not strong enough to effect radical changes of taste in any but the major Spanish American colonial cities: the love of ornament was too deep-rooted. In Mexico the first architect to reintroduce relatively plain columns into his façades was Francisco Antonio Guerrero y Torres (*c.*1740–92); he built the elegant Pocito chapel at the famous sanctuary of Guadalupe (1777–91), which is also interesting for its ground plan, reminiscent more of Brazilian than Spanish American designs. The purest neo-classical architecture was produced, not surprisingly perhaps, by Spaniards: Manuel Tolsá (1757–1816) in Mexico City and Matías Maestro in Lima. Both had some success in changing the prevailing style, but by and large the period of greatest architectural activity in Latin America coincided with a taste for rich elaborations and baroque effects.

PAINTING AND SCULPTURE

The successful 'spiritual conquest' of the New World required more than an appropriate architectural setting: it needed a new Christian iconography to replace the images of the various deities to whom the Indians had traditionally offered their prayers, and this need was initially met in two ways. Works of art were imported from Europe, and workshops were created in the monasteries where the friars could train Indians to execute suitable works in an approximately European representational mode, usually by setting them to copy imported engravings. The most famous of these schools were established by Franciscans, by Pedro de Gante in Mexico City in 1527, and by Pedro Gosseal in Quito, Ecuador, in about 1550. Fresco provided a cheap and easy way of producing Christian images, as well as of stimulating sculptured altars, coffered ceilings and architectural mouldings, and it had the added advantage of being familiar to

Detail from a fresco in the main church at Ixmiquilpán, Mexico, probably by Otomí Indians

Indian craftsmen from pre-conquest times. In Mexico at the Franciscan monastery of Huejotzingo (1550–60) the black and white murals are based on Flemish engravings, while the brightly coloured contemporary works at Ixmiquilpan demonstrate a strong native influence. Frescoes survive from the late sixteenth century in village churches around Cuzco, Peru, and the technique continued to be used in this area for over 200 years.

As with architecture, the Church remained the chief artistic patron throughout the colonial period for both the Indian and European populations. Religious art was the dominant, almost the only, genre to be practised. Of the other subjects open to artists in Europe – landscape, still-life, history, mythology and portraiture – only the last was of any importance; the others were virtually non-existent. By the later sixteenth century the demand for religious art was being supplied from a third source: craftsmen from several different countries had established workshops in the new Latin American towns and were producing works of art in a more consciously European style than most of that produced in the monastic workshops. Their sources, however, are often very heterogeneous: their own European training, imported paintings and sculptures, mostly from Seville and rarely of the highest quality, and engravings and illustrated books, most of which came from the Netherlands. Thus in 1566 Simon Pereyns (active 1566–88) arrived in Mexico from Antwerp and worked largely from engravings after Flemish artists, while Spaniards, such as Andrés de la Concha (active 1575–1612) and Balthasar de Echave Orio (c.1548–1620), worked in the Italian-influenced Sevillian style. Someone with a knowledge of French art must have been involved in the unique series of secular frescoes that decorated colonial mansions in Tunja, Colombia, around 1590–1610, and in the later sixteenth century several Italians were attracted to

Lima: Bernardo Bitti (1548–c.1620), Mateo Pérez de Alesio (1547–c.1628), a follower of Michelangelo, and Angelino de Medoro (c.1567–c.1631) who arrived in about 1600 having already worked in Bogotá, Tunja and Quito.

During the seventeenth century the influence of the flourishing Sevillian schools of painting is evident everywhere. During the 1640s and 1650s Zurbarán's workshop exported hundreds of canvases to America, and their powerful tenebrism was widely imitated. A few years later the soft sweet style of Murillo was adopted by several notable painters, including Cristóbal de Vilalpando (c.1652–1714) in Mexico, Gregorio Vézquez Ceballos (1638–1711) in Colombia, and Miguel de Santiago (c.1625–1706) in Ecuador. In the southern Andes, however, the influence of Flemish prints remained strong, as in the work of the Indian Diego Quispe Tito (1611–after 1681) in Cuzco, and of Melchor Pérez de Holguín (b.c.1660) and his followers in Bolivia.

During the eighteenth century few of the many documented painters stand out except in Mexico, where a lively school of portraiture challenged the supremacy of religious art. Portraits of nuns were especially popular: Sor Juana Inés de la Cruz, the nun-poetess, was depicted several times, serene and beautiful, surrounded by books, as in paintings of 1750 by Miguel Cabrera (1695–1768). Cabrera is also remembered for his plans to found an Academy in Mexico City which would exclude anyone who taught Indians to paint.

Genuine survivals of indigenous forms and techniques are most common in the field of pictorial representation, although only outside the jurisdiction of the stricter guilds, of course. In Mexico pre-conquest-style painted books containing information about native history and beliefs, as well as about the tributes due from different localities, continued to be produced, with some modifications, well into the

eighteenth century. Fine examples are the Codex
Mendoza (*c.*1520) and the curious, deliberately
archaizing Techialoyán manuscripts of the eighteenth century. In Peru in 1612 the Indian Guamán
Poma de Ayala completed an extensive history of the
Incas, which he illustrated throughout with drawings
that are a pleasing synthesis of European forms with
Incan themes, while in the Mexican feather paintings
of Christ and the Virgin, indigenous techniques are
applied to new subject matter.

Indigenous influence is present in one of the most
interesting schools of colonial painting, that of
Cuzco, which by the eighteenth century was exporting works all over South America. Contemporan-
eously with the Europe-oriented Quispe Tito, a more
provincial school of largely anonymous mestizo and
Indian artists developed, which, although generally
indebted compositionally to European sources, is
quite distinct in style. An evident lack of concern for
depth and contour is balanced here by an emphasis on
decorative detail: the Holy Family, the angels and
saints are dressed in richly embroidered costumes
with magnificent lace trimmings, over which gold
leaf is liberally applied in flat repeating patterns. The
backgrounds are often little Andean landscapes with
numerous local plants and birds dotted around, and
sometimes with scenes of village life or figures tending flocks of llamas.

This obvious pleasure in the multiplication of decorative detail for its own sake is a common feature of

the cult images which enjoyed (and enjoy) such popularity all over Latin America. Once a painting or
sculpture was recognized as having special powers,
like for example the seventeenth-century wooden
crucifix, *Cristo de los Temblores,* in Cuzco cathedral,
which was believed to be efficacious against earthquakes, or the sixteenth-century painting of the Virgin of Guadalupe in Mexico, the protectress of the
Indians, then it would be copied to enable devotees to
venerate it elsewhere. Statues were often copied on to
canvas or panel with the addition of the candles, cur-
tains and flowers that adorned the altar of the original. These copies were then often copied themselves,
each time becoming stiffer and more icon-like, but
with richer costumes and with ever more jewellery
and floral tributes.

Sculpture

In the field of European-style figure sculpture, only a
handful of the documented craftsmen are of especial
interest. The main influence throughout the colonial
period was the Sevillian school, and Martínez Mon-
táñez (1568–1649) in particular, who specialized in
stark crucifixions and passion figures in polychromed wood. He exported a few such statues to
America (although many more are attributed to him)
and the type was repeated again and again, by, for
example, Pedro de Lugo (active 1731–73) and Manuel
Chili, known as Caspicara (active late eighteenth

427

century) in Quito. Christ's Passion offered colonial artists a rare chance to depict the naked body and they made the most of it, stressing the beauty of the long limbs and smooth white skin and the ugliness of the wounds and rivulets of scarlet blood.

In the eighteenth century, Brazil was to produce the finest individual artist of the whole colonial period: the mulatto Antônio Francisco de Lisboa (1738–1814), called 'O Aleijadinho' ('the little cripple'). Both architect and sculptor, he has left ample testimony in the province of Minas Gerais of his outstanding ability to manipulate space in a dramatic and powerful way. The most famous of his many works are the sculptural groups in wood of the Stations of the Cross in the church of Bom Jesus, Congonhas do Campo (1797–9) and, above all, the twelve rugged stone prophets (1800–5) which watch over the monumental staircase that leads up to the same church.

Aleijadinho's genius apart, the most striking sculptural creations of the colonial period are the church interiors: the furnishings (choir-stalls, pulpits and retables), and the gold and polychromed stucco-work on the walls and ceilings, all largely anonymous. From as early as 1600 moulded stucco, particularly in the form of grotesques and entwined plants, predominantly in red, white and gold, was a special feature of the Dominican chapels of the Rosary, as for example at Puebla and Oaxaca in Mexico, both early seventeenth century. About fifty years later, the Jesuits used stucco to decorate many of their churches with flatter, more geometric forms, as in Quito and Córdoba, and by the eighteenth century the practice had become widespread. The general tendency was towards increasing unity between the stucco decorations of the walls and ceiling, and the church furnishings, especially the retables.

Main altar, church of São Francisco, Salvador, Brazil

A retable can include paintings and sculpture in both the round and relief, all organized within an architectural framework, usually of gilded wood. The central image is often an earlier work, a treasured sculpture from Spain, for example, or a popular miraculous image, and this forms the iconographical starting point for the figures and biblical scenes arranged around it. The stylistic development of the retable follows a similar pattern throughout Latin America from, to cite only one or two of the most splendid examples, one of the earliest surviving, that at Huejotzingo, with paintings by Simon Pereyns of 1586, through that in San Franscisco, Bogotá, designed by Ignacio García de Ascucha in 1623, which is still fundamentally classical in style, to the splendid baroque example in the Compañía, Cuzco, designed by Diego Martínez de Oviedo in 1670, and finally to the overwhelming richness of such eighteenth-century examples as that at São Francisco, Salvador, Brazil (1730s?) and San Martín, Tepotzotlán, Mexico of c.1755. It is interesting that the tendency throughout the seventeenth and eighteenth centuries to even more fanciful elaborations of the architectural framework of these retables in Latin America, as in Spain, often predates similar developments in the architecture of church façades. It is as if the designers, working on a smaller scale and in less durable materials, felt freer to experiment than those working in masonry.

By the end of the eighteenth century there was a reaction against this elaborate form of interior, led by the same men who were responsible for introducing the new taste in architecture: Manuel Tolsá in Mexico City, and Matías Maestro in Lima. In these two cities many churches were stripped bare, their retables burnt in an excess of neo-classical enthusiasm. Many more such interiors have been damaged or destroyed by earthquakes but enough survive in all their glittering splendour to make them among the most impressive monuments to colonial artistic achievement.   VF

Further Reading: V. Fraser, *The Architecture of Conquest: Building in the Viceroyalty of Peru, 1535–1635* (Cambridge, 1990); G. Kubler and M. Soria, *Art and Architecture of Spain and Portugal and their American Dominions* (Harmondsworth, 1959); P. Kelemen, *Baroque and Rococo in Latin America* (New York, 1951); H. E. Wethey, *Colonial Architecture and Sculpture in Peru* (Cambridge, Mass., 1949)

Painting and sculpture since 1830

ACADEMICISM AND LOCAL COLOUR

From the viewpoint of art, the period after independence in Latin America was somewhat poor in achievement. Painting and sculpture tended to be strongly derivative, with European (above all, French) models well to the fore. This was reinforced by the predominance of 'the academy', – i.e. the academies or schools of fine arts established in the various cities – where imported neo-classicism was the main orthodoxy. Yet even at this period local, 'national' influences were bound to seep into Latin American art, as painters strove to adapt neo-classicism or other European academic styles to the real world that surrounded them. The portraiture of the period, for instance, inevitably reflected local society (not least the Europeanizing aspirations of the creole elites, as shown, for instance, in their styles of dress). Works of art that evoked the growing national traditions of the new states – depictions on canvas of the battles of independence, statues of heroes, monumental sculptures – also bore an obvious Latin American stamp. The natural world of the American continent, in all its prodigality, was a further theme soon taken up by artists: this subject was affectionately cultivated by a number of foreign painters who lived and worked in the region – the most talented of these being a Bavarian, Johann Moritz Rugendas (1802–58) – and whose example proved contagious. Another foreigner who depicted Latin American (in this case, Ecuadorian) landscapes in an extraordinarily vivid way was the North American, Frederick Edwin Church (1826–1900), though he did not stay long enough to influence local artists. In paintings by foreigners and Latin Americans alike, it is easy to sense the special emotion with which exotic New World landscapes, typical rural characters, and the expanding urban scene were presented and interpreted on canvas. The three painters often considered as nineteenth-century Latin America's finest – Prilidiano Pueyrredón (Argentina, 1823–70), Juan Manuel Blanes (Uruguay, 1830–1901), and the remarkable José María Velasco (Mexico, 1840–1912) – all succeeded admirably in incorporating persuasive elements of 'local colour' into basically international styles. The remarkable military panoramas of the Paraguayan war by Cándido López (1840–1902) also deserve mention.

Despite the achievements of talented individuals such as these, the general artistic panorama remained somewhat conservative. But new influences gradually put in their appearance. Towards the end of the nineteenth century, French Impressionism began to leave its mark on certain Latin American artists. Among its most interesting exponents were a Mexican, Joaquín Clausell (1866–1935), a prolific Chilean, Juan Francisco González (1853–1933) – whose Impressionism was most pronounced during a productive twelve-year period (1888–1900) of residence at Limache, near Valparaíso – and, somewhat later on, the Venezuelan, Armando Reverón (1889–1954), whose later development was altogether remarkable. Some of Reverón's later canvases combine a luminosity reminiscent of Turner with the delicate allusiveness of some kinds of Chinese art.

It must also be remembered that a 'popular' tradition of 'naive' or 'primitive' art always existed alongside that of 'the academy' in the nineteenth century, and, indeed, beyond. (Twentieth–century Haiti was to see a particularly flourishing development of these forms.) From the mid-nineteenth century onwards, advances in lithography also provided artists with a definitely non-academic outlet for their talents. Easily the most extraordinary figure in this particular line was the Mexican, José Guadalupe Posada (1851–1913), the author of at least 15,000 prints and satirical woodcuts, whose compelling images of animated skeletons and skulls gave his art an utterly special stamp.

Soon after 1900, challenges to nineteenth-century academicism grew sharper. A notable part here was played by the Mexican artist (and energetic publicist) Gerardo Murillo (1875–1964), who changed his name to 'Dr Atl' ('atl' being the Nahuatl word for 'water'). Dr Atl and other rebel artists from the Academy of San Carlos – Mexico's main artistic institute, founded as far back as 1785 – mounted a highly successful exhibition of 'dissident' art in Mexico City in September 1910. The effects of this initiative were delayed by the start, a few weeks later, of the Mexican revolution, which, quite apart from its political importance, was to prove a decisive turning point for modern Latin American art.

MEXICAN MURALISM AND ITS INFLUENCE

The revolution shook Mexico to its foundation, and artists were completely caught up in its implications. They found that they had a choice of three courses of action: to become active combatants; to take part in the struggle through propaganda efforts; or to leave the country altogether for a while.

Once the violent years of upheaval were over, once thought was given to rebuilding the shattered nation, Mexican artists joined forces in pursuit of a common ideal: to contribute their art to a great programme of popular education. This programme, supported by the intelligentsia and by the governments of the day (especially that of President Alvaro Obregón, whose education minister was the philosopher José Vasconcelos), certainly had its roots in Dr Atl's pre-revolutionary criticisms of academic art. Following on from the dissident movement of 1910, artists now drew consciously on pre-Columbian and Spanish colonial traditions, and on the popular art of figures such as Posada; these indigenous elements were blended with the modern influences radiating from Europe to create a new and unique artistic trend – an essentially didactic pictorial language designed to further popular education, but one which soon transcended that simple aim. The result was a rich artistic movement, unprecedented and in many ways still unequalled in Latin America, in which a host of talented individuals played their part.

The key feature of the Mexican Renaissance (as it has been called) was its emphasis on *the painting of murals* – something that sets it apart, for instance, from post-revolutionary Soviet Russian art, which had similar didactic purposes. The three acknowledged 'giants' of Mexican muralism were Diego Rivera (1886–1957), José Clemente Orozco (1883–1949), and David Alfaro Siqueiros (1898–1974). It is difficult to exaggerate the importance of this trio – the first Latin American painters to enter the pantheon of modern art. All three were obsessed with large-scale nationalist visions of history and society (tinged with exuberant Marxism in the cases of Rivera and Siqueiros, with moralism and even mysticism in the case of Orozco), with the

Diego Rivera, 'Man the Controller of the Universe' fresco (Palacio de Bellas Artes, Mexico City).

Spanish conquest and the revolution itself as major and recurring themes in their work. This was an original, authentic Latin American form of art. Important differences of style are to be noted within the mainstream of muralism. Rivera's infatuation with Marxism, for instance, was given increasingly systematic expression, while Orozco's work was tinged with ambiguity and irony. A comparison could also be drawn between Rivera's crowded realism, relying sometimes on stock caricatures, and Orozco's increasingly dramatic and loose style (which became a significant influence on Abstract Expressionism in the United States).

The achievement of the muralists can best be studied, obviously, in Mexico – in Rivera's notable sequence in the National Preparatory School, the Secretariat of Education, and the National Palace, all in Mexico City, and in Orozco's magnificent series of frescoes in various public buildings in Guadalajara. Siqueiros's major Mexican works are to be found in the National Palace of Fine Arts, the University City, and the National History Museum in the Mexican capital. For lovers of modern art, pilgrimages to these places are obligatory. The great muralists were also sometimes in demand outside Mexico. Rivera himself did several major commissions in the United States, including some impressive murals in the Detroit Institute of Arts, appropriately enough on the theme of the automobile industry. (Another Rivera mural, for the Rockefeller Center in New York, proved too controversial, and was later obliterated, an unforgivable act of philistinism.) Orozco and Siqueiros, too, worked at times outside Mexico. This tradition has continued. As recently as the mid-1960s, to mention only one example, a later representative of the great tradition, Jorge González Camarena, executed a powerful mural ('Presence of Latin America') for the University of Concepción in Chile. The Mexican imprint, in fact, is to be found on numerous stretches of wall throughout the western hemisphere.

The Mexican muralist school was at its height in the 1920s and 1930s – years of unsurpassed achievement – and it has continued to inspire artists ever since. Its immediate impact on the rest of Latin America was considerable. Artists in several countries (sometimes through direct contact with Mexico) were prompted to develop their own 'indigenist' schools of modern painting. This trend was perhaps most conspicuous in the Andean republics (notably Ecuador, Peru and Bolivia), where strong indigenous traditions were to be found, and it clearly affected the work of modern Ecuador's most famous painter, Osvaldo Guayasamín (b. 1919). Guayasamín's work, which includes murals, strikes a rich vein of social protest while incorporating, also, the influence of

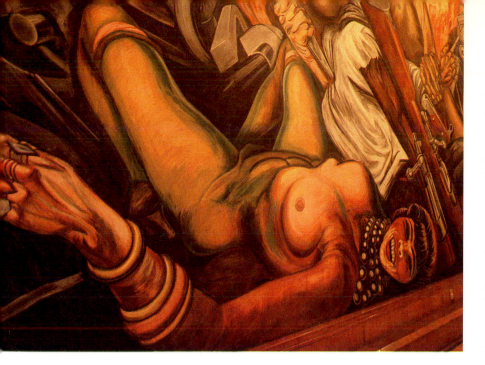

José Clemente Orzoco, 'Catharsis' (Palacio de Belles Artes, Mexico City)

tury's artistic endeavour. For while many Latin American artists have continued to emphasize the quest for authentic local values, others have eagerly embraced more cosmopolitan attitudes, striving to assert themselves (and Latin America) in the increasingly international marketplace of contemporary art.

The period after the *Semana de Arte Moderna* in Brazil – a country of key importance for modern Latin American art – was long dominated by the gentle nationalist genius Cândido Portinari. But there were others, like Tarsila do Amaral (1886–1973) and Emiliano di Cavalcanti (1897–1976) who also aimed at reflecting Brazilian realities in their art. (Brazil was large enough, too, to accommodate flourishing 'regionalist' schools of painting, based especially on Recife and Bahia.) In their very different ways – too varied to allow for instant classification – Pedro Figari (Uruguay, 1861–1938), Carlos Mérida (Guatemala 1891–1984), Raquel Forner (Argentina, 1902–89), Antonio Berni (Argentina, 1905–81) and Alejandro Obregón (Colombia, b. 1920) can, similarly, be regarded as representative artists who assimilated key features of early twentieth-century European styles – post-Impressionism, Fauvism, Cubism, Expressionism, and so on – in their distinctive explorations of Latin American, national, social and political (in Berni's case, left-wing) themes.

Picasso. It would be hard to deny that the Latin American penchant for mural-painting – including perhaps the propagandistic 'impromptu muralism' that has flourished during certain political episodes, for example the Allende government in Chile – stems to a large extent from the Mexican example, even where different styles have been used. Mexican influence was indirect in the work of the great Brazilian painter Cândido Portinari (1903–62), but this superb artist's quest for a genuinely national, Brazilian art *was* often expressed in large murals, although his style, traditional and modern at one and the same time, was all his own.

NATIONALISM AND INTERNATIONALISM

Mexican muralism, the single most notable phenomenon in modern Latin American art, was far from being the only effort made in the region to renew artistic traditions. In the early part of the twentieth century, various 'rebellions' against academicism took place in other countries. The most famous of these, undoubtedly, was the *Semana de Arte Moderna* (Modern Art Week) held in São Paulo, Brazil, in February 1922. This event, accompanied by noisy controversy, brought together writers and musicians as well as painters and sculptors, but its protagonists were all deeply committed to coming to terms with the twentieth century. Unlike the Mexicans with whom they were contemporary, the Brazilian promoters of the *Semana de Arte Moderna* did not have a precise or doctrinaire programme, over and above a keen desire for innovation. In this respect they can be seen to have set the tone for modern Latin American art as a whole, which has certainly shared in the extraordinary diversity of the present cen-

Right
Fernando Botero, 'Man with a Guitar'.

431

In Mexico a possibly understandable reaction to the programmatic nationalism of the muralists was embodied in the work of a very distinguished painter, Rufino Tamayo (b. 1899), in which the early influence of Picasso and Braque was soon transcended in a constantly developing personal style. Tamayo's rejection of the philosophical underpinnings of the muralist school was shown in his simple dictum: 'Painting is painting.' A further break with muralism came through Surrealism, whose principal French apologist, André Breton, visited Mexico in 1938. Among the Surrealists Breton 'discovered' in Mexico – though she had never heard of the movement before his visit – was a remarkable woman painter, Frida Kahlo (1910–54), twice married to Diego Rivera. Kahlo's tiny autobiographical paintings were based on the native tradition of the *retablo* (the naive, often anonymous paintings on tin made as offerings after miraculous deliverance). It cannot really be argued that Surrealism became a full-blooded Latin American school, but its influence, though diffuse, was strong. Two of the region's internationally most famous modern painters, the Cuban, Wilfredo Lam (1902–82), and the expatriate Chilean, Roberto Matta (b. 1912) were fundamentally influenced by the Surrealist aesthetic during their formative periods, and remained so thereafter. Lam's totemic canvases often express the magic 'primitivism' which Surrealists were always seeking.

Increasingly from the Second World War onwards, modern art's most radical innovation – abstract or non-figurative art – began to exercise a strong appeal throughout Latin America, with representatives in every country. An early figure in preparing the ground for this approach was the great Uruguayan, Joaquín Torres-García (1874–1949). In the 1920s Torres-García was active in Paris, where he was the co-founder of the Cercle et Carré group – responsible for organizing the world's first major international exhibition of abstract art (Paris, 1930). Torres-García returned to his native Montevideo in 1934. His extensively expounded theory of 'constructivist universalism' and his angular, geometrical style (using muted earth colours and retaining certain vaguely figurative aspects) had an immense influence in Uruguay. It was duly noted in neighbouring Argentina – a country where, following an early lead given by painters such as Emilio Pettoruti (1892–1971) and Xul Solar (1887–1963), abstractionism in all its successive forms was to gain a particularly strong following. This was also to prove true in Venezuela, where Alejandro Otero (b. 1921) developed, in his 'colour-rhythms' (first shown in 1955), a striking version of Op Art.

Yet by no means all Latin American painters adopted abstractionism. An extraordinary Colombian, Fernando Botero (b. 1932), struck out in a very different direction, elaborating a highly original, neo-figurative style based on exaggerated, parodistic reworkings of old masters. In Mexico, José Cuevas (b. 1933) has produced neo-figurative drawings of superb quality, rejecting the muralist school while acknowledging his debt to Orozco. Rafael Coronel (b. 1932) and (especially) Alberto Gironella (b. 1929) are two further Mexican artists whose striking neo-figurative work can be said to have anticipated – though in a lighter way, and with something of the 'bite' of Dada and Surrealism – the recent controversial German trend known as neo-expressionism.

MODERN SCULPTURE

The development of twentieth-century Latin American sculpture parallels that of painting in important respects, with modern figurative styles existing alongside a trend (increasingly powerful after the

Bruno Giorgi, 'The Meteorite' (Brasília)

1940s) towards the abstract. Among modern sculptors in the figurative tradition, Vítor Brecheret (Brazil, 1894–1956), Bruno Giorgi (Brazil, b. 1905) and Joaquin Roca Rey (Peru, b. 1923) all won considerable reputations both inside and outside their respective countries. Giorgi's work can be seen to good effect in Brasília. Sculptors and sculptresses who moved away from representation towards abstract, symbolic or 'totemic' forms include Edgar Negret (Colombia, b. 1920), who found a highly personal style, Marina Núñez del Prado (Bolivia, b. 1910), who was the creator of powerful semi-abstract 'interpretations of the Bolivian soul', María Martins (Brazil, 1900–73), Noemi Gerstein (Argentina, b. 1910) and Alicia Peñalba (Argentina, 1918–82). Latin American sculpture in recent times has sometimes attempted to reinterpret pre-Columbian forms in a modern idiom – with what degree of success is a matter of debate. Sculpture has also been imaginatively used to enhance some of the superb modern architecture of the region. Conspicuous examples of this 'integration of the plastic arts' are to be seen in Mexico City and Brasília.

The institutional framework for modern art in Latin America was greatly strengthened in the middle decades of the twentieth century. The opening of museums of contemporary art in major cities, combined with the proliferation of private galleries, did much to reinforce the triumph of the modern movement. The São Paulo Biennale (first held in 1951) quickly developed a well-deserved reputation as one of the important dates in the world's artistic calendar – a rival, indeed, to its European counterpart at Venice. In Argentina, in the 1960s, the Torcuato di Tella Institute for the Arts did much to promote experimentalism and to add to the cultural liveliness of Buenos Aires during that lively decade, though it fell a victim to the altogether harsher climate of the 1970s. Latin American art, whether consciously nationalist or consciously internationalist, or neither, has continued to share in the general ferment of the artistically agitated twentieth century. As contemporary art has become more international, Latin America has participated fully in universal trends, and yet, at the same time, its artists (or some of the most distinguished) have maintained a distinctive ability to reaffirm, in unusual ways, the vitality of the figurative tradition.   MD/SC

Further Reading: D. Ades, *Art in Latin America* (London, 1989); O. Baddeley and V. Fraser, *Drawing the Line: Art and Cultural Identity in Latin America* (London, 1989); J. Charlot, *The Mexican Mural Renaissance, 1920–1925* (New Haven, Conn., 1963); A. Rodríguez, *A History of Mexican Mural Painting* (London, 1969); *Bienal de São Paulo*. Catalogues (1951–)

Modern architecture in Latin America

Modern architecture in Latin America is perhaps best understood in contrast with its nineteenth-century counterpart. In general that was a lacklustre period, bearing little comparison with colonial times or with the twentieth century. The most cursory survey reveals that by the second quarter of the nineteenth century the early Mexican neo-classical style of Manuel Tolsá (1757–1816) and Francisco Eduardo Tresguerras (1759–1833) had been turned into one of the most sterile academic movements on record. Circumstances were similar in Brazil, where the work of two French architects, Grandjean de Montigny (1776–1850) and Louis Vauthier (c.1810–77), helped to encourage academic taste. To a greater or lesser degree, sooner or later comparable events developed throughout most of the continent. By the late 1870s and early 1880s a new preference had set in for rendering effusively the more ornate aspects of French Second Empire architecture, and this did little to improve architectural character in general. 'Europeanization' as a means of equating conspicuous splendour with urban decorum, as for instance in Manaus (on the River Amazon) in the 1890s, scarcely allowed for an opportunity to develop an architecture proper to the region.

It was almost exclusively in rural dwellings and in the anonymous residences of the provincial middle class that nineteenth-century Latin American builders remembered some of the lessons of their colonial past and showed some degree of sympathy for local conditions of climate, building tradition, and way of life in general. But these examples were shunned for the most part as hopelessly unfashionable, and there remained well into the twentieth century much enthusiasm for designs slavishly derived from a European high-bourgeois tradition. Better academic aesthetic standards, however, eventually replaced earlier and more exuberant ones. The early twentieth-century remodelling of Carlos Enrique Pellegrini's Teatro Colón in Buenos Aires, originally built in 1855–7, and Adamo Boari's Palacio de Bellas Artes in Mexico City, of 1904–34, find a place among the better examples of twentieth-century academic neo-classicism in Latin America.

In spite of the strength of the academic tradition, the architectural climate began to change remarkably in the early 1930s. At that time, when most modern European architects were attempting to create a universal style, an important group of avant-garde Latin American architects became concerned with expressing the specific character of their respective cultures. Such an interest in nationalism gives a particular flavour to modern Latin American architecture, and in general marks its importance. Although some of the objectives of avant-garde architecture in Latin America parallel similar ones in painting and literature, a modern nationalist architecture developed later that other arts. During the late 1920s and early 1930s the first examples of modern architecture in the area tended to follow stylistic patterns that Le Corbusier had developed earlier.

BRAZIL

One of the earliest expressions of modern architecture in Latin America appeared in Brazil in 1925 when Gregori Warchavchik, a young Russian émigré architect, published an important manifesto, 'Apropos of Modern Architecture', and subsequently built houses in a contemporary style in Rio de Janeiro and São Paulo in 1927 and in 1931. Shortly thereafter, Warchavchik entered into a partnership with the 28-year-old Lúcio Costa, who had just been forced to resign after only one year in office as Director of the National Academy of Fine Arts for having replaced a standard Beaux-Arts curriculum of instruction with Bauhaus teaching methods. As a result of these events, the fulcrum of avant-garde architecture in Brazil shifted almost exclusively to the office of Warchavchik and Costa, where students gathered to discuss the latest theories of the International Style.

In 1936, partly to advance the cause of modern architecture in Brazil, Gustavo Capanema, at the time Minister of Education, asked Costa to submit a design for a new building for the Ministry of Education and Health in Rio (designed in 1937 and finished in 1943). Costa was allowed to secure the consulting services of Le Corbusier, who came again to Brazil, following a first trip in 1929. The result of that association was a design of such quality that it brought modern Brazilian architecture to worldwide prominence. More importantly, with the design of this building Costa taught Brazilian architects how to turn Le Corbusier's plasticity into a means for evoking essential native rhythms without doing violence to a contemporary style.

Besides having an interest in creating a modern Brazilian architecture, Costa's circle worked also to record and restore colonial buildings, which they saw as a source of the national tradition they wished to continue. After its inception in 1936, the National Service of Historical and Artistic Patrimony (SPHAN) was headed by Costa himself. Pursuing their nationalist interests further, avant-garde architects came to consider that a modern Brazilian architecture should parallel colonial developments, and worked for an integration of the visual arts to revive the traditions of the eighteenth-century national baroque. It was partly to fulfil such an aim of subsuming all the arts into architecture that in his Ministry of Education Building Costa made use of sculpture by Bruno Giorgi, Antonio Celso, and Jacques Lipchitz, and commissioned two murals from Cândido Portinari. With such a decision Costa started a trend which became characteristic not only of modern Brazilian architecture, but of all twentieth-century Latin American architecture.

Oscar Niemeyer, by far the most outstanding student in Costa's circle, was allowed to collaborate in designing the building for the Ministry of Education. Moreover, he became Le Corbusier's draughtsman for three months. Such splendid beginnings led in time to a remarkable independent practice. By adding his own sensuous curvilinear rhythms to the spatial conceptions and methods of construction of Le Corbusier and Costa, Niemeyer established a new trend in Brazilian architecture that was fresher, more mature, and more characteristically national than Costa's. This early period in Niemeyer's career included among other designs the Brazilian Pavilion for the New York Fair, 1938 (in collaboration with Costa), the Casino at Pampulha (Minas Gerais), 1942, and the Church of Saint Francis of Assisi, also at Pampulha, of 1943. Adopting Costa's principle of integrating the visual arts and architecture, Niemeyer included in his work of this period murals by Portinari, by Roberto Burle Marx, and by himself. Just as it had been the case in his choice of architectural forms, art in his buildings always had a strong Brazilian flavour.

Brasília was undoubtedly the most important architectural event of the 1950s in Latin America. In 1956 an international jury awarded first prize to Lúcio Costa's scheme, in the shape of a bird with outspread wings. Concurrently, President Juscelino Kubitschek appointed Niemeyer technical advisor to NOVACAP, the governmental authority for the new capital of Brazil. In his new capacity, Niemeyer designed the buildings for the Congress, the presidential palace, the cathedral, a housing complex, and other major structures. His design for the Congress building was as forcefully symbolic as Costa's plan for the city; it included a concave dome for the Senate and a convex bowl for the Chamber of Deputies. He also made use of curvilinear forms for his cathedral, essentially a sheath of outward-opening concrete parabolas held together at their apex and forming a cone underneath. For the presidential palace, on the other hand, he chose an elongated parallelepiped

The Presidential Palace, one of the most striking buildings designed by Oscar Niemeyer for the new Brazilian capital

relieved by a colonnade in the shape of inverted parabolas. Brasília was supposed to be the crowning achievement in the development of modern Brazilian architecture, a cause that had the wholehearted support of President Kubitscheck. Although on paper the designs had created a complex of extraordinary elegance, reality was different. The scale of the city turned out to be too vast to be harmonious; moreover, Brasília has not aged well. Nevertheless, at the time that the designs were made known to the international architectural community, Brasília was hailed as one of the outstanding designs of the century.

Mexico

Mexico was another important leader in the development of modern Latin American architecture. Its early avant-garde architecture, however, was different from that of Brazil. During the 1930s Mexican architects, such as Juan O'Gorman and Luis Barragán, followed a stern international functionalist line exhibiting large expanses of glass and taut planes of white stucco. But already by the 1940s Barragán was investigating the possibilities of using vernacular elements of architecture in his residential work in the subdivision of El Pedregal in Mexico City.

By the end of the decade Mexican architecture was well on the way to creating a style that was as national as it was modern. The buildings of the University of Mexico (UNAM), a joint venture of gigantic proportions, reveal that fact splendidly. In the incredibly short span of three years, from 1950 to 1953, more than 150 architects, engineers, and technicians completed the basic portion of the overall plan for the University City, designed by Mario Pani and Enrique del Moral. This project made manifest an extraordinarily strong surge of nationalist sentiment. Not only did some of the shapes follow forms of pre-Columbian buildings, as was the case of Alberto Arai's handball courts in the shape of Toltec pyramids, but also, and for the first time, the work of Mexican muralists, with their powerful Indian themes, was extensively used for the exterior decoration of buildings. The Central Administration Building, by Mario Pani, Enrique del Moral, and Salvador Ortega, carried two murals by Siqueiros; the Central Library, by Juan O'Gorman, Gustavo Saavedra, and Juan Martínez de Velasco, was covered by murals by O'Gorman; and the Medical and Biological Sciences Building had murals by Francisco Eppens. The University of Mexico, with its vast scale, marked a new step in the development of Latin American architecture in the early 1950s, one that pointed to new possibilities of an almost heroic breadth. Brasília, it will be remembered, was first planned but a few years later.

Félix Candela, a Spaniard who fought on the Nationalist side during the Civil War and who arrived in Mexico in 1939, represents a different trend within the scope of Mexican architecture. Candela's work has always been coloured by an influence from Eduardo Torroja's sense of structure. As such, his work is characterized by the use of the *cascarón*, or concrete shells in the shape of hyperbolic paraboloids. The Pavilion for Cosmic Ray Research at the University of Mexico, the Church of Santa Mónica in Mexico City, of 1966, and the Sports Palace for the 1968 Olympics, in Mexico City, are among his outstanding works.

NATIONALISM AND THE INTERNATIONAL STYLE

The example of Mexico and Brazil was soon followed in other countries. In Venezuela, Carlos Raúl Villanueva, who had studied at the Ecole des Beaux-Arts in Paris and whose use of concrete has been greatly influenced by Auguste Perret, designed for Caracas the first low-cost public housing project in Latin America, El Silencio, of 1941–3. This was followed by El Paraíso, of 1952–4, and by the 23 de Enero Housing Complex of 1955–7. But the University of Caracas is by far Villanueva's best known works. There, his Olympic stadium (1950), and his Olympic swimming pool (1957), make a daring use of reinforced concrete. The unit of the Aula Magna (Great Hall) and the covered plaza is Villanueva's most famous work in the university complex. Alexander Calder, who designed the 'flying saucers' that not only deco-

Mexican muralism combines with modern architecture. Central Library, National Autonomous University of Mexico (UNAM), with mosaics designed by Juan O'Gorman, who was also one of the architects.

rate the interior of the hall, but more importantly regulate its acoustics to perfection, has said of it: 'None of my mobiles has met with a more extraordinary environment – more effective or more grandiose.'

In Havana, the Plaza de la República, designed in 1950–1, was a Cuban response to the new Latin American trend of vast monumental projects in a contemporary style. The Office of the Comptroller, by Aquiles Capablanca, of 1952, with murals by Amelia Peláez, is usually accepted as the best building in the complex. The Tropicana Night Club, by Max Borges, Jr, of 1952, a series of eccentric concrete arches and semicircular glass curtain walls telescoping down to a stage, was a very successful attempt at linking sensuous modern forms with the lush vegetation of a tropical garden. On another level, the residential work of Mario Romañach, especially the Alvarez Residence, of 1957, is a remarkable example of an important trend in Cuban architecture of the 1950s. It endeavoured to create a national style that would express an avant-garde mode at the same time that it would evoke the rhythms and colour of native colonial buildings. The composition is ordered about a central courtyard, a feature that Cuban architecture had abandoned for a good seventy years. Romañach put it to work not merely as a way of evoking the past but also, and more importantly, as a means of bringing the prevailing breezes into the house, which thus required no air-conditioning. Air flows from the courtyard into the rooms and then escapes through an upper clerestory after having been deflected by the reinforced concrete hyperbolic paraboloids that constitute the roof. The design of this house thus reflected an evocation of national culture and a clever use of local climatic conditions. Moreover, the sensuality of its forms was brought under control by a consistent use of the golden mean as a system of proportion – one example of the influence of Le Corbusier's *Modulor* in Cuban architecture.

After the Revolution of 1959, the complex of buildings for the teaching of the plastic and performing arts in the former Country Club of Havana is the one important attempt the government has made to continue the earlier nationalist style. Designed by Ricardo Porro as a school of plastic arts in 1961–2, the complex consists of a series of sensuous breast-like domes developing along sinuous contours. After Porro's defection in 1963, the project was finished in 1965 by Vittorio Garatti, who added to it a school of performing arts in Porro's style.

But not all important modern architecture in Latin America responds to nationalistic trends. In Colombia, for instance, the building for the Bank of Bogotá (1959), by Pablo Lanzetta and Reinaldo Valencia, followed the strict pattern of a North

Spanish American theatre

The theatre in Spanish America has been the Cinderella of the arts. While the subcontinent has produced poets of worldwide fame, such as Pablo Neruda and Octavio Paz, and writers of fiction as distinguished as Jorge Luis Borges and Gabriel García Márquez, no Spanish American dramatist has as yet achieved international recognition.

It seems to have been the case that something akin to theatre existed in pre-Columbian Indian cultures in Spanish America, but after the conquest the stage was taken over for a while as a means of spreading the Gospel. The Mexican nun, Sor Juana Inés de la Cruz (1648–95) is remembered as a prolific playwright within the conventions of the Spanish baroque theatre, but other dramatists from the colonial period and the nineteenth century are only of interest to specialists. In our own century we perceive a gradual acceleration of theatrical acitivity to a point at which in the mid-1980s there are probably about 150 working dramatists in Spanish America as well as a very large number of groups writing and staging 'collective' theatre.

THE EARLY TWENTIETH CENTURY

From the turn of the century we can postulate three fairly clearly defined generations of Spanish American dramatists, with a fourth now making its presence felt. The first of these generations was the pioneer group of men born approximately in the decade 1865–75. At this time, although Lima and one or two other capital cities had some sort of theatrical tradition, the main centres of dramatic activity were Buenos Aires and Mexico City. The year 1903 saw the success of the first really significant modern Spanish American play *M'hijo el dotor* (My Son, the Lawyer) in Buenos Aires by the Uruguayan dramatist Florencio Sánchez (1875–1910). Sánchez and his Argentine contemporary Roberto Payró (1867–1928) can be regarded as the founders of the theatre in the River Plate region. Theirs was a social theatre with a strong didactic and critical element designed to stir the awareness of their audiences to the rapidly changing reality of their countries and to the need for newer, less traditional attitudes among the middle class. Similarly in Mexico, Federico Gamboa (1864–1939) in *La venganza de la gleba* (1905; The

Aula Magna, National University, Caracas, Venezuela, with mobiles by Alexander Calder

American skyscraper. In fact, Skidmore, Owings and Merrill were retained as consultants for the project.

In the Southern Cone, architects generally followed the canons of the International Style during the 1940s and 1950s. Such is the case, for instance, of Jorge Ferrari and Amancio Williams, of Argentina. Among the outstanding modern buildings of Buenos Aires, the San Martín Municipal Theatre (1953–61), by Mario Roberto Alvarez and Macedonio Oscar Ruiz, and the Bank of London and South America Building (1960–6), by Clorindo Testa, Santiago Sánchez, and Alfredo Agostini, are to be especially noted. Of these, the latter already points to Brutalist sources. Earlier, in 1949–54, Le Corbusier had designed and built a residence in Argentina, the Curuchet House, in Mar del Plata.

Mainly because of economic conditions, and at times because of political developments, Latin American architecture has not paralleled of late the brilliant achievements of earlier decades. No new names have emerged to dazzle the international architectural community, and increasingly few architects from the earlier generation remain in practice. In 1980 the late Luis Barragán of Mexico received the Pritzker Prize; by that act the whole of the Latin American nationalist architectural movement received a belated but important accolade. NM

Further Reading: F. Bullrich, *New Directions in Latin American Architecture* (New York, 1969); M. L. Cetto, *Modern Architecture in Mexico* (New York, 1961); P. Goodwin, *Brazil Builds: Architecture New and Old* (New York, 1943); H. R. Hitchcock, *Latin American Architecture Since* 1945 (New York, 1955); S. Moholy-Nagy, *Carlos Raul Villanueva and the Architecture of Venezuela* (London, 1964); O. Niemeyer, *Oscar Niemeyer* (Milan, 1975)

Vengeance of the Serfs) seems to forecast the peasant uprising which was to be at the heart of the Mexican revolution a decade later. Unfortunately this pioneering activity was followed by a decline in drama production for some twenty years.

The second generation of twentieth-century Spanish American dramatists was composed of men born roughly between 1895 and 1905. It included in Argentina Samuel Eichelbaum (1894–1967), Roberto Arlt (1900–42) and Conrad Nalé Roxló (1898–1970), and in Mexico Xavier Villaurrutia (1903–50), Celestino Gorostiza (1904–67) and especially Rodolfo Usigli (1904–79). With their appearance in the 1930s we begin to see the emergence of fully professional dramatists, conscious of the evolution of the European theatre in their own time, and in some cases producing a large output. Between the two World Wars, Spanish American theatre was seeking to respond to two different imperatives. One was to explore new areas of specifically Spanish American reality; the other was to keep abreast of technical innovations, especially those which came in the aftermath of Surrealism. These imperatives can be seen clearly at work in Mexico where they produced a strongly nationalist tendency centred on the Comedia Mexicana (Mexican Theatre) group in the late 1920s and early 1930s, and alongside it the more important and innovatory Teatro Orientación (Orientation Theatre) group. The latter introduced Pirandello, Chekhov, Shaw, O'Neill, Strindberg and other influential European playwrights to Mexican audiences. Usigli, Bernard Shaw's greatest disciple in Spanish America, attempted to bestride both tendencies, but his most famous play *El gesticulador* (1937; The Impersonator) was so politically subversive that it could not be publicly performed for ten years and even then provoked a Cabinet crisis. Usigli was still having his plays prohibited in his old age. In contrast, Villaurrutia's *Invitación a la muerte* (1940; Invitation to die) is almost a 'black comedy' and was strikingly novel in its time. In Buenos Aires we see a similar split between the basically realist theatre of observation represented by Eichelbaum in *Un guapo del 900* (1940; A Tough of the Past) and the curiously distorted Pirandellianism of Arlt's theatre of ideas on the one hand and Nalé Roxló's fantasy and poetic drama on the other.

POST-WAR WRITERS

The third generation of modern Spanish American playwrights comprised writers born roughly between 1920 and 1930. They now form the dramatic Establishment. By the 1950s Buenos Aires and Mexico City had begun to lose their predominance as cen-

tres of dramatic activity and at the same time a fresh set of European influences was beginning to be felt. The theatre in Peru began a new phase with the appearance of Sebastián Salazar Bondy (b. 1924). René Marqués (1919–79) founded the experimental Ateneo theatre company in Puerto Rico. In Chile two famous university theatre groups, the University of Chile Theatre Institute and the University of Chile Experimental Theatre were founded in 1941 and 1943 respectively. Elsewhere, too, the theatre began to come to life. For the first time in the 1950s we can begin to talk meaningfully about a Spanish American theatre in the full geographical sense of the term.

If the output of the dramatists of this third generation has not made a significant impact outside Spanish America, the chief reason is undoubtedly its prevailing tone of rebellious and even revolutionary social commitment. As also happened with Spanish American novels and poetry of social protest, the tendency is to privilege 'message' by the use of often crude symbolism and deliberately loaded conflicts, so that even where an attempt is made at the same time to exploit new dramatic techniques the literary quality of the plays is usually severely compromised. Thus, whether we look at a play like *Por los caminos van los campesinos* (1946; Along the Roads go the Peasants) by the Nicaraguan Pablo Antonio Cuadra (b. 1912), or more famous plays like the Argentine Carlos Gorostiza's *El puente* (1949; The Bridge), René Marqés's *Là muerte no entrará en Palacio* (1957; Death Must not Get into the Governor's Palace) and the Chilean Egon Woolf's *Los invasores* (1962; The Invaders), we feel uneasily that as the sociopolitical situation changes these works will be in danger of becoming mere museum pieces.

This danger does not deter many younger Spanish American dramatists. For them the essential problem since the 1950s has been to combine commitment with increasingly complex vanguardist techniques. Here Brecht has been far and away the greatest influence. The solutions to the problem have taken various forms. Luis Rafael Sánchez of Puerto Rico in his play *La pasión según Antígona Pérez* (1968; The Passion of Antigone Pérez) uses the model of Sophocles's *Antigone* to attack political oppression in Spanish America. The Mexican Vicente Leñero's *Pueblo rechazado* (1968; The Rejects) uses German 'documentary theatre' techniques similar to those of Peter Weiss and Rolf Hochhuth to dramatize the real-life story of Prior Lemercier of Cuernavaca who came into conflict with reactionary Church authorities. Similarly Jorge Díaz, Alejandro Sieveking and Sergio Vodonovic in Chile strive towards a radical but innovatory style of playwriting. In Argentina, Osvaldo Dragún's *Historias para ser contadas* (1957; Stories for Telling)

Teatro Municipal, San José, Costa Rica

portended what has been called the 'theatre of dissent' of Victor de los Solares, Guillermo Gentile and Ricardo Monti, all of whom emerged in 1970. Their work moves away from documentalism towards symbolic stage-parables but the socio-political thrust remains. In a sense the climax of this tendency is to be seen in 'collective' theatre. Here a group studies a certain amount of material relating to a given episode and then uses it to improvise dramatic situations which may produce a collectively created text or one which is written *post facto* by a member of the group. The subject matter is almost always some very recent event. 'Collective' theatre is certainly the supreme example of 'living theatre' in contemporary Spanish America. In Chile, for instance, in the early 1970s there were some 600 such groups operating.

At the opposite extreme is the 'theatre of the absurd' in the tradition of Ionesco, Beckett, Adamov and Albee, together with the shock-effect 'theatre of cruelty' influenced by Artaud and Genet. A number of the most striking plays of the 1960s combine both absurdist and cruel elements. In the Chilean Jorge Díaz's *El cepillo de dientes* (1961; The Toothbrush) the two characters play a very elaborate game in order to avoid communicating with each other, symbolically destroy the set and ritually 'kill' each other. The Cuban José Triana's *La noche de los asesinos* (1966; The Night of the Assassins) again involves a monstrous and horrifying game, while his fellow Cuban Antón Arrufat's *Todos los domingos* (1965; Every Sunday) involves successive re-enactments of the same grotesque love-scene until, just as it becomes reality, one of the partners is stabbed to death. More consistently brutal is Griselda Gambaro's *El campo* (1967; The Camp). It is actually set in a prison camp and makes its impact through the representation of systematic degradation and terror. The

problem of this kind of theatre is less its minority interest than its derivativeness. As Brecht took over from Pirandello as a major influence, so more recently Gotowski's ideas came into vogue after a period of avant-garde theatre which took its orientations from Genet, Beckett or Albee.

At the end of the 1970s the Spanish American theatre was still feeling its way forward in three radically different directions. For one of these, that of extreme social and political commitment, we might point to the post-Allende Chilean theatre of Victor Torres, Jorge Díaz, Alejandro Sieveking and Sergio Vodanovic which rested on a mood of angry indictment of Chilean society (for example, Sieveking's *Pequeños animales abatidos*, 1975; The Beavers). The second, that of popular 'collective' theatre, is seen in the work of such a group as the Grupo Teatro Escambray operating in the backwoods among the peasant hill farmers of Cuba and dramatizing, for example, the problems of collectivizing the land. The third, that of uncompromising experimentalism, might be represented by the Centro de Cultura Experimental in Buenos Aires and the 'play' *El pan nuestro* (1977; Our Daily Bread) by its director Bruno Bert, in which the scenes or 'situations' alter from performance to performance. Despite constantly expanding dramatic activity, the 1980s saw little substantial change in the situation. It still remains to be seen whether a dramatist of international stature will emerge from the newcomers.   DLS

Further Reading: S. Albuquerque, *Violent Acts: A Study of Contemporary Latin American Theatre* (Detroit, 1990); L. F. Lyday and G. W. Woodyard, *Dramatists in Revolt: The New Latin American Theatre* (Austin, Texas and London, 1976); *The Latin American Theatre Review:* University of Kansas (especially no. 13/2, supplement for Summer 1980)

Brazilian theatre

The first manifestations of a dramatic character appear in Brazil in the Jesuit missions of the sixteenth century. José de Anchieta S. J. (1534–97) wrote *autos* or medieval morality plays with the intention of gaining converts to the Christian religion among the Amerindian population. The propaganda motive is so obvious that the plays are bilingual with passages both in Portuguese and Tupi to make them easily understood by a mixed audience. The oldest theatre in Brazil is located in Vila Rica (Ouro Preto) and dates from the early eighteenth century. But it was only after 1808 that the first permenant theatre, Teatro Real de S. João, was built in Rio de Janeiro by order of the Prince Regent João, with the move of the court from Portugal to Brazil. In 1855 the Ginásio Dramático was founded in Rio, where French drama was shown to the public. Gradually merchants, businessmen and landowners began to join the aristocracy and a lower middle class of civil servants in regular visits to the theatre. It was, however, only after the end of the Second World War, when many experimental theatres were born in São Paulo and Rio de Janeiro, that a larger urban public felt the attractions of the theatre.

The founder of the Brazilian theatre was J. Gonçalves de Magalhães (1811–82) – the first author to show in his work the influence of romanticism. He lived in Paris, where he helped launch a literary magazine, *Niterói* (1836), in order to promote the romantic style. On his return to Brazil, he was greatly assisted in his plans by the distinguished actor João Caetano, who had organized in Rio de Janeiro, in 1833, the National Drama Company. João Caetano staged Gonçalves de Magalhães's drama, *Antônio*

Municipal Theatre, Rio de Janeiro (1906–09)

José ou o poeta e a inquisição (1836; Antônio José or the Poet and the Inquisition). The play takes as its subject the story of Antônio José (1705–39), born in Rio of Jewish parents, who became a famous playwright in Lisbon and was burnt at the stake by the Inquisition, because of his pointed attacks on physical and intellectual repression. In accordance with the principles of romantic aesthetics, Magalhães chose a national subject for his play, but he still bowed to the earlier neo-classical tradition by writing a tragedy in blank verse. A large variety of themes, developed with great skill, is to be found in the twenty-six plays written by L. C. Martins Pena (1815–48). His one-act comedies are his best work; in these he captures the mood and explores the imbroglios of ordinary life, using the colloquial language of the lower-class districts where he sets the action. Some of his most famous plays are *Os três médicos* (1845; Three Doctors), *O cigano* (1845; The Gipsy), and *O inglês maquinista* (1845; The English Engineer). The genre created by Pena was successfully continued by Artur Azevedo (1855–1908), whose comedies – *Horas de humor* (1876; Humorous Hours), *A princesa dos cajueiros* (1880; The Cashewnut Princess), *A viúva Clark* (1900; The Widow Clark), *O dote* (1907; The Dowry) – were successfully staged until 1907.

A dramatic poetic style was attempted by Gonçalves Dias (1823–64), who improved on the model left by Gonçalves de Magalhães. Among his well-polished plays, *Leonor de Mendonça* (1847) takes pride of place, as a sensitive drama in verse that portrays the conflict between passion and intolerance, showing that fate is determined by men's actions rather than by God's will. Machado de Assis (1839–1908), the novelist, was also fascinated by the theatre. He translated French drama and wrote his own comedies – *O caminho da porta* (1862; The Way Out), *Os deuses de casaca* (1866; Gods in Dinner Jackets) – but his civilized plays did not seem to stir the public, who preferred Artur Azevedo. The audiences of Rio and São Paulo were content with a pure form of entertainment that made no intellectual demands. The modernist movement of the 1920s left the theatre untouched, and the dramas of Oswald de Andrade (1890–1954), such as *O homem e o cavalo* (1934; Man and Horse), were never staged, due to the technical limitations of the Brazilian theatre at the time.

The great renewal of the texts written for the theatre, and of staging techniques, started only in 1943, with the arrival of theatre experts among the European refugees from the Second World War. Brazilian theatre then experienced a radical change and soon achieved an extraordinary vitality and diversity of styles in the plays produced between that date and 1978. In the same period there was an increase in the number of small experimental theatres in Rio and São Paulo, in spite of the negative effects of official censorship. While Guilherme de Figueiredo (b. 1915) produced dramatic parables (*A raposa e as uvas*, 1949; the Fox and the Grapes), and Pedro Bloch (b. 1914) reworked Pirandello's techniques *(As mãos de Eurídice*, 1951; The Hands of Eurydice), a brilliant group of playwrights appeared on the scene. Nelson Rodrigues (1912–80) stripped bare the unconscious tensions of the upper-middle classes in expressionist plays, *Vestido de noiva* (1943; The Wedding Gown), *A serpente* (1978; The Serpent). Jorge Andrade (b. 1922) centred on the conflicts of a declining 'aristocracy' of coffee-planters – *A moratória* (1955; Moratorium), *Pedreira das almas* (1958; Quarry of Souls) – and dealt courageously with the question of torture and political persecution in *Milagre na cela* (1977; The Miracle in Jail).

All this theatre exposed and condemned poverty and social oppression. João Cabral de Melo Neto (b. 1920) rebelled against poverty and famine in his *auto* on the north-east, *Morte e vida Severina* (1956; Severino's Life and Death), and A. Suassuna (b. 1927) addressed the same problems from a Christian viewpoint, in a mocking vein, in his morality plays. The revolt in the city, in the megalopolis of São Paulo or Rio, was shown by Gianfrancesco Guarnieri (b. 1936) in his *Eles não usam black tie* (1958; They Don't Wear Black Tie) and *A semente* (1963; The Seed). Meanwhile Augusto Boal (b. 1931) staged a political play that revealed the anguish and the hopes of an oppressed continent in *Revolução na América do Sul* (1960; Revolution in South America). And in 1970, Chico Buarque de Holanda (b. 1944) achieved great success with his *Opera do Malandro* (The Villain's Opera), where music, song, acting and mime were combined to achieve an experience of 'total theatre'. Experimentation and audacious originality are thus the main features of the present-day Brazilian theatre. These qualities have combined admirably in the development of a new genre, the television play, which now attracts many of the greatest talents; Alfredo Dias Gomez (b. 1922), celebrated author of *O pagador de promessas* (Keeping a Promise), very successfully produced for television *O Bem amado* (The Beloved One), derived from an earlier play of his.

LSR

Further Reading: S. Albuquerque, *Violent Acts: A Study of Contemporary Latin American Theatre* (Detroit, 1991); L. Kirschenbaum, *History of the Brazilian Drama* (Los Angeles, 1954)

Latin American cinema

SPANISH AMERICAN

Cinema made an early appearance in Spanish America. Some months after Lumière first showed his historic 'cinématographe' in Paris in 1895, moving pictures could be seen in Mexico City, Buenos Aires and Havana. Picture houses soon spread through the various republics and attracted what would become one of the largest cinema audiences in the world. Figures for Cuba in the mid-twentieth century reveal that out of a population of 7 million, 1.5 million went to the cinema every week. (These figures have doubled since the revolution partly due to the increased access of the rural population.) Some numbers reveal a profitable market for distributors and exhibitors and, more importantly, point to film (before the advent of television) as being the most important artistic medium for influencing and shaping values and ideas. It was not just Lenin who understood film to be 'the most important of all the arts'. Hollywood, especially after the First World War, was to monopolize film production and distribution throughout the continent.

Early production in Spanish America was limited to newsreels and documentaries. The first fictional films, Mario Gallo's *El fusilamiento de Dorrego* (1909; The Shooting of Dorrego) in Argentina or *El grito de Dolores* (1908; The Cry of Dolores) in Mexico, presented historical dramas, which became refined in Argentina with the popular *Nobleza gaucha* (Gaucho Nobility) by Eduardo Martínez in 1915. Documentaries, historical reconstructions and contemporary social themes provided the main subject matter up to the 1920s – the work of Enrique Díaz Quesada in Cuba was exemplary in this respect. As yet there were no really national film industries, for the products were diffuse and sporadic, although the Mexican government made good use of film propaganda during the revolutionary period: Pancho Villa, in particular, became a film star in North America after signing an exclusive contract with Mutual Film Corporation to film 'him and his war'. Tastes in Spanish America were to change with the advent of Hollywood cinema in the 1910s, and especially after the First World War.

The Argentine writer (and also occasional film critic) Jorge Luis Borges has remarked 'To enter a cinema in Lavalle Street [Buenos Aires] and find myself (not without surprise) in the Gulf of Bengal or Wabash Avenue seems preferable to entering the same cinema and finding myself (not without surprise) in Lavalle Street.' The national product became increasingly replaced by the magic, but also the marketing of Hollywood. In 1925, Hollywood supplied nearly all the feature films shown in Latin America: 90 per cent in Argentina, 95 per cent in Mexico, taking the two countries with the most developed film culture. This dependence had been slightly reduced by 1937 (70 per cent in Argentina, 80 per cent in Mexico). The history of Spanish American cinema is that of small national industries trying to compete for markets with North American distributors and in some cases exhibitors. North American companies would undercut local producers and offer a range of films made with lavish budgets. This problem became more acute when the relatively cheap and easy-to-make silent movies were replaced by talking pictures. Few republics had the money to invest in the new technology. Chile, which had produced a large number of feature films in the 1920s, could not sustain this development, and Cuba became the exotic site for North American and Mexican film companies.

The extent of Hollywood cultural penetration was to be analysed in the 1960s by a group of Latin American film-makers and theoreticians who saw their task as opposing the Hollywood model and recovering 'national' culture. The system they sought to reject was established in this early period: the local market was saturated by foreign films which imposed their own styles and values. Control of the market could also be kept at government level. In 1944, during the Second World War, the United States attempted to put pressure on the then neutral Argentine government by imposing a package of measures which included cutting supplies of raw film stock to Argentina, while continuing to supply Mexico, thus damaging production. At the same time, the office of the Co-ordinator of Inter-American Affairs under Nelson Rockefeller provided a grant to help modernize the Mexican motion picture industry 'to support the war effort and hemispheric solidarity'.

The struggle against Hollywood domination

In these conditions, only Argentina and Mexico developed viable film industries. Both were aided by the advent of sound, which had crippled other, smaller industries. Hollywood adopted a policy which varied between dubbing its films ('Hollywood proposes monsters which combine the illustrious features of Greta Garbo with the voice of Aldonza Lorenzo', wrote Borges), using sub-titles, which excluded a large number of illiterates, or replacing its 'stars' with Spanish actors, none of which could successfully hamper local industries. By exploiting the market for 'talkies' and musical comedies, Latin America made fifty-six features in 1936 and ninety

in 1937. In 1937 Mexico made fifty-two, Argentina thirty, Brazil four, Peru two and Uruguay and Cuba one each. Mexico and Argentina also exported features to other Latin American republics and benefited from the war years. By 1948, each industry had more than 10 per cent of the market in Bolivia, Cuba, Chile, Ecuador, Paraguay, Uruguay and Venezuela.

Mexican cinema received state aid from Avila Camacho, who set up the Banco Cinematográfico. Early productions included melodramas starring the Chilean singer José Bohr, and the more sophisticated productions of the director Fernando de Fuentes who shot historic themes (*El Compadre Mendoza*, 1933; Compadre Mendoza; and *Vámonos con Pancho Villa*, 1935; Let's Go with Pancho Villa), literary classics (*Doña Bárbara*, 1943), and inaugurated a succession of *comedias rancheras* with *Allá en el rancho grande* (1936; Down on the Farm). The directors Emilio Fernández and Alejandro Galindo produced bucolic 'indigenous' films with local stars such as Dolores del Río, who appeared in all the productions of El Indio Fernández, including the famous *Maria Candelaria*. There were some successes (the comedies of Cantinflas and the influential films of the Spanish exiles Buñuel and Alcoriza) but also a welter of mediocre 'local colour' comedies, musicals and drama. The situation deteriorated with the unionization of the industry in 1945, which became increasingly monolithic and effectively barred new talent and new ideas. In 1951, the industry produced over 100 films, but by 1964 this was down to less than fifty. In Argentina a similar pattern emerged. Tango musicals and comedies predominated, with local stars such as Luis Sandrini, Libertad Lamarque and Pepe Arias. Some directors of note emerged – Luis Saslavsky, Mario Soffici and Lucas Demare whose nationalist *Guerra gaucha* (1942; Gaucho War) was a great success. From 1946 President Perón protected the local industry, yet enforced censorship, and the industry went into a long decline and only revived again (briefly) in the early 1970s and mid-1980s.

The 1950s saw the emergence of 'cine clubs' which began to create the conditions for the theoretical and practical 'break' with the dominant forms which occurred in the 1960s. One example is the development in Cuba of the groups Nuestro Tiempo and Visión, from which Tomás Gutiérrez Alea and Julio García Espinosa, amongst others, emerged.

The 'New Cinema'

The 1960s produced what has loosely been called the 'new cinema' of Latin America, reflecting the mood of political and social optimism in those years. The film-makers also became the theoreticians of the movement. Influential essays such as Julio García Espinosa's 'Imperfect Cinema', Getino and Solanas's

Still from 'Memories of Underdevelopment', a Cuban film directed by Tomás Gutiérrez Alea, 1968

'Third Cinema' and Glauber Rocha's 'Aesthetics of poverty' all criticized the dominant Hollywood model and in some cases the European *auteur* movement, and proposed in its place 'cinema as "process"', in which the relations of production and reception would be changed. Instead of passive 'mass' audiences, the film-makers sought to promote active popular participation, for, as Mattelart has pointed out, one cannot change the mass media just by inverting the message, making heroes revolutionaries rather than John Wayne.

Theory is often better developed than practice, though in these years there was a widespread cultural offensive. Cuba offered one model. The film industry ICAIC was founded within months of the seizure of power by Fidel Castro's revolutionary government and despite having to start from nothing, acquiring equipment and training directors after the flight of North American technology, it produced from 1959 to 1977 nearly 100 features, 600 documentaries and more than 800 weekly newsreels. Documentaries have a special significance in a revolutionary context and the work of Santiago Alvarez has been exemplary. Feature films have covered a wide range of historical and contemporary themes and in a great variety of styles. Notable feature films produced include Julio García Espinosa's *Adventuras de Juan Quin Quin* (1967; Adventures of Juan Quin Quin), Tomás Gutiérrez Alea's *La muerte de un burócrata* (1966; Death of a Bureaucrat), *Memorias del subdesarrollo*

(1968; Memories of Underdevelopment) and *La última cena* (1977; The Last Supper), Manuel Octavio Gómez's *La primera carga al machete* (1968; The First Machete Charge) and *Los días del agua* (1971; Days of Water), Humberto Solás's *Lucía* (1968) and *Cantata de Chile* (1976; Song of Chile), Pastor Vega's *Retrato de Teresa* (1979; Portrait of Teresa) and Sarah Gómez's *De Cierta Manera* (1974/77; One Way or Another). There is no dominant orthodoxy – the film-makers (Alea, García Espinosa, Solás, Octavio Gómez, Pastor Vega amongst others) act as a co-operative and are free to work within the limits of a budget. Audiences have increased and the rural population has been integrated for the first time through the mobile cinema. Chile under Allende was less successful in using film in its ideological struggle. Few films were produced in the Popular Unity period and the state corporation Chile Films was split by factionalism. In fact, the most productive period in Chile occurred in the late 1960s with Raúl Ruíz's *Tres tristes tigres*, Helvio Soto's *Caliche sangriente* (Bloody Nitrate), Aldo Francia's *Valparaíso mi amor* (I Love Valparaiso) and Miguel Littín's *El chacal de Nahualtoro* (The Jackal of Nahualtoro), which was seen by over 250,000 people in Chile. In the River Plate region, Mario Handler and Ugo Ulive made *Elecciones (*1967; Elections), an analysis of the corrupt Uruguayan political system, and Solanas's marathon *La hora de los hornos* (Hour of the Furnaces) explored the neo-colonial conditions of Argentina, and traced the history of Peronism. This had to be shown in clandestine sessions. When Perón returned, there was a brief burst of creativity with the national epic *Juan Moreira* and *La Patagonia rebelde* (Rebel Patagonia) being shown in major film theatres.

In Bolivia at this period Jorge Sanjines and his film co-operative Ukamau made films on the exploitation of the Indians and the miners (*Ukamau*, 1966; *Yawar Mallku*, 1969, Blood of the Condor; *El coraje del pueblo*, 1971; The Courage of the People). They lived with indigenous communities, learned Quechua and Aymara and attempted to convey this cultural difference in an appropriate language. The winds of change even reached Mexico, when young directors protested against the monolithic union structure and eventually received state support under President Echeverría. All these different groups met in festivals such as that of Viña del Mar (Chile) in 1967, but theirs was a 'permitted' cinema, caused by the expansive optimism of the 1960s and could not be sustained in the very different political climate of the mid-1970s. A wave of military regimes swept to power, and the intellectual community shared the same sufferings as others: imprisonment, torture, exile or severe censorship. However, some impressive films were made in exile, especially by Chilean cinéastes.

Developments in the 1980s, with its shift towards democracy, are too recent to keep in sharp focus. Film-makers still talk of the 'new Latin American cinema', though this covers an amorphous group of different practices. The economic problems of the 1980s were immense, and cinema was now also forced to fight against the other attractions of the mass entertainment industry, such as TV and the newly de-regulated world of satellite and cable. Latin American film-makers worked within very shaky support structures. In Peru, Colombia, Venezuela, Mexico and Argentina, the state drastically reduced its funding. Despite these difficulties, there still seems to be an unquenchable desire to make films, as was shown brilliantly in Argentina in the years 1984–6.

BRAZIL

Cinema came early to Brazil, and in the first decade of the century a great number of feature films and documentaries were produced, including a series on famous contemporary crime (Antonio Leal's *Os estranguladores*, 1908; The Stranglers), historical documentaries and local-colour realism. This vigorous industry could not, however, compete with the Hollywood films which entered the country in the 1910s and 1920s. As in Spanish America, the home market was saturated: Hollywood supplied 95 per cent of the market in 1925, and 85 per cent in 1928 and 1937. National production was sustained in the 1920s in various regional groups, so called '*ciclos*' (cycles) in Recife, Campinas, Manaus and especially Cataguazes, under Humberto Mauro. Mauro has been acclaimed as the pioneer of '*cinema novo*' ('new cinema') in his critical portrayal of regional life, using low budget, 'anti-industrial' techniques.

The advent of sound caused more money to be injected into the industry. Adhemar Gonzaga set up the Cinédia studios and allowed Mauro to produce his most eclectic and influential film *Ganga Bruta* (1933) but this success was not sustained. The Atlántida studios produced a series of films in the 1930s and 1940s, the *chanchadas*, which were a form of farce, interspersed with songs by popular entertainers. Carmen Miranda starred in features such as *Alô, alô carnaval* (1936; Hello, Carnival!), before leaving for Hollywood. The films were idealized and exotic, but attracted a mass audience who could listen to local songs and jokes. Another attempt to set up a studio system in São Paulo in the late 1940s – the Vera Cruz Company – failed, despite having Alberto Cavalcanti as director and producing the occasional popular success (Lima Barreto: *O cangaceiro*, 1953, reviled by later directors for its 'false' treatment of the north-east).

A clear national focus was offered by the directors of the *cinema novo* a movement which grew up in the brief optimistic years of Kubitscheck and Goulart. A precursor and 'father' of the movement, Nelson Pereira Dos Santos, made *Rio 40 Graus* (Rio 40 Degrees) in 1955 about poverty and social inequality in Rio. This led to a series of films which Glauber Rocha, the movement's main theoretician, has divided into three phases. The first, between 1960 and 1963, focused on the north-east, describing the feudal conditions, poverty and mystic religion of that region. Directors' styles ranged from the extravagances of Glauber Rocha's *Deus e o diabo na terra do sol* (Black God, White Devil), to the neo-realism of Ruy Guerra's *Os fuzis* (The Guns) and Pereira Dos Santos's *Vidas sêcas* (Barren Lives). The second phase, between 1964 and 1967, dealt with political disillusionment after the coup and included Glauber Rocha's *Terra em transe* (Land in Anguish) and Gustavo Dahl's *O bravo guerreiro* (Brave Warrior). In 1968, repression became more severe and directors were forced to work in more indirect, allegorical modes, in what has been called the 'tropicalist' phase. At the same time they attempted to reach a wider popular audience, setting up their own distribution network Difilm and producing such popular successes as *Macunaíma* and the 'cannibalist' nationalist *Como era gostoso o meu francês* (How Tasty my Little Frenchman Was). This period is said to have ended when a number of directors left the country in 1972.

From the early 1970s to the late 1980s conditions improved for film-makers. The state played an increasing role, supporting Embrafilme, which gave grants and has established an extensive distribution network. Legislation meant that cinemas had to show Brazilian films for at least a third of the year. The result was a relatively healthy climate in which quality films vie with commercial mediocrity and *pornochanchadas* (porno-farces). With the revolution at a distance, even radical film-makers such as Ruy Guerra made critical films (A *Queda*, 1977; The Fall) within the system. The successes and limitations of such a strategy were the subject of lively debate.   JK

Further Reading: E. Bradford Burns, *Latin American Cinema: Film and History* (Los Angeles, 1975); J. Burton, *The New Latin American Cinema: An Annotated Bibliography of English Language Sources* 1960–1976 (Cineaste Pamphlet 4, New York, 1976); R. Johnson and R. Stam, eds., *Brazilian Cinema* (New Jersey, 1982); J. King, *Magical Reels: A History of Cinema in Latin America* (London, 1990); C. Mora, *Mexican Cinema: Reflections of a Society, 1896–1980* (Los Angeles, 1982)

The Press

Many Latin American countries can trace back the history of their press to the appearance of commercial gazettes in the late colonial period. Of the existing newspapers, however, the oldest date back to the early years of independent life. Chile's *El Mercurio* (of Valparaíso) and Brazil's *Jornal do Comércio* were founded in 1827; Peru's *El Comercio* in 1839; Panama's *La Estrella de Panamá* in 1853 (its now defunct English-language parent, *The Star and Herald*, having appeared in 1849). In the Caribbean, Jamaica's *Daily Gleaner* dates back to 1834.

REVOLUTIONS AND CONTINUITY

In several countries, political upheavals interrupted such continuity. In Mexico (the country with the second largest number of newspapers in the region) the 1910 revolution led to a complete break with the past; the oldest existing newspapers (all still among the leaders) are *El Universla* (1916), *Excélsior* (1917) and *La Prensa* (1928). In Bolivia, three successive breaks left few survivors from the past: *El Diario* (1904) from when the tin barons emerged as the dominant force in the economy, *Ultima Hora* (1939) from the days of the populist experiment conducted by President Germán Busch, and *Presencia* (1952) from the time of the revolution led by Víctor Paz Estenssoro's Movimiento Nacionalista Revolucionario. Similarly, in Cuba the revolution headed by Fidel Castro in 1959 led to the disappearance of all pre-revolutionary newspapers; the oldest in existence now is *Granma*, founded in 1965.

In many other cases, political upheavals have not caused such complete breaks, but have been responsible for the birth and demise of journalistic booms, some of which have left a lasting mark on the development of the Latin American press. In Argentina, the country with the third largest number of newspapers even today, and with the highest indices of circulation per thousand inhabitants, the rise of *Yrigoyenismo* in the early twentieth century coincided with a publishing boom of which the best-remembered exponent was the newspaper *Crítica*. It was a remarkable experiment with a large circulation 'popular' daily whose writers included the leading intellectual lights of the time – echoes of which subsist in the present-day *Clarín* (1945), a daily with tabloid format and high circulation that ranks among the country's leading 'serious' newspapers.

Peronism in the late 1940s and early 1950s saw the creation of a huge state-controlled network of press media which was swept away by the military coup of 1955. Then came the boom of the late 1960s and early 1970s, which at one point made Buenos Aires the city with the largest number of magazines in the world. But it was dealt a crippling blow by the political violence of the mid–1970s, when many journalists were killed and most of the leading talents in the field were driven into exile.

In postwar Uruguay, 'the Switzerland of the Americas' saw the appearance of *Marcha*, once the most prestigious magazine of political analysis in the hemisphere, which vanished with the creeping military takeover of government in the early 1970s.

TRANS-NATIONAL PUBLICATIONS

The fact that most countries of the region share a common language (Spanish) and a common cultural heritage has repeatedly kindled the aspiration of developing region-wide publications. However, only one lasting success has been registered in this field: the newsmagazine *Visión*, founded in 1950. Better fortune has accompanied some more recent (1970s) ventures with a more limited, sub-regional scope. Leading exponents in this field are the Lima-based *Andean Report* (an English-language monthly covering economic news in the Andean countries) and the Guatemala-based *Inforpress Centroamericana* (with its English-language companion *Central America Report*, a weekly covering economic and political events in the isthmian countries).

If the common bond of the Spanish language has not provided strong enough foundations for the development of a region wide press, historical links with Britain and the United States have stimulated the growth of high-quality newspapers and journals in English. In Argentina, *The Buenos Aires Herald*, founded in 1876 occupies a position of great prestige. This has mainly been won by its editorial independence, maintained even through periods when other publications had fallen prey to censorship, self-censorship or the fear of violent reprisals. Also in Argentina, *The Review of the River Plate*, founded in 1891, has long been considered an authoritative journal of economic and commercial information. Venezuela's *Daily Journal* has equally long been considered one of the best exponents of the Caracas press. The above-mentioned *Andean Report* and *Central America Report* are also leading examples, and most capitals also have excellent examples of the classical newsletter. Paradoxically, in terms of news-gathering techniques and sophistication, the English-language press is far more developed on the Spanish-speaking mainland than in the English-speaking Caribbean.

PRESS FREEDOM

A side-effect of the political upheavals which have so marked the development of the Latin American newspapers has been the prevalence of constraints on press freedom in most countries. These, varying according to time and to place, have ranged from outright censorship to subtler methods of economic coercion and even institutionalized bribery. In the mid-1970s Argentina presented the extreme case of physical repression of the press: as a professional group journalists and publishers were leading targets of the campaign of assassinations, abductions ('disappearances'), imprisonment and enforced exile

TABLE 5
Press Freedom

Journalists killed

Country	1989[1]	1990[2]
Colombia[3]	20	6
Mexico[3]	2	4
Peru[3]	7	3
Chile[4]	–	2
Guatemala[3]	–	1
Haiti[5]	–	1
Jamaica[4]	–	1
El Salvador[3]	9	–
Brazil[3]	4	–
Ecuador[4]	1	–
Panama[4]	1	–

Notes: [1] Revised. [2] Data to 15 December. [3] 'Partly free' press. [4] 'Most free' press. [5] 'Least free' press.

Relative Press Freedom

Partly free	Least free
Colombia	Cuba
El Salvador	Guyana
Honduras	Haiti
Mexico	
Nicaragua	
Paraguay	
Peru	
Suriname	

All other countries are in the 'most free' category.

World Position Percentage of countries surveyed

Category	Latin America	World
Most free	61.3	38.9
Partly free	29.0	19.7
Least free	9.7	41.4

News-stand, Porto Velho, Brazil, mid-1980s

Source: *Freedom Review*

unleashed by the extreme right – and its counterpart, widespread self-censorship out of fear in the surviving media. The editor of the *Buenos Aires Herald*, Robert Cox, was forced to leave the country after threats were made against his life; the publisher and editor of *La Opinión*, Jacobo Timerman, was abducted, tortured and expelled from the country after having been stripped of his citizenship and his newspaper – his book *Prisoner Without a Name, Cell Without a Number* made his case known throughout the world.

Mexico has traditionally provided the best example of institutionalized 'indirect' constraints. Compliance by publishers was long ensured by a government monopoly of newsprint imports (and the threat to restrict them as a punitive measure), while the allegiance of journalists was 'bought' by bribery, in the form of a second paypacket from government institutions or agencies. Both practices have since been discontinued. In the Nicaragua of the Sandinista government (1979–90) a combination of outright censorship and 'indirect' pressures was used against the only opposition newspaper, *La Prensa*. In Cuba all press organs are controlled by the state, the party or their agencies.

After the period straddling the 1970s and 1980s in which a majority of countries were ruled by the military, the restoration of elected rule led to the easing of constraints on the press. Indeed, in several cases (Brazil, Argentina and Chile are good examples), the emergence of an increasingly free press preceded, and even helped expedite, the withdrawal of the military from power.

A survey published in 1990 by the New York-based Freedom House provides a mixed assessment of press freedom in Latin America at the start of the new decade. On the one hand the number of countries with a free press is higher than the world average; on the other, Latin America ranks high in the

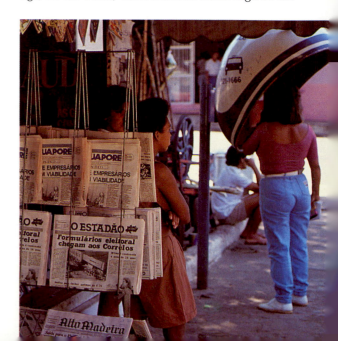

Display of magazines on sale, Mexico City, 1985

record of the killing of journalists. Out of the 157 countries surveyed worldwide, 38.9 per cent are listed under the heading of 'most free' press; among the thirty-one Latin American countries examined, 61.3 per cent are in that category. But in 1990, eighteen journalists in seven Latin American countries were killed: 42 per cent of the cases recorded worldwide. Indeed, of the four countries in the world with the highest rate of killings, three were Latin American: Colombia came second with six, Mexico third with four, Peru fourth with three. Overall the statistics were better than a year earlier, when forty-four journalists (60 per cent of the world total) were killed in Latin America. It is worth noting that the lives of journalists are not only, or even mainly, at risk from pro-establishment violence: most of the killings in Colombia (twenty-six in 1989–90) were perpetrated by drug-traffickers.

One disquieting feature of the survey was that not all the killings took place in countries whose press is listed in the 'least free' or 'partly free' categories: in 1990 three journalists were killed in two countries listed among those with the 'most free' media; in 1989 this was the fate of six journalists in three of the 'most free' countries.

JOURNALISTIC STYLE

It is only in the past thirty years that Latin American journalism has begun to break away from the traditional 'literary' style – wordy and not too concerned with factual reporting. The change was pioneered in the mid-1960s, in Argentina, by Jacobo Timerman. He introduced the first newsmagazines on the lines of the US publications *Time* and *Newsweek*. Timerman founded, first, *Primera Plana*, then its competitor, *Confirmado*. Though both of these have since disappeared, their 'newsier' style, hallmarked by a more economic use of the Spanish language, has lived on in Argentina (the weekly *Noticias* is a good example), and soon found emulators in the neighbouring countries, mainly in the Southern cone.

In Chile, Emilio Filippi switched the already existing magazine *Ercilla* to the new style and managed to maintain its tradition of (relative) editorial independence well into the years of General Pinochet's rule. When forced to relinquish the editorship of *Ercilla* in the late 1970s, Filippi founded the award-winning *Hoy* as its even more outspoken successor. The same style was adopted by newcomers to the field, such as *Análisis, Apsi* and *Qué Pasa*. These, together with a new venture of Filippi's, the newspaper *La Epoca*, helped create the political climate that led to the end of the military dictatorship.

Over the same period, similar changes were taking place in Brazil, which spawned a string of excellent newsmagazines such as *Veja, Exame* and *Isto E*. In spite of having to cope with the restrictions imposed by the military regime which came to power in 1964, the Brazilian press continued to develop professionally and technically, to the current position in

TABLE 6

Number of High Circulation Dailies (More Than 100,000 Copies) 1990

Country	No. of dailies	Circulation (000)
Mexico	10	2046
Venezuela	6	1190
Argentina	5	1236
Brazil	5	1112
Colombia	4	604
Peru	4	637
Chile	3	440
Ecuador	2	304
Puerto Rico	2	399
Costa Rica	1	100
El Salvador	1	97
Uruguay	1	130
TOTAL	44	8295

Number of dailies in top ten

Country	No. of dailies	Circulation (000)
Argentina	2	810
Mexico	2	700
Brazil	2	580
Venezuela	2	530
Peru	1	250
Colombia	1	215
TOTAL	10	3085

TABLE 7
Leading Daily Newspapers 1990

Title[1]	Country	Circulation[2]	Peak[3]
Clarín	Argentina	480,000	750,000s
Esto	Mexico	400,200	450,000w
O Globo	Brazil	350,000	520,000s
Cronica	Argentina	330,000	450,000s
La Prensa	Mexico	300,000	
Meridiano	Venezuela	300,000	
Ojo	Peru	250,000	
Ultimas Noticias	Venezuela	230,250	
O Estado de Sao Paulo	Brazil	230,000	460,000s
El Espectador	Colombia	215,000	
Folha de Sao Paulo	Brazil	211,900	314,830s
La Nación	Argentina	210,648	
Novedades	Mexico	210,000	240,000m
El Heraldo de México	Mexico	209,600	
El Vocero de P. Rico	Puerto Rico	209,000	
Ovaciones	Mexico	205,000	
El Tiempo	Colombia	200,000	350,000s
Jornal do Brasil	Brazil	200,000	325,000s
Excélsior	Mexico	200,000	
El Mundo	Venezuela	195,120	
El Nuevo Día	Puerto Rico	190,000	193,000s
El Universal	Mexico	181,375	197,681s
El Nacional	Venezuela	175,000	
El Universo (Guayaquil)	Ecuador	174,000	255,000s
La Tercera de la Hora	Chile	170,000	
El Comercio	Peru	150,000	220,000s
Las Ultimas Noticias	Chile	150,000	
2001	Venezuela	150,000	
El Universal	Venezuela	140,000	
El Comercio	Ecuador	130,000	
El País	Uruguay	130,000	
El Colombiano (Medellín)	Colombia	123,707	
Expreso	Peru	123,000	
El Mercurio	Chile	120,000	250,000s
Jornal da Tarde	Brazil	120,000	180,000m
El Norte (Nuevo León)	Mexico	120,000	150,000s
El Nacional	Mexico	120,000	
Ambito Financiero	Argentina	115,000	
La República	Peru	114,000	
El Cronista Comercial	Argentina	100,000	
Diario Extra	Costa Rica	100,000	
El Financiero	Mexico	100,000	
La Prensa Gráfica	El Salvador	97,312	115,564s
El País (Cali)	Colombia	65,071	108,304s

Notes [1] Unless otherwise indicated, published in the capital. In the case of Brazil, published in Rio de Janeiro.
[2] Normal weekday circulation.
[3] Day of highest circulation: s=Sunday; m=Monday.

which its quality is by far the highest in Latin America. This is in sharp contrast to Argentina, where the interruption of the press boom of the 1970s by the military coup of 1976 forced many of the country's best journalists into exile and caused a dramatic fall in quality from which the press was only beginning to recover in the late 1980s.

Daily newspapers took longer than the magazines to adapt to modern journalistic techniques and styles.

Here again one of the pioneers was Argentina's Jacobo Timerman, who in 1971 founded *La Opinión*, a daily newspaper divised on lines similar to those of France's *Le Monde*. *La Opinión* was a casualty of the 1976 coup, but its influence was felt in several other Spanish-speaking countries. Its mark, and that of some of its short-lived Argentine followers, is recognizable, for instance, in Mexico's *Unomásuno*. Argentina was breaking new ground again in 1987, with the appearance of *Página 12*, a daily newspaper which combines some of the best investigative reporting with daring design and a sharp sense of humour.

Another landmark in the modernization of the region's daily press was the apperance in Venezuela, in 1979, of *El Diario de Caracas,* founded by Rodolfo H. Terragno. Terragno is an exiled Argentine publisher who had earlier broken new ground in his home country with the magazine *Cuestionario* . Fellow-Argentines who accompanied Terragno to Caracas also contributed innovations in the field of the specialized press in Venezuela: Miguel Angel Diez with *Número*, Raúl Lotitto with *Producto*. This group was also involved in the 1982 takeover of the British-based *Latin American Newsletters* (founded in 1967), best known for its English-language publications that circulate in the northern hemisphere, but with three Spanish-language titles that circulate throughout Latin America.

CIRCULATION AND POPULATION

It is difficult to discern any clear pattern in the correlations between the development of the press and social indicators throughout the region. The three countries with the largest populations (Brazil, Mexico and Argentina, in that order) are also those with the largest number of daily newspapers (in the same order). Thereafter, however, the correlation breaks down. Uruguay, for example, ranks ninth in number of newspapers but sixteenth in size of population. When attention turns to circulation per thousand inhabitants, Argentina moves up to the top of the list, and Uruguay rises to second place (while Mexico falls to sixth place, Venezuela to eighth, Peru to ninth and Brazil all the way down to twenty-first).

Literacy rates do not offer any clearer correlation with circulation. Argentina and Uruguay rank, respectively, first and second on the literacy scale, matching their position regarding circulation. But Venezuela is in fifth place (eighth in circulation), Mexico in tenth (sixth in circulation) and Brazil in twelfth (twenty-first in circulation). Chile has the third highest literacy rate and ranks twelfth in circulation.

EC

Radio and television in Latin America

Radio and television stations proliferate throughout Latin America. According to the latest available estimates (*c.*1990) there are over 267 million radio receivers and more than 41 million TV sets in the eighteen Spanish-speaking countries of Latin America. For Brazil, the figures are 146 million radio receivers and 35 million TV sets.

Both in the vast thinly populated areas and in the great conurbations like Mexico City, São Paulo and Buenos Aires, broadcasting holds a commanding position as a vehicle of information and of entertainment. Several factors contribute to the penetration of radio and television, amongst them the generally low level of newspaper readership, the vigorous thrust of commercial interests, and the efforts of some governments to use the media for purposes of education and national integration.

In most Latin American countries broadcasting is under the control of a government department that is responsible for granting concessions for radio stations and television channels. In Mexico, for instance, it is the Directorate-General of Radio, Television and Cinematography, generally known as RTC. All commercial radio and TV stations in Mexico are compelled by law to cede one eighth of their broadcasting time to the government and it is the RTC that is responsible for planning and producing the material designed to fill that allocation, though it has not yet succeeded in taking up all the air and screen time to which it is entitled. RTC is also in charge of Radio México Internacional, the short wave external service, as well as 'La Hora Nacional', an official government bulletin carried on Sunday evening by all the radio stations in the country.

In Brazil, broadcasting is under the supervision of the Ministry of Infrastructure and the Ministry of Justice. Through Radiobrás, a state holding company established in 1976, the Ministry of Infrastructure co-ordinates the technical aspects of all the government-owned radio and television stations. Radiobrás was also designed to build up radio and television coverage in the north-east and in the Amazon region, both areas which had hitherto been poorly served by the Brazilian media. All radio stations in Brazil are compelled to broadcast a daily programme called 'A Hora do Brasil' (The Brazilian Hour), a bulletin of news and current affairs which is compiled by Radiobrás and broadcast between 19:00 and 20:00 hours.

In Argentina, to take a third example, the Communications Secretariat regulates the radio and television stations through the Broadcasting Directorate. The Federal Broadcasting Committee (COMFER) deals with administration, under the supervision of the Broadcasting Directorate.

RADIO

There are many thousands of radio stations in Latin America. Even the Dominican Republic, one of the smallest countries, has 120. In Brazil, the country with the most, there are about three thousand. Argentina has 190 and Venezuela 220. The majority of stations throughout the area are small commercial enterprises, in many cases virtually built around one man playing records, cassettes or CDs, interspersed with jingles and commercials. But in most of the larger cities there are also sophisticated organizations which operate several different programme streams, each designed to appeal to a particular section of the listening audience. Such networks are likely to include a news-type station which carries frequent short bulletins and perhaps three times a day (at breakfast time, at noon and in the evening) lengthy programmes of international and local news and comments; a stereo FM station (in all probability fully automated) presenting the latest international hits; and a medium- or long-wave station devoted to interminably lengthy soap operas (*radionovelas*) or the local brand of popular music, for example salsa or brassy ranchy style (*musica ranchera*) in the case of Mexico and Central America, tangos and milongas in the case of Argentina.

Advertising is selected to suit the appropriate stream. The first two types of stations described (news and Stereo FM) will carry commercials aimed at 'Class A' – that is, the more affluent consumer sector. The commercial message of the soap opera or local music station will be addressed to the 'Class B' or 'Class C' consumer.

National radio

In most countries there is also the national radio or the official state network. Often under-financed and ill-equipped, these stations are subject to the whim of the current political establishment, and the staff's often altruistic ideals are a poor defence against insecurity of tenure. With few exceptions – Brazil's Radiobrás is one – these stations do not make a great impact.

University stations

Several Latin American universities are active in broadcasting. Though by their very nature directed to the more discriminating minority audiences, university stations are sometimes run by enthusiasts who are able to offer surprisingly rich fare to listeners seeking refuge from the commercial battle of the air. Apart from broadly educational programmes supported by their own academic resources and classical music presented without concession, they tend to include in their output the choicest cultural programmes supplied by the leading international broadcasters such as the BBC, West Germany's Deutsche Welle, Netherlands Radio and the Voice of America. More recently, some university stations in Chile, for example, have started rebroadcasting from London – via satellite – news and current affairs programmes from the Latin American Service of the BBC. The best-endowed university station, and the one with the most ambitious output, is undoubtedly Radio UNAM, the broadcasting service of the National Autonomous University of Mexico.

Religious stations

Latin America has numerous religious broadcasting organizations, both Catholic and Protestant. Leading the field – and heard throughout the American continent and beyond – is HCJB (La Voz de los Andes), founded in Quito, Ecuador, in 1931. HCJB is a (Protestant) World Radio Missionary Fellowship station (of Florida, USA) which provides a wide-ranging service of news and cultural and evangelical material in sixteen different languages. Other important Protestant stations are the Adventist World Radio (AWR) in Costa Rica, and CAM International in Guatemala.

Among the many Catholic stations, Radio San Gabriel, which broadcasts in Aymara, the predominant language of the area surrounding Lake Titicaca,

aims to improve standards of literacy and self-reliance and also seeks to promote in its audience an awareness of Aymara culture and nationhood.

TELEVISION

There are about 400 TV stations in Latin America. The largest organization in the Spanish-speaking world is Mexico's Televisa, a privately owned commercial chain with four television channels. It dominates Mexico City as well as covering virtually the whole country. There are also forty-five stations that produce local programming which take Televisa programmes. Televisa's immense output of home-produced *telenovelas* (drama serials) and dubbed foreign programmes is marketed throughout Spanish-speaking America and gives Mexico an unrivalled preponderance in the medium.

Televisa also has a strong following among the millions of Spanish-speakers in the United States through Galavision, which is received either by satellite, cable or repeater stations. The satellite revolution has also made its impact in Latin America where TV dishes are now commonplace, with TV channels (mainly from the USA, but also from Europe and some Latin American countries) being received throughout the continent.

In Brazil, the most powerful TV organization is the Rede Globo (Globo Network), a Rio-based conglomerate which comprises TV, radio, the influential newspaper *O Globo*, a leading record company and various showbusiness interests. Globo claims the lion's share of TV audiences in Rio and São Paulo, but covers the whole country, including most of the Amazon region. It has offices in New York, Paris and

Scene from 'Amazon Sisters', a Brazilian television programme successfully exported

London, and has exported its programmes to many countries in Europe and Africa. (Great Britain's innovative Channel 4, established in 1982, has shown a variety of popular Brazilian material).

International broadcasting organizations

Of the various international bodies designed to promote cooperation between different broadcasting organizations and to represent their interests, the leading one in Latin America is AIR (Asociación Inter-Americana de Radiodifusión), which has its central office in Montevideo, Uruguay. Argentina, Brazil, Chile, Colombia, Mexico and Venezuela are also associate members of EBU, the European Broadcasting Union, which was founded in 1950 to support the interests of members and to assist the development of radio and television world-wide. The radio and TV organizations of the English-speaking Caribbean are grouped within the CBU, the Caribbean Broadcasting Union, an association of national broadcasting systems formed to promote interchange between member countries.   AMAP/DV

Further Reading: R. Atwood and E. McAnany, eds., *Communication and Latin American Society: Trends in Critical Research, 1960–1985* (Madison, Wisconsin, 1986); E. Fox, ed., *Media and Politics in Latin America: The Struggle for Democracy* (London, 1988); L. A. de Noriega and F. Leach, *Broadcasting in Mexico* (London 1979); J. Schwoch, *The American Radio Industry and its Latin American Activities, 1900–1939* (Urbana, Ill., 1990); T. E. Skidmore, ed., *Television, Politics and the Transition to Democracy in Latin America* (forthcoming)

History of Science in Latin America

SCIENCE IN EARLY COLONIAL TIMES

The scientific enterprise in Latin America has been closely linked to that of the western world from the Spanish conquest to the present. The Aztecs, Mayas and Incas had protoscientific accomplishments similar to those of the other high civilizations of antiquity (for example, numeration and astronomical observations related to calendrical computation, descriptive botany, pharmacology, metallurgy), elements of which were quickly assimilated by the Spaniards into the corpus of European science. The great expedition

of Francisco Hernández (1517–87) to New Spain from 1570 to 1577 was designed to recover and preserve Aztec natural history, particularly materia medica, towards which end Hernández learned Nahuatl. The result of his labours was a massive natural history of New Spain, unpublished in his lifetime. Prior to the Hernández expedition, a great store of the New World natural history had already been transferred to Europe in such treatises as the *Natural and General History of the Indies* (1535, a summary of which had appeared in 1526) of Gonzalo Fernández de Oviedo (1478–1557) and the *Medicinal History of the Indies* (1565) by Nicolás Monardes (*c.* 1493–1588), whose principal focus was the medicinal use of New World plants, animals and minerals.

At the same time, the geography of the New World was being integrated into the modified classical scheme based on the fifteenth-century recension of Ptolemy's geography. A conceptual breakthrough was achieved by Pedro Mártir de Anglería (1457–1526) who first posited the existence of a 'New' World as distinct from that which had been

Manuscript world map attributed to Juan de la Cosa (1500). This is one of the earliest maps to include the New World.

known to the ancients. The earliest general geography to synthesize a vision of old and new worlds conjoined was the *Suma de geografía* (1519) of Martín Fernández de Enciso. Early cartographic representations of the New World were found on maps drawn by Sebastian Cabot (1474–1557), Juan de la Cosa (d. 1510) and Francisco Domínguez, a Portuguese cartographer assigned to the Hernández Expedition.

In the seventeenth century, scientific activity domiciled in Latin America grew in importance, in part because of the growth of universities in the Spanish empire and in part a reflection of the density of urban populations and the growth of local economies which required technical personnel. Colonial men of science shared the age's characteristic enthusiasm for celestial observation, owing to the vogue of the telescope. Particularly noteworthy were Diego Rodríguez's (1596–1668) *Observation of the New Comet,* an astrological study of the comet of 1652 which cites observations by Galileo, and the observation of the comet of 1680 by Carlos Sigüenza y Góngora (1645–1700), another Mexican scientist, probably a student of Rodríguez. Siguenza was greatly influenced by the Spanish *novatores,* scientists who attempted to come to grips with the new science without breaking openly with official dogma. Accordingly, Sigüenza utilized elements of Copernican cosmology without championing it openly.

The accrued Spanish experience in practical metallurgy was synthesized in the work of seventeenth-century authors, particularly in the *Arte de los metales* (1640) of Alvaro Alonso Barba (*c.*1569–1662) which discusses amalgamation, founding and other processes used in the Peruvian silver mines.

THE EIGHTEENTH CENTURY

Science in eighteenth-century Latin America was characterized by a number of well-defined processes: first, the slow percolation of the New Science – represented by Copernicus, Galileo, Newton and Harvey – a process which took more than a century owing to the the scholasticism of official institutions of learning; second, the surveying of the natural history of Spanish America by a succession of expeditions sponsored by the crown, large-scale enterprises characteristic of the scientific programme of enlightened despotism and which reflected the period's zeal for taxonomy, typified by Linnaeus and his worldwide network of scientific informants; and third, the association of men of science with scientific nationalism and, later the movement for political independence.

In general, the open teaching of Copernicanism and Newtonian physics was delayed in Latin America by a full century or more. José Celestino Mutis (1732–1808) translated Newton's *Principia* into Spanish and espoused heliocentrism at the Colegio Mayor del Rosario in Bogotá in the 1770s. His disciple Juan Eloy Valenzuela (d. 1834) taught Newtonian physics there from 1777. Cosme Bueno (1711–98) had taught the doctrines of Newton at the University of San Marcos in Lima from 1758. There, as in Bogotá, however, the new science was mainly diffused outside the universities, where scholasticism was still entrenched. The Real Convictorio de San Carlos, founded in 1774, was Newtonian in orientation. In Mexico, Newtonian physics was not regularly taught until the first decades of the nineteenth century.

The circulation of the blood, another touchstone of the New Science, also arrived late, one of the earliest sources being a treatise on 'Evidence of the Circulation of the Blood' published in Lima in 1723 by Federico Bottoni, a Sicilian physican who had been in contact with Spanish *novatores* familiar with William Harvey. The great generation of Peruvian physicians of the end of the eighteenth century was introduced to Harvey through Bottoni's volume.

The first major expedition of the eighteenth century, one with primarily geodesic aims, was that of Charles Marie La Condamine to South America in 1735–44. This expedition was organized by the French government, but under strict controls imposed by the Spanish crown and with the participation of Spanish personnel. Its purpose was to measure the length of a degree in order to test Newton's assertion that the earth was not absolutely round. The group which carried out most of the geodesic measurements included La Condamine, Jorge Juan (1713–73), Antonio de Ulloa (1716–95) and Pedro Vicente Maldonado (b. 1704). The triangulation was completed in June 1739 when 3° of latitude had been covered. At the same time meteorological observations were made, as were studies of Newtonian attraction and the length of the beat of Huygens's pendulum at different altitudes above sea level. In Lima, La Condamine exchanged astronomical data with Pedro Peralta (1663–1743) and other members of the expedition (in particular, Joseph de Jussieu and Louis Godin) were instrumental in diffusing the ideas of Copernicus and Newton among the Peruvian intelligentsia. This expedition also produced botanical results, including the first accurate description of cinchona.

The persistent problem of establishing accurate boundary demarcations between Spanish and Portuguese territory produced a number of important expeditions in the eighteenth century. The northern boundary, in the region of the Orinoco River, was explored beginning in 1753 by a group led by José de Iturriaga (b. 1699) and which included Eugenio de

Drawings of Cinchona lanceifolia (left) *and* Aristolochia cordiflora Mutis (right) *from Mutis's* Expedición botánica

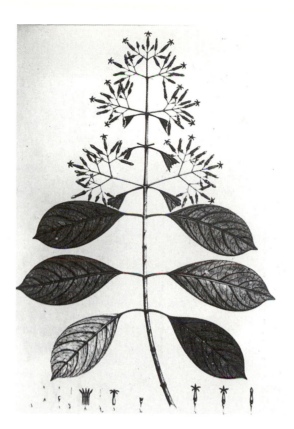
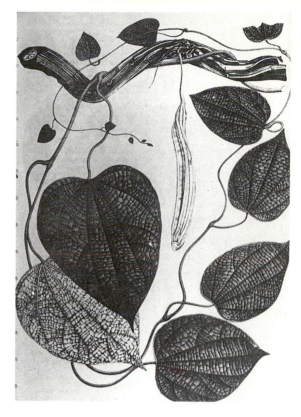

Alvarado (b.1715), Vicente Doz (c.1736–81), the instrument maker Apolinar Diez de la Fuente and José Solano (b. 1726), the latter a disciple of Jorge Juan. Linnaeus's disciple, Pehr Lofling (1729–56), was attached to the expedition as a botanist but the natural history component was largely forgotten after his premature death. Among the significant achievements of the expedition were Alvarado's expedition to Guyana, Solano's reconnaissance of the upper Orinoco and La Fuente's search for the source of that river. Solano, Doz and La Fuente all produced maps of the area which considerably clarified the geography of northern South America.

More varied was the work of demarcation teams in the River Plate, which included the geographers Juan de Aguirre (d.1811), Diego de Alvear (1749–1830) and Francisco Millau (1728–1805), as well as Félix de Azara (1746–1821), whose studies of flora and fauna resulted from, although were not officially part of, his service on the boundary commission.

First of the three botanical expeditions was that to Peru, led by Hipólito Ruíz (1752–1816), José Pavón (1754–1840) and the French botanist Joseph Dombey (1742–94). The expedition arrived in Lima in April 1778 and by the time its work ended in 1788 the botanists had amassed 589 drawings, 3000 plant descriptions and a herbarium of 1980 dried specimens. The most interesting scientific aspect of the Ruíz-Pavón expedition was its explicitly Linnaean

character. The decree establishing the expedition explicitly imposed the Linnaean system of classification, and Ruíz and Pavón personally diffused Linnaean concepts when they lectured on botany at the University of San Marcos in 1780.

The botanical expedition to New Granada was established in 1783 in Mariquita, under the direction of Mutis and his assistant Valenzuela. In 1791 the expedition moved to Bogotá where Mutis involved a number of young naturalists, including the geographer Francisco José de Caldas (1768–1816), the botanist Antonio Zea (1766–1822) and the zoologist Jorge Tadeo Lozano (1771–1816), in his labours and where in the first several years of the nineteenth century it was transformed into a genuine scientific institution, with the leadership passing to Mutis's nephew Sinforoso in 1808. The expedition's work included production of 6849 plates, of which 5393 survive. Mutis's preoccupation with cinchona has overshadowed the rich variety of the expedition's work, which included physical observations and the establishment of an observatory directed by Caldas.

The last of the great botanical expeditions, that to New Spain, was established in 1787 as an explicit continuation of the sixteenth-century enterprise: 'with the general and important objective of promoting the progress of physical science, banishing doubts and adulterations in medicine, dyeing and other useful arts, and to augment commerce, and also with the special end of supplementing illustrating and perfecting the original writings which Dr Francisco Hernández left in accord with the present state of these natural sciences' (Royal Order of 20 March 1787). The expedition included the director Martín de Sessé (1751–1808) and the creole botanist José de Mociño (1757–1819). Unlike the other botanical expeditions, that to New Spain was institutionalized immediately with the establishment of a botanical garden in Mexico City and a chair of botany, inaugurated in 1788 by Vicente Cervantes (1755–1829). The Linnaean spirit was also in evidence in colonial Brazil where the Franciscan José Mariano de Vellozo (1748–1811) collected a large herbarium and described around seventeen hundred plant species, published in 1827 as the *Flor fluminensis*.

Another expedition, headed by the Italian Alessandro Malaspina (1754–1809) was primarily hydrographic in aim, although its personnel included the naturalists Thaddaeus Haenke (1761–1817), Luis Née (1734–1803) and Antonio Pineda (1753–92). The expedition sailed in July 1789 and explored in the River Plate, Central America, Mexico and the Philippines, returning to Spain in 1795. A botanical expedition to western Cuba (1795–9) was organized by the Count of Mompox (1769–1807), with Baltasar Boldó as chief botanist. All these expeditions lent themselves to making astronomical observations, of which the most noteworthy were the observations of the transit of Venus across the solar disc by Doz and Joaquin Velázquez de León (1732–86) in Baja California (1769) and that of the transit of Mercury by Dionisio Alcalá Galiano (1762–1805) in Montevideo in 1789. A major expedition, with different aims, was

---

A plant-hunter's contribution to industry

Rubber, derived from the latex of a variety of plants, has been used by indigenous peoples in different parts of the world.

The modern rubber industry is based on the tree *Hevea brasiliensis*, Para rubber, although rubber used by the Aztecs and seen by Columbus was derived from Panama rubber, *Castilla elastica*, an unrelated American tree. La Condamine reported the use of local rubber for bottles and syringes in Ecuador in 1736, and the French began importing it under the vernacular name of 'caoutchouc'. The English chemist Priestley is often credited with the discovery (in 1770) of its property of rubbing out pencil marks – whence the modern English 'india-rubber' – and by the beginning of the nineteenth century the English had begun manufacturing rubber from the raw import of *Hevea* latex. This industry expanded with great rapidity after the discovery of the process of 'vulcanisation', which converted the raw rubber into the modern product with elastic qualities unaffected by temperatures between 0° and 100°C.

As with quinine, the expanding demand stimulated the European colonial powers to establish rubber plantations in Asia, and the role of Kew Gardens in effecting the transfer has often been cited (though the stories of illicit dealing are apparently much exaggerated!). There has been increased competition in recent times from new synthetic rubbers and from modern plastics.

A plant-hunter's contribution to the world's diet

Everyone knows the potato, *Solanum tuberosum*, the most important root vegetable in the world today. This plant is of Andean origin, and the English, patriotically but incorrectly, attribute its advent in Europe to Sir Walter Raleigh. In fact, the potato was known in Spain by about 1570, whereas its first record in England was not till 1586, though by 1597 the English botanist Gerard figured this remarkable new vegetable in his famous illustrated herbal.

Potatoes were widely cultivated by indigenous American peoples from what is now the Southern United States to Southern Chile, so the world expansion followed the straightforward transfer and selection of already existing native cultivated races. Modern plant breeding has done much to unravel the complex history of the truly native Andean species and the early cultivars derived from them.

---

the Royal Maritime Expedition of Vaccination, led by the physician Francisco Javier de Balmis (1753–1819), which visited the Caribbean, Mexico and the Philippines in 1803–6 to inoculate citizens against smallpox.

Colonial science was, by definition, dependent upon Europe. But scientists in Lima, Mexico City and Bogotá had, by the end of the eighteenth century, weaned themselves from dependence on Spain and were acquiring books and instruments from England and France. According to Alexander von Humboldt (1769–1859), only Joseph Banks, director of Kew Gardens in London, had a botanical library better than that of Mutis. Increasing participation in the mainstream of science tended paradoxically to heighten the creole naturalists' sense of isolation. An example is Caldas's confession that when he invented a barometric instrument, he was unsure whether or not it might already have been invented. Nevertheless, by the end of the century Spanish American naturalists had begun to think in terms of fully autonomous national schools of science, conducting research on a European level but without the necessity of direct European tutelage.

As a result, many of the creole scientists associated with Bourbon expeditions were later involved in the independence movements, particularly in New Granada, New Spain and Peru. When Humboldt toured Latin America (in 1799–1804) he stimulated naturalists there to examine the resources of their own countries with a view towards social and political reform. At the same time, creole scientists such as the Peruvians, José Hipólito Unánue (1755–1833) and José Manuel Dávalos (1758–1821) sought to defend the New World against charges of biotic and climatic inferiority levelled by the Count de Buffon and Cornelius de Pauw. This was the rationale of Unánue's famous *Observations on the Climate of Lima* (1802), whose exaggerated conclusions regarding the singularity of Lima's climate may actually have impeded the introduction of European medicaments which he believed to be inappropriate to Peruvian conditions. The nationalistic impulse in science was particuarly strong in Mexico where members of the botanical expedition sought to revive Aztec botany, so that 'Mexico might glory in having its own materia medica', in Mocino's words. Such impulses were easily converted into political ideology and scientists were highly visible in the independence movements, particularly in New Granada, where Caldas, Lozano and other disciples of Mutis were executed for revolutionary activities. The image of physical science among enlightened creoles was highly coloured by Benjamin Franklin, admired not only as a Newtonian and experimentalist, but also as a politicial example. Political leaders like Antonio Nariño of New Granada not only idealized Franklin and tinkered with electrical machines but also felt akin to the ideals of democracy which he represented.

THE AFTERMATH OF INDEPENDENCE

Science was a major casualty of the trauma of independence and although certain colonial institutions, such as the Observatory of Bogotá and the Real Seminario de Minería of Mexico, survived into the independence period, they did so at an impoverished level. The latter case is typical. Instruction at the Seminar, in the two decades prior to independence, had been at a European level, thanks to such professors as Fausto de Elhuyar (1754–1833) and Andrés Manuel del Río (1765–1849), discoverers of tungsten and vanadium respectively. As director, Elhuyar had introduced the new chemistry into the curriculum by commissioning a Spanish translation (1797) of Lavoisier's *Elementary Treatise of Chemistry*. During the war of independence mining engineers flocked to the Mexican side and lost their lives. The

Seminar itself fell into decay after 1810 and classes were not resumed until 1827, with only a handful of students.

Even European exploration declined, with but a few efforts such at that of Jean Baptiste Boussingault (1802–87), who had gone to Latin America at the behest of Humboldt, Charles Darwin's notable voyage on HMS *Beagle* (1831–5) and, later, the Spanish Pacific Commission (1862–6) which achieved interesting results in descriptive taxonomy.

The reception of Darwinism provides some insight into the status of the natural sciences in Spanish America in the late nineteenth century. With the exception of Argentina, Darwinism was received and discussed by physicians and social scientists, rather than naturalists, and the evolutionary debate was centred in medical schools and academies, anthropological societies and the literary lyceums and clubs where positivist social thinkers gathered. Although historians have promoted the notion that Spencerian positivists favoured Darwinism while Comtians opposed it, the actual situation was more complex. Spencerians did indeed raise Darwin's banner in Argentina and Uruguay (where positivist political control over education was strong enough to provide official support for Darwinism and to force Catholics to counterattack in the Congress) and in Mexico Comtians with strong links to France were, on the whole, opposed. In Venezuela, however, Comtian positivism and Darwinism were allied. Darwinian biology was first taught in the medical schools as, for example, by José Arechevaleta in Uruguay and in Venezuela by the anatomist Luis Razetti (1862–1932), who in 1905 manoeuvred the Academy of Medicine of Caracas into declaring itself in favour of Darwinism.

Argentina was the only country where naturalists bore the brunt of the Darwinian debate, because only in that country was there a large enough concentration of palaeontologists and other naturalists to forment a broad-based, informed discussion of Darwin's evidence. The natural history museums of Buenos Aires, La Plata and Paraná all had important collections of fossils whose contents were analysed in articles both in European and national journals, such as the *Revista Argentina de Historia Natural* (1891). At the centre of the Argentine debate was the palaeontologist Florentino Ameghino (1854–1911), author of a famous treatise on fossil mammals and a convinced evolutionist who waged a quixotic crusade to establish Argentina as the original home of the human species.

The recuperation of science in Latin America towards the end of the nineteenth century is associated with the influence of French science and scientific institutions. The Colombian botanist José Triana

(1826–90) collaborated with French and other European botanists on the flora of New Granada, published most of his research in France, and resided there from 1857 until his death. Later in the century, Paris became the pole of attraction for Latin American medical researchers. The Venezuelan José Gregorio Hernández (1864–1919) studied with Mathias Duval and Charles Richet in 1889–91, and imported a complete histological laboratory from France upon his return to Caracas. In Brazil, around the turn of the century, Osvaldo Cruz (1872–1917) established an Institute of Experimental Pathology explicitly modelled on the Pasteur Institute where he had studied from 1896 to 1899. His associate, Carlos Chagas (1879–1943), discovered an endemic parasitic disease, which now bears his name caused by a trypanosome infesting the huts of Brazilian villagers. Other physicians such as the Cuban Carlos Juan Finlay (1833–1915), who identified the vector of yellow fever, were educated in the United States.

The twentieth century

The early twentieth century witnessed the efforts of several Latin American governments both to improve the quality of scientific education and to vastly broaden the scope of scientific activities. In Argentina the government sought to implant German science directly at the University of La Plata where the physicist Emil Bose was installed as director of the Faculty of Exact Sciences in 1909. There he established a well-equipped institute of physics and lured from Germany a corps of distinguished faculty, including Richard Gans, an authority on electromagnetism, and Jakob Laub, Einstein's first collaborator who gave the first lectures on relativity in the New World. The institute produced a number of very talented Argentine physicists, yet after its initial burst of activity, the effort to establish German physics failed. To the north, the Mexican revolution stimulated the renaissance of some old institutions (such as the National Astronomical Observatory) and the creation of a host of new ones: the School of Chemistry, the Office of Geographical and Climatological Studies, and the Office of Biological Studies, the latter under the direction of Alfonso L. Herrera (1868–1942), an outstanding biologist, evolutionist and pioneer researcher into the origins of life.

The Spanish Civil War (1936–9) produced a substantial migration of Republican Spanish scientists to Latin America, where they had a positive impact. Indeed, in many countries Spanish refugees were responsible either for the founding or renovation of entire disciplines or sub-fields. Representative figures were Gustavo Pittaluga (1876–1955), for parasitology in Cuba; Emilio Mira y López (1890–1946), for clinical psychology in Brazil; Pau Vila (1881–1980), for geography in Venezuela; José Royo Gómez (1895–1961), for geology in Colombia and Venezuela. The Argentine Psychoanalytic Association was founded by another Spanish exile, Angel Garma (b.1904), together with two Argentines and a Jewish refugee. Medical research in Venezuela was put on a modern footing by three refugees from Europe: the Catalan physiologist August Pi i Sunyer (1879–1965) and two German Jews, Martin Meyer and Werner Jaffe.

The period after the Second World War really constitutes a sharply different phase in the history of Latin American science, marked by the massive influx of students from Latin countries into universities in the United States, the problems attendant upon their return to Latin America (including the 'brain drain'), and the establishment of major new research entities such as the Instituto Venezolano de Investigaciones Cientificas (1959) in Venezuela and national councils for higher scientific research, with both policy and research roles, in many other countries. Related to governmental efforts was the formation by scientists of national associations for the advancement of science: Peru (1920), Argentina (1933), Brazil (1948), Venezuela (1950).

A full range of scientific institutions, of inevitably varying size and quality, now exists across the region. Scientists and technologists are in increasing demand for a great variety of national projects, including significant nuclear power programmes in several countries. Governments, in the most recent period, have played a greater part in stimulating scientific research and in expanding education. The number of universities in Latin America approximately doubled between the end of the Second World War and the close of the 1960s. Both the natural sciences and engineering have benefited from this process of expansion, an important feature of which has been the creation of institutes for technology and applied science – the formation of Chile's State Technical University (in 1947) being an early example. Scientists, like other members of the academic community, have not always been able to escape the effects of political upheaval. General Juan Carlos Onganía's heavy-handed (and quite gratuitous) intervention in Argentine universities after the military coup of 1966 drove hundreds of well-qualified scientists into exile and virtually destroyed the departments of mathematics and physics at the University of Buenos Aires. Latin American scientists, like their counterparts elsewhere, often lament the inadequacy of laboratory facilities or of funding. There has also, at times, been debate as to the role of pure science in relation to the tasks of economic and social development. In general, however, the most recent phase has been marked by a growing aware-

The Butantan Institute, São Paulo, centre for biological and biochemical research

ness of science and technology as valuable components in the development of Latin America. Scientists themselves have been active in moves towards a greater degree of regional co-ordination of scientific activity.   TPG

Further Reading: I. H. W. Engstrand, *Spanish Scientists in the New World: The Eighteenth Century Expeditions* (Seattle, 1981); R. Hilton, *The Scientific Institutions of Latin America* (Stanford, 1970); R. R. Miller, *For Science and National Glory: the Spanish Scientific Expedition to America, 1862–1866* (Norman, Oklahoma, 1968); A. R. Steele, *Flowers for the King: The Expedition of Ruiz and Pavon and the Flora of Peru* (Durham, North Carolina, 1981).

Modern Science in Latin America

The absence in Latin America of a strong scientific tradition in basic research has proved difficult to overcome in the twentieth century: Argentina and Brazil are the only countries to achieve widespread distinction. The virtual absence of major private institutions (universities, foundations, etc) has further tied science to government control and funding. Since the 1950s scientific research has depended on national budgets and on multinational and binational aid, and has been victim to the weaknesses and vulnerabilities inherent in such dependence. With the possible exception of Cuba no country spends even one per cent of its GNP on research and development. Only in Brazil, Cuba, Venezuela, Mexico and Argentina can one observe progressive successes, and then only in a few fields.

With the ebbing of European influence after the Second World War and the rising demand for research facilities, the state became the primary sponsor through the creation of national scientific councils. Brazil's National Council for Research (1951) promoted scientific research in coordination with a range of public sector agencies. By the mid-1970s, after restructuring, the Council had developed a number of advisory organizations on national scientific policy. In Argentina Dr Bernardo Houssay (1887–1971), as president of the National Council for Scientific and Technical Research (1956), proved instrumental in shaping research commissions and stressing independence from the state. In Cuba the

National Centre for Scientific Research (1965) reflected the ideals of socialist perfectibility through scientific inquiry at advanced levels. Mexico's National Council for Science and Technology (1970) attempts to support both basic and applied research, emphasizing technological innovation.

CONTRIBUTIONS BY FIELD

Basic sciences

A major portion of all significant Latin American achievement is in the biological sciences. For his work on carbohydrate metabolism the Argentine Federico Leloir (1906–87) received the 1970 Nobel Prize for Chemistry. At the Butantan Institute (São Paulo, 1901) in Brazil, biological and biochemical research involves snake and toad venoms, cariotoxic steroids and enzymes in amphibians. Since the discovery (1939) of toxic protein in rattlesnake venom, scientists have described more than seventy new snake species from which vaccines are now produced for most of Latin America. Jayme Regallo Pereira (1893–1963) conducted basic research in plant venoms (e.g., curare, pereirina, digitalis and maconha), leading to the industrial development of a number of drugs. Cuba's commitment to biotechnology and genetic engineering since the early 1980s has enabled the copying and occasional modification of patented products developed in Japan, Europe and the USA. Principal among these are vaccines for hepatitis B and group B meningococcal meningitis, reagents, epideral growth factors, and AIDS diagnostic kits.

The leading research in physics occurs in Brazil and Argentina. Brazil's National Commission on Nuclear Energy (1956) sponsors studies and proposes standards. The Argentine National Commission for Atomic Energy (1950) centralizes research in the field. Drastic budget cuts in the 1980s brought nuclear developments to a virtual standstill. Elsewhere in Latin America, foreign nuclear technology dominates even more.

*Astronomical Observatory,
Quito, Ecuador*

Applied sciences

Research on ethanol began in Brazil in 1922 with the establishment of an experimental station dedicated to agricultural combustibles. By 1927 alcohol was proved to work as an industrial combustible and in 1931 the government decreed that all petrol contain at least five per cent alcohol. In the early 1970s, surpluses of domestic sugar (from which ethanol can be produced) and heavy government subsidization led to a massive alcohol production, thereby enabling it to serve as a major source of automotive fuel.

The digital area that includes microelectronics, automation, software and peripheral development is known as informatics in Brazil and since the early 1970s Brazilian law has reserved a significant share of the domestic market in it for locally manufactured products.

Brazil started its own aerospace engineering in the early 1960s, and among its achievements are a space-launch pad and earth station communications antenna for satellite relay. Matériel ranging from aircraft to rockets and missiles demonstrates inventiveness in adjusting and modifying technology for Brazilian conditions. The Argentines and Chileans have also demonstrated technical capacity with electronic warfare devices, communications intelligence equipment, and jammers, as well as aerospace and land warfare technologies.

Medicine

By focussing on preventative medicine, much Latin American research addresses public health concerns, but there is also some basic research, outstanding of which is Argentinian Bernardo Houssay's work in endocrinology, for which he received the Nobel Prize in 1947.

Tropical diseases have won attention from many Brazilian physicians. Carlos Ribeiro Justiniano das Chagas (1879–1934) described and studied malaria and its pathogenic mechanism in 1905. His research on the insect *panstrongylus megistus* verified the pathogenicity of what became known as Chagas disease. Oswaldo Cruz (1872–1917) identified the causative agent of the disease – *trypanosoma cruzi* – and launched sanitation campaigns prior to 1910 to eliminate bubonic plague, yellow fever and smallpox. Such research became the primary mission of the Oswaldo Cruz and Evandro Chagas Institutes. Vital Brazil (1885–1950) developed serums for snake venoms at his world-famous Butantan Institute. In 1912 Manuel Augusto Pirajá da Silva (1873–1961) described the evolutional cycle of *schistosoma mansoni*, the parasite responsible for schistosomiasis.

Transmission of yellow fever by the *aedes aegypti* mosquito was discovered (1881) by Carlos Finlay (1839–1915) in Cuba, but his announcement was initially ignored. It was not until 1900 that the finding was acted on, and by the next year Cuba had eradicated the fever. After 1959 Cuba's emphasis on medicine promoted education and development, and with the founding of MediCuba in 1978 the island became an exporter of medical goods and personnel.

The hygienist Eduardo Liceaga (1839–1920) founded modern public health care in Mexico, and was influential in establishing the Pan American Sanitary Bureau. Arturo Rosenblueth (1900–70), a world-class neurophysiologist, made important contributions to knowledge of the human nervous system, and also founded the Centre for Advanced Study at Mexico's National Polytechnic Institute. In Peru, Carlos Monge (1884–1970) revealed in 1925 the basis of chronic mountain sickness, suffered in high altitudes.

Agriculture

Until the mid-1950s the absence of stable financial support and inadequate coordination of research with agricultural policy severely hindered scientists in this area. From then on, decentralized institutes with autonomous administrations have brought improved assimilation of technology usually transferred from developed countries. Since the 1980s biotechnological research has been focussing on cell and tissue culture (particularly clonal propagation, disease elimination, germplasm conservation and exchange, and isolation of mutants), recombinant DNA and gene transfer, monoclonal antibodies, and bioconversion.

The International Centre for the Improvement of Maize and Wheat (Mexico 1966), initially funded by the Rockefeller Foundation (as were other similar ventures) conducts research and advises on improvements of grains. The International Potato Centre (Peru, 1971) offers a wide selection of biotypes and

OBSERVATORIES IN CHILE

The Inter-American Observatory, Cerro Tololo

Astronomy in the Norte Chico of Chile

The dry, semi-desert region of Chile known to Chileans as the Norte Chico possesses atmospheric conditions almost ideally suited to astronomical observation: 'the seeing,' as astronomers say, is as good in this particular area as anywhere on the earth's surface. The mountains in the vicinity of La Serena – the region's main city, situated at 30°S, some 400 km north of the Chilean capital, Santiago – have an average of 280 clear nights each year. Tucson, Arizona, the best place in the northern hemisphere from this standpoint, has no more than 200. Given the intrinsic interest of southern hemisphere skies – which contain, among other things, the galactic centre region and the two Magellanic Clouds (small galaxies accompanying our own, invisible from northerly latitudes) – it is not surprising that astronomers should have taken advantage of the favourable conditions of the Norte Chico. A number of important observatories have been installed there since the mid-1960s.

The INTER-AMERICAN OBSERVATORY has the largest telescope in the southern hemisphere, the 4 m reflector opened in 1976. The decision to build this observatory was taken in 1962, and it was dedicated in 1967. Used primarily by astronomers from the United States and Latin America, it is run by the US Association of Universities for Research in Astronomy (AURA), and stands on a dramatic mountain site at Cerro Tololo, some 35 km from the small town of Vicuña in the Elqui Valley – a valley traditionally celebrated for its production of good-quality pisco, a clear brandy. In addition to the 4 m instrument, the equipment at Cerro Tololo includes 1.5 m, 1 m, 0.9 m, 0.6m and 0.4 m reflectors.

The EUROPEAN SOUTHERN OBSERVATORY (ESO), operated by the Organisation Européene pour des Recherches Astronomiques dans l'Hémisphère Austral (whose member countries are France, West Germany, Italy, the Netherlands, Belgium, Denmark, Sweden and Switzerland), is located at Cerro La Silla, some 100 km north of La Serena. (The spot was chosen in 1964.) Its striking mountain-top position can be glimpsed unforgettably (in the distance) from Chile's main north–south highway. The largest of Cerro La Silla's thirteen telescopes in the 1980s was a 3.6 m reflector (like Cerro Tololo's largest, opened in 1976), the remaining instruments covering a range from 0.4 m to 2.2 m.

Other large telescopes in the area are maintained by the CARNEGIE INSTITUTION of Washington (2.5 m and 1 m) and the UNIVERSITY OF TORONTO (0.61 m). Plans for still more very large telescopes have been announced by the US and British governments and by Harvard and Cambridge Universities.

In less than three decades, in fact, the sleepy provincial city of La Serena (founded 1544) has become one of the astronomical centres of the world.

there genetic specimens; research focusses on frost resistancy and heat tolerance along with disease and pest controls. The International Centre for Tropical Agriculture (Colombia, 1966) pursues research on cassava, field beans, rice and animal forages for tropical pastures. These and similar research organizations coordinate their activities through the Consultative Group on International Agricultural Research.   PTJ

Further Reading: E. Adler, *The Power of Ideology: The Quest for Technological Autonomy in Argentina and Brazil* (Berkeley and London, 1987); M. Barzeley, *The Polticized Market Economy: Alcohol in Brazil's Energy Strategy* (Berkeley and London, 1986); Inter-American Development Bank, *Economic and Social Progress in Latin America: 1988 Report* (Washington DC, 1988): special section on science and technology; C. Roper and J. Silva, eds., *Science and Technology in Latin America* (London, 1983); S. Schwartzman, *A Space for Science: The Development of the Scientific Community in Brazil* (University Park, Pennsylvania, 1991); N. Stepan, *Beginnings of Brazilian Science: Oswaldo Cruz, Medical Research and Policy 1890–1920* (New York, 1976)

Medicine in Latin America

The discovery of the Spanish and Portuguese Americas by Christopher Columbus in 1492 and Pedro Alvares Cabral in 1500 respectively led to a holocaust of disease for the Amerindians and probably the worst demographic disaster in human history. During the very early years of colonization much was written about the salubrity of the New World. But this impression was decidedly ephemeral. The native Americans proved extraordinarily susceptible to epidemic Eurasian diseases such as smallpox, measles, diptheria and a host of other such illnesses that their conquerors had inadvertently introduced. The Iberians had either developed resistance to the illnesses in question over time or had gained immunity quickly by hosting the illnesses, usually as youngsters, but the native Americans had no immunity against them at all.

The massive scale of the deaths of the Indians caused the Iberians to look elsewhere for labour to colonize much of the Americas. They found their source in the black African, who was better able to resist Eurasian diseases. But with the importation of Africans came another onslaught of pestilence in the form of African diseases such as falciparum malaria and yellow fever to which the blacks were relatively resistant but which killed whites and Indians with equal vigour.

THE ARRIVAL OF EUROPEAN MEDICINE

Native healers, relying on medicines derived from plants as well as on magico-religious rites, were the first to combat these waves of plagues but were helpless against the onslaught. However, they probably did less damage to their patients than did European practitioners. During this transformation of Latin America into a pathogenic cauldron bubbling with all of the world's major illnesses, European medical practice was based on the Galenic system of the four humours, which was dedicated to removal of corrupt humours from the sick by a system of purging, bloodletting, vomiting, and sweating.

Iberian medicine reached the Americas with its discoverers. Sailing with Columbus in 1493 was one Dr Diego Alvarez de Chanca, a Seville physician, and accompanying Cabral to Brazil was a 'Mestre João', called a 'doctor' or 'physic'. Most of the early practitioners of medicine in both Spanish and Portuguese America were barber-surgeons, barbers, apothecaries and their apprentices. Some few held diplomas as physicians and thus had social status, while at the other end of the scale there were numerous irregular and illicit healers. Attempts to regulate medical practice in Spanish America led to the appointment of *protomedicatos*, or public health officers, to inspect the credentials of physicians and surgeons, to certify them and, frequently, to investigate the abilities of midwives and apothecaries as well.

In the early days in Brazil, the great majority of barber-surgeons and physicians were Jews or New Christians (converts), although later the professions of barber-surgeon and midwife came to be dominated by blacks. There, for most of the colonial period, the functions of *protomedicato* were shared between the local offices of *fisico-môr* and the First Medical House located in Lisbon, which had representatives in Brazil to examine and license physicians. In 1782 the *protomedicato* system was established in Brazil. Despite these attempts at regulation, however, forms of popular medicine like *curandismo* persisted among Indians and slaves. Moreover, complaints were constantly voiced about a lack of good physicians and a plethora of charlatans, barber-surgeons and bloodletters. Indeed many sick people prudently failed to consult any of these.

In Brazil and the Spanish Caribbean, where slavery prevailed, some doctors, both regular and irregular, specialized in providing health care for slaves. On the other hand, the slaves themselves often turned to their own for treatment when ill, and numerous aspects of African healing and magico-religious practices persist today in Latin America, sometimes to the exclusion of Western medicine.

Because of the epidemics that arrived with the slave ships, quarantining procedures were often implemented at ports with a system of medical inspectors, presumably with some prophylactic value. Quarantining was also often the *de facto* result of the scrutiny that representatives of the Inquisition gave to ships arriving in Spanish America.

Medical education began early in Spanish America. The first American faculty of medicine was established in Santo Domingo in 1583. This was followed by the establishment of chairs of medicine at the University of Mexico in 1575 and at the University of San Marcos in Lima, at about the same time. In Brazil, however, medical education had to await the arrival of the Portuguese Court in 1808, after which medical schools were authorized in 1808 for Bahia and Rio de Janeiro. Both were formally established in 1832 but had actually begun to function somewhat earlier.

In 1502 Nicolás Ovando in Hispaniola was instructed to build hospitals for both Indian and Christian poor, and throughout the first two centuries or so of colonial rule in Latin America numerous hospitals and foundling homes were established. Aid for them came from municipal governments, the church, alms, bequests, and from *cofradías*, or brotherhoods who served hospitals as volunteers and were especially important during epidemics. Religious orders, such as the Franciscans and the Dominicans in Spanish America and the Jesuits in Brazil, also played a large role in the health care of the colonists, as well as of the Indians and in the development of medicine generally. Some were physicians, others acted as nurses. They provided medicines and hospitalization, and often the only pharmacy in a town was connected with the church or the school. In addition, in Brazil 'Santa Casas', or Holy Houses of Mercy, sprang up modelled on those founded in Lisbon towards the end of the fifteenth century; together with the Jesuit infirmaries, these tended the ill during epidemics. Other hospitals were maintained for women, for the army, and for sailors, while still others (*lazarettos*) were established to house those believed to be lepers, as well as those people suffering from other contagious diseases.

STAGNATION

Yet because the colonizing of Latin America essentially consisted of the wholesale transferal of Iberian institutions to the Americas, those involving

medicine, like so many others, slipped into stagnation with the beginning of the isolation brought on by the Counter-Reformation. As a result, despite some intellecutal liveliness and new ideas during the eighteenth century, medicine in Latin America really never escaped inertia until after the independence movements. Thus in New Spain at the beginning of the nineteenth century, the *protomedicato* was still regulating medical practice, and no new hospitals had been established for some two hundred years. Indeed, frequent appeals to charity were required to keep the old ones open.

It is this stagnation that seems the most likely explanation for the relative dearth of important medical literature after the first century or two. Early in the colonial period, Gonzalo Fernández de Oviedo produced the *Natural and General History of the Indies (1535)*, which described many plants thought to be medicinal as well as the diseases of the natives. In 1570 Francisco Hernández was instructed by Philip II of Spain to study all plants of medicinal value in New Spain, reflecting both the interest of the Crown and the conviction of many that there were some miraculous cures to be found in the New World.

Some of this work found its way into print. Another such work of importance was the *Natural and Moral History of the Indies*, by José de Acosta (1590).

In Brazil, during the Dutch occupation, Willem Piso made notes and observations that led to his famous *Història Naturalis Brasiliae* published in 1648, and about a century later Luis Gomes Ferreira wrote the *Erário Mineral* (1735), which was greatly enlarged in 1755. In addition, in 1694 João Ferreira da Rosa published the *Tratado único da constituição pestilencial de Pernambuco*, a treatise on pestilence in Pernambuco, which seems to have been the first specialized study of yellow fever in international literature. But with these exceptions most of the medical literature produced in the Americas prior to the nineteenth century was undistinguished. The first medical journal in the New World, *Mercurio Volante* was founded in Mexico in 1772, but like other publications, medical journals did not flourish until the national period.

Most New World plants whose curing properties were loudly trumpeted at one time or another, such as arrowroot and sarsparilla, turned out over time to have few or none. Among the notable exceptions, however, were foxglove, which provided digitalis for sufferers of heart disease, ipecacuanha, in the treatment of amoebic dysentery, and most importantly, the *querango* or chinchona bark. Knowledge of it came from the Quito Indians, and as early as 1632 the Jesuit, Barnabé Cobo, was carrying the bark to Spain.

A plant-hunter's contribution to medicine

Quinine, an alkaloid obtained from the bark of species of *Cinchona*, was known for its anti-malarial medicinal properties to the indigenous peoples of the Andes from very early times, and was introduced to Europe by Jesuits as 'Peruvian bark' in the sixteenth century. The expedition led by La Condamine produced the first accurate botanical description of the genus *Cinchona*. By the middle of the nineteenth century the decline in production following unplanned exploitation of *Cinchona* trees in South America had led the Dutch and British to establish plantations in their South-East Asian colonies, and eventually, *via* India and Ceylon, into the former German African colonies now called Tanzania and Uganda. The height of world quinine production from natural sources was in the first half of the present century, but synthetic drugs have now largely replaced quinine from natural sources.

In 1812 Bernardino Antônio Gomes isolated quinine from it in Rio de Janeiro. The bark had proved effective to varying degrees in the treatment of malaria, but quinine was a much more valuable drug in combatting the disease.

NINETEENTH-CENTURY BREAKTHROUGHS

Major contributions to the international world of medicine – especially tropical medicine – began emerging from Latin America in the nineteenth century. In Rio de Janeiro, the French physician J. F. X. Sigaud, author of the classical epidemiological study *Du climat et des maladies du Brésil; ou statistique médicale de cet empire* (1844), was among those who founded the influential Academy of Medicine. He also was instrumental in publishing the *Annaes Brasilienses de Medicina,* one of the first Brazilian medical journals. In Bahia (Salvador) a remarkable trio of physicians combined to form what has been called the Bahian School of Tropical Medicine, with the *Gazeta Medica da Bahia* an important outlet for their research. This journal was founded in 1866, by the Scotsman John Paterson; he had been the first to identify yellow fever in Bahia after an outbreak in 1849. It was in the *Gazeta* that Dr Otto Wucherer, born of German and Dutch parents in Oporto, Portugal, announced the discovery of hookworm and hookworm anaemia in Brazil, described the filarial worm which causes filariasis, and identified its larval stage. The third of this international team, a Portuguese Dr José Francisco da Silva Lima, contributed systematic studies to the *Gazeta* which revealed to the world that beriberi was widespread in Brazil.

MEDICINE TODAY

In the first decades of the twentieth century, the Rockefeller Foundation launched a highly beneficial disease eradication programme aimed at yellow fever, hookworm and other tropical ailments. Today, medicine in Latin America is little different from medicine elsewhere in much of the West, meaning that it is mostly 'capitalist' medicine based on high technology and available to those who can afford it. (Heart transplants were carried out in several Latin American hospitals almost as soon as the technique was pioneered in South Africa.) This means, among other things, a lack of preventive medicine to aid those who do not have the money to pay, and thus many millions go without adequate medical care in Latin America today. This is especially true in rural areas because most hospitals and physicians are located in the large cities. Programmes such as those launched in Cuba after 1959 and Nicaragua after 1979, implemented largely by paramedics, concentrated on preventative medicine for those in rural areas and the poor in general. Such programmes have revealed how successful such efforts can be, if only governments will support them. KFK

Further Reading: D. B. Cooper, *Epidemic Diseases in Mexico City, 1761–1813* (Austin, Texas, 1965); J. T. Lanning, *The Royal Protomedicato: The Regulation of the Medical Professions in the Spanish Empire,* (Durham, New Hampshire 1985); A. Moll, *Aesculapius in Latin America* (Philadelphia, 1944); G. B. Risse, 'Medicine in New Spain' in Ronald L. Numbers, ed., *Medicine in the New World: New Spain, New France, and New England* (Knoxville, Tennessee 1987), pp. 12–63

Operating theatre in a Bogotá hospital

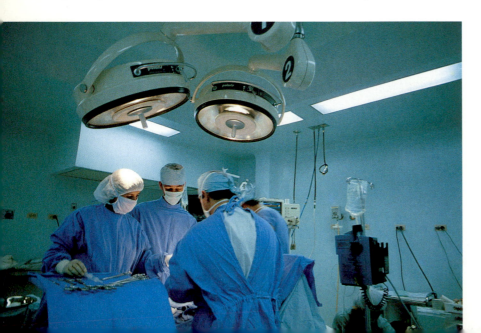

Sport in Latin America and the Caribbean

Despite the revered status of football (*fútbol* in Spanish, *futebol* in Portuguese, known only as soccer in the USA), across Latin America and the Caribbean the essence of participant and spectator sports is variety. Regional distribution of sports is determined by various factors: the physical environment (e.g. rowing and game fishing); the European colonial heritage (e.g., bullfighting and cricket); later immigration (e.g., Alpine skiing and bowling); neo-colonial influences from England (e.g., soccer, rugby, track and field), the United States (e.g., baseball, basketball, volleyball), and France (e.g., cycling and fencing), first through direct contacts and later through the media (e.g., American football); and relative wealth and technology (e.g., polo and motor racing).

When the Spanish arrived in the Americas they found such recreational activities as swimming, running, wrestling, and games of chance. Only in *chueca*, similar to field hockey and played in southern South America, and in the Mesoamerican ball games did they see anything resembling modern team games. But these games, like much of indigenous culture, possessed a sacred and ritualistic content, provoking the Spanish to try to suppress them by force. In their place, the Iberians introduced diversions brought from home, though gradually modified by local environmental and African and Amerindian influences to form a regionally diverse American sporting culture, often including animals and gambling.

The most prominent of these games/sports are bullfighting (especially in Mexico, Peru, Colombia, and Venezuela), cockfighting (Mexico and Central America), jai-alai and other Basque ball games (the Southern Cone and selected circum-Caribbean areas), and equestrian activities related to ranching. The most common of the latter are *charrería*, which is the source of North American rodeo, in Mexico, and various Argentine gaucho competitions such as *pato*, which is a bit like playing basketball on horseback!

MODERN SPORTS

By the mid-nineteenth century, three interrelated trends in the area of physical games and sports had become obvious. First, the few persisting indigenous forms continued to disappear. Second, folk culture was attacked as an impediment to progress. Finally, the first modern sports were arriving from Europe and North America. The suppression of folk sports was particularly noticeable. Bullfighting was temporarily banned in Mexico and it and cockfighting were prohibited elsewhere on grounds of cruelty and links to Spain. Pato and other gaucho diversions were suppressed in Argentina as part of an effort to impose capitalist control over the pampa and its labour force (in the twentieth century gaucho games would be revived as elite, folkloristic activities).

Following North Atlantic models, Latin Americans around 1900 began organizing athletic clubs, restructuring school curriculums, establishing national associations, and later forming physical education faculties which they argued would improve health and morals, teach discipline, cultivate national identity and integration, and earn them respect in the civilized world. They likewise affiliated with the emerging international sports network: the Olympics after 1896; FIFA, soccer's governing body, after 1904; and other sports' federations which appeared in later decades. Resources, however, rarely matched ambitions.

Institutionalization and commercialization of sport soon led to play for pay. Those countries with the closest ties to the North Atlantic economy (Mexico, Cuba, Brazil, the Southern Cone) and those sports with the broadest appeal among the masses (such as boxing, horse racing, baseball, soccer) combined to create the earliest forms of professionalism. The evolution of soccer caused the most trauma, as white, European-oriented elites sought to maintain their class preserve in the face of both rising skills among the masses and the desire to win and make profits on the part of club members and administrators. The result was several decades of semi-professionalism until open salaries for soccer players were permitted around 1930. (Argentina's professional regime began in 1931.)

In recent times Latin America has become a net exporter of sports talent. Soccer players, especially from the Southern Cone, play their peak years in Europe. Baseball players from the circum-Caribbean earn fame and fortune in the North American big leagues while stirring nationalistic pride back home: before 1959 Cuba was the major source, but since 1970 the mother lode has been the Dominican Republic. Other countries provide jockeys, boxers, and American football place kickers; on the amateur level they also help fill rosters of American university swimming, tennis, soccer, and track teams. Whatever their sport and wherever they choose to live, Latin America's best athletes have to perform abroad to earn major recognition and rewards.

INTERNATIONAL ACHIEVEMENTS

Today's most widely played and watched sports in Latin America are soccer and baseball, with basketball increasing at a notable rate. The region has made an impact internationally in all three. After dominating Olympic soccer in the 1920s, Uruguay won the World Cup twice (1930, 1950); Brazil permanently gained the Jules Rimet Cup for its victory in three championships (1958, 1962, 1970); Argentina won in 1978 and 1986 and finished second in 1990. Cuba, Nicaragua, Venezuela, and the Dominican Republic have each won the world series of amateur baseball. Brazil took the Pan American gold medal in men's basketball in 1987 and, along with Cuba, has been a world-level contender since the 1970s.

Further reflecting the diversity of sports in Latin America are, among many, the champion boxers from Argentina (Pascual Pérez, Justo Suárez, Carlos Monzón), Panama ('Panama' Al Brown, Roberto Durán), Nicaragua (Alexis Argüello), Colombia (Kid Pambelé, Rodrigo Valdés), Cuba (Kid Chocolate, Kid Tunero, Kid Gavilán), Brazil (Eder Jofre), and Mexico (José Luis Ramírez, Julio César Chávez). Argentina and Puerto Rico have produced talented golfers such as Roberto de Vicenzo and 'Chi Chi' Rodríguez. Tennis champions Pancho González (Mexico), Pancho Segura (Ecuador), Guillermo Vilas (Argentina), Alex Olmedo (Peru), and Andrés Gómez (Ecuador) have in their day established worldwide reputations. Brazilian runner Joaquim Cruz mined gold in the 1984 Olympic 800 metres. Both amateur and professional cycling remain popular in Colombia, Costa Rica, and Mexico; professional wrestling (more theatre than sport) attracts screaming thousands in Mexico; horse racing appeals to gamblers in an old English-type atmosphere in Argentina and Chile; Grand Prix and Formula-One racing features winners Emerson Fittipaldi (Brazil) and Juan Manuel Fangio, considered by some to be Argentina's greatest sportsman ever. Mexicans have earned Olympic medals in the sport of walking, while Cuba's José Raul Capablanca was a chess genius and grand master.

Unique to the English-speaking Caribbean is the dominance of cricket. What has made West Indian cricket distinctive has been its lively performance style and carnival-like performance context, and its ties to national identity, black ethnicity, and the pursuit of political independence. Though cricket, along with religion and education, were part of the white colonial regime, these three ultimately shaped the evolving culture of the transplanted African and mixed-blood population. With its emphasis on civility and recognition of achievement, cricket allowed West Indians a chance to emulate mainstream society while also challenging both British colonial rule and white domination.

Cricket matches between English and West Indian clubs began in the 1890s, though the first official Test Match was not held till 1928. While several blacks represented the West Indies then, the first black captain was not until Frank Worrell was named in 1959, following increasing criticism of white control of the sport in the islands. Later international Tests have earned the West Indians the reputation as the world's best for much of the last generation. If emotions surrounding such matches have engendered occasional riots among Caribbean fans, success has also stimulated great pride in such black stars as Frank Worrell, Learie Constantine, George Headley, and the great all-rounder Garfield (Gary) Sobers, 'the complete one-man cricket team'.

Despite these accomplishments, Latin America and the Caribbean have never been recognized as an internationally dominant sporting region. A partial exception is Cuba since 1959: abolishing professionalism in 1962, the country developed an interconnected sports programme for the masses and the training of world class athletes, winning more championships and medals per capita than the world's athletic giants. Although Castro's Cuba has spotlighted some of its individual champions (e.g. boxer Teófilo Stevenson and sprinter Alberto Juantorena), official ideology after 1961 emphasized the achievements of

Latin American World Champions

Motor Racing
Juan Manuel Fangio (Argentina) 1951, 1954, 1955, 1956, 1957
Emerson Fittipaldi (Brazil) 1974
Nelson Piquet (Brazil) 1981, 1983, 1987
Ayrton Senna (Brazil) 1988, 1990, 1991

Soccer World Cup
Uruguay 1930, 1950
Brazil 1958, 1962, 1970
Argentina 1978, 1986

Cricket World Cup
West Indies 1975, 1979

Tennis
Wimbledon (Women): Maria Bueno (Brazil)
    1959, 1960, 1964
US Open (Men): Raphael Osuna (Mexico) 1963
    Guillermo Vilas (Argentina) 1977
US Open (Women): Anita Linzana (Chile) 1937
    Maria Bueno (Brazil) 1959, 1963, 1964, 1966
    Gabriela Sabatini (Argentina) 1990
French Open (Men): Andrés Gómez (Ecuador)
    1990
Australian Open (Men): Guillermo Vilas
    (Argentina) 1978, 1979

Boxing
Heavyweight (WBC): Trevor Berbick (Jamaica)
    1986–9
Cruiserweight (WBA): Ossie Ocasio (Puerto Rico)
    1982–4
    (WBC): Carlos de Leon (Puerto Rico) 1980–82,
    1983–5, 1986–8, 1989
Light Heavyweight (undisputed): Jose Torres
    (Puerto Rico) 1965–6
    (WBA) Vincente Rondon (Venezuela) 1971–4
    Victor Galindez (Argentina) 1974–8, 1979
    Leslie Stewart (Jamaica) 1987
    (WBC) Miguel Cuello (Argentina) 1977–8

after 1973 used the soccer stadium as one of the few venues where they could meet and express emotions otherwise prohibited. Athletic club administrators often exploit their posts as stepping stones to political careers.

Latin American countries have also sought to increase their international prestige, legitimize incumbent regimes, and attract foreign aid, investment, and tourism by hosting international sporting competitions. Uruguayans gained satisfaction from both inaugurating and winning the soccer World Cup (1930). Later Brazil (1950), Chile (1962), Mexico (1970 and 1986), and Argentina (1978) prided themselves on their ability to organize this increasingly complicated event; Mexico also hosted the 1968 Olympic Games. Still, these events were never without major critics: the military's role in Argentina's 1978 glory failed to offset revelations of brutality, corruption, and incompetence, and few Colombians were seriously upset when their beleaguered government opted not to stage the 1986 Cup. Examples of more modest attempts to exploit such events include Mexico's inauguration of the Central American and Caribbean Games in 1926, at a time when the country was seeking reacceptance in the international community following its destructive Revolution (Mexico also sent small squads to the Olympic Games of 1924 and 1928 as part of this campaign). Similarly, Colombia held the first Bolivarian Games in 1938 on the four hundredth anniversary of the founding of Bogotá, and Peronist Argentina was invited to launch the Pan American Games in 1951. Even Fidel Castro perhaps viewed hosting the 1991 Pan Am Games as a way to regain international acceptance, harvest hard currency, and rejuvenate revolutionary fervour.

There are relatively few internationally famous Latin American female sports figures because of financial and social constraints. Brazil's Maria Bueno was one of the first exceptions, enjoying national stardom after winning Wimbledon in the 1960s; her tennis exploits have recently been exceeded by Gabriela Sabatini (Argentina). Nicaraguan born Silvia Poll was feted in her adopted Costa Rica by setting two records and winning eight medals at the 1987 Pan Am Games. Cuba's javelin thrower, María Caridad Colón, carried home gold from the 1980 Olympics. And Peru's major sporting triumphs of recent years have been delivered by its women's volleyball team (Olympic silver in 1988). Others, like swimmer Jeanette Campbell (Argentina), silver medalist at Berlin in 1936, won and were forgotten.

Although spectator and participant sports in Latin America are less developed than in North America or Europe, they have nonetheless penetrated the larger culture. Sports terminology, frequently in modified

the socialist system and saw the athlete as expression of the 'new man' within the larger community. Nicaragua's Sandinistas contemplated a similar programme in the 1980s, but lacked resources to implement much more than an end to professionalism.

Revolutionary Cuba and West Indies cricket are extreme illustrations of a common connection between sports and politics. Beyond hoping that sports can strengthen national identity and promote development, officials and interest groups have embraced them for varied political ends. Dominican dictator Rafael Trujillo promoted baseball and constructed sports facilities to solidify loyalty; the Brazilian military in 1970 embraced their nation's soccer heroes; opponents of the Chilean military

Gabriela Sabatini,
Argentine tennis star who
began to make sporting
headlines while a young
teenager in the mid-1980s

foreign form, permeates local languages. Sports magazines, (e.g., Brazil's *Placar* and Argentina's *El Gráfico)* enjoy large readerships. Popular songs praise the skills of Pele and Fernando Valenzuela; poems glorify the talents of Brazilian soccer star Garrincha, Puerto Rican baseballer Roberto Clemente, and the Argentinian jockey Irineo Leguisamo; works of art illustrate the physical beauty of athletics. Some of the region's best authors have expressed themselves through sports themes: Julio Cortázar (boxing), Antonio Skármeta (cycling), Andrés Eloy Blanco (baseball), C.L.R. James (cricket), Jorge Luis Borges (chess), and Miguel Angel Asturias, Isaac Goldemberg, Eduardo Galeano, Mario Benedetti, Mario Vargas Llosa, Silvia Lago, and more (soccer). In short, Latin America's sporting past evokes both pride and frustration.   JLA

Further Reading: J. L. Arbena, ed., *An Annotated Bibliography of Latin American Sport: Pre-Conquest to the Present* (Westport, Conn., 1989); J. L. Arbena, ed., *Sport and Society in Latin America: Diffusion, Dependency, and the Rise of Mass Culture* (Westport, Conn., 1988); C. L. R. James, *Beyond a Boundary* (London, 1963); J. Lever, *Soccer Madness* (Chicago, 1983); A. M. Klein, *Sugarball: The American Game, the Dominican Dream* (New Haven, Conn., 1991)

FINDING OUT MORE

General Reference Works

Helen Delpar, ed., *Encyclopedia of Latin America* (New York, 1974)
Barbara A. Tenenbaum, ed., *Encyclopedia of Latin American History*, 4 volumes (New York, forthcoming)

Bibliographical guides and bibliographies

Paula Covington, *Latin America and the Caribbean: a Critical Guide to Research Sources* (Westport, Conn., 1992)
Robert McNeil, *Latin American Bibliography* (Metuchen, N.J. 1990)
Charles Griffin, *Latin America: a Guide to the Historical Literature* (Austin, Texas, 1971)
Roberto Cortés Conde and Stanley Stein, eds., *Latin America: a Guide to Economic History 1830–1931* (Berkeley, Calif., 1977)
Meri Knaster, *Women in Spanish America: an Annotated Bibliography from pre-Conquest to Contemporary Times* (Boston, 1977)
Handbook of Latin American Studies (currently published by University of Texas Press). Annual publication from 1936 onwards, with volumes on Humanities and Social Sciences now appearing in alternate years

Periodical indexes

HAPI. Hispanic American Periodicals Index (Latin American Center, University of California, 1970–). Annual index to articles (including book-reviews) in over two hundred journals (in English, Spanish and Portuguese), covering humanities and social sciences, but not natural sciences
Bibliographie latinoaméricaine d'articles (Institut des Hautes Etudes de l'Amérique Latine, Paris 1975–). Twice-yearly index to journals in humanities and social sciences

Newsletters and newspapers

Latin America Weekly Report (Latin American Newsletters Ltd., London, 1979–)
Latin America Regional Reports (Latin American Newsletters Ltd., London, 1979–) *Andean Group, Brazil, The Caribbean, Mexico and Central America, Southern Cone*, each published roughly every five weeks

NEWSPAPERS Coverage of Latin American news in the main North American and European newspapers is often found unsatisfactory by people who are professionally concerned with the region. As of the start of the 1990s, three newspapers that can be recommended (though their emphases differ) are *The Financial Times* (London), *The Miami Herald* (Miami, Florida), *Le Monde* (Paris)

INDEX

Numbers in italics refer to illustrations

ACKNOWLEDGEMENTS

The editors and publishers are grateful to the following: Professor Dawn Ades (University of Essex) for advice on art history; Dr Tristan Platt (University of St Andrews) and Dr Valerie Fraser (University of Essex) for the Quechua text of the Lord's Prayer; Stephen Adamson for the boxed text on Latin American sporting champions, Dr Peter Richards for the boxed texts on El Niño, species diversity, the protection of the Amazonian Indians and the Mayan calendar, and Dr S. Max Walters for the boxed texts on Latin American plant contributions to world agriculture and medicine.

We are also grateful to the following for supplying pictures on the pages indicated:

Dr George Bankes 182, 197

Fernando Botero (© Fernando Botero/DACS, London/VAGA, New York 1992) 431R

Bridgeman Art Library 431R

British Film Institute 443

British Museum 229

Martin Chambi 258

Channel Four Television 450

Dr Colin Clarke 215, 339

Professor Simon Collier 145, 194, 270, 438, 457

Dr Peter Coy 436

Cuban Embassy, London 301

B. J. Darke 319

Dr J. P Dickenson 143, 210

Dr Robert Gwynne 77, 78

Hulton Picture Company 263, 299, 314, 410

Manchester Museum 181

Mansell Collection 141, 197, 208, 226, 245, 386

Museo Naval, Madrid 451

Museu Marítim de Barcelona 177

National Optical Astronomy Observatories, Chile 459

Organization of American States 119, 124, 148, 184, 216, 220, 221, 224, 237, 239, 243, 247R, 267L, 267R, 269, 272B, 272T, 277, 278, 281, 288, 289, 291, 297, 304, 305, 327, 389, 391, 393, 397, 398, 411, 413, 437

Penguin Books 401

Popperfoto 125, 248, 331, 464

South American Pictures/Tony and Marion Morrison 13, 25, 28, 29, 33, 37, 44, 48, 54, 55, 56, 57, 58, 59, 61, 67, 71, 82, 85, 86, 87, 89, 91, 95, 100, 102, 106, 107, 109, 110, 112, 116, 126, 138, 143, 147, 152, 157, 158, 159, 160, 161, 162, 163, 164, 165, 166-7, 171, 173, 174, 177, 178, 183, 184, 186, 190, 191, 192, 193, 206, 215, 224, 229, 232, 241, 243, 247L, 251, 253, 261, 262, 268, 271, 275, 280, 295, 310, 319, 321, 323, 330, 333, 342, 349, 351, 353, 355, 356, 362, 366, 367, 380, 384, 407, 408, 409, 413, 415, 417L, 417R, 418, 419, 421, 423, 424L, 424R, 425, 426, 427L, 427R, 428, 430, 431L, 432, 435, 446, 447, 453, 458, title page

South American Pictures/Nicholas Bright 75, 462

South American Pictures/Robert Francis 50, 126, 335

South American Pictures/Bill Leimbach 126 BL

Sygma/C. Carrion 268

Sygma/John Hillelson 324

Trip/John Batten 99

Trip/Peter Blake 466

Trip/L. Fordyce 98, 176

Trip/Felix Kerr 313

Trip/Ian Mursell 405

Trip/David Oliver 24

Trip/N.D. Price 40

Trip/Dave Saunders 214, 343

Trip/Julia Waterlow 99, 292